L'EUROPE

DÉPARTEMENTS ET TERRITOIRES D'OUTRE-MER

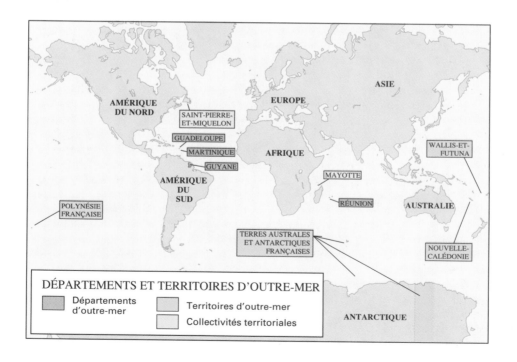

Mais oui!

INSTRUCTOR'S ANNOTATED EDITION

CHANTAL P. THOMPSON
Brigham Young University

ELAINE M. PHILLIPS
Southwest Educational Development Laboratory

HOUGHTON MIFFLIN COMPANY

Boston   New York

Director, Modern Language Programs: Kristina E. Baer
Development Manager: Beth Kramer
Senior Development Editor: Cécile Strugnell
Senior Project Editor: Rosemary R. Jaffe
Editorial Assistant: Jane Lee
Senior Production/Design Coordinator: Jennifer Waddell
Senior Designer: Henry Rachlin
Senior Manufacturing Coordinator: Priscilla Bailey
Associate Marketing Manager: Tina Crowley Desprez

Cover design by Diana Coe/ko Studio

Credits for texts, illustrations, and photographs are found following the index at the back of the book.

Houghton Mifflin Company has provided this book free of charge to instructors considering it for classroom use. Selling free examination copies contributes to rising textbook prices for students and denies textbook authors fair royalties for their work.

Printed in the U.S.A.

Student Text ISBN: 0-395-95600-5

Instructor's Annotated Edition ISBN: 0-395-95601-3

Library of Congress Catalog Card Number: 99-71894

23456789-VH-03 02 01 00

Instructor's Annotated Edition

Instructor's Guide
Contents

Introduction

I. TO THE INSTRUCTOR

The *Mais oui!* Approach

Welcome to the second edition of **Mais oui!,** a complete program for beginning college French. What makes **Mais oui!** different and unique? First and foremost, its approach to learning. Rather than perpetuating lower-order thinking through rote memorization and repetition, **Mais oui!**—which means "But of course! It's logical! I understand!"— calls on students to use their higher-order thinking skills and participate actively in the process of discovering the French language and the French-speaking world.

- **Real-world input.** Carefully selected real-world listening and reading materials are used as entry into the language. The Instructor's Annotated Edition comes with a sixty-minute cassette containing the listening segments as well as the pronunciation activities for each chapter. (The Student Edition comes with either an audio CD *or* a cassette containing this material.) The readings in the text are actual magazine articles or literary passages. The **Mais oui!** Video, with accompanying activities in the Video Manual, and the CD-ROM provide additional exposure to authentic materials. The Web Activities expand opportunities for learning about francophone cultures. Through a hierarchy of tasks, students develop strategies that enable them to process this input successfully, which serves as a natural stage for the introduction of vocabulary, structures, cultural concepts, and the practice of language functions. Through this wealth of real-world input, students not only learn to understand "real" French, but they embark on a journey of discovery.

- **Critical thinking.** The journey turns the travelers into reflective observers who use the input to discover the French way of saying things. Through a process of *Observez et déduisez,* then *Vérifiez,* students are led to figure out on their own how the language works. They observe, infer, verify and acquire the language in a stimulating environment conducive to long-term retention. They are also led to understand new social and cultural realities, for a new way of saying things is often a new way of seeing things. Take the word *bread* for example. When you think of bread, what images come to your mind? A loaf of evenly-sliced bread wrapped in plastic? Other images? To the French, the word *pain* is likely to evoke the taste and smell of a warm baguette or the heavier texture of a *pain de campagne.* Language learning is not simply a matter of learning different words, but one of acquiring a new set of concepts associated with the words—a chance to expand one's horizons, inquisitively.

- **Realistic expectations.** The discovery process may sound challenging, but fortunately, the journey is a guided tour. The tasks are kept simple, and, one small step at a time, students are guided from receptive to productive activities. Chances to create with the language abound, and functions are recycled from chapter to chapter in everexpanding contexts. By the end of the **Mais oui!** program, students can reasonably expect to be able to express personal meaning about a variety of simple topics, to ask and answer questions, and to deal with most common everyday situations in French.

New to the Second Edition

Based on extensive input from instructors and students alike, we have implemented a number of changes in the second edition, without altering the essence of **Mais oui!**

- The *Interludes culturels* have been replaced by cultural information about the francophone world that is now integrated into each chapter. A new, full-page feature, *Culture et réflexion,* presents written and visual information about some aspects of the francophone world relating to the chapter theme. Then, true to the critical thinking approach of **Mais oui!,** it provides opportunities for students to reflect and draw their own conclusions on cultural differences and similarities. For example, in the preliminary chapter where students are taught how to greet people in French, *Culture et réflexion* takes a look at the presence or absence of physical contact during greetings and leave-takings: what does it reveal about a culture? In other chapters, attitudes towards privacy, education, dating, vacations, social roles and other issues are examined.

- One of the challenges of presenting the language through real-world input is keeping track of active vocabulary. Convenient *Vocabulaire actif* boxes are now placed throughout the chapter to help students take note of the new vocabulary as it occurs in context. For further reference, the vocabulary is glossed at the end of the chapter.

- The development of listening and reading strategies is crucial to **Mais oui!** To help students focus on global understanding, the *En général* activities now precede the readings, indicating how important it is to get a global picture of a text before trying to make sense of the details.

- Some readings have been replaced by selections that are more accessible to the students. In chapitre 2, the «En famille» advertisement has been replaced by «Les médias d'abord,» a survey of leisure activities in France, and «Par derrière chez mon père» has been replaced by «L'homme qui te ressemble,» a poem by a writer from Cameroon, René Philombe. In chapitre 6, «La télévision» has been replaced by «Les zappeurs,» a comic strip. In chapitre 8, «L'amour et le mariage en France» has been updated to include current practices in France. In chapitre 10, «Astérix» has been replaced by «Arithmétique de la mode,» some clever suggestions from a popular magazine on how to make the most of your wardrobe. And, in chapitre 11, «Vie professionnelle» has been replaced by «L'image du travail,» an article about French people's perceptions of work and professional success.

- To enhance the problem-solving approach to the presentation of grammar, the questions and tasks formerly featured in *Déduisez* now stand out in boxed format.

- To emphasize the importance of interaction among students, role-plays in attractive boxes have been added as the culminating activity of each *étape.*

- The last *étape* in each chapter is now called *Intégration* to emphasize that it is designed to help students synthesize the language functions and content of the chapter.

- The last chapter, *chapitre complémentaire,* has been reduced to include only one reading selection and one listening passage as preludes to the function of stating an opinion. Seeds of abstractions are being planted, but mostly for recognition purposes. The authors' intent is to have students leave the course feeling challenged but comfortable with what they have learned to do with the language.

- Web Activities relating to the chapter theme motivate students to make further discoveries about the francophone world on the Internet.

Teaching Suggestions for the Textbook

Chapter Openers

Ask students to make statements about the chapter opening photograph to activate their background knowledge about the chapter topic and to introduce a few key vocabulary items. As you progress through the chapters, you can also review previously studied vocabulary and structures by asking students to describe a person or place in the photograph, to imagine what has gone on before, or to imagine what a person in the photograph is feeling. Go over the chapter objectives with students and ask them to predict the kinds of things they will need to learn in order to accomplish the objectives. Finally, at the end of the chapter, return to the opener and use the *Et vous?* questions to review and to point out to students that they have been able to accomplish the stated goals.

Chapitre préliminaire

Listening comprehension is often the skill that most frustrates students. Consequently, this mini-chapter focuses on that skill, showing students from day one that they can learn to understand authentic, spoken French through a step-by-step approach. Follow carefully the suggestions given under *À l'écoute* in this Instructor's Guide, and spend as much time as necessary replaying the recorded segments on the student cassette in class to accustom students to the listening passages and to get them comfortable with the task types assigned.

The structures and vocabulary presented in the *chapitre préliminaire* are relatively easy, everyday items. However, since some students may be more reticent to speak than others, allow responses from *volunteers* and provide intensive practice with a partner or small group work rather than requiring individuals to respond in front of the whole class.

À l'écoute

The development of the listening comprehension skill is an integral part of—not a supplement to—the **Mais oui!** program; essential vocabulary, structures, and cultural information are introduced in each listening excerpt. These sections occur at the beginning of the first and third *étapes* in chapters 2–12 and once in the *chapitre complémentaire*. (In chapter 1, they occur at the beginning of the first and second *étapes*.) There are two suggestions of vital importance in the utilization of this section. First, tell students frequently that they are *not expected to understand everything they hear*. Train them to read each individual listening task before they listen to the audio CD or cassette, and to listen as often as necessary, but only for information pertinent to the task at hand. Challenge them to infer the unknown from the known. Second, train students to *follow the sequence of tasks* laid out in the section; no task should be skipped because each one builds on the preceding tasks. For example, the *Avant d'écouter* activities are designed to prepare students to understand more easily the vocabulary and structures of the listening input, and the vocabulary of one task often depends on the foundation laid in the previous task. These tasks also provide a chance for the instructor to model pronunciation of new words that students need to recognize and then learn as *vocabulaire actif*. Once students are comfortable with the step-by-step inductive approach, portions of these sections can be assigned as homework. To make sure students take the assignments seriously, however, it is important to spend a few minutes *in class* reviewing their responses, answering questions, and checking on the *vocabulaire actif*.

Prononciation

Here again, students go through the steps of higher-order learning as they are called on to infer, from the listening input, how the sound system and various prosodic elements of the language work. Because the samples and the activities are recorded on the audio CD or cassette, most of the *Prononciation* sections can be assigned as homework. In class, check answers to the *Écoutez* activities as needed, and monitor students' pronunciation through the *Essayez!* exercises.

Lecture

These authentic cultural readings open the second *étape* in chapters 2–12. The *chapitre complémentaire* also has a reading section. (In chapter 1, the *Lecture* section occurs at the beginning of the third *étape*.) Like *À l'écoute*, this is an input section that introduces students to essential vocabulary, structures, and cultural information and that serves as a foundation for understanding the sections that follow it. Many of the teaching suggestions listed under *À l'écoute* apply to the *Lecture* sections as well. Students learn to first skim over the text to get a general idea; with the global picture in place, it is then easier to infer the meaning of specific words and sentences. One task at a time, students develop reading strategies that they can also apply to other texts. To facilitate students' ability to transfer strategy use from one text to the next, we suggest you discuss *explicitly* such techniques as skimming, scanning, and recognizing cognates, root words, parts of speech, and discourse markers. Occasionally ask students to explain *how* they were able to infer meaning without recourse to a dictionary. Remind students often to follow the planned sequence of activities. To set proper habits, take the time to complete *all* tasks in the first few *Lecture* sections with students, in class. As students strengthen their reading skills, portions of this section can be assigned as homework. A sound approach is to do the *Avant de lire* (pre-reading) activities and the *En général* (global) tasks in class the day before the reading is scheduled, to assign the *En détail* section (and parts of *Et vous?* as appropriate) as homework, and then to check and expand on those tasks the next day in class.

Structure

Most students are used to a deductive learning approach in which they are given a rule and asked to apply it. The problem-solving approach used in this section provides students with examples of speech taken from or based on the listening/reading input and asks them to infer the rules. It is designed to engage students' critical thinking and to teach them to predict meaning, form, and function by responding to specific questions and hypothesizing about language samples. Because the approach may be unfamiliar to students, it is important to take the time to complete all materials in the *Observez et déduisez* sections *with* them for at least the first few weeks of the course. To help students develop their powers of linguistic observation, always have them cover up the *Vérifiez* sections with a piece of paper until they have answered the questions in the box. Each time they "figure out" an answer, and even when they can't, they will learn something new about French, making the next step easier. Once students are comfortable with the inductive approach, this section can be assigned as homework. As with *À l'écoute* and *Lecture*, however, it is always important to spend a few minutes in class reviewing student responses and answering questions.

Structures and vocabulary introduced in the reading and listening input sections of the chapters can be brought to students' attention again through "teacher talk." This term refers to the simplified, iterative, somewhat slower speech often used by teachers when speaking with their classes. Teacher talk, accompanied by pictures and/or realia lends itself neatly to introducing the material in *Observez et déduisez*. Teachers may use that language sample specifically or personalize the topic as suggested on page 49 of the Instructor's Annotated Edition.

Vocabulaire

All vocabulary words introduced in these sections are active items, so there is no *Vocabulaire actif* box. The illustrations frequently used to present the vocabulary are reproduced on overhead transparencies, so that you can use them for the initial presentation. Then students open their books and continue with the in-text activities. Through the illustrations and activities, they discover the meaning of the vocabulary items actively without the need to refer to English translations.

Stratégie de communication

This section occurs once in each chapter. A short introduction presents the communicative purpose and asks students to find expressions that fulfill the function of the *Stratégie* in the language samples that follow. Students should be told to cover up the box of functional expressions as they work to identify examples using context, cognates, and their knowledge of French. To summarize this section, the functional expressions are listed in a box for students to study. These are active vocabulary items though no reminder boxes are included.

Notes culturelles

This floating feature appears as appropriate to facilitate students' understanding of concepts mentioned in the listening inputs, the reading selections, and the strategy sections and to support students' study of the language being presented. In the early chapters of the text, you may want to expand in English on the cultural notes and, as students become more proficient, switch to French. If the *Notes* are assigned for homework, check students' understanding the next day by asking them questions, having them infer differences and similarities, and encouraging them not to overgeneralize or engage in stereotyping.

Activités

Each *Structure, Vocabulaire,* and *Stratégie de communication* section is followed by activities supporting communicative practice of these materials. In keeping with **Mais oui!**'s emphasis on communication, many of the activities are designed for pair and small group work. They also relate to the topics presented in the preceding *À l'écoute* or *Lecture* section, providing a smooth, contextualized transition from input to output. For instructors who choose to use them, drills and listening discrimination activities are included in the marginal annotations of the Instructor's Annotated Edition.

The first activities ask students to process the relevant structure or vocabulary through listening or reading comprehension without having to produce it immediately. These activities include matching, sentence completion, word association, multiple-choice or true/false questions, etc., all of which check comprehension.

The activities that follow move along a continuum from those providing more support to those that are more open-ended and personalized. Activity types include interviews, surveys, signature searches, games, task-based activities, eliciting personal responses or creative responses based on pictures or written cues, role-playing, and information gap activities. The latter are explained in the Instructor's Resource Manual where worksheets are provided. Students are encouraged, at all times, to personalize their answers and to inject humor into the situation. In group activities, accountability can be ensured by having students report on their "findings," asking follow-up questions, or completing charts with their responses.

Culture et réflexion

True to the critical thinking approach of **Mais oui!,** this section is designed to help students develop cultural analytical skills. As they discover and reflect upon various aspects of francophone cultures, they may understand things about their own culture they had never considered. How do they feel about smiling at strangers? What is their concept of private space? Do they agree with the attitude that «une famille qui mange ensemble reste ensemble»? Such are the questions posed in *Culture et réflexion*. The short texts and the photos introduce students to other cultural realities. Instructors may expand on this information as they see fit. But the focus of this section is the process of cultural analysis, through the questions students are asked to consider—not in terms of what is better or worse, but what is different or similar, and why. In the early chapters (P–3), the discussion will be conducted in English. From chapter 4 on, everything can be done in French. To help students expand their thinking and elaborate, use brainstorming, review vocabulary as needed, and generate lists of ideas on the board before you put students in pairs or small groups. Group discussion reduces anxiety and helps students formulate their ideas more effectively before they share them with the rest of the class. During group work, as you circulate from group to group, take mental notes of the major language mistakes students are making, and discuss those mistakes before you ask for reports. This will enable students to incorporate some of the corrections in the general discussion and feel more confident about sharing their ideas. Any time cultural issues are analyzed, it is important to keep the discussion open and allow students to draw their own conclusions. To further explore the cultural issues presented in *Culture et réflexion,* assign some of the Web Activities and have students report on their findings to the class (see p. IAE 16.)

Littérature

The beauty of literature is that it provides authentic texts that engage the reader beyond sheer comprehension. Literature has a way of talking to the imagination and of enabling learners to overcome linguistic obstacles that might be considered too great in less involving material.[1] Thus, literature does indeed belong in the first-year curriculum—*if* the texts are carefully chosen, and *if* they are made accessible through manageable, enjoyable tasks.

Mais oui! uses literature as a culminating point in each chapter's *Intégration,* to stretch and enhance students' reading skills, to synthesize the chapter's content, and to bring closure to the chapter's theme in a motivating, innovative fashion. As with other readings, the *Avant de lire* and *En général* activities should be done in class the day before the reading is scheduled. Assign the *En détail* section and parts of the *Et vous?* section as homework, then check and expand on those tasks the next day in class.

Par écrit

Work through the *Avant d'écrire* activities in class with students, especially in the early chapters where they need the most guidance and where tasks are short. In later chapters, these sections may be assigned as homework, but encourage students to share their responses to the *Application* activities with the class. *Écrivez* assignments can be done in class or as homework as time allows. Use anonymous examples from student writings to illustrate "good" uses of structures, vocabulary, and strategies as well as to correct the most common types of errors. When responding to student assignments, focus your comments on *content,* discussing how ideas are developed, and asking probing questions that encourage students to think more critically. You are encouraged to point out grammatical errors related to the particular structures studied in the chapter and to ask students to revise both the content and the form of their papers. You may also wish to have students keep all their *Par écrit* work in a portfolio, choosing two or three writing samples to revise for final grading at the end of the semester.

---

[1] See Collie and Slater, *Literature in the Language Classroom.* Cambridge: Cambridge University Press, 1987, p. 6.

Supplementary Materials for the Instructor

Instructor's Annotated Edition	• Packaged with student cassette • Preface to the instructor with valuable explanations and suggestions • Transcript of the textbook's *À l'écoute* listening passages • On-page marginal notes with numerous optional drills and specific suggestions for implementing or supplementing the chapter's materials • Icons referencing the ancillaries, including Information Gap Activities found in the Instructor's Resource Manual
Mais oui! Video	• Filmed in Aix-en-Provence and other parts of France • Three distinct types of footage for each chapter: scripted situations; realia shots of everyday life; and unrehearsed interviews with native speakers • On-screen cues to help students find corresponding activities in Video Manual
Instructor's Resource Kit	• Includes Instructor's Resource Manual, Instructor's Test Cassette, Overhead Transparencies, and Situation Cards Kit
Instructor's Resource Manual	• Information Gap Activities (instructions and worksheets) • Complete Testing Program: chapter tests plus two comprehensive final exams; chapter culture quizzes containing multiple-choice or true-false items on cultural content from the chapter; script for listening sections on the Instructor's Test Cassette; answer keys; suggestions for grading for oral testing • Complete transcripts of Audio Program and **Mais oui!** Video
Overhead Transparencies	• Colorful reproductions of art found in textbook to present/ review vocabulary • Full-color maps of the French-speaking world • «Un plan du métro» with supplementary activities to be used with ch. 3 or ch. 7
Houghton Mifflin home page: http://www.hmco.com/college/	• Web Activities related to the cultural theme of each chapter • **Mais oui!** Web Site: extensive suggestions for chapter planning and detailed lesson plans; ideal for teaching assistants and new teachers • Generic web resources for French teachers, including links, maps, and transparencies that can be downloaded
Computer Study Module 2.0 Lab Disk	• Permits instructor to author questions and monitor student progress with use of Computer Study Modules

Teaching Suggestions for Selected Components

The Workbook/Laboratory Manual/Video Manual

The workbook activities are organized by *étapes* to enable you to assign individual activities as you work through the chapter or to assign all of the activities in a section once you have completed that *étape*. The laboratory manual activities are meant to provide students with a cumulative listening experience that integrates the structures, vocabulary, cultural information, and communicative strategies presented in the first three *étapes* of the corresponding textbook chapter. Therefore, it is recommended that you assign the laboratory manual activities *after* the third *étape* of a chapter has been completed. Likewise, the video and Video Manual can be used as summative activities after students are thoroughly familiar with the first three *étapes*.

Most of the activities in the Workbook/Laboratory Manual/Video Manual are designed to be self-correcting so that students can work on them on their own, reinforcing what they have done in class. However, you can add variety to the lesson by choosing some of the more open-ended activities in class.

The Information Gap Activities

The Information Gap Activities are cued in the annotations of the Instructor's textbook, and the directions and worksheets are found in the Instructor's Resource Manual. These are valuable as a regular feature to be used in class, as they allow students to practice structures, vocabulary, and communicative strategies in a game-like atmosphere with a partner. This alleviates the anxiety associated with speaking in front of the whole class. Be sure that students exchange information *orally*, and always save time for "reporting" to ensure that students stay on task.

The *Mais oui!* Video

The thirteen text-specific video modules and their accompanying video manual activities are cross-referenced in the textbook with a special reminder at the end of the third *étape*. They may be used in class, in whole or in part, so that students learn to work through the activity sequences—the *Préparez-vous!* pre-viewing sections, the *Regardez!* viewing sections, and the *Récapitulez* post-viewing sections—as they do for the various sections of the textbook. The video activities are carefully sequenced to focus on one task at a time so that students are soon able to work through them on their own if you wish to assign them for homework or lab work, however.

The *Mais oui!* CD-ROM

The **Mais oui!** CD-ROM provides direct exposure to authentic input, presenting unrehearsed interview clips of native speakers as they talk about topics covered in the corresponding chapters. Two or four activities provide an opportunity to interact further with the input. Listening comprehension is checked using a multiple-choice format or click-and-drag exercises. A writing task focuses on the same topic and provides cues and helpful hints related to vocabulary and structures in the chapter. Finally, students can record their own responses to questions asked by a native speaker and listen to their "conversation" at the end. The video clip and comprehension activities can be used with the whole class when the required equipment is available, or students can complete all activities individually or in small groups in the language lab or on their personal computers.

The *Mais oui!* Web Site

Cues to Web Activities are included on the *Culture et réflexion* page. To access the **Mais oui!** Web site, students select *French* at the Houghton Mifflin College Division home page, http://www.hmco.com/college/. The site includes links to web sites and related activities that will help students explore further the topics of the *Culture et réflexion* section. After completing the activities, they will share their findings and discuss them with fellow students in class.

The Overhead Transparencies

Use the overhead transparencies to present or review vocabulary, structures, and cultural information. To present material, show and discuss the transparency in general terms, pointing to the transparency, writing cognates on the board, and using "teacher talk" (redundancies, repetitions, synonyms, etc.) and mime in order to make your meaning clear to students. Confirm student comprehension by asking true/false questions about what you have told them. Comprehension can be checked by having students respond physically (raise a hand, stand up), give a one-word answer *(oui/non, vrai/faux),* or reply to either/or questions regarding what you have told them.

The Testing Program and Instructor's Test Cassette

The testing program consists of twelve chapter tests, two short exams for the *chapitre préliminaire* and the *chapitre complémentaire,* thirteen chapter culture quizzes, and two end-of-semester tests. The chapter tests allow you to monitor students' progress in the domains of listening comprehension, vocabulary, structures, communicative strategies, writing, and reading comprehension. Each begins with a listening comprehension section and ends with a short, open-ended writing and reading comprehension section. A variety of question types are used to test vocabulary, cultural context, structures, and communicative strategies; many require more than filling in a blank and ask students to create their own sentences. The chapter culture quizzes are designed to briefly test recall of the cultural content most often found in the chapter's *Notes Culturelles, Culture et réflexion,* and the introduction to the *Littérature* section. Each quiz consists of four multiple-choice or true-false items, to allow for quick administration and correction at the end of the chapter. The two end-of-semester tests consist of a series of multiple-choice questions focused on skills and concepts covered in chapters *préliminaire*–6 and chapters 7–*complémentaire,* respectively. The multiple-choice format permits instructors to collect data and compare group performances. All tests in the testing program are meant to be used as measures of achievement, as well as proficiency.

The testing program should be viewed as a source of evaluation materials. While the tests are given in their entirety in the Instructor's Resource Manual, we hope you will customize them for your classes by selecting, deleting, and adding items or sections. If class schedules do not allow time for a test after each chapter, two chapter tests can be combined into one that has a listening comprehension, open-ended writing section, and a reading comprehension section, along with selected items or sections testing vocabulary, structures, and communicative strategies. The results from the testing program, when considered in conjunction with instructor-administered oral examinations, provide a comprehensive view of a student's level of mastery of concepts covered in **Mais oui!**

II. COURSE PLANNING

This section on course planning includes suggested syllabi for various configurations of semester and quarter courses, as well as alternative schedules for false beginners or for programs that spread the introductory-level curriculum over three semesters. **Extensive suggestions for chapter planning and detailed lesson plans can be found at the Mais oui! Web Site http://www.hmco.com/college/.**

Suggested Syllabi

Two Fifteen-Week Semesters Meeting Four Times Per Week

This suggested syllabus is based on 60 contact hours per semester, for a total of 120 hours. The first semester covers the *chapitre préliminaire* and chapters 1–6. The second semester covers chapters 7–12 and *chapitre complémentaire*. The following list breaks out the suggested coverage by number of days.

- 3 days for the *chapitre préliminaire*
- 8–9 days each for chapters 1–12
- 3–4 days for the *chapitre complémentaire*
- 12 days for exams

Two Fifteen-Week Semesters Meeting Three Times Per Week

This suggested syllabus is based on 45 contact hours per semester for a total of 90 contact hours. The coverage each semester would be the same as described above, but with the following breakouts by number of days:

- 2 days for the *chapitre préliminaire*
- 6–7 days each for chapters 1–12
- 2 days for the *chapitre complémentaire*
- 7–8 days for exams

If there is a testing center at your institution, where students can take the exams outside of class, spend the additional time on some of the chapters and/or review.

Two Fifteen-Week Semesters Meeting Five Times Per Week

Two-semester courses meeting five times per week offer even more flexibility. You and your students will have increased opportunities to spend additional time on the chapters, and you will be able to work more thoroughly with the text's components such as the video and video activities, the information gap activities, and the overhead transparencies. The following suggested syllabus is based on 75 contact hours per semester for a total of 150 contact hours.

- 4 days for the *chapitre préliminaire*
- 10–11 days each for chapters 1–12
- 4 days for the *chapitre complémentaire*
- 12–13 days for exams

Three Ten-Week Quarters Meeting Three Times Per Week

This suggested syllabus is based on 30 contact hours per quarter for a total of 90 contact hours. The first quarter covers the *chapitre préliminaire* and chapters 1–4, the second quarter covers chapters 5–8, and the third quarter covers chapters 9–12 and the *chapitre complémentaire*. This suggested syllabus would entail the same number of days of coverage for the text's elements as shown in the list for two semester courses meeting three times per week.

Alternative Schedules

False Beginners

Some students beginning first semester French will already have had some exposure to the French language. **Mais oui!** is ideally suited for use with *faux débutants* as well as with true beginners. False beginners will often have a foundation in the structures of the language but be far less advanced in their ability to produce the language orally or in writing, and their ability to comprehend the spoken or written language may also lag behind their knowledge of grammatical structures. Because of this, such students will benefit from **Mais oui!**'s preliminary chapter with its emphasis on listening skills and its coverage of high frequency, basic items that they may not have internalized during their previous exposure to French. It is also recommended that you focus on the *À l'écoute, Lecture, Littérature,* and *Par écrit* sections of the first few chapters, as well as the video modules, in order to strengthen the false beginners' listening, reading, and writing skills. Once students have learned how to use the problem-solving approach in the *Observez et déduisez* and *Vérifiez* sections, this material, which for them is principally review material, may be assigned for homework. In class, oral practice should then concentrate on the information gap and the other open-ended and interactive activities.

The Expanded Syllabus

At some institutions, the introductory-level curriculum occurs over three semesters. **Mais oui!** with its abundant exercises and activities, its attention to building the four skills and culture, and its wealth of components is also well suited for use in this type of extended program. The first semester would cover the *chapitre préliminaire* and chapters 1–4, the second semester would cover chapters 5–8, and the third semester would cover chapters 9–12 and the *chapitre complémentaire*. The following list of the coverage of the text's sections and materials by number of days assumes that classes meet three times per week over three 15-week semesters for a total of 135 contact hours. It also permits the integrated use of the complete components package.

- 4 days for the *chapitre préliminaire*
- 9–10 days each for chapters 1–12
- 4–5 days for the *chapitre complémentaire*
- 8–9 days for exams

If your classes have the advantage of meeting four times per week over three 15-week semesters for a total of 180 contact hours, the following is the recommended breakout by number of days for the text's sections and materials. This configuration also permits the integrated use of the complete components package.

- 4 days for the *chapitre préliminaire*
- 12–13 days each for chapters 1–12
- 5 days for the *chapitre complémentaire*
- 10–12 days for exams

III. SCRIPT OF THE *À L'ÉCOUTE* LISTENING TEXTS

(The script for the *Prononciation* sections is in the text.)

Chapitre préliminaire

À l'écoute

A. Attention!

Attention, s'il vous plaît. Madame Duchesnay, Madame Duchesnay est priée de se présenter au bureau de la compagnie Air France. Mme Duchesnay, s'il vous plaît.

À l'écoute

B. Votre nom?

— Bonjour, mademoiselle... euh... Je suis Madame Duchesnay...
— Ah oui... Votre nom s'écrit bien D-u-c-h-e-s-n-a-y?
— Oui.
— Alors, voici un message pour vous.
— Merci. Au revoir, mademoiselle!
— Au revoir, madame!

Chapitre 1

Première étape

À l'écoute: Qui suis-je?

1. Je suis française; je suis actrice; mon prénom est Catherine. Qui suis-je?
2. Je suis français; je suis un peintre impressionniste; mon prénom est Auguste. Qui suis-je?
3. Je suis allemand; je suis musicien; mon prénom est Jean-Sébastien. Qui suis-je?
4. Je suis anglais; je suis écrivain; je suis l'auteur de *Roméo et Juliette*. Qui suis-je?
5. Je suis américaine; je suis avocate; je suis la femme d'un président qui s'appelle Bill. Qui suis-je?
6. Je suis russe; je suis politicien; mon prénom est Boris. Qui suis-je?

Deuxième étape

À l'écoute: Tu connais... ?

— Tu connais Nicolas?
— Nicolas... Nicolas... Comment est-il?
— Il est petit, brun, intelligent...
— Timide?
— Non, non, au contraire! Il est très sociable et très actif, très amusant aussi...
— C'est le copain d'Alceste?
— Exactement!
— Ah oui, le petit Nicolas! Il est un peu fou, mais c'est un garçon très sympathique.

Chapitre 2

Première étape

À l'écoute: Une photo de famille

— Oh, Véronique, c'est une photo de ta famille? J'adore les photos de famille! Voyons... ici, c'est toi, bien sûr, et là, c'est ta mère et ton père, n'est-ce pas? Tu ressembles à ta mère.
— Oui, un peu.
— Et là, c'est qui?
— C'est mon frère Paul, et ici mon autre frère, Fabien.
— Paul ressemble à son père et Fabien ressemble à sa mère, je crois, non?
— Oui.
— Tu as deux sœurs?
— Non, une, ici. Ma sœur s'appelle Olivia. Là, c'est ma belle-sœur, la femme de Paul, et leurs deux enfants, mes petits neveux.
— Ils sont adorables!

Troisième étape

À l'écoute: Quel âge avez-vous?

1. Je m'appelle Nathalie. J'ai 5 ans. J'ai les cheveux bruns et les yeux bleus, comme ma maman.
2. Je suis Renaud. J'ai 16 ans. J'ai les cheveux blonds et les yeux bruns.
3. Je m'appelle Driss. J'ai 21 ans. J'ai les cheveux noirs et les yeux bruns.
4. Je m'appelle Brigitte. J'ai les cheveux roux et les yeux verts. Mon âge? Oh... 29, 30, 31, 32... je ne compte plus. Je n'aime pas les anniversaires.
5. Je m'appelle Léon. J'ai les yeux bruns et je n'ai pas beaucoup de cheveux! Aujourd'hui c'est mon anniversaire. J'ai 48 ans.
6. Je m'appelle Marguerite Folin. J'ai 62 ans. J'ai les yeux bleus et les cheveux gris.

Chapitre 3

Première étape

À l'écoute: Un studio

— Allô? C'est bien le 04.42.26.09.11?
— Oui.
— Je téléphone au sujet de l'annonce dans le journal. Est-ce que le studio est déjà loué?
— Non.
— Il est comment, le studio?
— Eh bien, il y a une chambre qui est très spacieuse, très agréable, et puis il y a une petite cuisine et une salle de bains avec douche, lavabo, W.C.
— C'est meublé?
— Non, ce n'est pas meublé.
— Et les charges sont comprises, n'est-ce pas?
— C'est ça.
— Et l'adresse?
— C'est sur le boulevard de la République, au numéro 16.
— Ah oui, c'est vraiment le centre-ville, c'est idéal. Est-ce que je pourrais le voir?
— Mais, bien sûr.

Troisième étape

À l'écoute: Je cherche la rue...

— Pardon, monsieur, je cherche la rue Clémenceau.
— La rue Clémenceau... voyons... Comment vous expliquer... ? Vous connaissez un peu Aix?
— Non, pas du tout.
— Bon, là, devant vous, c'est l'avenue Victor Hugo. Vous allez tout droit dans l'avenue Victor Hugo jusqu'à la Rotonde. Vous allez voir, c'est une grande place avec une grande fontaine et sur la droite, il y a une grande avenue qui s'appelle le cours Mirabeau. Alors vous tournez à droite sur le cours Mirabeau et après ça, la rue Clémenceau c'est la troisième ou quatrième rue à gauche.
— Voyons si j'ai bien compris: je vais tout droit dans l'avenue Victor Hugo jusqu'à la Rotonde, puis je tourne à droite sur le cours Mirabeau et à gauche dans la rue Clémenceau.
— C'est ça!
— Merci, monsieur.
— Je vous en prie.

Chapitre 4

Première étape

A l'écoute: Ça te plaît, l'école?

— Audrey, tu as quel âge?
— Neuf ans.
— Et ça te plaît, l'école?
— Oui.
— À quelle heure est-ce que tu vas à l'école?
— On commence à huit heures et demie et on finit à quatre heures et demie. De onze heures et demie à une heure et demie, on a deux heures pour manger et pour jouer.
— Qu'est-ce que tu as comme matières à l'école?
— Eh ben, le français, les maths, les sciences, l'histoire, la géographie, et puis, euh... la musique, le dessin et la gymnastique.
— Et quelle est ta matière préférée?
— Le français.
— Pourquoi?
— Parce que j'aime lire et écrire.
— Et l'institutrice est gentille?
— Oh oui! Elle est super!

Troisième étape

À l'écoute: La fac

— Stéphane, tu vas passer ton bac cette année, n'est-ce pas?
— Oui.
— Tu as peur?
— Ben oui, un peu, parce que c'est un examen vachement important. Sans le bac, on peut pas entrer à l'université.
— Tu sais ce que tu veux faire après?
— Je voudrais faire des études supérieures de chimie à la Fac des Sciences.
— Pour préparer quels diplômes?
— Ben, d'abord la licence, une licence de chimie, quoi, et puis sans doute la maîtrise, et peut-être le doctorat, je ne sais pas, on verra.

Chapitre 5

Première étape

À l'écoute: Vous désirez?

— J'ai faim! et toi?
— Ouais... mais j'ai surtout soif!
— Qu'est-ce que tu vas prendre?
— Une bière.
— Oui, mais pour manger?
— Bof, un hamburger, peut-être, avec des frites, ou bien un sandwich-brochette, mais il n'y a pas de frites avec... j'ai envie de frites... Qu'est-ce que tu prends, toi?
— Une salade. J'hésite entre la Niçoise et la Louisiane...

(*Male waiter arrives*)

— M'sieur-dame! Vous désirez?
— Ben, moi, je vais prendre une salade niçoise.
— Une salade niçoise! et pour monsieur?
— Je vais prendre une brochette, mais je voudrais aussi des frites, c'est possible?
— Oui, c'est 5 francs pour un supplément frites.
— Bon, alors brochette et frites.
— Et comme boissons?
— Une bière pour moi, Heineken si vous avez.
— Une bière Heineken, oui, et pour mademoiselle?
— Un coca, s'il vous plaît.

Troisième étape

À l'écoute: Les courses

— Il n'y a plus de lait?
— Mince! J'ai fait les courses mais j'ai complètement oublié le lait!
— Tu as pris du pain?
— Oui, oui, j'ai pris deux baguettes à la boulangerie, et puis à l'épicerie j'ai acheté des légumes, des fruits, des pâtes, du fromage et du beurre.
— Et la viande, tu n'as pas oublié la viande?
— Non, non, j'ai acheté du bifteck à la boucherie, et puis j'ai pris du jambon et du pâté à la charcuterie.

— Qu'est-ce que c'est que ça?
— Oh, c'est quelque chose que j'ai trouvé à l'épicerie, ça s'appelle des tacos.
— Des tacos?
— Ouais, ce sont des chips de maïs, c'est une spécialité mexicaine, qu'on mange avec de la salsita...
— De la quoi?
— De la salsita, c'est une sauce mexicaine à la tomate et au piment.
— Ça me semble très exotique!

Chapitre 6

Première étape

À l'écoute: Le bulletin météo

Messieurs dames, bonjour! Les nouvelles du ciel ne sont pas très bonnes. Les pluies qui continuent sur notre pays depuis lundi ont touché une grande partie de l'Europe: le nord de l'Espagne, la France, les îles Britanniques, l'Allemagne et la Scandinavie ont enregistré des précipitations en ce début de semaine. Cette zone de perturbation se déplace lentement vers l'est, mais elle détermine encore le temps en Suisse. Les températures vont rester fraîches pour la saison: entre 12 et 16 degrés. Un temps donc très nuageux pour toute la Suisse, avec des pluies, des orages, et même en montagne quelques chutes de neige avec un vent d'ouest modéré. Pour trouver le soleil, il faut aller bien au sud de l'Europe: 28 degrés à Madrid, 32 degrés à Rome...

Troisième étape

À l'écoute: Sport et culture

— Tiens, j'ai lu quelque chose d'intéressant sur le sport.
— Ah bon?
— Oui, c'est un article qui dit que chaque sport est le reflet d'une culture.
— Comme quoi, par exemple?
— Ben, le hockey au Canada, par exemple. Le hockey est comme le climat du Canada—rigoureux et froid.
— Tiens, c'est intéressant, ça. Et qu'est-ce qu'ils disent sur le football?
— Ben, le football américain d'abord, ils disent que c'est comme la conquête de l'Ouest...
— La conquête de l'Ouest?
— Oui, une conquête progressive du territoire par la tactique et la force. Ils disent aussi que c'est caractéristique d'une société de plus en plus violente.
— Est-ce qu'ils parlent de la violence aux matchs de football en Europe?
— Oui, mais là, ce sont les spectateurs qui sont violents!
— Oh, justement, on m'a dit qu'il y a eu un autre incident de violence au match d'hier, entre la France et l'Italie. C'est vrai?
— Il paraît, oui.

Chapitre 7

Première étape

À l'écoute: À l'hôtel

— Pardon, madame, vous avez une chambre libre, s'il vous plaît?
— Pour quand, monsieur?
— Pour ce soir.
— Pour combien de temps?
— Euh, je ne sais pas encore... au moins deux nuits.
— Une chambre pour une personne?
— Non, pour deux personnes, avec baignoire ou douche si possible.
— Alors, il me reste une chambre avec baignoire à 340 francs la nuit. Ça vous convient?
— Oui, c'est parfait. Le petit déjeuner est-il compris?
— Oui, monsieur. Nous servons le petit déjeuner dans la salle de restaurant de sept heures à neuf heures et demie. C'est à quel nom, monsieur?
— Chesnel, Alain Chesnel, C-h-e-s-n-e-l.
— Vous pouvez payer la première nuit tout de suite?
— Vous prenez la carte Visa?
— Bien sûr... Alors voici votre clé, monsieur, c'est la chambre numéro 27, au premier étage. L'ascenseur est là, à gauche.
— Merci, madame.

Troisième étape

À l'écoute

A. À la gare

— Tiens! mais c'est Monsieur Godot! Comment ça va?
— Monsieur Estragon, quelle surprise! Ça va bien, et vous-même?
— Ça va, ça va. Mais qu'est-ce que vous faites ici?
— Eh bien, j'attends. J'ai raté le train de 15 h 40, alors j'attends le prochain TGV pour Marseille, qui est à 16 h 53.
— Vous avez toujours votre petite maison à côté de Marseille?
— Oui, à Cassis. Ma femme et les enfants y sont déjà, alors je les rejoins pour les vacances. Et vous, un autre voyage d'affaires?
— Eh oui! À Lyon cette fois. Peut-être qu'on va être dans le même train. Attendez, je vais prendre mon billet.

À l'écoute

B. Au guichet

— Un billet pour Lyon, s'il vous plaît. Vous avez toujours des places dans le train de 16 h 53?
— Oui. Un aller-retour ou un aller simple?
— Un aller-retour.
— Première ou deuxième classe?
— Deuxième, non-fumeurs, s'il vous plaît.
— Et le retour?
— Demain soir. Qu'est-ce qu'il y a comme trains après 18 h?
— Il y a un TGV qui part de Lyon à 18 h 47 et qui arrive à Paris à 20 h 49.
— C'est parfait!

Chapitre 8

Première étape

À l'écoute: L'amitié

L'amitié? Voyons... En fait, mon meilleur ami, c'est quelqu'un que je connais depuis mon enfance. Il habitait à côté de chez moi, alors, on allait à l'école ensemble, on revenait de l'école ensemble. On parlait de tout, de rien, on racontait des blagues, on riait beaucoup. Qu'est-ce qu'on faisait d'autre? Euh... on regardait la télé ensemble, on jouait au foot, on faisait du vélo, on jouait aux cow-boys et aux Indiens. Quelquefois on avait des petites disputes, mais pas souvent.

Plus tard, quand on était au lycée et même à la fac, on faisait toujours un tas de choses ensemble. On retrouvait des copains au café ou au ciné. Le samedi soir on allait en boîte. On dansait, on discutait jusqu'à trois heures du matin—on s'amusait, quoi.

Maintenant, euh... évidemment, ce n'est plus pareil parce que la vie nous a séparés, mais on continue à se voir de temps en temps, et quand on se voit, bon, ben, on rit, on raconte des blagues, on parle de tout, de rien—comme avant, quoi!

Troisième étape

À l'écoute: Le bonheur

A.

— Larmé, vous venez du Tchad, n'est-ce pas?
— Oui, je viens de Pala, un petit village au sud du Tchad, mais j'ai fait mes études à N'Djamena, la capitale du Tchad.
— Larmé, quel est votre concept du bonheur?
— Alors, là... le bonheur... eh ben, le bonheur, ça dépend de l'individu. Pour moi, le bonheur, c'est le fait de se sentir libre.
— Libre? Dans quel sens?
— Libre de choisir ce qu'on veut faire dans la vie, libre d'arriver à ses objectifs.
— Est-ce que les relations humaines jouent un rôle important dans votre bonheur?
— Ah oui, très important. On a besoin des autres pour être heureux. D'ailleurs en Afrique, les autres jouent un rôle plus important qu'en Europe. En Europe, et aux États-Unis c'est pareil, on est très individualiste, ou bien quand on partage, c'est avec sa famille ou quelques amis. En Afrique, quand quelque chose se passe, tout le village le sait, tout le monde participe.

B.

— Nayat, vous êtes algérienne...
— En fait, je suis née en Algérie, mais j'ai grandi en France.
— Qu'est-ce que c'est que le bonheur pour vous, Nayat?
— Le bonheur... ben, quand j'étais petite, je me sentais inférieure parce que j'étais déchirée entre deux cultures. Y avait la culture arabe à la maison, et y avait la culture française à l'école. Alors moi, j'avais deux identités, ou bien pas d'identité du tout. Mais maintenant, pour moi le bonheur c'est de trouver mon identité dans ces deux cultures, et d'apprécier la richesse d'un double héritage.
— Est-ce que l'amitié, l'amour, c'est essentiel au bonheur?
— Ah oui! Sans l'amour, on est isolé et on ne peut pas vraiment se développer. Pour pouvoir trouver son identité et se développer, il faut être aimé. On a besoin des autres pour apprendre à s'accepter, quoi. C'est ça le bonheur—s'accepter, et partager.

Chapitre 9

Première étape

À l'écoute: Un souvenir d'école

— Joëlle, est-ce que tu as un souvenir d'école à nous raconter?

— Ben, en fait, la première chose dont je me souvienne vraiment bien dans mon enfance, c'est un souvenir d'école. Je crois que j'avais cinq ans à l'époque, j'étais donc à l'école maternelle. Je me souviens très bien de la salle de classe. J'étais assise à côté d'une petite fille qui s'appelait Solange. Et Solange... enfin, disons que Solange n'aimait pas trop l'école et elle ne travaillait pas trop bien, quoi. Mais moi, j'aimais bien l'école, et j'aimais bien répondre aux questions de la maîtresse, parce que quand on répondait bien, la maîtresse nous donnait des images, et moi je faisais la collection de ces images. Et puis un jour, la maîtresse a dû penser que je répondais trop souvent, alors elle a arrêté de m'interroger. Cinq ou six fois de suite, j'ai levé le doigt, sans succès. Mais j'ai murmuré les réponses, et ma voisine Solange m'a entendue. Alors cinq ou six fois de suite, Solange a levé le doigt, la maîtresse a interrogé Solange, et Solange a eu des images, avec *mes* réponses. Ce n'était pas juste! C'était moi qui savais les réponses, et c'était à Solange qu'on donnait les images! J'étais tellement fâchée, ce jour-là, que j'ai attrapé Solange par les cheveux, et j'ai commencé à la battre.

— La battre?

— Ben, je n'avais que cinq ans, et j'étais vraiment fâchée... Enfin, bref, la maîtresse nous a séparées tout de suite, évidemment, et puis j'ai été punie—une punition très sévère que je n'ai jamais oubliée...

— Ah bon?

— J'ai dû rester debout, au coin de la classe, avec la tête contre le mur et les mains derrière le dos, pendant plus de deux heures! Je n'ai jamais oublié la honte et l'humiliation... mais ça m'a appris quelque chose, parce que je n'ai plus jamais attaqué personne en classe!

Troisième étape

À l'écoute: Un souvenir de voyage

— Édith, parle-nous de ton voyage à Tahiti...

— Ben, j'arrivais de Paris, et quand je suis descendue de l'avion à Papeete, ce qui m'a frappée, c'était la chaleur et l'humidité—j'avais l'impression d'être dans un sauna. En sortant de l'aéroport, j'ai été éblouie par la lumière et la végétation, les fleurs exotiques, les palmiers, les cocotiers... C'était... j'sais pas comment dire, c'était comme un décor de film, c'était trop beau pour être vrai. Et puis j'ai fait un tour de la ville, Papeete, et j'ai vu que la plupart des Tahitiens vivaient très simplement. Les maisons étaient très modestes, et il n'y avait pas de portes, ou alors les portes étaient ouvertes en permanence...

— Tu as été invitée chez des Tahitiens?

— Plusieurs fois, et la première fois, en fait, c'était vraiment intéressant.

— Qu'est-ce qui s'est passé?

— Eh bien, j'ai été invitée, avec quelques amis, à un *tama'ara'a*, c'est-à-dire un repas, dans une famille tahitienne très traditionnelle. Alors avant d'entrer, nous avons retiré nos chaussures, comme c'est l'usage à Tahiti, puis on nous a fait asseoir à une grande table couverte de plats traditionnels tahitiens. C'était un vrai festin—y avait des poissons cuits, du poisson cru, des bananes cuites, du poulet, du taro, des œufs de tortue et d'autres choses que je ne reconnaissais pas. Mais la chose la plus curieuse, c'est qu'il y avait seulement assez d'assiettes pour les invités. Nos hôtes et leur famille n'ont pas mangé avec nous. En fait, seuls les parents se sont assis à table avec nous, et ils nous ont regardés manger. Alors nous avons mangé, avec les doigts, car c'est la coutume à Tahiti, et plus on mangeait, plus ils étaient contents. Ils répétaient constamment: *A amu! Tama'a!* Mangez! mangez!

— Ils n'ont pas mangé du tout?

— Pas devant nous. C'était leur façon de montrer leur respect.

Chapitre 10

Première étape

À l'écoute: La routine quotidienne

— Larmé, est-ce que vous pouvez nous parler de la vie de tous les jours dans un village africain?

— Eh bien, dans mon village, au sud du Tchad, on se lève vers cinq ou six heures du matin, on se lave, on s'habille et puis on va aux champs, ou plus exactement les hommes vont aux champs et les femmes préparent à manger. Plus tard, les femmes arrivent aux champs avec le petit déjeuner.

— Quel genre de petit déjeuner?

— C'est ce qu'on appelle «la boule». C'est une sorte de pâte qu'on mange avec de la sauce.

— Après ça, les femmes rentrent au village?

— Ah non! Elles restent aux champs et elles travaillent toute la journée. En fait, elles travaillent plus dur que les hommes, parce qu'après le travail des champs, les hommes se reposent, mais pour les femmes ça continue. Il faut aller chercher du bois pour le feu, préparer à manger, tout ça.

— Et le repas du soir, comment ça se passe?

— Eh bien, on mange vers dix-neuf ou vingt heures. Les hommes mangent ensemble et les femmes mangent ensemble...

— Vous voulez dire que les hommes et les femmes mangent séparément?

— Bien sûr!

— Pourquoi?

— Ben, parce que les hommes ont leurs causeries et les femmes ont leurs causeries, c'est mieux comme ça...

— Et les enfants, avec qui est-ce qu'ils mangent?

— Les petits mangent avec les femmes, mais à partir de l'âge de dix à douze ans, les garçons mangent séparément, et les filles continuent à manger avec les femmes.

— Et quand est-ce qu'on se couche?

— Ça dépend de la lune. Comme y a pas d'électricité, on se couche quand il fait trop noir pour y voir, en général c'est vers vingt-deux heures.

Troisième étape

À l'écoute: La forme

— Madame, nous faisons un sondage sur la popularité de l'exercice physique. Vous avez quelques minutes?

— Bof, pourquoi pas!

— Je vous remercie, madame, c'est bien gentil! Alors, dites-nous, madame, est-ce que vous faites de l'exercice physique?

— De l'exercice physique? Mais bien sûr, tous les jours!

— C'est formidable, ça! Est-ce que vous faites de l'aérobic?

— Oh non! L'aérobic, ça fait mal aux jambes, au dos, aux bras... Ça fait mal partout!

— Vous faites du jogging?

— Oh non! Le jogging, c'est très mauvais pour les genoux, vous savez.

— De la marche?

— Oh non! La marche, ça fait mal aux pieds. Voyez-vous, j'ai les pieds très sensibles.

— Vous faites de la musculation? des abdominaux, peut-être?

— Oh non! Les abdominaux, ça fait mal au ventre et au dos, ça fait mal partout!

— Mais quel genre d'exercice physique faites-vous donc?

— Eh bien, tous les matins à la radio, il y a un petit programme de gymnastique: «Levez! Baissez! Levez! Baissez! Et maintenant, l'autre paupière!... »

Chapitre 11

Première étape

À l'écoute: Le monde du travail

— Allô? Bonjour, madame. Je téléphone au sujet de l'annonce dans le journal.

— Vous êtes infirmière diplômée?

— Oui.

— Quel genre d'expérience est-ce que vous avez?

— Ben, je viens de sortir de l'école d'infirmières, mais j'ai fait un stage de trois mois dans un bloc opératoire à l'hôpital Lariboisière à Paris.

— Et vous cherchez un poste à plein temps ou à mi-temps?

— À plein temps.

— Bon, écoutez, envoyez-nous votre curriculum vitae, et puis vous prendrez rendez-vous pour un entretien. Il faudra aussi remplir une demande d'emploi quand vous viendrez pour votre entretien.

— Si je suis embauchée, quand est-ce que je pourrai commencer?

— Le premier du mois. Je vous passe mon assistante pour prendre rendez-vous, d'accord?

— Merci, madame.

Troisième étape

À l'écoute: Hommes et femmes—l'égalité?

— (*interviewer*) Mesdames et messieurs, j'ai devant moi deux personnalités politiques—Françoise Brasseur, député socialiste, et Philippe Aubry, député républicain. La question que je voudrais leur poser est la suivante: Est-ce qu'on peut parler d'égalité entre les hommes et les femmes dans la France des années 90?

— (*Françoise Brasseur*) Ben, on peut en parler, oui, en théorie!

— (*Philippe Aubry*) C'est plus que de la théorie! Les femmes constituent aujourd'hui 46 pour cent de la population active, elles peuvent entrer dans toutes les professions, euh...

— (*Françoise Brasseur*) Entrer, peut-être, mais monter, non. Le pouvoir économique et politique est encore réservé aux hommes. Qui c'est qui dirige toutes les grandes banques, toutes les grandes entreprises? Des hommes, évidemment! Une femme en position numéro un dans le milieu professionnel, c'est l'exception! Et les salaires... savez-vous qu'en France, à profession égale, les femmes gagnent en moyenne 25 pour cent de moins que les hommes? Vous appelez ça l'égalité? Prenons le monde politique... combien de femmes est-ce qu'il y a au Parlement français? Six pour cent! Six pour cent de représentation féminine! Franchement, vous appelez ça l'égalité?

— (*Philippe Aubry*) Oui, mais dites-moi, depuis combien de temps est-ce que les femmes ont le droit de voter? Depuis cinquante ans. Eh bien, cinquante ans, ce n'est pas beaucoup. Il faut du temps pour changer les institutions. Il faut du temps pour changer les mentalités—des hommes et des femmes, de la société en général. Dans cinquante ans, la situation sera très différente, vous verrez.

Chapitre 12

Première étape

À l'écoute: Ça ne va pas du tout

— Odile, ça va mieux aujourd'hui?

— Non, ça ne va pas du tout.

— Qu'est-ce qui ne va pas?

— J'ai le nez bouché, j'ai mal à la gorge, j'ai mal à la tête...

— Tu as peut-être attrapé un rhume.

— Oui, peut-être, mais je tousse aussi, et j'ai mal partout...

— C'est peut-être la bronchite, ou la grippe.

— Tu crois que j'ai de la fièvre? Touche mon front.

— Voyons... hum, non, ta température me semble normale.

(*Odile éternue très fort—Atchoum!*)

— Tu as entendu?

— Quoi?

— J'ai éternué.

— Ben, c'est assez normal quand on a un rhume. À ta place, je ne m'inquiéterais pas pour ça.

(*Odile tousse*)

— Tu as entendu?

— Quoi?

— Ma toux. Ce n'était pas une toux étrange?

— Non, c'était une toux normale. Ça arrive à tout le monde de tousser. Tu as du sirop?

— Non. Tu crois que j'devrais appeler l'médecin?

— Oui, à ta place, j'appellerais un médecin. Il te prescrirait des médicaments, et surtout tu serais plus tranquille... Et nous, on aurait la paix!

Troisième étape

À l'écoute: Peurs et phobies

— Peur? Voyons... ? qu'est-ce qui me fait peur... ? Parce que je ne suis plus très jeune, je dois dire que c'est la maladie qui me fait peur—le cancer, ou les attaques cérébrales. J'ai peur de perdre mes facultés, de devenir un fardeau pour les autres, voilà.

— Ce qui me fait peur? Ben, je finis mes études, là, et j'ai peur de ne pas pouvoir trouver de travail. Y a tellement de chômage en France, surtout chez les jeunes. Vous connaissez les statistiques? Des chômeurs, y en a 10 pour cent pour l'ensemble de la population active, mais 20 pour cent chez les jeunes. Vous imaginez un peu? Vingt pour cent des jeunes de moins de 25 ans qui cherchent un emploi! Alors le chômage, bien sûr que j'en ai peur...

— Peur? Moi? Non... Y a rien dont j'aie vraiment peur, mais j'ai un copain, par contre, qui a peur de tout. Il a peur du noir. Il a peur des araignées, des chiens et j'sais pas quoi encore. Il a peur des espaces clos...

— Il est claustrophobe?

— Tout à fait. Il peut pas supporter les portes fermées, les pièces dont les fenêtres ne s'ouvrent pas, les avions, tout ça.

— Moi, j'ai peur des ascenseurs.

— Des ascenseurs? Pourquoi?

— Ben parce que... parce que quand j'avais cinq ans, j'étais avec ma maman et on était dans un grand bâtiment avec plein d'étages, et j'suis rentrée dans l'ascenseur et les portes se sont fermées très vite, et l'ascenseur il est parti, sans ma maman. J'étais toute seule dans l'ascenseur et je savais pas quoi faire...

— Mais t'as retrouvé ta maman?

— Oui, mais j'ai eu peur, et j'ai pleuré, et ma maman elle a pleuré. J'aime pas les ascenseurs.

Chapitre complémentaire

À l'écoute: L'appel de l'abbé Pierre

(*L'abbé Pierre*) Mes amis, réveillons-nous! Assez d'indifférence. C'est la guerre. La guerre de défense contre la misère qui attaque l'univers total des hommes. En Europe—le savez-vous?—quarante millions de personnes vivent en dessous du seuil de la pauvreté. Dans les banlieues, dans les cités de nos grandes villes, des générations de jeunes sont laissées à l'abandon, sans espoir de logement, sans projet, sans avenir. Est-ce qu'il faut attendre des catastrophes bien visibles, bien filmées, pour enfin se mobiliser? Ce cri s'adresse à chacun d'entre nous et en premier à vous, mes compagnons et amis, à vous tous qui écoutez, et surtout, à vous les plus jeunes. Ensemble, nous avons à détruire la misère qui agresse la planète entière. Elle surgit de partout. À chacun de nous, à nous tous ensemble—audacieux, sans merci, sans repos—de la vaincre. Beaucoup de municipalités, et plus que toutes, celles de certaines grandes villes, trahissent, oui, trahissent, en refusant leurs gîtes aux plus faibles. La France ne doit plus laisser de logis vides ni de bureaux vides, ni surtout laisser détruire des lieux habitables sans immédiate nécessité. Commander cela est abominable et peut être criminel. La France doit bâtir immédiatement et pour tous. Elle en a les moyens: l'argent, la technique, la main-d'œuvre, le sol. Vous, les élus, il est temps d'agir, pour que tout le monde ait un logement. Je vous l'ai déjà tant demandé, par parole et par écrit, et en actes. Vous, tous les citoyens, écrivez à votre maire, lancez des pétitions, déposez-les dans vos mairies avant le 15 mars pour qu'elles précèdent nos prochaines initiatives communes.*

---

* Reprinted by permission of Mr. Claude Duverlie.

Mais oui!

CHANTAL P. THOMPSON
Brigham Young University

ELAINE M. PHILLIPS
Southwest Educational Development Laboratory

HOUGHTON MIFFLIN COMPANY
Boston   New York

Director, Modern Language Programs: Kristina E. Baer
Development Manager: Beth Kramer
Senior Development Editor: Cécile Strugnell
Senior Project Editor: Rosemary R. Jaffe
Editorial Assistant: Jane Lee
Senior Production/Design Coordinator: Jennifer Waddell
Senior Designer: Henry Rachlin
Senior Manufacturing Coordinator: Priscilla Bailey
Associate Marketing Manager: Tina Crowley Desprez

Cover design by Diana Coe/ko Studio

Credits for texts, illustrations, and photographs are found following the index at the back of the book.

Printed in the U.S.A.

Student Text ISBN: 0-395-95600-5

Instructor's Annotated Edition ISBN: 0-395-95601-3

Library of Congress Catalog Card Number: 99-71894

23456789-VH-03 02 01 00

To the Student

Welcome to the second edition of **Mais oui!,** a complete program for beginning college French. What makes **Mais oui!** different and unique? First and foremost, its approach to learning. Rather than perpetuating lower-order thinking through rote memorization and repetition, **Mais oui!**—which means "But of course! It's logical! I understand"—will have you use your higher-order thinking skills and participate actively in the process of discovering the French language and the French-speaking world.

- **Real-world input.** Carefully selected real-world listening and reading materials are used as entry into the language. The text comes with a sixty-minute audio CD or cassette containing the listening segments as well as the pronunciation activities for each chapter. The readings in the text are actual magazine articles or literary passages. The **Mais oui!** Video, with accompanying activities in the Video Manual, and the CD-ROM provide additional exposure to authentic materials. The Web Activities expand opportunities for learning about francophone cultures. Through a hierarchy of tasks, you will develop strategies that will enable you to process this input successfully. A natural stage will thus be set for the introduction of vocabulary, structures, cultural concepts, and the practice of language functions. Through this wealth of real-world input, you will not only learn to understand "real" French, but you will embark on a journey of discovery.

- **Critical thinking.** The journey turns the traveler into a reflective observer who uses the input to discover the French way of saying things. Through a process of *Observez* and *Déduisez,* then *Vérifiez,* you will be led to figure out on your own how the language works. You will observe, infer, verify and acquire the language in a stimulating environment conducive to long-term retention. You will also be led to understand new social and cultural realities, for a new way of saying things is often a new way of seeing things. Take the word *bread* for example. When you think of bread, what images come to your mind? A loaf of evenly-sliced bread wrapped in plastic? Other images? To the French, the word *pain* is likely to evoke the taste and smell of a warm baguette or the heavier texture of a *pain de campagne (country bread).* Language learning is not simply a matter of learning different words, but one of acquiring a new set of concepts associated with the words—a chance to expand one's horizons, inquisitively.

- **Realistic expectations.** The discovery process may sound challenging, but fortunately, the journey is a guided tour. The tasks are kept simple, and one small step at a time, you will be guided from receptive to productive activities. Chances to create with the language abound, and functions (or language tasks) are recycled from chapter to chapter in ever-expanding contexts. By the end of the **Mais oui!** program, you can reasonably expect to be able to express personal meaning about a variety of simple topics, to ask and answer questions, and to deal with most common everyday situations in French.

Organization of *Mais oui!*

Mais oui! contains a brief preliminary chapter, twelve regular chapters, and a complementary chapter designed to provide a glimpse of higher functions. Organized around a cultural theme, each regular chapter is divided into five sections. The first three *étapes* begin with an authentic listening or reading selection that previews vocabulary, grammar and cultural concepts; then a section using examples from this input expands on vocabulary, structures and communicative strategies, with ample opportunities for communicative practice. In the middle of the chapter, *Culture et réflexion* explores the cultural theme(s) of the chapter, inviting students to reflect on cultural differences and similarities. The last section, *Intégration,* opens with a literary reading and concludes with a writing section; the activities synthesize the language functions of the chapter.

Here is an overview of the chapter sections and other salient features of **Mais oui!**

Chapter Opener   Each chapter opens with a listing of the chapter's objectives and a theme-setting photograph accompanied by preview questions.

À l'écoute   The first and the third *étapes* start with a listening comprehension section. Pre-listening tasks in *Avant d'écouter* set the scene for the listening passage, introduce new vocabulary as needed, and activate your expectations of what you will hear. A series of carefully sequenced, manageable listening tasks in *Écoutons* then guides you step-by-step as you listen to the segment on the audio CD or cassette, moving from global understanding to specific details. The real-world listening passages include a variety of materials such as public announcements and conversations between natives of all ages from various parts of the francophone world.

Prononciation   These sections appear in chapters 1–8 and present the basic elements of the French sound system and intonation patterns. Sample words or sentences are taken from the preceding listening input section, providing continuity and a familiar context for your work. In the *Écoutez* section, you will be led to discover for yourself the pronunciation rules. In *Essayez!,* you will practice the sounds and other aspects of French pronunciation.

Lecture   The second *étape* begins with a reading input section that features a cultural or journalistic text taken from publications from around the French-speaking world. Pre-reading tasks in the *Avant de lire* section activate your expectations of the text and background knowledge of the topic. The *En général* tasks train you to realize that if you start with a global picture of the text, it is much easier to make sense of the details. The *En détail* activities engage you in a closer examination of the text. Concluding *Et vous?* activities relate the reading's content to your own experiences.

The *Structures, Vocabulaire,* and *Stratégies de communication* sections expand on your insights and understanding of the vocabulary and structures introduced in the input and present related communicative strategies.

Structures   These sections take a unique three-step, problem-solving approach to the presentation of grammar. The *Observez et déduisez* section features examples of new structures from the preceding listening or reading input followed by questions and tasks that lead you to examine and infer from the examples the forms and uses of the structures. In the *Vérifiez* section, you'll check your conclusions by comparing them with numerous examples and studying clear, concise grammar explanations supported by charts.

Vocabulaire   These sections are used to introduce vocabulary important to the chapter theme—for example, food, clothing, or parts of the body. Photos, drawings, and creative mini-activities based on previously taught language and cognates make you an active participant in inferring the meanings of new words and phrases.

Stratégie de communication   This section appears once per chapter and presents high-frequency expressions used in daily communication. Mini-dialogues demonstrate the expressions' uses in realistic contexts, and background information in English explains their cultural usage.

Activités   Following each *Structure, Vocabulaire,* and *Stratégie de communication* section, these activities provide abundant opportunities for the development of speaking skills. The activities progress from comprehension checks to guided practice to open-ended, communicative work in which you reuse previously learned language as you practice and apply the new grammar, vocabulary, and strategies. All activities are set in contexts related to the theme of the *étape,* and they emphasize personalized interactions with classmates.

Notes culturelles   These notes occur where pertinent to provide important, interesting information about the French-speaking world and the everyday lives and behaviors of French-speaking people as the information relates to the materials being studied.

Culture et réflexion   Through photos and brief descriptions, this feature, placed in the middle of the chapter before the third *étape,* presents cultural information about various aspects of the francophone world and asks you to reflect and draw your own conclusions on cultural differences and similarities. For example, what does the presence or absence of physical contact during greetings and leave-takings reveal about a culture? Comparing attitudes towards privacy, education, dating, vacations, social roles and other issues can be quite revealing!

Littérature   The *Intégration* section of the chapter opens with a literary selection illustrating various genres—excerpts from novels, short stories, poems and scenes from plays—from diverse French-speaking countries—France, Canada, Cameroon, Senegal, Morocco and Martinique. Why literature? Because literature has a way of talking to the imagination and of enabling learners to overcome many linguistic obstacles. Carefully chosen and made accessible through manageable, enjoyable tasks, literary texts become the culminating point of the chapter, synthesizing the chapter's content and bringing closure to the theme in a motivating, innovative fashion.

Par écrit   This second part of *Intégration* is designed to help develop your writing skills in French through a process-oriented approach. It provides pre-writing support and opportunities to use new vocabulary, structures, and communicative strategies in a variety of ways.
- The *Avant d'écrire* section presents two writing strategies such as brainstorming, outlining, adding variety to sentences, or ordering a narrative. Each strategy is immediately reinforced in an *Application* exercise set off with a pen icon.
- The *Écrivez* section provides a wide range of writing tasks—interviews, letters, messages, photo captions, journal entries, and brief paragraphs—related to the chapter theme.

Vocabulaire actif   One of the challenges of discovering the language through real-world input is keeping track of active vocabulary. Convenient *Vocabulaire actif* boxes are placed throughout the chapter to help you take note of the new vocabulary as it is introduced in context. At the end of the chapter, all new active vocabulary, as well as expressions needed to understand the direction lines of activities, are listed and translated.

Reference Materials   The following materials provide students with useful reference tools throughout the course:
- *Maps*   On the front and back inside covers of the textbook, five vivid full-color maps show France, French territories around the world, and countries where French is spoken in Europe, Africa, the Americas, and the Caribbean.

- *Appendix*   The appendix contains conjugation charts of regular and irregular verbs.
- *End vocabularies*   French-English and English-French end vocabularies follow the conjugation charts. The French-English end vocabulary lists all active words and identifies the number of the chapter in which the word or phrase first appears. It also includes the classroom expressions vocabulary featured in the end-of-chapter *Vocabulaire actif* sections and all vocabulary included in the *À l'écoute, Lecture,* and *Littérature* input.

Supplementary Materials for the Student

The Student Audio CD/Cassette   A free copy of the sixty-minute audio CD or cassette containing the textbook's *À l'écoute* listening passages, the *Écoutez* pronunciation samples, and the items of the *Essayez!* exercises is packaged with each copy of the student's text. This recording is designed to maximize your exposure to the speech of native speakers from a variety of regions. It also allows you to listen to the recorded passages as often as you wish and to improve your pronunciation.

The Workbook/Laboratory Manual/Video Manual   The *Workbook* section of this manual provides structured, written practice of the materials introduced in the corresponding chapters and additional reading comprehension based on cultural and journalistic topics. Each chapter of the *Laboratory Manual,* designed for use with the audio program, contains pronunciation practice and a variety of listening comprehension tasks, all focused on the language presented in the chapter. The *Video Manual* section guides you through the thirteen modules of the **Mais oui!** Video with activities structured to help you understand authentic speech one step at a time. An *Answer Key* for *Workbook, Laboratory Manual,* and *Video Activities* is provided for self-correction.

The Audio Program   The complete Audio Program that accompanies the *Laboratory Manual* section of the **Mais oui!** Workbook/Laboratory Manual/Video Manual is available for student purchase (in the form of audio CDs or cassettes). It includes the *À l'écoute* listening passages, the pronunciation exercises, and the recorded materials for the listening comprehension activities and dictations.

The *Mais oui!* CD-ROM   This interactive CD-ROM features unrehearsed interviews with native speakers focused on the topics of the corresponding textbook chapters. For each interview, two or four activities provide you with opportunities to interact further with the oral text and practice all four skills. Listening comprehension is checked through multiple-choice questions and a click-and-drag activity. An interactive speaking task asks you to answer the questions of the native speaker, record your voice, and listen to your "conversation." A writing task focuses on the same topic and provides cues and helpful hints related to vocabulary and structures in the chapter. You can print out this writing assignment and hand it in to your instructor.

The *Mais oui!* Web Site   Cues to Web Activities are included on the *Culture et réflexion* page. To access the **Mais oui!** Web Site, select *French* at the Houghton Mifflin College Division home page, http://www.hmco.com/college/. Here, under Web Activities, you will find several links to web sites and related activities that will help you explore further the topics of the *Culture et réflexion* section. After completing the activities, you will share your findings and discuss them with fellow students in class.

The *Mais oui!* Video   The complete **Mais oui!** Video is available for student purchase at an attractive, discounted price.

The *Mais oui!* Computer Study Modules 2.0   Available in Macintosh®, and Windows® versions, this software provides computer-aided practice correlated to the chapters of the textbook.

A Final Word

We hope that instructors and students alike will find their experience with **Mais oui!** enjoyable, rewarding, and motivating and that the meaning of *Mais oui!*—"But of course! It's logical! I understand!"—will become the watchword of students' success.

Acknowledgments

A book is the work of many people: its authors, yes, but also those who have accepted its concept, bettered its manner of expression, and nurtured its development. For this we thank Kristina Baer, Beth Kramer, Cécile Strugnell, Rosemary Jaffe, and the whole team at Houghton Mifflin. They have shared our vision, supported our efforts, and provided invaluable guidance.

We also wish to thank the following colleagues for the many useful suggestions they offered in their reviews of **Mais oui!** during various stages of development:

Laura Anderson, University of Wisconsin, Platteville
Patricia Applevich, University of Waterloo
Karen S. Begley, Asbury College
Michelle Chilcoat, Colby College
Robert R. Daniel, Saint Joseph's University
Robert G. Erickson, Brigham Young University
Scarlett Gani, Los Angeles Pierce College
Dr. Lana E. Hamon, Drew University
Mary Jane Highfield, Cornell University
Catherine A. Jolivet, George Washington University
Jacqueline Konan, Columbus State University
Anna Krauth, College of Charleston
Dr. Michèle K. Langford, Pepperdine University
Véronique Maisier, Southern Illinois University
Patricia Kyle Mosele, Michigan State University
Renée Norrell, Birmingham-Southern College
Dr. Genevieve M. Peden, Eastern Michigan University
Dr. Norman R. Savoie, Utah State University
Jacqueline Simons, University of California, Santa Barbara
Dana Strand, Carleton College
Colette Theallier, Trident Technical College
Bonnie L. Youngs, Carnegie Mellon University

Finally, we want to express our appreciation to our families (Bill Thompson, Nick, Erica, and Natalie; Bob Phillips and Jonathan), whose patience, confidence, and love sustain us. We dedicate this book to them.

Chantal P. Thompson
Elaine M. Phillips

Scope and Sequence

Langue

Langue

Langue

Bonjour!

What do you think
these people are
saying to one
another?

This chapter will enable you to
- **understand an announcement and a short conversation at an airport**
- **understand basic classroom terms**

- **greet people formally and informally**
- **introduce people**
- **spell in French**
- **identify people and things**

1

À l'écoute: Attention!

PRELIMINARY ACTIVITY: Go around the class, greeting students (with handshake if desired) and asking their names. «Bonjour! Je m'appelle _____ . Et vous, comment vous appelez-vous? Classe, comment s'appelle-t-il? Comment s'appelle-t-elle?» In addition to exposing students to French right off, this activity helps create a bond among class members.

You are about to listen to an audio segment on the student audio CD that is shrink-wrapped with your text. You will hear an announcement made over the public address system at a French airport. Prepare yourself by doing the activity that follows.

Avant d'écouter

1   Brainstorm with the class; list answers on the board in one or two columns.

First name of the person	Who is paging the person
Last name of the person	Reason for paging
?	?

Écoutons

2   Play the **À l'écoute** segment from the student audio CD as often as necessary for students to answer the questions.

3   Model the words in the list, then have students repeat them so they can identify them in the listening passage. Have students work in pairs, then have them report on their conclusions and explain their choice of answer. Lead them to understand that if they use logic, background knowledge, and cognates, French is not so hard!

1 Imagine that you are at a French airport, and someone is being paged. What do you expect to hear in this announcement?

Attention!   Before you listen to the announcement, read the numbered tasks outlined in the **Écoutons** section below. You will probably not understand everything you hear, but these tasks will guide you step by step. For each task, focus only on what you are asked to do. As you learn various strategies for listening, authentic speech will become increasingly easier for you to understand.

2 Listen a first time and check the information you had anticipated in **Avant d'écouter** that is actually mentioned in the announcement.

3 Listen again. In the following list, circle the words used in the announcement, and then guess their meaning.

⟨attention⟩	merci	⟨s'il vous plaît⟩
Monsieur	⟨Madame⟩	Mademoiselle
⟨bureau⟩	⟨compagnie⟩	société
⟨Air France⟩	Airbus	Air Inter

L'aéroport international de Nice.

4 Listen a final time to infer the meaning of **est priée de se présenter** from the following choices.

    a. is asked to call
    (b.) is asked to come in person
    c. is asked to give a present

À l'écoute: Votre nom?

Avant d'écouter

1 The woman being paged comes to the airline counter. What do you expect will be included in the conversation?

Écoutons

1 Brainstorm with the class. List answers on the board, along the following lines.

  greetings identifying oneself

  thanking leave-taking

  ?   ?

Audio CD

3 Model the words first and have students repeat them. With a class of true beginners, have students do this activity in pairs.

5 ANSWER: Duchesnay

6 As students identify the pause filler, write **euh...** on the board. From now on, as students hesitate in class, make sure they use **euh...**

2 Listen a first time and check the information you had anticipated in **Avant d'écouter.** What is actually included in the conversation?

3 Listen again. Match the French expressions on the left with the categories on the right.

  1. je suis   a. greetings
  2. au revoir b. identifying oneself
  3. bonjour   c. thanking
  4. merci   d. leave-taking

4 Now that you have heard the conversation twice, indicate why the woman is being paged.

  (a.) There was a message for her.
  b. There was a problem with her ticket.
  c. She had lost her passport.

5 Listen a final time, paying close attention to the woman's name. How is it spelled? Unscramble the following letters to spell her name.

      U E A H S D C Y N

6 In English, we use *um* as a pause filler in conversation. Having heard this conversation three times, can you identify the pause filler that French speakers use to mark hesitation?

Notes culturelles

«Bonjour, madame.»   In formal situations, French people generally add **monsieur, madame,** or **mademoiselle** (abbreviated **M., Mme,** and **Mlle** respectively) to **bonjour, au revoir,** and **merci.** Note that the last name is not used.

Salutations et gestes.   When greeting or saying good-bye to a colleague or an acquaintance, French people always shake hands. Close friends and family members exchange kisses on the cheeks **(des bises)**—two, three, or even four kisses, depending on regional customs.

> **Au revoir?**   If you expect to see the person again in the near future, you may say **À bientôt!** *(See you soon!)* instead of **au revoir**. To say good-bye, French Canadians may say **bonjour** or **salut** rather than **au revoir**.
>
> **Merci et la politesse.**   **Je vous en prie** is a formal way to say *you're welcome*. **De rien** or **il n'y a pas de quoi** are less formal. French Canadians use the expression **Bienvenue!** *(Welcome!)*

STRATÉGIE DE COMMUNICATION
Greetings, introductions, and basic courtesy

Cue to Video Module 1 (00:01:46) for examples of greetings and introductions, and also to street interviews (00:03:49) where people give their names.

All vocabulary introduced in **Stratégie de communication** is active vocabulary.

VOCABULAIRE ACTIF
à bientôt
au revoir
bonjour
de rien
il n'y a pas de quoi
je suis
je vous en prie
madame
mademoiselle
merci
monsieur
s'il vous plaît

Greetings and introductions in French, as in English, usually involve a great deal of social ritual. Study the examples that follow; then answer the following questions.

- In formal situations, do French speakers use **tu** or **vous?**
- What expressions are used to do the following?

  Greet a new student
  Give your name and find out his
  Introduce him to a classmate
  Respond to an elderly neighbor's greeting
  Ask how she is doing
  Say you're doing fine

- What are the French equivalents for the following expressions?

name	first name	last name
My name is . . .	Good evening.	I'm fine.
Not too good.	And you? *(formal)*	And you? *(informal)*

— Bonjour, madame. Comment allez-vous?
— Je vais bien, merci. Et vous?
— Très bien, merci.

— Bonsoir, monsieur. Vous allez bien?
— Oh, comme ci comme ça... les rhumatismes, vous savez...

— Salut! Ça va?
— Oui, et toi?
— Ça va!

— Simone, je vous présente
   Monsieur LeBlanc. Monsieur
   LeBlanc, Madame Bichon.
— Enchanté, madame.
— Enchantée.

Point out that if a woman says it,
enchantée takes an **-e** to mark feminine agreement. Pronunciation is the
same.

— Tiens, Claire, je te présente
   Naima.
— Bonjour.

— Bonjour, monsieur. Comment
   vous appelez-vous?
— Je m'appelle Cacharel.
— Pardon? Votre nom?
— Cacharel.
— Votre prénom?
— Alain.

— Comment tu t'appelles?
— Mohammed.
— Et ton nom de famille?
— Belhaj. Mohammed Belhaj.

Greetings and introductions

To greet someone		To respond
formel	Bonjour, madame.	Bonjour, monsieur.
familier	Salut, Jean.	Bonsoir, Marie.

To ask how someone's doing		To respond
formel	Comment allez-vous?	Je vais bien, merci. Et vous?
	Vous allez bien?	Très bien, merci. Et vous?
		Comme ci comme ça.
familier	Comment vas-tu?	Ça va bien, et toi?
	Comment ça va?	Oh, pas mal.
		Comme ci comme ça. Et toi?

To introduce someone		To respond
formel	Je vous présente...	Enchanté(e).
		Bonjour, monsieur (madame).
familier	Je te présente...	Bonjour.

To ask someone's name		To respond
formel	Comment vous appelez-vous?	Je m'appelle...
	Votre nom? / Votre prénom?	Cacharel. / Alain.
familier	Comment tu t'appelles?	Je m'appelle...
	Ton nom? / Ton nom de famille?	Mohammed. / Belhaj.

ACTIVITÉS

A. Options.   Choose the most appropriate response to the following.

1. Comment vous appelez-vous?

   _____ Très bien, merci.   _____ Je m'appelle Caroline.

2. Je vous présente Monsieur Carel.

   _____ Il n'y a pas de quoi.   _____ Enchanté.

3. Comment allez-vous?

   _____ Ça va bien.   _____ Je vais bien, merci.

4. Ton prénom?

   _____ Jacques.   _____ Chirac.

5. Bonjour, mademoiselle.

   _____ Bonjour, monsieur.   _____ Salut.

6. Merci, monsieur.

   _____ Comme ci comme ça.   _____ Je vous en prie.

7. Au revoir, Caroline.

   _____ À bientôt!   _____ De rien.

Note culturelle

Tu ou vous?   The decision to use **tu** or **vous** is often a delicate one, even for native speakers of French. In general, the pronoun **tu** is used in familiar contexts (with family, friends, children, and students your own age). Use **vous** with people you address by their last name, new acquaintances, people with whom you maintain a professional distance, or people who are older than you. French Canadians use **tu** more readily than the French, as do younger people throughout the francophone world. However, if you have any doubt, use **vous!**

B. Students should do **B** in pairs. First they write the missing expressions, then they practice the exchange. Finally, have various pairs act out the dialogues.

B. Complétez.   Now complete the following dialogues with the appropriate expressions.

1. — <u>Bonsoir</u>   , monsieur.

    — <u>Bonsoir</u>   , madame,

      <u>comment allez-vous</u> ?

    — <u>Très bien merci</u>   !

2. — <u>Comment tu t'appelles</u> ?

    —Samuel.

    — <u>Et ton nom de famille</u>   ?

    —Beynet.

3. — <u>Comment vous appelez-vous</u> ?

    — <u>Je m'appelle</u>   Letort.

    — <u>Votre prénom</u>   ?

    — Suzanne. Suzanne Letort.

4. — Salut, Michelle,

      <u>ça va</u>   ?

    — Oui, <u>et toi</u>   ?

    — <u>Comme ci comme ça</u>   , je suis

      fatiguée...

5. — Paul, *je te présente* _____ Jean-
   Michel. Jean-Michel, Paul.

   __ *Bonjour* _____ .

   __ *Bonjour/Salut* _____ .

6. — Charles, *je vous présente* _____
   Madame Beynet. Madame
   Beynet, Monsieur Duval.

   __ *Enchanté* _____ , madame.

   __ *Enchantée* _____ , monsieur.

STRATÉGIE DE COMMUNICATION
Spelling in French

Cue to Video Module 1, street interviews (00:04:32), where people say their names and spell them.

When you meet new people, you may need to spell your name or ask them to spell their names (**Comment ça s'écrit?**). Although French and English use the same alphabet, the sounds corresponding to many of the letters are different.

A	B	C	D	E	F	G	H	I	J	K	L	M
[a]	[be]	[se]	[de]	[ə]	[ɛf]	[ʒe]	[aʃ]	[i]	[ʒi]	[ka]	[ɛl]	[ɛm]
N	O	P	Q	R	S	T	U	V	W	X	Y	Z
[ɛn]	[o]	[pe]	[ky]	[ɛr]	[ɛs]	[te]	[y]	[ve]	[dublə ve]	[iks]	[i grɛk]	[zɛd]

C. Repeat the activity several times using both first and last names of students in the class. FOLLOW-UP: Have students spell their name for a partner who writes it down. Then have students check that the spelling is correct.

D. FOLLOW-UP: Introduce these useful expressions: un autre mot, deux m (mm), deux l (ll), deux p (pp), point d'interrogation. Have students write the following expressions as you spell them out. CUES: 1. compagnie 2. prénom 3. bureau 4. monsieur 5. euh 6. salut 7. pardon 8. je vous en prie 9. Comment allez-vous? 10. Tu t'appelles?

E. If time is a problem, give students a time limit and see who can meet the most people and get the most names. FOLLOW-UP: Make sure you allow time for students to report on their lists.

accent aigu   André
accent grave   Irène
accent circonflexe   Benoît
c cédille   François
tréma   Joëlle
trait d'union   Marie-France, Jean-Paul
apostrophe   M'hammed

Teach the students the pronunciation of the letters.

ACTIVITÉS

C. C'est qui? Stand with your classmates and listen carefully as your teacher spells a name—either a first name or a last name. Sit down when you are sure s/he is *not* spelling *your* name.

D. Comment ça s'écrit? You are making tour reservations for a group of tourists. Spell out their names to make sure there are no mistakes!

1. Jean-Pierre Segond   3. Mariama Bâ   5. Hélène Leroux
2. Yambo Hazoumé   4. Françoise Gracq   6. Aïcha Al'Kassem

E. Faisons connaissance. Circulate in the class, exchanging greetings and asking people's first and last names and how they spell their names. Arrange the names alphabetically. Does your list match the teacher's roll?

CULTURE ET RÉFLEXION

Internet

■ **Les salutations et les gestes.** Greetings and leave-takings in France and many francophone countries must include physical contact. As mentioned in the **Note culturelle** on pages 3–4, close friends and family members exchange **des bises** (kisses on the cheeks). Colleagues and acquaintances shake hands, and if one's hands are dirty or holding other things, a finger, wrist, elbow, or arm is offered to shake instead. Some type of physical salutation must be offered to each individual present in order to be polite; when leaving a group of ten or twelve people, for example, each person in the group would receive a handshake or a kiss, even if doing so is time consuming! A bank director in Paris reports that he clocks 20 minutes of handshaking per day for most of his personnel.[1] You shake hello, and you shake good-bye, adding the first name of the person if you are on first-name terms (**«Bonjour, Martine,» «Au revoir, Robert»**) or adding **madame** or **monsieur** with formal acquaintances or strangers.

Do you usually shake hands when you meet someone for the first time? When you meet a friend or acquaintance in a public place? Do you exchange hugs or kisses when you greet or leave family members in the morning or at night? In what situations do such greetings make you feel uncomfortable? What does the presence or the absence of physical contact

Les bises rituelles. Bonjour, Carine!

during greetings and leave-takings reveal about a culture?

■ **Le sourire.** Nothing separates Americans and French people more than their smile codes.[2] Americans smile to strangers; French people don't. This may explain why tourists sometimes label the French as rude and arrogant. True, the French don't smile without a reason, and stumbling into someone's stare is not one of them. Smiles usually come if you bump into each other by mistake, or if you both witness an event worth smiling at, but when you walk down the street or sit in the subway **(le métro),** don't take the French **mine d'enterrement** (funeral expression) personally! How do you feel

La poignée de mains—une obligation culturelle.

about smiling to strangers? Is it hypocritical? Does it banalize the smile?

---

[1]Polly Platt, *French or Foe* (London: Culture Crossings, 1998), p. 34.   [2]Ibid, p. 24.

À l'écoute: La salle de classe

You will watch and listen as your teacher points out and names items around the classroom. But first prepare yourself by reading these explanations.

Avant d'écouter

In French, nouns are either feminine or masculine. **Accent,** for example, is masculine—**un accent; apostrophe** is feminine—**une apostrophe.** The article that accompanies the noun indicates its gender; **un** is used with masculine nouns, **une** with feminine nouns.

Écoutons

The listening input for this **À l'écoute** is not on the student audio CD. Provide the listening material for the students by going around the room, pointing out items in random order: Qu'est-ce que c'est? C'est une porte, etc. See the list on p. 10. Add other items as you see fit. The first time around, students just listen with their books closed.

Name and point out the classroom items a second time. Have students repeat the answers, still with their books closed.

Now ask students to open their books and identify the items in the picture. They should write the number of each item next to its name in the list below the picture.

1 First, simply watch and listen to your teacher. What are the French names for some familiar classroom items? Which article goes with each name?

2 Listen again, and repeat each word with its article.

3 Now look at the following picture and words, and match the number of each item with its name.

VOCABULAIRE ACTIF
La salle de classe
   un livre..., etc.

9	un livre	17	une serviette	18	un professeur
1	un cahier	4	un tableau	16	un sac à dos
8	une feuille de papier	5	un morceau de craie	19	une carte
11	un crayon	13	une porte	23	une cassette
10	un stylo	15	une fenêtre	24	un CD
12	une gomme	14	un mur	22	un classeur
2	un bureau	6	un étudiant	20	une horloge
3	une chaise	7	une étudiante	21	une table

STRUCTURES: Identifying people and things (I)

*Les expressions **Qu'est-ce que c'est? Qui est-ce?** • **C'est / Ce sont** • Le genre et le nombre • Les articles indéfinis*

Observez et déduisez

— Qu'est-ce que c'est?

— Qui est-ce?

VOCABULAIRE ACTIF
c'est / ce sont
des
Qu'est-ce que c'est?
Qui est-ce?
un / une

— C'est un bureau.

— C'est un professeur.

— Ce sont des chaises.

— Ce sont des étudiants.

Always cover the **Vérifiez** section before answering the questions in **Observez et déduisez.**

- ■ Which question refers to people? Which question refers to things?
- ■ What expression is used to identify one person or thing? What expression is used to identify more than one person or thing?
- ■ What is the plural form of **un?** of **une?** How is a noun made plural?

Vérifiez *Les expressions **Qu'est-ce que c'est? Qui est-ce?***

OPTIONAL DRILL: Singulier? Pluriel? Give students the following cues while you point to either one or two of the items. For example, you say **C'est un livre?** and point to one book. Students say: **Oui, c'est un livre.** If you point to two books, they say **Non, ce sont des livres.**
CUES: 1. une feuille de papier 2. des crayons 3. un stylo 4. des chaises 5. un tableau 6. une porte 7. des étudiants

- ■ Use **qui est-ce?** to ask about a person. Use **qu'est-ce que c'est?** to ask about a thing.   Give students a picture of either a person or an object, then have each one ask you the appropriate question: **Qu'est-ce que c'est?** or **Qui est-ce?**

*L'expression **C'est / Ce sont***

- ■ Use **c'est un (une)** to identify one person or thing. Use **ce sont des** to identify more than one person or thing.

Le genre et le nombre

- ■ In French, nouns usually occur with articles that indicate number (singular or plural) and gender (masculine or feminine). Most nouns form their plural

OPTIONAL DRILL: Point to various classroom items as you say their names, and ask students to identify gender by adding the correct article: livre? → un livre.

OPTIONAL DRILL: Read the cues, and have students indicate number by choosing the correct expression: **C'est un(e)...** or **Ce sont des...** For plural, either point to two of the items or hold up two fingers. Cassettes? → Ce sont des cassettes.   CUES: classeur, étudiantes, étudiants, horloge, gomme, feuilles de papier, professeur, cahier

by adding an **-s**, but since the plural **-s** never changes the pronunciation of a word, you must listen carefully to the article to determine number.

■ As you saw in **À l'écoute,** all nouns—even inanimate objects—have gender. Since gender distinction cannot always be determined logically, it is best to associate each noun you learn with an appropriate article: **une porte** rather than just **porte.**

Les articles indéfinis

■ The indefinite articles **un** and **une** correspond to *a/an* in English and are used with nouns identifying things that can be counted. **Un** is used with masculine singular nouns, and **une** with feminine singular nouns.

    un classeur   **une** gomme

■ **Des** *(some, any)* is the indefinite article for all plural nouns, masculine *and* feminine. In French, the article *must* be expressed.

    Ce sont **des** stylos et **des** crayons.   *These are (some) pens and pencils.*

ACTIVITÉS

F. Chassez l'intrus.   Find the word in each line that does not belong with the others.

1. un stylo, un crayon, un morceau de craie, un cahier
2. un mur, un sac à dos, une porte, une fenêtre
3. une serviette, un étudiant, un professeur, une étudiante
4. un livre, une gomme, un classeur, une feuille de papier

G. This may be used as a pair, small-group, or whole-class activity. Encourage students to use all vocabulary items, mixing people and objects.

G. Identifiez.   Point to an object or person in the room and ask a classmate what or who it is. Respond when someone asks you a question.

  ➡ — Qu'est-ce que c'est?   — Qui est-ce?
     — C'est une fenêtre.   — C'est Marie.

H. Singulier? Pluriel?   Change the following expressions to the singular or the plural.

  ➡ C'est un professeur.   *Ce sont des professeurs.*
    Ce sont des étudiantes.   *C'est une étudiante.*

1. C'est une gomme.
2. C'est un sac à dos.
3. Ce sont des CD.
4. Ce sont des serviettes.
5. C'est un mur.
6. Ce sont des cartes.
7. C'est une fenêtre.
8. Ce sont des horloges.

VOCABULAIRE
Expressions pour la classe

■ Study the following expressions and divide them into two categories: those you would most likely hear the teacher say and those you would most likely hear a student say.

Ouvrez vos livres.	*Open your books.*
Fermez vos livres.	*Close your books.*
Prenez une feuille de papier.	*Take out a sheet of paper.*
Écrivez (la phrase, le mot).	*Write (the sentence, the word).*
Lisez (les instructions, le chapitre).	*Read (the instructions, the chapter).*
Écoutez (le professeur, la cassette, la réponse).	*Listen (to the teacher, the cassette, the answer).*
Comment?	*What?*
Répétez, s'il vous plaît.	*Please repeat.*
Vous comprenez?	*Do you understand?*
(Oui) Je comprends.	*(Yes) I understand.*
(Non) Je ne comprends pas.	*(No) I don't understand.*
Comment dit-on ... en français?	*How do you say . . . in French?*
Je ne sais pas.	*I don't know.*
Que veut dire... ?	*What does . . . mean?*
Comment ça s'écrit?	*How is that spelled?*

Les nombres

0	zéro	6	six
1	un(e)	7	sept
2	deux	8	huit
3	trois	9	neuf
4	quatre	10	dix
5	cinq		

ACTIVITÉS

I. Options.   Choose the most logical completion for each sentence beginning.

1. Écrivez...

   _____ le livre   _____ le mot   _____ le mur

2. Prenez...

   _____ la réponse   _____ un crayon   _____ les instructions

3. Ouvrez...

   _____ la porte   _____ la cassette   _____ la chaise

4. Écoutez...

   _____ les instructions   _____ le chapitre   _____ le livre

5. Lisez...

   _____ le professeur   _____ la phrase   _____ le CD

J. **Complétez les phrases.**   Look back at the commands in activity I. With a partner, find as many ways as you can to complete each sentence.

➡ Fermez...
Fermez la porte, le livre, le cahier, la fenêtre, le sac à dos...

K. **Expressions pour la classe.**   Using the classroom expressions and commands above, decide what you or the teacher should say in the following situations.

1. You want to know how to say *homework* in French.
2. You can't hear what the teacher is saying.
3. You don't understand an explanation.
4. You don't know the answer to a question.
5. The teacher wants to know if you understand a question.
6. The teacher wants you to open your book.
7. The teacher wants you to take out a pen.
8. The teacher wants you to listen to the cassette tape.
9. You want to know how to spell something.

L. CUES: trois horloges, neuf classeurs, six crayons, huit cassettes, deux étudiantes, dix sacs à dos, cinq tables, sept fenêtres, deux feuilles de papier, quatre cahiers, une serviette, quatre murs.

L. **Combien?**   Listen to the instructor and write down the correct number of the items mentioned. Cross out the **-s** on any word that is not plural.

_____ horloges   _____ tables

_____ classeurs   _____ fenêtres

_____ crayons   _____ feuilles de papier

_____ cassettes   _____ cahiers

_____ étudiantes   _____ serviettes

_____ sacs à dos   _____ murs

M. Explain the irregular plural for the last two items only if students inquire. Add other vocabulary items if numbers do not exceed ten, e.g., étudiants? étudiantes?

M. **Votre salle de classe.**   Say how many of the following items are in your classroom: portes? fenêtres? murs? professeurs? CD? tables? horloges? cartes? tableaux? morceaux de craie?

VOCABULAIRE ACTIF

Les salutations *(Greetings)*

FORMEL

Bonjour / Bonsoir, monsieur / madame / mademoiselle. *Hello / Good evening, sir / ma'am / miss.*
Comment allez-vous? / Vous allez bien? *How are you? / Are you well?*
Je vais bien, merci. Et vous? *I'm fine, thank you. And you?*
Très bien, merci. *Very well, thank you.*

FAMILIER

Salut, Robert! *Hi, Robert!*
Comment ça va? / Comment vas-tu? *How are you?*
Ça va? *How is it going?*
Oui, et toi? *Fine, how about you?*
Ça va (bien)! *I'm fine!*
Oh, pas mal. *Oh, not bad.*
Comme ci comme ça. *So-so.*

Le nom *(Name)*

FORMEL

		FAMILIER
Comment vous appelez-vous?	*What's your name?*	Comment tu t'appelles?
Votre nom?	*Your last name?*	Ton nom de famille?
Votre prénom?	*Your first name?*	
Je m'appelle... / Je suis...	*My name is . . .*	
Comment s'appelle-t-il / elle?	*What's his / her name?*	

Les présentations *(Introductions)*

FORMEL

FAMILIER

Je vous présente... *May I introduce . . .*   Je te présente... *This is . . .*
Enchanté(e). *Pleased to meet you.*   Bonjour! *Hello / Glad to meet you.*

Les formules de politesse *(Polite expressions)*

S'il vous plaît / S'il te plaît *Please*
Merci (monsieur / madame / mademoiselle) *Thank you (sir / ma'am / miss)*
Je vous en prie (je t'en prie) / De rien / Il n'y a pas de quoi *You're welcome*

Pour partir *(Leave-taking)*

Au revoir (monsieur / madame / mademoiselle) *Good-bye*
A bientôt *See you soon*

Pour hésiter

euh...

Pour demander une répétition

Pardon? Comment? *Pardon me? What?*

Comment ça s'écrit?

Les lettres de l'alphabet	une cédille	un trait d'union
un accent aigu / grave / circonflexe	une apostrophe	un tréma

La salle de classe

un bureau *a desk*	une horloge *a clock*
un cahier *a notebook*	un livre *a book*
une carte *a map*	un morceau de craie *a piece of chalk*
une cassette	un mur *a wall*
un CD	une porte *a door*
une chaise *a chair*	un professeur *a teacher*
un classeur *a binder*	un sac à dos *a backpack*
un crayon *a pencil*	une serviette *a briefcase*
un étudiant / une étudiante *a student*	un stylo *a pen*
une fenêtre *a window*	une table
une feuille de papier *a sheet of paper*	un tableau *a blackboard*
une gomme *an eraser*	

Les nombres

zéro	quatre	huit
un	cinq	neuf
deux	six	dix
trois	sept	

Les articles indéfinis

un / une *a, an*
des *some*

Questions

Qu'est-ce que c'est? *What is it?*
Qui est-ce? *Who is it?*

Expressions verbales

C'est / Ce sont *It is, this is, these are*

EXPRESSIONS POUR LA CLASSE

Ouvrez vos livres (à la page...) *Turn to page . . .*
Fermez vos livres. *Close your books.*
Prenez une feuille de papier. *Take out a sheet of paper.*
Écrivez (la phrase, le mot) *Write down (the sentence, the word)*
Comment? *What?*
Complétez... / Devinez... / Identifiez... *Complete . . . / Guess . . . / Identify . . .*
Lisez (les instructions, le chapitre). *Read (the instructions, the chapter).*

Écoutez (le professeur, la réponse). *Listen (to the teacher, the answer).*
Répétez, s'il vous plaît. *Repeat, please.*
Vous comprenez? (Oui / Non) *Do you understand? (Yes / No)*
Je comprends / Je ne comprends pas. *I understand / I don't understand.*
Comment dit-on... (en français)? *How do you say . . . (in French)?*
Que veut dire... ? *What does . . . mean?*
Je ne sais pas. *I don't know.*
Singulier / Pluriel *Singular / Plural*

Qui êtes-vous?

Qui sont-ils?
Quelle est leur
profession?
Quelle est leur
nationalité?
Comment sont-ils?
Et vous?
Qui êtes-vous?
Comment êtes-
vous?

This chapter will enable you to
- **understand some riddles and a brief conversation between native speakers**
- **read a French cartoon and a mini-play**

- **identify and describe yourself and others**
- **ask and answer yes/no questions**
- **discuss where people are from**

Première étape

À l'écoute: Qui suis-je?

*This input section presents basic ways to talk about nationalities and professions. It introduces the verb **être** and forms of adjectives and nouns.*

As you listen to the student audio CD, you will hear some famous people introduce themselves, then ask **Qui suis-je?** *(Who am I?)*. Try to guess who they are.

Avant d'écouter

1 In a guessing game about famous people's identity, what clues are you likely to hear?

Écoutons

Audio CD

1 Brainstorm (in English) with the class; list answers on the board: nationality, occupation, physical description, famous accomplishment(s), etc.

Attention! As you listen to this segment, remember that you don't need to understand every word. Before the first listening, read task 2 and focus only on what you are asked to listen for. Then read task 3 and listen again with that task in mind. Repeat the process for the other tasks. One step at a time, your ability to understand will increase.

2 Listen first to determine how many of the descriptions mention nationality. What are those nationalities? Circle them in the following list.

VOCABULAIRE ACTIF
Les nationalités
allemand, etc.
Les professions
avocat, etc.

For activities 2–4, model the words in the lists first, then have students repeat them, to make those words easier to identify in the listening passage.

2 ANSWER: All six mention nationality.

allemand / allemande
anglais / anglaise
français / française
espagnol / espagnole
canadien / canadienne
belge
américain / américaine
chinois / chinoise
japonais / japonaise
africain / africaine
italien / italienne
russe

3 Listen again. Circle the occupations mentioned.

avocat / avocate   acteur / actrice
médecin   écrivain
musicien / musicienne   politicien / politicienne
chanteur / chanteuse   journaliste
peintre

4 Brainstorm together in English to infer the meaning of both words.

4 Listen for the following words. Using the context and logic, can you guess their meaning?

la femme (Je suis **la femme** d'un président.)
l'auteur (Je suis **l'auteur**...)

18

5 As students justify their answers, ask for the clues. For example, #1: Pourquoi Deneuve? (write **pourquoi?** [why?] on the board) → Française (féminin), actrice, prénom Catherine   #2: Pourquoi pas Picasso? Picasso est peintre? Quelle est sa nationalité? Et Botticelli, il est français? etc. Students may answer in French with single words, or in English.

5 Listen a final time to decide who each person is. Be ready to justify your answers.

1.   a. G. Depardieu   (b.) C. Deneuve   c. Madame Curie
2.   (a.) Renoir   b. Picasso   c. Botticelli
3.   a. Mozart   (b.) Bach   c. Tchaïkovski
4.   a. Victor Hugo   b. Cervantes   (c.) Shakespeare
5.   (a.) Hillary Clinton   b. Jane Fonda   c. George Bush
6.   a. Tolstoï   b. Mao Zedong   (c.) Boris Eltsine

Prononciation   *Les consonnes finales et la liaison*

Écoutez

Audio CD

Listen to the following sentences on the student audio CD, paying close attention to the pronunciation of the words in bold. You will hear the pairs of sentences twice. Then, turn off the CD and answer the two questions that follow.

Je **suis française;** je **suis actrice.**
Je **suis français;** je **suis un** peintre impressionniste.

1. When is the **s** of **français / française** pronounced?
2. What happens when **suis** is followed by a word beginning with a vowel?

Note the following rules.

■ Consonants at the end of words are generally silent.

Je suis̸ français̸.

■ When a word ends with a consonant + **e,** the consonant is pronounced.

avoca̸t   avoca̲t̲e̲

■ Note that an **s** between two vowels is pronounced [z].

françai̲s̲e

■ When a final consonant that is normally silent is followed by a word beginning with a vowel, it is often pronounced as part of the next word. This linking of two words is called **liaison.**

Je suis‿actrice.
Je suis‿un peintre impressionniste.

Essayez! *(Try it!)*

Encourage students to practice aloud at home with the audio CD and to do the additional pronunciation activities provided in the lab program.

In the following sentences, look at the final consonants in bold. Cross out the ones that should be silent, underline the ones that should be pronounced, and indicate the **liaisons** with a link mark (‿).

➡ Je sui**s**‿alleman**d**.

1. Je sui**s** avocate.
2. Je sui**s** la femme d'un présiden**t**.
3. Commen**t** allez-vous**?**
4. Commen**t** vous appelez-vous**?**
5. C'est un étudian**t**.
6. Ce son**t** de**s** étudiantes.

Now listen to the sentences on the student audio CD. Repeat each sentence, and listen again to verify your pronunciation.

STRUCTURES: Identifying oneself and others (I)

*Le verbe **être** et les pronoms sujets*

Observez et déduisez

VOCABULAIRE ACTIF

D'où es-tu?
D'où êtes-vous?
être (de)
voici
voilà

Cue to Video Module 1 (00:01:02), as Élisabeth states where she and her friend Fatima are from. Cue also to street interviews (00:04:57), for people saying where they are from.

Qui suis-je? Je suis Cécile, une étudiante. Je suis d'Aurillac.

Et voici Léopold. Il est ingénieur; il est de Dakar.

Monsieur et Madame Bonal sont français. Ils sont de Saint-Simon.

Voilà Naïma. Elle est d'Alger.

- The verb **être** *(to be)* can be used to describe oneself and others and to say where someone is from. What forms of this verb do you see above?
- What word (pronoun) is used to refer to oneself? to a man? to a woman? to a man and a woman?

Vérifiez *Le verbe **être** et les pronoms sujets*

Le verbe être	
je suis	nous sommes
tu es	vous êtes
il / elle / on est	ils / elles sont

■ The pronoun **ils** refers to any group that includes a male; **elles** refers to groups composed of females only. You already know that **vous** is the formal *you*. It is also the plural *you*—both formal and familiar.

> Alors, Mike et Sally, vous êtes américains?

■ In spoken English, the noun *people* and the pronouns *one*, *you*, and *they* often refer to a general, unspecified person or group:

> To learn another language, *one* has to study regularly.
> If *you* are enthusiastic, language learning can be fun!
> If you travel to another country, *people* will appreciate your efforts to speak their language.
> In France, *they* are very proud of the French language.

In French, the pronoun **on** is used in these instances, and although it usually refers to a group of people, it requires a singular verb.

> En France, on parle *(speak)* français.

■ To tell what city someone is from, use the appropriate form of the verb **être** followed by **de** and the city. Use **d'où es-tu?** or **d'où êtes-vous?** to ask where someone is from.

> — D'où es-tu?   — D'où êtes-vous?
> — Je suis de Boston.   — Nous sommes de Montréal.

ACTIVITÉS

A. D'où sont-ils? Match the names in the column on the left with a logical city on the right.

Jacques Chirac	Salt Lake City
Boris Eltsine	Hollywood
Céline Dion	Londres
Julia Roberts et Demi Moore	Paris
Bill et Hillary Clinton	Québec
Spice Girls	Little Rock
Karl Malone et John Stockton	Moscou

Now say where these people are from.

> ➡ *Jacques Chirac? Il est de Paris.*

B. D'où es-tu? Conduct a survey to find out where your classmates are from. Make a list of the different hometowns represented in the class.

> ➡ *— D'où es-tu?*
> *— Je suis de Toronto. Et toi?*

STRUCTURES: Identifying oneself and others (II)
Le genre et le nombre

Observez et déduisez

Cue to Video Module 1, street interviews (00:04:57), where people state their nationalities. Cue also to Module 11, street interviews (00:55:25), where people talk about their professions. Help students as necessary with vocabulary.

Have students infer meaning of new vocabulary based on cognates. Allow them a few minutes to work with a partner, then discuss their answers and rationale as a class.

1. Voilà Juliette. Elle est française. Elle est mécanicienne.

2. Mohammed est dentiste. Il est marocain.

3. Mariama est sénégalaise. Elle est ingénieur.

4. Voici María et Juan. Ils sont architectes. Ils sont mexicains.

Remind students to cover **Vérifiez** as they do the chart.

If students have difficulty with this activity, tell them to look at the pages mentioned and find words with the same endings.

■ You learned in the Chapitre préliminaire that, in French, nouns have gender (masculine or feminine) and number (singular or plural). The adjectives that describe them are also masculine or feminine, singular or plural. Keeping in mind the examples above and in the **À l'écoute** section on page 18, can you infer the feminine and plural forms of the following nouns and adjectives?

masculin singulier	masculin pluriel	féminin singulier	féminin pluriel
président			
secrétaire			
espagnol			
algérien			

Vérifiez *Le genre et le nombre*

■ Most adjectives and nouns can be made feminine by adding an **e** to the masculine form. This **e** is not pronounced, but the consonant that precedes it *is* pronounced. In most cases, you can listen for the sound of the final consonant to distinguish feminine from masculine.

> Il est présiden*t*. (final **t** *not* pronounced)   Elle est présiden<u>t</u>e. (final **t** *is* pronounced)

■ If the masculine form already ends with an unaccented **e**, there is no change for the feminine, and both are pronounced alike.

> Il est artiste (suisse).   Elle est artiste (suisse).

■ If the masculine form ends in **-ien,** the feminine ending is **-ienne.**

> Il est brésilien.   Elle est brésilienne.   Point out that the **n** is not doubled when the word ends in **ain.**

■ The plurals of most nouns and adjectives are formed by adding an **-s** to the singular. However, there is no change if the singular already ends in an **s, x,** or **z.**

> Il est anglai<u>s</u>.   Ils sont anglai<u>s</u>.

■ Nouns ending in **-eau** form their plurals by adding an **-x.**

> un morceau de craie   des morceau<u>x</u> de craie

Notes culturelles

Le féminin des professions. Many professions were typically practiced by men only until fairly recently. Consequently, the masculine form of some professions is used for both sexes. To distinguish between a man and a woman, the word **femme** *(woman)* may be added: **une femme écrivain, une femme ingénieur.** In popular culture in France and more frequently in Canada, an **e** is sometimes added to the masculine form (**écrivaine, auteure**) but this usage is not yet widely accepted.

Professions et prestige? According to a recent survey, the occupations French people admired most were: medical doctor 56%, schoolteacher 27%, farmer 26%, business executive 21%, engineer 18%, judge 14%.

ACTIVITÉS

C. Des partenaires célèbres. Identify the partners of the people on the left.

Elizabeth est anglaise.	Roxanne
Cyrano est français.	Juliette
Gretel est allemande.	Scarlett
Rhett est américain.	Philip
Carmen est espagnole.	Hänsel
Roméo est italien.	Don José

Now give the nationality of each partner, paying careful attention to pronunciation.

➡ *Clyde est américain; Bonnie est américaine aussi.*

DISCRIMINATION DRILL: Masculin? Féminin? Begin by eliciting ways to recognize masculine/feminine forms (**Anglais** est masculin ou féminin? Et **anglaise?**). As you read the following cues, have students respond orally or write "masculin/féminin/Je ne sais pas" on a piece of paper. CUES: africain, brésilienne, japonaise, suisse, mexicain, chinois, actrice, secrétaire, mécanicien, ingénieur, journaliste, présidente.

OPTIONAL DRILL: Give sentences with masculine or feminine form; students give the alternate form. Il est mécanicien. Et elle? CUES: 1. mécanicien 2. dentiste 3. ingénieur 4. président 5. secrétaire 6. musicien 7. médecin 8. auteur You might prefer to have students list several professions mixing masculine and feminine forms. They then read their list to a partner who gives the alternate form for each profession.

Discuss **Professions et prestige** with the class. Would responses be the same if the poll were conducted in the U.S. or Canada? Do your personal feelings mirror those of the French? Why / Why not?

C. Students can work with a partner, alternately reading the statement and giving the nationality.

D. I. M. Pei is the American architect who designed the glass pyramid erected as a new entrance to the Musée du Louvre in Paris.

D. Professions.   Identify the people below who have the same profession.

➡ *Juliette Binoche et Julia Roberts sont actrices.*

Johnny Cochran   Gérard Depardieu
Jacques Chirac   George Clooney
Hillary Clinton   Diane Sawyer
I. M. Pei   Céline Dion
Elizabeth Dole   Madonna
Peter Jennings   ?
Frank Lloyd Wright

Now name others who have the same professions.

➡ *Sophie Marceau est actrice aussi.*

E. ANSWERS: 1. espagnol, peintre/artiste 2. italien, chanteur 3. sénégalais, écrivain/auteur et politicien 4. américaine, politicienne 5. allemand, écrivain/auteur. (Senghor was president of the Republic of Senegal from 1960 to 1980. Together with Aimé Césaire, he founded the Négritude movement in literature. He was elected to the French Academy in 1983.)

E. Identité.   Identify the following people, giving their profession and nationality.

➡ *Margaret Thatcher est politicienne; elle est anglaise.*

1. Pablo Picasso
2. Luciano Pavarotti
3. Léopold Senghor
4. Madeleine Albright
5. Johann Wolfgang von Goethe

 Jeu de rôle

Play the role of a "mystery person"—living or dead—and describe yourself. Your classmates will try to guess your name. If they need an additional clue, give them your first name.

➡ *Je suis français. Je suis de Paris. Je suis politicien. (Je m'appelle Jacques.)*

Deuxième étape

À l'écoute: Tu connais... ?

This input section introduces personal description with a variety of adjectives.

Tu connais Nicolas? *(Do you know Nicolas?)* When you're not sure who a certain person is, a description of that person can be helpful. As you listen to the student audio CD, you will hear two people talking about someone you will get to know in this chapter.

1 The purpose of activity 1 is to encourage independent thinking and the ability to analyze and infer meaning instead of relying on rote memorization. Read the words aloud, have students repeat them with proper pronunciation, then give

Avant d'écouter

students a few minutes to work out meanings in small groups. Knowing that these pairs are opposites, students should be able to deduce the meaning of all noncognates. Ask: "If **blond** means *blonde,* then what does **brun** mean? What is the opposite of *blonde?*" For **mince/ fort, gros,** and **triste/heureux,** illustrate meanings using stick figures or happy/sad faces on the board. If students don't get **égoïste,** act it out **(moi! moi! moi!).**

3 Point out the **liaison:** très actif, très amusant. ANSWERS: **Très:** 4 times; **peu:** 1 time.

1 Look at the pairs of adjectives below. They are opposites. Many of them are cognates **(mots apparentés),** that is, words that are similar in spelling and meaning to English words. Can you infer their meaning?

grand	petit	intéressant	ennuyeux
blond	brun	intelligent	bête, stupide
mince	fort, gros	optimiste	pessimiste
actif	paresseux, passif	patient	impatient
calme	nerveux	raisonnable	fou
égoïste	altruiste	riche	pauvre
fatigué	énergique	sympathique	désagréable
généreux	avare	timide	sociable
idéaliste	réaliste	triste	heureux
individualiste	conformiste	sérieux	amusant

Écoutons

4 If students need additional help, ask them to recall the adjectives in context—is there opposition between **sociable/ actif/amusant?** between **fou/sympathique?** What is the meaning of **et? aussi? mais?**

Audio CD

2 As you listen to the conversation for the first time, look at the list of adjectives in **Avant d'écouter** and circle the ones that are mentioned.

3 **Un peu** *(a little)* and **très** *(very)* are adverbs used to modify adjectives. Listen to the conversation again, writing down how many times each adverb is mentioned.

4 Have students infer the meaning of **de/d'** in **le copain d'Alceste.**

4 Now focus on some new words **(des mots nouveaux).**

1. Listen to the conversation again. Listen for the words **le copain** and **un garçon.** From the context, which one do you think means *boy?* Which one means *friend?*
2. Listen once more. This time listen for the words **et, aussi,** and **mais.** Using the context and logic, can you guess which one introduces an opposite? Which ones introduce an additional item?

VOCABULAIRE ACTIF

Les adjectifs
   grand, petit, etc.
aussi
un copain
et
un garçon
mais
un peu
très

5 Listen to the conversation a final time in order to answer the question **Comment est Nicolas?** Listen for words that tell what Nicolas is like, and then describe him. **5** For this task, instruct students to take notes as they listen one last time.

Prononciation   *Le rythme et l'accentuation*

■ In the acquisition of a good accent in French, even more important than the mastery of any particular sound is the development of proper habits as far as the rhythm of the language is concerned.

■ The rhythm of English is uneven:

Some SYLlables reCEIVE GREATer EMphasis than OTHers.

■ The rhythm of French, however, is very even. French words are spoken in groups, and each syllable but the last one receives equal emphasis. This accentuation in French is not a change in force, but a lengthening of the last syllable in the group and a change in intonation. Compare the following:

English: NIColas is inTELligent.
French: Nicolas est intelliGENT.

■ Word groups consist of short sentences or single ideas within longer sentences; punctuation and linking words such as **et** and **mais** generally indicate a word group.

Écoutez   Listen to the following sentences on the student audio CD, paying close atten-
Audio CD   tion to the rhythm you hear as each sentence is pronounced. Use a slash to indi-
cate the end of word groups you hear and underline the accented syllables.
Then turn off the student CD.

ANSWERS: 1. Non, <u>non</u>,/ au
contraire!/ Il est très so<u>ciable</u>/ et très
ac<u>tif</u>,/ très amusant au<u>ssi</u>.../   2. C'est
le copain d'Al<u>ceste</u>?/   3. Il est un
peu <u>fou</u>,/ mais c'est un garçon très
sympa<u>thique</u>./ (*or:* mais c'est un
gar<u>çon</u>/ très sympa<u>thique</u>./)

➡ Il est pe<u>tit</u>, / <u>brun</u>, / intelli<u>gent</u>... /

1. Non, non, au contraire! Il est très sociable et très actif, très amusant aussi...
2. C'est le copain d'Alceste?
3. Il est un peu fou, mais c'est un garçon très sympathique.

Now practice saying the sentences aloud, using the rhythm and accentuation you just indicated. Then, play the student audio CD again and listen to the sentences to verify your pronunciation.

Essayez!   Pronounce the following sentences to yourself, paying attention to word groups. Make sure you say each syllable evenly, and that you make the last syllable slightly longer.

1. Nicolas est français.
2. Nicolas est un garçon.
3. Nicolas est un garçon très amusant.
4. Alceste est grand.
5. Alceste est grand et fort.
6. Alceste est un peu paresseux, mais très sympathique.
7. Alceste est le copain de Nicolas.

Now listen to the sentences on the student audio CD. Repeat each sentence, and listen again to verify your pronunciation.

STRUCTURE: Describing people
L'accord des adjectifs

Cue to Video Module 1 (00:02:51) where Nicolas and Fatima describe their teacher.

Le petit Nicolas

Les copains

Marie-Edwige

Observez et déduisez

Comment sont Nicolas et ses copains?

Nicolas est heureux et sportif.
Il adore le football.

Les copains de Nicolas sont paresseux?
Non, ils sont très actifs.

Marie-Edwige est heureuse. Louisette
est active! Elles sont sportives? nerveuses?

Louisette

■ What is the feminine form of masculine adjectives ending in **-f?** in **-x?**

■ When an adjective ends in **-x,** how is the plural formed?

■ How would you say that Nicolas's friends are athletic and happy?

Tell students to cover **Vérifiez** before they answer the questions.

Vérifiez *L'accord des adjectifs*

VOCABULAIRE ACTIF

Comment est-il?
Comment sont-ils?
sportif/ve
typique

■ Masculine adjectives ending in **-f** and **-x** form their feminine in **-ve** and **-se** respectively.

     Il est **sportif** et **sérieux.**   Elle est **sportive** et **sérieuse.**

■ The plural of adjectives ending in **-x** does not change.

     Il est **ennuyeux.**   Ils sont **ennuyeux.**

■ Some adjectives have irregular feminine forms.

     Il est **fou.**   Elle est **folle.**

OPTIONAL DRILL: Have students say how Christiane is like her twin Christian. Write the example on the board: blond → Christian est blond et Christiane est blonde aussi.
CUES: 1. grand   2. sportif
3. intelligent   4. petit   5. heureux
6. sympathique   7. raisonnable

L'accord des adjectifs

masculin singulier	masculin pluriel	féminin singulier	féminin pluriel
grand	grand**s**	grand**e**	grand**es**
typique	typique**s**	typique	typique**s**
sportif	sportif**s**	spor**tive**	spor**tives**
ennuyeux	ennuyeu**x**	ennuyeu**se**	ennuyeu**ses**

ACTIVITÉS

A. Read cues a first time as students check off their answers. The second time, have students name the person referred to. Ask: «Vous êtes d'accord ou pas d'accord? Et Louisette, elle est petite aussi?»   CUES: 1. petit
2. riche   3. sportive   4. ennuyeux
5. actif   6. sérieuse   7. sociable
8. intelligente

A. Opinions.   Listen as the teacher describes some of the following people. Decide if she or he is referring to the man or the woman in each pair. Check both, if the word can refer to the man *or* the woman. Do you agree with the descriptions?

				d'accord	pas d'accord
1.	_____ Louisette	_____ Nicolas		_____	_____
2.	_____ Oprah Winfrey	_____ Bill Gates		_____	_____
3.	_____ Martina Hingis	_____ Michael Jordan		_____	_____
4.	_____ Maya Angelou	_____ Dave Letterman		_____	_____
5.	_____ Martha Stewart	_____ Gregory Hines		_____	_____
6.	_____ Meg Ryan	_____ Tom Hanks		_____	_____
7.	_____ Rosie O'Donnell	_____ Jay Leno		_____	_____
8.	_____ Elizabeth Dole	_____ Bob Dole		_____	_____

B. Students should work with a partner. They will need to choose opposites since they have not had the negative.

B. C'est à vous de décider.   Agree or disagree with the statements below and on page 29 based on the accompanying drawings. Correct the comments that are not accurate.

➡ Jacques est blond.
   Oui, il est blond.
   Jacques est brun.
   Non, il est blond.

1. Jacqueline est blonde.

2. Paul est grand.

3. Pierre est sérieux.

4. Marie est énergique.   5. Annick est conformiste.   6. Paul est sociable.

7. Hélène est triste.   8. Babette est fatiguée.

C. Do this activity as a chain. Begin by asking a student, «Tu es énergique?» The student responds and asks another student the question but using a different adjective. Go around the room without repeating adjectives, if possible. The last student asks you the question.

D. Assign different descriptions to pairs or small groups. Collect the descriptions and read them to the class («Cette personne est... »). Have students guess who is being described from the categories listed.

C. **Comment êtes-vous?**   How would you describe yourself?

➡ Tu es énergique?   *Oui, je suis énergique.*   ou   *Non, je suis fatigué(e).*

D. **Comment sont-ils?**   With a partner, prepare a description of one of the following people.

1. Le professeur idéal
2. Le professeur typique
3. L'étudiant(e) idéal(e)
4. L'étudiant(e) typique
5. L'acteur/L'actrice idéal(e)
6. Le copain idéal
7. Le politicien typique
8. ?

E. **Vrai ou faux?**   First write down some words that describe you and some that do not. Then share your "self-portrait" with a partner who will guess what is true and what is false.

➡ — *Je suis un peu paresseux.*
— *C'est vrai.*   ou   — *Toi? Non, tu es très énergique!*

STRUCTURES: Identifying people and things (II)
Les articles définis

Observez et déduisez   Tu connais les copains de Nicolas?

Voilà Clotaire, le copain de Nicolas.
C'est un garçon heureux.

Et voici Louisette. C'est... euh...
la copine de Nicolas?

DISCRIMINATION DRILL: As you read the following cues, have students determine the number and gender of each and respond orally or in writing. Students answer «Je ne sais pas» if gender cannot be determined by the sound. (Unfamiliar vocabulary is used to force attention to the definite articles.)   CUES: 1. le frère   2. la tante   3. l'hôtel 4. les pères   5. le cousin   6. les amis   7. la mère   8. l'hôpital

> ■ How do you account for the difference in the articles **le, la,** and **les** in the captions above?

Vérifiez   *Les articles définis*

VOCABULAIRE ACTIF

Les articles
    le, la, l', les
une copine
une dame
une femme
une fille
un homme
un monsieur

- ■ In French, the definite articles **le, la,** and **les** (*the* in English) agree in number and gender with the nouns they modify.

    masculin: le monsieur
    féminin: la dame, la femme, la fille
    masc./fém. pluriel: les copains, les copines, les étudiant(e)s

- ■ **Le** and **la** become **l'** when followed by a word beginning with a vowel sound. Since the letter **h** is usually silent in French, most words beginning with **h** take **l'**.

    l'avocate   l'homme

OPTIONAL DRILL: Now have students add the appropriate definite articles to the following words. Hold up one finger to indicate singular, two for plural. Put the following examples on the board: étudiants → les étudiants.   CUES: copains, dames, garçons, homme, monsieur, chanteuse, copines, étudiante, tableau, cassette, médecin

- ■ The definite articles **le, la, l',** and **les** identify more specifically than the indefinite articles—**un, une, des**—that you studied in the last chapter.

    Qu'est-ce que c'est?   C'est **un** livre. *(a book)*
                            C'est **le** livre *(the book)* de Nicolas.

Les articles		
	Articles définis	**Articles indéfinis**
masculin singulier	le, l'	un
féminin singulier	la, l'	une
masculin pluriel	les	des
féminin pluriel	les	des

F. Have students avoid items that have no recognizable owner, or claim ownership of these items yourself, e.g., le tableau de madame/monsieur. To reinforce the use of **voici / voilà,** be sure students are actually pointing.

ACTIVITÉS

F. Votre salle de classe. Point out various objects in the classroom, then say to whom they belong.

➡ *Voici **un** livre. C'est **le** livre de Nicolas!*

STRUCTURE: Identifying people and things (III)
*Les expressions **C'est / Il (Elle) est***

Observez et déduisez Tu connais le monsieur là-bas *(over there)?* C'est un Français. C'est Monsieur Courteplaque, le papa de Marie-Edwige. Il est sérieux et intelligent. Et voilà la femme de Monsieur Courteplaque. Elle est française aussi. Elle est très sympathique. C'est une journaliste.

VOCABULAIRE ACTIF
là-bas

> ■ Is the expression **c'est** followed by a noun or an adjective? And the expression **il / elle est?**

Vérifiez *Les expressions **C'est / Il (Elle) est***

■ **Il / Elle est** is used with adjectives and is used to describe.

> **Il est** intelligent.   **Elles sont** actives.

■ **C'est** occurs with nouns and is used to identify. Except with proper names, use an article before the noun.

> **C'est** un étudiant.   **Ce sont** des filles.
> **C'est** Madame Courteplaque.

■ Nationalities can be either adjectives or nouns. When a nationality is an adjective, no article is used, and the word is *not* capitalized.

> Elle est française. *(adjective)*

When a nationality is a noun, an article must be used, and the word *is* capitalized.

> C'est **une** Française. *(noun)*

■ Professions are treated like adjectives when they follow **il (elle) est** or **ils (elles) sont.** *No* article is used.

> **Il est** professeur.   **Elle est** actrice.

With **c'est / ce sont,** professions are treated like nouns and must be preceded by an article.

> **C'est un** médecin.   **Ce sont des** avocates.

OPTIONAL DRILL: 1. To reinforce the rules for article use, have students state the profession of the following people using **il (elle) est:** Madeleine Albright, Benjamin Spock, Garth Brooks, Georgia O'Keefe, Diane Keaton. ANSWERS: Il/Elle est... politicienne, médecin, chanteur/ musicien, peintre, actrice. 2. Now have students respond using **C'est un(e)...** : Tom Clancy, Jacques Chirac, Barbara Walters, Madonna, [your name]. ANSWERS: C'est un(e)... écrivain/auteur, politicien, journaliste, chanteuse, professeur.

G. Read the cues and have students write "vrai" or "faux." Then repeat the cues and elicit their answers. Help students correct false statements orally, e.g., (#1) «Elle est triste?» ⟶ «Non, elle est heureuse.»

ACTIVITÉS

G. **Vrai ou faux?**   Decide if the descriptions match the pictures. Correct the statements that do not match.

1. C'est une journaliste. Elle est triste.

2. Ce sont des copines. Elles sont paresseuses.

3. C'est une fille. Elle est énergique.

4. C'est le petit Nicolas. Il est sérieux.

5. Ce sont des hommes. Ils sont tristes.

6. Ce sont des acteurs. Ils sont amusants.

H. Discuss variables affecting choice: noun vs. adjective and, with nationality and profession, use of article or capital letter. Have students work in groups and present their answers.

H. **C'est? Il est?**   Which of the following expressions would you use with each word listed below?

c'est / ce sont   il / elle est   ils / elles sont

➡ une Espagnole   *C'est une Espagnole.*
   petite   *Elle est petite.*

1. un homme
2. timide
3. écrivain
4. une Allemande

5. amusantes
6. des politiciens
7. désagréables

8. une femme
9. un cahier
10. des stylos

I. Adjectives may vary but should correspond to the picture. Do as a whole-class activity or have partners collaborate and present the results to the class.   FOLLOW-UP: Use pictures from magazines or have students bring in pictures to discuss.

I. **Qui est-ce?**   Identify and describe the following people using at least two adjectives you know.

➡ *C'est un professeur!*
   Il est intelligent, amusant, énergique!

1.

2.

3.

4.

5.

6.

J. You may want to assign this ahead of time and allow students to bring magazine pictures, or photos if they prefer.

J. **Un dessin** *(drawing).* Draw a picture of someone—stick figures are okay! Invent character traits for this person, then identify and describe the picture to the class.

➡ *C'est une étudiante.*
Elle est sérieuse et intelligente.
Elle est fatiguée.
C'est la copine de Claire.

 Jeu de rôle

You and your classmate seem to have opposing opinions about a lot of different people! Role-play a scene in which you discuss the latest issue of *People* or another magazine. First make a list of the people you will discuss. For each opinion you express about someone on the list, your friend will disagree, and vice versa.

**W
B**

CULTURE ET RÉFLEXION

Internet

■ **L'identité québécoise.** Settled by French explorers in 1534, the eastern part of Canada was known as **la Nouvelle-France** for over two centuries before Great Britain took it over in 1763. **Les Canadiens français,** however, held firmly to their language and traditions, forming the province of Quebec, the only French-speaking province in English-speaking Canada. Linguistic and cultural tensions between Anglophones and Francophones are still very much an issue, as many of the 7 million **Québécois** still talk of independence. What is a **Québécois(e)?** Here are a couple of answers from some **Québécois.** "Surrounded by English speakers, a **Québécois** defies cultural assimilation through personal inner strength—strong emotions, a strong will to preserve one's heritage, and a good sense of humor!" (I.L., student). "The **Québécois** can never rest on

their laurels, for the survival of their culture is never assured. This pressure brings on a sense of insecurity at times, but most often an abundance of energy and creativity" (H.D.F., university professor). Let us imagine . . . If your neighborhood were the only one for miles around that spoke your language, how would it affect your lifestyle? What would you do to preserve your heritage?

■ **Nationalités et immigration.** Like the United States, France has a long tradi- tion of being a melting pot for immigrants from around the world who seek a new home in a demo- cratic nation that

professes **«liberté, égalité, fraternité»** for all. The most recent count estimated close to 4 million immigrants living in France, totaling 6.3% of the French population. Where do you think these immigrants come from? What influence do immigrants have on a culture? Give some specific examples from your own experience.

Au Québec, en français!

Un boucher algérien en France.

Refer students to chart p. 451 *after* they have made some guesses.

Troisième étape

Lecture: Le petit Nicolas est malade

Avant de lire

This input section introduces an authentic reading passage. Although the passage contains unfamiliar words, students can use pre-reading and reading strategies to understand the text and to infer how to form questions and negative statements.

1 **Le petit Nicolas** is a popular cartoon character in France. As you look at the three cartoons below and on the next page, can you guess what this little schoolboy is up to? Do you think he is really sick **(vraiment malade)?**

2 As you have seen before, identifying cognates can greatly facilitate your comprehension. Before you actually read the text that accompanies the cartoons, can you pick out some words that look familiar? Considering those words, do you think the captions will confirm your guess above?

En général

List cognates on the board and model their pronunciation as students find them; discuss probable meaning (prescrit, chocolat, allergique, visite, adore).

The key to success in reading in a foreign language is the realization that you don't have to understand every word in order to understand the text. The best way to approach a text is first to skim over it to get a general idea, using cognates and familiar words as anchors.

3 Review the text and cartoons below and on the next page as you consider this question: **Quel est le problème de Nicolas?** *(What is Nicolas's problem?)* Check the correct answer(s).

VOCABULAIRE ACTIF

allergique
le chocolat
l'école (f.)
malade
vraiment

_____ Il est vraiment malade.

_____ Il est allergique à l'école.

_____ Il est allergique au chocolat.

3 If students cannot infer the meaning of **l'école,** provide an explanation: Le professeur et les étudiants sont à l'école; l'université est une école.

Le petit Nicolas est malade

Pauvre Nicolas... Il est malade. Le médecin prescrit une journée de repos et surtout pas de chocolat.

Nicolas est malade? Hum... Est-ce qu'il est vraiment malade? ou est-il allergique à l'école?

Le copain de Nicolas vient lui rendre visite après l'école.
Alceste adore les chocolats mais il n'aime pas partager.
— Tu n'es pas vraiment malade, hein?
— Non, et je ne suis pas allergique au chocolat non plus...

Extrait de *Le petit Nicolas* (Jean-Jacques Sempé et René Goscinny)

Once you have a general idea of what the text is about, it is easier to infer the meaning of specific words and sentences.

4 **Les mots.**   Using the context as your guide, can you find the French words that express the following ideas?

1. a day of rest
2. no chocolate!
3. after school
4. but he doesn't like to share

5 **Le texte.**   Answer the following questions using sentences from the text.

1. Qu'est-ce que le médecin prescrit?
2. Le narrateur est sceptique (*skeptical*). Quelles sont les questions du narrateur?
3. Quel est le problème d'Alceste?
4. La visite d'Alceste: est-ce que Nicolas est heureux?

Have you ever skipped school? What excuse did you use? **(malade? fatigué(e)? une obligation familiale?)**

STRUCTURE: Asking questions
L'interrogation

Observez et déduisez   Nicolas est malade? Est-ce qu'il est vraiment malade? Ou est-il allergique à l'école?

> Look at the questions above. Find several ways to ask a question in French. How would you ask, "Is he allergic to chocolate?"

Vérifiez *L'interrogation*

■ The simplest and most common way to ask a question is to use rising intonation with a declarative statement.

Nicolas est malade.   Nicolas est malade?

■ **Est-ce que** (**Est-ce qu'** before a vowel) can also be added to the beginning of a statement to signal a question. This expression has no English equivalent.

Est-ce que Nicolas est malade?   **Est-ce qu'**il est vraiment malade?

■ If you seek a simple confirmation, a "tag" question such as **n'est-ce pas?** or **hein?** (familiar) can be added at the end of a declarative sentence.

Il est malade, **n'est-ce pas?**   *He's sick, isn't he?*
Tu es vraiment malade, **hein?**   *You're really sick, aren't you?*

■ A question can also be formed by inverting the subject pronoun and the verb, and placing a hyphen between them.

Est-il malade?   Sont-ils allergiques à l'école?

■ If the subject of the sentence is a noun, both the noun *and* a pronoun must be used, with the noun preceding the inverted pronoun and verb.

Nicolas est-il heureux?   Les étudiants sont-ils heureux?

■ Inversion is most often used in written and formal spoken French and occasionally in familiar speech for certain common questions such as **Comment vas-tu?** or **Comment t'appelles-tu?**

Focus on the active use of the more common interrogative forms: intonation and **est-ce que.** Introduce inversion primarily for recognition and for use in high-frequency questions.

OPTIONAL DRILL: Have students repeat these questions using **est-ce que:** Nicolas est-il malade? Êtes-vous fatigué? Tes copines sont-elles amusantes? Es-tu conformiste ou individualiste?

DISCRIMINATION DRILL: As you read the cues, have students indicate if they hear **une question** or **une déclaration.** CUES: 1. Il est malade, n'est-ce pas? 2. Il est allergique à l'école. 3. Est-ce qu'il est vraiment malade? 4. Vous êtes étudiants. 5. Vous êtes étudiants? 6. Est-ce qu'il est professeur? 7. Elle est médecin. 8. Il est avocat, hein? 9. Es-tu architecte?

L'interrogation	
intonation	Nicolas est amusant?
est-ce que	Est-ce qu'il est amusant?
tag question	Il est amusant, n'est-ce pas?
inversion	(Nicolas) est-il amusant?

ACTIVITÉS

A. À mon avis. First give your opinion about your class and friends by checking either **oui** or **non** for the questions that follow.

	oui	non
1. La classe est intéressante, n'est-ce pas?	___	___
2. Est-ce que le professeur est patient?	___	___
3. Est-ce que les étudiants sont amusants?	___	___
4. Les étudiants et le professeur sont intelligents?	___	___
5. Tes copains et toi, êtes-vous heureux?	___	___
6. Tes copains sont sympathiques?	___	___

Now interview a partner, placing a second check mark beside his/her responses. Are your opinions the same or different?

B. Students circulate, asking questions of as many classmates as possible. If you wish your students to actively practice inversion, have them use it in this activity or in activity F below.

B. Je suis...   Write down five adjectives that describe you, then ask questions to find your "soulmate"—a classmate who has listed the same five adjectives you have.

➡ *Est-ce que tu es patiente? Tu es sociable, n'est-ce pas? etc.*

Remember, you can only respond "yes" if the word is on your list!

STRUCTURE: Answering negatively
ne... pas

Observez et déduisez

— Tu n'es pas vraiment malade, hein?
— Non, et je ne suis pas allergique au chocolat non plus...

VOCABULAIRE ACTIF
ne... pas

■ From the exchange above, can you infer how to answer a question negatively in French ?
■ Can you answer the following question negatively?

  Est-ce que Nicolas est allergique à l'école?

Vérifiez   *ne... pas*

Other negative expressions are taught in this chapter on p. 39 and in Chapters 5 and 9.

OPTIONAL DRILL: Ask students to make the following sentences negative.   1. Je suis algérien/(ne). 2. Nicolas est bête.   3. Vous êtes réalistes.   4. C'est un professeur. 5. Ce sont des journalistes.

■ A sentence is made negative by placing **ne** before the verb and **pas** after it.

  Je **ne** suis **pas** malade.

■ **Ne** becomes **n'** before a vowel.

  Tu **n'**es **pas** vraiment malade, hein?

ACTIVITÉS

C. Have students work in groups, writing some original sentences for #8—some true, some false. As a group reads its statements, others respond «c'est vrai» or «c'est faux» and correct the false statements.

C. Vrai ou faux?   Decide if the following sentences are true or false. Correct the ones that are false. Add statements of your own and have classmates say if they are true or not.

➡ La maman de Nicolas est désagréable.
  C'est faux. Elle n'est pas désagréable.

1. Nicolas est allergique à l'école.
2. Il est allergique au chocolat.
3. Il est amusant.
4. Il est grand.
5. Il est triste.
6. Alceste est timide.
7. Le médecin est blond.
8. ?

D. FOLLOW-UP: Have partners brainstorm additional statements and infer the corresponding French understatement. (Bill Gates est riche. Jim Carrey est amusant. Dennis Rodman est individualiste.)

D. À la française.   The French tend to use understatements when they describe people and things. Agree with the sentences on the next page the way a French person might do.

➡ Nicolas est sociable.
  C'est vrai. Il n'est pas timide!

1. Alceste est avare.
2. Louisette est sympathique.
3. Le professeur est intelligent.
4. Les étudiants de la classe sont actifs.
5. Mes copains sont sociables.

E. Madame Mystère. Try to guess the identity of Madame Mystère. Only your instructor knows for sure!

➡ Est-ce que Madame Mystère est journaliste?
   Non, elle n'est pas journaliste.

STRATÉGIE DE COMMUNICATION
Responding to questions and comments

In French, just as in English, you can respond noncommittally to questions and comments, or you can answer in the affirmative or the negative with various degrees of emphasis. Study these examples and find useful expressions to do the following:

- to add emphasis to **oui** or **non**
- to respond in the affirmative to a negative question
- to avoid a direct answer
- to say something is true (or not) for you also

— Comment est Nicolas? Il est amusant?
— Mais oui, bien sûr!
— Il n'est pas ennuyeux?
— Non, pas du tout!

— Louisette est sympathique, n'est-ce pas?
— Euh, ça dépend.

— Nicolas est allergique à l'école.
— Moi aussi!
— Mais il n'est pas allergique au chocolat.
— Moi non plus!

— Les copains de Nicolas ne sont pas actifs?
— Si, si! Ils sont très actifs!

Responding to questions and comments

	Affirmative response	Negative response
Affirmative questions	Oui. Mais oui! Bien sûr!	Non. Mais non! Pas du tout!
Negative questions	Si, si. Mais si!	Non. Pas du tout! Mais non!
Remaining noncommittal	Ben, je ne sais pas... Peut-être... Euh, ça dépend.	
Affirming comments	Moi aussi.	Moi non plus.

F. Say you are or are not the following: 1. sociable 2. patient 3. avare 4. calme 5. raisonnable 6. triste 7. égoïste 8. pessimiste FOLLOW-UP: Continue with this activity, but have volunteers make statements about themselves.

Use **games and information gap (IG) activities** as a regular classroom feature. The *Instructor's Resource Manual* contains at least one game or information gap activity for each chapter of the textbook. For IG activities, a student must work with a partner to solve a puzzle or complete a "fact" sheet for which s/he holds only part of the clues. Game cards, fact sheets, and instructions for IG activities are found in the *Instructor's Resource Manual*.

For Chapter 1, you will find two activities, **Espion/Espionne,** and **Le Club International,** in which students practice describing, identifying, and asking questions about nationalities, professions, and personalities.

The *Mais oui!* video was specially developed to accompany the *Mais oui!* textbook. Pre-viewing, viewing, and post-viewing activities for each of the thirteen video modules are provided in the *Workbook/Laboratory Manual/Video Manual.*

ACTIVITÉS

F. Moi aussi! Moi non plus! Listen to the comments your instructor makes about himself or herself. Indicate if the statements are true for you also or not.

G. Opinions. Write five questions, then interview two partners to get their opinions. Answer their survey questions using expressions to agree or disagree.

➡ *Dennis Rodman est intéressant?* *Mais oui! / Non, pas du tout!*

Share your group's questions and findings with the class.

 Jeu de rôle

> With two classmates, role-play a scene between roommates who are just getting to know one another. Ask questions to find out what your new roommates are like. Are you similar in personality or very different? Perform the scene for the class and let other students indicate if they think you'll get along. Use a variety of expressions to respond to your roommates' questions and to concur with their comments.

Now that you have finished the Troisième étape of this chapter, do your Lab Manual activities with the audio program. Explore chapter topics further with the Mais oui! Video and CD-ROM. Viewing and comprehension activities are in the video section of your *Workbook/Lab Manual/Video Manual.*

Intégration

Littérature: L'accent grave

Jacques Prévert (1900–1977) was a popular French poet who chose to depict the modern world in its "ordinariness," with simplicity, understatements, and a delightful sense of humor. Several of his poems have been set to music. *L'accent grave* is a mini-play on words.

Avant de lire

1 One of the characters in the mini-play you are about to read is named Hamlet. When you think of Hamlet, what famous line comes to your mind? Can you predict which verb is likely to be a key word in this text?

2 An accent mark can make a big difference. Take the little word **ou:** without an accent, **ou** means *or;* with **un accent grave, où** means *where.* With a text entitled *L'accent grave*, and a character named Hamlet, what do you anticipate?

En général

Identifying the organization of a text can make comprehension easier. In this mini-play, who are the characters **(les personnages)?** What happens? Try to answer these questions as you read.

3 Look over the text, focusing on the characters. Who is talking to Hamlet? Using logic, can you infer the meaning of **l'élève?**

4 Now skim through the text paying attention to the action **(l'action).** Using words that you recognize and the punctuation as anchors, put the sequence of events in the proper order (1–7).

_____ Hamlet is startled.

_____ Hamlet plays on the meaning of the words **ou / où.**

_____ The teacher wants Hamlet to conjugate a verb.

__1__ The teacher calls on Hamlet.

_____ The teacher is unhappy with Hamlet.

_____ The teacher is *extremely* unhappy with Hamlet.

_____ Hamlet conjugates his favorite verb in an untraditional fashion.

L'accent grave

LE PROFESSEUR:	Élève Hamlet!
L'ÉLÈVE HAMLET:	*(sursautant)* ... Hein ... Quoi ... Pardon ... Qu'est-ce qui se passe ... Qu'est-ce qu'il y a ... Qu'est-ce que c'est?...
LE PROFESSEUR:	*(mécontent)* Vous ne pouvez pas° répondre «présent» comme tout le monde°? Pas possible, vous êtes encore dans les nuages°.
L'ÉLÈVE HAMLET:	Être ou ne pas être dans les nuages!
LE PROFESSEUR:	Suffit. Pas tant de manières. Et conjuguez-moi le verbe être, comme tout le monde, c'est tout ce que je vous demande.
L'ÉLÈVE HAMLET:	To be...
LE PROFESSEUR:	En français, s'il vous plaît, comme tout le monde.
L'ÉLÈVE HAMLET:	Bien, monsieur. *(Il conjugue:)* Je suis ou je ne suis pas Tu es ou tu n'es pas Il est ou il n'est pas Nous sommes ou nous ne sommes pas...
LE PROFESSEUR:	*(excessivement mécontent)* Mais c'est vous qui n'y êtes pas°, mon pauvre ami!
L'ÉLÈVE HAMLET:	C'est exact, monsieur le professeur, Je suis «où» je ne suis pas Et, dans le fond°, hein, à la réflexion, Être «où» ne pas être C'est peut-être° aussi la question.

Vous... Can't you
comme... like everyone else
encore... again in the clouds

Mais... But you are the one who's out of it

dans... in the end

perhaps

En détail

5 **Expressions de surprise.** Find in the text six ways to express surprise in French.

6 **Comme tout le monde...** What are the three things the teacher wants Hamlet to do "like everyone else"?

7 **Deux mondes différents** *(Two different worlds).* Where are the teacher and Hamlet? Check the answers in the grid below.

	le professeur		Hamlet	
	oui	non	oui	non
dans les nuages				
dans la réalité ordinaire				
dans le conformisme				
dans les réflexions philosophiques				

8 **Etre** *où* **ne pas être...**   Complete the following sentences.

1. Physiquement, Hamlet est
   a. dans la salle de classe   b. dans les nuages

2. Mentalement, Hamlet est
   a. absent   b. présent

3. La situation est
   a. tragique   b. comique   c. tragique et comique

Have students discuss the questions in **Et vous?** in small groups (in English) and find at least 3 answers in common with their partner(s).

Et vous?

Do you ever feel like Hamlet? When do you feel like this? Why?

Par écrit: Celebrities in town!

Avant d'écrire

A. **Strategy: Keeping purpose in mind.**   Each type of writing serves a purpose that influences what is included in the written text and what is not. If you were a newspaper reporter interviewing a celebrity, for example, you'd want to ask questions that would enable you to *inform* your readers.

Application.   Jot down some questions that would get you the information your readers would want to know about an international star.

VOCABULAIRE ACTIF
ou

B. **Strategy: Avoiding repetition.**   Use **et** and **aussi** to introduce an additional point and **mais** or **ou** to indicate contrast.

➡ Hamlet est amusant. Il est un peu paresseux. Il n'est pas bête.
   Hamlet est amusant et un peu paresseux aussi, mais il n'est pas bête.
   Vous êtes très raisonnable? Vous êtes un peu fou?
   Vous êtes très raisonnable ou un peu fou?

Application.   Use the following words to write a sentence that avoids repetition by using **et, mais,** or **ou.** You may use negation as well.

Pierre / amusant / sympathique / heureux

ÉCRIVEZ

1. The pictures above represent famous people visiting your city. You, as chief reporter for the local newspaper, will interview them. Make a list

of questions you will ask the woman and a list of questions you will ask the man in order to inform your readers about who they are, where they're from, what they do professionally, and what they are like.

2. Imagine you have now interviewed the celebrities above. Write captions that will appear in the paper under each photo stating name, profession, hometown, and character traits for each.

➡ *Voici Mme Robert. C'est une Canadienne. Elle est de Montréal. Elle est musicienne et écrivain. Elle est grande et brune et très amusante, mais elle n'est pas sportive. Elle est un peu nerveuse.*

Put a few of the students' captions on a transparency and critique them together. Are adjectives grouped logically (physical characteristics vs. personality traits)? Where/How could repetition be avoided?

VOCABULAIRE ACTIF

Verbes / expressions verbales
être *to be*
Je suis de... *I'm from . . .*
Voici / Voilà *Here is / There is*
Tu connais... ? *Do you know (so and so)?*

Les nationalités
africain(e) *African*
algérien(ne) *Algerian*
allemand(e) *German*
américain(e) *American*
anglais(e) *English*
belge *Belgian*
brésilien(ne) *Brazilian*
canadien(ne) *Canadian*
chinois(e) *Chinese*
espagnol(e) *Spanish*
français(e) *French*
italien(ne) *Italian*
japonais(e) *Japanese*
marocain(e) *Moroccan*
mexicain(e) *Mexican*
russe *Russian*
sénégalais(e) *Senegalese*
suisse *Swiss*

Les professions
acteur / actrice *actor / actress*
architecte *architect*
artiste *artist*
avocat(e) *lawyer*
chanteur (chanteuse) *singer*
dentiste *dentist*
écrivain *writer*
ingénieur *engineer*
journaliste *journalist*
mécanicien(ne) *mechanic*
médecin *doctor*
musicien(ne) *musician*
peintre *painter*
politicien(ne) *politician*
président(e) *president*
secrétaire *secretary*

Les gens *(People)*
un copain / une copine *a friend, a pal*
un(e) élève *a student (elementary through high school)*
un garçon / une fille *a boy / a girl*
un homme / une femme *a man / a woman*
un monsieur / une dame *a gentleman / a lady*

Adjectifs pour décrire les gens
actif / active ≠ paresseux / paresseuse, passif / passive *active, lazy, passive*
allergique *allergic*
blond(e) ≠ brun(e) *blond, brunette*
calme ≠ nerveux / nerveuse *calm, nervous*
égoïste ≠ altruiste *selfish, altruistic*
fatigué(e) ≠ énergique *tired, energetic*
généreux / généreuse ≠ avare *generous, stingy*
grand(e) ≠ petit(e) *tall (big), short (small)*
idéal(e) ≠ typique *ideal, typical*
idéaliste ≠ réaliste *idealistic, realistic*
individualiste ≠ conformiste *nonconformist, conformist*
intelligent(e) ≠ bête, stupide *intelligent, stupid (dumb)*
intéressant(e) ≠ ennuyeux / ennuyeuse *interesting, boring*
malade *sick, ill*

mince ≠ fort(e), gros (grosse) *thin, heavyset*
optimiste ≠ pessimiste *optimistic, pessimistic*
patient(e) ≠ impatient(e) *patient, impatient*
raisonnable ≠ fou / folle *reasonable, crazy*
riche ≠ pauvre *rich, poor*

sérieux / sérieuse ≠ amusant(e) *serious, funny*
sportif / sportive *athletic*
sympathique ≠ désagréable *nice, rude*
timide ≠ sociable *shy, friendly (outgoing)*
triste ≠ heureux / heureuse *sad, happy*

Adverbes
là-bas *over there*   un peu *a little*   très *very*   vraiment *really*

Mots-liens *(Connectors)*
aussi *also, too*   et *and*   mais *but*   ou *or*

La négation
ne... pas

Articles définis
le, la, l', les *the*

Questions
Qui suis-je? *Who am I?*
Comment est-il / elle? *What is he / she like?*
D'où es-tu? / D'où êtes-vous? *Where are you from?*
Est-ce que... ?
N'est-ce pas? / Hein?

Expressions pour répondre et réagir *(react)*
peut-être *maybe*
Mais oui / Mais non *But of course (well, yes) / Of course not*
Bien sûr / Pas du tout *Of course / Not at all*
Si! / Mais si! *Yes! (after negative question) / Well, yes!*

Moi aussi / Moi non plus *Me too / Me neither*
Ben, je ne sais pas *Well, I don't know*
Euh, ça dépend *Well, it depends*

Divers
le chocolat *chocolate*   une école *a school*

EXPRESSIONS POUR LA CLASSE
un(e) camarade de classe *a classmate*
un dessin; dessinez *a drawing; draw*
un mot apparenté *a cognate*
des mots nouveaux *new words*

un sondage *a poll*
Décidez *Decide*
Essayez *Try*
semblable *similar*

absent(e) ≠ présent(e) *absent, present (here!)*
masculin ≠ féminin *masculine, feminine*
vrai ≠ faux *true, false*

These words and expressions in this last section are found in the chapter in explanations and direction lines. They will be used throughout the book, so they should become part of your active vocabulary.

2 La famille

Qui sont les membres de cette famille?

Quel âge ont-ils?

Quelle est la couleur de leurs cheveux et de leurs yeux?

Quelles sont leurs activités préférées?

Et vous?

Qui sont les membres de votre famille?

Quelles sont vos activités préférées?

This chapter will enable you to
- **understand native speakers talking about themselves and their families**
- **read a survey of leisure activities in France and a poem by an author from Cameroon**
- **identify family members and their relationships**
- **ask about people's ages and physical characteristics**
- **talk about leisure activities you like or dislike**

Première étape

À l'écoute: Une photo de famille

This listening section introduces students to vocabulary about the family and to possessive adjectives.

As you listen to the student audio CD, you will hear two people talking about a family picture. Do the following tasks one by one, focusing only on what you are asked to do for each task.

Avant d'écouter

1 Who is likely to be in a family picture? Look at the words below. Can you infer their meaning? Place them in the family tree.

le père (le papa)   la mère (la maman)
le frère   la sœur

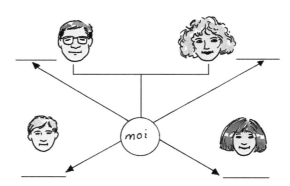

moi

Écoutons

Model the new words and have students repeat them, to facilitate comprehension when you play the audio segment.

Audio CD

3 Two listenings may be required. (**Sœur** includes **belle-sœur.**)

2 Listen to the conversation a first time to identify who is talking. Then, justify your answer.

(a.) two friends
b. a mother and her daughter
c. two sisters

3 Listen again, noting how many times the following words are mentioned: une fois? deux fois? trois fois? quatre fois?

père _2_   frère _2_   mère _3_   sœur _3_

4 Listen again to determine how the following people are related to Véronique (père? frère? mère? sœur?).

Paul _frère_   Fabien _frère_   Olivia _sœur_

47

5 Model the words and have students repeat them. Have students infer meaning in pairs, then have them report on how they reached their conclusions.

5 Now that you have heard the conversation several times, from the context, can you infer the meaning of the words in the left-hand column? Match them with items in the right-hand column and justify your choices.

1. belle-sœur
2. femme
3. enfants
4. neveux

a. *wife*
b. *half-sister*
c. *sister-in-law*
d. *parents*
e. *children*
f. *nephews*
g. *cousins*

6 Help students by asking questions such as: Combien de pères? Combien de mères? Combien de sœurs? Combien de belles-sœurs? Combien de neveux? Write answers or draw pictures on the board as you go.   ANSWERS: «moi», 1 père, 1 mère, 2 frères, 1 sœur, 1 belle-sœur, 2 neveux = 9 personnes

> **VOCABULAIRE ACTIF**
> **une belle-sœur**
> **combien**
> **un enfant**
> **la famille**
> **une femme**
> **un frère**
> **une mère**
> **un neveu**
> **un père**
> **ressembler (à)**
> **une sœur**

6 Based on your repeated listenings to the conversation, answer the following questions.

Combien *(How many)* de personnes y a-t-il sur la photo?
Qui sont ces personnes?

7 Listen one last time to note family resemblances **(Qui ressemble à qui?).**

1. Véronique ressemble à son/<u>sa</u>... mère
2. Paul ressemble à <u>son</u>/sa... père
3. Fabien ressemble à son/<u>sa</u>... mère

Prononciation

Le son [r]

■ The French [r] is very different from its English counterpart. There are three keys to pronouncing a French [r] correctly.

1. Keep the tip of your tongue against your lower front teeth.
2. Arch the back of your tongue toward the back of your mouth, as for the sounds [k] (<u>c</u>at) or [g] (<u>g</u>et).

→ Practice saying [go], then **gros** [gro]; **gant** [gã] → **grand** [grã].

*Practice with other vowels, for example: [ge] (as in **gué**) → [gre] (**gré**); [gɛ̃] (**gain**) → [grɛ̃] (**grain**); [gy] (as in **aigu**) → [gry] (**grue**); [gu] (**goût**) → [gru] (as in **groupe**).*

3. Keep your lips from moving! Set your lips in position for the vowel that comes before or after the [r], and make sure they don't move for the [r].

→ Pronounce the following sound combinations, checking the corners of your mouth with your fingers to make sure your lips don't move.

k [ka] → **car** [kar]   **qui** [ki] → **cri** [kri]

Écoutez

Audio CD

Note: From this point on, the directions for the **Prononciation** are not recorded. You should read the directions in the text.

Listen again to **À l'écoute: Une photo de famille,** paying close attention to the pronunciation of the **r**'s occurring in the following expressions. Listen to the segment a second time if necessary.

1. Vé<u>r</u>onique
2. j'ado<u>r</u>e
3. bien sû<u>r</u>
4. mè<u>r</u>e
5. pè<u>r</u>e
6. tu <u>r</u>essembles à ta mère
7. mon f<u>r</u>è<u>r</u>e
8. mon aut<u>r</u>e f<u>r</u>è<u>r</u>e
9. Paul <u>r</u>essemble à son pè<u>r</u>e
10. Fabien <u>r</u>essemble à sa mè<u>r</u>e, je c<u>r</u>ois
11. deux sœu<u>r</u>s
12. ma belle-sœur
13. leu<u>r</u>s deux enfants
14. ado<u>r</u>ables

Essayez

Audio CD

Now listen again to the words and expressions in the preceding section. Repeat each one, keeping in mind the three key directions for pronouncing the French [r]. Then listen again to verify your pronunciation.

VOCABULAIRE
La famille

Cue to Video Module 2 (00:07:31), where Nicolas and Élisabeth talk about their families. Also to street interviews (00:09:27), where people describe their families.

■ **Regardez** *(Look at)* la photo de famille.

— Combien de grands-parents est-ce qu'il y a?
— **Il y a** *(There are)* trois grands-parents.
— Combien d'enfants? Combien de personnes est-ce qu'il y a?

Point out that **il y a** is invariable whether used in the singular or the plural. Give examples.

Using teacher talk (see the Introduction to the Instructor's Annotated Edition), introduce your own family with photographs (or a well-known family using magazine pictures) to present the vocabulary. «Voici ma mère; elle s'appelle Helen. C'est la femme de mon père. Et voici mon père; il s'appelle Curtis. C'est le mari de Helen.» After each vocabulary "pair," ask students a series of yes/no questions («Helen est ma mère?»), then short-answer questions («Qui est-ce? C'est ma mère ou mon père?») to check understanding and familiarize students with the new words. Then have partners work on the first set of sentences, reporting on their conclusions before repeating the process for the second set of statements.

■ Using logic and cognates, figure out the meaning of the following words. Then complete the sentences below and on page 50.

oncle *(m.)*	**tante** *(f.)*
grand-père *(m.)*	**grand-mère** *(f.)*
fils *(m.)*	**fille** *(f.)*
grands-parents *(m.)*	**mari** *(m.)*

1. Le père de mon père est mon _____ .

2. La mère de mon père est ma _____ .

3. Les parents de mes parents sont mes _____ .

4. La sœur de ma mère est ma _____ .

5. Le frère de ma mère est mon _____ .

6. Un enfant du sexe féminin est une _____ .

7. Un enfant du sexe masculin est un _____ .

8. Mon père est le _____ de ma mère.

neveu *(m.)*   **nièce** *(f.)*   **beau-frère** *(m.)*   **belle-sœur** *(f.)*
cousin *(m.)*   **cousine** *(f.)*   **petit-fils** *(m.)*   **petite-fille** *(f.)*

9. Le fils de mon oncle et de ma tante est mon _____ .

10. La fille de mon oncle et de ma tante est ma _____ .

11. La sœur de mon neveu est ma _____ .

12. Le fils de mon fils est mon _____ .

13. La fille de mon fils est ma _____ .

14. Le mari de ma sœur est mon _____ .

Note culturelle

La famille française.   Today there are probably more similarities than differences between families in France and families in the United States and Canada. For example, couples in France today tend to share authority as well as household chores. A majority of French women now work outside the home, and young children whose parents both work may spend time in daycare. As in the United States and Canada, the single-parent family and couples who live together outside marriage are not uncommon. In France, however, cohabitation is given a legal status.

ACTIVITÉS

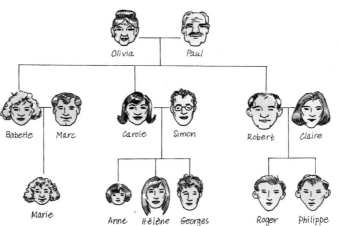

La famille d'Hélène

A. Combien de... ?   Regardez l'arbre généalogique d'Hélène. Qui sont les sœurs? les mères? les oncles? les frères? Combien de tantes est-ce qu'il y a? de pères? de fils? de maris?

B. D'autres liens de parenté.   Parlez de *(Talk about)* tous les liens de parenté *(relationships)* possibles pour les membres de la famille d'Hélène.

➡ *Anne est la sœur de Georges et d'Hélène, la fille de Carole et de Simon, la nièce..., la cousine..., la petite-fille...*

STRUCTURE: Expressing possession
Les adjectifs possessifs

Observez et déduisez

DISCRIMINATION DRILL: Replay the audio segment **Une photo de famille** from the student audio CD. Have students write down each possessive adjective they hear (**ta, ta, ton, ta, mon, mon, son, sa, ma, ma, leurs, mes**).

Ici, c'est Marie, la fille de mon oncle et de ma tante. C'est ma cousine. Et là, ce sont Olivia et Paul, les parents de ma mère. Ce sont mes grands-parents.

> ■ In the paragraph above, how many ways do you find to say *my?* Based on your understanding of adjective/noun agreement, what conclusions can you draw about the various forms of *my?*

Vérifiez   *Les adjectifs possessifs*

VOCABULAIRE ACTIF
Les adjectifs possessifs
mon, ma, etc.

■ The possessive adjective agrees in number and gender with the noun following it.

| oncle (masculin) → **son** | tante (féminin) → **sa** |
| parents (masc./pluriel) → **ses** | cousines (fém./pluriel) → **ses** |

Notice that *it does not matter* whether the possessor is a male or a female. The adjective agrees with the noun that *follows* it.

son frère (*his/her* brother)   **sa** sœur (*his/her* sister)

DISCRIMINATION DRILL: **Singulier ou Pluriel?** First discuss with students how to recognize singular and plural possessive adjectives. (Be sure to mention the liaison between **leurs** and a noun beginning with a vowel, e.g., **leurs enfants.**) As you read the cues, have students write "singulier/ pluriel" or a question mark if number cannot be determined. Then repeat the cues and check responses. (You may also have students hold up one or two fingers as you read the cues the first time.) CUES: 1. notre tante 2. votre mère 3. tes cousins 4. son avocate 5. leurs secrétaires 6. mes frères 7. leurs oncles 8. nos professeurs 9. ma grand-mère 10. ses étudiants

■ For singular words beginning with a vowel sound, always use the masculine adjective even if the noun is feminine.

son avocat**e**   **mon** étudiant**e**

Les adjectifs possessifs			
	masculin	**féminin**	**pluriel**
my	**mon** oncle	**ma** tante	**mes** parents
your	**ton** oncle	**ta** tante	**tes** parents
his/her/its	**son** oncle	**sa** tante	**ses** parents
our	**notre** oncle	**notre** tante	**nos** parents
your	**votre** oncle	**votre** tante	**vos** parents
their	**leur** oncle	**leur** tante	**leurs** parents

OPTIONAL DRILL: Changez les mots du singulier au pluriel. mon neveu → mes neveux CUES: 1. sa cousine 2. leur professeur 3. notre médecin 4. ta belle-sœur 5. votre nièce

OPTIONAL DRILL: Changez les mots du pluriel au singulier. nos grands-pères → notre grand-père CUES: 1. tes cousines 2. mes tantes 3. ses oncles 4. leurs sœurs 5. vos frères

ACTIVITÉS

C. Vrai ou faux? Lisez les phrases suivantes et indiquez si (*if*) elles sont vraies ou fausses selon l'arbre généalogique d'Hélène. Corrigez (*Correct*) les phrases si elles sont fausses.

➡ (Hélène)   Roger est son frère.
     C'est faux. Roger est son cousin.

The activity **C'est à qui?** in the *Instructor's Resource Manual* practices possessive adjectives and recycles classroom vocabulary from the Chapitre préliminaire.

La famille d'Hélène

1. Olivia est sa mère.
2. Roger et Philippe sont ses cousins.
3. Simon est son père.
4. Marc est sa tante.
5. Georges est son frère.

La famille d'Olivia et de Paul

6. Babette, Carole et Hélène sont leurs filles.
7. Marie est leur petite-fille.
8. Robert est leur fils.
9. Georges et Roger sont leurs fils aussi.
10. Babette est leur sœur.

Note culturelle

Des questions personnelles.   Although it may seem perfectly natural for you to discuss your family with a partner in French class, such would not necessarily be the case in France, where topics such as the number of members in the family or their occupation are often considered private matters to be broached only with close friends, not acquaintances. In many African cultures, asking parents how many children they have is taboo for two reasons: it would be a breach of privacy, and it might also invite fate to strike one of the children. The notion of privacy exists in all cultures; however, its manifestations vary from culture to culture.

D. Have volunteers ask you questions about your family.

D. Interview. Posez *(Ask)* les questions suivantes à un(e) partenaire et répondez à ses questions.

1. Il y a combien de personnes dans ta famille?
2. Qui sont les membres de ta famille?
3. Comment s'appelle ta mère? ton frère? etc.
4. Comment est ton oncle? (ta tante, etc.)
5. D'où est ton cousin? (ta cousine, etc.)

STRUCTURE: Pointing out people and things
Les adjectifs démonstratifs

Observez et déduisez

OPTIONAL DRILL: Have students write the appropriate demonstrative adjective as you read the cues. Hold up two fingers to indicate plural nouns. CUES: 1. oncle 2. femme 3. garçons 4. monsieur 5. étudiante 6. professeur 7. avocat 8. cahiers. Reread the list, then

— Qui est cette femme, là-bas?
— C'est ma tante. Et ce monsieur-là, c'est mon oncle.

■ What is the meaning of **ce/cette?** Why the difference in form?

Vérifiez   *Les adjectifs démonstratifs*

■ Demonstrative adjectives are used to point out or clarify, and, like all adjectives, they agree in number and gender with the noun they modify.

have volunteers give answers and explain simply, e.g., «ce—masculin», «cet—voyelle».

cette dame (fém./sing.)	**ce** monsieur (masc./sing.)
ces filles (fém./pluriel)	**ces** garçons (masc./pluriel)

■ **Cet** is the form used before masculine words beginning with a vowel sound.

cet h̲omme   **cet** a̲vocat   **cet** é̲tudiant

VOCABULAIRE ACTIF

Les adjectifs démonstratifs
   ce, cet, cette, ces
   -ci / -là

■ **-ci** and **-là** may be added to the noun to distinguish between *this* and *that* or between *these* and *those*.

ce monsieur**-ci**   **cette** femme**-là**
ces garçons**-ci**   **ces** filles**-là**

ACTIVITÉS

E. Have pairs/groups make three sentences for each person, including at least one adjective not listed above. Have volunteers share answers, then ask students to make negative statements about each picture: «Ce papa n'est pas... »

E. Comment est cette famille?   Décrivez *(Describe)* la famille en employant le vocabulaire ci-dessous.

➡ *Ces enfants sont heureux...*

		grand(e)(s)
Ces enfants		amusant(e)(s)
Cette mère	est/sont	sociable(s)
Ce père		blond(e)(s)
		?

F. To do this as a whole-class activity, use Transparency 18. Have volunteers point to various people and call on classmates to respond.

F. Qui est-ce? Posez des questions à un(e) partenaire au sujet des *(about)* personnes suivantes. Répondez en regardant l'arbre généalogique (page 50).

➡ homme / Marc   — *Qui est cet homme?*
                  — *C'est Marc, le mari de Babette (le père de Marie, etc.).*

1. homme / Paul   3. garçon / Georges   5. femme / Carole
2. enfant / Marie   4. homme / Robert   6. enfant / Roger

 Jeu de rôle

Play the role of a client who has hired a genealogist (your partner) to research and develop your family tree. Give a brief description of your immediate family, including names and relationships. Your partner will ask follow-up questions about other relatives. Share as much information as you can while your partner sketches your **arbre généalogique.** Check to be sure it's correct before the genealogist leaves to begin his/her research.

**W
B**

Deuxième étape

Lecture: Les loisirs et la famille

Avant de lire

This reading section introduces students to the topic of leisure activities. From this input, they will learn pertinent vocabulary, many **-er** verbs, some adverbs, and cultural information.

Read expressions aloud to model pronunciation, then put students in groups of 2 or 3 to infer meaning. Check meaning together, then resume group work to fill out the chart. Discuss answers.

1 What leisure activities do you associate with family life? Infer the meaning of the expressions below, then indicate whether you and your family practice these activities often **(souvent),** sometimes **(quelquefois),** or never **(jamais).**

Activités de loisirs	souvent	quelquefois	jamais
manger au restaurant			
regarder la télévision			
écouter de la musique (radio, cassettes, CD)			
aller au cinéma			
aller au concert			
aller à des matchs de football, de basket, etc.			
jouer au tennis, au foot, au basket, etc.			
visiter des musées			

Un pique-nique en famille.

2 Look at the chart below entitled "Les médias d'abord". What is this chart about?

    a. the evolution of media options in France between 1973 and 1992
    (b.) the evolution of leisure activities among French people over the last three decades
    c. a comparison of leisure activities among various segments of the population

3 The chart is divided into two parts. What is examined in each part? Check the proper column.

Leisure activities practiced . . .	First part	Second part
at least once a week **(par semaine)**	✓	
at least once in the last twelve months		✓
every day or almost every day	✓	

Now can you find the French word or expression for the following?

    • month   • every day   • almost   • at least

Les médias d'abord			
Évolution de quelques pratiques de loisirs (en %):	**1973**	**1981**	**1992**
Proportion de Français ayant pratiqué l'activité suivante:			
• Regarder la télévision tous les jours ou presque	65	69	73*
• Écouter la radio tous les jours ou presque	72	72	66*
• Écouter des disques ou cassettes au moins une fois par semaine	66	75	73*
Au moins une fois au cours des 12 derniers mois:			
• Lire un livre	70	74	75*
• Acheter un livre	51	56	62*
• Aller au cinéma	52	50	49
• Aller dans une fête foraine	47	43	34
• Visiter un musée	27	30	28
• Visiter un monument historique	32	32	30
• Assister à un spectacle sportif (payant)	24	20	17
• Aller à une exposition (peinture, sculpture)	19	21	23
• Aller dans un zoo	30	23	24
• Aller à un spectacle:			
— théâtre	12	10	12
— music-hall	11	10	9
— cirque	11	10	14
— danse	6	5	5
— opéra	3	2	3
• Aller à un concert:			
— rock ou jazz	7	10	14
— musique classique	7	7	8

Ministère de la Culture

* 1989

VOCABULAIRE ACTIF

Activités
acheter
aller *(infinitive only)*
    (au cinéma, à un
    match de football, de
    basket, à un concert)
écouter de la musique
    (de rock, de jazz,
    de la musique
    classique), la radio
jouer (au tennis, au
    foot)
lire *(infinitive only)*
manger (au restaurant)
regarder (la télévision)

Adverbes
au moins, jamais,
presque, quelquefois,
souvent, tous les jours,
une fois

4 **Les mots.**   Using the context and logic, can you infer the meaning of the words in the left-hand column? Choose the correct answers from the right-hand column.

1. acheter
2. assister (à)
3. une fête foraine
4. un spectacle
5. une exposition
6. une peinture
7. un zoo
8. un cirque

a. *to assist*
b. *to attend*
c. *to buy*
d. *a circus*
e. *a zoo*
f. *a show/an event*
g. *an exhibit*
h. *an opera*
i. *a carnival*
j. *a painting*

4   Have students infer meaning in groups of 2 or 3, then report on conclusions and strategies used. Model/practice pronunciation of each word before group work, and again as students report. Note: **zoo** is pronounced [zo] in French.   **5**   Students can list activities in French, but allow further discussion in English.   ANSWERS: 1. regarder la télévision, écouter des disques ou cassettes, lire un livre, acheter un livre, aller à un concert de rock ou jazz   2. aller au cinéma, visiter un musée, visiter un monument historique, aller à une exposition, théâtre, music-hall, cirque, danse, opéra, concert de musique classique   3. écouter la radio, aller dans une fête foraine, assister à un spectacle sportif, aller dans un zoo

5 **Les résultats.**   Make a list of

1. the leisure activities that increased by 5% or more from 1973 to 1992.
2. the activities that remained fairly constant (within 1 to 4%).
3. the activities that decreased by 5% or more.

How do you explain the changes?

2. As students walk around the room, make sure they use French only. Quelles activités? visiter un musée? (oui? non?) aller à un spectacle de théâtre? un spectacle d'opéra? un concert de rock? etc. Reports can be done in French as well, since no numbers should exceed 10: visiter un musée, 4 oui, 6 non; aller dans un zoo, 2 oui, 8 non.

1. **Des différences culturelles?**   Would this poll look the same in North America? In groups of four or five students, estimate the percentage of Americans (or other nationality) who would currently practice the activities mentioned in the chart. Then compare your answers with those of other groups. Quelles sont les différences?
2. **Un sondage** *(A poll).*   With a partner, pick from the bottom part of the chart five activities that can be done **en famille,** then poll five classmates each to see how many of them have done these activities with their family at least once in the last twelve months. Compile your results and share them with the rest of the class.

Cue to Video Module 2 (00:06:44), where Nicolas and Élisabeth discuss their families' favorite activities. Cue also to Module 6 (00:27:06), where Élisabeth, Fatima, and Nicolas discuss what to do on a rainy Saturday. Also to street interviews (00:28:41), where people talk about their leisure activities. Help students with vocabulary as needed.

STRUCTURE: Talking about leisure activities
Les verbes en -er

Have students pick out the cognates they recognize.

Observez et déduisez   Ma sœur et moi, nous aimons les médias. Nous aimons regarder la télévision, écouter de la musique: le jazz, le rock, la musique classique. Nous aimons aussi aller au cinéma. J'aime bien les films d'aventure et les comédies. Sophie aime les films d'amour. Mes parents aiment les sports—le tennis, le volley—et ils aiment aller à des matchs de foot le week-end. Mon grand-père, par contre, n'aime pas le sport, mais il aime beaucoup lire, surtout les romans historiques, pas les romans policiers. Est-ce que nous sommes une famille typique? (La réponse à cette question se trouve dans le sondage de la page 55.)

- The verb **aimer** is used to express preferences. How many different forms of the verb do you see in the preceding paragraph? How do you explain these differences?
- What kind of article follows the verb **aimer:** definite or indefinite?
- How would you say "I like movies"? How would you say "I don't like sports"?

Vérifiez *Les verbes en -er*

- Many French verbs are formed like **aimer.** The written stem is found by dropping the **-er** from the infinitive: **aim-.** Add the following endings to the stem to form the present tense of **-er** verbs.

Le verbe aimer	
j'aim**e**	nous aim**ons**
tu aim**es**	vous aim**ez**
il / elle / on aim**e**	ils / elles aim**ent**

Note that **je** becomes **j'** before a vowel.

J'adore le français. J'étudie la littérature.

Although there are five written endings for **-er** verbs, only two are pronounced: those for **nous** and **vous.** *All other endings are silent.*

je regarde	nous regard**ons**
tu regardes	vous regard**ez**
il / elle / on regarde	ils / elles regardent

Liaison occurs when **nous, vous, ils,** and **elles** are followed by a verb beginning with a vowel.

nous‿écoutons vous‿étudiez elles‿adorent
       z   z   z

DISCRIMINATION DRILL: To focus attention on liaison, read the cues and have students indicate «singulier» or «pluriel.» CUES: 1. Ils aiment les vacances. 2. Elle adore la télé. 3. Ils étudient le français. 4. Il écoute la radio. 5. Ils invitent leurs copains. 6. Ils habitent à Paris. 7. Elle admire le professeur.

- A simple (one word) present tense is used in French to express actions in progress:

Nous **écoutons** la radio. *We are listening to the radio.*

as well as habitual actions:

Nous **écoutons** toujours la radio. *We always listen to the radio.*

■ Spelling changes occur in the stems of some **-er** verbs.

Some stem-changing verbs		
é → è before a silent ending		
nous préférons	BUT	ils préfèrent
vous préférez	BUT	elle préfère
mute e → è before a silent ending		
nous achetons	BUT	ils achètent
vous achetez	BUT	elle achète
g → ge before -ons		
nous mangeons		
c → ç before -ons		
je commence	BUT	nous commençons

VOCABULAIRE ACTIF

un(e) ami(e)
un(e) camarade de
   chambre
une comédie
une discothèque
dormir
écrire
un film d'amour/
   d'aventure
la littérature
un magazine
des parents (m.)
un restaurant
un roman historique/
   policier
le sport
surtout
Les verbes en -er
   aimer, etc.
le volley

■ Many **-er** verbs are easily recognizable cognates. They are often used in the following situations:

a. in directions in this textbook

   compléter (la phrase)   comparer (les réponses)

b. to discuss pastimes and activities

chanter (bien, mal)   *to sing well/ badly*
danser (dans une discothèque)
dîner (au restaurant)
donner (un stylo à un copain)   *to give*
étudier (la littérature)   *to study (a subject)*
habiter (à Toronto)   *to live*

inviter (ses amis)
parler (à une amie/de Paul/ avec Marie)
penser (à sa sœur/à Noël)   *to think about*
retrouver (son camarade de chambre)   *to meet; get together with*
travailler (pour un avocat)   *to work*
voyager (à Montréal)

c. to discuss likes and dislikes

   admirer (ses parents)   détester (la télévision)
   adorer (les vacances)   préférer (le cinéma français)

■ Verbs of preference (**aimer, adorer, préférer, détester**) can be followed by a noun or by another verb. When followed by a noun, a definite article *must* be used.

   Mon frère aime **les** romans, et il adore **les** films. Il déteste **les** sports.

When followed by another verb, the second verb is always an *infinitive*.

   J'aime **regarder** les films, mais je préfère **aller** au cinéma.

In the negative, the *conjugated* verb is negated.

   Je **n'**aime **pas** lire les magazines.

A few verbs you may want to use in this chapter are not conjugated like **aimer.** For now, use only the infinitives of the verbs **aller, lire,** and **dormir** *(to sleep).*

ACTIVITÉS

A. Les activités.   Écoutez le professeur. Est-ce que les phrases correspondent aux images ci-dessous *(below)?* Écrivez *vrai* ou *faux.*

➡ (Elle travaille.)   *faux*

1. _____

2. _____

3. _____

4. _____

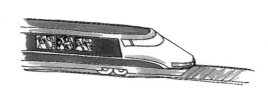

5. _____

6. _____

Écoutez encore et décidez quelle image correspond à la phrase que vous entendez *(hear).* Si la phrase ne correspond pas à une image, écrivez X.

➡ (Ils mangent.)   *4*

1. _____   5. _____

2. _____   6. _____

3. _____   7. _____

4. _____

B. Préférences.   Regardez les images ci-dessous et parlez des activités et préférences de Paul et de Marie.

➡ *Paul aime aller au cinéma.*
   Il aime regarder des films.
   Marie préfère écouter la radio.
   Elle adore la musique. Elle
   aime chanter aussi!

1.

2.

3.

4.

5.

C. Habitudes.   À quelles activités participez-vous toujours? souvent? quelquefois? jamais? Cochez la bonne réponse selon vos expériences personnelles.

	toujours	souvent	quelquefois	jamais
1. Je regarde des films français.	_____	_____	_____	_____
2. J'invite mes copains au café.	_____	_____	_____	_____
3. Je dîne au restaurant.	_____	_____	_____	_____
4. Je chante avec la radio.	_____	_____	_____	_____
5. Je danse dans une discothèque.	_____	_____	_____	_____
6. Je joue au volley.	_____	_____	_____	_____
7. Je parle à mes parents.	_____	_____	_____	_____
8. Je pense à Noël.	_____	_____	_____	_____
9. Je retrouve mes amis.	_____	_____	_____	_____
10. Je voyage.	_____	_____	_____	_____

Maintenant *(Now)*, posez des questions à un(e) partenaire. Êtes-vous semblables ou différent(e)s?

➡ *Tu regardes des films français?*
Oui, quelquefois. ou *Non, jamais.*

Comment est l'étudiant(e) typique de votre classe?

STRATÉGIE DE COMMUNICATION
Pour hésiter et pour gagner du temps

French uses expressions for hesitating and marking pauses similar to *so* and *well* and *"ya know"* in English.

■ Find the French expressions in the paragraph below used to hesitate or fill pauses.

Mes passe-temps préférés, hein? Eh bien... euh... j'aime beaucoup la musique, euh... le rock et le rap surtout, euh... pas la musique classique! Et bon, ben, j'aime les sports, voyons... la gymnastique, le foot. Et puis j'aime retrouver mes copains au café. On s'amuse bien, quoi!

Since beginning students usually hesitate a lot, encourage the use of these fillers in all classroom interactions. Also draw their attention to or have them find some of these expressions in the video and CD-ROM interviews.

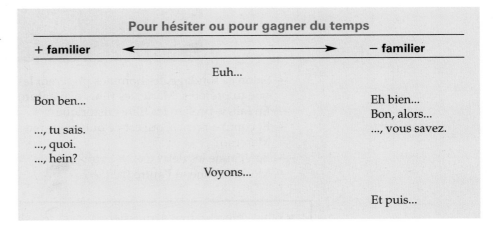

Pour hésiter ou pour gagner du temps		
+ familier ⟵――――――――――⟶		**– familier**
	Euh...	
Bon ben...		Eh bien...
		Bon, alors...
..., tu sais.		..., vous savez.
..., quoi.		
..., hein?		
	Voyons...	
		Et puis...

ACTIVITÉS

D. Opinions. Lisez les commentaires et les questions suivantes, puis parlez de vos opinions en groupes de trois ou quatre étudiants. Employez des expressions pour hésiter et pour gagner du temps.

1. Vous aimez la musique classique?
2. Les films de Woody Allen sont amusants.
3. Vous n'aimez pas danser?
4. J'adore retrouver mes copains au café.
5. Vous aimez aller au cinéma?
6. Vous ne jouez pas au tennis?

STRUCTURE: Asking about people and things
Les pronoms interrogatifs

Observez et déduisez

— Selon ce sondage, les hommes préfèrent les films d'aventure. Qu'est-ce
que tu préfères, Marie, les films d'aventure ou les comédies?
— En fait, je préfère les films historiques.
— Et comme actrice, qui est-ce que tu préfères, Juliette Binoche ou Sophie
Marceau?
— Bof, j'aime les deux *(both)*. Et toi?
— Moi? Ni l'une ni l'autre *(neither)*.

- What interrogative expression is used to ask questions about people?
  What interrogative expression is used to ask questions about things?

- How would you ask these questions: Whom do you like? What do you
  like?

Vérifiez *Les pronoms interrogatifs*

You may wish to explain that **qui** is
the subject of a verb and **qui est-ce
que** is an object.

- The interrogative pronoun **qu'est-ce que** *(what?)* refers to things and is followed by a subject noun or pronoun. Note that **que** becomes **qu'** before a
  word beginning with a vowel.

  Qu'est-ce que Marie aime?   Elle aime les vacances.
  Qu'est-ce qu'elle regarde?   Elle regarde la télé.

■ The interrogative pronoun **qui est-ce qu(e)** (*who/whom?*) refers to people and is followed by a subject noun or pronoun.

> **Qui est-ce que** Marie écoute? Elle écoute ses parents.
> **Qui est-ce qu'**elle admire? Elle admire le professeur, bien sûr!

Rappel

■ You have already used **qui est / qui sont** to ask for identification of people.

> Qui est-ce? Qui est cette femme? Qui sont vos copains?

Qui can also be followed by any of the **-er** verbs presented in this étape to ask who does or is doing something.

> **Qui joue** au tennis? **Qui danse** avec Rémi?

■ Remember that questions beginning with **est-ce que** have "yes" or "no" as an answer. Do not confuse **est-ce que** with **qu'est-ce que** (*what*) and **qui est-ce que** (*whom*).

> Est-ce que tu aimes le cinéma? → Oui.
> Qu'est-ce que tu aimes? → Le cinéma.
> Qui est-ce que tu aimes? → Maman!

ACTIVITÉS

E. Personne ou chose? Écoutez le professeur lire les réponses. Cochez (*Check*) la bonne question.

1. _____ Qu'est-ce que tu aimes?   _____ Qui est-ce que tu aimes?

2. _____ Qu'est-ce que tu admires?   _____ Qui est-ce que tu admires?

3. _____ Qu'est-ce que tu préfères?   _____ Qui est-ce que tu préfères?

4. _____ Qu'est-ce que tu regardes?   _____ Qui est-ce que tu regardes?

5. _____ Qu'est-ce que tu étudies?   _____ Qui est-ce que tu étudies?

6. _____ Qu'est-ce que tu écoutes?   _____ Qui est-ce que tu écoutes?

F. Nos préférences. Regardez les choix suivants et à la page 64, et indiquez vos préférences.

1. _____ Demi Moore / _____ Meryl Streep

2. _____ Sting / _____ George Straight

3. _____ le golf / _____ le tennis

4. _____ les romans policiers / _____ les romans historiques

5. _____ la télé / _____ le cinéma

6. _____ Michael Jordan / _____ Dennis Rodman

7. _____ aller au cinéma / _____ aller au restaurant

8. _____ ? / _____ ?

Maintenant, posez des questions à un(e) partenaire et comparez vos réponses.

➡ — *Qui est-ce que tu préfères, Whitney Houston ou Madonna?*
 — *Moi, je préfère Madonna.*   ou   *J'aime les deux.*   ou   *Ni l'une ni l'autre.*

G. First have students work in pairs/groups to come up with "questions" for the answers given. Encourage students to use as many new verbs as possible. As groups share answers, students may want to vote for the most original questions. FOLLOW-UP: Have teams write several "answers" to questions and use their answers to continue the game.

A *Jeopardy* game in the *Instructor's Resource Manual* provides practice with a variety of question types studied so far.

G. Jeopardy!   Regardez les réponses ci-dessous. Quelles sont les questions? Employez les verbes suivants pour les questions:

admirer   retrouver   chanter   écouter   inviter   manger   regarder

➡ (réponse)   (question)
la télévision   *Qu'est-ce que tu regardes?*
ma sœur   *Qui est-ce que tu admires?*

1. mes copains
2. de la musique classique
3. un hamburger
4. mes professeurs
5. *Don't Cry for Me, Argentina*
6. mon (ma) camarade de chambre
7. le président
8. la vidéo *Mais oui!*

Jeu de rôle

You and three classmates are each looking for a new roommate. First write down seven questions you feel are essential in helping you make a decision. Then role-play a scene in which you each ask and answer questions to decide who is compatible with whom.

Have students write questions for homework before doing the role-play in class.

**W
B**

CULTURE ET RÉFLEXION

■ **Le mariage et la famille.** The number of marriages in France has decreased 35% since 1975. A large portion of the French population is single (35% of men and 28% of women over 18), and 13% of France's total population practices **la cohabitation** (living together outside of marriage). However, 94% of French people recently surveyed said they consider the family to be an essential ingredient for happiness. What do these statistics tell you? Do they reflect a reality found elsewhere?

■ **Les allocations familiales.** To help families with the high cost of raising children and to encourage demographic growth in a country where the fertility rate is 1.7 children per woman (versus 2.0 in the United States), the French government offers subsidies to families. **L'allocation jeune enfant,** the equivalent of $175 per month, is given to low-income families starting with the fifth month of pregnancy through the third birthday of each child. Families with two children or more, regardless of income, receive **des allocations familiales** through the eighteenth birthday of each child. This amounts to the equivalent of $120 per month for two children, $280 for three children, $430 for four, and $600 for five. In Canada, the

Vive les mariés!

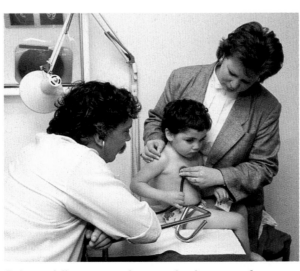

Soins médicaux gratuits pour les jeunes enfants.

government allocates **des prestations fiscales pour enfants** (tax-deductible benefits for children) of up to $1,000 per month to low-income families. How do you feel about such programs?

■ **Des enfants «bien élevés».** Americans often find French parents quite strict with their children about manners. By two and a half or three, French children shake hands with grown-ups and say **«Bonjour, monsieur»** or **«Bonjour, madame».** By five or six, they are expected to sit with their families at restaurants for hours at a time. Should children be caught running wild through a restaurant or a store, the parents are expected to immediately inflict punishment, ranging from verbal reprimands to facial slaps or spanking in public. That's all part of being **bien élevé,** or well brought up. Proper behavior will often take precedence over a child's ego or "blossoming self-expression." How do you feel about disciplining children? Should a five-year-old be allowed to "run wild" in a public place or should he be expected to sit still for hours? What qualities and/or problems do the two types of upbringing foster?

À l'écoute: Quel âge avez-vous?

From this listening section, students will learn how to talk about age and about people's physical characteristics.

As you listen to the student audio CD, you will hear six people giving their age (**âge**) and a brief description of themselves.

Avant d'écouter

Model pronunciation before doing the activity.

1 If the people in the following pictures were talking about their age, what numbers would they be likely to mention? Match the approximate age with the letter of the correct picture.

A   B   C

D   E   F

Âge approximatif

A _____ 4–6 ans (quatre à six ans)

C _____ 30–35 ans (trente à trente-cinq ans)

E _____ 15–16 ans (quinze ou seize ans)

B _____ 40–50 ans (quarante à cinquante ans)

F _____ 20–25 ans (vingt à vingt-cinq ans)

D _____ 60–65 ans (soixante à soixante-cinq ans)

Écoutons

Audio CD

Remind students to focus on one task at a time as they listen.

2 Listen first to identify which description corresponds to which picture (**image**) in **Avant d'écouter.** Fill in the letter of the picture in the following chart and add the name of each person (*Renaud, Brigitte, Driss, Nathalie, Marguerite* ou *Léon*).

description	image	nom
1	A	Nathalie
2	E	Renaud
3	F	Driss
4	C	Brigitte
5	B	Léon
6	D	Marguerite

3 Model/practice pronunciation of all numbers as you work through this activity. Point out that the numbers from 21 through 69 follow a regular pattern. 21, 31, 41, 51, and 61 all use **et;** other numbers use a hyphen. Make sure students pronounce the **t** of **vingt** in 21 through 29 (vingt-deux [vɛ̃tdø], etc.). Stress proper pronunciation of **soixante,** in which the **x** is pronounced like an *s,* not a *z:* [swasɑ̃t].

3 Listen again to the people as they give their age. Circle all the numbers you hear in the following list.

⑤ cinq	19 dix-neuf	41 quarante et un
6 six	20 vingt	
	㉑ vingt et un	㊽ quarante-huit
11 onze	22 vingt-deux	49 quarante-neuf
12 douze		50 cinquante
13 treize	㉙ vingt-neuf	51 cinquante et un
14 quatorze	㉚ trente	52 cinquante-deux
15 quinze	㉛ trente et un	
⑯ seize	㉜ trente-deux	60 soixante
17 dix-sept		61 soixante et un
18 dix-huit	40 quarante	㉒ soixante-deux

VOCABULAIRE ACTIF

L'âge: (avoir) _____ ans
Les nombres: 11–69
La description physique
  (avoir) les cheveux
  blonds, bruns, roux,
  noirs, gris
  (avoir) les yeux bleus,
  verts, bruns
beaucoup / pas beaucoup
un anniversaire

4 Listen a final time, paying attention to the people's descriptions of their hair and eyes (**les cheveux et les yeux**). Number the following words to show the order in which they are mentioned. If a word is mentioned several times, account for it the first time only.

a. les cheveux
  3 _____ blonds
  1 _____ bruns
  6 _____ roux
  5 _____ noirs
  8 _____ gris

b. les yeux
  2 _____ bleus
  7 _____ verts
  4 _____ bruns

4 Model/practice pronunciation and recap meaning of each word as you check students' answers. If meaning is not clear, refer students to pictures.

5 From memory, or after an additional listening, recap the age and physical attributes of each person. Who doesn't have much hair **(pas beaucoup de cheveux)**? Whose birthday **(anniversaire)** is it today?

nom	âge	cheveux	yeux
Nathalie	5 ans	bruns	bleus
Brigitte	?	roux	verts
Marguerite	62 ans	gris	bleus
Renaud	16 ans	blonds	bruns
Driss	21 ans	noirs	bruns
Léon	48 ans	pas beaucoup	bruns

Prononciation

L'intonation

■ Intonation refers to the rising (⟋) and the falling (⟍) of the voice.

Écoutez
Audio CD

Look at the five sentences that follow. On the student audio CD, listen again to **À l'écoute: Quel âge avez-vous?** Notice the intonation patterns for each sentence, and circle the letter of the option that best represents the pattern you hear. Then, turn off the student audio CD.

1. a. Quel âge avez-vous?
   (b.) Quel âge avez-vous?

2. a. J'ai cinq ans.
   (b.) J'ai cinq ans.

3. a. J'ai les cheveux bruns et les yeux bleus, comme ma maman.
   b. J'ai les cheveux bruns et les yeux bleus, comme ma maman.
   (c.) J'ai les cheveux bruns et les yeux bleus, comme ma maman.

4. a. Mon âge?
   (b.) Mon âge?

5. (a.) Aujourd'hui, c'est mon anniversaire.
   b. Aujourd'hui, c'est mon anniversaire.

■ As you can hear, French intonation patterns are determined by the length of word groups (short sentences or single ideas within longer sentences) and by the type of utterance (question or declarative statement). Such patterns can be summarized as follows.

1. Short statements have a falling intonation.

   → Practice saying sentence 2b in **Écoutez**.

2. In longer declarative sentences
   a. each word group before the last one has a rising intonation (indicates that the sentence is not over).

b. the last word group has a falling intonation (marks the end of the sentence).

→ Practice saying sentences 3c and 5a in **Écoutez.**

■ Information questions (starting with an interrogative word, such as **quel, comment, qui, qu'est-ce que,** etc.), have a falling intonation.

→ Practice saying sentence 1b in **Écoutez.**

■ Yes/no questions (those starting with **est-ce que** or anything but an interrogative word) have a rising intonation.

→ Practice saying sentence 4b in **Écoutez.**

Essayez!

Audio CD

Read the following sentences aloud with the proper intonation. Then listen to them on the student audio CD to verify your pronunciation.

1. Tu connais Marguerite Folin?
2. Elle a les yeux bleus et les cheveux gris.
3. Comment est-elle?
4. Est-ce qu'elle est sympathique?
5. Elle aime beaucoup la musique.
6. Elle aime aussi le cinéma, les romans historiques et les sorties en famille.
7. Et vous? Comment êtes-vous? Quel âge avez-vous?

STRUCTURES: Talking/asking about age and physical characteristics

*Le verbe **avoir** • L'adjectif interrogatif **quel***

Observez et déduisez

Cue to Video Module 2, street interviews (00:09:27), where people describe their families.

Using teacher talk, comment on the photo to introduce students to the structures. «Quel âge ont ces enfants? Vingt ans? Non, ils n'ont pas vingt ans. Est-ce qu'ils ont trente ans? Non, ils ont peut-être quatre ou cinq ans, n'est-ce pas? Et cette petite fille, elle a quel âge? Un an ou quatre ans? Et vous, quel âge avez-vous?»

— Quel âge avez-vous?
— J'ai dix-neuf ans.
— Et vos frères et sœurs, quel âge ont-ils?
— J'ai un frère qui a vingt-deux ans et une sœur qui a quatorze ans.
— Et votre tante, quel âge a-t-elle?
— Elle a peut-être 45 ans.

Quel âge ont-ils?

■ Based on the preceding dialogue, what verb is used in French to express age? What forms of the verb do you see?

■ What new interrogative word do you notice? What type of word does it precede: a verb? a noun? a pronoun?

■ What do you notice about the inversion form with **elle**?

■ How would you say "My father is forty"?

Vérifiez   *Le verbe **avoir***

Model pronunciation of the verb. Help students to distinguish between **ils ont** and **ils sont**.

Le verbe avoir	
j'ai	nous avons
tu as	vous avez
il / elle / on a	ils / elles ont

Ask several volunteers to state their age, then ask other students to remember what was said: «Quel âge a Carol?»

Ask several comprehension questions regarding hair and eye color: «Qui a les cheveux noirs? Oui, Thomas a les cheveux noirs. Et Erica? Elle a les cheveux noirs? Non, elle a les cheveux roux.» Then describe yourself and ask volunteers to do the same.

Give a personal example based on your family, then ask volunteers to do the same: «J'ai deux frères; je n'ai pas de sœur.»

DISCRIMINATION DRILL: **Être ou avoir?** Have students indicate whether the verb they hear is **être** or **avoir**.   CUES: 1. tu es 2. nous avons 3. elle a 4. ils ont 5. j'ai 6. il est 7. vous avez 8. elles sont 9. nous sommes

OPTIONAL DRILL: Change the subject pronouns as directed.   Elle a les cheveux roux. (tu) ⟶ Tu as les cheveux roux.   CUES: 1. Elle a les cheveux roux. (je, nous, ils, on, vous, elles) 2. Je n'ai pas de sœurs. (nous, on, tu, elles, il, vous, ils)

■ Use the verb **avoir** *(to have)* to express age in French. **An(s)** must be stated after the number.

   Elle **a** trente **ans.**

■ **Avoir** is also used with a definite article to state eye and hair color.

   Ils **ont les** cheveux noirs et **les** yeux bruns.

■ Use the verb **avoir** to express possession. To say you do *not* have something, the indefinite article **(un, une, des)** becomes **de/d'** in the negative.

   J'ai **une** sœur; je n'ai pas **de** frère.
   Tu as **un** fils? Non, je n'ai pas **d'**enfants.

■ Notice that in questions with inversion, **-t-** is inserted between any verb form ending with a vowel and the subject pronouns **il, elle,** or **on.**

   Quel âge a-**t**-il/elle/on?   Aim**e-t-**il les enfants?

L'adjectif interrogatif **quel**

■ **Quel** means *which* or *what.* It is used to clarify or to ask for a choice. It is an interrogative adjective and agrees in number and gender with the noun it modifies.

A   B   A   B

Quel homme n'a pas beaucoup   **Quelle** femme a quarante ans?
   de cheveux?

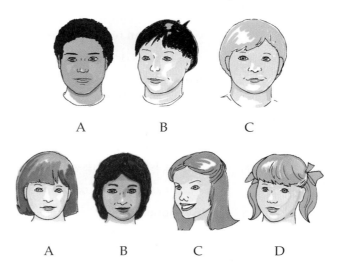

A   B   C

A   B   C   D

Quels garçons ont les cheveux noirs?   **Quelles** filles ont les yeux bruns?

ACTIVITÉS

A. CUES: 1. Il a 60 ans. 2. Elle a 42 ans. 3. Elle a 10 ans. 4. Il a 25 ans. 5. Elle a 63 ans. 6. Il a 51 ans. 7. Elles ont 29 ans. 8. Il a 20 ans.

Les nombres. A game called **«machin»** (thingie; doohickey) may be used to practice numbers to sixty. Begin with all students standing in a circle or in rows. The first student begins counting with the number one, and others follow in order; however, every third (or fifth) number must be replaced by **"machin."** For example: «un, deux, machin, quatre, cinq, machin, sept...» Any student who fails to say either the correct number or **«machin»** when appropriate, sits down. Play continues until only one student remains standing.

A. Quel âge ont-ils? Écoutez le professeur et décidez si les phrases correspondent à la scène. Choisissez «possible» ou «pas possible».

➡ (Il a 60 ans.)   *pas possible*

Maintenant, à votre avis, quel âge ont-ils?

➡ 1. *Il a peut-être 16 ans.*

B. Remind students that in searching for signatures they must (1) speak only French, (2) ask, not point to the question, and (3) interview only one person at a time (no groups). The person who answers **«oui»** signs his or her initials. Students should try to get a different signature for each question.

 See the *Instructor's Resource Manual* for an information gap activity (**La famille d'Hélène**) in which students practice asking questions, giving physical descriptions, telling ages, and talking about preferences using -**er** verbs and **avoir.**

C. Have students take turns or repeat the exercise twice, changing roles.

B. Cherchez quelqu'un.   Posez ces questions à des camarades de classe. La personne qui répond «oui» met ses initiales sur la ligne.

➡ — Tu as des cousins?   _____CT_____
   — *Bien sûr!*   ou   — *Non, je n'ai pas de cousins.*

1. Tu as un frère qui s'appelle Matt? _____

2. Tu ressembles à ton père? _____

3. Tu as des grands-parents? _____

4. Tu as les cheveux (vraiment) blonds? _____

5. Tu as les yeux verts? _____

6. Tu as 24 ans? _____

7. Tu as trois sœurs? _____

C. Précisons.   Interviewez votre partenaire au sujet de ses préférences, selon l'exemple. Répondez à ses questions.

➡ films: les comédies, les films d'amour, les films d'aventure
   — *Est-ce que tu aimes les films?*
   — *Quels films?*
   — *Les films d'aventure.*
   — *Non, je préfère les comédies.*   ou   *Oui, j'aime les films d'aventure.*

1. le sport: le tennis, le foot, le basket
2. la musique: le jazz, le rock, la musique classique, la musique de Billy Joel
3. les sorties: avec des copains, en ville, à la campagne, avec la famille
4. la cuisine: chinoise, française, américaine, italienne
5. les romans: d'amour, historiques, policiers, de Steven King

Jeu de rôle

Quelle coïncidence! As you and your classmate discuss your new boyfriends or girlfriends (physical appearance, personalities, age, family) and their favorite pastimes, you discover that they are remarkably similar. Is it possible you are dating the same person? Role-play the scene with a partner.

CD-ROM

Now that you have finished the Troisième étape of this chapter, do your Lab Manual activities with the audio program. Explore chapter topics further with the *Mais oui!* Video and CD-ROM. Viewing and comprehension activities are in the video section of your *Workbook/Lab Manual/Video Manual*.

W
B

Intégration

Littérature: L'homme qui te ressemble

Many fine literary works come from the former French colonies. Writers from these countries choose to write in French for a variety of reasons: their countries have no truly national language, the writers themselves have been educated in French schools, or they want to address a larger audience than it would be possible to do in their native tongue. The poem you are about to read comes from Cameroon **(le Cameroun),** a country in Equatorial Africa that was colonized first by the Germans, then by the British and the French. It became an independent republic in 1960.

When René Philombe (1930–   ) took up writing in 1956, after a short career in the colonial police administration in Yaoundé, **le mouvement de la négritude** was sending tremors throughout Black Africa. Begun by a group of African students in Paris in the 1930s (including Léopold Sédar Senghor, the future president of Senegal), this movement was an affirmation of the cultural heritage and values of the Black African civilization. It encompassed a sense of pride in one's race and background, a protest against being attributed second-class status, and a rebellious refusal to conform to the norms of colonial powers. Imprisoned on several occasions for his subversive writings, René Philombe has published tales, short stories, plays, and poems. The following poem is a hymn to the human family.

Avant de lire

Model/practice pronunciation of new words as you go through the factors listed. Students may use English for additional ideas.

1 «L'homme qui te ressemble»—*The man that looks like you.* Within the human family, what are resemblances and differences based on? Check the factors that are most commonly used to compare people from different parts of the world, and add other ideas as needed.

_____ La race et la couleur de la peau *(skin)*

noir   blanc   jaune   rouge

_____ Les traits physiques: les cheveux, les yeux, le nez *(nose)*, la bouche *(mouth)*

_____ Les caractéristiques universelles (la nécessité d'aimer et d'être aimé, etc.)

_____ La taille (grand, petit)   _____ La religion

_____ La langue   _____ Le statut économique et social

_____ La nationalité   _____ Le caractère, le cœur *(heart)*

          _____ ?

2 Skim the poem briefly to determine how the poet approaches his subject.

    a. As a prayer to God **(Dieu)**

    b. As a prayer to his fellow man

    c. As an accusation in a court of law

3 Among the categories of resemblances and differences listed in **Avant de lire,** which ones are actually mentioned in the poem?

L'homme qui te ressemble

J'ai frappé à ta porte
j'ai frappé à ton cœur
pour avoir bon lit°   bon... *good bedding*
pour avoir bon feu°   *fire*
pourquoi me repousser?
Ouvre-moi mon frère!...

Pourquoi me demander
si je suis d'Afrique
si je suis d'Amérique
si je suis d'Asie
si je suis d'Europe?
Ouvre-moi mon frère!...

Pourquoi me demander
la longueur° de mon nez   *length*
l'épaisseur° de ma bouche   *thickness*
la couleur de ma peau
et le nom de mes dieux?
Ouvre-moi mon frère!...

Je ne suis pas un noir
je ne suis pas un rouge
je ne suis pas un jaune
je ne suis pas un blanc
mais je ne suis qu'°un homme   ne... que *only*
Ouvre-moi mon frère!...

Ouvre-moi ta porte
Ouvre-moi ton cœur
car je suis un homme
L'homme de tous les temps°   de tous... *of all times*
L'homme de tous les cieux°   *all heavens*
L'homme qui te ressemble!...

René Philombe (*Petites gouttes de chant pour créer l'homme,* Éditions Semences Africaines, 1977)

4 **Les mots.** Using the context and logic, infer the meaning of the words in bold.

1. **J'ai frappé à** ta porte
   a. I closed   b. I knocked on
2. **pour** avoir
   a. in order to   b. even though
3. pourquoi **me repousser**
   a. push me away   b. invite me in
4. pourquoi **me demander si**
   a. ask me if   b. insist that
5. **car** je suis un homme
   a. for   b. whereas

5 **Le texte.** Vrai ou faux?

1. Le poète demande à son «frère» d'ouvrir sa porte et son cœur.
2. Le «frère» ouvre immédiatement sa porte.
3. Le poète pense que la nationalité n'est pas importante.
4. Il pense que les traits physiques ne sont pas importants.
5. Il pense que la religion justifie la discrimination.
6. Il pense que tous les hommes sont frères.

1. **Un dialogue.** Imaginez un dialogue entre le poète et son «frère».

— Bonjour, mon frère. Ouvre-moi ta porte...
— Es-tu d'Afrique?
— Pourquoi demandes-tu?
— Es-tu noir?
   etc. Continuez!

2. Poetry is the music of literature, and to enjoy the full impact of a poem, it should be read aloud. With a partner, prepare a unique reading of Philombe's poem, then present it to the class.

Par écrit: To be or not to be the same

Avant d'écrire

A. Strategy: Visualizing relation-ships. In order to compare two people, you need to describe them not only as individuals but also as they relate to each other. One way of visualizing this relationship is through the use of a Venn diagram, a pair of overlapping circles that can be used to compare and contrast characteristics.

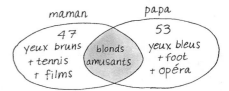

Application. Choose two people you know well and draw your own Venn diagram to help you organize your ideas. In the left circle, list traits exclusive to one of the people; in the right circle, the other. In the middle where the circles overlap, list traits shared by both people.

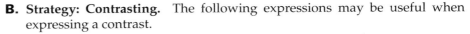

VOCABULAIRE ACTIF
alors
par contre
plutôt

B. Strategy: Contrasting. The following expressions may be useful when expressing a contrast.

mais	*but*
par contre	*on the other hand*
plutôt	*instead, rather*
alors que	*whereas*

Maman aime les sports, **mais** tante Marie aime **plutôt** les livres.
Paul est brun. Pierre, **par contre**, est blond.
Paul ressemble à maman **alors que** Pierre ressemble **plutôt** à papa.

Application. Write three sentences contrasting the same two people you described in activity A using **mais, par contre, plutôt,** and **alors que.**

ÉCRIVEZ

Refer students to the expressions for avoiding repetition in Ch. 1, **Intégration.**

1. Using the Venn diagram you constructed for the first strategy above, write a paragraph comparing and contrasting the two people you selected. Tell about their physical characteristics, ages, professions, personality traits, and their likes and dislikes. Remember to use appropriate expressions to avoid repetition and to show contrast.
2. Review *L'accent grave,* page 42. Write a paragraph comparing and contrasting Hamlet and his teacher. Begin with a Venn diagram. Physical contrasts may be obvious (**grand/petit,** etc.), but what about personality traits? preferred activities? Use your imagination and appropriate expressions to enhance your writing style.

➡ Le professeur aime étudier, mais Hamlet préfère jouer au foot...

VOCABULAIRE ACTIF

La famille

les parents (m.) *parents, relatives*	les enfants *children*
le mari *husband*	la femme *wife*
le père *father*	la mère *mother*
le fils *son*	la fille *daughter*
le frère *brother*	la sœur *sister*
le beau-frère *brother-in-law*	la belle-sœur *sister-in-law*
l'oncle *uncle*	la tante *aunt*
le neveu *nephew*	la nièce *niece*
le cousin / la cousine *cousin*	les grands-parents *grandparents*
le grand-père *grandfather*	la grand-mère *grandmother*
le petit-fils *grandson*	la petite-fille *granddaughter*
une photo de famille *a family picture*	un anniversaire *a birthday*

Les amis

un ami / une amie *a friend*   un(e) camarade de chambre *a roommate*

La description physique
avoir _____ ans *to be _____ years old*
avoir les cheveux blonds / bruns / roux / noirs / gris *to have blond / brown / red / black / gray hair*
avoir les yeux bleus / bruns / verts *to have blue / brown / green eyes*
pas beaucoup de cheveux *not much hair*

Les nombres
11–69
les deux *both*   ni l'un(e) ni l'autre *neither one*

Les loisirs
le cinéma *movies*
une comédie *a comedy*
un concert *a concert*
une discothèque
un film d'amour *a romantic film*
un film d'aventure *an action film*
la littérature: un roman (historique / policier)
   literature: a novel (historical / detective)
un magazine

un match de foot *a (soccer) game*
la musique: le jazz, la musique classique, le rock
la radio
un restaurant
le sport: le basket, le base-ball, le foot(ball), le
   tennis, le volley
la télévision (la télé)
les vacances (f.) *vacation*

Les verbes
acheter *to buy*
admirer *to admire*
adorer *to adore*
aimer *to like, love*
avoir (irrég.) *to have*
chanter *to sing*
danser *to dance*
détester *to detest, hate*
dîner *to have dinner*
donner *to give*
écouter *to listen*

étudier *to study*
habiter *to live (in, at)*
inviter *to invite*
jouer *to play*
manger *to eat*
parler *to speak, talk*
penser (à) *to think (about)*
préférer *to prefer*
regarder *to look at, to watch*
ressembler (à) *to look like,*
   resemble

retrouver (des amis) *to*
   meet with
travailler *to work*
voyager *to travel*

Infinitives only: aller *(to go),*
   dormir *(to sleep),* lire *(to*
   read)

il y a *there is, there are*

Les questions
Combien... ? *How much / How many?*
Quel(s) / Quelle(s)... *Which . . . ?*
Quel âge avez-vous / as-tu? *How old are you?*

Qu'est-ce que... *What . . . ?*
Qui est-ce que... *Who . . . ?*

Adjectifs démonstratifs
ce, cet, cette... -ci / là *this / that*   ces *these / those*

Adjectifs possessifs
mon, ma, mes *my*
ton, ta, tes *your (familiar)*

son, sa, ses *his / her*
notre, nos *our*

votre, vos *your (formal, plural)*
leur, leurs *their*

Adverbes de quantité et de qualité
beaucoup / pas beaucoup *much (many) / not much (not many)*
bien / mal *well / badly*

Adverbes de fréquence

jamais *never*	souvent *often*	tous les jours *every day*
quelquefois *sometimes*	toujours *always*	une fois, deux fois *once, twice*

Expressions pour nuancer la pensée

alors que *whereas*	par contre *on the other hand*	presque *almost*
au moins *at least*	plutôt *rather*	surtout *especially*

Expressions pour hésiter

Bon, alors / Bon, ben / Eh bien... *Well . . .*
c'est-à-dire que *that is to say*
Et puis *And then*
quoi / hein *you know*
Tu sais / Vous savez *You know*
voyons *let's see*

EXPRESSIONS POUR LA CLASSE

à votre avis *in your opinion*
au sujet de *about*
choisissez *choose*
un choix *a choice*
ci-dessous *below*
commencez *begin*
comparez *compare*
complétez *complete*
corrigez *correct*
décrivez *describe*
demandez (à) *ask*
employez *use*
en employant *using*

une image *a picture*
indiquez *indicate*
interviewez *interview*
maintenant *now*
participez *participate*
posez une question *ask a question*
présentez *present*
la réponse:
    la bonne réponse (*the right answer),*
    la réponse qui convient (*appropriate),*
    la meilleure réponse (*the best answer)*
selon *according to*
suivant(e) / qui suivent *following*

La maison et la ville

3

EPP 6005

EPP 6005

Quel type de logement est-ce?

Imaginez les pièces.

Et vous?

Quel type de logement avez-vous?

Où se trouve ce logement?

Comment est votre chambre?

This chapter will enable you to
- understand native speakers having a phone conversation and asking for directions
- read an opinion poll and travel with *le petit Nicolas* to a country home
- inquire about and discuss lodging options
- use the telephone in French
- ask for, give, and receive street directions
- talk about future plans

Première étape

À l'écoute: Un studio

Cue to Video Module 3 (00:12:16), as Fatima's friend, Flore, looks for housing.

You are going to hear a telephone conversation between a prospective renter and a landlady. Do the activities in **Avant d'écouter,** then listen to the student audio CD and do the tasks in **Écoutons.**

Avant d'écouter

Model pronunciation as you go over the activity.

This listening section introduces students to telephone expressions and vocabulary for describing a house/apartment.

1 Imagine that you are going to attend the university in Aix-en-Provence in the south of France. Of course, you need housing. What sort would you like to have? Circle your choices.

1. Le type de logement:

   un appartement meublé / non meublé *(furnished/unfurnished)*
   un studio   une maison   une résidence universitaire

2. Les pièces:

   une chambre   une entrée   un salon / un séjour
   une cuisine   une salle à manger une salle de bains
                                         les W.C.

VOCABULAIRE ACTIF

une petite annonce
le centre-ville
les charges (comprises)
une douche
idéal(e)
un lavabo
Un logement
  un appartement
  une maison
  une résidence
    universitaire
  un studio
  meublé(e)/
    non meublé(e)
louer
Une pièce
  une chambre
  une cuisine
  une entrée
  une salle à manger
  une salle de bains
  un salon/un séjour
  les toilettes (f.)/
    les W.C. (m.)
un(e) propriétaire
trouver
voir (infinitif)

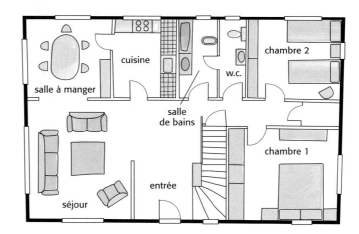

2 Now look at the following **petites annonces** *(classified ads).*

1. Aix centre. 2 pièces, cuisine, s.d.b.,
   W.C. séparés, terrasse, garage,
   3 200F + charges.
   Tél. 04.42.39.06.58

2. Avenue Victor Hugo. Studio meublé,
   idéal étudiant(e), 1 800F + charges.
   Tél. 04.42.20.11.65

3. Aix centre. Studio tout confort, cuisine,
    salle de bains, 1 950F charges comprises.
    Tél. 04.42.26.09.11

4. Boulevard Carnot. Chambre meublée
    dans villa, entrée indépendante.
    1 200F + électricité.
    Tél. 04.42.38.64.29

1. What do you think the following words and abbreviations mean?

    s.d.b.   W.C. séparés   charges comprises   Tél.

Notes culturelles

Les W.C.   In a French home or apartment, the toilet is usually in its own little room, called **les W.C.** or **les waters** (pronounced *ouatair*), apart from the bathroom. The bathroom typically contains a sink, a bathtub and/or a shower, and a bidet. Restrooms can also be called **les toilettes,** particularly in public places. In Quebec, the restroom is called **la toilette,** rather than **les W.C.**

Les logements étudiants.   In France, students typically live at home and attend a university nearby. If they choose, they may live in subsidized university housing **(les résidences universitaires),** but openings are limited. They are more likely to rent a room **chez un particulier** (in someone's house), with a sink in the room and access to the family's bathroom; or they may rent a studio apartment. The concept of roommate(s) or living in an apartment with several other students is not common to French culture but is becoming increasingly accepted.

2. **What do you notice about French phone numbers (les numéros de téléphone)?** What is the area code for southeastern France? What is the city code for Aix-en-Provence?
3. **Où préférez-vous habiter?** Which of the four housing accommodations would you choose? Why?
4. **Pour trouver** *(to find)* **un appartement...** Now imagine that you are calling about the ad of your choice. Formulate in French two or three questions you would like to ask of the **propriétaire** *(landlord/owner)*.

➡ *Est-ce que l'appartement est meublé?*

Écoutons

Audio CD

3 Listen first to identify which of the ads in **Avant d'écouter** is referred to in this telephone conversation.

C'est l'annonce # <u>3</u> pour les raisons suivantes: tél. 04.42.26.09.11; studio; centre-ville; charges comprises	
Ce n'est pas l'annonce	parce que les éléments suivants sont différents:
# <u>1</u>	tél.; appartement; charges non-comprises
# <u>2</u>	meublé; charges non-comprises
# <u>4</u>	chambre meublée; + électricité

4 Listen to the conversation a final time. From the context, can you infer the meaning of the words in the left-hand column? Choose the correct answers from the right-hand column, then justify your choice.

1. louer
2. une douche
3. un lavabo
4. le centre-ville
5. voir

a. *downtown*
b. *to see*
c. *to buy*
d. *to rent*
e. *a sink*
f. *a refrigerator*
g. *a shower*

5 As you listened to the conversation, what expression did you hear used before a telephone number to confirm that the right number was called?

a. C'est bien le...
b. Voilà...
c. Est-ce que j'ai...

Prononciation   *Les voyelles nasales*

French purists may shudder at the thought of pronouncing **un** [ɛ̃] instead of [œ̃], but since more and more French speakers no longer make the distinction between [œ̃] and [ɛ̃], [œ̃] will not be presented at this level.

■ Nasal vowels are produced by diverting air into the nose. There are three nasal vowels in French, represented by the following phonetic symbols.

[ɑ̃] as in **étudiant, parents**
[ɔ̃] as in **bonjour, nom**
[ɛ̃] as in **américain, bien, mince, un**

Écoutez

Audio CD

Listen to the student audio CD as the following words are read twice. Pay close attention to the way they are pronounced, and in the chart check the nasal sounds you hear.

To help students identify the various nasal sounds in the audio segment, have them practice repeating the sample words (**étudiant, parents,** etc.) before doing the listening task.

	[ɑ̃]	[ɔ̃]	[ɛ̃]
quarante	✔		
vingt-six			✔
onze		✔	
l'annonce		✔	
non		✔	
comment	✔		
chambre	✔		
salle de bains			✔
sont		✔	
comprises		✔	
vraiment	✔		
centre	✔		

ANSWERS: en, om, in

Using the examples in the chart, can you complete the following summary of spellings that correspond to each nasal vowel?

[ɑ̃]   an, am, _____

[ɔ̃]   on, _____

[ɛ̃]   ain, ien, un, _____

■ Note that these spellings correspond to a nasal sound only when they are followed by a consonant or occur at the end of a word. If the **n** or the **m** is followed by a vowel or another **n** or **m,** the vowel is not nasal.

nasal	not nasal
<u>un</u>	<u>un</u>e
canad<u>ien</u>	ca<u>n</u>ad<u>ien</u>ne
ann<u>on</u>ce	téléph<u>on</u>e

Exception: <u>en</u>nuyeux *(nasal)*

Essayez!   Underline the nasal vowels in the following expressions.

Audio CD

1. un appartement intéressant
2. une salle à manger française
3. un salon marocain
4. une famille marocaine
5. un politicien ennuyeux à la télévision
6. la salle de bains des enfants
7. la maison de mon oncle et de ma tante
8. les chambres de mes cousins et de mes cousines

Now practice saying each expression aloud, then listen to the expressions on the student audio CD to verify your pronunciation.

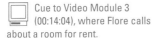
STRATÉGIE DE COMMUNICATION
Pour parler au téléphone

Cue to Video Module 3 (00:14:04), where Flore calls about a room for rent.

Certain expressions are routinely used to make phone calls. Study the dialogues below and find the words or expressions used in French to

- answer the phone
- identify yourself
- politely request to speak with someone

Au téléphone (1)

— Allô?
— Allô, bonjour, madame. Je voudrais parler à Madame Cacharel, s'il vous plaît.
— Qui est à l'appareil?
— Sylvie Dupont. Je téléphone au sujet de l'annonce.
— Un moment, s'il vous plaît. Ne quittez pas.

Au téléphone (2)

— Allô?
— Allô, bonjour, madame. Ici Sylvie Dupont. Je téléphone au sujet de l'appartement. Est-ce que je pourrais parler à Monsieur Picard, s'il vous plaît?
— Je suis désolée. Monsieur Picard n'est pas là *(isn't in)*. Est-ce que vous pouvez téléphoner plus tard *(later)*?
— Bon, d'accord! Merci, madame.

Pour parler au téléphone	
Pour commencer	
Allô?	Allô, bonjour...
Pour demander qui c'est	**Pour s'identifier**
Qui est à l'appareil, s'il vous plaît?	Ici Sylvie Dupont. C'est Sylvie Dupont.
C'est de la part de qui?	De Sylvie Dupont.
Pour demander quelqu'un	**Pour répondre**
Je voudrais parler à...	Un moment, s'il vous plaît. Ne quittez pas.
Est-ce que je pourrais parler à...	Je suis désolé(e). Il n'est pas là. Est-ce que vous pouvez téléphoner plus tard?
Pour expliquer pourquoi vous téléphonez	
Je téléphone au sujet de...	

Although **allô** is the equivalent of *hello,* it is used only in answering the phone, not in greeting people in person. The expressions **je voudrais** *(I would like)* and **Est-ce que je pourrais** *(Could I)* are the most common ways to make a polite request. Both are generally followed by infinitives.

Est-ce que je pourrais parler à Monsieur Picard?
Je voudrais parler à Monsieur Picard.

VOCABULAIRE ACTIF
un répondeur
un téléphone

Note culturelle

Les télécommunications. Phone cards **(les télécartes)** have long been required for computerized pay phones in France. These cards may be purchased at a post office, a **bureau de tabac** (newsstand/tobacco store), or at other authorized shops. Answering machines and fax machines **(les répondeurs; les télécopieurs)** are not yet very common in homes, but cordless phones and cell phones **(les téléphones sans fil; les téléphones mobiles)** are becoming more and more popular.

TRANSFERT D'APPEL

FRANCE TELECOM

TELECARTE 50

ACTIVITÉS

A. Have pairs present dialogues to the class as time allows.

A. Dialogues. Complétez le dialogue en choisissant parmi les expressions de la liste *Pour parler au téléphone* page 84.

— Allô?

— _____ . Je voudrais _____ .

— C'est de la part de qui?

— _____ . Je téléphone _____ .

— Un moment, s'il vous plaît. _____ .

Maintenant, inventez un dialogue original avec un(e) partenaire. À qui est-ce que vous téléphonez? (À votre camarade de chambre? À votre professeur? À Madame Cacharel?) Au sujet de quoi téléphonez-vous? (D'un studio à louer? De votre classe de français? D'une fête *(party)*?) Imaginez la situation.

B. Have students compare their sentences in pairs or in groups, or have a whole-class discussion.

B. Je voudrais... Indiquez vos préférences en matière de logement. Écrivez huit phrases avec les mots et les expressions des colonnes ci-dessous.

➡ *Je voudrais... / Je ne voudrais pas...*

		avec une petite (grande) cuisine
	une maison	au centre-ville
avoir	un appartement	avec une entrée indépendante
louer	un studio	meublé(e) / non meublé(e)
habiter	une chambre	dans une résidence universitaire
		chez un particulier

VOCABULAIRE
Les meubles et les objets personnels

First review vocabulary for rooms of a house using the drawing on p. 80 or transparency 21. Then use transparency 22 or the drawings on pp. 85–86 to introduce room vocabulary. Reinforce use of **voici/voilà** as you introduce new words: «Voici une chambre d'étudiant...»

des rideaux *(m.)*   des étagères *(f.)*   des posters *(m.)*

une commode

un ordinateur

un placard

une radio

un lit

Voici l'appartement de Marie. Dans sa chambre, il y a un lit, une commode et un ordinateur.

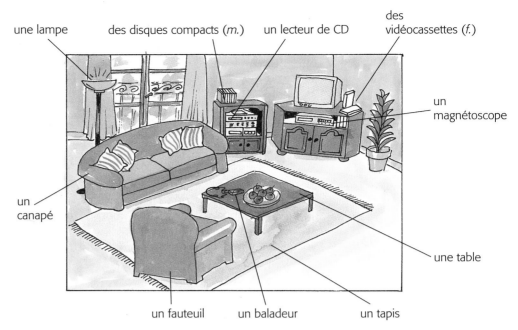

une lampe   des disques compacts (m.)   un lecteur de CD   des vidéocassettes (f.)   un magnétoscope   un canapé   une table   un fauteuil   un baladeur   un tapis

Dans le salon, il y a un canapé, un fauteuil, un lecteur de CD et un magnétoscope.

 Quels autres objets est-ce qu'il y a dans son appartement? Trouvez au moins cinq autres choses dans la chambre et trouvez cinq autres choses dans le salon.

Note culturelle

Les appareils électroniques.   According to a survey in the magazine *Le Français dans le monde,* 59% of French 15- to 25-year-olds own a Walkman, 53% a television set, 52% a stereo, 19% a VCR, 16% a computer, and 14% a CD player. Some 7% of French 15- to 25-year-olds own none of these appliances. How do you think these figures would compare with those for Americans and Canadians in the same age group?

ACTIVITÉS

C. Chambres d'étudiants.   Trouvez les chambres (page 87) qui correspondent aux cinq descriptions suivantes. Quelle description ne correspond pas à une image? Quels sont les objets qui sont communs à toutes (*all*) les chambres?

3 _____   Dans la chambre d'Anne, il y a un lit, des rideaux, un poster, une lampe, une chaise, un magnétoscope et une radio.

4 _____   Dans la chambre de Babette il y a un lit, un placard, une commode, un tapis, un fauteuil, un magnétoscope, des étagères.

_____   Dans la chambre de Robert, il y a un lit, un ordinateur, une table, un tapis, un lecteur de CD, un magnétoscope, des vidéocassettes.

1 _____ Dans la chambre de Georges, il y a un lit, des rideaux, un poster, une lampe, une chaise, un ordinateur et une radio.

2 _____ Dans la chambre de Paul, il y a un lit, un placard, une lampe, un fauteuil, un poster, un magnétoscope et une radio.

1.

2.

3.

4.

D. Des objets personnels.   Développez deux listes: (1) des objets personnels que vous avez dans votre chambre/appartement et (2) des objets personnels que vous n'avez pas mais que vous voudriez avoir.

➡ *J'ai...   Je voudrais avoir...*
  un baladeur...   un magnétoscope...

Maintenant, comparez vos listes avec celles d'un(e) partenaire. Cochez les objets que vous avez en commun, et partagez vos réponses avec la classe. Quels objets l'étudiant typique a-t-il? Qu'est-ce qu'il voudrait avoir?

➡ *L'étudiant typique de la classe a un(e)... Il voudrait avoir un(e)...*

Êtes-vous typique?

E. Un logement à louer.   Vous avez un logement à louer. (1) Écrivez une petite annonce pour ce logement «idéal». (Regardez les exemples aux pages 80–81.) (2) Décrivez le logement à vos camarades de classe. (Quels sont les avantages? Combien de pièces est-ce qu'il y a? Quels meubles est-ce qu'il y a? etc.) (3) Écoutez les descriptions de vos camarades de classe. Quel logement préférez-vous? Pourquoi?

➡ *Je préfère le logement de Matt. Il y a trois chambres; c'est idéal pour trois personnes.*

STRUCTURE: Asking information questions
Les adverbes interrogatifs

Observez et déduisez   *Des questions indiscrètes...*

... Et vous? Où est-ce que vous habitez? Dans une maison ou dans un apparte-ment? Comment est votre chambre? Grande? Petite? Pourquoi est-ce que vous aimez votre chambre? Parce qu'elle est confortable? Combien de disques com-pacts est-ce que vous avez? 10? 20? Quand est-ce que vous voudriez écouter vos disques compacts? Aujourd'hui *(today)*? Maintenant? Demain *(tomorrow)*?

> ■ What are the interrogative words used in the preceding questions?
> Which interrogative adverb refers to
>
> an amount   a place   a description
> a time   a reason

Vérifiez   *Les adverbes interrogatifs*

Point out that **qu'est-ce que** and **qui est-ce que,** studied in Chapter 2, fit this same pattern.

■ Information questions with interrogative adverbs like **où, quand, combien de, comment,** and **pourquoi** usually follow this pattern:

Interrogative word + est-ce que + subject + verb
Où est-ce que tu habites?
Quand est-ce que tu étudies?
Combien de CD est-ce que tu as?

Teach inversion for recognition only.

■ These adverbs can also be used with inversion.

Interrogative word + verb + subject pronoun
Combien de posters as-tu?
Pourquoi étudies-tu?

VOCABULAIRE ACTIF
Comment... ?
Où... ?
Pourquoi... ?
... parce que...
Quand... ?
... aujourd'hui
... demain
... maintenant
visiter

■ **Où** and **comment** can be followed directly by **être** + a noun subject.

Où est ta chambre?
Comment est ton appartement?

■ To answer a question with **pourquoi,** begin with **parce que.**

Pourquoi est-ce que tu n'as pas de vidéocassettes?
Parce que je n'ai pas de magnétoscope!

■ To answer a question with **quand,** the following adverbs are useful: **aujourd'hui, demain, maintenant.**

Quand est-ce que je peux visiter l'appartement?
Oh, **aujourd'hui, maintenant,** si vous voulez.

F. EXEMPLE: (1) Oui, il y a des lits, des tables, un canapé, des rideaux. CUES: 2. Non, il n'est pas loué.   3. Il est grand et agréable.   4. Il y a deux chambres, une cuisine, un salon, une salle de bains et les W.C.   5. Aujour-d'hui.   6. Il est sur le boulevard de la République.

ACTIVITÉS

F. Je cherche un appartement.   Voici des questions que vous posez au sujet d'une petite annonce. Écoutez les réponses du professeur et décidez à quelle question il/elle répond.

➡ (1. Oui, il y a des lits, des tables, un canapé, des rideaux, etc.)

_____1_____ L'appartement est meublé?

_____4_____ Combien de pièces est-ce qu'il y a?

_____6_____ Où est l'appartement?

_____5_____ Quand est-ce que je pourrais voir l'appartement?

_____2_____ Est-ce que l'appartement est loué?

_____3_____ Comment est l'appartement?

G. If students are ready, have them supply their own answers as they read the questions.

G. Une petite annonce. Deux copains discutent d'une petite annonce. Reliez les questions et les réponses logiques des colonnes ci-dessous.

Questions

_e_____ 1. Pourquoi est-ce que tu cherches un appartement? Pourquoi pas un studio?

_c_____ 2. C'est vrai. Alors, où est cet appartement?

_d_____ 3. Et comment est-il, selon l'annonce?

_b_____ 4. Ah, bon? Et il y a combien de chambres?

_a_____ 5. Et quand est-ce que tu téléphones au propriétaire?

Réponses

a. Demain.
b. Trois, je pense.
c. Sur le boulevard Manet.
d. Il est grand et confortable.
e. Parce qu'ils sont trop petits.

Maintenant, jouez le rôle des deux copains, et lisez le dialogue avec un(e) partenaire.

H. Encourage students to ask yes/no questions and to use **qui, qui est-ce que,** and **qu'est-ce que** as well as interrogative adverbs.

H. Curiosité. Est-ce qu'une chambre reflète la vie de la personne qui y habite? Posez des questions au sujet de la (des) personne(s) qui habite(nt) cette chambre.

➡ Où est-ce qu'elle travaille? (étudie? habite?)

Jeu de rôle

You've rented a room near the university, and you're discussing your ideas with the landlord. Tell him some things you'd like to do, and ask if you are allowed to do other things (_Je voudrais..., Est-ce que je pourrais... ?_). The landlord is very curious (perhaps nosy!) and asks many questions (_Où... ? Quand... ? Qui... ?_ etc.).

Help students get started by recycling **-er** verbs and brainstorming a few ideas with the class: Je voudrais/ Est-ce que je pourrais... inviter mes copains, écouter la radio, regarder la télévision, manger avec la famille, parler au téléphone, étudier dans le salon, etc.

W B

Deuxième étape

Lecture: Les Français et leur logement

This input presents cultural information and previews numbers over 60 as well as adjective placement/agreement.

You are going to read a survey taken from *Le Journal Français d'Amérique* about housing in France. What kind of information do you expect to find in such a survey?

Avant de lire

1 This is critical thinking at work! For the matching activity, do 70, 80, and 90 with the whole class. (Soixante-dix, qu'est-ce que c'est? et quatre-vingts? quatre-vingt-dix? Maintenant avec un(e) partenaire, trouvez les autres réponses!) If students seem to struggle, do the whole matching activity together; save group work for the guessing game. You may mention that in Belgium, 70 = **septante**, 90 = **nonante**; 91, 92 = **nonante et un, nonante-deux**, etc. In Switzerland, 80 = **octante.**

Cue to Video Module 3, street interviews (00:14:23), where people describe where they live.

1 Surveys include numbers and percentages **(les nombres et les pourcentages).** French numbers between 70 and 99 follow a pattern that is a remnant of the system used by the Celts, who counted by twenties. Knowing this, can you match the numbers on the left with their French form on the right?

1. 70	a. soixante-dix
2. 71	b. quatre-vingts
3. 72	c. quatre-vingt-dix
4. 80	d. soixante et onze
5. 81	e. soixante-douze
6. 85	f. quatre-vingt-onze
7. 90	g. quatre-vingt-dix-huit
8. 91	h. quatre-vingt-un
9. 98	i. quatre-vingt-cinq

Now, can you guess how to say the following numbers?

73   76   84   87   95   99

2 **Un sondage.** Interview ten of your classmates. Ask them the following questions and note their answers.

1. Où est-ce que tu préfères habiter?

 a. _____ dans une maison individuelle   _____ dans un appartement

 b. _____ dans une grande ville   _____ dans une petite ville ou une commune rurale

2. Qu'est-ce qui est plus (+) important dans la sélection d'un logement?

 a. _____ le prix *(price)*

 b. _____ l'emplacement *(location)*

Après le sondage, transformez les résultats en pourcentages.

➡ *Six personnes sur dix, ou 60% (soixante pour cent), préfèrent habiter dans une grande ville. Pour 70%, le prix est plus important.*

3 Skim the text that follows and match each section with an appropriate title.

section 1   a. «Le type de logement des Français»
section 2   b. «L'attitude des Français vis à vis de leur logement»
section 3   c. «Les facteurs importants pour sélectionner un
logement»

SONDAGE

86 % DES FRANÇAIS sont satisfaits de leur logement. Les propriétaires sont plus satisfaits que les locataires (96 % contre 74 %), les habitants de maisons individuelles plus satisfaits que ceux qui habitent un appartement (94 % contre 75 %), et les provinciaux plus heureux que les Parisiens (88 % contre 76 %).

55 % DES FRANÇAIS HABITENT dans une maison individuelle (ils étaient 48 % en 1962), 45 % dans un appartement. 52 % des ménages sont propriétaires de leur logement (67 % dans les communes rurales, 34 % à Paris).

LES PRINCIPAUX CRITÈRES de choix d'un logement sont, par ordre décroissant: le calme (27 %), la proximité du lieu de travail (26 %), le prix (22 %), la proximité des commerces (18 %), la proximité des écoles (17 %).

Adapté de «Les Français sur le vif», *Journal Français d'Amérique,* 17–30 mai, 1991, p. 3.

En détail

4 **Les mots.**   Using context and logic, can you infer the meaning of the words that follow? Match the words on the left with their synonyms or definitions on the right.

1. les habitants
2. les locataires
3. les Parisiens
4. les provinciaux
5. satisfaits
6. le choix
7. l'ordre
8. le lieu
9. les ménages
10. le calme

a. les personnes qui louent (une maison, un appartement)
b. les personnes qui habitent les diverses régions de France
c. les personnes qui habitent (une maison, une ville, etc.)
d. les personnes qui habitent à Paris
e. les familles
f. la place, l'emplacement
g. la tranquillité
h. heureux
i. la hiérarchie, l'organisation
j. la sélection

VOCABULAIRE ACTIF

calme
une commune rurale
un emplacement
individuel(le)
un lieu
un locataire
le prix
satisfait(e)

5 **Le sondage**

A. **Les pourcentages.**   Indiquez les pourcentages donnés dans l'article.

satisfaction   74%____ des locataires aiment leur logement.

88%____ des provinciaux aiment leur logement.

75%____ des habitants d'appartements aiment leur logement.

possession   52%____ des familles françaises sont propriétaires de leur logement.

34%____ des Parisiens sont propriétaires de leur logement.

type de logement   45%____ des Français habitent dans un appartement.

55%____ des Français habitent dans une maison individuelle.

B. **Plus (+) ou moins (−).**   Décidez si les phrases suivantes sont vraies ou fausses, selon l'article. Si elles sont fausses, corrigez-les.

1. Plus de Français habitent dans une maison individuelle que dans un appartement.
2. La proximité des écoles est plus importante que la proximité du lieu de travail.
3. Le prix est moins important que la proximité des commerces.
4. Le calme est plus important que l'emplacement.

Additional activity if time allows: À la base d'un sondage, il y a des questions. Formulez les questions qui sont à la base de ce sondage.

Et vous?

Le sondage présente l'ordre des critères de choix d'un logement pour les Français. Est-ce que cet ordre est le même *(the same)* pour vous? pour les Américains en général?

VOCABULAIRE
Les nombres

Combien coûte *(costs)* un logement typique?

Begin by reviewing numbers to 69, from Chapter 2. Use the following drill to practice numbers introduced on p. 90. COMPREHENSION DRILL: Write numbers from 70 to 100 on note cards and pass out to students. Ask, e.g., «Qui a soixante-quinze?» and have the student hold up the note card.

Loyer d'un appartement au centre d'Aix-en-Provence

Loyer d'une chambre meublée à Lyon

Prix d'un appartement à Paris, 3ᵉ arrondissement

Show students that it is easy to read large numbers if they simply begin from the left and break them down into millions, thousands, hundreds, etc. Use the following numbers as examples: 994; 1 246; 300 333; 80 867; 1 220 751.

Other than when writing checks, one seldom writes out large numbers. Still, you should notice in the preceding examples that **vingt** and **cent** are written with an **-s** when they are preceded but not followed by another number. **Mille** never takes an **-s,** and no hyphen is used with **cent** or **mille.** A space or period is used to separate groups of thousands: **1 000** or **1.000.**

Numbers 100 and above follow a simple pattern.

100	cent	200	deux cents
101	cent un	301	trois cent un
102	cent deux	402	quatre cent deux
1 000	mille	1 500	mille cinq cents
1 001	mille un	1 515	mille cinq cent quinze
2 000	deux mille	3 620	trois mille six cent vingt
10 000	dix mille	100 000	cent mille
1 000 000	un million	1 000 000 000	un milliard

ACTIVITÉS

A. Combien?   Combien coûtent les meubles que votre professeur voudrait pour sa maison? Écoutez les prix et identifiez les objets ci-dessous. Numérotez-les dans l'ordre que vous entendez.

LAMPE **190**F▷

LA COMMODE **1350**F

1290F

LITS SUPERPOSÉS

LE CANAPÉ + 1 FAUTEUIL **4490**F

ÉTAGÈRES **1150**F▷

ORDINATEUR **7590**F▽

BUREAU △**850**F

_____ lampe	_____ commode	_____ canapé et fauteuil
_____ étagères	_____ ordinateur	_____ lits superposés
__1__ bureau		

B. Les prix. Regardez les objets du catalogue. Combien coûtent les objets que vous voudriez avoir pour votre chambre ou appartement? En tout *(For everything)* ça coûte combien?

➡ *Je voudrais avoir _____ et _____ . _____*

coûte _____ francs et _____ coûte _____

francs. En tout, ça coûte _____ francs.

C. Quel logement? (1) Choisissez le logement que vous préférez parmi les petites annonces suivantes. (2) Dites à votre partenaire combien coûte le logement et quel est le numéro de téléphone. (3) Votre partenaire écrit les nombres et identifie votre choix.

➡ — *Ça coûte ... par mois. Je téléphone au numéro...*
— *Ah bon. C'est le logement numéro...*

Maintenant, changez de rôle et répétez.

Le long d'un canal à Strasbourg.

IMMOBILIER

▼ **ventes**
APPARTEMENTS

3ᵉ arrondt
RUE CHARLOT IIIᵉ
COMME UNE MAISON
159 m² + 70 m² cour privative
Parfait état – 3 750 000 F
AGENCE DU MUSÉE
01-42-78-08-02

11ᵉ arrondt
Pptaire vd beaux appts
REFAITS A NEUF
– stud. 34 m² s/jd   493 000 F
– 2 P 52 m² s/jd   712 000 F
– 2 P. 54 m² s/jd   772 000 F
– 2 P 57 m²   799 000 F
53, AV. PARMENTIER
Visites mercredi et jeudi
de 11 à 13 h et de 14 à 19 h.
SEFIMEG 01-48-06-22-96

14ᵉ arrondt

ALESIA
Voie privée s/ verdure,
2 chbres, séj. terrasse,
originalité, calme,
1 540 000 F   01-45-42-49-26

province

NÎMES
80 m², vue sur golf, cuis. et
salle de bains équipées,
chauf. gaz, terrasse, gar,
Parf. état. Expo sud, vue.
Prix : 820 000 F
Tél. : 04-66-64-12-82-HR

PROPRIÉTÉS
Marseille
Part. vd
PROPRIÉTÉ PROVENÇALE
12 ha. Site d'exception vallon
colline et pins. Calme.
Bâtisse rustique,
130 m² + studio indép., grd
gar. 1,5 MF.
Tél. : 04-91-45-35-38

D. Have students report on distances before beginning their search for vacation partners.

D. Une maison de vacances. D'abord imaginez que vous habitez à Paris et que vous voulez passer vos vacances «en province». Vous décidez entre les villes suivantes, des lieux de vacances populaires. Trouvez les villes sur la carte de France, au début du livre. Puis calculez les distances entre ces villes et Paris en employant le tableau suivant.

➡ *Montpellier est à 766 kilomètres de Paris.*

Dijon								
293	Grenoble							
578	668	La Rochelle						
249	317	839	Marseille					
493	302	683	156	Montpellier				
661	336	992	190	309	Nice			
310	566	468	771	766	934	Paris		
450	711	467	910	905	1073	139	Rouen	
312	507	875	756	741	909	455	576	Strasbourg

Maintenant, décidez dans quelle ville vous voudriez passer vos vacances selon la distance et l'emplacement. Cherchez des camarades de classe qui désirent passer leurs vacances dans le même endroit.

STRUCTURES: Describing people and things
La place des adjectifs • Quelques adjectifs irréguliers

Observez et déduisez Eh bien, nous sommes les propriétaires satisfaits d'une belle maison dans une commune rurale. C'est une communauté calme et agréable, pas trop loin d'une grande ville. Pour nous, c'est un logement idéal.

■ Can you find six noun-adjective combinations in the preceding paragraph?

➡ *un logement idéal*

■ Based on the examples that you found in the text, what can you infer about the placement of adjectives in relationship to the nouns they modify?

■ You have already seen that some adjectives are irregular, for example, **fou/folle.** Based on what you know about adjective agreement, can you fill in the chart of irregular adjectives below?

masculin singulier	masculin pluriel	féminin singulier	féminin pluriel
beau	beaux	belle	belles
nouveau			
	bons	bonne	
vieux			vieilles

Vérifiez   *La place des adjectifs; les adjectifs irréguliers*

■ In general, adjectives follow the nouns they modify.

une commune rurale
des rideaux rouges

■ A few adjectives precede the nouns they modify.

beau *(good-looking; lovely)*	un beau salon
joli *(pretty)*	une jolie maison
jeune *(young)*	un jeune locataire
vieux *(old)*	un vieux propriétaire
nouveau *(new)*	un nouveau studio
mauvais *(bad)*	un mauvais emplacement
bon *(good)*	un bon prix
petit	un petit appartement
grand	une grande chambre
autre *(other)*	un autre logement

■ In careful speech, the indefinite article **des** becomes **de** before a plural adjective preceding a noun. This change is mandatory with **autres.**

des maisons spacieuses
de/des belles maisons
d'autres maisons

■ Adjectives can be placed before *and* after a single noun.

une **petite** maison **blanche***
un **vieux** tapis **jaune**

---

*Blanc is the masculine form: **un tapis blanc.**

VOCABULAIRE ACTIF

agréable
autre
beau (belle)
blanc (blanche)
bon(ne)
confortable
jeune
joli(e)
mauvais(e)
nouveau (nouvelle)
rouge
spacieux (spacieuse)
vieux (vieille)

E. Ask volunteers to explain their answers.

■ In addition to the patterns you identified earlier, three adjectives have special forms for the masculine singular used before words beginning with a vowel or a silent **h:**

> un **bel** emplacement
> un **nouvel** appartement confortable
> un **vieil** hôtel

■ The plural form of these adjectives is regular.

> de **beaux** appartements
> les **vieux** hôtels

ACTIVITÉS

E. Une description.   Les adjectifs suivants décrivent un logement ou la personne associée au logement. Remarquez la forme des adjectifs et décidez à quoi ou à qui ils se réfèrent. **Soulignez** la bonne réponse.

1. nouvel   la maison / l'appartement
2. mauvais   l'emplacement / la commune
3. grands et vieux   les chambres / les fauteuils
4. petite mais agréable le salon / la cuisine
5. jolies   les pièces / les meubles
6. jeune et beau   la locataire / le propriétaire

Maintenant, dites comment est ce logement selon vos réponses.

➡ *La cuisine est...*

Voudriez-vous habiter ce logement?

F. Comparaisons.   Cochez les adjectifs qui décrivent votre logement, etc., ou ajoutez un adjectif approprié.

1. ma maison
    ____ blanche   ____ vieille   ____ idéale   ____ belle   ____ ?
2. mon fauteuil
    ____ bleu   ____ bon   ____ vieux   ____ confortable   ____ ?
3. mon salon
    ____ meublé   ____ typique   ____ agréable   ____ grand   ____ ?
4. ma chambre
    ____ petite   ____ bonne   ____ belle   ____ intéressante   ____ ?
5. mes copains
    ____ jeunes   ____ patients   ____ beaux   ____ optimistes   ____ ?

Maintenant, interviewez un(e) camarade de classe. Soulignez les adjectifs qui décrivent *son* logement, etc., et répondez à ses questions.

➡ — *Comment est ta maison?*   _____ belle

Ensuite écrivez un paragraphe où vous comparez vos logements.

➡ *J'ai une vieille maison blanche, mais Frédéric a...*

G. Des préférences différentes. Complétez les phrases avec les adjectifs suivants. Attention à l'accord et au placement!

calme   grande   nouvel   vieilles
sympathique   beaux   individuelles   jeune
petite   agréable   rurale   vieux
chinois

1. Moi, je préfère les _____ maisons _____ .
2. J'habite une _____ commune _____ au Québec.
3. Je préfère un emplacement _____ et _____ .
4. Ma copine, par contre, a un _____ appartement dans une _____ ville.
5. Dans l'appartement, elle a de _____ meubles et un _____ tapis _____ .
6. Elle a un _____ propriétaire _____ aussi.

Est-ce que ces phrases sont vraies pour vous?

H. Imaginons. Décrivez un logement idéal pour les personnes suivantes, selon leur personnalité.

une personne qui aime le calme   votre professeur
Picasso   le président des Etats-Unis

 Jeu de rôle

You and your partner play the roles of an interior decorator and a client who wishes to renovate an old, three-bedroom apartment. The decorator asks questions to understand the client's needs (family, pastimes), personality, and color preferences. There are three children in the family, and money *is* an object, so the client asks questions about costs. The decorator offers suggestions for renovation until the client is satisfied.

CULTURE ET RÉFLEXION

Internet

■ **La vie privée.** Privacy is sacred to French people, and a home is a private domain, reserved for family and close friends. The French rarely invite acquaintances to their home. They invite them to a restaurant or a café instead. What do you think of this custom? Is it a good idea to invite people you don't know too well to your home?

■ **Fenêtres, portes et murs.** For the sake of privacy again, French houses have shutters that are closed at nightfall. A French person in a house without shutters in the evening feels like a fish in a fish tank, exposed to the public eye. Inside the house, the doors to the various rooms are generally kept shut, especially the door to «**le petit coin**», which is *never* left open, not even to indicate that the bathroom is unoccupied. Outside the house, walls and gates generally separate the yard from the neighbors' and from the street. What is your concept of private space? Do you close your curtains or drapes at night? Are there doors inside your house or apartment that you keep closed? How do you define private space in your culture?

■ **Les concessions.** African villagers live with their extended family in **concessions**, which consist of small dwellings (**les cases**) built around a common courtyard. Young children generally live in their mother's **case**. Teenage boys live in a separate **case**.

La vie privée, c'est sacré.

Une concession dans un village du Burkina Faso.

Teenage girls may share a **case** with their grandmother. The head of the family often has **sa case personnelle**. Most family activities take place outside, in the courtyard. Where do most family activities take place in your home?

Troisième étape

À l'écoute: Je cherche la rue...

Being able to ask for and give directions is essential to surviving in a foreign country. As you listen to the student audio CD, you will hear just how this is done in French. Do the activities in **Avant d'écouter,** then read the tasks in **Écoutons** before you listen.

Avant d'écouter

1 Imagine you have just arrived in Aix-en-Provence. You are at the train station **(la gare SNCF)** and you need directions to get to a certain street. First look at the map **(le plan de la ville)** on page 102. What are the different words that precede street names? Which one probably means *street?* What is the abbreviation for **le boulevard? l'avenue? la place?**

2 When you *ask* for directions, you may begin by saying **Je cherche...** *(I'm looking for . . .).* What other words can you expect to use when you *give* directions? Look at the following expressions and match them with the correct pictures, using cognates and logic.

a. Allez tout droit.
b. Traversez la rue.
c. Tournez à droite dans l'avenue Louis Pasteur.
d. Tournez à gauche dans la rue Espariat.

101

Écoutons

Audio CD

3 Listen to the conversation a first time and identify on the map the streets or places mentioned. Then listen again and trace with your finger the woman's route on the map, from start to finish. Begin at **la gare SNCF.**

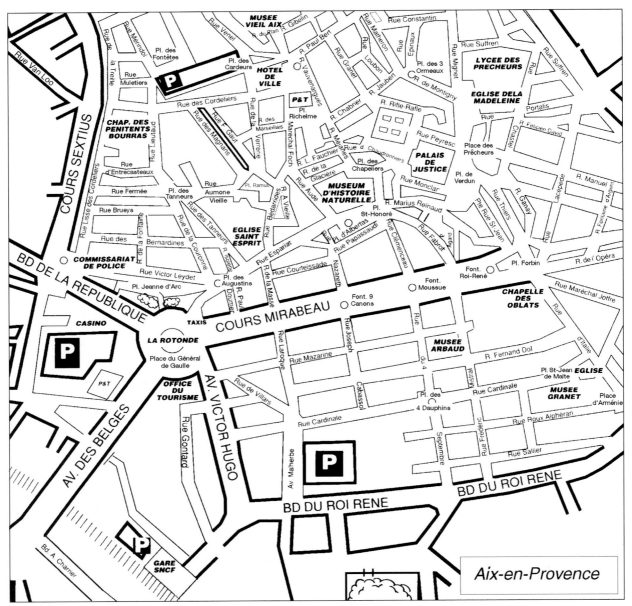

Aix-en-Provence

3 More than two listenings may be necessary for this task. Encourage students to work in groups. If they need help, write proper names (Mirabeau, Clémenceau) on the board. ANSWER: Av. V. Hugo → Rotonde → Cours Mirabeau → rue Clémenceau.

4 Listen to the conversation a final time, focusing on the following words. From the context, and using the map to follow along, can you infer their meaning? Select the proper English equivalent.

1. devant
2. jusqu'à

a. *to, until*
b. *from*
c. *behind*
d. *in front of*

5 ANSWER: quatrième.

5 According to the map, which is correct: la troisième ou la quatrième rue? Can you now infer how to form an ordinal number (i.e., *three* → *third*)? Complete the following chart. Irregular forms are already provided.

un →	premier/première	six →	
deux →		sept →	
trois →		huit →	
quatre →		neuf →	neuvième
cinq →	cinquième	dix →	

Les sons [u] *et* [y]

■ [u] is the vowel sound in **vous.** It is spelled **ou,** and unlike its English counterpart, it is never pronounced as a diphthong, that is, two vowel sounds in the same syllable. Compare the following:

English: new [nuʷ] *French:* nous [nu]
two [tuʷ] tout [tu]

■ To pronounce a French [u] correctly, say it as a single sound, with your mouth almost closed.

■ [y] is the vowel sound in **tu.** It is spelled **u,** and has no equivalent sound in English. To produce it, say [i], with your tongue pressed firmly against your lower front teeth, then round your lips like for [u]. Again, there is no diphthong.

tu sal**ut**

ANSWERS to **Écoutez:** 1. r**u**e 2. v**ou**s 3. aven**u**e, H**u**go 5. **u**ne, aven**u**e, c**ou**rs 6. v**ou**s, t**ou**rnez, s**u**r, c**ou**rs 7. **ou**, r**u**e Point out that the **u** in **qu** does not represent an [y] sound, and that **au** is pronounced [o].

Écoutez

Audio CD

Listen to the following expressions from **À l'écoute: Je cherche la rue** on your student audio CD. Each expression will be read twice. In the chart, write the words that contain the sounds [u] or [y]. The chart has been started for you. If you need to, turn off the audio CD after each item in order to write your answers.

VOCABULAIRE ACTIF
aller
chercher
devant
Les directions
à gauche
à droite
tout droit
jusqu'à
Les nombres ordinaux
premier, deuxième, etc.
tourner
traverser
La ville
une avenue
un boulevard
la gare
une place
un plan de la ville
une rue

	[u]	[y]
1. la rue Clémenceau		
2. comment vous expliquer		
3. l'avenue Victor Hugo		
4. vous allez tout droit jusqu'à La Rotonde	vous, tout	jusqu'à
5. une grande avenue qui s'appelle le cours Mirabeau		
6. vous tournez à droite sur le cours Mirabeau		
7. c'est la troisième ou quatrième rue à gauche		

Essayez!

Audio CD

B. To help students with the challenging combination of [r] and [y], remind them to keep the tip of their tongue firmly pressed against their lower front teeth for both [r] and [y], and to keep their mouth almost closed, with their lips rounded as if drinking through a straw.

A. Prononcez. Practice saying the expressions in the **Écoutez** section aloud. Then listen to the expressions on the student audio CD to verify your pronunciation.

B. [u] **et** [y].   For additional practice, say the following pairs of words aloud. Then listen to the words on the student audio CD to verify your pronunciation.

1. vous / vu
2. tout / tu
3. nous / nu

4. roux / rue
5. rousse / russe
6. cours / cure

7. rouge / mur
8. beaucoup / bureau

STRUCTURES: Asking for and giving directions

*Le verbe **aller*** • *L'impératif*

Observez et déduisez

Cue to Video Module 3 (00:12:48), where Fatima gives her friend directions to the room she wants to visit.

— Pardon, monsieur, pourriez-vous me dire où se trouve (où est) le boulevard de la République?
— Euh, voyons, vous allez tout droit dans l'avenue Victor Hugo jusqu'à la place du Général de Gaulle. Tournez à gauche sur la place. Le boulevard de la République est la deuxième rue à gauche.
— Ah bon, je vais tout droit, puis je tourne à gauche sur la place du Général de Gaulle?
— C'est ça!

■ Find a polite expression in the dialogue for asking directions.

■ Can you identify two forms of the verb **aller?**

■ Why, do you think, the verb **tournez** has no subject pronoun?

Vérifiez   *Le verbe **aller***

OPTIONAL DRILL: Changez les pronoms sujets. Tu vas tout droit. (nous) → Nous allons tout droit. CUES: 1. Tu vas tout droit. (vous, ils, nous, je, le professeur) 2. Il va dans la rue Cardinale. (nous, je, les garçons, vous, elle) 3. Nous allons jusqu'à la place. (tu, vous, les touristes, je, il)

■ The verb **aller** *(to go)* is irregular. You have seen it used to say or ask how someone is doing.

Comment-allez vous?   Ça va bien.

Le verbe aller	
je vais	nous allons
tu vas	vous allez
il / elle / on va	ils / elles vont

Contractions with **à** and **de** are introduced in the next **Structure** section.

■ **Aller** is frequently followed by the preposition **à** to indicate movement toward a place.

Vous **allez à** La Rotonde et vous tournez à gauche.

■ Use the preposition **dans** with **avenue** and **rue**. Use **sur** with **place** and **boulevard.**

Vous allez **dans** l'avenue des Belges (**dans** la rue d'Italie).
Vous allez **sur** le boulevard du Roi René (**sur** la place du Général de Gaulle).

The imperative is recycled in Ch. 10, 2ᵉ étape.

VOCABULAIRE ACTIF

continuer
dans
une église
Pardon, monsieur...
prenez
Pourriez-vous me dire...
se trouver
sur

OPTIONAL DRILL: Mettez les phrases à l'impératif. Tu vas tout droit. → Va tout droit! CUES: 1. Tu traverses la rue. 2. Vous prenez la rue Ganay. 3. Vous allez jusqu'à la place. 4. Tu cherches le cours Mirabeau. 5. Vous tournez à gauche. 6. Tu ne vas pas tout droit. 7. Tu tournes à droite. 8. Vous ne traversez pas la rue.

A. Students may work with a partner. Check answers and ask volunteers to correct false statements, e.g., #6 «Non, La Rotonde.» ANSWERS: 1. vrai 2. faux—le cours Mirabeau 3. faux—à gauche 4. faux—l'avenue Victor Hugo 5. faux—la place St-Honoré 6. faux—La Rotonde 7. faux—la cinquième à gauche.

B. Students find the appropriate square and produce only the correct form of **aller**. Have all students complete the exercise individually or in groups before sharing answers. They should be able to infer unfamiliar vocabulary in the cues.

C. Begin by brainstorming relevant verbs and prepositions for giving directions as you list the words on the board. Do an example with the class, eliciting several ways to reach the same location. Finish as a paired activity.

L'impératif

■ The imperative, or command form, is also used in giving directions. It is formed by dropping the subject pronoun.

Vous prenez *(take)* le cours Mirabeau.   →   **Prenez** le cours Mirabeau.

■ For the familiar **(tu)** form of the imperative, the **-s** of **-er** verbs and of **aller** is dropped.

Tu ne tourn**es** pas à gauche.   →   Ne tourn**e** pas à gauche.
Tu v**as** tout droit.   →   V**a** tout droit.

■ In giving directions, you will frequently use a subject *and* the verb instead of the imperative.

Vous continuez tout droit pour aller à l'église.

■ The following expression is commonly used to ask for directions politely.

Pourriez-vous me dire où est (où se trouve) le musée?
Could you tell me where the museum is (is located)?

ACTIVITÉS

A. Vrai ou faux? Décidez si les phrases suivantes sont vraies ou fausses selon le plan d'Aix, page 102.

1. Le Palais de Justice est sur la place de Verdun.
2. Vous êtes à La Rotonde. Pour aller à la place Forbin, vous allez dans l'avenue Victor Hugo.
3. Vous êtes au musée Granet. Pour aller à la place des Quatre-Dauphins, vous allez à droite dans la rue Cardinale.
4. Si vous êtes à la gare, le cours Mirabeau est tout droit devant vous.
5. Le Muséum d'histoire naturelle se trouve sur la place des Augustins.
6. Si vous allez de la gare à la place Jeanne d'Arc, vous traversez la place de Verdun.
7. Vous êtes à La Rotonde et vous prenez le cours Mirabeau. La rue Fabrot est la quatrième rue à droite.

B. À quelle place? Vous êtes à Aix avec votre professeur et vos camarades de classe! Dites à quelle place vont les personnes suivantes selon leur situation.

Pl. Jeanne d'Arc	Pl. Richelme	Pl. St-Jean de Malte
Pl. St-Honoré	Pl. du Général de Gaulle	Pl. de Verdun

➡ Nous cherchons un taxi.
Nous allons sur la place du Général de Gaulle.

1. Le professeur aime beaucoup les sciences naturelles.
2. Deux étudiantes s'intéressent au système judiciaire.
3. Vous cherchez des renseignements touristiques.
4. Une copine et moi, nous sommes catholiques pratiquantes.
5. Je perds *(lose)* mon passeport.
6. Tu voudrais poster une lettre.

C. Devinez! *(Guess!)* Choisissez un endroit sur le plan d'Aix. Donnez des directions pour aller à cet endroit à un(e) camarade de classe. Il/Elle va deviner le nom de l'endroit. Commencez à la gare!

STRUCTURES: Saying where you're going and what you're going to do

Le futur proche • Les contractions

Observez et déduisez   Je vais traverser La Rotonde pour aller à la poste dans l'avenue des Belges. Ensuite, je vais acheter des CD et des livres aux magasins sur le cours Mirabeau. Finalement, je vais manger au café près du cinéma.

> ■ What do you notice about the form of the verbs that immediately follow **aller** in the preceding paragraph?
>
> ■ What happens to the preposition **à** before **magasins** and **café?** What happens to **de** before **cinéma?** Can you think of a reason for the changes?

Vérifiez   *Le futur proche*

OPTIONAL DRILL: **Du présent au futur.** Je tourne à droite. ⟶ Je vais tourner à droite.   CUES: 1. Je continue tout droit.   2. Tu tournes à gauche.   3. Elle traverse la place.   4. Nous visitons le musée.   5. Vous cherchez La Rotonde.   6. Ils vont dans l'avenue Victor Hugo.

■ The verb **aller** is frequently followed by an infinitive to say what one is *going to do*. This is called the **futur proche,** the *near* future.

   Nous **allons manger** au café sur le cours Mirabeau.

■ In the negative, place **ne ... pas** around the conjugated verb **aller.** The infinitive follows.

   Nous **n'allons pas visiter** le musée Granet.

Les contractions

OPTIONAL DRILL: **Les contractions.** Hold up one finger for singular nouns, two for plural.   CUES: 1. Nous allons à (cinéma, magasins, musées, églises, poste).   2. L'église est près de (hôtel, églises, parc, maisons, poste).

■ The prepositions **à** and **de** contract with **le** and **les** as follows:

   Elles vont **au** cinéma près **du** parc.
   Nous allons **aux** magasins près **des** restaurants.

■ There is no contraction with **la** or **l'.**

   Les étudiants sont **à l'**hôtel près **de la** poste.

VOCABULAIRE ACTIF

un café
un magasin
un musée
un parc
la poste
près de

Les contractions	
à + le = **au**	de + le = **du**
à + les = **aux**	de + les = **des**

ACTIVITÉS

D. Projets.   Anne voyage à Aix avec des copains. Jouez le rôle d'un copain ou d'une copine et indiquez si vous avez les mêmes projets qu'Anne. Si non, dites ce que vous allez faire *(to do).*

   ➡ ANNE: Je vais chercher un hôtel dans l'avenue Victor Hugo.
      VOUS: *Moi aussi!*   ou   *Pas moi. Je vais chercher un hôtel dans l'avenue des Belges.*

1. Je vais visiter l'Office de Tourisme.
2. Je vais chercher un taxi à La Rotonde.
3. Je vais aller à l'église de la Madeleine.
4. Je vais voir une exposition au musée Granet.
5. Je vais retrouver mes copains sur la place Forbin.
6. Je vais dîner au restaurant sur le cours Mirabeau.

E. Où va-t-on? Les membres de la famille ont des destinations différentes. Dites où ils vont, probablement, en employant le futur proche.

➡ Maman voudrait poster une lettre.
Alors, elle va aller à la poste.

1. Papa et moi, nous voudrions manger.
2. Je voudrais acheter un livre.
3. Mes sœurs adorent l'art et la sculpture.
4. Mon frère voudrait voir le nouveau film de Juliette Binoche.
5. Maman voudrait acheter une télécarte.
6. Mes grands-parents voudraient voyager de Villeneuve à Paris.

VOCABULAIRE
La ville et les prépositions de lieu

Hélène est sur la place Bonaparte devant l'église. Elle cherche le cinéma qui est au coin de l'avenue Victor Hugo et de la rue Mazarin, à côté du restaurant La Bonne Cuisine. La banque est en face du musée, entre le café et l'Hôtel Crécy. Hélène est près de l'école mais loin de l'université. Plus tard, elle va aller au parc derrière la pharmacie.

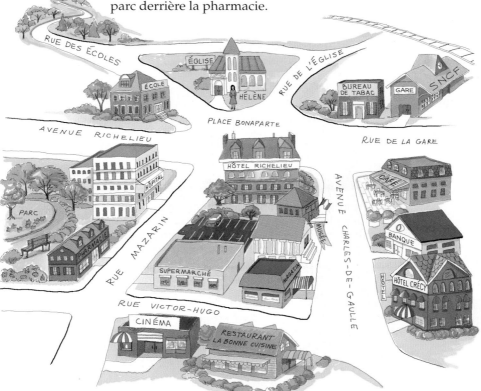

For additional practice with directions, you may wish to use the transparency of Métro de Paris, provide the following cultural information, and have students work in pairs on the tasks given.

Le métro de Paris is one of the best-developed subway systems in the world. The lines are designated by the **directions,** or stations at the end of each line. For example, one of the purple lines is referred to as **Porte d'Orléans-Porte de Clignancourt.** To determine your route on the **Plan du métro,** find the station where you want to get off and the station at the end of the line beyond it. If you need to change lines *(faire la correspondance),* identify the station where you will change trains and the new direction. Do not confuse subway lines with the thicker **RER** lines for trains that run between Paris and its suburbs. «Imaginez que vous êtes à la Sorbonne (Cluny-Sorbonne) et vous voudriez aller à la Tour Eiffel. Trouvez ces deux stations sur le plan du métro, puis identifiez la direction de la première ligne (Boulogne-Pont de Saint-Cloud) et de la deuxième ligne (Charles de Gaulle-Étoile). Où allez-vous faire la correpondance? (La Motte-Picquet). Maintenant, en groupes de deux, identifiez les itinéraires suivants (s'il y a plusieurs possibilités, identifiez la possibilité la plus directe):»
1. Point de départ: Gare Montparnasse; destination: Le Louvre
2. Point de départ: L'Arc de triomphe (Place de l'Étoile); destination: le cimetière du Père Lachaise.   3. Point de départ: Rue Montmartre; destination: la Sorbonne. (Help students as needed.)

Based on the clues in the paragraph and the map, match the prepositions on the left with the terms on the right.

_____ 1. entre	a. *in front of*	
_____ 2. derrière	b. *beside*	
_____ 3. en face de	c. *far from*	
_____ 4. loin de	d. *facing*	
_____ 5. devant	e. *at the corner of*	
_____ 6. près de	f. *behind*	
_____ 7. à côté de	g. *near*	
_____ 8. au coin de	h. *between*	

F. CUES: Je suis... 1. derrière le magasin 2. à côté du cinéma 3. en face du supermarché 4. près de la gare 5. entre la poste et le magasin 6. au coin de l'avenue Richelieu et de la rue des Écoles. To correct, reread the cues and have students respond.

G. You may do this as a whole-class activity using the corresponding transparency. Continue by asking volunteers to mention other spatial relationships.

Can you identify the following buildings **(bâtiments)** on the map: la banque? la pharmacie? le supermarché? le bureau de tabac? l'hôpital? le café?

ACTIVITÉS

F. Bâtiments.   Écoutez le professeur expliquer où il/elle est. Numérotez les bâtiments dans l'ordre où vous les entendez.

➡ (1. Je suis derrière le magasin. Où suis-je?)

² _____ au restaurant	⁴ _____ au bureau de tabac	_____ à l'université
³ _____ à la pharmacie	_____ à l'hôpital	¹ _____ au super-marché
⁶ _____ à l'école	⁵ _____ au musée	

G. Les endroits.   Situez cinq bâtiments de la liste de l'activité F d'après le plan de la page 107.

➡ *Le supermarché? Il est au coin de... / près de (du)... / loin de (du)...*

 Practice prepositions of place using **Le Plan de la ville** in the *Instructor's Resource Manual.* **La Maison idéale** also practices prepositions of place and recycles vocabulary **(les pièces et les meubles).** For intensive vocabulary practice, use **Concentration.**

 Jeu de rôle

You and your classmates are bragging about your hometowns. Mention the various places of interest (museums, shops, cinemas, restaurants) and their locations relative to one another. Ask your partners where various sites (hospitals, universities, hotels) are located in their hometowns.

CD-ROM

Now that you have finished the Troisième étape of this chapter, do your Lab Manual activities with the audio program. Explore chapter topics further with the Mais oui! Video and CD-ROM. Viewing and comprehension activities are in the video section of your *Workbook/Lab Manual/Video Manual.*

Intégration

Littérature: Le chouette bol d'air

You have already met **le petit Nicolas** in Chapter 1. The story you are about to read is taken from *Le petit Nicolas et ses copains*, first published in 1963. Popular with both adults and children, **le petit Nicolas** was created by Jean-Jacques Sempé (1932–), a cartoonist whose own son is named Nicolas, and René Goscinny (1926–1977), who also authored the famous cartoon series *Astérix*. Nicolas's simple words hide funny and sometimes profound observations about the adult world. One of his favorite words is **chouette** *(cool, neat)*. Here it applies to **un bol d'air**—a breath of fresh air.

Avant de lire

1 What words come to your mind when you think of town and country **(la ville et la campagne)?** Choose from the list below or add your own.

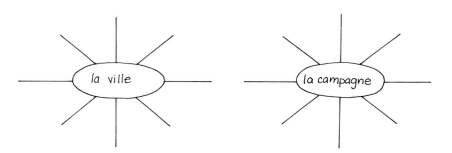

le bruit *(noise)*   le calme, le silence
l'air pur   la pollution
la détente, la relaxation   le stress
les immeubles *(apartment buildings)*   la nature
les routes   les rues
les embouteillages *(traffic jams)*   la solitude
?   ?

2 What are the benefits of a country home **(une maison de campagne)?** Judging from the drawing on page 111, is Monsieur Bongrain enjoying his country home?

3 Skim over the text and choose a title for each paragraph or group of paragraphs.

paragraphe	titre
1. «Nous sommes invités... »	a. Où est Corentin?
2. «Moi, je suis bien content... »	b. Qui est Monsieur Bongrain?
3. «On part... »	c. L'opinion de Monsieur Bongrain sur les maisons de campagne
4–6. «Elle est chouette... »	
7–9. «Mais parce que je suis là... »	d. Les directions pour arriver chez Monsieur Bongrain
10–11. «Après le déjeuner... »	e. Les difficultés pour arriver chez Monsieur Bongrain
12–14. «Corentin et moi... »	
15–16. «Papa décide... »	f. La tragédie de la balle
	g. Première tentative de jouer dehors (à l'extérieur)
	h. Deuxième tentative de jouer dehors

Le chouette bol d'air

1   Nous sommes invités à passer le dimanche° dans la nouvelle maison de campagne de M. Bongrain. M. Bongrain travaille avec Papa et il a un petit garçon qui a mon âge et qui s'appelle Corentin.

2   Moi, je suis bien content parce que j'aime beaucoup aller à la campagne. M. Bongrain a dit que ce n'est pas loin de la ville. Il a donné tous les détails à Papa par téléphone. C'est tout droit, on tourne à gauche au premier feu rouge, ensuite c'est encore tout droit jusqu'au carrefour°, où on tourne à gauche, et puis encore à gauche jusqu'à une grande ferme° blanche, et puis on tourne à droite par une petite route en terre, et là c'est tout droit et à gauche après la station-service.

3   On part, Papa, Maman et moi, assez tôt le matin° dans la voiture°, et Papa chante°, et puis il s'arrête de chanter à cause de toutes les voitures qu'il y a sur la route. On ne peut pas avancer°. Et puis Papa rate le feu rouge où il devait° tourner, et au carrefour suivant il y a une pancarte où c'est écrit «Détour», et nous nous perdons°; et Papa crie après Maman parce qu'elle lit° mal° les indications qu'il y a sur le papier; et Papa demande son chemin° à beaucoup de gens qui ne savent pas°; et nous arrivons chez M. Bongrain à l'heure du déjeuner, et nous arrêtons de nous disputer.

4   Elle est chouette, la maison de M. Bongrain! Pas très grande, mais chouette.

5   — Corentin n'est pas là? demande Papa.

6   — Mais oui, il est là, répond M. Bongrain; mais ce petit crétin est puni dans sa chambre parce qu'il est monté dans un arbre. Vous imaginez un peu? Chacun° de ces arbres m'a coûté une fortune!

7   Mais parce que je suis là, M. Bongrain appelle Corentin. Il a l'air assez° chouette.

8   — On va jouer dans le jardin? je demande à Corentin.

Sunday

intersection
farm

tôt... early in the morning / car
sings
progresser / *was supposed to*

nous... *we get lost* / vous lisez →
elle lit / ≠ bien / demande...
asks his way / je ne sais pas →
ils ne savent pas

Each one

a... *seems rather*

9 Corentin regarde son papa et son papa dit non, parce qu'on va bientôt manger.

10 Après le déjeuner, qui est très rustique, je demande à Corentin si on peut° aller jouer dehors°. Corentin regarde son papa et M. Bongrain dit:

may
outside

11 — Mais bien sûr les enfants! Mais ne jouez pas sur la pelouse!

12 Corentin et moi on commence à jouer à la balle et bientôt la balle va sur la pelouse. La fenêtre de la maison s'ouvre° immédiatement et M. Bongrain crie:

vous ouvrez → elle s'ouvre

13 — Corentin! Je t'ai déjà° dit plusieurs° fois de faire attention à la pelouse! Cette pelouse représente un travail fou! Tu es impossible quand on est à la campagne! Allez! dans ta chambre jusqu'à ce soir°!

already / several

ce... tonight

14 Corentin commence à pleurer et il rentre° dans la maison.

goes back

15 Papa décide qu'il est temps° de partir, à cause des embouteillages.

il... it's time

16 — Pourquoi n'achètes-tu pas une maison de campagne, comme moi? dit M. Bongrain à Papa. Pour les enfants, c'est formidable cette détente et ce bol d'air, tous les dimanches!

Extrait de *Le petit Nicolas et ses copains* (Jean-Jacques Sempé et René Goscinny)

4 **Les mots.**   Using the context, background knowledge, and logic, can you guess what the following words mean? Choose a or b.

¶2	une route en terre	a. *a paved road*	b. *a dirt road*
¶3	part (partir)	a. *to leave*	b. *to share*
	arrêter	a. *to start*	b. *to stop*
	à cause de	a. *because of*	b. *because*
	rater	a. *to miss*	b. *to take*
	une pancarte	a. *a sign*	b. *a card*
	crier après	a. *to yell at*	b. *to cry*
	l'heure du déjeuner	a. *lunch time*	b. *dinner time*
	se disputer	a. *to argue*	b. *to sing*
¶6	puni	a. *puny, small*	b. *punished*
	est monté	a. *climbed*	b. *planted*
¶11	la pelouse	a. *the farm*	b. *the lawn*
¶13	faire attention (à)	a. *to be careful (with)*	b. *to listen (to)*
¶14	pleurer	a. *to cry*	b. *to fall*

ANSWERS: 1. V 2. F (très compliquées!) 3. F (il chante en voiture mais pas dans les embouteillages) 4. F (il crie après maman) 5. F (ils trouvent la maison) 6. F (il est dans sa chambre parce qu'il est puni) 7. V 8. V 9. V 10. F (il est toujours puni dans sa chambre!)

5 **Le texte.**   Vrai ou faux? Si c'est faux, corrigez.

1. Monsieur Bongrain est le papa de Corentin.
2. Les directions pour arriver à la maison de Monsieur Bongrain sont très simples.
3. Le papa de Nicolas commence à chanter quand il y a des embouteillages.
4. Papa est un exemple de calme et de patience quand il cherche la maison de Monsieur Bongrain.
5. La maman de Nicolas téléphone à M. Bongrain pour avoir des directions plus précises.
6. Corentin est dans un arbre quand la famille de Nicolas arrive.
7. Nicolas voudrait jouer dehors.
8. M. Bongrain regarde Corentin et Nicolas quand ils jouent à la balle.
9. La pelouse de M. Bongrain est sacrée *(sacred)!*
10. Corentin peut apprécier l'air pur de la campagne!

6 **L'humour.**   What is funny about the following aspects of the story? Do you see other funny parts? Discuss in English.

1. The directions to M. Bongrain's house.
2. «Une grande ferme blanche, une petite route en terre, [puis une] station-service»
3. «Papa chante et puis il s'arrête de chanter.»
4. «Nous arrivons chez M. Bongrain et nous arrêtons de nous disputer.»
5. «Ce petit crétin est puni dans sa chambre parce qu'il est monté dans un arbre.» «Ne jouez pas sur la pelouse!» «Allez! dans ta chambre jusqu'à ce soir!»
6. «Pour les enfants, c'est formidable cette détente et ce bol d'air, tous les dimanches!» (Where does Corentin spend most of his time in the country?!)
7. The drawing: What is in the background? Is it really «la campagne»?
8. The name of the Bongrains' property, as indicated on the sign by the gate, is Sam Suffi, which is pronounced the same way as **ça me suffit** *(it's all I need).* Do you think Corentin would give it the same name?

Et vous?   Imaginez le dialogue entre le papa et la maman de Nicolas dans la voiture. Le papa pose des questions, la maman donne les directions, et les deux sont très impatients! Relisez le deuxième et le troisième paragraphes du texte, puis, avec un(e) camarade de classe, composez un dialogue original. Ensuite, jouez votre dialogue devant la classe.

Expressions utiles

Qu'est-ce que ça dit sur le papier? *(What does it say . . . ?)*
Où est-ce que je vais/tourne?
Où est le feu rouge?
Fais attention! Regarde!
Imbécile!
Ne crie pas! / Mais je ne crie pas!
Silence!

Par écrit: Well worth the money!

Avant d'écrire

A. Strategy: Listing.   Listing is a very common form of prewriting activity. If you wanted to describe your house, for example, you might first make a list of the rooms and then add some descriptive words beside each one. However, your writing may become predictable if your lists are always sequential or "logical." Developing lists in unexpected ways may lead you to surprising or provocative ideas.

Application.   Prepare to write a description of your house by developing a list in a unique way: Group rooms by adjective, by mood, by activity. Or think of each room as a painting or a musical composition—who is the artist or composer? Or develop your own method for bringing out the uniqueness of your home.

B. Strategy: Adding variety.   Improve a choppy writing style by varying sentence construction. For example, use adjectives or a sentence with **qui** to describe.

➡ J'ai une maison. La maison est spacieuse et belle.
J'ai une maison qui est spacieuse et belle.
ou: *J'ai une belle maison spacieuse.*

Application.   Write two sentences describing your house or room. Use an adjective in one and a clause with **qui** in the other.

Begin the letter with: *Monsieur/Madame, Je vous écris au sujet de...* Conclude with: *Veuillez agréer, Monsieur/Madame, l'expression de mes sentiments distingués.* Write your address in the top right-hand corner, followed by the date. The recipient's address should be written below, flush left above the greeting.

ÉCRIVEZ

1. Would you like to exchange lodging for the summer with a person in southern France? in Martinique? Write a letter describing your house/apartment/studio that would entice someone to make the exchange. Provide as many details as possible to convince the other party your place is ideal.

2. You have an apartment in Montreal that you want to exchange or rent out for the semester. Using the following ads as a model, write an ad for the local newspaper to try to rent your apartment.

CANNES/SUQUET, bordure mer : living, 2 chambres, 2 sdb, grande terrasse/jardinet, cuisine, téléphone, TV. Août-sept. 10.000/7.000 quinzaine. 4/6 personnes. (33-1) 46.28.23.13 soir.

ECHANGE JUILLET ou août, appt. 120 m², très grand standing, Avenue Montaigne, 1 chambre, 1 très grand salon, 1 bureau, grande cuisine complètement équipée, contre maison avec piscine à Los Angeles, de Beverly Hills à Malibu. (1) 47.23.41.28.

JH FRANÇAIS, 23, cherche à partager studio avec jeune Américaine à Los Angeles ou Miami pour apprendre anglais et visite à partir du mois d'août et pour plusieurs mois. Sérieux, merci. FUSAC réf: 4405.

ARTISTE peintre cherche à louer pour 6 mois atelier avec appt à New York, loyer raisonnable, possibilité échange en France. Tél Strasbourg : 88.36.60.30/Fax 88.36.70.24.

VOCABULAIRE ACTIF

Le logement
une petite annonce *a classified ad*
un appartement *an apartment*
un bâtiment *a building*
les charges (f.) *utilities*
le lieu, l'emplacement (m.) *place, location*

un(e) locataire *a renter*
une maison *a house*
le prix *price*
un(e) propriétaire *landlord, landlady*
une résidence universitaire *a dorm*
un studio *a studio*

Les pièces (f.)
une chambre *a bedroom*
la cuisine *the kitchen*
la douche *the shower*
l'entrée (f.) *the entry*
le lavabo *the bathroom sink*

la salle à manger *the dining room*
la salle de bains *the bathroom*
le salon / le séjour *the living room*
les toilettes (f.) / les W.C. (m.) *the restroom*

Les meubles (m.)
un canapé *a couch, sofa*
une commode *a chest of drawers*
des étagères (f.) *(book)shelves*
un fauteuil *an armchair*
une lampe *a lamp*

un lit *a bed*
un placard *a closet*
des rideaux (m.) *curtains, drapes*
un tapis *a rug*

Les objets personnels

un baladeur *a Walkman*
un lecteur de CD *a CD player*
un magnétoscope *a VCR*
un ordinateur *a computer*

un poster
un répondeur *an answering machine*
un téléphone
une vidéocassette

La ville

une avenue
une banque *a bank*
un boulevard
un bureau de tabac *tobacco / magazine shop*
un café
le centre-ville *downtown*
une commune rurale *a rural community; a small town*
une église *a church*
la gare *the train station*

un hôpital (des hôpitaux) *a hospital*
un hôtel
un magasin *a store*
un musée *a museum*
un parc *a park*
une pharmacie *a pharmacy / drugstore*
une place *a city square*
un plan (de la ville) *a city map*
la poste *the post office*
une rue *a street*
un supermarché *a supermarket*

Les directions

à côté de *next to*
à droite *to (on) the right*
à gauche *to (on) the left*
au coin de *at the corner of*
dans *in (on)*
derrière *behind*
devant *in front of*

en face de *across from*
entre *between*
jusqu'à *to, until*
loin de *far from*
près de *close to*
sur *on (in)*
tout droit *straight ahead*

Pour demander des directions

Pardon, monsieur / madame *Excuse me, sir / ma'am*
Je cherche... *I'm looking for . . .*
Pourriez-vous me dire...? *Could you tell me . . . ?*
Où se trouve...? / Où est...? *Where is . . . ?*

Au téléphone

Allô? *Hello?*
Qui est à l'appareil? / C'est de la part de qui? *May I ask who's calling?*
Ici... *This is . . .*
Je voudrais... *I would like . . .*
Est-ce que je pourrais...? *Could I . . .*
Je téléphone au sujet de... *I'm calling about . . .*
Un moment, s'il vous plaît / Ne quittez pas *Just a minute, please*
Je suis désolé(e) *I'm sorry*
Il (Elle) est là / n'est pas là *He (She) is in / isn't in*
Est-ce que vous pouvez téléphoner plus tard? *Can you call later?*
D'accord *Okay*

Questions

Comment? *How?*
Où? *Where?*
Parce que *Because*
Pourquoi? *Why?*
Quand? *When?*

Adjectifs

agréable *nice*
autre *other*
beau (bel, belle, beaux, belles)
   beautiful
blanc (blanche) *white*
bon(ne) *good*
calme *calm, peaceful*
compris(e) *included*
confortable *comfortable*
individuel(le) *individual*
jaune *yellow*

jeune *young*
joli(e) *pretty*
mauvais(e) *bad*
meublé(e) / non meublé(e) *furnished /*
   unfurnished
nouveau (nouvel, nouvelle, nouveaux,
   nouvelles) *new*
rouge *red*
satisfait(e) *satisfied, content*
spacieux (-euse) *spacious*
vieux (vieil, vieille, vieux, vieilles) *old*

Verbes

aller *to go*
chercher *to look for*
continuer *to continue*
coûter *to cost*
louer *to rent*
prendre (prenez) *to take*
téléphoner *to call, to phone*

tourner *to turn*
traverser *to cross*
trouver *to find*
se trouver *to be located*
visiter *to visit (a place)*
voir (infinitif) *to see*

Adverbes

aujourd'hui *today*
demain *tomorrow*

maintenant *now*
plus tard *later*

Les nombres

70 → un milliard *(a billion)*
Les nombres ordinaux: premier, deuxième, etc. *(first, second, etc.)*

EXPRESSIONS POUR LA CLASSE

ajoutez *add*
ci-dessus *above*
cochez *check*
développez *develop*
devinez *guess*
discutez *discuss*
dites *say*
expliquez *explain*

imaginez *imagine*
inventez *invent, make up*
numérotez *number*
partagez *share*
reliez *link, connect*
remarquez *note, notice*
soulignez *underline*

L'école

À quel genre d'école vont ces jeunes gens?

Quel diplôme est-ce qu'ils préparent?

Et après, qu'est-ce qu'ils vont faire?

Et vous?

Qu'est-ce que vous étudiez?

Comment sont vos cours?

This chapter will enable you to

- understand French children speaking about their school program
- read an article about the school week in France and a humorous text about a little boy who learns to read

- talk about studies and schedules
- express your personal reactions
- talk about activities you enjoy

117

Première étape

À l'écoute: Ça te plaît, l'école?

This listening section presents cultural information and introduces telling time as well as school vocabulary.

Vous allez entendre une conversation avec une petite fille qui parle de son école en France. **Avant d'écouter** et les autres activités vont vous aider à comprendre la conversation.

Avant d'écouter

1 Quels souvenirs est-ce que vous associez à l'école primaire? Cochez toutes les réponses appropriées et ajoutez des réponses personnelles.

L'école primaire, c'est

_____ les copains/copines

_____ les instituteurs/institutrices (les «professeurs» dans les écoles primaires)

_____ la salle de classe

_____ les matières qu'on étudie: les maths, l'histoire, etc.

_____ les récréations (quand on joue)

_____ ?

Écoutons

Audio CD

2 Écoutez la conversation une première fois et numérotez les sujets (*topics*) dans l'ordre où ils sont mentionnés.

2 _____ l'emploi du temps (*schedule*) d'Audrey

1 _____ l'âge d'Audrey

5 _____ son opinion de son institutrice

3 _____ les matières qu'elle étudie

4 _____ sa matière préférée

Sur le chemin de l'école.

3 Écoutez une deuxième fois et faites attention aux heures *(times)* mentionnées.

1. À quelle heure commence l'école?

huit heures   (huit heures et demie)   neuf heures

2. À quelle heure finit l'école?

deux heures   quatre heures   (quatre heures et demie)

3. À quelle heure finit la session du matin *(morning)?*

onze heures et quart   (onze heures et demie)   midi moins le quart

VOCABULAIRE ACTIF

Les heures (f.)
  et demie
  et quart
  moins le quart
  midi
  de l'après-midi
  du matin

4. À quelle heure commence la session de l'après-midi *(afternoon)?*

une heure moins le quart   une heure et quart   (une heure et demie)

4 Écoutez une troisième fois et cochez les matières mentionnées.

✓ les mathématiques (maths)	_____ la biologie
✓ le français	_____ l'économie
_____ l'anglais	_____ l'informatique
_____ l'allemand	*(computer science)*
✓ l'histoire	✓ la musique
✓ la géographie	✓ le dessin, l'art
✓ les sciences	✓ la gymnastique
	(l'éducation physique)

5 D'après le contexte, quel est le sens *(meaning)* de «ça te plaît?»?

   a. tu aimes?   b. tu étudies?   c. tu détestes?

6 Répondez aux questions suivantes.

   1. Quelle est la matière préférée d'Audrey? Pourquoi?

   2. Comment est l'institutrice d'Audrey?

      a. gentille *(nice)*   b. stricte   c. jeune   (d.) super

Note culturelle

L'école en France.   The French school system starts with **l'école mater-nelle** *(kindergarten),* available to children ages two through six. School becomes mandatory at age six, when children enter **l'école primaire** for five years. At age eleven, they go to **le collège** for four years, then on to **le lycée** for three years. At age fourteen, midway through **le collège,** students may choose a professional track instead of the traditional academic track; **le lycée d'enseignement professionnel** allows them to prepare, in two or three years, technical degrees in construction, cooking, office work, and other fields.

Les sons [e] *et* [ɛ]

■ [e] is the sound in **et** or **étudier;** it is pronounced with your mouth almost closed, and your lips stretched like for an [i].

■ [ɛ] is the sound in **elle** or **aime;** it is a more open sound, similar to the vowel in the English word *bet.*

Écoutez

Audio CD

Listen to the following excerpts from **À l'écoute: Ça te plaît, l'école?** on the student audio CD, and in the chart, write the words that contain the sounds [e] or [ɛ]. Each excerpt will be read twice. The first excerpt has been done for you. If you need to, turn off the audio CD after each item in order to write your answers.

	[e]	[ɛ]
1. Et ça te plaît, l'école?	<u>et</u>, l'éc<u>o</u>le	pl<u>aî</u>t
2. À quelle heure est-ce que tu vas à l'école?	éc<u>o</u>le	q<u>ue</u>lle, <u>est</u>-ce
3. On a deux heures pour manger et pour jouer.	mang<u>er</u>, jou<u>er</u>	
4. Qu'est-ce que tu as comme matières à l'école?	<u>é</u>cole	Qu'<u>est</u>-ce, mati<u>è</u>res
5. Eh ben, le français, les maths, la géographie...	<u>Eh</u>, l<u>es</u>, g<u>é</u>ographie	fran<u>ç</u>ais
6. Et quelle est ta matière préférée?	<u>Et</u>, pr<u>é</u>f<u>é</u>r<u>é</u>e	q<u>ue</u>lle, <u>est</u>, mati<u>è</u>re
7. Parce que j'aime lire et écrire.	<u>et</u> <u>é</u>crire	j'<u>ai</u>me
8. Elle est super!		<u>E</u>lle <u>est</u> sup<u>er</u>

Now, underline the [e] and [ɛ] sounds in the words you entered in the chart, then practice pronouncing them.

Essayez!

Audio CD

A. Prononcez. Practice saying the following words aloud, paying particular attention to the highlighted sounds. Then listen to them on the student audio CD to verify your pronunciation.

1. [e] **ré**p**é**tez, enchant**é**, à côt**é**, caf**é**, mus**é**e, t**é**l**é**phon**er**, d**é**solé
   all**ez**, ouvr**ez**, ferm**ez**, lis**ez**, écout**ez**, écriv**ez**
   trouv**er**, habit**er**, donn**er**, papi**er**
   l**es**, m**es**, t**es**, c**es**

2. [ɛ] m**è**re, p**è**re, fr**è**re, derri**è**re, deuxi**è**me, tr**ès**
   être, fen**ê**tre, f**ê**te
   m**ai**s, s'il vous pl**aî**t, ch**ai**se, cr**ai**e, angl**ai**s, japon**ai**se, propri**é**t**ai**re
   m**er**ci, s**er**viette, prof**e**sseur, hôt**e**l, canadi**e**nne, ch**er**, un post**er**

B. [e] ou [ɛ]? In the following sentences, underline the [e] sounds with one line, and the [ɛ] sounds with two lines.

1. La b<u>e</u>lle H<u><u>é</u></u>l<u><u>è</u></u>ne pr<u>é</u>f<u><u>è</u></u>re regard<u>er</u> la t<u>é</u>l<u>é</u>vision.

2. La secr<u>é</u>t<u><u>ai</u></u>re de l'archit<u>e</u>cte <u>est</u> am<u>é</u>ric<u><u>ai</u></u>ne.

3. Il y a d<u>es</u> <u>é</u>tudiants à l'université; à l'<u>é</u>cole prim<u><u>ai</u></u>re, au coll<u><u>è</u></u>ge et au lyc<u>é</u>e, il y a d<u>es</u> <u><u>é</u>l<u>è</u></u>ves.

Now practice saying the sentences aloud, then listen to them on the student audio CD to verify your pronunciation.

VOCABULAIRE
Les matières

For **Vocabulaire** and **Structure** cue to Video Module 4 (00:17:04), where Nicolas and Élisabeth discuss their courses and schedules. Also cue to street interviews (00:19:42) for students talking about the courses they take.

Have groups brainstorm names and then share their answers with the class. Encourage students to think of French-speaking celebrities, or introduce them to some they may not know.

Quelles personnes ou quelles choses associez-vous avec les matières suivantes? Travaillez en groupes et complétez la liste.

➡ les langues étrangères   *mon prof de français; Mais oui!*
    la littérature   *Victor Hugo, Les Misérables*

    la peinture, l'art   _____

    les sciences politiques   _____

    la philosophie   _____

    la psychologie   _____

    l'architecture   _____

    la physique   _____

    la chimie   _____

    la littérature   _____

    les langues étrangères   _____

A. Have students brainstorm possible categories: easy/hard, interesting/boring, related subject matters. See who can come up with the longest lists or the most original categories.

B. As an alternative to a paired activity, do a chain. Going in order around the room, each student asks another about a different course. For larger classes, have two or three chains.

ACTIVITÉS

A. Catégories. Groupez les matières mentionnées ci-dessus et à la page 120 en trois catégories. Inventez des catégories: les cours qu'on aime, qu'on n'aime pas...

B. Ça me plaît. Ça te plaît? Posez des questions à votre partenaire sur les matières qu'il/elle préfère.

➡   — *La chimie, ça te plaît?*
     — *Mais oui, ça me plaît (un peu / beaucoup).*
ou   — *Non, ça ne me plaît pas (beaucoup / du tout).*

STRUCTURE: Telling time
L'heure

Observez et déduisez

À quelle heure commence l'école?
L'école commence à huit heures
et demie (du matin).

Quelle heure est-il
maintenant? Il est
neuf heures vingt.

Et maintenant?
Il est midi.

Il est deux heures et quart
(de l'après-midi).

Il est huit heures moins
le quart (du soir).

Il est onze heures
moins vingt.

Maintenant, il
est minuit.

VOCABULAIRE ACTIF

À quelle heure... ?
un cours
un examen
minuit
occupé(e)
Quelle heure est-il?
du soir
tard
tôt

■ Review the preceding examples and infer the correct way to state the following times. How do you distinguish between A.M. and P.M.?

Quelle heure est-il?   Il est...

6 h 30 (A.M.)	6 h 30 (P.M.)	7 h 25 (A.M.)
12 h 15 (P.M.)	9 h 50 (P.M.)	3 h 35 (P.M.)
10 h 45 (A.M.)	8 h 20 (A.M.)	12 h (A.M.)

Vérifiez   *L'heure*

■ Note that **Quelle heure est-il?** means *What time is it?* whereas **À quelle heure... ?** means *At what time . . . ?*

— **À quelle heure** est-ce que tu vas retrouver Djamila?
— Très tôt *(early)*. À trois heures et demie.

■ Use **de** and **à** to indicate the time frame *(from . . . to . . .)*.

— Quand est-ce que tu as ton cours de biologie demain?
— **De** neuf heures **à** dix heures et demie. Et j'ai un examen **de** onze heures **à** midi.

■ When necessary, the expressions **du matin, de l'après-midi,** and **du soir** are used to denote *morning, afternoon,* and *evening.*

Chantal a un emploi du temps chargé *(full)*. Elle est occupée de sept heures **du matin** à huit heures **du soir!**

■ If you want to say you regularly do something *in the morning, in the afternoon,* or *in the evening,* use the definite article with the appropriate expression. **Le matin** means *in the morning.*

J'ai mon cours de maths **le matin** et mon cours de français tard *(late)* **l'après-midi. Le soir** je travaille.

Note culturelle

L'heure officielle.   A twenty-four-hour clock is commonly used on television and in listing times for public events (concerts, films) and schedules (trains, buses). To express hours from noon to midnight, add 12 to the hour. For example, 1:00 P.M. becomes **13.00** or **13 h 00 (treize heures)**; 7:30 P.M. becomes **19.30** or **19 h 30 (dix-neuf heures trente)**. Expressions for half hours and quarter hours (e.g., **et demie, et quart**) and time of day (e.g., **du matin**) are not necessary. The number of hours and number of minutes past the hour are used instead (20 h 15 = vingt heures quinze).

OPTIONAL DRILL: Change the official times to conversational times: 17.25 → Il est 5 h 25 de l'après midi. CUES: 1. 14.15 2. 20.20 3. 8.30 4. 16.45 5. 24.00 6. 19.35

ACTIVITÉS

C. Remind students that although the agendas use official time, you are using conversational time. CUES: Cette personne... 1. a un cours à 9 h 2. a un cours de géographie à 10 h 30 3. va au café à minuit 4. a son cours de géographie à 10 h 45 5. a son cours de français à 1 h 45 6. va au cours de gymnastique à 5 h 30 7. mange à 12 h 45 8. a son cours de maths à 8 h 30 ANSWERS: 1. Malick 2. Malick 3. ni … ni 4. ni … ni 5. Catherine 6. Malick 7. Catherine 8. Catherine

C. Qui est-ce?   Regardez les emplois du temps qui suivent. Écoutez le professeur et décidez s'il/si elle parle de Catherine, de Malick, ou de ni l'un ni l'autre.

Catherine	
8	8h30 maths
9	
10	histoire
11	11h45 géo
12	12h45 café avec Hélène
13	13h45 français
14	
15	pause café
16	16h15 gymnastique
17	

Malick	
8	
9	histoire
10	10h30 géo
11	
12	Resto-U avec Mariama
13	
14	14h45 français
15	
16	maths
17	17h30 gymnastique

1. ＿＿ C'est Catherine.   ＿＿ C'est Malick.   ＿＿ Ni l'un ni l'autre

2. ＿＿ C'est Catherine.   ＿＿ C'est Malick.   ＿＿ Ni l'un ni l'autre

3. ＿＿ C'est Catherine.   ＿＿ C'est Malick.   ＿＿ Ni l'un ni l'autre

4. ＿＿ C'est Catherine.   ＿＿ C'est Malick.   ＿＿ Ni l'un ni l'autre

5. ＿＿ C'est Catherine.   ＿＿ C'est Malick.   ＿＿ Ni l'un ni l'autre

6. _____ C'est Catherine.   _____ C'est Malick.   _____ Ni l'un ni l'autre

7. _____ C'est Catherine.   _____ C'est Malick.   _____ Ni l'un ni l'autre

8. _____ C'est Catherine.   _____ C'est Malick.   _____ Ni l'un ni l'autre

Maintenant, parlez de l'emploi du temps de Catherine en mélangeant (mixing) des phrases vraies et des phrases fausses. Votre partenaire va corriger vos «erreurs».

➡ — _Catherine a son cours de maths à huit heures._
— _Mais non. Son cours de maths est à huit heures et demie._

Ensuite, changez de rôle et répétez l'activité avec l'emploi du temps de Malick.

D. D'habitude. Dites quand vous faites les activités suivantes: le matin? l'après-midi? le soir? Ensuite, trouvez un(e) partenaire pour chaque activité. Parlez-en avec vos camarades de classe!

➡ — _D'habitude je retrouve mes copains l'après-midi. Et toi?_
— _Moi aussi!_   ou   — _Moi, je retrouve mes copains le soir._

danser	regarder la télé
arriver en classe	jouer au... (tennis, etc.)
manger	retrouver mes copains
parler au téléphone	écouter de la musique
préparer mes cours	aller au cinéma
aller à la bibliothèque	aller au supermarché

E. Et vous? Êtes-vous très occupé(e)? Parlez de votre emploi du temps pour une journée «typique».

➡ _J'ai mon cours de français de huit heures à neuf heures moins dix..._

(avoir le petit déjeuner, avoir mon cours de _____ , manger, aller à la bibliothèque, regarder la télévision..., etc.)

D. Insist on the correct use of the definite article. (You may also add **«le week-end»** as a possibility.) This may also be done as a signature activity. FOLLOW-UP: Solicit reports from volunteers: «Sue et moi, nous allons en classe le matin.»

E. Have students practice with a partner before volunteers share with the class. You may also use this activity as a written homework assignment.

STRATÉGIE DE COMMUNICATION
Reacting to news and information

People often react in different ways to the same news. These students have found a note on the door telling them that their teacher has canceled class and has postponed their test until next week. Study the examples on the next page and answer the following questions.

What expressions can be used to express

• surprise? _____

• indifference? _____

• pleasure? _____

• irritation? _____

Formidable! Quelle chance!
Maintenant je vais aller au
cinéma.

C'est incroyable! Madame
Chamier n'annule jamais la
classe!

Zut, alors! C'est embêtant!
J'ai déjà deux autres
examens à préparer pour
la semaine prochaine.

Je m'en fiche, moi. Je ne
fais pas mes devoirs de
toute façon (*anyway*).

Verify your answers in the chart that follows. Can you tell anything about the
attitude of these students toward the test, the teacher, or the class, based on
their reactions?

Tell students that more than one
expression can be used at the
same time, e.g., «Zut, alors. C'est
embêtant!»

Point out that in casual speech, the
ne of negative expressions is often
dropped.

Encourage the use of these
expressions in all classroom
interactions.

Expressions pour réagir

l'intérêt	l'indifférence
Ah, bon?	Et alors?
Vraiment?	Tant pis!
Ah oui?	Bof!
C'est vrai?	Je m'en fiche!

la surprise	l'irritation
Tiens!	Mince!
C'est pas vrai!	C'est embêtant!
Tu plaisantes!	J'en ai marre!*
C'est incroyable!	Zut, alors!

l'enthousiasme

C'est chouette!	Formidable!	C'est génial!
Super!	Quelle chance!	

***J'en ai marre** is the equivalent of *I'm fed up!*

ACTIVITÉS

F. FOLLOW-UP: Have students work in groups of 2–3 to come up with original situations. As they share them with the class, others can react using appropriate expressions.

F. Les réactions. Quelle est votre réaction aux situations suivantes? Employez des expressions pour réagir.

1. Votre professeur de français dit *(says):*
   a. La classe est annulée demain.
   b. Vous allez avoir un examen la semaine prochaine.
   c. Aujourd'hui nous étudions les matières et l'heure.
   d. Tous les étudiants ont un A à l'examen.

2. Une camarade de classe qui n'aime pas travailler dit:
   a. Moi, j'adore travailler.
   b. Nous n'avons pas d'exercices à préparer aujourd'hui.
   c. Moi, j'ai beaucoup de cours difficiles.
   d. Je déteste mes cours.

3. Votre nouveau (nouvelle) camarade de chambre dit:
   a. Ce semestre, j'ai cours à huit heures du matin tous les jours.
   b. Je ne vais pas en cours aujourd'hui.
   c. J'ai un nouveau lecteur de CD.
   d. Je préfère écouter la musique classique.

 Jeu de rôle

You and two friends are complaining about your courses and your busy schedules, and exaggerating quite a bit! Tell them when you have classes, when you study, when you work, and so on. Use expressions for reacting to your classmates' comments. Present the skit to others in the class, and let them decide who is the worst off.

Deuxième étape

Lecture: La semaine scolaire

This reading section will have students infer how to talk about days and dates.

1 Le calendrier

A. C'est différent? Regardez le calendrier français ci-dessous. Comment est-il différent d'un calendrier américain?

JANVIER ☉ 7 h 46 à 16 h 03	FÉVRIER ☉ 7 h 23 à 16 h 46	MARS ☉ 6 h 35 à 17 h 32	AVRIL ☉ 5 h 30 à 18 h 20	MAI ☉ 4 h 32 à 19 h 04	JUIN ☉ 3 h 54 à 19 h 44
1 S JOUR de l'AN	1 M Sᵉ Ella	1 M S. Aubin	1 V S. Hugues	1 D FÊTE du TRAVAIL	1 M S. Justin
2 D Épiphanie	2 M Présentation	2 M S. Charles le B.	2 S Sᵉ Sandrine	2 L S. Boris	2 J Sᵉ Blandine
3 L Sᵉ Geneviève	3 J S. Blaise	3 J S. Guénolé	3 D PAQUES	3 M SS. Phil., Jacq.	3 V S. Kévin
4 M S. Odilon	4 V Sᵉ Véronique	4 V S. Casimir	4 L S. Isidore	4 M S. Sylvain	4 S Sᵉ Clotilde
5 M S. Édouard	5 S Sᵉ Agathe	5 S S. Olive	5 M Sᵉ Irène	5 J Sᵉ Judith	5 D Fête Dieu
6 J S. Mélaine	6 D S. Gaston	6 D Sᵉ Colette	6 M S. Marcellin	6 V Sᵉ Prudence	6 L S. Norbert
7 V S. Raymond	7 L Sᵉ Eugénie	7 L Sᵉ Félicité	7 J S. J.-B. de la S.	7 S Sᵉ Gisèle	7 M S. Gilbert
8 S S. Lucien	8 M Sᵉ Jacqueline	8 M S. Jean de D.	8 V Sᵉ Julie	8 D VICT. 1945/F.J.-d'Arc	8 M S. Médard
9 D Sᵉ Alix	9 M Sᵉ Apolline	9 M Sᵉ Françoise	9 S S. Gautier	9 L S. Pacôme	9 J Sᵉ Diane
10 L S. Guillaume	10 J S. Arnaud	10 J S. Vivien	10 D S. Fulbert	10 M Sᵉ Solange	10 V S. Landry
11 M S. Paulin	11 V N.-D. Lourdes	11 V Sᵉ Rosine	11 L S. Stanislas	11 M Sᵉ Estelle	11 S S. Barnabé
12 M Sᵉ Tatiana	12 S S. Félix	12 S Sᵉ Justine	12 M S. Jules	12 J ASCENSION	12 D S. Guy
13 J Sᵉ Yvette	13 D Sᵉ Béatrice	13 D S. Rodrigue	13 M Sᵉ Ida	13 V Sᵉ Rolande	13 L S. Antoine de P.
14 V Sᵉ Nina	14 L S. Valentin	14 L Sᵉ Mathilde	14 J S. Maxime	14 S S. Matthias	14 M S. Elisée
15 S S. Remi	15 M Mardi-Gras	15 M Sᵉ Louise	15 V S. Paterne	15 D Sᵉ Denise	15 M Sᵉ Germaine
16 D S. Marcel	16 M Cendres	16 M Sᵉ Bénédicte	16 S S. Benoît-J.	16 L S. Honoré	16 J S. J.F. Régis
17 L Sᵉ Roseline	17 J S. Alexis	17 J S. Patrice	17 D S. Anicet	17 M S. Pascal	17 V S. Hervé
18 M Sᵉ Prisca	18 V Sᵉ Bernadette	18 V S. Cyrille	18 L S. Parfait	18 M S. Eric	18 S S. Léonce
19 M S. Marius	19 S S. Gabin	19 S S. Joseph	19 M Sᵉ Emma	19 J S. Yves	19 D S. Romuald
20 J S. Sébastien	20 D Carême	20 D PRINTEMPS	20 M Sᵉ Odette	20 V S. Bernardin	20 L S. Silvère
21 V Sᵉ Agnès	21 L S. P. Damien	21 L Sᵉ Clémence	21 J S. Anselme	21 S S. Constantin	21 M ÉTÉ
22 S S. Vincent	22 M Sᵉ Isabelle	22 M Sᵉ Léa	22 V S. Alexandre	22 D PENTECÔTE	22 M S. Alban
23 D S. Barnard	23 M S. Lazare	23 M S. Georges	23 S S. Georges	23 L S. Didier	23 J Sᵉ Audrey
24 L S. Fr. de Sales	24 J S. Modeste	24 J Sᵉ Cath. de Su.	24 D Jour du Souvenir	24 M S. Donatien	24 V S. Jean-Bapt.
25 M Conv. S. Paul	25 V S. Roméo	25 V Annonciation	25 L S. Marc	25 M Sᵉ Sophie	25 S S. Prosper
26 M Sᵉ Paule	26 S S. Nestor	26 S Sᵉ Larissa	26 M Sᵉ Alida	26 J S. Bérenger	26 D S. Anthelme
27 J Sᵉ Angèle	27 D Sᵉ Honorine	27 D Rameaux	27 M Sᵉ Zita	27 V S. Augustin	27 L S. Fernand
28 V S. Th. d'Aquin	28 L S. Romain	28 L S. Gontran	28 J Sᵉ Valérie	28 S S. Germain	28 M Sᵉ Irénée
29 S S. Gildas		29 M Sᵉ Gwladys	29 V Sᵉ Cath. de Si.	29 D Fête des Mères	29 M SS. Pierre, Paul
30 D Sᵉ Martine		30 M S. Amédée	30 S S. Robert	30 L S. Ferdinand	30 J S. Martial
31 L Sᵉ Marcelle	Epacte 17 / Lettre dominicale B / Cycle solaire 15 / Nbre d'or 19 / Indiction romaine 2	31 J S. Benjamin		31 M Visitation	CASLON - Paris (1) 45 42 13 20

JUILLET ☉ 3 h 53 à 19 h 56	AOUT ☉ 4 h 25 à 19 h 28	SEPTEMBRE ☉ 5 h 08 à 18 h 32	OCTOBRE ☉ 5 h 51 à 17 h 29	NOVEMBRE ☉ 6 h 38 à 16 h 29	DÉCEMBRE ☉ 7 h 24 à 15 h 55
1 V S. Thierry	1 S S. Alphonse	1 J S. Gilles	1 J Sᵉ Th. de l'E.J.	1 M TOUSSAINT	1 J Sᵉ Florence
2 S S. Martinien	2 M S. Julien-Ey.	2 V Sᵉ Ingrid	2 D S. Léger	2 M Défunts	2 V Sᵉ Viviane
3 D S. Thomas	3 M Sᵉ Lydie	3 S S. Grégoire	3 L S. Gérard	3 J S. Hubert	3 S S. Xavier
4 L S. Florent	4 J S. J.M. Vianney	4 D Sᵉ Rosalie	4 M S. Fr. d'Assise	4 V S. Charles	4 D Sᵉ Barbara
5 M S. Antoine	5 V S. Abel	5 L Sᵉ Raïssa	5 M Sᵉ Fleur	5 S Sᵉ Sylvie	5 L S. Gérald
6 M Sᵉ Mariette	6 S Transfiguration	6 M S. Bertrand	6 J S. Bruno	6 D Sᵉ Bertille	6 M S. Nicolas
7 J S. Raoul	7 D S. Gaëtan	7 M Sᵉ Reine	7 V S. Serge	7 L Sᵉ Carine	7 M S. Ambroise
8 V S. Thibaut	8 L S. Dominique	8 J Nativité N.D.	8 S Sᵉ Pélagie	8 M S. Geoffroy	8 J Imm. Concept.
9 S Sᵉ Amandine	9 M S. Amour	9 V S. Alain	9 D S. Denis	9 M S. Théodore	9 V S. P. Fourier
10 D S. Ulrich	10 M S. Laurent	10 S Sᵉ Inès	10 L S. Ghislain	10 J S. Léon	10 S S. Romaric
11 L S. Benoît	11 J Sᵉ Claire	11 D Sᵉ Adelphe	11 M S. Firmin	11 V ARMISTICE 1918	11 D S. Daniel
12 M S. Olivier	12 V Sᵉ Clarisse	12 L S. Apollinaire	12 M S. Wilfried	12 S S. Christian	12 L Sᵉ Jeanne F.C.
13 M SS. Henri, Joël	13 S S. Hippolyte	13 M S. Aimé	13 J S. Géraud	13 D S. Brice	13 M Sᵉ Lucie
14 J FÊTE NATIONALE	14 D S. Evrard	14 M La Sᵉ Croix	14 V S. Juste	14 L S. Sidoine	14 M Sᵉ Odile
15 V S. Donald	15 L ASSOMPTION	15 J S. Roland	15 S Sᵉ Th. d'Avila	15 M S. Albert	15 J Sᵉ Ninon
16 S N.D.Mt-Carmel	16 M S. Armel	16 V Sᵉ Edith	16 D Sᵉ Edwige	16 M Sᵉ Marguerite	16 V Sᵉ Alice
17 D Sᵉ Charlotte	17 M S. Hyacinthe	17 S S. Renaud	17 L S. Baudouin	17 J Sᵉ Elisabeth	17 S S. Gaël
18 L S. Frédéric	18 J Sᵉ Hélène	18 D Sᵉ Nadège	18 M S. Luc	18 V Sᵉ Aude	18 D S. Gatien
19 M S. Arsène	19 V S. Jean Eudes	19 L Sᵉ Emilie	19 M S. René	19 S S. Tanguy	19 L S. Urbain
20 M Sᵉ Marina	20 S S. Bernard	20 M S. Davy	20 J Sᵉ Adeline	20 D S. Edmond	20 M S. Abraham
21 J S. Victor	21 D S. Christophe	21 M S. Matthieu	21 V Sᵉ Céline	21 L Prés. Marie	21 M S. Pierre C.
22 V Sᵉ Marie-Mad.	22 L S. Fabrice	22 J S. Maurice	22 S Sᵉ Elodie	22 M Sᵉ Cécile	22 J HIVER
23 S Sᵉ Brigitte	23 M Sᵉ Rose de L.	23 V S. Constant	23 D S. Jean de C.	23 M S. Clément	23 V S. Armand
24 D Sᵉ Christine	24 M S. Barthélemy	24 S Sᵉ Thècle	24 L S. Florentin	24 J Sᵉ Flora	24 S Sᵉ Adèle
25 L S. Jacques	25 J S. Louis	25 D S. Hermann	25 M S. Crépin	25 V Sᵉ Catherine L.	25 D NOËL
26 M SS. Anne, Joa.	26 V Sᵉ Natacha	26 L SS. Côme, Dam.	26 M S. Dimitri	26 S Sᵉ Delphine	26 L S. Etienne
27 M Sᵉ Nathalie	27 S Sᵉ Monique	27 M S. Vinc. de Paul	27 J Sᵉ Emeline	27 D Avent	27 M S. Jean
28 J S. Samson	28 D S. Augustin	28 M S. Venceslas	28 V SS. Sim., Jude	28 L S. Jacq. de la M.	28 M SS. Innocents
29 V Sᵉ Marthe	29 L Sᵉ Sabine	29 J S. Michel	29 S S. Narcisse	29 M S. Saturnin	29 J S. David
30 S Sᵉ Juliette	30 M S. Fiacre	30 V S. Jérôme	30 D Sᵉ Bienvenue	30 M S. André	30 V S. Roger
31 D S. Ignace de L.	31 M S. Aristide		31 L S. Quentin		31 S S. Sylvestre
			CASLON - Paris (1) 45 42 13 20		

Allow students to brainstorm in English as needed.

Point out that months are not capitalized in French. Model pronunciation as you work through these activities. Days of the week will be seen later, in the reading below. Have students guess the meaning of **Pâques**.

B. La fête.   Chaque date du calendrier français est la fête d'un saint ou d'une sainte. Le 5 janvier, par exemple, est la Saint-Édouard. Si vous vous appelez Édouard, votre fête est le 5 janvier! Quelles sont les dates des fêtes suivantes?

➡ *La date de la Saint-Édouard est le 5 janvier.*

1. Sainte-Jacqueline   3. Sainte-Audrey   5. Saint-Nicolas
2. Saint-Joseph   4. Saint-Christophe   6. Pâques

C. Les jours, les semaines, les mois et les années

Le 5 janvier 1994

le jour   le mois   l'année

1. Quelle est la date de votre anniversaire *(birthday)?*
2. Selon le calendrier, il y a, au mois de janvier, quatre semaines et trois jours. Combien de semaines complètes y a-t-il au mois de février?

2 **Le calendrier scolaire**

A. L'année scolaire.   Quelle est la date du premier jour et du dernier jour de classe pour les écoles de votre ville?

B. La semaine scolaire.   Combien de jours par semaine est-ce que les enfants vont à l'école—quatre ou cinq?

En général   **3** D'après le titre et une lecture rapide du texte, quel est le sujet principal de ce texte?

a. La semaine traditionnelle dans les écoles françaises
b. Une réforme expérimentale du calendrier scolaire
c. Une analyse de trois formules possibles pour le calendrier scolaire

École: La semaine des quatre jours

Philippe Durand est un instituteur heureux: comme 93% des écoliers du Rhône°, ses élèves du cours élémentaire font la semaine de quatre jours. Les enfants travaillent le lundi, mardi, jeudi et vendredi. «Nous sommes beaucoup moins fatigués qu'avant, explique Philippe Durand. Nous ne voulions pas° abandonner la coupure° traditionnelle du mercredi: elle nous permet de souffler°. Le samedi est maintenant consacré à la vie de famille, et le dimanche, nous préparons les cours de la semaine suivante.»

Cette semaine de quatre jours est de plus en plus populaire depuis que le ministre de l'Éducation nationale a autorisé, par un décret d'avril 1991, les inspecteurs d'académie° à modifier le calendrier scolaire, au cas par cas, dans chaque académie. Trois conditions: l'inspecteur d'académie consulte les conseils° d'école, la municipalité et les parents d'élèves; le nouveau calendrier scolaire doit garder° le même volume annuel de cours; et la journée ne peut pas excéder six heures. Pour rattraper° les samedis matins libérés, soit° douze journées de classe, les vacances sont écourtées°: l'école commence une semaine plus tôt° en septembre, et il y a deux jours de vacances en moins à Noël, en février et à Pâques.

région de Lyon en France

ne... *didn't want to* / interruption
breathe

district scolaire

councils
doit... *must keep*
make up for
i.e. / *shortened*
earlier

Officiellement, cette formule est seulement une expérience. «C'est un mouvement culturel et sociologique inévitable: 90% des adultes qui travaillent disposent aujourd'hui de leur week-end. Il est logique que les enfants suivent° le même rythme», affirme Florence Balay, adjointe au maire° de Lyon pour les affaires scolaires.

follow
mayor
key / better

Question clé°: les écoliers apprennent-ils mieux° en quatre ou en cinq jours? Médecins et enseignants sont divisés, mais tous sont unanimes pour accuser la journée scolaire—six heures de classe—d'être trop longue.

COMBIEN DE JOURS D'ÉCOLE

	par semaine	dont le samedi	par an
JAPON	6 ou 5	4 samedis sur 5	210
ALLEMAGNE	6 ou 5	1 samedi sur 2	200–226
GRANDE-BRETAGNE	5		200
ITALIE	5		200–210
ÉTATS-UNIS	5		173
FRANCE	5 ou 4	matin (1)	180

Les écoliers français–seuls avec les américains–ont, par an, plus de jours de vacances que de jours de classe, mais des journées scolaires plus longues que celles de leurs voisins.

(1) Pour la semaine de cinq jours et pas dans certaines écoles privées, qui font classe le mercredi matin.

Adapté de *L'Express*, 11 décembre 1992.

En détail   **4** **Les jours de la semaine.** Lisez attentivement le premier paragraphe. Quels sont les jours de la semaine? Complétez la liste qui correspond aux abréviations du calendrier.

L = _____   V = _____

M = _____   S = _____

M = _mercredi_   D = _____

J = _____

Quel est le premier jour de la semaine française? Et le dernier jour?

5 **La semaine scolaire en France.** Selon la formule traditionnelle française, les enfants vont à l'école le lundi, le mardi, le jeudi et le vendredi pour toute la journée, et le samedi matin. Il n'y a pas classe le mercredi. Quelle

Le gymnase—lieu privilégié du mercredi.

VOCABULAIRE ACTIF

un an
une année
un anniversaire
le calendrier
une date
dernier (-ère)
une fête
Les jours (m.)
   lundi, mardi, etc.
long (-gue)
Les mois (m.)
   janvier, février, etc.
une semaine

est la formule expérimentale proposée? Relisez le texte en fonction des questions suivantes.

1. Quels sont les jours de classe et quels sont les jours de repos *(rest)* dans la formule expérimentale?
2. Comment est-il possible d'avoir une semaine de quatre jours et de garder le même volume annuel de cours?
   a. Les vacances sont écourtées.
   b. Les journées de classe sont plus longues.
   c. Les vacances sont écourtées *et* les journées de classe sont plus longues.

6 **Les autres détails du texte.** Vrai ou faux? Si c'est faux, corrigez.

1. Le ministre de l'Éducation nationale impose le nouveau calendrier scolaire à toutes les académies.
2. 90% des adultes travaillent le samedi.
3. Les médecins et les enseignants sont unanimes en faveur de la semaine de quatre jours.
4. Les médecins et les enseignants pensent que six heures de classe par jour, c'est trop long.
5. Les vacances de Pâques sont au mois d'avril. (Consultez le calendrier.)

7 **Les illustrations**

1. Quel pays a le moins *(the fewest)* de jours d'école par an?
2. Quels sont les pays où le samedi est un jour d'école?
3. Quelle est l'activité favorite des enfants français le mercredi?

Et vous? Que pensez-vous de la semaine de quatre jours pour les écoles publiques? pour les universités? pour le monde professionnel? Est-ce une bonne idée?

STRUCTURE: Talking about days and dates

Articles et prépositions avec le jour et la date

Observez et déduisez Dans mon école, on a la semaine de quatre jours. C'est chouette! Le mercredi est libre pour nos passe-temps préférés, et le samedi on fait des choses en famille. Cette semaine, mercredi je vais au gymnase avec mes copains, et samedi papa et moi, on va acheter un cadeau pour maman pour son anniversaire le 14 novembre. Est-ce que votre anniversaire est aussi en novembre?

- Which of the preceding sentences refers to a specific Wednesday and Saturday? Which one refers to Wednesdays and Saturdays in general? In which case is the day preceded by the definite article?
- What preposition is used to express *in* with the name of a month?

Vérifiez *Articles et prépositions avec le jour et la date*

- Use an article with a weekday to talk about what you do every week on that day, e.g., **le samedi** (*Saturdays, on Saturdays*).

  Le samedi est consacré à la vie de famille.

VOCABULAIRE ACTIF
un cadeau
des projets (m.)

Do *not* use an article with a weekday if it refers to one specific day.

> Nous avons des projets pour **samedi** après-midi. *(this coming Saturday)*

■ To say *in* what month (January, etc.), use **en** or **au mois de.**

> L'école commence une semaine plus tôt **en septembre (au mois de septembre).**

Notice that in French the names of months and days are *not* capitalized.

■ To express dates, use **le premier** for the first day of the month, but use cardinal numbers for all other dates.

> le **premier** avril   le **23** (vingt-trois) avril

Do *not* use the preposition **de** when giving dates in French.

> le 5 (cinq) janvier

⚠ **Attention!**   When expressing the date numerically, in French you place the day *before* the month: le 3 avril   →   3/4

■ The year can be expressed as follows:

> 1999   →   mille neuf cent quatre-vingt-dix-neuf
> →   dix-neuf cent quatre-vingt-dix-neuf
> 2000   →   l'an deux mille

Point out that this is the way the date is expressed orally also.

ACTIVITÉS

A. Une chaîne.   Quelle est la date de votre anniversaire? Et l'anniversaire de votre camarade de classe?

➡ — *Mon anniversaire est le 5 septembre. Et toi?*

B. Associations.   Êtes-vous bon(ne) en histoire? Dites quelle date vous associez aux événements *(events)* suivants.

➡ Guillaume le Conquérant   *1066*

1. Jeanne d'Arc	a.	1914
2. la Déclaration d'indépendance	b.	1789
3. la guerre de Sécession	c.	1431
4. Christophe Colomb	d.	1492
5. la Révolution française	e.	1963
6. la Première Guerre mondiale	f.	1864
7. le premier homme sur la lune	g.	1776
8. l'assassinat de John F. Kennedy	h.	1969

C. La semaine de quatre jours.   Vous participez à la semaine scolaire de quatre jours. Avec vos camarades de classe, imaginez comment vous allez passer votre temps libre.

➡ *Samedi matin, nous allons...*

A. Begin the activity by giving your birthday and asking a student his/hers. «... Et toi, Carol, quelle est la date de ton anniversaire?» The student answers, then asks the next person until everyone has given his/her birthday. Write birth dates on the board, commenting on dates shared by students, months with many birthdays, etc. For large classes, divide into two or three groups.   ALTERNATE FORMAT: Have everyone write their birthday on a note card. Shuffle and distribute the cards. Students circulate, inquiring about birthdays to try to find the person whose card they hold.

In Canada, a birthday is known as «une fête» and one sings «Bonne fête à toi.»

B. Allow students time to match names and dates, then ask, «Quelle date est-ce que vous associez avec Guillaume le Conquérant?» Students only need to answer with the date. (Make sure they say the date—not the letter.)   ANSWERS: 1. 1431 2. 1776   3. 1864   4. 1492   5. 1789 6. 1914   7. 1969   8. 1963

C. For classes with nontraditional students, discuss the 4-day work week. Students may discuss in small groups, or you may use this as a short written assignment.

STRUCTURE: Talking about activities
*Le verbe **faire***

Observez et déduisez   Ces jeunes gens ont la semaine de quatre jours. Qu'est-ce qu'ils font quand ils ont du temps libre?

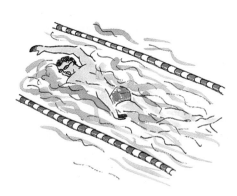

D'habitude, Kofi fait de la natation.

Nathalie et Erica font souvent de la marche.

Quelquefois Hang fait la cuisine.

Geneviève fait toujours ses devoirs.

— Et vous? Qu'est-ce que vous faites quand vous avez du temps libre?
— Nous? Nous ne faisons jamais nos devoirs!

Remind students to cover up **Vérifiez** while they answer the questions in **Observez et déduisez.**

■ What different forms of the verb **faire** do you find in the preceding examples?

Vérifiez　*Le verbe **faire***

VOCABULAIRE ACTIF

VOCABULAIRE ACTIF

**Les expressions
　avec *faire***
d'habitude
du temps libre
ne... jamais

Le verbe **faire**	
je fais	nous faisons
tu fais	vous faites
il / elle / on fait	ils / elles font

■ The verb **faire** means *to make* or *to do* and is used idiomatically with many different activities.

> Le dimanche, il **fait** toujours ses devoirs.
> Ils ne **font** jamais leur lit.
> Ils **font** la sieste *(take a nap)* ou ils **font** la grasse matinée *(sleep in)*.
> Il **fait** souvent du sport.
> Elle **fait** quelquefois du ski (du golf, du vélo, du foot, du basket, du volley, du tennis, du jogging, de la gymnastique, de l'exercice).*
> Elles **font** de la musique (des courses, un voyage, la cuisine...).
> **Faisons** une promenade *(walk)!*

■ Notice that questions with **faire** do not always require an answer with **faire**.

> — Qu'est-ce que vous **faites** quand vous avez du temps libre?
> — Je joue au golf.
> — Qu'est-ce que vous allez **faire** aujourd'hui?
> — Je vais travailler.

OPTIONAL DRILL:　Que faire? Changez le sujet ou l'objet de la phrase.　CUES:　1. Je fais mes devoirs. (Georges, nous, les étudiants, vous, tu)　2. Nous faisons un voyage en voiture. (elles, tu, vous, Roger et Philippe, je)　3. Hélène fait du ski. (tennis, volley, natation, gymnastique, promenade, voyage, marche, courses, devoirs, cuisine)

D. CUES:　Thomas est un peu paresseux. Il fait souvent la grasse matinée et il ne fait pas souvent ses devoirs. Mais Nora, elle est très active. Elle fait de la natation le matin et de la marche l'après-midi. Et elle fait toujours ses devoirs! Thomas fait du sport aussi. Il aime le golf et le foot, par exemple, et il fait la cuisine quelquefois, mais il ne fait jamais les courses. C'est Nora qui fait ça.

A **loto** game in the *Instructor's Resource Manual* provides practice for speaking about activities.

ACTIVITÉS

D. Que font-ils?　Écoutez le professeur, et indiquez qui fait les activités mentionnées. Ensuite, dites si vous faites les mêmes activités.

➡ — <u>Thomas</u> / Nora fait du golf.　　✓ moi aussi　　_____ pas moi
　 — *Thomas fait du golf, et moi aussi.*

1. Thomas / Nora fait la grasse matinée.　　_____ moi aussi　　_____ pas moi

2. Thomas / Nora fait toujours ses devoirs.　　_____ moi aussi　　_____ pas moi

3. Thomas / Nora fait de la natation.　　_____ moi aussi　　_____ pas moi

4. Thomas / Nora fait de la marche.　　_____ moi aussi　　_____ pas moi

5. Thomas / Nora fait du foot.　　_____ moi aussi　　_____ pas moi

6. Thomas / Nora fait la cuisine.　　_____ moi aussi　　_____ pas moi

7. Thomas / Nora fait des courses.　　_____ moi aussi　　_____ pas moi

---

*The verb **jouer à** can also be used with games: Je **joue au** tennis et mon frère **joue au** basket, mais notre sœur fait de la gymnastique. Names of sports like football are often shortened, as in the example.

E. Réponses personnelles.   Lisez les phrases suivantes et répondez selon vos habitudes personnelles.

	toujours	souvent	quelquefois	jamais
1. Le matin, je fais mon lit.	——	——	——	——
2. Le mardi, je fais de la musique.	——	——	——	——
3. Le samedi, je fais des courses.	——	——	——	——
4. Le mercredi, mes amis font du volley.	——	——	——	——
5. Le week-end, nous faisons une promenade.	——	——	——	——
6. Le soir, nous faisons nos devoirs.	——	——	——	——
7. Le… , je…	——	——	——	——

Maintenant partagez *(share)* vos réponses avec un(e) partenaire.

➡ — *Tu fais ton lit le matin?*
— *Jamais! Je n'ai pas le temps. J'ai un cours à huit heures.*

Prenez des notes sur ses réponses et écrivez un paragraphe au sujet de ses habitudes.

Jeu de rôle

> You and a prospective roommate have different interests and abilities. One of you is athletically inclined and likes music. The other dislikes physical activity intensely and prefers intellectual endeavors like learning languages! Discuss your pastime preferences. You may discover that the rooming arrangement would not work out! Use expressions with **faire** to talk about what you like or do not like to do.

**W
B**

CULTURE ET RÉFLEXION

Internet

■ **La maternelle.** Les enfants en France commencent l'école à un très jeune âge: 99,6% des enfants de 3 ans vont à la maternelle, et 36% des enfants de 2 ans. Comment expliquez-vous ces statistiques? À votre avis, est-ce une bonne idée de commencer l'école à l'âge de 2 ou 3 ans?

■ **Le bac.** À la fin de leur dernière année de lycée, les jeunes Français passent[1] un grand examen national qui s'appelle **le baccalauréat**, ou **le bac**. Les résultats à cet examen déterminent la possibilité de faire des études supérieures. Seulement[2] 63% des élèves qui passent le bac réussissent[3]. Les élèves qui ratent[4] l'examen peuvent refaire la dernière année de lycée et repasser le bac l'année suivante. Que pensez-vous de ce système? Préférez-vous un système de contrôle continu comme dans les lycées américains? À votre avis, quels sont les effets d'un grand examen national à la fin des études secondaires sur (a) la qualité des programmes scolaires, (b) l'attitude des élèves et des professeurs vis-à-vis de l'éducation, et (c) l'idée de réserver l'accès aux études supérieures à une sorte d'élite intellectuelle?

■ **Éducation et sacrifices.** Dans la majorité des pays africains francophones, le système scolaire est basé sur le système français, l'instruction est en français, mais les ressources sont souvent très limitées. Imaginez une salle de classe dans un village comme

À la maternelle.

Une école primaire au Sénégal.

Toubacouta, au Sénégal: il y a 60 à 70 enfants dans une seule classe, et ces enfants doivent partager[5] une douzaine (10–12) de livres, de cahiers, de stylos... Dans d'autres villages, il n'y a pas d'école. Dans l'ensemble d'un pays comme le Sénégal, seulement 44% des enfants vont à l'école, et seulement 10% à 15% des enfants qui finissent l'école primaire continuent au collège, car les collèges sont peu nombreux et situés exclusivement dans les villes. Les études universitaires sont réservées à une très petite minorité; certains obtiennent des bourses[6] pour continuer leurs études en France. L'éducation vient donc au prix de grands sacrifices. À votre avis, est-il justifié de demander à un enfant de quitter[7] sa famille à l'âge de 11 ans pour continuer ses études en ville? Est-ce que des sacrifices, financiers et autres, sont nécessaires pour obtenir une formation universitaire chez vous? Quels sacrifices faites-vous pour votre éducation?

1. *take*　2. *only*　3. *pass*　4. *fail*　5. *share*　6. *scholarships*　7. *leave*

Troisième étape

À l'écoute: La fac

This listening section introduces students to university life in France.

Décisions, décisions! La conversation que vous allez entendre illustre les décisions que les jeunes Français doivent prendre *(must make)* pour leurs études. Lisez **Avant d'écouter,** puis écoutez selon les instructions données.

Avant d'écouter

1 On dit qu'en France il n'y a «pas de fac sans bac». Comme l'explique la page culturelle (p. 137), il est nécessaire d'avoir le baccalauréat, ou le bac, pour entrer à l'université ou dans une école supérieure.

Jour d'examen dans une fac française.

Note culturelle

Le bac. This cumulative exam covers several years of study in one of three major tracks: **la série littéraire** (language, literature, philosophy), **la série économique et sociale** (social sciences, economics, applied mathematics), and **la série scientifique** (mathematics, physics, chemistry, natural sciences, industrial technology). The exam, which lasts several days, has oral as well as written components.

La fac est un autre terme pour l'université, qui se divise en facultés (facs).

Exemples de facs	Pour les études de/d'
La fac des lettres et sciences humaines	histoire, géographie, littérature, langues étrangères, philosophie, sociologie, psychologie
La fac des sciences	biologie, chimie, géologie, maths, physique
La fac de droit et sciences économiques	droit *(law)*, relations internationales, sciences politiques, économie, gestion *(business)*, commerce

Écoutons

Audio CD

2 Écoutez une première fois. Est-ce que Stéphane est

   a. au lycée?
   b. à la fac?

3 Écoutez encore et répondez aux questions suivantes.

   1. **Passer, réussir** ou **rater:** quel verbe est-ce que la dame utilise quand elle pose sa question à Stéphane sur le bac?
   2. Quelles sont les intentions de Stéphane? Il va faire des études de ___chimie___ à la fac ___des sciences___ .
   3. Stéphane **a peur** du bac, «parce que c'est un examen **vachement** important.» En utilisant le contexte et la logique, déduisez le sens de **avoir peur** (être nerveux ou calme?) et **vachement** (très ou un peu?).

Explain that **vachement** is used for emphasis; it is a familiar equivalent of **très**.

4 Quels diplômes est-ce que Stéphane va préparer? Écoutez encore et reliez les adverbes et les diplômes.

   la maîtrise   d'abord
   la licence   peut-être
   le doctorat   sans doute

Déduisez: quel est le terme français pour l'équivalent du *bachelor's degree? master's degree? Ph.D.?* Comment dit-on *first? probably?*

5 Écoutez une dernière fois en faisant attention au contexte de **on peut pas** et **tu veux.** Quel verbe signifie *to want*, et quel verbe signifie *can / to be able to?*

Notes culturelles

L'enseignement supérieur. After **le bac,** l'enseignement supérieur offers several options:

■ **Les instituts universitaires de technologie (IUT),** where students can obtain technical degrees in such fields of specialization as engineering, business, computer science, accounting **(la comptabilité),** and so on.

VOCABULAIRE ACTIF

un amphithéâtre
avoir peur
la bibliothèque
le campus
la comptabilité
un diplôme
le droit
la fac
la gestion
la médecine
passer un examen
rater
le restaurant
  universitaire
réussir (infinitive only)
la sociologie

■ **Les universités,** where it generally takes three years to obtain **une licence,** one more year for **une maîtrise,** and three to five additional years for **un doctorat. Les études de médecine** take a minimum of seven years, and **les études dentaires** five years.

■ **Les grandes écoles,** which are prestigious institutions specializing in engineering, business, education, or the sciences. The entrance exam takes one to two years to prepare for, and only the intellectual elite are admitted to these three-year schools.

All public schools of higher learning are free. The concept of liberal arts education at the university level is not part of the French school system. Liberal arts courses are taught at the secondary level, and students specialize immediately at the university.

French universities, especially the older ones, may not have **un campus** per se—various **facultés** may be housed in different parts of town. Students go to **la bibliothèque** (library) mostly to check out books or do research. Large classes are held in **des amphithéâtres. Les restaurants universitaires** are subsidized by the government and provide students with inexpensive meals.

Prononciation

Les sons [ø] *et* [œ]

Have students practice saying **euh/heure** and **deux/neuf** several times in a row, to feel the difference between the closed [ø] and the open [œ].

■ [ø] is the sound in **euh** and **deux.** To pronounce this vowel sound, say [e], then round your lips like for an [o], without moving your tongue or the opening of your mouth.

■ [œ] is the sound in **heure** and **neuf.** To pronounce it, say [ɛ], then round your lips, again without moving your tongue or the opening of your mouth.

Écoutez

Audio CD

Listen to the following phrases from **À l'écoute: La fac** on the student audio CD, and in the chart, check the sounds you hear. Each phrase will be read twice.

	[ø]	[œ]
1. Tu as p**eu**r?		✓
2. un p**eu**	✓	
3. tu v**eu**x	✓	
4. on p**eu**t pas	✓	
5. des études supéri**eu**res		✓
6. p**eu**t-être	✓	

Now practice saying the phrases aloud. Then listen to the phrases again to verify your pronunciation.

Essayez!

Audio CD

A. Prononcez. Practice saying the following words aloud, paying particular attention to the highlighted sounds. Then listen to the words on the student audio CD to verify your pronunciation.

1. [ø] mons**ieu**r, paress**eu**x, paress**eu**se, sér**ieu**x, sér**ieu**se, ennuy**eu**x, ennuy**eu**se, h**eu**r**eu**x, h**eu**r**eu**se, v**ieu**x, les chev**eu**x, les y**eu**x, bl**eu**

2. [œ] un profess**eu**r, un act**eu**r, un ingén**ieu**r, une f**eu**ille, un faut**eu**il, un ordinat**eu**r, les m**eu**bles, j**eu**ne, l**eu**r, s**œu**r

Remind students that the **f** of **neuf** is pronounced [v] when followed by **heures** and **ans: le neuf avril** (with [f]), but **neuf heures, neuf ans** (with [v]).

B. [ø] et [œ]. Now practice saying aloud the following expressions that contain both [ø] and [œ]. Then listen to them on the student audio CD to verify your pronunciation.

1. J'ai un p**eu** p**eu**r.
2. Le mons**ieu**r aux y**eu**x bl**eu**s est profess**eu**r.
3. Il est n**eu**f h**eu**res moins d**eu**x.

STRUCTURE: Saying what you can and want to do
*Les verbes **pouvoir** et **vouloir***

Observez et déduisez

Cue to Video Module 4 (00:19:00), where Élisabeth and Nicolas talk of what they will do after their studies. Also cue to street interviews (00:20:21), where some students talk of their future plans.

— Tu vas passer ton bac cette année, n'est-ce pas?
— Bien sûr! Sans le bac, on ne peut pas entrer à la fac.
— Tu sais ce que tu veux faire après?
— Je pense que je voudrais faire des études supérieures de chimie l'année prochaine.
— Ah, bon. Tu veux préparer la licence?
— Oui. Et la maîtrise et le doctorat si je peux.

■ You have already learned to use the polite expressions **je voudrais** and **pourriez-vous** in Chapter 3. What other forms of the verb **vouloir** and **pouvoir** do you see in the dialogue above?

ESG

La Grande École parisienne leader pour l'emploi et les salaires

CONCOURS PARALLÈLE
d'entrée en 1ère année
les 8 et 9 septembre 1997
ouvert aux étudiants de niveau
BAC + 2

3 options de concours : • DROIT-SCES ECO.GESTION • LETTRES • SCIENCES

École Supérieure de Gestion

RECONNUE PAR L'ÉTAT
DIPLÔME HOMOLOGUE PAR L'ÉTAT
25, RUE ST-AMBROISE 75011 PARIS

Renseignements : 01 43 55 44 44

Vérifiez *Les verbes **pouvoir** et **vouloir***

■ The verb **vouloir** is used to express desire. It is often followed directly by another verb in the infinitive.

Je ne **veux** pas rater le bac. Je **veux faire** des études supérieures.

■ **Vouloir bien** is often used to accept an invitation or to express willingness.

— Tu veux aller à la bibliothèque avec moi?
— Oui, je **veux bien.**

■ The verb **pouvoir** is used to express ability or permission and is commonly followed by an infinitive.

> Le prof est gentil. Nous **pouvons** toujours **poser** des questions.
> Claire et Lise ne **peuvent** pas **faire** leurs devoirs. Elles n'ont pas le temps *(time)*.
> Je ne **peux** pas **faire** de courses. Je n'ai pas d'argent *(money)*.

Draw students' attention to the differences in both the oral and the written forms. Ask how many forms they see, then read the conjugation and ask how many forms they hear.

DISCRIMINATION DRILL: To further focus learners' attention on differences in third-person forms, read the following and have students indicate singular/plural by holding up one finger or two.   CUES: 1. Ils veulent faire une maîtrise.   2. Elle veut étudier à la fac.   3. Elles ne peuvent pas travailler ce soir.   4. Il ne veut pas rater son examen.   5. Il ne peut pas faire ses devoirs.   6. Elles peuvent entrer à la fac.

OPTIONAL DRILL: **Vouloir/ pouvoir.** Marie veut faire son doctorat. —→ Marie peut faire son doctorat.   CUES: 1. Les enfants veulent aller à l'école.   2. Nous voulons entrer à la fac.   3. Tu veux habiter dans la résidence universitaire.   4. Vous pouvez étudier le français.   5. Je peux faire une maîtrise.   6. Elle peut préparer son bac.

A. Refer students to the **Notes culturelles** on pp. 120 and 139–140.

B. Do the first task with the whole class, then have students work in pairs on the second task.

Les verbes **vouloir** et **pouvoir**	
je veux	nous voulons
tu veux	vous voulez
il / elle / on veut	ils / elles veulent
je peux	nous pouvons
tu peux	vous pouvez
il / elle / on peut	ils / elles peuvent

ACTIVITÉS

A. L'enseignement en France.   Complétez les phrases de la colonne de gauche avec une expression logique de la colonne de droite.

1. Alain n'a pas son bac. Il ne peut pas...
2. Tu veux aller dans une grande école? Tu vas...
3. Nous voulons être avocats. Nous allons...
4. Mes copains veulent étudier la physique. Ils vont...
5. J'étudie la littérature. Je suis...
6. Vous étudiez dans un IUT. Vous pouvez...

a. à la faculté des lettres.
b. faire de la comptabilité.
c. faire la série scientifique.
d. entrer à la fac.
e. à la faculté de droit.
f. préparer des concours pendant deux ans.

B. Obligations/Préférences.   Qu'est-ce que ces gens ne veulent pas faire? Qu'est-ce qu'ils préfèrent faire?

➡ *Il ne veut pas passer un examen; il veut faire de la natation.*

Et vous? Qu'est-ce que vous ne voulez pas faire? Qu'est-ce que vous voulez bien faire? Discutez avec un(e) partenaire. Vos réponses sont-elles semblables?

C. **La permission.** C'est le premier jour de votre cours de français. Jouez le rôle du professeur. Dites aux étudiants ce qu'ils peuvent faire en classe et ce qu'ils ne peuvent pas faire.

➡ manger? *Vous ne pouvez pas manger en classe.*

1. regarder une vidéocassette?
2. parler espagnol?
3. faire des exercices?
4. poser des questions?
5. étudier la chimie?
6. ?

C. Have pairs/groups come up with 3 additional things they *can* do in class and 3 things they *can't* do.

D. **Invitations.** Vous faites vos devoirs depuis des heures et vous êtes fatigué(e). Qu'est-ce que vous voulez faire, alors? Cochez les activités qui vous intéressent et ajoutez trois autres activités.

_____ faire des courses	_____ dîner au restaurant	_____ jouer au tennis
_____ écouter un nouveau CD	_____ regarder une vidéocassette	_____ faire de la marche
_____	_____	_____

Maintenant invitez votre partenaire à faire les activités qui vous intéressent. Il/Elle va accepter ou refuser.

➡ — *Tu veux faire des courses?*
— *Oui, je veux bien!* ou *Non, je ne peux pas.*

E. **Ni le temps ni l'argent?** *(Neither time nor money?)* Qu'est-ce que vos amis et vous voulez faire ce week-end? Est-ce possible? Si ce n'est pas possible, dites pourquoi.

➡ *Mes amis et moi, nous voulons jouer au foot, mais nous ne pouvons pas parce que nous n'avons pas le temps.*

STRUCTURE: Talking about classes
*Les verbes **prendre, apprendre** et **comprendre***

Observez et déduisez

Ces étudiants **prennent** des notes
en classe.

Ces étudiants **apprennent** à
parler français.

Cet étudiant ne **comprend** pas l'exercice.

Et vous? Vous **apprenez** le français aussi, n'est-ce pas? Est-ce que vous
comprenez les exercices? Est-ce que vous **prenez** des notes en classe?
Est-ce que vous **prenez** souvent le temps d'étudier?

> ■ You learned the expression **je ne comprends pas** in the Chapitre
> préliminaire, and you used the verb **prendre** *(Prenez la rue Victor Hugo...)*
> in Chapter 3. Can you infer the meaning of **apprendre** from the examples
> in **Observez et déduisez?**
>
> ■ **Apprendre** and **comprendre** are both compounds of **prendre**. Using
> what you already know and the examples above, can you infer the **tu**
> and **nous** forms of these verbs?

Vérifiez   *Les verbes **prendre, apprendre** et **comprendre***

VOCABULAIRE ACTIF

apprendre
comprendre
prendre...
le temps de...

■ **Prendre** *(to take)* can be used in a variety of contexts:

Les étudiants **prennent** des notes en classe.
Jean-Michel **prend** son vélo pour aller en classe.
Pour aller à la fac, **prenez** la rue de l'Université.

Have volunteers say one thing they take the time to do every day.

Ask volunteers to say something they're learning to do. Emphasize the use of the preposition before the infinitive. This may be a good time to review uses of the infinitive after **aller, vouloir, pouvoir.** Contrast these verbs with the two new expressions: **prendre le temps de** and **apprendre à.**

■ **Prendre un cours** is used for extracurricular or private lessons. For school contexts, use **avoir un cours.**

> Il **prend un cours** de gymnastique.   J'**ai un cours** de maths.

■ **Prendre le temps de** + an infinitive means *to take the time to* do something.

> Je **prends le temps d'**étudier tous les jours.

■ The verb **apprendre** *(to learn)* may be followed by a noun or by the preposition **à** and an infinitive to say one is learning to *do* something.

> Nous **apprenons** le vocabulaire.
> Nous **apprenons à parler** français.

■ **Comprendre** may be followed by a direct object, or it may stand alone.

> Tu **comprends** la grammaire?
> Oui, je **comprends.**
> Les étudiants **comprennent** le professeur.

OPTIONAL DRILL: Prendre/apprendre/comprendre. CUES: 1. Marie apprend à parler français. (nous, tu, je, on, les étudiants) 2. Nous prenons des notes. (les étudiants, Marie, tu, vous, je) 3. Les profs ne comprennent pas! (les hommes, je, tu, les femmes, nous, les parents, on) 4. Est-ce qu'il comprend le professeur? (tu, les étudiants, vous, Hélène)

Le verbe prendre	
je prends	nous prenons
tu prends	vous prenez
il / elle / on prend	ils / elles prennent

ACTIVITÉS

F. Interview.   Interviewez un(e) partenaire en vous posant *(asking each other)* les questions suivantes.

1. Tu comprends le professeur de français?
2. Les étudiants dans la classe comprennent les CD?
3. Est-ce qu'ils prennent des notes en classe?
4. Tes copains apprennent à parler espagnol?
5. Tes copains et toi, vous prenez des leçons de tennis?
6. Tu apprends la chimie, toi?
7. Tu prends ton vélo pour aller en cours?

G. Have students work in groups or assign as homework. Ask students to come up with 7–8 suggestions using as much of the vocabulary as possible. Brainstorm additional useful vocabulary on the board if needed.

G. Pour réussir en français, on...   Utilisez le vocabulaire suivant pour dire ce qui est nécessaire pour réussir en français.

➡ *Pour réussir en français, on apprend le vocabulaire.*

les verbes	les noms
étudier	la grammaire
parler	le vocabulaire
écouter	le professeur
apprendre	des notes
comprendre	des exercices
prendre le temps de	le cahier
poser des questions	les CD
faire ses devoirs tous les jours	
préparer/passer des examens	

Jeu de rôle

You have an acquaintance with an annoying personality who is forever invit-ing you out. Prepare a skit with a classmate in which she or he invites you and continues to insist even though you refuse (you can't, don't have the time, and so on). Your friend tries tennis, studying, a movie—any pretext to get together. You have to find several excuses because you have no desire to go anywhere with this person.

CD-ROM

Now that you have finished the Troisième étape of this chapter, do your Lab Man-ual activities with the audio program. Explore chapter topics further with the *Mais oui!* Video and CD-ROM. Viewing and comprehension activities are in the video section of your *Workbook/Lab Manual/Video Manual*.

Intégration

Littérature: «Ils vont lui faire éclater le cerveau... »

Marcel Pagnol (1895–1974) is the author of *Jean de Florette* and *Manon des sources,* made famous in recent years through the award-winning movies with Yves Montand. Born and raised in the south of France, Marcel Pagnol has immortalized both in print and on film the charm of the sun-drenched hills of Provence and the singing accent of its people. First a playwright with acclaimed plays such as *Topaze* (1928), *Marius* (1929), and *Fanny* (1931), Pagnol turned to the screen as early as 1936 when he wrote and directed *César,* which has become a classic in the world of film. Pagnol then devoted much of his life to filmmaking. In 1957, he published the first volume of his autobiography, *La Gloire de mon père,* followed in 1958 by *Le Château de ma mère,* which were both made into movies in 1990. Son of Joseph, a schoolteacher, and Augustine, a sweet-natured woman, Marcel recounts with much humor and tenderness the early days of a magical childhood in Provence. The following piece is an excerpt from *La Gloire de mon père.*

Avant de lire

Remind students that they are not expected to understand every word. They will be guided through the text one activity at a time, and will understand what they need to understand to handle the given tasks.

1 Dans le texte, la concierge dit, «Ils vont lui faire éclater le cerveau... » *(They are going to make his brain burst . . .).* Quelle horreur! «Ils», ce sont les instituteurs d'une petite école primaire. La victime: le petit Marcel. À votre avis, quelles sont les causes possibles d'une «explosion cérébrale»? Cochez la réponse qui vous semble la plus probable.

_____ Une expérience scientifique sur le cerveau des enfants

_____ Une expérience psychologique sur les capacités cérébrales des enfants

_____ Un enfant très intelligent encouragé à apprendre trop de choses *(too much)* trop vite *(too fast)*

_____ Un enfant paresseux forcé d'étudier

_____ La punition d'un enfant qui n'est pas sage *(quiet, good)*

_____ Une réaction causée par une grande peur *(fear)*

En général

2 Parcourez le texte une première fois. Parmi *(Among)* les possibilités proposées dans **Avant de lire,** quelle est la réponse correcte?

147

3 Parcourez le texte une deuxième fois pour identifier les paragraphes qui correspondent aux titres suivants. Attention, il y a un titre supplémentaire qu'on ne peut pas utiliser!

paragraphe	titre
1. «Quand ma mère va faire... »	a. Le papa comprend que Marcel sait lire.
2. «Un beau matin... »	b. Le papa confirme avec un livre que Marcel sait lire.
3. «Mon père se retourne... »	c. La maman appelle un docteur.
15. «Alors il va prendre... »	d. Marcel va souvent dans la classe de son père.
16. «Quand ma mère arrive... »	e. Le papa écrit une phrase sur un petit garçon qui a été puni.
17. «Sur la porte de la classe... »	f. La maman observe la condition physique de Marcel.
18. «À la maison... »	g. Marcel de quatre à six ans.
19. «Non je n'ai pas mal... »	h. La réaction immédiate de la maman.
	i. La réaction de la concierge.

«Ils vont lui faire éclater le cerveau... »

1 **Q**uand ma mère va faire ses courses, elle me laisse° souvent dans la classe de mon père, qui apprend à lire à des enfants de six ou sept ans. Je reste assis°, bien sage, au premier rang° et j'admire mon père qui, avec une baguette° de bambou, montre les lettres et les mots qu'il écrit au tableau noir.

me... leaves me

seated / row / stick

2 Un beau matin—j'ai à peine quatre ans à l'époque—ma mère me dépose à ma place pendant que mon père écrit magnifiquement sur le tableau: «La maman a puni° son petit garçon qui n'était pas sage.» Et moi de crier: «Non! Ce n'est pas vrai!»

punished

3 Mon père se retourne soudain, me regarde stupéfait, et demande: «Qu'est-ce que tu dis?»

4 — Maman ne m'a pas puni! Ce n'est pas vrai!

5 Il s'avance vers moi:

6 — Qui dit qu'on t'a puni?

7 — C'est écrit.

8 Sa surprise est totale.

9 — Mais... mais... est-ce que tu sais lire?

10 — Oui.

11 — Voyons°, voyons...

let's see

12 Et puis il dirige° son bambou vers le tableau noir.

points

13 — Eh bien, lis°.

*du verbe **lire** (lisez)*

14 Et je lis la phrase à haute voix.

15 Alors il va prendre un livre, et je lis sans difficulté plusieurs° pages... La surprise initiale de mon père est vite remplacée par une grande joie et une grande fierté.

several

16 Quand ma mère arrive, elle me trouve au milieu de° quatre instituteurs, qui ont envoyé° leurs élèves dans la cour de récréation, et qui m'écoutent lire

avec

sent

lentement° l'histoire du Petit Poucet°... Mais au lieu d'admirer cet exploit, elle   *slowly / Tom Thumb*
pâlit°, ferme brusquement le livre, et me prend dans ses bras, en disant: «Mon   *turns pale*
Dieu°! mon Dieu!... »   *God*

17 Sur la porte de la classe, il y a la concierge, une vieille femme corse°, qui   *from Corsica*
répète avec effroi°: «Ils vont lui faire éclater le cerveau.... Mon Dieu, ils vont lui   *peur*
faire éclater le cerveau... » C'est elle qui est allée chercher ma mère.

18 À la maison, mon père affirme que ce sont des superstitions ridicules, mais
ma mère n'est pas convaincue, et de temps en temps elle pose sa main° sur   *hand*
mon front° et me demande: «Tu n'as pas mal à la tête°?»   *forehead /* mal... *a headache*

19 Non, je n'ai pas mal à la tête, mais jusqu'à l'âge de six ans, je n'ai plus° la   ne... plus: *no longer*
permission d'entrer dans une classe, ni d'ouvrir un livre, par crainte° d'une   *peur*
explosion cérébrale. Elle va être rassurée quand, à la fin de mon premier
trimestre à l'école, mon institutrice va déclarer que j'ai une mémoire exception-
nelle, mais que j'ai la maturité d'un bébé.

Extrait de *La Gloire de mon père* (Marcel Pagnol)

En détail

4 Have students report on how they
inferred meaning. What were the
clues?

4 **Les mots.** D'après le contexte, quel est le sens des mots suivants? Choisissez a ou b.

¶1	apprendre (ici)	a. to learn	b. to teach
¶2	à peine	a. painfully	b. barely
¶14	à haute voix	a. quietly	b. aloud
¶15	fierté	a. fear	b. pride
¶16	cour de récréation	a. playground	b. principal's office
¶18	convaincue	a. convinced	b. convalescent
¶19	rassurée	a. worried	b. reassured

5 **Le texte**

A. Vrai ou faux?   Indiquez si la phrase est vraie (V) ou fausse (F). Corrigez les phrases fausses.

1. Marcel va généralement faire les courses avec sa mère.
2. Quand Marcel est dans la classe de son père, il admire les autres élèves.
3. Quand Monsieur Pagnol écrit que «la maman a puni son petit garçon qui n'était pas sage», Marcel prend cette phrase très personnellement.
4. Monsieur Pagnol veut des évidences supplémentaires que son fils sait lire.
5. Après la surprise initiale, Monsieur Pagnol téléphone à sa femme.
6. Les autres instituteurs veulent que leurs élèves écoutent Marcel lire.
7. La réaction de Madame Pagnol est très différente de la réaction de Monsieur Pagnol.
8. La vieille concierge est superstitieuse.
9. Madame Pagnol a peur pour son fils.
10. Madame Pagnol encourage son fils à lire.

B. Allow students to discuss this in English or provide needed vocabulary. C'est une preuve que... normal... précoce... etc.

B. Pourquoi?   Pourquoi Madame Pagnol est-elle «rassurée» quand elle apprend que son fils, à l'âge de six ans, a la maturité d'un bébé?

Et vous?

Question 1 can be done with the whole class. Before group work for question 2, you may wish to brainstorm ideas, writing vocabulary on the board as students suggest circumstances.   FOLLOW-UP: Have various groups report on their lists, and have the class compare and discuss.

1. Imaginez que Marcel est votre fils de quatre ans. Vous apprenez avec surprise qu'il sait lire! Qu'est-ce que vous allez faire? Est-ce que vous allez être content(e) comme le père de Marcel, ou est-ce que vous allez avoir peur, comme sa mère? Est-ce que vous allez encourager Marcel à lire?
2. Est-ce que vous avez parfois l'impression que votre cerveau va éclater? Dans quelles circonstances? Avec un(e) partenaire, faites une liste de ces circonstances.

Par écrit: I like school but I'm *so* busy!

Avant d'écrire

A. Strategy: Brainstorming.   To prepare a writing assignment, begin brainstorming by jotting down lists of ideas and vocabulary related to the proposed task. For instance, what ideas would you be likely to use in a letter discussing your weekly activities? What would you tell a prospective student about your university?

Application.   To prepare for the writing assignments that follow, develop two lists: (1) your activities and classes in an average week, and (2) opportunities for students at your university.

B. Strategy: Writing to a friend.   Begin a friendly letter with a salutation such as:

    Cher Pierre,   Chère Natalie,   Salut les amis!

Close letters to friends with an expression like:

    Bien amicalement,   Amitiés,

More familiar expressions (similar to "hugs and kisses") used with family and close friends include:

    Grosses bises!   Je t'embrasse, / Je vous embrasse,

ÉCRIVEZ

1. En vous basant sur les listes 1 et 2 dans **Avant d'écrire A,** écrivez une lettre à votre ami(e) québécois(e) au sujet de votre vie à l'université. Parlez d'une semaine typique—vos cours, votre emploi du temps, vos activités. Qu'est-ce que vous faites pendant la semaine? le week-end? etc.

➡ *Cher/Chère...*
   La vie à l'université est très fatigante mais aussi très intéressante...

2. Vous aidez votre université à préparer de la publicité destinée aux étudiants francophones. Écrivez un paragraphe où vous décrivez les avantages d'être étudiant(e) à votre fac. Parlez des cours et des emplois du temps, des professeurs, des activités et du campus.

VOCABULAIRE ACTIF

Le temps

un an, une année *a year*
le calendrier *the calendar*
la date *the date*

une fête *a holiday, celebration*
un emploi du temps *a schedule*
du temps libre *free time*

Les mois (m.)

janvier *January*
février *February*
mars *March*
avril *April*
mai *May*
juin *June*

juillet *July*
août *August*
septembre *September*
octobre *October*
novembre *November*
décembre *December*

Les jours (m.) de la semaine

lundi *Monday*
mardi *Tuesday*
mercredi *Wednesday*
jeudi *Thursday*

vendredi *Friday*
samedi *Saturday*
dimanche *Sunday*

La journée

le matin *morning*
l'après-midi *afternoon*
le soir *evening*

L'heure (f.)

Quelle heure est-il? *What time is it?*
À quelle heure? *At what time?*
neuf heures du matin *9:00 A.M. / 9:00 in the morning*
deux heures de l'après-midi *2:00 P.M. / 2:00 in the afternoon*
du soir P.M. */ in the evening*

... et quart *a quarter after*
... moins le quart *a quarter to*
... et demie *-thirty, half past*
midi *noon*
minuit *midnight*

Les matières (f.) / les études (f.)

l'allemand (m.)
l'anglais (m.)
l'architecture (f.)
l'art (m.)
la biologie *biology*
la chimie *chemistry*
la comptabilité *accounting*
le dessin *drawing, design*
le droit *law*
l'économie (f.) *economics*
le français
la géographie
la gestion *business management*
la gymnastique / l'éducation physique (f.) *physical
  education, gym*

l'histoire (f.) *history*
l'informatique (f.) *computer science*
les langues étrangères *foreign languages*
la littérature *literature*
les maths (f.)
la médecine *medicine*
la musique
la peinture *painting*
la philosophie *philosophy*
la physique *physics*
la psychologie *psychology*
les sciences (f.)
les sciences politiques (sciences po) *political science*
la sociologie *sociology*

Les écoles

l'école maternelle *kindergarten*
l'école primaire *elementary school*
le collège *junior high / middle school*

le lycée *high school*
la fac / l'université *college / university*

un cours *a class*
les devoirs (m.) *homework*
un diplôme *a diploma, degree*
un examen *an exam, a test*

passer un examen *to take an exam*
rater un examen *to fail an exam*
réussir à un examen (*infinitive only*)
  to pass an exam

Le campus

un amphithéâtre *an amphitheater*
la bibliothèque *the library*
le restaurant universitaire *university cafeteria*

Verbes

apprendre *to learn*
comprendre *to understand*
entrer (à la fac) *to enter*
faire *to do, to make*
penser *to think*

pouvoir *to be able to, can*
prendre *to take*
préparer *to prepare*
vouloir *to want*

Expressions avec faire

faire des courses *to go shopping*
faire la cuisine *to cook*
faire ses devoirs *to do homework*
faire du golf *to play golf*
faire la grasse matinée *to sleep in*
faire de la gymnastique / de l'exercice
  to exercise
faire du jogging / de la marche
  to go jogging / walking
faire son lit *to make one's bed*

faire de la musique *to practice music*
faire de la natation *to swim*
faire une promenade *to go for a walk*
faire la sieste *to take a nap*
faire du ski *to ski*
faire du sport *to play sports*
faire du vélo *to go biking*
faire du volley *to play volleyball*
faire un voyage *to go on a trip*

Expressions verbales

avoir peur (de) *to be afraid*
avoir le temps (de) / prendre le temps (de) *to have / take the time (to)*
Ça me plaît *I like it*
Ça te plaît? *Do you like it?*

Expressions pour réagir

Ah bon? Vraiment? *Oh really?*
C'est vrai? *Is that right?*
Bof... *Well . . .*
Et alors? *So what?*
Tant pis! *Too bad!*
Tiens... *Oh . . .*
C'est pas vrai! *No! / I can't believe it!*
Tu plaisantes! *You're kidding!*

C'est chouette! / génial! *That's cool!*
Formidable! / Super! *Great!*
Quelle chance! *How lucky!*
C'est embêtant! *That's too bad!*
C'est incroyable! *Unbelievable!*
Je m'en fiche *I don't give a darn*
J'en ai marre *I'm fed up*
Mince! / Zut alors! *Darn it!*

Adverbes de temps

d'habitude *usually*
ne... jamais *never*
tard *late*
tôt *early*

Adjectifs

dernier (dernière) *last*
gentil(le) *nice*
libre *free*
long (longue) *long*

occupé(e) *busy*
prochain(e) *next*
strict(e) *strict*
super *super, great*

Divers

l'argent (m.) *money*
un cadeau *a gift*
des projets *plans*

EXPRESSIONS POUR LA CLASSE

aider *to help*
accepter *to accept*
associer *to associate*
à tour de rôle *in turn*
circulez dans la classe *walk around the classroom*
entendre *to hear*
grouper *to group together*

Quel est le sens de... ? *What is the meaning of . . . ?*
n'oubliez pas *don't forget*
refuser *to refuse*
selon le cas *whatever the case may be*
selon vous *according to you*
un sketch *a skit*

5 À table!

Comparez les aliments sur cette photo.

Qu'est-ce qui est meilleur? plus sain? moins cher?

Et vous?

Quels sont vos aliments préférés?

This chapter will enable you to

- **understand conversations about food**
- **read about eating habits in France**
- **read an excerpt from an African play**

- **talk about what you like to eat and drink**
- **know what to say in a restaurant**
- **compare people and things**
- **ask for and give explanations**
- **talk about what happened**

À l'écoute: Vous désirez?

This listening section serves as entry into the function of ordering food and drink in a restaurant.

La conversation de cette étape a lieu *(takes place)* à La Belle Époque, un café-snack-bar à Aix-en-Provence. Faites d'abord l'activité 1, **Avant d'écouter,** puis écoutez en suivant les instructions données. **1** Model the pronunciation of the words in the list before pairs begin the task. Point out the change in pronunciation from **un œuf** to **des œufs.**

Avant d'écouter

1 Voici une page du menu (ou de la carte) de La Belle Époque. Avec un(e) partenaire, examinez les photos et les descriptions, puis déduisez le sens des mots suivants.

de la salade
une tomate
un œuf
du maïs
du jambon
une saucisse
un avocat
de la viande (bœuf, porc, etc.)

3 ANSWERS: *Mentionnés:* hamburger, frites, sandwich-brochette, salade (niçoise, Louisiane); *commandés:* salade niçoise, brochette, frites.

Écoutons

Audio CD

2 Écoutez une première fois pour déterminer qui parle.

a. deux clients et une serveuse *(waitress)*
b. deux clients et un serveur *(waiter)*
c. trois clients

3 Écoutez une deuxième fois en regardant le menu et notez sur une feuille

les plats *(dishes)* mentionnés
les plats commandés *(ordered)*

4 Qu'est-ce que le jeune homme commande en supplément?

a. une salade   b. des frites   c. de la soupe

_____
thon *tuna*   brochette *skewer*

SNACK La Belle Epoque
spécialités chaudes

La Niçoise
salade, tomates, thon, œuf
35,00 F

Hamburger Œuf à cheval
35,00 F

La Louisiane
salade, tomates, maïs, jambon
35,00 F

Coppacabana
Saucisse, Tomate, Avocat
28,00 F

Sandwich
Brochette viande
18,00 F

5 Quel est le sens de **j'ai faim** et **j'ai soif?** Complétez les phrases de gauche avec les explications à droite.

1. Quand on a faim...   a. on prend une boisson.
2. Quand on a soif...   b. on mange.

6 Écoutez encore une fois et identifiez les boissons commandées.

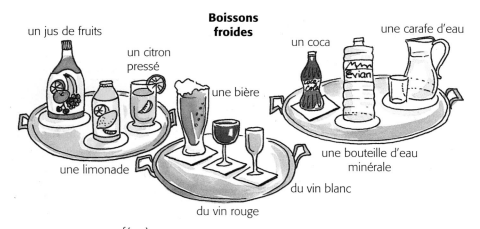

Boissons froides

un jus de fruits — un citron pressé — un coca — une carafe d'eau — une bière — une limonade — une bouteille d'eau minérale — du vin blanc — du vin rouge

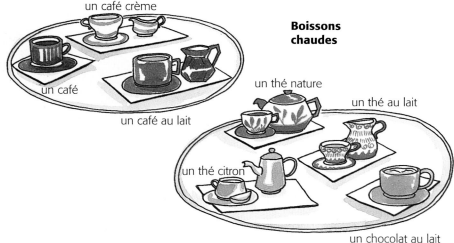

Boissons chaudes

un café crème — un café — un café au lait — un thé nature — un thé au lait — un thé citron — un chocolat au lait

Notes culturelles

Les boissons. In most French cafés and restaurants, if you order water, you will get **de l'eau minérale,** i.e., bottled mineral water, which you will have to pay for. If you just want (free) tap water, you must specify **une carafe d'eau** or **de l'eau ordinaire. Un citron pressé** is a lemonade made from fresh-squeezed lemons; **une limonade** is a sweet carbonated drink very much like 7-Up. **Le café au lait,** half coffee, half milk, is generally served for breakfast.

Les repas (meals). Breakfast (**le petit déjeuner**) is quite simple, usually consisting of coffee (**café au lait**), tea, or hot chocolate with toast (**du pain grillé**) or **un croissant.** The French call eggs and bacon **le petit déjeuner**

anglais. Although Canadians and Americans tend to associate French cuisine with very elaborate meals, some French city dwellers today have lunch, **le déjeuner,** at self-service or fast-food restaurants where they may have **une pizza, de la quiche,** or **une omelette** on the run. Most, however, still have a full sit-down meal at lunch, often in an employee cafeteria **(une cantine).** Sundays and holidays are reserved for the traditional family meal, which can last two to three hours. This "real" French meal is like a play in five acts: **les hors-d'œuvre ou une soupe; le plat principal—la viande** *(meat)* **et les légumes; la salade; le fromage; et le dessert (de la mousse au chocolat, de la glace à la vanille...).** Note that the green salad *follows* the main dish, and cheeses are commonly eaten just before dessert. Many households still have a shortened version of this meal, **le dîner en famille,** each evening as the entire family gathers around to discuss the day's events.

Prononciation   *Le e caduc*

■ An unaccented **e** is not pronounced at the end of words. This type of **e** is called **le** *e* **muet,** or mute **e.**

> un̸ serveus̸   cett̸ bièr̸   ell̸ mang̸

■ But in monosyllables such as **je, que, le, ne,** and other words where the unaccented **e** is not in final position **(demain, samedi),** the **e** is called **le** *e* **caduc,** or unstable **e,** because sometimes it is pronounced, and sometimes not.

Écoutez
Audio CD

Listen to the following excerpts from **À l'écoute: Vous désirez?** on the student audio CD, paying close attention to the *e* **caducs** in bold. How are these expressions pronounced by native speakers? Indicate which pronunciation you hear, a or b. An underlined **e** represents a pronounced **e;** an **e** with a slash through it represents a silent **e.** Each item will be read twice.

1. a. Qu'est-c̸ qu<u>e</u> tu vas prendre?
   b. Qu'est-c̸ qu̸ tu vas prendre?
2. a. il n'y a pas d<u>e</u> frites avec...
   b. il n'y a pas d̸ frites avec...
3. a. Ben moi, j<u>e</u> vais prendre une salade niçoise.
   b. Ben moi, j̸ vais prendre une salade niçoise.
4. a. mais j<u>e</u> voudrais aussi des frites.
   b. mais j̸ voudrais aussi des frites.
5. a. et pour mad<u>e</u>moiselle?
   b. et pour mad̸moiselle?

■ The *e* **caduc** is usually not pronounced if you can drop it without bringing too many consonant sounds together.

> j̸ vais prendre...   mad̸moiselle   sam̸di

■ When there are two *e* **caducs** in a row, usually the second one is dropped, except in the case of **que,** which is normally retained.

> J<u>e</u> n̸ comprends pas.   Qu'est-c̸ qu<u>e</u> tu veux?

■ The *e* **caduc** is pronounced when it is preceded by two or more consonant sounds.

> vendr<u>e</u>di (d, r)   une brochette d<u>e</u> bœuf (t, d)

Essayez!

Audio CD

A. Prononcez.   Practice saying the following sentences aloud, dropping the **e** when it is crossed out, and retaining it when it is underlined. Then listen to the sentences on the student audio CD to verify your pronunciation.

1. Qu'est-c~e~ qu~e~ tu r~e~gardes?
2. J~e~ n'aime pas l~e~ coca; j~e~ préfère les jus d~e~ fruits.
3. Nous n~e~ pr~e~nons pas d~e~ café cette s~e~maine.
4. Elle d~e~mande de l'eau minérale; moi, j~e~ vais d~e~mander d~e~ l'eau ordinaire.

ANSWERS: 1. ... d~e~ Paris. 2. Je n~e~ suis pas d~e~ Paris, mais j~e~ viens d'une petite... côté d~e~ Paris. 3. Il y a d~e~ bons p~e~tits... près d~e~...

B. *e* caduc.   In the following sentences, cross out the *e* **caducs** that would normally be dropped, and underline the ones that must be pronounced.

1. Vous êtes d~e~ Paris?
2. Je n~e~ suis pas d~e~ Paris, mais j~e~ viens d'une p~e~tite ville à côté d~e~ Paris.
3. Il y a d~e~ bons p~e~tits restaurants près d~e~ chez moi.

Now practice saying the sentences aloud. Then listen to them on the student audio CD to verify your pronunciation.

VOCABULAIRE
Pour commander au restaurant

Cue to Video Module 5 (00:23:10) where Élisabeth and Fatima order dinner in a restaurant.

Write the functional expressions on the board as students find them in the dialogue: Monsieur, s'il vous plaît; je voudrais... ; moi, je vais prendre... ; et pour moi... Have them infer the meaning of **commander** from the photo.

— Monsieur, s'il vous plaît.
— Oui, monsieur. Vous désirez?
— Je voudrais un sandwich au jambon et un citron pressé.
— Moi, je vais prendre* une pizza et un coca.
— Et pour moi, un steak frites et une bière, s'il vous plaît.

Plus tard...

— Monsieur, l'addition, s'il vous plaît.

■ Si vous voulez parler au serveur ou à la serveuse, qu'est-ce que vous dites? Quelles sont les expressions pour commander? Pour demander à payer?

Vous désirez?

---

*The verb **prendre** is often used to express the idea of having something to eat or drink. **Prendre** (not **manger**) is used with meals, e.g., Quand je **prends** le petit déjeuner, je **prends** du pain et du café.

L'alimentation: Ce qu'on achète* au magasin

To present the illustrated vocabulary that follows, name a food item and have students respond, «J'aime le (la, les)... » or «Je n'aime pas le (la, les)... » This allows you to model pronunciation and reinforces the use of the definite article to express preferences (p. 58).

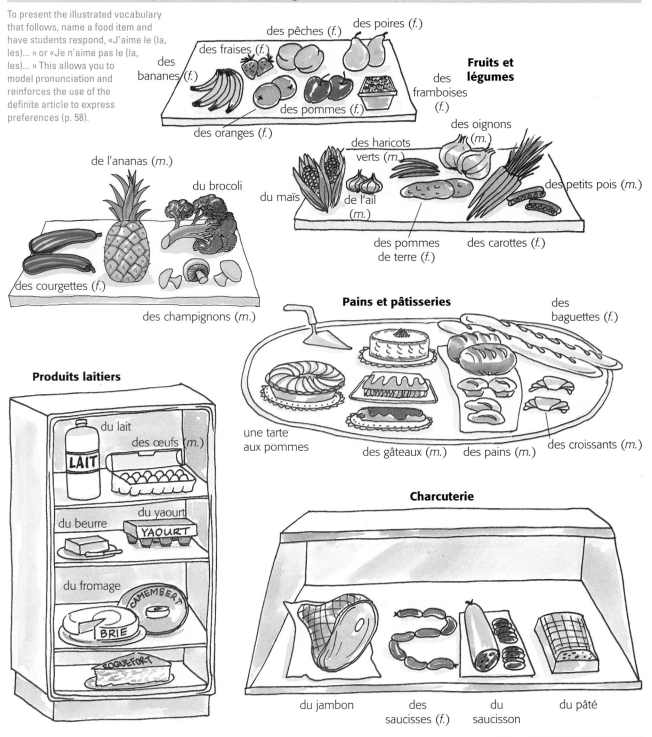

des pêches (f.) des poires (f.)

des fraises (f.)

des bananes (f.)

Fruits et légumes

des framboises (f.)

des pommes (f.)

des oranges (f.)

de l'ananas (m.)

du brocoli

des haricots verts (m.)

des oignons (m.)

du maïs

de l'ail (m.)

des petits pois (m.)

des courgettes (f.)

des champignons (m.)

des pommes de terre (f.)

des carottes (f.)

Pains et pâtisseries

des baguettes (f.)

Produits laitiers

du lait

des œufs (m.)

LAIT

une tarte aux pommes

des gâteaux (m.)

des pains (m.)

des croissants (m.)

du yaourt

YAOURT

du beurre

du fromage

CAMEMBERT

BRIE

ROQUEFORT

Charcuterie

du jambon

des saucisses (f.)

du saucisson

du pâté

****Acheter** (to buy) is a stem-changing verb like **préférer** (Chapter 2, deuxième étape): j'achète, tu achètes, il/elle/on achète, ils/elles achètent; but, nous achetons, vous achetez.

Produits énergétiques

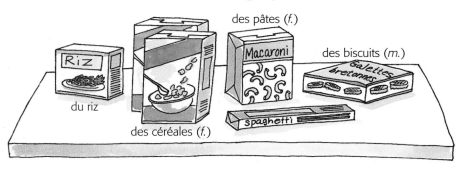

des pâtes (f.)

des biscuits (m.)

du riz

des céréales (f.)

Poissons et fruits de mer

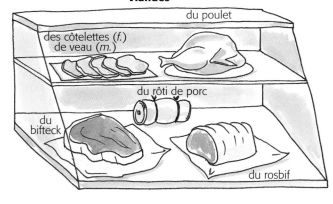

du poisson   des huîtres (f.)   des crevettes (f.)   du homard

Viandes

du poulet

des côtelettes (f.) de veau (m.)

du rôti de porc

du bifteck

du rosbif

Pour manger à la maison: le couvert

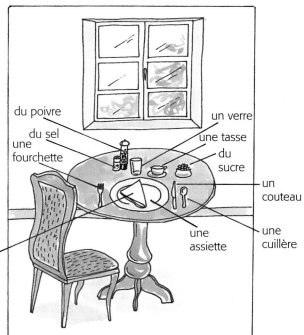

une salière
une poivrière

du poivre

du sel
une fourchette

un verre

une tasse

du sucre

un couteau

une assiette

une cuillère

une serviette

VOCABULAIRE ACTIF
Les petits magasins
   la boucherie du coin...
les produits surgelés
Le rayon...
   fromages, etc.
le supermarché

See the *Instructor's Resource Manual* for a concentration game to practice food vocabulary and an information gap activity to practice table setting vocabulary.

A. Read the cues as students write their answers. Then repeat and have volunteers indicate their responses. CUES: des crevettes, du rosbif, du yaourt, du saucisson, des oignons, du pain, du beurre, du pâté, du riz, des bananes, une tarte aux pommes, du homard, du poulet

B. Refer students to the **Notes culturelles** on pp. 156–157 and above.

Notes culturelles

Les magasins alimentaires. Most French people go grocery shopping more often than Americans. They like fresh foods to be truly fresh, and will generally prefer to drop by a small neighborhood bakery **(une boulangerie)** to buy their bread fresh and hot each day, rather than buy it wrapped and cold in a supermarket. A **boulangerie** is often also a **pâtisserie**, selling delicious pastries made fresh each day. Meat, likewise, is considered fresher if cut right in front of you at the **boucherie du coin**. A **charcuterie** is like a delicatessen; it sells cold cuts, salamis, and prepared foods, made fresh daily. **La poissonnerie** sells fresh fish and seafood. **L'épicerie du coin** is usually more convenient than **un supermarché** to pick up a last-minute item such as milk or lettuce; it's also the perfect place to catch up on the latest news with the owner, **l'épicier** or **l'épicière**. French supermarkets are very similar to their North American counterparts, with various departments—**le rayon boucherie, le rayon boulangerie,** etc. The main differences are that in France, the frozen food department **(les produits surgelés)** is generally smaller, the **rayon fromages** is much larger, and there is a greater selection of wines and mineral water.

ACTIVITÉS

A. Quel magasin? Écoutez le professeur et dites dans quels magasins on trouve les produits mentionnés: à la boucherie? la boulangerie/pâtisserie? la charcuterie? la poissonnerie? l'épicerie?

B. Traditions culinaires. Indiquez si les habitudes suivantes caractérisent plutôt les Français ou les Nord-Américains.

Cette personne...	Français	Nord-Amér.
prend une omelette, du bacon et du pain grillé au petit déjeuner.		
a un grand repas à midi dans la cantine du bureau.		
achète du pain tous les jours.		
commence le repas par une salade.		
va faire les courses uniquement au supermarché.		
mange fréquemment dans un restaurant fast-food.		
achète très peu de produits surgelés.		
termine souvent le repas par du fromage.		
boit du lait avec le déjeuner.		
préfère les petits magasins du coin.		

C. Chassez l'intrus. Dans chaque groupe, trouvez le mot qui ne va pas et expliquez pourquoi.

➡ du homard, du brie, du thon, des crevettes
du brie. Ce n'est pas un poisson ou un fruit de mer.

1. du maïs, des haricots verts, des pommes, des petits pois
2. de la glace, de la mousse au chocolat, de la tarte, de la quiche
3. du bifteck, du veau, du poulet, des poires
4. de l'eau minérale, de la bière, du poivre, du café
5. des saucisses, du jambon, du pâté, du beurre
6. des tomates, des céréales, du riz, des pâtes

D. Repas. Complétez les listes suivantes, puis comparez-les avec celles d'un(e) partenaire. Avez-vous les mêmes goûts *(tastes)*?

Au petit déjeuner je prends...	Au déjeuner je prends...	Au dîner je prends...	Comme dessert je prends...
?	?	?	?

D. Ask several volunteers to say what they have for each meal. Have the class decide on «les plats les plus communs, les plus bizarres», etc.

STRUCTURES: Talking about food and drink
*Le verbe **boire** • Les articles partitifs*

Observez et déduisez

Cue to Video Module 5 (00:22:08), where Élisabeth and Fatima discuss with the waiter what they will eat at the restaurant.

Quand on a soif, on veut boire, n'est-ce pas? Moi, je bois du coca ou je prends de la limonade. Paul, lui, boit souvent du café et de l'eau minérale, mais il ne boit pas de coca. Et vous, qu'est-ce que vous buvez? Du jus de fruits? De la bière?

> ■ What forms of the verb **boire** do you see in the paragraph above? What do you think the verb means? Calling to mind other irregular verbs you know, infer the following forms of **boire:**
> tu _____ nous _____
>
> ■ In the paragraph, there are four different ways of expressing an indefinite quantity (the idea of *some*). What are they?

Vérifiez *Le verbe **boire***

■ The verb **boire** *(to drink)* is irregular.

OPTIONAL DRILL: CUES: 1. Carole boit souvent de l'eau minérale. (nous, tu, les étudiants, on) 2. Quelquefois nous buvons du vin. (le prof, les parents, mon copain, vous) 3. Je ne bois pas de bière. (les enfants, nous, mes sœurs, tu)

Le verbe boire	
je bois	nous buvons
tu bois	vous buvez
il / elle / on boit	ils / elles boivent

Les articles partitifs

■ A partitive article is used before mass (uncountable) nouns to refer to an unspecified amount, a part or portion of the whole *(some)*. It agrees in number and gender with the noun.

Je prends du café
    ... de la tarte   *(some* coffee / pie / water—
    ... de l'eau   an unspecified amount)

■ Note that the partitive article is often used after verbs such as **manger, boire, prendre, vouloir,** and **avoir,** since one frequently uses these verbs to refer to portions or unspecified amounts.

— Tu veux **du** chocolat?
— Non, je prends **de la** tarte au citron.

To illustrate the difference, point out that in English, one may say simply, "Mineral water for me, please," without expressing *some.*

■ The partitive article is always expressed in French, even though at times no article at all is used in English.

Pour moi, de l'eau minérale, s'il vous plaît.

■ After a negative expression, the partitive article is **de/d'.**

Paul boit du café, mais il **ne** boit **pas d'**eau minérale ou **de** thé.

Rappel!

■ The *indefinite* articles that you studied on page 11—**un, une, des**—are used only with nouns that can be counted. Compare the use of the indefinite and the partitive article in French:

indefinite: Tu veux un (verre de) coca? (*a* glass of cola)
partitive: Tu veux du coca? (*some* cola)

■ *Definite* articles—**le, la, l', les**—(p. 30) refer to specific objects or persons.

— Quel gâteau?   — Quelle serviette?
— **Le** gâteau sur la table.   — **La** serviette de Claire.

In French, definite articles are required after verbs of preference (p. 58).

J'aime **la** glace au chocolat.   *I like chocolate ice cream.*
Je déteste **les** oignons.   *I hate onions.*

VOCABULAIRE ACTIF
boire
Les articles partitifs
  du, de la, etc.

Les articles			
	masculin	**féminin**	**m./f. pluriel**	**après un verbe négatif**
article défini	le, l'	la, l'	les	le, la, les, l'
article indéfini	un	une	des	de, d'
article partitif	du, de l'	de la, de l'	—	de, d'

ACTIVITÉS

E. Les boissons.   Complétez les phrases de la colonne de gauche avec des boissons logiques.

boissons

jus d'orange
citron pressé
eau minérale
chocolat au lait
thé nature
vin rouge
bière
café crème

1. Mon frère ne prend pas de caféine, alors il ne

   boit pas de _____ .

2. Mes parents n'aiment pas les boissons alcoolisées,

   alors ils ne boivent pas de _____ .

3. Je préfère les boissons froides, et je bois souvent

   _____ .

4. Dans ma famille, nous détestons les fruits; nous

   ne buvons pas de _____ .

5. Mes sœurs sont allergiques au lait, alors elles

   boivent _____ .

6. Vous aimez bien les boissons chaudes, et vous

   buvez beaucoup de _____ .

F. Des goûts différents.   Décrivez les aliments et les boissons que ces personnes prennent souvent. Employez les articles partitifs qui correspondent.

1. Maman: poisson, petits pois, riz, poires
2. Papa: frites, pâtes, homard, tartes aux pommes
3. Nicolas: fromage, pain, huîtres, quiche
4. Nathalie: pâté, crevettes, poulet, oranges
5. les parents: thé, café au lait, eau minérale, bière
6. les enfants: jus de fruit, lait, eau minérale, coca

G. On ne prend pas de...   Lisez encore les listes de l'activité F. Nommez trois choses que chaque personne ne prend pas souvent.

➡ *Papa ne prend pas souvent de pizza ou de chocolat. Il ne boit pas souvent de lait.*

H. On mange ce qu'on aime.   Indiquez les préférences des personnes mentionnées, puis décidez quel aliment ou quelle boisson elles vont prendre ou ne pas prendre. Employez des articles définis et des articles partitifs.

➡ Roger / viande +
Roger aime la viande, alors il mange du porc.

Roger / boissons alcoolisées −
Roger n'aime pas les boissons alcoolisées, alors il ne boit pas de vin.

1. Philippe / dessert +
2. Babette / caféine −
3. Simon / boissons froides +
4. Paul / viande −
5. Claire / légumes −
6. Olivia / œufs +
7. Marc / fruits −

Jeu de rôle

For expressions, refer students to the photo and dialogue in the **Vocabulaire** section (pp.158–160).

You and some friends are ordering a meal in the restaurant Chez Jo. Prepare a skit using the following menu. Vary the polite expressions for ordering and asking for the bill.

See the *Instructor's Resource Manual* for two communicative activities to practice vocabulary items and partitive/definite articles: **Sondage: les aliments,** and an information gap game called **Qui dîne avec moi?**

Chez Jo
Ouvert tous les soirs jusqu'à 2 heures du matin

NOS PIZZAS	Petites	Grandes
Anchois	28 Fr	46 Fr
Fromage	30 "	48 "
Jambon	30 "	48 "
Champignons	30 "	50 "

NOS PLATS CUISINÉS

Spaghettis sauce bolognaise	42 Francs
Lasagnes au four	44 "
Pâtes à la Carbonara	44 "
Raviolis au four	44 "
Steak tartare	64 "
Filet de bœuf au poivre	82 "

NOS HORS-D'ŒUVRE

Salade niçoise	30 Francs
Cœurs d'artichauts vinaigrette	28 "
Poivrons marinés à l'ail	40 "
Jambon de Paris	28 "
Gratinée à l'oignon	38 "
Melon à l'italienne (en saison)	42 "

NOS LÉGUMES

Haricots verts persillade	20 Francs
Pommes allumettes	18 "
Salade verte	20 "
Tomates provençales	22 "
Gratin de légumes	22 "

NOS GRILLADES au FEU de BOIS

Entrecôte de bœuf grillée	66 Francs
Filet de bœuf	78 "
Brochette	72 "

NOS DESSERTS

Plateau de fromages	24 Francs
Tarte maison	22 "
Salade de fruits frais	22 "
Glaces et Sorbets	22 "
Mousse au chocolat	22 "
Crème caramel	22 "
Fraises et Framboises (en saison)	24 "

• Toutes nos viandes sont garnies • Prix nets—Service compris—Boissons non comprises •

W B

Deuxième étape

Lecture: Que mangent les Français?

Avant de lire

This reading section recycles food vocabulary, introduces cultural information, and presents comparisons.

Cue to Video Module 5, street interviews (00:24:09), where different people say what they eat at different meals.

1 Encourage students to add to the list.

1 Que mangent les Français? Quand vous pensez à cette question, qu'est-ce que vous imaginez? Cochez les réponses qui vous semblent caractéristiques de l'alimentation de tous les jours pour le Français typique.

_____ des produits naturels

_____ des produits surgelés

_____ des plats cuisinés (préparés commercialement)

_____ des produits frais (*fresh*)

_____ des produits en boîte (*canned*)

_____ des produits diététiques

_____ beaucoup de produits énergétiques (pain, pâtes, etc.)

_____ beaucoup de desserts

_____ des escargots

_____ ?

2 Allow students to brainstorm in small groups.

2 Maintenant pensez aux groupes sociaux mentionnés dans la liste suivante. Selon votre expérience, qu'est-ce qu'ils mangent? Utilisez le vocabulaire de la Première étape.

	mangent plus (+) de	mangent moins (−) de
les étudiants		
les hommes		
les femmes		
les célibataires (personnes non mariées)		

Parmi ces groupes, qui, à votre avis, va acheter les produits les plus chers? Les moins chers (*expensive*)?

3 Est-ce que vous préférez manger à la maison ou au restaurant? Combien de fois par mois mangez-vous au restaurant?

Des crevettes et des poissons—tout frais!

En général

5   Have students identify paragraphs by first words, or number the paragraphs.

4 Lisez l'introduction du texte. D'après cette introduction, quel est le sujet principal du texte?

> a. les traditions alimentaires en France
> b. l'évolution de l'alimentation en France
> c. une comparaison de la structure alimentaire dans les différents pays d'Europe

VOCABULAIRE ACTIF
cher (chère)
diététique
en boîte
frais (fraîche)
sain(e)

5 La structure du texte: parcourez le texte une deuxième fois pour identifier les sections qui correspondent aux idées principales suivantes.

L'alimentation des femmes   ¶ 4
L'alimentation des hommes   ¶ 3
Le rôle des restaurants   ¶s 5–7
Un petit résumé des transformations dans l'alimentation à domicile (à la maison)   ¶ 6

QUE MANGENT LES FRANÇAIS?

1   Une enquête° de l'INSEE° sur la période 1979–1989 fait apparaître° une «lente déformation°» de la structure de l'alimentation depuis dix ans; les hommes consomment plus de produits énergétiques tandis que les femmes, elles, font° des «extras».

2   Les ménages° abandonnent les produits traditionnels ruraux et énergé-tiques au profit° des produits plus élaborés, plus diététiques, plus rapides à préparer (surgelés, plats cuisinés) et souvent plus chers.

3   L'enquête souligne les différences de comportement alimentaire entre hommes et femmes. À domicile, les hommes célibataires dépensent plus que les femmes pour les produits énergétiques (pâtes, riz, pain) et certains produits élaborés (soupes en boîte, charcuterie, plats préparés).

4   Les femmes, elles, font des «extras» (chocolat, gâteaux, glaces) qu'elles compensent par d'autres aliments plus «sains°» ou plus légers°, comme les

survey / l'Institut national de la statistique et des études économiques / *fait... shows* / *lente... transformation progressive* / *mangent* / *households* / *in favor of*

healthy / light

fruits et légumes, les yaourts, le poisson, la margarine, le jambon, le veau, le thé et les tisanes°.   *herb teas*

Moins à la maison, plus au resto

5 Les Français dépensent de moins en moins pour leurs repas à la maison mais de plus en plus pour leur alimentation hors du domicile—à la cantine, au café ou au restaurant—d'après l'étude de l'INSEE.

6   L'alimentation à domicile coûte désormais en moyenne° 840 francs ($153) par mois et par personne, soit 17% du budget familial. Les dépenses de sorties au restaurant, repas à la cantine ou consommations prises au café occupent une place grandissante°; désormais les repas dehors absorbent 1/5ème du budget alimentaire des Français.   *en... an average of*

growing

7   Les citadins° sont les plus fidèles adeptes des sorties, pratiquement les deux tiers° des Parisiens ne déjeunent pas chez eux. Les plus gros° clients des restaurants sont les célibataires, en particulier les hommes.   *habitants de la ville*
two-thirds / biggest

Adapté de «Que mangent les Français?» *Journal Français d'Amérique.*

En détail

6 **Les mots.**   D'après le contexte, quel est le sens des mots en caractères gras?

Les Français **dépensent de moins en moins** pour leurs repas à la maison, mais **de plus en plus** pour leur alimentation **hors du** domicile—à la cantine, au café ou au restaurant.[...] ... les repas **dehors** absorbent 1/5ème du budget alimentaire.

7 **Le texte.**

A. **Que mangent les Français?** Complétez le tableau suivant.

les Français en général (plus de... moins de...)	les hommes	les femmes

B. **L'alimentation et les restaurants.**   Répondez aux questions suivantes.

1. Selon cet article, quel pourcentage du budget familial français est consacré à l'alimentation à domicile?
2. Quelle proportion du budget alimentaire est consacrée aux repas au restaurant?
3. Est-ce pour le déjeuner ou le dîner que les restaurants de Paris sont les plus populaires?
4. Qui sont les plus gros clients des restaurants?

Et vous?

Students can do this activity in groups of three, or circulate in the class. FOLLOW-UP: Have several students report on answers they have or don't have in common with their classmates. If time allows, you may wish to compile a list on the board of the most frequently mentioned items in each category (**plus/moins/autant**).

1. Comparez l'alimentation des hommes et des femmes en France et dans votre pays. À votre avis, y a-t-il des différences?

2. Et vous? Est-ce que vous mangez les mêmes choses aujourd'hui qu'il y a cinq ans? Faites d'abord une liste personnelle, puis interviewez deux camarades de classe. Ensuite comparez vos réponses—est-ce que vous avez des réponses en commun?

	plus de (+)	moins de (−)	autant de (=)
Moi			
Camarade 1			
Camarade 2			

STRUCTURE: Saying what you no longer or never do
*Les expressions **ne... plus; ne... jamais***

Observez et déduisez

Tiens! On dit que les Français ne mangent plus comme avant. C'est vrai dans ma famille aussi. Nous pensons à notre santé *(health)*. Nous ne mangeons plus de porc ou de bœuf et nous ne mangeons jamais de produits surgelés.

- Where are **ne... plus** and **ne... jamais** placed in relation to the verbs?
- What article follows these expressions?
- How would you say "I never eat fish"?

Vérifiez *Les expressions **ne... plus; ne... jamais***

VOCABULAIRE ACTIF

être au régime
ne... plus
ne... jamais
la santé

- The negative expressions **ne... plus** *(no longer, not . . . anymore)* and **ne... jamais** *(never)* are treated like the expression **ne... pas;** that is, **ne** precedes the verb and **plus** or **jamais** follows the verb.

    Nous sommes au régime, alors nous **ne** mangeons **plus** de porc, et nous **ne** mangeons **jamais** de dessert.

- To talk about the future, place the negative expression around **aller.**

    Demain je commence mon régime. Je **ne** vais **plus** manger de sucre.

- Remember that the partitive article following a *negative expression* is **de/d'** (page 163).

    Les bébés boivent du lait. Ils **ne** boivent **jamais de** vin.

ACTIVITÉS

A. Jamais!   Dites ce que les personnes suivantes ne mangent jamais.

➡ (une personne qui déteste les fruits de mer)
Elle ne mange jamais de crevettes ou de homard!

1. un(e) végétarien(ne)
2. une personne qui n'aime pas le bœuf
3. un enfant de quatre ans
4. une personne qui est allergique au sucre

B. De mauvaises habitudes.   Dites ce que vous n'allez plus manger ou boire dans les circonstances suivantes.

➡ Vous voulez participer au Tour de France.
Je ne vais plus boire de vin ou de café et je ne vais plus manger de gâteaux ou de glace.

1. Vous voulez être en très bonne santé.
2. Vous êtes au régime.
3. Vous êtes très nerveux (-euse).
4. Vous apprenez que votre cholestérol est trop élevé *(high)*.
5. Vous apprenez que vous êtes diabétique.

C. Have students work with a partner or in small groups taking turns suggesting and refusing food items. Have them expand their answers by giving an explanation.

C. Des goûts incompatibles.   Votre copain (copine) et vous allez manger ensemble, mais vous avez des goûts différents. Chaque fois que vous proposez quelque chose, votre partenaire refuse et vice versa. Expliquez pourquoi vous refusez.

➡ — *On peut manger un hamburger?*
— *Non, je ne mange plus de hamburger. Je n'aime pas les sandwichs.*
ou: — *Non, je ne mange jamais de viande. Je préfère les légumes.*

VOCABULAIRE
Les expressions de quantité

Give students time to study the chart, then ask volunteers for comments.

■ In Chapter 2, you learned to use **combien de** to ask questions about quantity. Besides numbers, a variety of expressions can be used to answer such questions. Use the following expressions of quantity to give your opinion on the information in the food chart on the next page.

trop de *(too much)*
trop peu de *(too little, too few)*
beaucoup de
(ne... pas) assez *(enough)* **de**
un peu de
pas du tout de

➡ *Les Français mangent beaucoup de pain.*

■ Note that, as with negative expressions, the article that follows *all* expressions of quantity is **de/d'.**

Tout ce que nous mangeons dans une vie

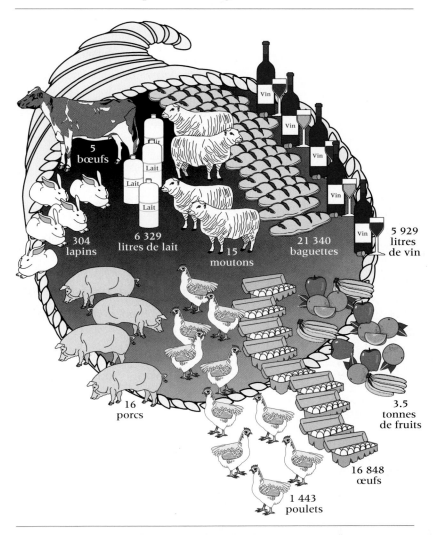

5 bœufs

304 lapins

6 329 litres de lait

15 moutons

21 340 baguettes

5 929 litres de vin

16 porcs

3.5 tonnes de fruits

16 848 œufs

1 443 poulets

■ What kinds of food items do you associate with the following quantities?

➡ un bol *(bowl)* de   *céréales, riz, glace...*

une assiette de
une tasse de
un verre de
une boîte de *(box / can)*
une bouteille de
une carafe de
une douzaine de
un kilo de
100 grammes de
un litre de
une tranche de *(slice)*
un morceau de *(piece)*

VOCABULAIRE ACTIF

Les expressions de quantité
une livre (de)
pas du tout (de)
un peu (de)
un verre (de), etc.

If time is short, assign different expressions to individual students or small groups. Have them report to the class, allowing others to add to the lists if desired.

Note culturelle

Le système métrique.   France and most francophone countries use the metric system of weights and measures. In order to make purchases of food items, you'll need to know that **un kilogramme (un kilo)** is just over 2 pounds and **un litre** is just over a quart. More specifically:

1 ounce = 28.5 grams
1 kilogram = 1000 grams = 2.2 pounds
1/2 kilogram = 500 grams (also called **une livre**) = 1.1 pounds
4 liters = 1.2 gallons

ACTIVITÉS

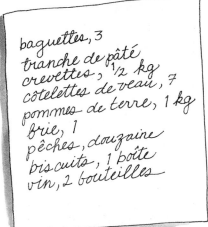

D. Achats.   Votre copine invite six amis à dîner chez elle. Regardez sa liste d'achats, et dites si elle a assez (trop, trop peu, etc.) pour sept personnes.

➡ *Elle achète trop peu de pâté pour sept personnes.*

Maintenant préparez votre propre liste d'achats. Qu'est-ce que vous allez acheter?

➡ *Je vais acheter trois tranches de pâté...*

E. Le repas favori.   Vous préparez le repas préféré de votre famille. Dites ce que vous allez préparer et combien de chaque aliment vous allez acheter.

➡ *Je vais préparer un beau rosbif avec des pommes de terre et des carottes. Je vais acheter 750 grammes de rosbif, un kilo de pommes de terre...*

E. Allow students time to prepare an answer, then let them practice with a partner before calling on several volunteers to share their answers with the class.

STRUCTURE: Making comparisons (I)

Le comparatif

Observez et déduisez   Selon l'INSEE, l'alimentation des Français a beaucoup changé depuis dix ans. Ils mangent moins de bœuf et de beurre et plus de poisson et de légumes. Ils mangent maintenant des repas plus sains et plus équilibrés que leurs voisins européens.

- What expression is used above to make a comparison of superiority *(more)*?
- What expression is used to make a comparison of inferiority *(less)*?
- How would you say "I eat more fruit; I eat less cheese"?

Ce que révèlent les comparaisons internationales
La France, patrie de l'équilibre

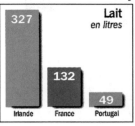

Lait *en litres*

Irlande	France	Portugal
327	132	49

Les Français l'aiment peu. Mais ils compensent avec le fromage et les yaourts.

Poisson et produits de la mer *en kilogrammes*

Danemark	France	Grèce
56	22	6

Grâce au hareng, les Danois sont champions, devant les Portugais.

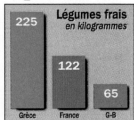

Légumes frais *en kilogrammes*

Grèce	France	G-B
225	122	65

Partout on en mange plus. Seuls les Britanniques les préfèrent en boîte.

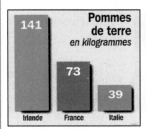

Pommes de terre *en kilogrammes*

Irlande	France	Italie
141	73	39

Malgré leurs frites, les Belges en consomment moins que les Irlandais.

La consommation de viande en Europe

Pays	Bœuf	Veau	Porc
France	25	7	37
Belgique/Luxembourg	21	3	46
Danemark	15	0	66
Espagne	8	4	39
Allemagne	22	2	62
Grèce	24	2	24
Irlande	21	0	3
Italie	23	4	29
Pays-Bas	18	2	44
Portugal	11	1	25
Royaume-Uni	23	0	25

SOURCE : EUROSTAT

Avec le vin, la viande est le seul aliment dont les Français soient de très gros consommateurs. Ils sont les champions d'Europe pour le bœuf et le veau.

Vérifiez *Le comparatif*

■ When comparing with *nouns,* use **plus de... que** to indicate superiority, **moins de... que** to indicate inferiority, and **autant de... que** to indicate equivalency.

> Les Français mangent **plus de** pommes de terre **que** les Italiens.
> Les Portugais boivent **moins de** lait **que** les Irlandais.
> Les Belges consomment **autant de** bœuf **que** les Irlandais.

■ When comparing with *adjectives* or *adverbs,* use the expressions **plus... que, moins... que,** and **aussi... que.**

> Les fruits sont **plus** sucrés **que** les légumes.
> Le riz est **moins** gras **que** les frites.
> La quiche est **aussi** bonne **que** la pizza.
> Les jeunes mangent **plus** souvent **que** les adultes.
> Quelquefois les jeunes mangent **moins** bien **que** les adultes.
> Les jeunes mangent **aussi** vite **que** les adultes.

■ **Bon,** an adjective, has an irregular comparison of superiority: **meilleur(e)(s)** *(better).*

> Le poulet est **meilleur que** le bœuf.

Bien, an adverb, has an irregular comparison of superiority: **mieux** *(better).*

> Les Français mangent **mieux que** les autres Européens.

Les comparaisons	
quality	**quantity**
+ **plus** cher **que**	**plus de** pain **que**
− **moins** cher **que**	**moins de** pain **que**
= **aussi** cher **que**	**autant de** pain **que**
BUT: **bon(ne)(s)** → + **meilleur(e)(s) que**	
bien → + **mieux que**	

ACTIVITÉS

F. Vrai ou faux?   Dites si les phrases suivantes sont vraies ou fausses. Expliquez pourquoi.

➡ Je mange moins de viande que mes parents.
C'est vrai. Mes parents aiment beaucoup le bœuf, et moi, je suis végétarien.

ou: *Mais non! Moi, je mange plus de viande que mes parents. Ils sont végétariens.*

1. Je mange mieux que mes copains.
2. Je bois moins de café que mes copines.
3. Je prends plus de fruits que ma sœur (mon frère).
4. Je mange aussi souvent que mon/ma camarade de chambre.
5. Les légumes sont meilleurs que les fruits.
6. Le riz est moins bon que les pâtes.

G. Des comparaisons internationales.   Comparez la consommation alimentaire des pays européens en regardant le tableau à la page 173. Travaillez avec un(e) partenaire.

1. La Belgique consomme plus de _____ que _____ .

2. La Grèce consomme moins de _____ que _____ .

3. L'Irlande consomme autant de _____ que _____ .

4. ?

H. Opinion ou fait *(fact)?*   Comparez quelques aliments mentionnés pages 159–160 puis dites si votre comparaison est une opinion ou un fait. (Pour comparer: **bon, cher, sucré, gras(se), sain, diététique.**)

➡ *Les haricots verts sont plus sains que les frites.*

I. Des habitudes alimentaires. Combinez les mots et les expressions des colonnes ci-dessous pour parler des habitudes alimentaires des personnes mentionnées dans la colonne de gauche.

➡ *Dans ma famille, on mange beaucoup de sucre, et on ne boit jamais de vin.*

Je	manger	beaucoup	plats préparés
Mes camarades	prendre	trop	pain
Dans ma famille, on	boire	assez	vin
En général, les		peu	pêches
Américains		ne... plus	hors-d'œuvre
		ne... pas	sucre
		ne... jamais	citron pressé
		plus de... que	poisson
		autant de... que	porc
		moins de... que	yaourt
		?	?

 Jeu de rôle

You and a couple of friends are preparing a dinner. One of you is a vegetarian; another is on a diet; another is allergic to dairy products. Discuss what you want and don't want to eat. Compare your preferences and come to a consensus about what you're going to prepare.

W
B

CULTURE ET RÉFLEXION

■ Les repas. Un proverbe français dit qu' «il faut manger pour vivre et non pas vivre pour manger» *(you must eat to live and not live to eat)* mais les Français ont souvent la réputation de vivre pour manger, car les repas sont très importants pour eux. Un repas ordinaire, pris en famille à la maison pendant la semaine, dure[1] aujourd'hui une moyenne de 33 minutes pour le déjeuner et 38 minutes pour le dîner (contre 40 et 45 minutes en 1975). Les repas sont-ils importants pour vous? Combien de temps dure un repas typique dans votre famille? Y a-t-il une relation entre la durée des repas et l'attitude des gens vis-à-vis de la famille ou de la vie en général?

■ L'art de manger. Un autre proverbe français dit que «la présentation, c'est la moitié du goût» *(presentation is half the taste).* La disposition des aliments sur les plats est donc un art où les mélanges[2] de couleurs et de goûts ont une valeur esthétique autant que nutritive. C'est pourquoi on ne sert qu'une ou deux choses à la fois[3] et on ne mélange jamais les hors-d'œuvre et le plat principal! Est-ce qu'il vous arrive de mettre la salade et le plat principal en même temps sur votre assiette? La présentation des plats est-elle importante pour vous? Qu'est-ce qui caractérise un «bon» repas pour vous?

■ Les boulettes *(balls).* «Le plaisir de la main accroît le plaisir du palais» *(The pleasure of the hand increases the*

La présentation, c'est la moitié du goût...

Le couscous se mange avec la main droite.

pleasure of the palate), disent les Africains qui mangent avec les doigts[4]. Dans la plupart des pays francophones d'Afrique, en effet, le repas traditionnel est un grand bol de riz ou de couscous avec du bouillon de viande et de légumes. Les membres de la famille sont assis par terre[5] autour de ce bol commun et chacun fait des «boulettes» avec sa

portion. Parfois les hommes mangent séparément des femmes et des enfants, mais l'acte de manger est considéré comme un acte de communion avec la nature et avec ceux qui partagent[6] le repas. À votre avis, quels sont les avantages et les désavantages de manger de cette façon?

■ Des révélations... «Dis-moi ce que tu manges et je te dirai qui tu es» *(Tell me what you eat and I'll tell you who you are).* Est-ce vrai? Trouvez des exemples pour illustrer votre opinion.

---

1. *lasts*   2. *mixtures*   3. *at a time*   4. *fingers*   5. *on the ground*   6. *share*

Troisième étape

À l'écoute: Les courses

This listening section serves as entry into past narration and valuable communication strategies, such as circumlocution.

Vous allez écouter une conversation entre un mari et une femme qui font l'inventaire de leurs courses. Faites d'abord l'activité 1, **Avant d'écouter,** puis écoutez en suivant les instructions données.

Avant d'écouter

1 Où est-ce que vous faites vos courses, dans un supermarché ou dans des petits magasins? Préférez-vous les supermarchés ou les petits magasins spécialisés quand vous êtes pressé(e) *(in a hurry)?* quand vous cherchez un produit exotique?

Écoutons

Audio CD

2 Écoutez d'abord en fonction des questions suivantes.

1. Où est-ce que le monsieur a fait ses courses? Dans un supermarché ou dans des petits magasins?

2. Il a «oublié» quelque chose. D'après le contexte, que veut dire **oublier?**
   a. prendre   b. ne pas prendre

3. Qu'est-ce qu'il a oublié?
   a. le lait   b. le pain   c. une spécialité mexicaine

4. ANSWER: les tacos   4. Qu'est-ce qui est exotique, selon la dame?

À la charcuterie.

3 Écoutez encore en faisant particulièrement attention aux magasins mentionnés. Qu'est-ce que le monsieur a acheté dans chaque magasin?

magasins	produits
la boulangerie	deux baguettes
l'épicerie	des légumes, des fruits, des pâtes, du fromage, du beurre
la boucherie	du bifteck
la charcuterie	du jambon, du pâté

4 Écoutez encore en faisant attention aux expressions communicatives.

1. Quels sont les mots utilisés dans la conversation pour

   ■ demander une explication:
   a. Quelle chose?
   b. Quelque chose?
   c. Qu'est-ce que c'est que ça?
   ■ donner une explication:
   a. C'est ça.
   b. C'est quelque chose que...
   c. Ça me semble...

2. ANSWERS: des chips de maïs, la salsita

2. Selon la conversation, qu'est-ce que c'est que des tacos? Et comment s'appelle la sauce mexicaine à la tomate et au piment?

5 **Le passé.** Écoutez une dernière fois en faisant attention aux verbes. Encerclez les formes que vous entendez. Quel est l'infinitif de **pris**?

j'ai fait   j'ai acheté   j'ai trouvé
tu as fait   tu as acheté   tu as trouvé

j'ai pris   j'ai oublié   je n'ai pas oublié
tu as pris   tu as oublié   tu n'as pas oublié

Prononciation   *Les articles et l'articulation*

■ Because it is so common in English to reduce unstressed vowels to an *uh* sound (for example, VISta, proFESsor, CApital), Anglophones often have the tendency to reduce the vowels in French articles to a brief **e,** thus making **le** and **la,** or **du** and **de** sound alike. It is important to remember that in French, only the *e* **caduc** can be reduced or dropped; all other vowels must be pronounced distinctly, with equal stress.

Écoutez

Audio CD

Listen to the following sentences from **À l'écoute: Les courses** on the student audio CD, and fill in the articles you hear. Then cross out the *e caducs* that are not pronounced in the articles or in boldface in other words. Each sentence will be read twice.

1. Il n'y a plus <u>de</u> lait?

2. Mince! J'ai fait <u>les</u> courses mais j'ai complètement oublié

   <u>le</u> lait!

3. Tu as pris du____ pain?

4. Oui, oui, j'ai pris deux baguettes à la____ boulangerie, et puis à

l'____ épicerie j'ai acheté des____ légumes, des____ fruits,

des____ pâtes, du____ fromage et du____ beurre.

5. Et la____ viande, tu n'as pas oublié la____ viande?

6. Non, non, j'ai acheté du bifteck à la____ boucherie; et puis j'ai pris

du____ jambon et du____ pâté à la____ charcuterie.

Essayez   Practice saying the sentences in **Écoutez** at fluent speed, making sure you drop
the *e* **caducs** where necessary, and pronounce all other vowels distinctly. Then
Audio CD   listen to the sentences to verify your pronunciation.

STRUCTURE: Saying what happened (I)
Le passé composé

Observez et déduisez   — Mince! J'ai fait les courses mais j'ai oublié le lait.
— Et la viande, tu n'as pas oublié la viande?
— Non, j'ai acheté du bifteck à la boucherie.

> ■ Based on the examples, can you infer how to form the past tense in
> French?
> ■ How would you say, "We forgot the ice cream!"?

Vérifiez   *Le passé composé*

■ This common past tense is used in French for narrating—telling what happened. It has several English equivalents.

Tu as mangé?   *Did you eat? / Have you eaten?*
Oui, j'ai mangé.   *Yes, I ate. / Yes, I've eaten.*

■ The passé composé is called a compound tense because it is composed of two
parts—an auxiliary (helping) verb and a past participle. The auxiliary verb
(**avoir** in most cases) is conjugated in the present. To form the past participle
of **-er** verbs, drop the final **r (aimeṛ)** and add an **accent aigu** to the **e (aimé)**.

Nous **avons mangé** au restaurant.   Ils **ont payé** mon dîner.

■ Negative expressions go around the auxiliary verb; the participle follows.

Claude **n'**a **pas** oublié les baguettes.
Claudine **n'**a **jamais** mangé de chips ou de salsita.

■ Irregular verbs have irregular past participles which must be learned as they
are introduced.

Elle n'**a** pas **pris** de pain hier (*yesterday*).
J'**ai fait** les courses la semaine dernière.

Irregular participles for verbs like
avoir, être, vouloir, etc., are
presented in Ch. 9.

Le passé composé avec **avoir**	
manger	
j' ai mangé	nous avons mangé
tu as mangé	vous avez mangé
il / elle / on a mangé	ils / elles ont mangé
prendre	
j' ai pris	nous avons pris
tu as pris	vous avez pris
il / elle / on a pris	ils / elles ont pris

regular participles: acheté, oublié, payé, cherché, voyagé, étudié, travaillé, etc.
irregular participles: fait (faire), pris (prendre), appris, compris, bu (boire)

ACTIVITÉS

A. Replay the audio CD for students to refresh their memories.

A. Une histoire. Numérotez les phrases suivantes dans l'ordre chronologique selon **À l'écoute: Les courses.**

_6_____ Le monsieur a acheté du jambon à la charcuterie.

_1_____ Il a fait les courses.

_8_____ Il a expliqué ce que c'est que la salsita et les tacos à sa femme.

_3_____ Il a acheté du pain à la boulangerie.

_5_____ Il a acheté du bifteck.

_4_____ Il a pris des fruits et des légumes à l'épicerie.

_2_____ Il a oublié le lait.

_7_____ Il a trouvé des tacos aussi.

B. After partners compare responses, elicit comments on their findings: «Nous avons fait les courses. J'ai pris de la salsita, mais elle a acheté des fruits.»

B. Et vous? Qu'est-ce que vous avez fait la semaine dernière? Complétez les phrases suivantes selon vos expériences personnelles.

1. J'ai... / je n'ai pas...
   a. oublié le lait.
   b. acheté des (de) fruits et des (de) légumes.

2. J'ai... / je n'ai pas...
   a. trouvé des (de) tacos.
   b. pris de la (de) salsita.

3. J'ai... / je n'ai pas...
   a. fait les courses.
   b. préparé un (de) gâteau.

4. J'ai... / je n'ai pas...
   a. bu de l'eau (d'eau) minérale.
   b. cherché du (de) jambon.

5. J'ai... / je n'ai pas...
   a. mangé au restaurant.
   b. payé mon dîner.

Maintenant, comparez vos réponses avec celles d'un(e) partenaire. Avez-vous fait les mêmes choses la semaine dernière?

C. Une journée chargée. Christine, étudiante à la fac, a fait beaucoup de choses hier. Regardez les images suivantes et parlez de ce qu'elle a fait.

1.

2.

3.

4.

5.

6.

C. Do this as a whole-class activity. Have students suggest as many verbs as possible for each picture. Suggestions: 1. acheter, faire les courses 2. travailler 3. faire ses devoirs 4. boire, parler 5. prendre, manger 6. faire du sport, jouer au foot

D. Give students time to prepare answers (or assign as homework) before asking volunteers to share with the class. FOLLOW-UP: Have groups brainstorm what they think you did last weekend, then have them ask you questions to confirm their hunches: «Vous avez regardé un film en français?»

D. La semaine dernière? Qu'est-ce que les personnes suivantes ont fait la semaine dernière? Si vous n'êtes pas sûr(e), imaginez!

➡ *Ma camarade de chambre a téléphoné à ses amis, et elle a oublié de faire ses devoirs. Elle a mangé au restaurant; elle a pris du bifteck.*

1. mon/ma camarade de chambre
2. mes amis
3. ma mère/mon père
4. le président des États-Unis

STRATÉGIES DE COMMUNICATION
Asking for clarification • Explaining

Point out that **Comment?** is the generic way to ask for clarification or repetition, but when the question applies to a specific word, the article is repeated and is followed by **quoi?** e.g., –Des tacos. –Des quoi? –Du couscous. –Du quoi? (**Quoi?** used by itself is considered familiar. **Comment?** is more polite.)

As you learn a language, you will undoubtedly find yourself asking for an explanation of unfamiliar words at times. Study the dialogues that follow and answer the following questions.

■ What expressions are used to ask what something is?

■ What expressions are used to give explanations about things, people, or places **(endroits)?**

— **Qu'est-ce que c'est que ça?**
— **C'est quelque chose que** j'ai trouvé à l'épicerie:
ça s'appelle des tacos. **Ce sont** des chips de maïs.
C'est une spécialité mexicaine qu'on mange avec
de la salsita.
— **De la quoi?**
— De la salsita. **C'est une espèce de** sauce mexicaine
à la tomate et au piment.

— **Qu'est-ce que c'est qu'**un boucher?
— **C'est quelqu'un qui** travaille dans une boucherie.
— **Une quoi?**
— Une boucherie. **C'est là où** on achète de la viande.

Verify your answers in the chart that follows.

Explications	
Pour demander une explication	**Pour donner des explications sur**
Qu'est-ce que c'est qu'un (qu'une)... ?	*une personne* C'est quelqu'un qui... C'est une personne qui...
Qu'est-ce que c'est que ça? Qui est-ce? Un quoi? Une quoi?	*un endroit* C'est là où...
De la quoi? Du quoi? Des quoi?	*une chose* C'est... / Ce sont... C'est quelque chose que... C'est une espèce de... Ça s'appelle...

Les Chaussons aux Fruits

Le Hamburger

La Niçoise
Salade, tomates, thon, œuf

Paëlla Andalouse "Sauffier"

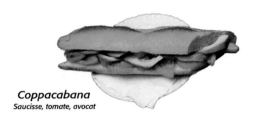

Coppacabana
Saucisse, tomate, avocat

Macédoine de Légumes

ACTIVITÉS

E. Les Martiens sont arrivés! Vous discutez la vie terrestre *(life on earth)* avec des Martiens. Selon votre expérience ou les photos ci-dessus, expliquez ce que sont ces aliments à vos amis de Mars! Regardez les illustrations pour les numéros 6–10.

➡ hamburger
 — *Qu'est-ce que c'est que ça?*
 — *Ça s'appelle un hamburger. C'est quelque chose qu'on peut manger vite. C'est un sandwich avec de la viande, de la tomate, et de la salade. C'est une spécialité américaine.*

1. une poissonnerie
2. une quiche
3. une pizza
4. un dessert
5. une boulangerie
6. une salade niçoise
7. le Coppacabana
8. des chaussons aux fruits
9. la paëlla andalouse
10. la macédoine de légumes

F. Les humains. Maintenant expliquez ce que sont ces personnes à vos nouveaux amis extraterrestres.

➡ étudiant(e)
 — *Qu'est-ce que c'est qu'un étudiant ou une étudiante?*
 — *C'est une personne qui va à l'université pour apprendre. Elle a des cours de maths, de science, et de philosophie, par exemple.*

1. une mère
2. un(e) camarade de chambre
3. un(e) ami(e)
4. un cuisinier
5. une actrice
6. un professeur

Jeu de rôle

You've just returned from a vacation spot where you ate in several "exotic" restaurants. Prepare a skit in which you tell your partner about the unusual dishes you had to eat. Your partner will ask you questions about the foods that you mention. Do your best to describe them using the expressions in the **Stratégies de communication**.

CD-ROM

Now that you have finished the Troisième étape of this chapter, do your Lab Manual activities with the audio program. Explore chapter topics further with the Mais oui! Video and CD-ROM. Viewing and comprehension activities are in the video section of your *Workbook/Lab Manual/Video Manual*.

Intégration

Littérature: Du camembert, chéri...

The literary excerpt you are about to read comes from Cameroon (**le Came-roun**), West Africa. Although Cameroon has been an independent republic since 1960, its colonial past, first German, then both British and French, has left an indelible mark. The language of most of Cameroon is French; French culture and French products are present everywhere. Caught between ancestral traditions and the commercial and social appeal of foreign modernism, small countries such as Cameroon have struggled over the years to define their national identity. Writer Guillaume Oyônô Mbia has portrayed this struggle.

Born in 1939 in Cameroon, Guillaume Oyônô Mbia studied in England and France before becoming a professor at the University of Yaoundé, the capital of Cameroon, where he still teaches. He is known for his tales, his plays, and his sense of humor.

The following scene, taken from *Notre fille ne se mariera pas (Our daughter won't get married)*, a play first performed on the French radio network in 1971, portrays a "modern" family in Yaoundé. Colette Atangana is trying to educate her ten-year-old son, Jean-Pierre, but experiences a few frustrations, which she expresses to a friend, Charlotte.

Avant de lire

1 Qu'est-ce qu'on fait au nom des bonnes manières à table? Cochez toutes les réponses qui vous semblent appropriées.

_____ On accepte de manger des choses qu'on n'aime pas.

_____ On mange avec le couteau dans la main droite et la fourchette dans la main gauche.

_____ On ne parle pas quand on mange.

_____ On refuse de manger des produits qui sont nouveaux ou exotiques.

Encourage students to add their own ideas.

_____ ?

En général

2 Parcourez le texte une première fois en fonction des questions suivantes.

1. *Du camembert, chéri...* c'est l'histoire d'une mère qui
   a. demande à son fils d'aller chercher du camembert.
   b. demande à son fils de manger moins de camembert parce que ça coûte cher.
   c. veut forcer son fils à manger du camembert.
   d. ne veut pas que son fils mange du camembert parce que c'est réservé aux adultes.
2. Parmi les bonnes manières mentionnées dans **Avant de lire,** laquelle/lesquelles Colette veut-elle apprendre à son fils?

185

Du camembert, chéri...

COLETTE: C'est vrai que tu refuses de manger ton camembert, chéri?

JEAN-PIERRE: Je n'aime pas le camembert!

COLETTE: La question n'est pas là! Il ne s'agit pas° d'aimer le camembert: il s'agit de le manger comme un bon petit garçon! *(L'en-
traînant° de force vers la table)* Viens!

Il... Ce n'est pas une question

dragging him

JEAN-PIERRE: *(qui commence à pleurer)* J'aime pas le camembert!

COLETTE: *(tendre mais ferme)* Il faut° le manger, chéri! Apprends à
manger le camembert pendant que° tu es encore jeune! C'est
comme ça qu'on acquiert° du goût°! Onambelé!

Il est nécessaire de
quand
développe / *taste*

ONAMBELÉ: Madame?

COLETTE: Apporte-nous un couvert! Apporte-nous aussi la bouteille de
Châteauneuf-du-Pape° que nous avons commencée! *(Onambelé apporte le couvert et le vin.)*

vin français

JEAN-PIERRE: *(pleurant toujours)* J'veux pas de camembert!

COLETTE: *(toujours tendre et ferme)* Il faut vouloir le manger, chéri! C'est
la culture!

JEAN-PIERRE: *(obstiné)* J'veux pas manger de culture! *(Tous les adultes éclatent
de rire°.)*

burst out laughing

COLETTE: Dis donc, Charlotte, pourquoi est-ce qu'il n'a pas de goût,
cet enfant? Je fais pourtant tout ce que je peux pour lui
apprendre à vivre°! Le chauffeur va le déposer° à l'école
urbaine chaque matin pour éviter° que les autres enfants
ne lui parlent une langue vernaculaire. J'ai déjà renvoyé trois
ou quatre maîtres d'hôtel parce qu'ils servaient des mangues,

*live / drop him off
avoid*

des ananas et d'autres fruits du pays au lieu de lui donner des produits importés d'Europe, ou, à la rigueur, des fruits africains mis en conserve en Europe, et réimportés. Je ne l'autorise presque° jamais à aller rendre visite à la famille de son père, parce que les gens de la brousse° boivent de l'eau non filtrée. Enfin, je fais tout ce qu'une Africaine moderne peut faire pour éduquer son enfant, et il refuse de manger du camembert! Écoute, mon chéri! Tu vas manger ton camembert!

almost

bush country

JEAN-PIERRE: *(criant)* Mais puisque je te dis que j'aime pas le camembert!

COLETTE: *(doucement°)* Je te répète qu'on ne te demande pas de l'aimer. On te demande de le manger!... Comme ceci, regarde! *(Elle prend un peu de camembert et de pain, et commence à le manger.)* Je le mange! Je le... *(Elle s'étrangle° un peu.)* Zut!... Donne-moi un verre de vin, Onambelé! *(Colette boit le vin et tousse°.)* Tu as vu? Tu crois que j'aime le camembert, moi?

softly

chokes

coughs

JEAN-PIERRE: *(naïvement)* Pourquoi tu le manges, alors?

Extrait de *Notre fille ne se mariera pas* (Guillaume Oyônô Mbia)

En détail

3 **Les mots.** Pouvez-vous déduire le sens des mots en caractères gras dans le contexte suivant?

J'ai déjà **renvoyé** trois ou quatre **maîtres d'hôtel** parce qu'ils servaient des **mangues**, des ananas et d'autres fruits du pays **au lieu de** lui donner des produits importés d'Europe, ou, **à la rigueur,** des fruits africains **mis en conserve** en Europe, et réimportés.

3 Students can do the matching activity in small groups, then report on findings and clues.

1. renvoyé
2. un maître d'hôtel
3. une mangue
4. au lieu de
5. à la rigueur
6. mis en conserve

a. canned, processed
b. instead of
c. if need be
d. mango
e. type of servant
f. fired, dismissed

4 **Le texte**

ANSWERS: 1. F (seulement le manger) 2. V 3. V 4. F (pas de «langue vernaculaire» à son école) 5. V 6. F (presque jamais) 7. V 8. V

A. Vrai ou faux? Si c'est faux, corrigez.

1. Colette veut que son fils *aime* le camembert.
2. Selon Colette, c'est plus facile d'acquérir du goût quand on est jeune.
3. Jean-Pierre pense que la culture, c'est quelque chose à manger.
4. Jean-Pierre a l'occasion de parler en langue africaine avec les autres enfants quand il va à l'école.
5. Selon Colette, les produits importés d'Europe sont meilleurs que les produits africains.
6. Jean-Pierre va souvent rendre visite à la famille de son père.
7. Colette a besoin d'un verre de vin pour cacher *(hide)* le goût du camembert.
8. Jean-Pierre ne comprend pas sa mère.

B. L'éducation de Jean-Pierre.   Qu'est-ce qu'il faut ou ne faut pas faire, selon Colette? Complétez le tableau.

Il faut	Il ne faut pas
manger du camembert	*manger des mangues fraîches*

C. Le symbolisme.   Qu'est-ce que le camembert symbolise dans ce texte? Et les produits africains?

1. Quel est le message de ce texte pour vous? Est-ce un message positif? négatif?
2. Est-ce que Colette Atangana existe dans la société américaine? Décrivez-la.
3. Avec un(e) partenaire, préparez un petit sketch où une maman veut forcer son enfant à manger quelque chose. Déterminez d'abord le produit alimentaire que vous allez utiliser et les raisons de la mère (c'est bon pour la santé, c'est la culture, tout le monde le fait *[everybody does it]*, quand on a de bonnes manières... etc.). Ensuite, en imitant le style de Guillaume Oyônô Mbia, écrivez votre sketch, et puis jouez-le devant la classe!

Par écrit: Eat, drink, and be merry!

Avant d'écrire

A. Strategy: Anticipating readers' questions.   Written communication is more difficult than oral communication because the other party is not present to ask for clarification or elaboration. You must anticipate the questions that your reader will likely have about the topic you are discussing. Try jotting down possible questions before you begin writing to help you better organize your thoughts.

Application.   If you sent your family the menu from La Ciboulette on the next page, what questions might they have about your dining experience there? If you were cooking a special dinner for friends and your roommate was to do the shopping, what questions might s/he have about those errands? Write two sets of questions.

Questions: *menu, repas à La Ciboulette*   Questions: *les courses*

VOCABULAIRE ACTIF
après
d'abord
enfin
ensuite
finalement
premièrement
puis

B. Strategy: Organizing a narrative.   Use transitional words when describing a sequence of events to avoid a choppy writing style.

to introduce a sequence:	premièrement, d'abord
to connect the events:	puis, ensuite, après
to show contrast:	mais, par contre
to conclude:	enfin, finalement

Application. Look at the first set of questions you prepared in A. Imagine how you might describe dinner at La Ciboulette. Write four sentences that you could use in your letter, beginning each sentence with a transitional word from among those listed above.

ÉCRIVEZ

La Ciboulette is in the city of St-Pierre. The islands of St-Pierre-et-Miquelon are a territorial collectivity of France located a few miles off the coast of Newfoundland in North America.

1. Vous avez mangé hier soir au restaurant La Ciboulette avec vos amis. Le repas? Magnifique! Écrivez une lettre à vos parents en vous inspirant du menu à 130 francs ci-dessous. Parlez de ce que vous avez mangé et bu. Décrivez les plats à l'aide de circonlocutions et d'imagination! Rappelez-vous les questions que votre famille va avoir en lisant le menu. N'oubliez pas d'employer des expressions de transition.

➡ *Chers parents,*
   Hier soir, j'ai mangé un repas magnifique au restaurant La Ciboulette...

2. Votre camarade de chambre et vous invitez des amis à dîner ce soir. Vous allez préparer le repas, et votre camarade va faire les courses. Écrivez-lui un message en anticipant ses questions et en expliquant ce qu'il/elle a besoin *(needs)* d'acheter et où. (Structure utile: l'impératif, chapitre 3, page 105.)

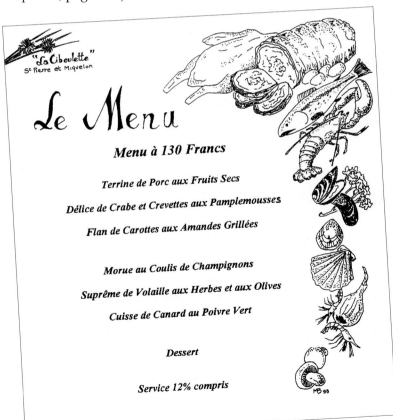

VOCABULAIRE ACTIF

Au restaurant / au café
un client / une cliente *a customer*
le menu / la carte *the menu*

un serveur / une serveuse *a waiter / a waitress*

Pour commander
Monsieur / Mademoiselle, s'il vous plaît?
  Sir / Miss, please?
Vous désirez? *Are you ready to order?*
Je voudrais... *I would like . . .*

Je vais prendre... *I'm going to have . . .*
Et pour moi... *For me . . .*
L'addition, s'il vous plaît. *The check,*
  please.

Les boissons froides
une bière *a beer*
une bouteille d'eau minérale *a bottle of*
  mineral water
une carafe d'eau *a pitcher of water*
un citron pressé *fresh lemonade*

un coca *a cola*
un jus de fruits *fruit juice*
une limonade *lemon soda*
du vin rouge / blanc *red / white wine*

Les boissons chaudes
un café *coffee*
un café crème *coffee with cream*
du café au lait *coffee with milk*
un chocolat *hot chocolate*

un thé nature *tea*
un thé au lait *tea with milk*
un thé citron *tea with lemon*

Les repas (m.)
le petit déjeuner *breakfast*
le déjeuner *lunch*

le dîner *dinner*

Les plats (m.)
un hors-d'œuvre *starter, hors d'oeuvre*
la soupe *soup*
le plat principal *main dish, entree*

la salade *salad*
le dessert *dessert*

Les aliments (m.)

LES PRODUITS (M.) ÉNERGÉTIQUES

une baguette
des biscuits (m.) *cookies*
des céréales (f.) *cereals*
un croissant

le pain *bread*
du pain grillé *toast*
des pâtes (f.) *pasta*
du riz *rice*

LES FRUITS (M.)

de l'ananas (m.) *pineapple*
une banane *a banana*
une fraise *a strawberry*
une framboise *a raspberry*

une orange *an orange*
une pêche *a peach*
une poire *a pear*
une pomme *an apple*

LES LÉGUMES (M.)

de l'ail (m.) *garlic*
du broccoli
une carotte *a carrot*
des champignons (m.) *mushrooms*
des courgettes (f.) *squash*
des haricots (m.) verts *green beans*

du maïs *corn*
un oignon *an onion*
des petits pois (m.) *peas*
une pomme de terre *a potato*
une tomate *a tomato*

LA VIANDE

un bifteck *a steak*
du bœuf *beef*
une côtelette de veau *a veal chop*
du jambon *ham*

du porc *pork*
du poulet *chicken*
du rosbif *roast beef*
du rôti de porc *pork roast*

LE POISSON ET LES FRUITS DE MER

des crevettes (f.) *shrimp*
du homard *lobster*

des huîtres (f.) *oysters*
du thon *tuna*

LES PLATS PRÉPARÉS

des frites *French fries*
une omelette *an omelet*
du pâté
une pizza

une quiche
un sandwich
une saucisse *a sausage*
du saucisson *hard salami*

LES FROMAGES (M.)

le brie   le camembert   le roquefort

LES DESSERTS

un gâteau *a cake*
une glace (à la vanille, au chocolat) *ice cream*
la mousse au chocolat *chocolate mousse*

une tarte (aux pommes, aux fraises) *a tart*
un yaourt *a yogurt*

DIVERS

du beurre *butter*   du poivre *pepper*
du lait *milk*   du sel *salt*
un œuf *an egg*   du sucre *sugar*

Les rayons (m.) et les magasins

la boucherie (du coin)
   the (neighborhood) butcher shop
la boulangerie *bakery*
la charcuterie *deli*

l'épicerie *grocery store*
la pâtisserie *pastry shop*
la poissonnerie *fish market*
le rayon (fromages, etc.) *(cheese) section*

Le couvert

une assiette *a plate*
un couteau *a knife*
une cuillère *a spoon*
une fourchette *a fork*

une serviette *a napkin*
une tasse *a cup*
un verre *a glass*

Adjectifs

cher (chère) *expensive*
diététique
en boîte *canned*
frais (fraîche) *fresh*

gras (grasse) *fatty, greasy*
sain(e) *healthy*
sucré(e) *sweet*
surgelé(e) *frozen*

Verbes et expressions verbales

avoir faim *to be hungry*
avoir soif *to be thirsty*
boire *to drink*
commander *to order*
être au régime *to be on a diet*

faire les courses *to go grocery shopping*
être pressé(e) *to be in a hurry*
oublier *to forget*
payer *to pay*

Expressions négatives

ne... jamais *never*   ne... plus *not . . . anymore, no longer*

Expressions de quantité

assez (de) *enough*
une boîte (de) *a can, a box*
une douzaine (de) *a dozen*
100 grammes (de)
un kilo (de) *a kilo (2.2 lbs)*
un litre (de) *a liter*
une livre (de) *a pound*

un morceau (de) *a piece*
pas du tout (de) *not at all*
un peu (de) *a little*
une tranche (de) *a slice*
trop (de) *too much*
trop peu (de) *too little*

Expressions de comparaison

aussi... que *as . . . as*
moins... que *less . . . than*
plus... que *more . . . than*
meilleur(e) *better (adj.)*

mieux *better (adv.)*
autant de... que *as much/as many (+ noun) as*
moins de... que *less (+ noun) than*
plus de... que *more (+ noun) than*

Expressions communicatives

Qu'est-ce que c'est que ça? *What's that?*
Qu'est-ce que c'est que... ? *What is . . . ?*
C'est quelque chose que... *It's something that . . .*
C'est quelqu'un qui... *It's someone who . . .*
C'est une espèce de... *It's a kind of . . .*

C'est là où... *It's where . . .*
De la (Du) quoi? *Some what?*
Un(e) quoi? *A what?*
Ça s'appelle... *It's called . . .*

Mots de transition

premièrement, d'abord *first*
puis, ensuite *then*

après *after that*
enfin, finalement *finally*

Divers

hier *yesterday*
un régime *a diet*

la santé *health*

EXPRESSIONS POUR LA CLASSE

avoir lieu *to take place*
examinez *examine*

utilisez *use*

Le temps et les passe-temps

Où le patinage sur glace est-il un passe-temps favori?

Et vous?

Quels sont vos passe-temps préférés aux différentes saisons?

Est-ce que vous aimez lire? regarder la télévision?

This chapter will enable you to
- **understand a weather report and a conversation about sports**
- **read humorous texts about a family's reactions to television and to the weather**

- **describe the weather**
- **talk about your favorite pastimes in the present and in the past**
- **extend, accept, and decline invitations**
- **avoid repetition through the use of pronouns**

Première étape

À l'écoute: Le bulletin météo

Imaginez que vous écoutez la radio, et voici le bulletin météorologique! Pour bien le comprendre, faites les activités 1 et 2 avant d'écouter, puis écoutez en suivant les instructions données.

Avant d'écouter

1 To clarify **brumes et brouillards,** say, «Les Anglais connaissent bien le brouillard; à Los Angeles il y a souvent de la brume causée par la pollution.»

1 Quel temps fait-il? Voici les possibilités, dans le langage des bulletins météo.

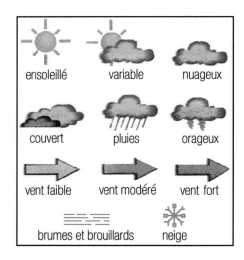

En langage ordinaire, les expressions suivantes sont plus communes. Avec quels symboles peut-on les associer?

Il fait du soleil.	**Il fait du vent.**
Il pleut.	**Il neige.**
Le ciel est couvert.	**Il y a des nuages. / Le temps est nuageux.**
Il fait du brouillard.	**Il fait mauvais.**
Il fait beau.	

En matière de **températures,** c'est une question de degrés, n'est-ce pas?

30°	**Il fait chaud.**
20°	**Il fait bon.**
10°	**Il fait frais.**
0°	**Il fait froid.**

2 Choose a city, Paris for example, and speculate with the class about the weather (Le temps est nuageux, peut-être qu'il pleut; il fait frais—peut-être 15 degrés). Repeat with other cities, or have small groups discuss weather possibilities for different cities, with reports afterwards. Remind students that August temperatures in most of western Europe are generally cooler than in most of the United States.

2 Vous allez entendre un bulletin météo du mois d'août. En regardant la carte qui l'accompagne, qu'est-ce que vous anticipez pour les grandes villes mentionnées? Où est-ce qu'il pleut? Où est-ce qu'il fait du soleil? Est-ce qu'il va faire frais ou chaud sur la plus grande partie de l'Europe?

LE TEMPS

MERCREDI 25 AOÛT 1993, 34ᵉ semaine, 237ᵉ jour de l'année, saint Louis

PHOTO EUMETSAT PRISE LE 24 AOÛT 1993 À 12 h 30 GMT.

Note culturelle

Les températures. Temperatures used in the francophone world are given on the Celsius, or centigrade, scale. 0° Celsius = 32° Fahrenheit (freezing point of water); 10°C = 50°F; 20°C = 68°F; 30°C = 86°F; 40°C = 104°F.

Écoutons

3 ANSWER: pluies (2 fois), nuageux, orages, neige, vent modéré, températures fraîches.

Audio CD

4 A separate listening may be required for this task. ANSWERS: entre 12° et 16° (températures fraîches pour la saison); 28° à Madrid; 32° à Rome.

3 Écoutez une ou deux fois en regardant les possibilités météorologiques données dans **Avant d'écouter.** Lesquelles sont mentionnées dans ce bulletin météo?

4 Quelles sont les températures mentionnées dans ce bulletin météo pour la plus grande partie de l'Europe? Est-ce que ce sont des températures normales pour la saison? Quelles sont les températures mentionnées pour Madrid et Rome?

5 **L'Europe**

1. Écoutez encore pour identifier les pays qui sont mentionnés. Encerclez les noms que vous entendez.

l'Espagne (Madrid)
la France (Paris)
la Pologne (Varsovie)
la Belgique (Bruxelles)
l'Italie (Rome)
la Suisse (Genève)
la Scandinavie (Stockholm, etc.)
les Îles Britanniques (Londres)
l'Autriche (Vienne)
l'Allemagne (Berlin)

2. Quel est le pays d'origine de ce bulletin météo?   ANSWER: la Suisse

6 Écoutez une dernière fois pour identifier les points cardinaux qui sont mentionnés.

Les pluies ont touché le _nord_____ de l'Espagne...

Cette zone de perturbation se déplace (progresse) lentement

vers _l'est_____ . En montagne, quelques chutes de neige

(*snowfalls*) avec un vent d'_ouest_____ . Pour trouver le

soleil, il faut aller bien au _sud_____ de l'Europe.

Have students infer the meaning of **montagne**; if additional clues are needed, say: «Les montagnes qu'il y a en Suisse s'appellent les Alpes, n'est-ce pas? On fait du ski en montagne.»

Prononciation   *Les sons* [o] *et* [ɔ]

■ [o] is the closed *o* sound in **mét<u>é</u>o** and **b<u>eau</u>**.
  [ɔ] is the open *o* sound in **al<u>ors</u>** and **c<u>o</u>mme**.

Écoutez   Listen to the following expressions from **À l'écoute: Le bulletin météo** on the student audio CD, and in the chart, indicate the *o* sounds you hear. Each expression will be read twice. The first expression has been done for you.

	[o]	[ɔ]
1. Les nouvelles ne sont pas très b<u>o</u>nnes.		✔
2. n<u>o</u>tre pays		✔
3. une grande partie de l'Eur<u>o</u>pe		✔
4. le n<u>o</u>rd de l'Espagne		✔
5. Cette z<u>o</u>ne de perturbation	✔	

	[o]	[ɔ]
6. des **o**rages		✔
7. un vent d'ouest m**o**déré		✔
8. Pour trouver le s**o**leil,		✔
9. il f**au**t aller bien **au** sud	✔ ✔	
10. 32 degrés à R**o**me		✔

Now practice saying the expressions aloud. Then listen to the expressions again to verify your pronunciation.

■ As you can tell, the open [ɔ] is more common in French. The closed [o] occurs only in the following cases:

as the final sound in a word	m**o**t, styl**o**
when followed by a [z] sound	ch**o**se, p**o**ser
when spelled ô	hô**tel, diplô**me
when spelled **au** or **eau**	ch**au**d, b**eau**coup
in a few isolated words	z**o**ne

Exception: au + [r] = [ɔ]: rest**au**rant, **au** revoir.

Essayez! Practice saying and contrasting the following pairs of *o* sounds. Then listen to them on the student audio CD to verify your pronunciation.

Audio CD

A. Prononcez.

[o]	[ɔ]
nos	notre
vos	votre
allô	alors
beau	bonne
faux	folle

B. [o] ou [ɔ]? In the following sentences, underline the [o] sounds with one line, and the [ɔ] sounds with two lines.

1. Zut al<u>o</u>rs! j'ai oublié les c<u>ô</u>telettes de v**<u>eau</u>** et le ch<u>o</u>c<u>o</u>lat!
2. Mais j'ai pris un kil<u>o</u> de p<u>o</u>mmes et un morc**<u>eau</u>** de r<u>o</u>quef<u>o</u>rt.
3. Le magnét<u>o</u>sc<u>o</u>pe et la radi<u>o</u> sont sur la c<u>o</u>mm<u>o</u>de, à c<u>ô</u>té de la p<u>o</u>rte.
4. Il ne fait pas tr<u>o</u>p ch**<u>au</u>**d en <u>o</u>ct<u>o</u>bre.
5. Quand il fait b**<u>eau</u>,** on joue **<u>au</u>** g<u>o</u>lf ou on fait du vél<u>o</u>.

Now practice saying the sentences aloud, then listen to them on the student audio CD to verify your pronunciation.

VOCABULAIRE
Le temps et les saisons

Le célèbre Bonhomme du Carnaval de Québec.

Comment est **le climat** au Québec?

1. **En hiver,** il fait très froid (entre $-10°$ et $-30°$), et le temps est souvent nuageux.
2. **Au printemps,** il fait bon, mais le temps est variable.
3. **En été,** les températures varient entre $20°$ et $35°$.
4. **En automne,** les arbres sont magnifiques avec leurs feuilles jaunes et rouges.

À quelle phrase correspond la photo?

Note culturelle

Festivals québécois. **Les Québécois** celebrate the winter season during the Quebec Winter Carnival, eleven days of festivities each February. The festival mascot, **Bonhomme Carnaval,** oversees a parade, canoe races on the Saint Lawrence, snow-sculpting contests, and other winter activities. In the summer you can attend the **Festival international d'été de Québec,** the largest francophone cultural event in North America, lasting eleven days and offering over four hundred free musical and street-performance events.

A. Begin by reviewing the **Note culturelle** on p. 195 and the active vocabulary corresponding to the meteorological symbols on p. 194. Since multiple answers are usually possible, have students work in pairs and then compare responses. Finally, ask volunteers to give a forecast for several cities.

ACTIVITÉS

A. Le temps au Canada. Regardez la carte météorologique à la page 199, puis complétez les phrases avec le nom d'une ville logique.

1. Le ciel est couvert à _____ .

2. Il neige à _____ .

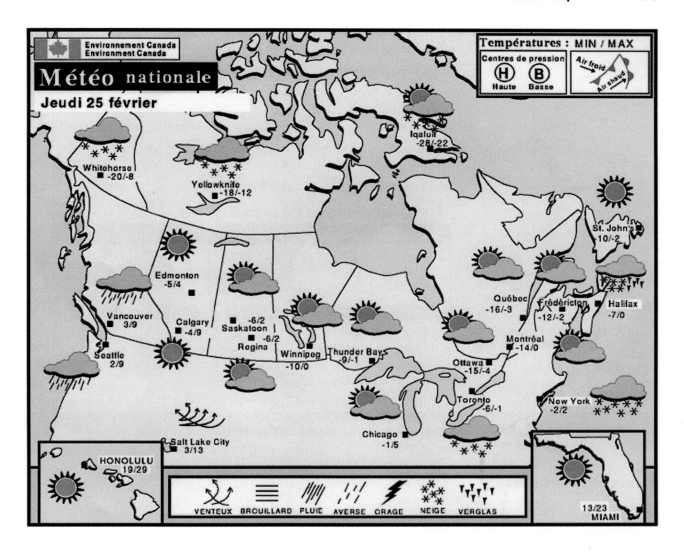

3. À _____ il fait du soleil, mais il ne fait pas chaud.

4. Il pleut à _____ .

5. Le temps est variable à _____ .

6. Il fait assez frais à _____ .

7. Il fait beau à _____ .

8. La température est entre 0 et −7 degrés à _____ .

Maintenant, choisissez deux villes et parlez du temps qu'il y fait.

➡ *À Whitehorse il fait très froid et il ne fait pas de soleil. Le ciel est couvert et il neige. La température est entre −20 et −8 degrés.*

B. After students have practiced with a partner, compare descriptions of the weather from different regions represented in the class for several of the cues, e.g., summer in Montréal, in Montana, in Texas, etc.

B. Le climat chez vous. Expliquez à votre partenaire le temps qu'il fait chez vous selon les indications.

➡ au mois d'avril
Au mois d'avril il fait du soleil et il fait très bon. Il ne pleut pas souvent.

1. aujourd'hui   3. en été   5. en hiver
2. au printemps   4. en automne   6. le jour de votre anniversaire

C. Remind students to use the futur proche for this activity.

C. Et demain? Regardez les images et dites quel temps il **va** faire cette semaine.

➡ *Aujourd'hui le temps est variable mais il va faire bon.*

Prévision à long terme pour **Québec**

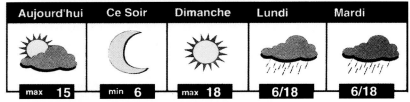

Aujourd'hui	Ce Soir	Dimanche	Lundi	Mardi
max **15**	min **6**	max **18**	**6/18**	**6/18**

D. To make a game of the activity and challenge students to be precise, have partners prepare a weather report for a particular place and date. Then, as the report is read, have classmates try to guess the location.

D. Un bulletin météorologique. Préparez un bulletin météorologique. Parlez du temps qu'il fait aujourd'hui et du temps qu'il va faire demain, puis présentez-le à la classe.

STRUCTURE: Saying what happened (II)
*Le passé composé avec **être***

Observez et déduisez

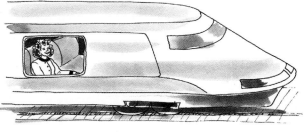

1. Anne est allée à Genève* vendredi.

2. Le train est arrivé à neuf heures du matin, sous la pluie.

---

*Use the preposition **à** with the names of cities: Je vais souvent **à** Paris parce que mon ami habite **à** Paris.

Point out that **rester** is a false cognate. If students are unclear about the meaning of **rentrer**, write **rentrer = retourner (à la maison)** on the board.

3. Anne est restée à Genève toute la journée pour faire des courses—sous la pluie! Elle est entrée dans beaucoup de magasins...

VOCABULAIRE ACTIF
arriver
entrer
monter
passer
rentrer
rester
retourner
tomber

4. ... et elle est rentrée le soir— sous la pluie.

- How does the past tense of the verbs in the examples above differ from the past tense of verbs you learned in Chapter 5?
- In #1, 3, and 4, the second part of the verb ends in **ée,** but in #2, it ends in **é.** Can you think of a logical explanation for the difference?

Vérifiez

Have students compare **je vais aller** *(I'm going to go)* with **je suis allé** *(I have gone; I went).* Point out that **je suis allé** does *not* mean *I am going.*

OPTIONAL DRILL: **Demain? Non, hier!** Claire va aller à New York demain? → Mais non, elle est allée à New York hier. CUES: 1. Thomas va aller au cinéma demain? (Et les filles? Et maman?) 2. Vous allez arriver de bonne heure demain? (Et les étudiants? Et le professeur? Et toi?) 3. Tu vas rentrer à l'heure demain? (Et les étudiants? Et tes parents? Et vous? Et Caroline?) 4. Il va rester à la maison demain? (Et tes amis? Et vous?)

Le passé composé avec **être**

- A few verbs like **aller** use **être** as the auxiliary in the passé composé.

— Il est allé à Genève?   *Did he go to Geneva?*
                              Has he gone to Geneva?

— Non, il est allé à Bruxelles.   *No, he went to Brussels.*
                              No, he's gone to Brussels.

- Some other verbs requiring **être** in the passé composé include **arriver, entrer, monter** *(to go up, get on),* **passer par, rentrer, rester, retourner,** and **tomber** *(to fall).*   Other verbs requiring **être** will be introduced in Ch. 7.

- The past participle of verbs conjugated with **être** agrees in number and gender with the *subject* of the verb.

Anne et Cécile sont all**ées** en ville, mais Paul est rest**é** à la maison.
Et toi, Nicole? Tu es rest**ée** à la maison?

ACTIVITÉS

E. Voyages.   Écoutez Anne parler des voyages de sa famille. Écrivez la bonne destination pour chaque personne, puis indiquez si le voyage est présent, passé ou futur.

Bruxelles   Londres   Genève   chez grand-mère   Vienne   Rome

	destination?	présent / passé / futur?
Claude	_____	_____
Marie/Claire	_____	_____
Maman	_____	_____
Paul	_____	_____
Papa/Michelle	_____	_____
les garçons	_____	_____

Maintenant parlez du temps qu'il fait à chaque destination selon la carte météorologique à la page 195.

F. Quelle journée!   En regardant l'image ci-dessous et les verbes suivants, dites ce que Driss a fait et n'a pas fait aujourd'hui.

rester à la maison   monter dans un taxi   rester une heure au musée
aller au cinéma   tomber dans la rue   passer par l'épicerie
rentrer à 5 h du soir   entrer dans des   ?
                         magasins

➡ *Il n'est pas resté à la maison.*

VOCABULAIRE
Pour parler du passé, du futur et de la ponctualité

The chart below contains some useful expressions for referring to past and future times. Fill in the blanks by studying the expression used in the opposite column and writing its counterpart for expressing the past or future as required.

aujourd'hui
mardi le 9

hier lundi le 8	⟵⟶	demain mercredi le 10

	demain matin
hier après-midi	
	demain soir
vendredi (dernier)	vendredi (prochain)
	la semaine prochaine
le mois dernier	
l'année dernière	

Draw students' attention to adjective agreement with **prochain / dernier**. Point out that context usually indicates whether days of the week are past, present, or future, but that **prochain** and **dernier** may be added for clarity.

■ Read the following paragraph and infer the meaning of the boldfaced time expressions using cognates and context.

Remind students of the expressions **tôt** and **tard,** which they learned in Ch. 4; they refer to the hour, not to people.

> Anne a un rendez-vous à 9 h 30 ce matin, alors elle a pris le train **il y a** une heure et demie (à 8 h). Si elle arrive au bureau à 9 h 30, elle est **à l'heure.** Si elle arrive à 10 h, elle est **en retard.** Si elle arrive à 9 h, elle est **en avance.**

1. il y a   a. on time
2. à l'heure   b. early
3. en retard   c. ago
4. en avance   d. late

ACTIVITÉS

G. Before beginning, ask students to identify the verbs that use **être** in the passé composé and those that use **avoir.**

G. Il y a longtemps?   Dites la dernière fois *(time)* que vous avez fait les activités suivantes.

➡ aller en vacances   *Je suis allé(e) en vacances il y a 7 mois.*

aller au cinéma
arriver en classe en avance
rentrer à 9 h un samedi soir
regarder la télé
rester à la maison toute la journée
arriver en classe en retard
manger au restaurant

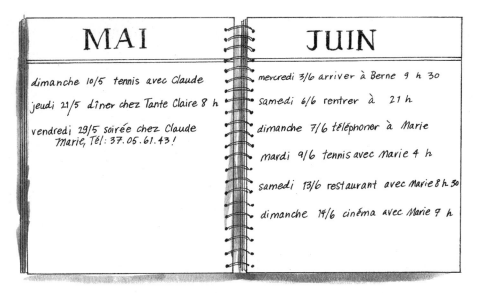

H. Begin by having students identify which activities are in the past (before June 8) and which are in the future. Ask them to identify verbs that take **être** and verbs that take **avoir** in the passé composé.

I. Encourage students to practice saying as much as possible about their trip with a partner, then ask volunteers to share their travel stories with the class. Ask members of the audience to ask follow-up questions.

The *Instructor's Resource Manual* contains an activity, **Anecdote embrouillée,** to practice the **passé composé** with **être** and **avoir.**

H. Calendrier. Nous sommes aujourd'hui le 8 juin... Dites ce qu'Ahmed a fait récemment et ce qu'il *va* faire en employant le calendrier ci-dessus.

I. Discussion. Discutez avec un(e) partenaire d'un voyage mémorable que vous avez fait. Où est-ce que vous êtes allé(e)? Est-ce qu'il a fait beau? mauvais? Combien de temps est-ce que vous êtes resté(e)? Qu'est-ce que vous avez fait? etc.

➡ *L'été dernier je suis allé(e) à Montréal...*

Jeu de rôle

Weekend plans vary with personal preferences and according to the weather. With two classmates, play the roles of three friends who have different preferences. One of you likes sports; another music, movies, and videos; the third likes to stroll around town and eat in restaurants. One is always late; another likes to arrive early. Discuss what you did last weekend, then decide on something different for this weekend. Make two sets of plans: what will you do if the weather's nice? What will you do if it rains?

Deuxième étape

Lecture: La télévision

Avant de lire

This reading section introduces cultural information and vocabulary about television.

Cue to Video Module 2 (00:06:15), where Nicolas talks about his family's love of watching TV. Cue also to Module 6 (00:27:06), where Nicolas proposes that Élisabeth and Fatima come and watch TV at his house.

1 Encourage students to give titles of (American) TV programs as you discuss each type. This will clarify meaning for all students. **Une émission** is a TV program or show, and **un programme de télé** generally refers to TV listings, or TV guide; however, the two terms are starting to be used synonymously.

1 Quelles sortes d'émissions aimez-vous regarder à la télévision? Numérotez les émissions suivantes dans l'ordre de vos préférences (de 1 à 8).

_____ les films

_____ les jeux télévisés (comme *La Roue de la Fortune*)

_____ le journal télévisé (les informations)

_____ les magazines et documents

_____ les sports

_____ les variétés (musiciens, comédiens)

_____ les dessins animés (comme *Winnie l'Ourson* ou *Les Tortues Ninja*)

_____ les feuilletons (les séries en épisodes, comme *Beverly Hills 90210*)

2 Chez vous, qui contrôle la télé-commande *(remote control)*? Êtes-vous un «zappeur»? Quand changez-vous de chaîne *(channel)*? Cochez les réponses appropriées et ajoutez d'autres possibilités.

_____ quand il y a des pubs (publicités)

_____ quand il y a deux émissions intéressantes en même temps

_____ quand il n'y a rien *(nothing)* d'intéressant à voir

_____ quand les nouvelles sont trop déprimantes *(depressing)*

_____ quand vous êtes morose (triste)

_____ ?

En général

3 Parcourez le texte une première fois pour identifier l'idée principale. **Les zappeurs,** c'est l'histoire d'une famille qui

    a. achète une nouvelle télévision et la regarde pour la première fois.
    b. n'est pas contente parce que la nouvelle télé ne fonctionne pas bien.
    c. regarde une nouvelle chaîne de télé et ne l'aime pas.
    d. aime beaucoup la chaîne «anti-morosité».

205

LES ZAPPEURS

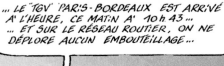

4 **Les images et le texte.** Les paraphrases suivantes sont-elles vraies ou fausses selon les images? Corrigez les fausses, puis indiquez à quelle(s) image(s) elles correspondent.

image(s)

1. Le programme de télé annonce une nouvelle chaîne.   1

2. La réaction à l'idée d'une chaîne «anti-morosité» est très positive chez les enfants et très négative chez les parents.   1, 2

3. La nouvelle chaîne donne seulement de mauvaises nouvelles.   4, 5, 6

4. Le père veut «zapper» mais le fils ne veut pas.   7

5. Les nouvelles traditionnelles sont plus intéressantes!   8

5 **Les mots.** D'après le contexte, quel est le sens des mots suivants? Choisissez a ou b.

1. génial!
   a. cool!   b. too bad!

2. je me réjouis
   a. I rejoice, I'm happy   b. I fear, I'm afraid

3. manquer
   a. to watch   b. to miss

4. Bienvenue
   a. Welcome   b. Hello again

5. aucun (embouteillage)
   a. no (traffic jams)   b. many (traffic jams)

6. se porte bien
   a. is being carried   b. is doing well

7. un biberon
   a. a glass   b. a baby bottle

8. nul!
   a. no good!   b. none!

6 **L'histoire.** Résumez en trois ou quatre phrases l'histoire des zappeurs!

A. Qu'en pensez-vous? Discutez avec deux ou trois camarades de classe.

1. Les médias semblent nous bombarder de mauvaises nouvelles. À votre avis, pourquoi les mauvaises nouvelles sont-elles plus populaires que les bonnes nouvelles? Qu'est-ce que cela indique au sujet de notre société?

2. Les bonnes nouvelles peuvent-elles être intéressantes? Préparez un journal télévisé «anti-morosité» avec au moins quatre bonnes nouvelles se rapportant à l'actualité locale, nationale ou internationale. Comment allez-vous présenter ces nouvelles pour garder l'intérêt de votre public? Essayez vos techniques devant la classe!

B. La télé en France. Voici un extrait du programme de télé français du 15 août.

Dimanche 15 août

TF1	2 France	France 3
12.25 Le Juste Prix. **12.50** À vrai dire. **12.55** Météo - Trafic infos. **13.00** Journal. **13.55** Spécial sport. **16.05** Starsky et Hutch. **16.50** Tarzan. **17.15** Disney parade. **18.20** Des millions de copains. **19.10** Duo d'enfer. **20.00** Journal. **20.30** Spécial sport. **20.45** Météo.	**12.00** Envoyé spécial. *Le Rire du médecin. Des hommes en colère.* **13.00** Le journal. **13.15** Météo. **17.40** Championnats du monde d'athlétisme à Stuttgart. **18.55** Stade 2. *Présenté par Patrick Chêne.* **20.00** Le journal. **20.40** Journal des courses. **20.45** Météo.	**12.45** Journal. **13.00** Le Poney rouge. *Téléfilm américain avec Henri Fonda.* **14.40** Des gorilles et des hommes. *Document.* **15.30** Sports 3 dimanche. **17.35** Les Simpson. **19.10** Editions régionales. **19.35** 19/20 - Météo (suite). **20.10** 4es championnats d'athlétisme à Stuttgart.
20.50 CINéMA **SIERRA TORRIDE** *Film américain de Don Siegel. Avec Shirley MacLaine, Clint Eastwood*	*20.50 CINéMA* **UN ESPION DE TROP** *Film américain de Don Siegel. Avec Charles Bronson, Lee Remick.* **22.20** *L'Idole d'Acapulco. Film de Richard Thorpe. Avec Elvis Presley, Ursula Andress.* **23.45** *Journal de la nuit.*	*21.05 DIVERTISSEMENT* **LE CIRQUE DU SOLEIL Le cirque réinventé.** *La pyramide des chaises; Contorsionniste; Le clown mécanique; Fildeféristes; Tango; Trapézistes; Acrobaties sur cycles.* **22.05** Le Soir 3 - Météo.

CANAL+	arte	M6
13.30 Décode pas Bunny. **14.25** Animaux superstars. **14.30** L'Odyssée des Eulakanes. **14.50** Surprises. **15.00** L'homme qui racontait des histoires. **16.30** L'Œil du cyclone. **17.00** La Harley-Davidson. **18.00** Le Dimanche de préférence. **19.35** Flash infos. **20.15** Football.	**19.00** American Supermarket *(R). Les affaires sont les affaires.* **19.35** Megamix *(R). Magazine musical. Proposé par Martin Messonier. Invité : Michel Redolfi.* **20.40** Soirée thématique: Le Ring de Wagner. *Éclats de voix, Bayreuth 1976. Document réalisé par Jean-Luc Léon.*	**11.50** Mariés deux enfants. *Série.* **12.20** Ma Sorcière bien aimée *(R). Série.* **12.55** Equalizer. *Série.* **13.50** Cosmos 1999. *(1/2). Série.* **16.10** Fréquenstar. *Invitée : Véronique Sanson.* **18.00** Clair de lune. *Série.* **19.00** Booker. *Série.* **19.54** 6 Minutes - Météo. **20.00** Loin de ce monde. *Série.* **20.35** Sport 6. *Magazine.*
20.30 FOOTBALL **MARSEILLE/PSG** *Commenté par Thierry Gilardi et Pierre Sled. 5e journée du championnat de France de D1.* **22.30** Flash infos.	*21.40 OPERA* **LE RING L'Or du Rhin.** *1re partie. Tétralogie de Richard Wagner. Chef d'orchestre: Pierre Boulez. Avec Donald McIntyre, Martin Egel, Siegfried Jerusalem, Heinz Zednik, Hanna Schwarz, Carmen Reppel, Ortrun Wenkel.*	*20.45 CINÉMA* **SÉNÉCHAL LE MAGNIFIQUE** *Film français de Jean Boyer. (1957). Avec Fernandel, Nadia Frey, Armontel, Albert Dinan.*

1. Combien de chaînes publiques y a-t-il? Que remarquez-vous concernant les heures? Quelles émissions reconnaissez-vous?
2. Avec un(e) partenaire, cherchez dans le programme de télé du 15 août les renseignements nécessaires pour compléter le tableau suivant.

type d'émission ou titre	chaîne	heure
Tarzan	TF1	16.50
Journal	TF1 / France 2	20.00
Météo	TF1 / France 2	20.45

If your class likes competition, make a game out of this activity—who can find the answers the fastest? As you go over answers, ask students what strikes them as different in a French TV guide. (Les émissions ne commencent pas nécessairement toutes les heures ou demi-heures, etc.)

type d'émission ou titre	chaîne	heure
Document: *Des gorilles et des hommes*	France 3	14.40
Les Simpson	France 3	17.35
Football	Canal +	20.30
Opéra (Wagner)	Arte	21.40
Série: *Mariés deux enfants*	M6	11.50
Film américain avec Shirley MacLaine et Clint Eastwood	TF1	20.50

FOLLOW-UP: Have a few groups report and/or see which **émissions** were the most popular.

3. Maintenant imaginez qu'on est le dimanche 15 août. Qu'est-ce que vous allez regarder à la télé? Avec un(e) partenaire, discutez ce qui vous intéresse et faites une liste des émissions que vous allez regarder (1) l'après-midi et (2) le soir.

Note culturelle

La télévision en France. In addition to the free channels, there is an ever growing number of cable TV channels in various categories: *Généralistes (Monte-Carlo), Sports (Eurosport), Cinéma (Cinéstar), Jeunesse (Disney Channel), Documentaires (Planète), Fiction (Série Club), À la carte (Kiosque), Musique (MTV), Étrangères (BBC Prime),* and *Information (Euro News, CNN).* A recent survey reports that 96% of households in France own a television and that adults spend an average of 3 hours and 19 minutes per day in front of the TV set. Commercials appear only *between* shows on French TV— never in the middle of a program!

STRUCTURE: Talking about favorite pastimes
*Les verbes **lire**, **dire**, **voir** et **écrire***

Observez et déduisez *Les passe-temps préférés*

Cue to Video Module 2 (00:06:44), where Nicolas and Élisabeth talk about their families' favorite activities. Cue also to Module 6 (00:27:06), where the three friends discuss what to do on a rainy Saturday. Also to the street interviews (00:28:41) where people say what they like to do in their free time.

Moi, je ne passe pas mon temps libre à regarder la télé—et surtout pas la chaîne anti-morosité! Quand j'ai du temps libre, j'aime lire—des romans, des magazines, des journaux. Hier, j'ai lu des bandes dessinées vraiment comiques dans le journal. J'aime aussi écrire—des lettres, des histoires, des rapports pour mes cours ou même des poèmes. Et puis bien sûr, j'aime les sorties avec mes amis, Danielle et Patrick. Samedi nous sommes allés voir deux films ensemble. Nous avons vu *Ponette,* un drame, et *The English Patient* avec Juliette Binoche. Patrick a dit que ce sont deux excellents films; Danielle a dit la même chose, et moi, je suis d'accord!

- From the context, what do you think the verbs **lire, écrire, dire,** and **voir** mean?
- What are the past participles of **voir, lire,** and **dire?**
- How would you say, "I saw *Ponette*"? "We read *Madame Bovary*"?

Quel genre *(type)* de film préférez-vous? Les films policiers ou...

les films d'amour?   les films d'aventure?

les films d'épouvante?   les comédies?

ou les drames?

Vérifiez *Les verbes **lire, dire, voir** et **écrire***

■ You have now learned several verbs that have irregular past participles in the passé composé. **Lire, dire, voir,** and **écrire** are all conjugated in the passé composé with **avoir.**

— Tu **as vu** *Ponette?*
— Non, mais Claire **a dit** que c'est bien.

— Tu **as lu** les histoires (*stories*) de Pierre?
— Il **a écrit** des histoires?!

Les verbes lire, écrire, dire, voir	
je lis	j'écris
tu lis	tu écris
il / elle / on lit	il / elle / on écrit
nous lisons	nous écrivons
vous lisez	vous écrivez
ils / elles lisent	ils / elles écrivent
je dis	je vois
tu dis	tu vois
il / elle / on dit	il / elle / on voit
nous disons	nous voyons
vous dites*	vous voyez
ils / elles disent	ils / elles voient

Participes passés: lu, écrit, dit, vu

ACTIVITÉS

A. Nos activités. Complétez les phrases en cochant toutes les réponses logiques.

1. Les étudiants lisent...

   _____ des bandes dessinées   _____ les variétés   _____ le journal télévisé

2. J'écris quelquefois...

   _____ des jeux télévisés   _____ des poèmes   _____ des dessins animés

3. La classe a lu...

   _____ des variétés   _____ des magazines   _____ des histoires

4. Hier, j'ai vu...

   _____ la chaîne anti-morosité   _____ mes copains   _____ un film policier

5. Mes amis et moi, nous lisons souvent...

   _____ des journaux   _____ des romans   _____ des films d'épouvante

*Note irregular form.

B. Allow time for students to prepare answers (individually or in pairs) before asking volunteers to report on their responses. Have students ask you questions about your preferences to practice the **vous** form of the verbs.

B. Préférences. Complétez les phrases avec une des réponses indiquées ou avec une réponse originale.

➡ *Mes parents lisent des magazines.*

Mes parents lisent...	des B.D.	le journal télévisé
Mes ami(e)s écrivent...	des poèmes	des choses intéressantes
Ma (mon) camarade de	des drames	«bonjour» aux étudiants
chambre a vu...	des lettres	des magazines
Le professeur dit...	des comédies	des feuilletons
	des rapports	«Faites vos devoirs»
	des journaux	?
	des romans	

C. Quel genre? Complétez le tableau suivant avec vos préférences pour chaque catégorie.

	Moi	Mes camarades de classe
Genre de film		
Genre d'émission		
Genre de lectures		
Ce que j'aime écrire		

Maintenant cherchez des camarades de classe qui aiment les mêmes passe-temps que vous et écrivez leur nom.

➡ *Moi, j'aime les films policiers. Quel genre de film est-ce que tu aimes voir?*
Ou: *Moi, je n'aime pas lire. Et toi? Qu'est-ce que tu aimes lire?*

STRUCTURE: Avoiding repetition (I)
Les pronoms d'objet direct: le, la, l' et les

Observez et déduisez

— Dis, tu as vu la nouvelle chaîne anti-morosité?
— Non, je ne **l'**ai pas vue, mais je voudrais **la** voir. On dit que les émissions sont géniales!
— Pas du tout! Moi, je **les** trouve ennuyeuses!

> ■ To what words do the boldfaced pronouns in the preceding dialogue refer?
> ■ Where is the pronoun placed when the verb is in the present tense? when the verb is in the passé composé? when there are two verbs?
> ■ Where is **ne... pas** placed in relation to the pronoun and verb?

Vérifiez   *Les pronoms d'objet direct:* **le, la, l'** *et* **les**

- A direct object is a noun that "receives" the action of the verb. It comes immediately after the verb.

    J'ai regardé **la chaîne anti-morosité** hier soir.

Compare with the use of subject pronouns to replace subject nouns.

- A direct object *pronoun* is used to avoid repeating the noun if the direct object—a person or thing—has already been mentioned.

    — Tu as vu **le journal télévisé?**
    — Oui, je **l'**ai vu.

Have students compare English usage: *to look* **for,** *to look* **at,** *to listen* **to.**

- Certain French verbs require a direct object, unlike their English equivalents.

    Je cherche **la télé-commande.**
    Je regarde **le documentaire sur les gorilles.**
    J'écoute **les informations à la radio.**

- The direct object pronouns **le, la, l',** and **les** agree in number and gender with the nouns they replace. The direct object pronoun directly *precedes* the verb of which it is the object. In a negative sentence, **ne** precedes the object pronoun.

    — Tu vois **mon journal?**
    — Oui, je **le** vois.

    — Tu vois **mes amis?**
    — Non, je ne **les** vois pas.

- In the futur proche, the direct object pronoun precedes the *infinitive.* (It is the object of the infinitive.)

Point out that **le** is the object of **voir,** *not* **aller.**

    — Tu vas voir le film?
    — Oui, je vais **le** voir.
    — Moi, je ne vais pas **le** voir.

- In the passé composé, the pronoun directly precedes the auxiliary verb.

    — Tu as vu le film?
    — Oui, je **l'**ai vu.
    — Moi, je ne **l'**ai pas vu.

OPTIONAL DRILL: Replace the nouns with direct object pronouns.
1. Je regarde le journal télévisé.
2. Il regarde *La Roue de la Fortune.*
3. Ils aiment les dessins animés.
4. Tu as regardé la télé hier.   5. Nous avons vu les sports.   6. Voulez-vous voir le nouveau film de Spielberg?

- Note that in the passé composé, the past participle agrees in number and gender with the preceding direct object pronoun.

    — Tu as vu **la** chaîne anti-morosité?
    — Oui, je **l'**ai vu<u>e</u>.

    — Tu as vu **mes amis?**
    — Oui, je **les** ai vu<u>s</u>.

ACTIVITÉS

D. Have students work in pairs/
groups to identify all possible
responses. Then, as they share
their answers with the class, make
sure everyone understands why
only certain answers are correct,
especially for #4–6. Finally, to be
sure students focus on meaning,
have volunteers read the sentences,
substituting nouns for the pronouns,
as others respond, «C'est vrai pour
moi aussi», «Ce n'est pas vrai pour
moi».

D. Préférences des téléspectateurs.   De quoi parle-t-on dans les phrases de
gauche? Choisissez parmi les expressions de la colonne de droite.

➡ «Je vais le regarder ce soir.»   *le journal télévisé*

1. «Je les regarde souvent.»   a. la télé-commande
2. «Je la regarde tous les jours.»   b. la chaîne anti-morosité
3. «Je ne le regarde jamais.»   c. le programme de télévision
4. «Je les ai regardés hier.»   d. les sports
5. «Je ne l'ai pas vue.»   e. le journal télévisé
6. «Je ne l'ai pas aimé.»   f. *La Roue de La Fortune*
                                        g. les informations
                                        h. le document sur les gorilles

Maintenant dites si les phrases sont vraies pour vous aussi. Faites un
sondage des préférences de la classe en matière de télévision.

E. CUES: 1. Tu vois souvent tes
copains? 2. Tu regardes la télé?
3. Tu écoutes le jazz? 4. Tu as lu les
poèmes de Jacques? 5. Tu as vu ta
sœur le week-end dernier? 6. Tu as
écrit le rapport pour le cours de
français?

E. Toujours «oui».   Écoutez les questions du professeur, et complétez les
réponses avec le pronom qui convient: **le, la, l'** ou **les.**

➡ (Tu aimes les histoires comiques?)
   Oui, je les aime.

1. Oui, je _____ vois souvent.
2. Oui, je _____ regarde.
3. Oui, je _____ écoute.
4. Oui, je _____ ai lus.
5. Oui, je _____ ai vue.
6. Oui, je _____ ai écrit.

F. Go over both examples to review
pronoun placement before students
begin this activity.

F. Interview.   À tour de rôle, posez les questions suivantes à un(e) partenaire. Répondez en employant un pronom d'objet direct.

➡ Tu as vu le match de foot samedi dernier?
   Oui, je l'ai vu.   ou: *Non, je ne l'ai pas vu.*

1. Tu as fait tes devoirs?
2. Tu as vu le nouveau film de Depardieu?
3. Tu as commencé la leçon de français?
4. Tu as fait ton lit?
5. Tu as écouté la musique de Céline Dion?

Maintenant parlez de vos préférences pour samedi *prochain*.

➡ Tu veux voir le match de foot samedi?
   Oui, je veux le voir.   ou: *Non, je ne veux pas le voir.*

The *Instructor's Resource
Manual* contains an information gap activity, **Des copains,**
providing students practice in asking
questions and answering with direct
object pronouns.

6. Tu vas voir tes copains?
7. Tu veux faire les courses?
8. Tu veux lire le roman de Pagnol?
9. Tu vas écrire les exercices?
10. Tu veux payer mon dîner au restaurant?

Jeu de rôle

Today is August 15. You and your "family" want to watch television, but each person likes a different show. Create a skit where you all look at the TV guide (p. 208) together and discuss possibilities. Each person explains why his/her choice is the best. Who will be the most convincing? Which show will you watch?

CULTURE ET RÉFLEXION

Internet

■ **Le climat et la vie.** Quels sont les effets du climat sur la vie personnelle? Au Québec, où les hivers sont très longs et rigoureux, on dit que les familles sont très proches[1] et quand on parle de famille, il s'agit de la famille nucléaire. Mais en Polynésie, où il fait entre 21 et 32° C toute l'année, la «famille» qui assume la responsabilité des enfants inclut les grands-parents, les oncles, les tantes et même les voisins! Comment expliquez-vous cela? Dans un pays comme la France, où les climats sont variés, on dit aussi que les gens du Nord sont plus froids et plus fermés que les gens du Midi, qui sont plus ouverts, plus gais. Est-ce la même chose aux États-Unis? Donnez des exemples de différences culturelles qui peuvent être liées (associées) au climat.

■ **Les loisirs et l'école.** En France, la vie sportive et sociale est complètement séparée de la vie scolaire. Les lycées et les universités n'ont pas d'équipes[2] sportives et n'organisent pas de bals[3] pour les jeunes. Les sports et les activités sociales se font à l'extérieur de l'école, car l'école est considérée comme une institution purement académique. À votre avis, quels sont les avantages et les désavantages de cette séparation?

■ **Sports individuels ou collectifs?** Un Français sur trois pratique un sport individuel (le jogging, l'aérobic, le ski, le cyclisme) mais seulement un sur quinze pratique un sport collectif (le football, le volley-ball, le rugby). Trouvez-vous ces statistiques surprenantes? Comment les expliquez-vous?

■ **Les vacances.** «Fermeture pour congés annuels»[4]. C'est ce qu'on voit en France sur les portes de beaucoup de magasins ou d'entreprises pendant les mois de juillet et août. Une fermeture d'un mois! Eh oui, l'activité économique française baisse (diminue) de 25% en été, mais ce sont les vacances, et pour les Français, les vacances sont sacrées! La loi[5] française garantit cinq semaines de congés payés par an, et les Français sont prêts à faire toutes sortes de sacrifices pour avoir de bonnes vacances. Qu'est-ce que cela révèle sur les Français? Le fait que les vacances sont beaucoup moins importantes aux États-Unis est-il révélateur? De quoi?

FERMETURE ANNUELLE
DU
31 juillet 1993
AU
16 août 1993

LES VINS DU PANTHÉON

REOUVERTURE
MARDI 17 AOUT

Les vacances sont sacrées.

En famille en Polynésie française.

---

1. *close*   2. *teams*   3. *dances*   4. *closed for annual vacation*   5. *law*

Troisième étape

À l'écoute: Sport et culture

This listening section presents cultural information and new vocabulary about sports.

Le sport comme passe-temps ou comme profession est-il le reflet d'une culture? La conversation que vous allez écouter dans cette étape va proposer des idées très intéressantes. Pour bien les comprendre, faites la tâche 1 avant d'écouter, puis écoutez en suivant les instructions données.

Avant d'écouter

1 On associe traditionnellement certains sports avec certains pays. Regardez les photos, puis reliez les sports et les pays suivants.

les pays d'Europe de l'Ouest	le judo
le Canada	le football
le Japon	le football américain
les États-Unis	la gymnastique
l'Afrique	le hockey
les pays d'Europe de l'Est	la course

Avec quel(s) pays associez-vous les sports suivants: le patinage sur glace (*ice skating*)? le cyclisme? le ski? le base-ball? Y a-t-il d'autres sports liés à des pays particuliers?

2 Écoutez d'abord pour identifier les sports qui sont mentionnés.

3 Écoutez encore et complétez.

1. Le <u>hockey</u> est caractéristique du climat du <u>Canada</u> : rigoureux et <u>froid</u> .

2. Le <u>football américain</u> est une conquête progressive du territoire par la tactique et la force, comme la conquête de <u>l'Ouest</u> .

3. Ce sont les spectateurs qui sont violents aux matchs de <u>football</u> en <u>Europe</u> .

4 Vrai ou faux? Si c'est faux, corrigez.

1. Selon cette conversation, la société canadienne est de plus en plus violente.
2. Hier, il y a eu un incident de violence entre spectateurs au match entre l'Allemagne et la Belgique.

5 Est-ce que vous êtes d'accord avec les idées exprimées dans cette conversation sur le hockey et le football américain? Est-ce que les sports sont vraiment le reflet des cultures?

Prononciation   *Les consonnes s et c*

■ The letter **s** can be pronounced [s] or [z] in French.

Écoutez   **A.** Listen to the following sentences from **À l'écoute: Sport et culture** on the

Audio CD

student audio CD, underlining the [s] sounds with one line, and the [z] sounds with two lines. You will hear each sentence twice.

1. J'ai lu quelque chose d'intéressant sur le sport.
2. Ils disent aussi que c'est caractéristique d'une société de plus en plus violente.

Now can you infer when the **s** is pronounced [z]? Fill in the following chart.

	[s]	[z]
a single **s** between two vowels		
s in a liaison		
s at the beginning of words		
s between a vowel and a consonant		
spelled **-ss-**		

■ The letter **c** can be pronounced [s] or [k] in French.

B. [s] ou [k]? Listen to the following words from **À l'écoute: Sport et culture** on the student audio CD, and in the chart check [s] or [k] for each sound you hear. You will hear each word twice.

le climat   c'est
la tactique   la force
le Canada   la société
la conquête   un incident
la culture   ça

	[s]	[k]
c + consonant		
c + **a, o, u**		
c + **e, i**		
ç + **a, o, u**		

Essayez!   **Prononcez.** Practice saying the following words aloud, then listen to them on the student audio CD to verify your pronunciation.

Audio CD

1. inversion; maison; saison; conversion; télévision; émission
2. ils lisent; nous disons; vous dansez; on traverse; tu plaisantes
3. les loisirs; le cyclisme; un musée; un dessin; la philosophie
4. une bicyclette; de toute façon; un concert; les vacances; le cœur; un morceau

STRUCTURE: Avoiding repetition (II)
*Les pronoms d'objet indirect: **lui** et **leur***

Observez et déduisez

— Il y a un match de hockey cet après-midi. Tu veux y aller avec moi?
— Ah non. Le hockey est trop violent. Je préfère aller voir le match de foot. Et Jean-Claude, on va l'inviter?
— Bonne idée! Je sais qu'il aime beaucoup le foot. Je vais lui téléphoner. Et pourquoi pas inviter Caroline et Marianne aussi?
— D'accord, je leur téléphone.

Once students have identified the nouns to which the pronouns refer, write the following on the board and point out the different verb/object constructions: On va inviter Jean-Claude. / Je vais téléphoner à Jean-Claude. / Je téléphone à Caroline et à Marianne.

■ To whom does the pronoun **l'** refer to in the preceding conversation? And the pronouns **lui** and **leur**?

■ What can you infer about the placement of **lui** and **leur** in the passé composé based on the dialogue and what you learned about the placement of **le, la, les, l'** in the preceding étape?

Vérifiez   *Les pronoms d'objet indirect:* **lui** *et* **leur**

Refer students to p. 213.

VOCABULAIRE ACTIF
un message électronique
la vérité

■ The difference between direct and indirect object *pronouns* is similar to the difference between the direct and indirect objects they replace. In French a direct object immediately follows the verb and receives the action of the verb.

> Il a écrit **ce message électronique.**   Qui a dit **cette bêtise** *(nonsense)?*

■ An indirect object also follows the verb but is *preceded* by the preposition **à.** The corresponding sentence in English does not always use *to.*

> J'ai téléphoné **à mes amis.**   J'écris des lettres **à mes parents.**

Students have seen similar verbs in instructions: «Demandez/Expliquez à votre partenaire... » To reinforce French usage, have students provide several conclusions to these sentences: Je téléphone à... ; Je pose une question à... ; Je donne... à...

■ Verbs that involve an interchange of objects or information often require an indirect object.

> parler de la télévision *à ma famille*
> donner la télé-commande *à mon frère*
> écrire un message électronique *à ma copine*
> téléphoner *à mes parents*
> poser une question *au professeur*
> dire au revoir *à Étienne*

Remember that if the object is preceded by **à,** it is indirect and can be replaced only by an indirect object pronoun **(lui, leur).**

Point out that direct object pronouns are used for people and objects, but indirect object pronouns refer only to people.

■ An indirect object pronoun refers to a person already mentioned and is used to avoid repeating the noun.

> — J'ai dit la vérité **au professeur.**
> — Tu **lui** as dit la vérité *(truth)?*
> — Oui, je ne **lui** dis jamais de bêtises.

■ The third-person pronouns **lui** and **leur** agree in number with the nouns they replace. No distinction in gender is made; that is, **lui** *(him/her)* and **leur** *(them)* refer to both males and females.

> J'ai téléphoné à ma mère (à mon père). Je ne **lui** ai pas écrit de lettres.
> Je veux parler à mes amis (amies). Je vais **leur** téléphoner demain.

The first- and second-person object pronouns will be presented in Ch. 8. Point out that the indirect object pronoun **leur,** as opposed to the possessive adjective, never adds an **s.**

■ Note that the placement of indirect object pronouns is the same as that of direct object pronouns in all tenses and that there is no agreement of the past participle with *indirect* object pronouns.

Les pronoms d'objet direct et indirect	
objet direct	**objet indirect**
Paul? Je **le** vois rarement.	Je **lui** téléphone ce soir.
Marie? Je **la** vois rarement.	Je **lui** téléphone ce soir aussi.
Mes cousins? Je **les** ai vus hier.	Je ne vais pas **leur** téléphoner.
Mes amies? Je **les** ai vues mardi.	Je **leur** ai téléphoné ce matin.

ACTIVITÉS

A. Réponses personnelles. Écoutez le professeur et répondez selon votre expérience personnelle. Choisissez toutes les réponses qui conviennent pour chaque cas.

➡ (1. Je leur parle de sport.)

parents	copains (copines)	professeurs	prof de français	camarade de chambre	meilleur(e) ami(e)
1. ✔	✔				

B. Interview. Interviewez un(e) partenaire et répondez à ses questions en employant un pronom d'objet indirect (**lui** ou **leur**).

➡ Tu parles de sport à tes amis?
Oui, je leur parle de sport. ou: *Non, je ne leur parle pas de sport.*

1. Tu dis toujours la vérité à tes parents? à ton professeur? à tes amis?
2. Tu écris des messages électroniques à ton (ta) cousin(e)? à tes professeurs? au Président des États-Unis?
3. Est-ce que les étudiants posent des questions au professeur? à leurs parents? à leur(s) camarade(s) de chambre?
4. Le professeur apprend le français aux étudiants? à ses collègues? au président de l'université?

C. Le match de hockey. Paul est allé voir un match de hockey. Racontez (dites) son histoire en évitant la répétition. Choisissez le pronom d'objet direct *ou* indirect qui convient pour remplacer les mots soulignés (*replace the underlined words*). Attention au placement des pronoms.

➡ Paul a invité <u>Claudine</u> au match de foot. Paul *l'*a invitée.

L'autre jour, j'ai décidé d'inviter mes amies, Claudine et Marianne, au match de hockey. Alors j'ai téléphoné <u>à mes amies</u> pour inviter <u>mes amies</u> au match. J'ai demandé <u>à mes amies</u>, «Vous aimez le hockey?» et elles ont dit «Oui». Alors, j'ai invité <u>Claudine et Marianne</u> à aller au match et j'ai dit <u>à mes amies</u> d'être prêtes (*ready*) à 13 h 30.

Cet après-midi-là, nous avons rencontré un autre ami, Jean-Claude, au stade, et nous avons parlé <u>à Jean-Claude</u> pendant le match. Marianne et Claudine ont dit <u>à Jean-Claude</u> que le hockey est un peu trop violent. Jean-Claude a dit <u>à Marianne et à Claudine</u> que le sport est un véhicule très positif pour extérioriser des frustrations naturelles. Moi, j'ai dit <u>à Jean-Claude, à Marianne et à Claudine</u>: «Vous êtes trop sérieux! Un sport, c'est un sport!»

STRATÉGIE DE COMMUNICATION
Inviting and responding to invitations

Cue to Video Module 6 (00:27:06), where the three friends in turn suggest various activities to the others.

Bonne idée! Allons au cinéma!

You can also ask students to identify other parts of the ritual, such as confirming and expressing regret.

Every speech act carries with it an implied ritual that is understood by all the parties involved. With invitations, for example, first the invitation is extended, then if it is accepted, details (time, place, etc.) are negotiated and confirmed. If the invitation is declined, an excuse is made, and regrets are expressed.

Study the following dialogues and identify the expressions used to

- invite
- accept an invitation
- decline an invitation
- suggest
- confirm
- make excuses
- express regret

— J'ai envie *(feel like)* d'aller au match de foot cet après-midi. Ça t'intéresse?
— Oui, je veux bien! À quelle heure?
— Rendez-vous devant le stade à trois heures, d'accord?
— Entendu! À trois heures!

— J'ai une idée. Allons manger au restaurant! Je t'invite.
— Oh, c'est gentil, mais je ne peux pas. J'ai des courses à faire.
— Dommage. Une autre fois, alors.

— Veux-tu aller au cinéma avec moi? Je t'invite!

— Volontiers! C'est génial!

Now verify your answers in the table below.

Les invitations	
pour inviter	
J'ai envie de...	Tu veux aller avec moi? (Vous voulez aller... ?)
J'ai une idée!	Ça t'intéresse? (Ça vous intéresse?)
Je voudrais...	Je t'invite. (Je vous invite.)
	Ça te dit? (Ça vous dit?)
	Veux-tu... ? (Voulez-vous... ?)
pour accepter	
Bonne idée!	C'est gentil, volontiers!
Je veux bien.	Avec plaisir.
	C'est génial!
pour refuser	
Malheureusement, je n'ai pas le temps.	
C'est gentil, mais je ne peux pas...	
Je suis désolé(e), mais je ne suis pas libre.	
pour confirmer	
Entendu.	Ça va.
D'accord.	C'est parfait!

ACTIVITÉS

D. Dialogues. Complétez les dialogues en employant des expressions pour inviter, refuser, accepter et confirmer.

1. — J'ai une idée! Allons jouer au tennis.

   — _____

   — À trois heures?

   — _____

2. — Tu veux déjeuner au restaurant?

   — _____

   — Dommage.

3. — _____

   — Avec plaisir. C'est gentil.

   — Rendez-vous devant le stade?

   — _____

4. — _____ . Ça t'intéresse?

   — _____

Jeu de rôle

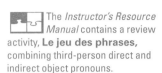
The *Instructor's Resource Manual* contains a review activity, **Le jeu des phrases,** combining third-person direct and indirect object pronouns.

Read the film descriptions that follow and decide which film you'd like to see. Then develop a skit in which you invite your partner to go to the movies. Discuss which film you'd like to see and when you can meet. If you don't agree on the film or time, try to find a compromise.

PLACE LONGUEUIL: 825, St-Laurent O. (679-7451) — **Miracle de la 34e rue** sam. dim. 13 h 30, 16 h, 19 h — **Le spécialiste** 21 h 15 — **La cloche et l'idiot** sam. dim. 14 h 20, 16 h 35, 21 h 30.

PLAZA CÔTE DES NEIGES: 6700, Côte-des-neiges — **Prêt-à-porter** jeu. ven. 19 h 30 — **Sans parole** 19 h 10 sem.; 18 h 10, 21 h 30 sam. dim. — **Parc Jurassic** sam. dim. mer. 13 h 15.

PLACE CHAREST: Startrek 13 h 55, 19 h 20 — **Entretien avec un vampire** 16 h 15 — **Anna** 13 h 15, 16 h 15 — **Le professionnel** 19 h, 21 h 25 — Samedi programme double **Nell** 19 h, **Le professionnel** 21 h 25.

À L'ÉCRAN

NELL *** De Michael Apted, Jodie Foster incarne ici une femme sauvage, élevée par une mère ermite et aphasique qui s'est inventée un univers et un langage. Ses rapports avec deux thérapeutes venus l'observer seront la trame du film. Liam Neeson joue le médecin transformé par sa rencontre avec cet être libre.

PRÊT-À-PORTER *** 1/2
De Robert Altman, le film très attendu du plus acide des cinéastes américains, penché cette fois sur les dessous de la mode parisienne. Une pléthore de vedettes et de célébrités de tout poil, des gags drôles, une finale éblouissante.

SANS PAROLE ** 1/2   De Ron Underwood. La comédie comico-romantique du temps des Fêtes place le duo Geena Davis–Michael Keaton dans un amour à la Roméo et Juliette, mais sur le mode rigolo. Ils appartiennent en pleine campagne électorale à des camps rivaux, possè-dent des partenaires respectifs. L'amour sera-t-il plus fort que tout?

LA CLOCHE ET L'IDIOT *** De Peter Farrely. Deux amis aussi bêtes l'un que l'autre sont lancés dans une série de mésaventures truculentes dont la grossièreté n'a d'égale que l'astuce des auteurs et des interprètes de ce film qui savent jusqu'où on peut aller trop loin. Cela devrait faire rire de bon cœur les enfants de sept à soixante-dix-sept ans. J'ai bien dit les enfants.

ANNA, 6–18 **** Nikita Mikhalkov a chaque année filmé sa fille en lui posant les mêmes questions. De six à dix-huit ans, nous suivons donc l'évolution d'Anna mais aussi et surtout, à travers des documents d'archives extrêmement variés, nous survolons l'histoire d'une décade prodigieuse avec comme guide le cinéaste qui se fait commentateur.

CD-ROM

Now that you have finished the Troisième étape of this chapter, do your Lab Man-ual activities with the audio program. Explore chapter topics further with the Mais oui! Video and CD-ROM. Viewing and comprehension activities are in the video section of your *Workbook/Lab Manual/Video Manual.*

Intégration

Littérature: M. Bordenave n'aime pas le soleil

Vous connaissez déjà le petit Nicolas et son mot favori, **chouette** *(cool)*. Voici un autre épisode dans la vie du petit Nicolas...

Avant de lire

This text is longer than previous readings, but students should find it fairly easy, especially if they don't skip any of the tasks designed to make it accessible.

1 Brainstorm quickly with the whole class, or have students do the task in small groups first.

1 Regardez l'illustration qui accompagne cette histoire. Le monsieur en noir est M. Bordenave. Son travail? Il est surveillant, c'est-à-dire qu'il surveille *(watches)* et discipline les enfants à la récréation. À votre avis, pourquoi n'aime-t-il pas le soleil?

2 Les mots suivants sont des mots-clés dans l'histoire.

> la cour de récréation *(school playground)*
> se battre *(to fight)*
> crier *(to yell)*
> mettre au piquet *(to put someone in the corner, as a punishment)*
> un sandwich à la confiture *(jam)*
> une balle
> l'infirmerie *(nurse's office)*
> boiter *(to limp)*
> jouer
> tomber par terre *(to fall on the ground)*
> pleurer
> se fâcher *(to get mad)*
> pousser *(to push)*
> glisser *(to slip)*
> désespéré *(desperate)*

D'après ces mots-clés, qu'est-ce que vous anticipez comme histoire?

 Attention: In this text, you will see verbs in another past tense, *l'imparfait*, or the imperfect (**il parlait, ils jouaient,** etc.). This tense indicates past circumstances or actions in progress *(he was speaking, they were playing, etc.)*. **C'était** is the imperfect of **être.**

En général

3 Parcourez le texte une première fois pour vérifier vos prédictions.

4 Parcourez le texte une deuxième fois pour identifier les paragraphes qui correspondent aux titres suivants. Attention, il y a un titre supplémentaire qu'on ne peut pas utiliser!

paragraphe	titre
1. «Moi, je ne comprends pas... »	a. Nicolas, la balle et M. Bordenave
2. «Aujourd'hui, par exemple... »	b. La fin de la récréation
3. «Et mon sandwich... »	c. Comment Alceste a perdu *(lost)* son sandwich
4. «Et alors, qu'est-ce qu'on fait... »	d. Les avantages et les désavantages de la pluie
5. «Pendant l'absence... »	e. L'accident d'Agnan
6. «M. Bordenave s'est relevé... »	f. La tragédie à l'infirmerie
7. «Alors, mon vieux... »	g. La bataille *(fight)* avec les grands
	h. Dialogue entre les deux surveillants

M. Bordenave n'aime pas le soleil

1 Moi, je ne comprends pas monsieur Bordenave quand il dit qu'il n'aime pas le beau temps. C'est vrai que la pluie ce n'est pas chouette. Bien sûr, on peut s'amuser aussi quand il pleut. On peut marcher dans l'eau, on peut boire la pluie, et à la maison c'est bien, parce qu'il fait chaud et on joue avec le train électrique et maman fait du chocolat avec des gâteaux. Mais quand il pleut, on n'a pas de récré° à l'école, parce qu'on ne peut pas descendre dans la cour. C'est pour ça que je ne comprends pas M. Bordenave, puisque° lui aussi profite du beau temps, c'est lui qui nous surveille à la récré.

récréation
parce que

2 Aujourd'hui, par exemple, il a fait très beau, avec beaucoup de soleil et on a eu une récré terrible°. Après trois jours de pluie, c'était vraiment chouette. On est arrivés dans la cour et Rufus et Eudes ont commencé à se battre. Rufus est tombé sur Alceste qui était en train de manger un sandwich à la confiture et le sandwich est tombé par terre et Alceste a commencé à crier. Monsieur Bordenave est arrivé en courant°, il a séparé Eudes et Rufus et il les a mis au piquet.

(ici) formidable

running

3 «Et mon sandwich, a demandé Alceste, qui va me le rendre°?» —«Tu veux aller au piquet aussi?» a dit monsieur Bordenave. «Non, moi je veux mon sandwich à la confiture», a dit Alceste qui mangeait un autre sandwich à la confiture. «Mais tu es en train d'en manger un!» a dit monsieur Bordenave. «Ce n'est pas une raison, a crié Alceste, j'apporte quatre sandwichs pour la récré et je veux manger quatre sandwichs!» Monsieur Bordenave n'a pas eu le temps de se fâcher, parce qu'il a reçu une balle sur la tête, pof! «Qui a fait ça?» a crié monsieur Bordenave. «C'est Nicolas, monsieur, je l'ai vu!» a dit Agnan. Agnan c'est le meilleur élève de la classe et le chouchou de la maîtresse°, nous, on ne l'aime pas trop, mais il a des lunettes° et on ne peut pas le battre aussi souvent qu'on veut. «Je confisque la balle! Et toi, tu vas au piquet!» il m'a dit, monsieur

donner

l'institutrice
glasses

Bordenave. Moi je lui ai dit que c'était injuste parce que c'était un accident. Agnan a eu l'air tout content et il est parti avec son livre. Agnan ne joue pas pendant la récré, il lit. Il est fou, Agnan!

4   «Et alors, qu'est-ce qu'on fait pour le sandwich à la confiture?» a demandé Alceste. Il n'a pas pu répondre parce qu'Agnan était par terre et poussait des cris terribles. «Quoi encore?» a demandé monsieur Bordenave. «C'est Geoffroy! Il m'a poussé! Mes lunettes! Je meurs°!» a dit Agnan qui saignait du nez° et qui pleurait. M. Bordenave l'a emmené à l'infirmerie, suivi d'Alceste qui lui parlait de son sandwich à la confiture.

I'm dying / qui... whose nose was bleeding

5   Pendant l'absence de monsieur Bordenave, nous on a décidé de jouer au foot. Le problème c'est que les grands jouaient déjà au foot dans la cour et on a commencé à se battre. M. Bordenave qui revenait de l'infirmerie avec Agnan et Alceste est venu en courant mais il n'est pas arrivé, parce qu'il a glissé sur le sandwich à la confiture d'Alceste et il est tombé. «Bravo, a dit Alceste, marchez-lui dessus°, à mon sandwich à la confiture!»

marchez... step on it

6   Monsieur Bordenave s'est relevé et il s'est frotté le pantalon° et il s'est mis plein de° confiture sur la main. Nous on avait recommencé à se battre et c'était une récré vraiment chouette, mais monsieur Bordenave a regardé sa montre° et il est allé en boitant sonner la cloche°. La récré était finie.

s'est... brushed his pants off
mis... put lots of
watch
sonner... ring the bell

7   «Alors, mon vieux Bordenave, a dit un autre surveillant, ça s'est bien passé°? —Comme d'habitude, a dit monsieur Bordenave, qu'est-ce que tu veux, moi, je prie pour la pluie, et quand je me lève le matin et que je vois qu'il fait beau, je suis désespéré!»

ça... did it go well?

8   Non, vraiment, moi je ne comprends pas monsieur Bordenave, quand il dit qu'il n'aime pas le soleil!

Extrait de *Le petit Nicolas* (Jean-Jacques Sempé et René Goscinny)

5 Les mots.   D'après le contexte, quel est le sens des mots suivants? Choisissez a ou b.

¶1	s'amuser	a. to have fun	b. to be bored
	profiter (de)	a. to take advantage (of)	b. to suffer (from)
¶2	en train de	a. on a train	b. in the process of
¶3	le chouchou	a. teacher's pet	b. class clown
	avoir l'air	a. to breathe	b. to seem
¶4	emmener	a. to call	b. to take
¶5	revenir (revenait)	a. to go back	b. to come back
¶6	se relever (s'est relevé)	a. to pick oneself up	b. to lie down
¶7	comme d'habitude	a. as usual	b. for once
	prier	a. to pray	b. to choose
	se lever (je me lève)	a. to go to bed	b. to get up

6 Le texte.   Complétez selon l'histoire avec le ou les mots qui conviennent.

1. Quand il pleut, on peut _s'amuser_ , _marcher dans l'eau_ et _boire la pluie_ , mais on ne peut pas _descendre dans la cour_ .

2. Alceste a commencé à _crier_ parce que son sandwich _est tombé par terre_ . Alors M. Bordenave a puni (*punished*) _Eudes_ et _Rufus_ .

3. Alceste a trois autres _sandwichs_ mais il insiste pour en avoir _quatre_ .

4. Nicolas et ses copains n'aiment pas beaucoup _Agnan_ mais ils ne peuvent pas le battre aussi souvent qu'ils veulent parce qu'il a des _lunettes_ —peut-être aussi parce que c'est _le chouchou_ de la maîtresse.

5. Agnan a dit à M. Bordenave que c'est _Nicolas_ qui lui a jeté une balle sur la tête.

6. Agnan est fou parce qu'il _lit_ pendant la récré.

7. _Agnan_ a besoin d'aller à l'infirmerie parce que _Geoffroy_ l'a poussé et il est tombé par terre.

8. Alceste, qui continue à parler de son _sandwich_ , accompagne _Agnan_ et _M. Bordenave_ à l'infirmerie.

9. Quand Nicolas et ses copains ont décidé de jouer au _foot_ ils ont commencé à se battre avec _les grands_ .

10. M. Bordenave a glissé sur _le sandwich_ . Après, il avait _de la confiture_ sur son pantalon et sur sa main.

11. Nicolas et ses copains pensent qu'une récré est vraiment
    __chouette_____ quand on peut se battre.

12. __M. Bordenave_____ est désespéré quand __il fait beau_____ .

Encourage students to work on this in small groups, then have various groups read their report. Compare, discuss, edit together.

1. Est-ce que vous comprenez M. Bordenave quand il dit qu'il n'aime pas le soleil? Expliquez.

2. Imaginez que M. Bordenave fait un rapport au directeur de l'école sur cette récréation. Écrivez ce rapport, selon le point de vue de M. Bordenave, avec tous les détails nécessaires.

Par écrit: It depends on your point of view . . .

Avant d'écrire

Have student groups brainstorm part 1 and share their responses with the class. Then, in part 2, have students make notes on their personal experiences.

To facilitate understanding, have students say what they're going to do this month using the futur proche and the adverbs in the left-hand column (and others as appropriate). List the infinitives and adverbs on the board. Now ask them to imagine it's a month later and have them relate what they did—in the past—using the passé composé and the adverbs in the right-hand column.

A. Strategy: Taking a point of view.   The stories of **petit Nicolas** are recognized and loved world-wide, in part, because their commentary on the adult world is presented from the naive (hence humorous) viewpoint of a child. Differences in point of view occur because different narrators focus on different aspects of an event, and sometimes a single narrator's viewpoint changes because of circumstances.

Application.   (1) Imagine the story, *Monsieur Bordenave n'aime pas le soleil*, if told by the **surveillant** years later, after Nicolas has become an internationally known celebrity. How would the story differ? (2) Think back to a memorable vacation or day trip you took as a small child and make some notes. What events were most memorable to you? Would your parents answer in the same way? Were your feelings about the trip any different after it than they were before?

B. Strategy: Expressing time.   When you talk about the future in a present context, for instance when you state your plans, you use the *futur proche*. When you talk about the future in a past context, for instance when you tell a story, you use the past tense. The adverbial time expressions for each instance vary. See the following table.

VOCABULAIRE ACTIF

après
le lendemain
suivant(e)

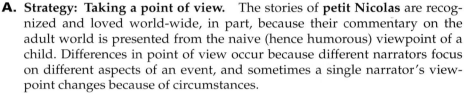

To talk about the future	
in a present context	**in a past context**
demain	le lendemain (*the next day*)
dans une semaine	une semaine après (*a week later*)
samedi prochain	le samedi suivant (*the next Saturday*)

Application.   Write three pairs of sentences using the preceding expressions to talk about the future in a present and then a past context.

➡ *Samedi prochain nous allons voir un match de hockey.*
   Le samedi suivant nous sommes allés voir un match de hockey.

ÉCRIVEZ

1. Racontez l'histoire, *Monsieur Bordenave n'aime pas le soleil,* selon le point de vue d'un copain de Nicolas, Alceste ou Agnan, par exemple.
2. Regardez les images suivantes. Selon vous, qu'est-ce qui s'est passé *(what happened)* pendant les vacances de cette famille? Mettez-vous *(Put yourself)* à la place d'un des enfants ou d'un des parents, puis écrivez deux paragraphes de son point de vue: le premier «avant les vacances»; le deuxième «après les vacances». N'oubliez pas d'employer des expressions de transition et, pour éviter la répétition, des pronoms d'objet direct ou indirect. À mentionner: destination, temps, activités et réactions pour chaque personne, autres détails.

➡ (Avant) *Nous allons passer des vacances...* (vraiment chouettes? intéressantes?)
(Après) *Nous avons passé des vacances...* (horribles? vraiment chouettes?)

VOCABULAIRE ACTIF

Le climat et le temps

Il fait du soleil / du vent / du brouillard *It is sunny / windy / foggy*
Il fait beau / bon / mauvais / chaud / frais / froid *The weather is nice / pleasant / bad / hot / cool / cold*
Le temps est ensoleillé / variable / nuageux / orageux *The weather is sunny / changing / cloudy / stormy*
Le ciel est couvert. *It's cloudy, overcast.*
Il pleut. *It's raining.*
Il neige. *It's snowing.*
la neige *snow*
un nuage *a cloud*
un orage *a thunderstorm*
la pluie *rain*
la température

Les points cardinaux et la géographie

le nord *north*   l'ouest *west*
le sud *south*   une montagne *a mountain*
l'est (m.) *east*   un pays *a country*

Les saisons (f.)

le printemps *spring*   l'été (m.) *summer*   l'automne (m.) *fall*   l'hiver (m.) *winter*

Les passe-temps (m.)

LA LECTURE

une bande dessinée / une B.D.
   a cartoon, a comic strip
une histoire *a story*
un journal *a newspaper*

une lettre *a letter*
un poème *a poem*
un rapport *a report*
un roman *a novel*

LA TÉLÉVISION

une chaîne *a channel*
changer de chaîne *to change the channel*
un dessin animé *a cartoon*
une émission *a show, a program*
un feuilleton *a soap opera, a series*
un jeu télévisé *a game show*
le journal télévisé (les informations) *the news*

un programme *a TV guide*
une pub *a commercial*
la télé-commande *the remote control*
les variétés (f.) *a variety show*
zapper *to channel surf*
un zappeur

LE CINÉMA

un drame psychologique *a psychological
   drama*
un film d'épouvante *a horror movie*

un film policier *a detective film*
le genre (de film) *the kind (of film)*

LES SPORTS

le base-ball
la course *running*
le cyclisme *cycling*
le hockey

le judo
le patinage *skating*
le ski
le stade *a stadium*

Verbes et expressions verbales

arriver *to arrive*
avoir envie (de) *to feel like*
dire *to say*
écrire *to write*
entrer *to enter, to come in*
lire *to read*
monter *to go up, to get on*

passer (par) *to pass (through, by)*
rentrer *to come home*
rester *to stay*
retourner *to go back*
tomber *to fall*
voir *to see*

Expressions de temps

à l'heure *on time*
l'année prochaine / dernière *next year / last year*
dans une semaine *in a week*
demain matin, après-midi, soir *tomorrow
   morning, afternoon, evening*
hier matin, après-midi, soir *yesterday
   morning, afternoon, evening*

en avance *early*
en retard *late*
il y a (trois jours) *(three days) ago*
le lendemain *the next day*
le samedi suivant *the following Saturday*
une semaine après *a week later*
la semaine prochaine / dernière *next week / last week*

Les invitations

POUR INVITER

Ça t'intéresse? / Ça te dit? / Ça vous intéresse? *Are you interested?*
Je t'invite / Je vous invite *I'm inviting you (My treat!)*
Tu veux... / Voudriez-vous... ? *Would you like to . . .*

POUR ACCEPTER

Avec plaisir *I'd love to*	D'accord *Okay*
Bonne idée! *Good idea!*	Entendu! *Good!*
C'est parfait! *It's perfect!*	Je veux bien *I'd be glad to*
C'est génial! *That's cool!*	Volontiers *Gladly*

POUR S'EXCUSER

C'est gentil, mais je ne peux pas *It's very nice of you, but I can't*
Je suis désolé(e), mais je ne suis pas libre *I'm sorry, but I'm not available*
Malheureusement, je n'ai pas le temps *Unfortunately, I don't have time*

Les pronoms d'objet direct et indirect

le, la, l' *it, him, her*	lui *(to) him, her*
les *them*	leur *(to) them*

Divers

un message électronique *an e-mail*
une sortie *an outing, a night out*
la vérité *the truth*

Voyages et transports

EPP 6005

EPP 6005

Ces gens reviennent de vacances.

Où sont-ils allés?

Qu'ont-ils fait?

Et vous?

Quand allez-vous partir en vacances?

Où voulez-vous aller?

Pendant combien de temps allez-vous y rester?

Comment allez-vous voyager?

This chapter will enable you to

- **understand conversations related to travel**
- **read travel brochures and an excerpt from *Le Petit Prince***
- **talk about places you've been or would like to visit**
- **discuss vacation activities**
- **ask for information or help**

Première étape

À l'écoute: À l'hôtel

Cue to Video Module 7 (00:31:19), where Élisabeth and Fatima make travel plans and hotel reservations.

Dans cette étape, vous allez entendre une conversation qui a lieu dans un hôtel de Quimper, en Bretagne.

Avant d'écouter

This input section introduces students to hotel vocabulary and transactions.

1 Imaginez que vous voyagez en Bretagne, une province de l'ouest de la France. Vous arrivez à Quimper, une ville touristique connue pour sa cathédrale et ses vieux quartiers, et vous cherchez un hôtel. Vous consultez donc un guide. Avec un(e) partenaire, étudiez ce guide et la légende des abréviations qui l'accompagne, puis remplissez le tableau à la page suivante.

LÉGENDE DES ABRÉVIATIONS

❦	= Jardin		📺	= Télévision dans la chambre
⚲	= Tennis		≈	= Vue sur lac, rivière, canal
⚱	= Piscine		M	= Vue sur mer
🅿	= Parking		☆	= Petit déjeuner
🚗	= Garage		S.R.	= Sans restaurant
🐕	= Chiens admis		L.F.	= Logis de France
↕	= Ascenseur			
♿	= Chambres accessibles aux handicapés physiques			
☎	= Téléphone dans la chambre			

LOCALITÉS HOTELS-ADRESSES CONFORT	Téléphone	Nbre de chambres	PRIX	
			Chambre mini/maxi	R
9000 QUIMPER - C2				
★★★ HOTEL GRADLON 30, RUE DE BREST LF ❦ 🚗 ☎ 📺	02.98.95.04.39	24	315/395	S.R.
★★★ HOTEL LE GRIFFON 131, ROUTE DE BENODET ⚱ 🅿 ☎ 🐕 📺	02.98.90.33.33	49	330/450	☆
★★★ NOVOTEL QUIMPER 2, RUE DU POHER ⚱ ❦ 🅿 ☎ 🐕 ♿ 📺 ↕	02.98.90.46.26	92	470/520	☆
★★ HOTEL ARCADE 21BIS, AVENUE DE LA GARE ❦ 🚗 ☎ 🐕 ♿ 📺 ↕	02.98.90.31.71	63	290/355	S.R.
★★ HOTEL DUPLEIX 34, BOULEVARD DUPLEIX 🚗 ☎ ≈ ♿ 📺 ↕	02.98.90.53.35	29	330/400	☆
★★ HOTEL IBIS RUE GUSTAVE EIFFEL 🅿 ☎ 🐕 ♿ 📺	02.98.90.53.80	72	290/320	☆
★★ HOTEL LA SAPINIERE 286, ROUTE DE BENODET Tx 940 034 ⚲ 🅿 ☎ ♿ 📺	02.98.90.39.63	39	125/260	S.R.
★ HOTEL BALLADINS (ERGUE GABERIC) 🅿 ☎ 🐕 ♿ 📺	02.98.59.55.00	38	195/219	☆
★ HOTEL PASCAL 17, AVENUE DE LA GARE 🅿 ☎ 🐕 📺	02.98.90.00.81	20	140/240	☆

Vous préférez un hôtel...	Vos choix possibles sont... (Donnez le nom des hôtels)
avec une piscine	Novotel
avec un jardin	Gradlon, Novotel, Arcade
avec un ascenseur *(elevator)*	Novotel, Arcade, Dupleix
avec un garage	Gradlon, Arcade, Dupleix
où les chiens sont admis	Le Griffon, Novotel, Arcade, Ibis, Balladins, Pascal
qui sert le petit déjeuner	Le Griffon, Novotel, Dupleix, Ibis, Balladins, Pascal
qui coûte moins de 250 F la nuit (prix maximum)	Balladins, Pascal

Écoutons

2 ANSWERS: 1a. V
1b. F (Elle ne mentionne
pas les bagages.) 1c. V
2a. F (au moins deux nuits)
2b. F (deux personnes) 2c. V

Audio CD

2 Écoutez une ou deux fois en fonction des questions suivantes. Les phrases suivantes sont-elles vraies ou fausses? Si elles sont fausses, corrigez-les.

1. La réceptionniste demande au client
   a. combien de temps il veut rester à l'hôtel.
   b. s'il a des bagages.
   c. de payer tout de suite (immédiatement).
2. Le client veut
   a. rester seulement une nuit *(one night only).*
   b. une chambre pour une personne.
   c. payer avec une carte de crédit.

3 ANSWERS: 1. 340 F 2. Alain
Chesnel 3. 27

3 Écoutez encore et répondez aux questions suivantes.

1. Combien coûte la chambre que prend le monsieur?
2. Comment s'appelle le monsieur?
3. Quel est le numéro de sa chambre?

4 Students can do this activity
in pairs, then report on their
conclusions and the clues that led
them to the conclusions (context,
background knowledge, etc.).

4 Écoutez une dernière fois et complétez les phrases suivantes, puis déduisez le sens des mots en caractères gras.

1. Quand on entre dans un hôtel, on demande: «_Pardon_____, madame (monsieur), vous avez _une chambre_____ **libre,** s'il vous plaît?»

2. Le monsieur veut une chambre avec **baignoire** ou _douche_____, si possible.

3. Il demande si le _petit déjeuner_____ est **compris.**

4. La dame lui donne sa **clé** et lui indique que sa chambre est au _premier_____ **étage.**

5 ANSWER: Hôtel Dupleix.
Seulement trois hôtels ont un
ascenseur. Le Novotel Quimper
coûte plus cher (prix minimum
470 F); l'hôtel Arcade n'a pas de
restaurant.

5 Maintenant consultez encore le guide des hôtels de Quimper. De quel hôtel s'agit-il? Justifiez votre réponse.

6 Imaginez que vous voulez réserver une chambre dans un hôtel de Quimper. Jouez les rôles suivants avec un(e) partenaire: l'un(e) de vous est le/la touriste, l'autre le/la réceptionniste. D'abord, sélectionnez ensemble un hôtel qui vous plaît, puis jouez la situation au téléphone. «Allô?...»

Note culturelle

Les hôtels. A star system is used to categorize hotels in France. Four-star hotels **(quatre étoiles)** are the most luxurious. **Une étoile** indicates more basic accommodations, which means that each room has **un lavabo** *(sink)*, but the toilet and the shower may be down the hall. Several chains of inexpensive hotels, such as **Formule 1** or **Nuit d'Hôtel** are springing up all over France, near freeway exits. Rooms are small, but cost under 150 francs ($20–$30) for one to three people. If you stay in a French hotel, don't be surprised if the clerk tells you your room is **au premier étage** and points you to the stairs **(l'escalier)** or the elevator **(l'ascenseur)**. In France, the first floor is called **le rez-de-chaussée**, the second floor **le premier étage**, and so on.

VOCABULAIRE ACTIF

un ascenseur
les bagages (m.)
une baignoire
une carte de crédit
(une chambre) libre
un chien
une clé
un escalier
un garage
un jardin
un lavabo
la nuit
le petit déjeuner
   compris
une piscine
le premier étage, etc.
un(e) réceptionniste
le rez-de-chaussée
tout de suite

La rue Kéréon à Quimper.

Prononciation *Les semi-voyelles* [w] *et* [ɥ]

■ A semi-vowel is a short vowel sound that is combined with another vowel in the same syllable.

■ [w] is the initial sound in **oui** [wi]; it is a short [u] sound that is also found in **soir** [swar].

■ [ɥ] is the initial sound in **huit** [ɥit]; it is a short [y] sound that glides into the following vowel, in this case [i].

Écoutez   Listen to the following expressions from **À l'écoute: À l'hôtel** on the student audio CD and in the following chart check the [w] and [ɥ] sounds you hear. The first expression is done for you. You will hear each expression twice.

Audio CD

	[w]	[ɥ]
au m**oi**ns	✔	
deux n**ui**ts		
avec baign**oi**re		
tout de s**ui**te		
v**oi**ci		

Now can you match the following spelling combinations with the appropriate phonetic symbols?

    ou + vowel   [ɥ]
    oi/oy   [w]
    u + vowel*   [wa]

Essayez!   **A. Prononcez.**   Practice pronouncing and contrasting the sounds [w] and [ɥ] in the following pairs. Then listen to them on the student audio CD to verify your pronunciation.

Audio CD

    [w]   [ɥ]
  1. oui   huit
  2. Louis   lui
  3. moins juin

B. [w] ou [ɥ]?   In the following sentences, underline the [w] sounds with one line, and the [ɥ] sounds with two lines.

  1. Quand Marie-Louise voyage, elle prend toujours des fruits et des biscuits.
  2. L'Hôtel des Trois Suisses? Continuez jusqu'au coin de la rue, puis tournez à droite.
  3. Chouette! Il n'y a pas de nuages aujourd'hui. C'est ennuyeux, des vacances sous la pluie.
  4. Je suis fatigué; bonne nuit!

Now practice saying the sentences aloud, then listen to them on the student audio CD to verify your pronunciation.

---

*Exception: after a **q** or a **g,** the **u** is generally not pronounced: qui [ki]; quel [kɛl]; Guy [gi]; guerre *(war)* [gɛr].

STRUCTURE: Talking about travel (I)
*Les verbes comme **sortir***

Observez et déduisez   Angèle Martin fait un séjour à l'Hôtel Dupleix, le même hôtel qu'Alain Chesnel. On lui sert le petit déjeuner à 8 h 30; après ça, elle sort pour visiter les vieux quartiers. Aujourd'hui, elle est rentrée à onze heures du soir, et elle est allée au lit tout de suite. Après cette longue journée, elle a bien dormi! Demain elle part pour Bruxelles.

> ■ Look at the present tense forms of the verbs **servir**, **sortir**, and **partir** in the preceding paragraph. What would be the third-person singular form of the verb **dormir?**
>
> ■ Look at the past participle of **dormir.** What would be the past participles of **partir**, **servir**, and **sortir?**

Vérifiez   *Les verbes comme **sortir***

VOCABULAIRE ACTIF

dormir
faire un séjour
partir
servir
sortir

Les verbes comme **sortir**	
servir	**dormir**
je sers	je dors
tu sers	tu dors
il /elle / on sert	il / elle / on dort
nous servons	nous dormons
vous servez	vous dormez
ils / elles servent	ils / elles dorment

OPTIONAL DRILL: Draw students' attention to the different oral and written forms. Ask how many forms they see, then read the conjugation and ask how many forms they hear. Ask which endings are not pronounced. Point out the consonant sound in the plural. As you read cues, have students hold up either one finger for singular or two fingers for plural. CUES: 1. Il sert le petit déjeuner. 2. Elles partent à dix heures. 3. Ils ne sortent pas de l'hôtel. 4. Elle part pour Paris. 5. Il dort bien le soir. 6. Elles ne servent pas de vin. 7. Il sort l'après-midi. 8. Elles dorment jusqu'à midi.

Les verbes comme **sortir**	
partir	**sortir**
je pars	je sors
tu pars	tu sors
il / elle / on part	il / elle / on sort
nous partons	nous sortons
vous partez	vous sortez
ils / elles partent	ils / elles sortent

Passé composé

j'ai servi   j'ai dormi   je **suis** parti(e)   je **suis** sorti(e)

■ Verbs like **sortir** have two stems. The plural stem is formed by dropping the **-ir** of the infinitive. The singular stem drops the consonant preceding the **-ir** as well.

plural: nous **sort**-ons   singular: je **sor**-s

Elicit other verbs that are conjugated with **être** (**aller, arriver, rester, rentrer, entrer, monter, passer, retourner, tomber**). A summary chart appears on p. 250.

■ Notice that in the passé composé, **sortir** and **partir** are conjugated with **être**. This means that the past participle must agree with the subject in number and gender.

Angèle **est sortie** tôt.   Les filles **sont parties** le 15 mai.

OPTIONAL DRILL: Transformez les phrases en remplaçant le sujet. CUES: 1. On sert le dîner à 20 h? (nous, les restaurants, maman, tu) 2. Les touristes partent à midi. (je, vous, nous, Claire) 3. Tu sors souvent? (les étudiants, vous, ton professeur, tu) 4. Nous dormons bien. (je, mes parents, vous, tu)

■ Both **sortir** and **partir** can be used alone or with a preposition, but to convey the idea of leaving a particular place, both verbs must be followed by **de**.

Angèle **sort**. *(is going out)*   Elle **sort de** l'hôtel. (du supermarché, de sa chambre)

Elle **part** demain. *(is leaving)*   Elle **part de** Quimper. (de la gare, du musée)

■ Other prepositions are also used with these verbs.

Elle sort **avec** ses amis.   Elle part **pour** Paris.

ACTIVITÉS

A. After students work in pairs, have a volunteer read the statements to the class and record responses on the board. Elicit summary statements based on those responses, e.g., «L'étudiant typique ne sort pas le dimanche.» FOLLOW-UP: Ask questions: «Vous ne sortez pas le dimanche? Alors, quand est-ce que vous sortez? Qu'est-ce que vous faites le dimanche si vous ne sortez pas?... »

A. Vrai ou faux? Malheureusement, vous n'êtes pas en vacances comme Mme Martin. D'abord, indiquez si ces phrases sont vraies ou fausses pour votre vie de tous les jours, puis interviewez un(e) camarade de classe pour comparer vos réponses.

	moi	partenaire
1. Mes copains et moi, nous sortons souvent le dimanche.	_____	_____
2. Mes parents ne sortent jamais.	_____	_____
3. Le matin, je pars pour mes cours avant neuf heures.	_____	_____
4. Mon/Ma camarade de chambre part toujours à la dernière minute.	_____	_____

5. Au restaurant universitaire, on sert de bons _____ _____
repas.

6. Chez moi, nous ne servons jamais de poisson. _____ _____

7. Après un bon dîner, moi, je dors tout de suite. _____ _____

8. Je dors huit heures par nuit. _____ _____

Maintenant, partagez vos réponses avec vos camarades de classe. Comment est la vie de l'étudiant typique?

B. Help students with follow-up questions by brainstorming question words (**où, avec qui, pourquoi, à quelle heure, quel(le),** etc.) before beginning the activity.

B. Curiosité. Qu'est-ce que vos camarades de classe ont fait récemment? Pour chaque question que vous posez, trouvez une personne différente qui répond affirmativement. Posez une question complémentaire *(follow-up)*—même si la personne répond négativement.

➡ — *Tu es sorti(e) hier soir?*   — *Tu es sorti(e) hier soir?*
— *Oui, je suis sorti(e).*   — *Non, je ne suis pas sorti(e).*
— *Où est-ce que tu es allé(e)?*   — *Pourquoi pas?*
— *Je suis allé(e) à la bibliothèque.*   — *J'ai fait mes devoirs.*

1. Tu es sorti(e) hier soir?
2. Tu es rentré(e) très tard?
3. Tu as bien dormi?
4. Tu es resté(e) à la maison samedi dernier?
5. Tu es allé(e) voir un bon film récemment?
6. Tu es parti(e) pour tes cours avant huit heures ce matin?
7. Tu es arrivé(e) à l'heure au cours de français?
8. Tu as servi du gâteau au professeur?

STRUCTURES: Saying how long or how long ago
Depuis / Il y a / Pendant

Observez et déduisez Angèle Martin est partie en vacances il y a une semaine pour un voyage en France. Elle a voyagé pendant onze heures pour arriver à Quimper. Maintenant, elle est à l'hôtel Dupleix depuis huit jours.

> ■ Three time expressions are used in the preceding **Observez et déduisez.** Which one suggests how long an activity *has been going on?* Which one is used to state *how long ago* something happened? Which one indicates how long an activity *lasted?*

Vérifiez *Depuis*

Tell students that English uses *for* or *since,* but the main criterion for **depuis** is that the action *is still going on.* Give students several personal examples, e.g., «Je suis professeur depuis... ; j'habite à _____ depuis... ; je parle français depuis... »

■ Use **depuis** and an expression of time to indicate *how long something has been going on.* Although the activity began in the past, it is still going on, so use the *present* tense of the verb.

On sert le petit déjeuner **depuis** une heure.
Angèle est à l'hôtel **depuis** lundi dernier.

If students ask about the difference between the two expressions, explain that although **depuis quand** requires a date for a response and **depuis combien de temps** requires a period of time, in the spoken language **depuis quand** is often used in both cases.

Remind students that this expression has a completely different meaning and use than **il y a** as introduced in Ch. 2, 1ᵉ étape, where **il y a** is followed by an indefinite article and a noun.

■ To ask how long something has been going on, use the expression **depuis quand?** *(since when)* or **depuis combien de temps?** *(for how long).*

> **Depuis quand** est-elle à l'hôtel? **Depuis** samedi dernier.
> **Depuis combien de temps** est-ce qu'elle est à l'hôtel? **Depuis** une semaine.

Il y a

■ You learned in Chapter 6 that **il y a** can be used with a period of time to say *how long ago something happened.* Since the activity has been completed, use the past tense.

> Elle est arrivée **il y a** huit jours. (trois minutes, un an, etc.)

■ To ask how long ago something happened, use **Quand?**

> — **Quand** est-ce qu'elle est arrivée?
> — Il y a une heure.

Pendant

VOCABULAIRE ACTIF

Depuis combien de temps?
Depuis quand?
Pendant combien de temps?

■ Use **pendant** to indicate *the duration of an event* in the past, present, or future.

> Après son voyage, elle a dormi **pendant** dix heures.
> On sert le petit déjeuner **pendant** une heure et demie.
> Elle va voyager **pendant** toute la nuit.

■ To ask about the duration of an event or activity, use the interrogative expression **pendant combien de temps?**

> **Pendant combien de temps** est-ce qu'il a dormi?
> est-ce qu'il dort d'habitude?
> est-ce qu'il va dormir?

Des expressions de temps	
Question	**Réponse**
Depuis quand est-il à l'hôtel?	**Depuis** hier. (**Depuis** 15 h.)
Depuis combien de temps est-il à l'hôtel?	**Depuis** deux jours. (**Depuis** vingt minutes.)
Quand est-ce qu'il est arrivé à l'hôtel?	Il est arrivé **il y a** vingt minutes. (... **il y a** trois jours.)
Pendant combien de temps va-t-il rester à l'hôtel?	**Pendant** une semaine.

ACTIVITÉS

C. Clients. Indiquez de qui on parle selon le registre de l'hôtel Dupleix ci-dessous. *(Aujourd'hui c'est le mardi 15 mai.)*

1. Cette personne est à l'hôtel depuis deux jours. C'est Henri Duclos .

2. Cette personne va être à l'hôtel pendant dix jours. C'est
   Claude Grimmer .

3. Cette personne est arrivée il y a huit jours. C'est Angèle Martin .

4. Cette personne est partie il y a trois jours. C'est Antoine Bonal .

5. Cette personne part aujourd'hui. C'est Mme Mystère .

6. Cette personne est à l'hôtel depuis lundi. C'est Mme Péron .

7. Ces personnes vont être à Quimper pendant deux semaines. C'est
   Angèle Martin et Mme Mystère .

Chambre N°	Clients	Arrivée	Départ prévu
10	Claude Grimmer	1 mai	11 mai
27	Mme Mystère	1 mai	15 mai
32	Angèle Martin	7 mai	21 mai
35	Antoine Bonal	9 mai	12 mai
15	Henri Duclos	13 mai	19 mai
44	Mme Péron	14 mai	18 mai
	Nouradine Charfi	8 mai	18 mai
	Pierre Bonnet	13 mai	20 mai

Maintenant, complétez le registre avec les dates d'arrivée et de départ prévues pour les deux autres clients:

- Nouradine Charfi est à l'hôtel depuis une semaine. Il va être à Quimper pendant dix jours.
- Pierre Bonnet est arrivé à Quimper il y a deux jours. Il va rester à l'hôtel pendant une semaine.

D. Students can use names of classmates/friends for the guests. By using the current date as a point of reference along with the arrival and departure dates they choose, students can say how long a guest has been at the hotel and how long s/he will be there. The goal is to complete the partner's "register" as accurately as possible by asking questions.

D. Un jeu. Imaginez que vous travaillez dans un hôtel. D'abord inventez tous les renseignements pour compléter le registre à gauche ci-dessous. Votre partenaire va faire la même chose. Ensuite, posez des questions à votre partenaire pour compléter *son* registre, à droite.

➡ *Comment s'appelle le client dans la chambre numéro... ?*
Depuis combien de temps est-ce qu'il/elle est à l'hôtel?
Pendant combien de temps est-ce qu'il/elle va être à l'hôtel?

Mon hôtel

Chambre Nº	Client	Arrivée	Départ prévu
15			
23			
25			
31			

L'hôtel de mon/ma partenaire

Chambre Nº	Client	Arrivée	Départ prévu
15			
23			
25			
31			

Maintenant comparez vos registres. Avez-vous bien noté les renseignements?

Jeu de rôle

You're a guest at the Hotel Dupleix, and you're spending a few moments visiting with other guests (two classmates) as you wait for breakfast. One person is in Quimper on a business trip **(un voyage d'affaires),** the second is there on vacation, and the third is moving there and looking for a house to rent. Ask one another the reasons for your visit, when you arrived, how long you've been there, how long you're staying, when you're leaving, etc. If you enjoy your conversation, you might want to invite the others to go out. Discuss some possible outings.

Deuxième étape

Lecture: Un voyage en Afrique

1 Qu'est-ce que vous aimez faire pendant les vacances? Regardez les deux illustrations, puis cochez les activités que vous aimez et ajoutez d'autres options si vous le désirez.

This input section introduces students to vocabulary about vacations and prepositions with geographical names.

1 Model the pronunciation of the expressions and make sure their meaning is clear; then have students discuss their preferences in small groups and report on them afterwards.

une voiture — une montagne — une promenade à pied

une forêt

la chasse

un vélo

la pêche

un lac

_____ voyager en train

_____ voyager en avion

_____ découvrir une région en voiture

_____ faire des promenades à pied ou en vélo

_____ explorer la nature—la montagne, le désert, la forêt

_____ faire du camping

_____ aller à la pêche ou à la chasse

_____ aller à la plage

_____ nager dans la mer, dans un lac ou dans une piscine

_____ faire du bateau ou du ski nautique

_____ visiter des villes historiques avec leurs vieux quartiers et leurs monuments

_____ visiter des châteaux, des musées, des églises et des cathédrales

_____ acheter des souvenirs

_____ manger des plats exotiques

_____ danser dans une discothèque

_____ ?

un bateau   un avion   le ski nautique   la mer   nager   la plage

2 Regardez la carte du monde francophone au début du livre. Quels sont les trois pays francophones d'Afrique du Nord? Quels sont les pays francophones de l'Afrique occidentale (de l'ouest)?

3 Maintenant imaginez qu'on vous offre la possibilité de passer une semaine en Tunisie ou au Sénégal. Comment imaginez-vous ces pays?

The description on the left applies to Senegal. Clues for Tunisia (on the right): **méditerranéen, le Sahara.**

1. À votre avis, laquelle des descriptions suivantes s'applique au climat de la Tunisie? du Sénégal?

Climat très agréable et sec *(dry)* de novembre à mars. Très chaud (plus de 30°) de juin à septembre avec précipitations.

Climat méditerranéen, doux et humide en hiver. Pas d'intersaison; été sec et chaud (25°–28°), très chaud dans le Sahara.

2. Parmi les activités touristiques mentionnées dans **Avant de lire,** lesquelles, à votre avis, peut-on faire dans ces deux pays?

En général

4 Parcourez rapidement les deux textes. De quel genre de textes s'agit-il? Cochez toutes les réponses correctes.

✔ Des extraits d'une brochure d'une agence de voyages

_____ Des renseignements distribués par l'office de tourisme de la Tunisie et du Sénégal sur l'histoire et la géographie de leur pays

✔ Une description de voyages organisés

_____ Des renseignements sur les safaris et la chasse au lion

5 ANSWERS: découvrir une région en voiture, visiter des villes et des monuments, manger des plats exotiques, faire du bateau, explorer la nature, faire des promenades, aller à la plage.

5 Reprenez la liste des activités touristiques donnée dans **Avant de lire.** Lesquelles de ces activités sont mentionnées dans les textes?

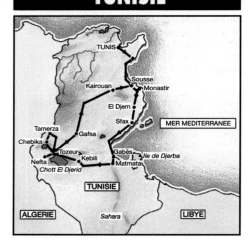

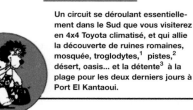

L'AVIS DU LION

Un circuit se déroulant essentiellement dans le Sud que vous visiterez en 4x4 Toyota climatisé, et qui allie la découverte de ruines romaines, mosquée, troglodytes,[1] pistes,[2] désert, oasis... et la détente[3] à la plage pour les deux derniers jours à Port El Kantaoui.

EL DJEM - GABES - MATMATA - TOZEUR - NEFTA - TAMERZA - GAFSA - KAIROUAN

Départ de France les dimanches.

1er jour: France - Tunis- Sousse. Accueil[4] à l'aéroport et transfert à Sousse. Dîner et nuit à l'hôtel El Mouradi.

2e jour: Port El Kantaoui. Journée de détente en pension complète[5] à l'hôtel El Mouradi.

3e jour: Sousse - El Djem - Gabès - Matmata - Kébili. Départ pour le Sud en 4x4 Toyota climatisé. Visite de l'amphithéâtre romain d'El Djem. Arrêt à Sfax, arrivée à Gabès et visite de l'oasis de Chenini. Déjeuner à Matmata et visite des maisons troglodytiques. Dîner et nuit à Kébili, hôtel Al Fouar, situé au milieu des dunes de sable.

4e jour: Chott El Djerid - Tozeur - Nefta. Traversée du Chott El Djerid. Déjeuner à Nefta, visite de l'oasis et route sur Tozeur pour la visite du zoo du désert. Dîner et nuit à Nefta, hôtel Les Nomades.

5e jour: Chebika - Tamerza - Gafsa - Kairouan - Sousse. Le matin, visite des oasis de montagne Chebika et Tamerza. Continuation sur Gafsa. Déjeuner. Route sur Kairouan, ville sainte de l'Islam. Dîner et nuit à l'hôtel El Mouradi de Port El Kantaoui.

6e jour: Nabeul - Port El Kantaoui. Le matin, excursion à Nabeul, ville célèbre pour ses poteries. Visite du marché. Retour à l'hôtel pour déjeuner. Après-midi libre. Le soir, départ pour un dîner spécial tunisien avec fête bédouine. Nuit hôtel El Mouradi.

7e jour: Port El Kantaoui. Journée libre de détente à l'hôtel El Mouradi en pension complète.

8e jour: Tunis - France. Petit déjeuner, transfert à l'aéroport de Tunis et envol pour la France (repas à bord).

_____

1. _cave dwellings_   2. _trails_   3. _relaxation_   4. _welcome_   5. chambre et trois repas inclus

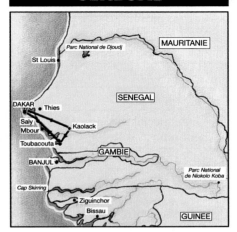

SENEGAL

DAKAR - TOUBACOUTA - NDANGANE TOUTI - SALOUM - SALY

1er jour: France - Dakar. Vol pour Dakar.

2e jour: Dakar. Arrivée matinale à l'aéroport de Yoff, transfert à votre hôtel sur la presqu'île[1] de Ngor. Excursion au lac Rose puis départ pour l'île Gorée, émouvant centre de la traite des esclaves[2] jusqu'au siècle dernier.[3] Déjeuner au restaurant Le Chevalier de Boufflers puis retour vers Dakar. Dîner et nuit à l'hôtel Le Calao, Ngor, Diarama ou similaire.

3e jour: Dakar - Toubacouta. Départ le matin pour Toubacouta. Déjeuner en route. Promenade en pirogue[4] l'après-midi dans le delta du Saloum. Dîner et nuit à l'hôtel-campement Les Palétuviers ou similaire.

4e jour: Toubacouta - Ndangane Touti. Départ après le petit déjeuner, en pirogue, pour l'île de Ndangane Touti. Déjeuner. Promenade en pirogue l'après-midi dans le delta du Saloum. Dîner et nuit au campement.

5e jour: Ndangane Touti - Toubacouta. Retour par la mer à l'hôtel Les Palétuviers. Déjeuner. Après-midi libre, promenade en brousse[5] dans le pays Sérère. Dîner et nuit à l'hôtel Les Palétuviers.

6e jour: Toubacouta - Saly. Petit déjeuner, puis visite d'un marché et de villages africains. Route pour Saly. Arrivée en fin de matinée. Déjeuner libre. Dîner et nuit au Club du Lion Saly.

7e et 8e jours: Saly. Séjour libre en demipension au Club du Lion Saly.

9e jour: Saly - France. Transfert à l'aéroport de Dakar tôt le matin et vol pour la France.

L'AVIS DU LION

Le circuit du Lion vous propose 3 journées de séjour libre sur les plages de la Petite Côte en fin de voyage. Vous découvrirez tout particulièrement la région du Siné Saloum à la richesse souvent ignorée des circuits habituels. Détente et découverte sont soigneusement dosées et le tout pour un prix attractif.

---

1. péninsule   2. *slave market*   3. *last century*   4. type de bateau   5. *brush country*

En détail

6 Have students infer meaning in small groups, then report on findings and clues.

VOCABULAIRE ACTIF

Les moyens de transport
à pied, en avion, en bateau, en train, en vélo, en voiture
l'aéroport
un vol

6 Les mots. En utilisant les mots apparentés, le contexte et la logique, pouvez-vous déduire le sens des mots en caractères gras?

1. Texte sur la Tunisie: «en 4×4 Toyota **climatisé**»; «découverte de **ruines romaines, mosquée**»; «des dunes de **sable**»; «ville **sainte** de l'Islam»; «ville **célèbre** pour ses **poteries**»

2. Texte sur le Sénégal: «3 journées de **séjour** libre»; «**Vol** pour Dakar»; «**Arrivée** matinale à **l'aéroport... départ** pour **l'île** Gorée... puis **retour** vers Dakar»

7 Les textes. Complétez les tableaux suivants selon les renseignements donnés dans les textes.

VOCABULAIRE ACTIF

La nature
le désert, la forêt, une île, un lac, la mer, la plage

Les vacances
acheter des souvenirs
une agence de voyages
aller à la chasse/à la pêche
célèbre
faire du bateau, du camping, du ski nautique
un lieu
nager
passer (une semaine, ses vacances)
un séjour
visiter une cathédrale, un château, un monument, des vieux quartiers
un voyage organisé

Et vous?

Before pair work, brainstorm with the class details that could be added; refer students to vocabulary on pp. 244–245, and review other vocabulary and structures as needed. Instruct students that they will have to report on their partner's trip. FOLLOW-UP: Students give as many reports as time allows. Partners are allowed to interrupt to add missing details (Tu as oublié quelque chose... tu n'as pas dit que...).

1. En Tunisie

jour	lieu *(place)*	activité
2e jour	Port El Kantaoui	détente
3e jour	Gabès	visite de l'oasis de Chenini
4e jour	Tozeur	visite du zoo
6e jour	Nabeul	visite du marché
6e jour	Port El Kantaoui	dîner spécial tunisien, fête bédouine

2. Au Sénégal

jour	lieu	activité
2e jour	île Gorée	visite du centre de la traite des esclaves
3e et 4e jours	delta du Saloum	promenades en pirogue
5e jour	pays Sérère	promenade en brousse
6e jour	Toubacouta	visite du marché et des villages
7e et 8e jours	Saly	séjour libre

1. Quel circuit préférez-vous? Pourquoi?
2. Imaginez que ce voyage en Afrique est un fait accompli. En groupes de deux, racontez ce que vous avez fait chaque jour en Tunisie (étudiant/e A) et au Sénégal (étudiant/e B). Comparez vos aventures, posez des questions, ajoutez des détails—et n'hésitez pas à exagérer!

Notes culturelles

La Tunisie. Tunisia, Algeria, and Morocco form the Maghreb, an Arab region in North Africa once colonized by France. Most of the population of Tunisia lives in the northern third of the country, where the land is more fertile. The history of Tunisia goes back to the ninth century B.C., when the Phoenicians founded the city of Carthage, near present-day Tunis, the capital of Tunisia. Carthage was under Roman rule from 146 B.C. until the fifth century A.D., which explains the presence of Roman ruins. Tunisia was a French protectorate from 1881 to 1956. Although Arabic is the official language of Tunisia, French is still widely used.

Le Sénégal. Senegal was France's oldest colony in West Africa. The French founded the city of Saint-Louis, at the mouth of the Senegal River, in 1659. In 1902, Dakar, Senegal's chief port, became the capital of **l'Afrique occidentale française (l'AOF),** a federation of eight French territories in West Africa. Senegal became an independent republic in 1960, with poet Léopold Sédar Senghor as its first president. Senegal is a predominantly Muslim country with six national languages, including **le ouolof,** but French has remained the official language.

STRUCTURES: Referring to places

Le verbe (re)venir • Les prépositions avec les noms géographiques

Cue to Video Module 7, street interviews (00:33:28), where people say where they went on vacation.

Observez et déduisez

Elles reviennent du Luxembourg.   Il revient de Tunisie.

Pour entendre parler français, bien sûr, on peut voyager en France. Mais on peut aller aussi au Maroc ou au Mali ou même aux États-Unis, par exemple, en Louisiane. Regardez les cartes au début du livre. Quel pays ou région du monde francophone voudriez-vous visiter? La Guyane? Le Sénégal? Les Antilles?

Point out that **États-Unis** is plural if students fail to notice.

- If the verb **venir** means *to come,* what do you think **revenir** means?
- What three prepositions do you notice in the preceding paragraph that express the idea of being *in* or going *to* a country or region? Can you think of a reason why the prepositions are different?
- Geographical names, like all nouns, have a gender. **France** is feminine. Can you find the other feminine names in **Observez et déduisez?** What is the last letter in each of those names? Which names are masculine?
- From the preceding paragraph and the following example, can you infer which prepositions to use in the blanks below?

  Je suis **en** Suisse, mais je pars **au** Mali la semaine prochaine et ensuite je vais **aux** Antilles.

  Nous allons... _____ Espagne _____ Tunisie _____ Philippines

  _____ Portugal _____ Canada _____ Allemagne

  (Germany)

Vérifiez *Le verbe (re)venir*

Draw students' attention to the different oral and written forms. Ask how many forms they see, then read the conjugation and ask how many forms they hear.

OPTIONAL DRILL: 1. Je viens de Dallas. (nous, le professeur, vous, mes cousins, tu) 2. Nous revenons de Mexico. (je, mes parents, le président, vous, tu)

Les verbes **venir/revenir**	
je (re)viens	nous (re)venons
tu (re)viens	vous (re)venez
il / elle / on (re)vient	ils / elles (re)viennent

Passé composé

il / elle / on est (re)venu(e)	nous sommes (re)venu(e)s

Other verbs that use **être** will be noted as they occur. Reflexive verbs are introduced in Ch. 10.

■ Both **venir** and **revenir** *(to come back)* require **être** in the passé composé, as do several other verbs you have already studied. Below is a summary chart of these verbs.

Quelques verbes avec être au passé composé		
aller	passer	revenir
arriver	rentrer	sortir
entrer	rester	tomber
monter	retourner	venir
partir		

VOCABULAIRE ACTIF

le monde
Les pays
   l'Algérie, etc.
revenir
venir

Les prépositions avec les noms géographiques

■ You have already seen that **de** means *from* when referring to cities (page 21) and that **à** is used to express the idea of being *in* or going *to* a city (page 200).

  — D'où es-tu? — Où est-elle allée?
  — Je suis **de** Dakar. — Elle est allée **à** Bruxelles.

■ Most countries with names ending in **e** are feminine, and those ending in other letters are usually masculine.*

  la Belgique le Maroc

■ The choice of preposition to express *going to* or *being in* a place or *coming from* a place depends on gender, number, and whether or not the place name begins with a vowel. Study the examples in the chart below.

Prepositions with geographical names		
	going *to* / being *in*	coming *from*
	à	de / d'
names of cities	je vais... / je suis... à Dakar	je viens... d'Alger
	en	de / d'
feminine names; *masculine names* *beginning with a vowel*	je vais... / je suis... en Suisse en Irak	je viens... de Suisse d'Irak
	au	du
all other masculine *place names*	je vais... / je suis... au Canada	je viens... du Portugal
	aux	des
all plural place names	je vais... / je suis... aux Antilles	je viens... des États-Unis

*__Le Mexique__ is an exception to this rule.

■ The same rules for choosing prepositions apply to continents (e.g., **en Asie**) and to regions (e.g., **en Provence, au Québec**). Most states will also follow these rules (**au** Texas, **en** Floride), although usage varies. **Dans l'état de...** can be used with any state.

Il habite **dans l'état de** New York.   Elle habite **dans l'état d'**Ohio.

■ When no preposition is indicated, use a definite article to refer to countries, continents, and regions.

L'Algérie est **le** pays voisin *(neighboring)* **du** Maroc.
Avez-vous visité **l'**Algérie ou **le** Maroc?

Des noms géographiques

l'Afrique	**l'Amérique du Nord**	**l'Europe**
l'Afrique du Sud	le Canada	l'Allemagne
l'Algérie	les États-Unis	l'Angleterre
le Cameroun	le Mexique	la Belgique
la Côte-d'Ivoire		le Danemark
la Libye	**l'Amérique du Sud**	l'Espagne
le Mali	l'Argentine	la France
le Maroc	le Brésil	la Fédération Russe
la Mauritanie	le Chili	l'Italie
le Sénégal	la Colombie	le Luxembourg
la Tunisie	la Guyane	les Pays-Bas
	le Vénézuéla	le Portugal
		la Suisse
l'Asie	**le Proche-Orient**	**l'Océanie**
la Chine	l'Égypte	l'Australie
la Corée	l'Irak	la Nouvelle-Zélande
l'Inde	l'Iran	les Philippines
le Japon	Israël	
le Viêt-nam		
	La mer des Antilles	
	la Guadeloupe	
	Haïti (f.)	
	la Martinique	

OPTIONAL DRILL: Have students find several countries on the maps at the front of the book. Ask them to name the neighboring countries. Les États-Unis? → Les pays voisins sont le Canada et le Mexique.

ACTIVITÉS

A. Allow time for students to use the maps at the front of the book and write answers, then have volunteers read the questions to the class and elicit as many suggestions as possible:

— Qu'est-ce que vous recommandez pour une personne qui...?
— Je recommande le Mexique.
— Et moi, le Brésil.

A. Agent de voyage. Vous organisez des voyages selon les préférences de vos client(e)s. Quel pays est-ce que vous recommandez pour...

➡ une personne qui aime aller à la chasse?
Je recommande l'Afrique du Sud ou le/la...

Quel pays est-ce que vous recommandez pour...

une personne qui veut aller à la plage?
une personne qui aime faire du bateau et du ski nautique?
une personne qui s'intéresse aux châteaux?

une personne qui adore manger des plats exotiques?
une personne qui veut faire des promenades à pied en montagne?
une personne qui s'intéresse à l'histoire ancienne?
une personne qui parle couramment l'espagnol?
une personne qui s'intéresse à l'art de la Renaissance?
une personne qui étudie la forêt tropicale?

B. Have students first work with a partner to locate cities with which they are not familiar.

B. Arrivée à Tunis.   Vous êtes guide d'une visite organisée en Tunisie. Selon votre registre, d'où viennent les membres du groupe?

➡ *Mustapha vient d'Algérie.*

passager	provenance
A. Mustapha	Alger
M/Mᵐᵉ Martin	Montréal
Y. Mikimoto	Tokyo
M. Wéry	Bruxelles
M/Mᵐᵉ Clark	Chicago
Mlle Sabouri	Téhéran
A. Bergen	Amsterdam
J. Maier	Jérusalem

C. Personalize by having students say where they'd like to go and what languages they'd like to study.

C. Des stages linguistiques.   Plusieurs étudiants veulent faire des stages linguistiques. Où vont-ils aller pour apprendre les langues suivantes? Vous êtes chargé des réservations!

➡ l'espagnol?
Ils vont aller en Espagne ou...

l'anglais?   le chinois?   le français?   le portugais?   l'arabe?

D. Les sites touristiques.   Testez vos connaissances culturelles. Dites où se trouvent les sites touristiques suivants.

➡ *L'abbaye de Westminster se trouve à Londres.*

sites	villes
le palais de Buckingham	Québec
le Louvre	Jérusalem
le Kremlin	Pékin
le Parthénon	Londres
le mur des Lamentations	Moscou
la place Tien-an-men	Paris
le château Frontenac	Athènes

See the *Instructor's Resource Manual* for an information gap activity, **Des étudiants de l'école internationale,** in which students practice prepositions with place names and the verb **venir.**

Maintenant, écrivez d'autres exemples de sites touristiques, et testez les connaissances de vos camarades de classe.

➡ *Où se trouve l'Alamo?*

STRATÉGIE DE COMMUNICATION
Asking for information or help

When you travel, you will certainly need to ask for help or information from strangers. Doing so politely makes a good impression and facilitates the task. Study the examples below and find polite expressions French speakers use to

- get someone's attention
- ask for information
- ask for help

— Pardon, madame. Je voudrais savoir à quelle heure arrive l'avion de Dakar, s'il vous plaît.

— Je suis désolée, madame. Demandez au bureau de renseignements *(information)*.

— Excusez-moi de vous déranger, monsieur. Est-ce que vous pourriez m'aider à descendre *(get down)* ma valise?
— Avec plaisir.

— Pardon, monsieur. Pourriez vous m'indiquer la consigne *(baggage claim)*?
— Bien sûr. Vous continuez tout droit. C'est à gauche, juste après le bureau des objets trouvés.

Now verify your answers in the chart on the next page.

Remind students they used **pourriez-vous** to ask for directions (Ch. 3).

Pour demander de l'aide/des renseignements

Pour attirer l'attention

Pardon, madame.
Excusez-moi de vous déranger, monsieur.

Pour demander

Pourriez-vous...
    me donner un coup de main?
    m'indiquer... la consigne? le bureau de renseignements?
    m'aider... à descendre ma valise? à trouver la consigne?
Je voudrais savoir... s'il vous plaît.
    l'heure
    à quelle heure arrive le train (l'avion)
    où se trouve(nt)... la consigne, les toilettes, le restaurant

Pour accepter	**Pour refuser**
Avec plaisir.	Je regrette, mais...
Bien sûr. / Certainement.	Je suis désolé(e)...
Volontiers.	

Note culturelle

La politesse. In their quest for efficiency, North Americans like to get right to the point: *Could you help me . . .* This directness, however, may be perceived as bluntness by a French person. In her book *French or Foe*, Polly Platt insists that the five most important words in the French language are **Excusez-moi de vous déranger...** The next five, **mais j'ai un petit problème,** will guarantee, she insists, a quick, thorough response to any request. Try it!

ACTIVITÉS

E. Soyez poli(e)! Complétez les dialogues suivants avec des expressions polies.

1. — Est-ce que vous pourriez m'aider à trouver mes valises?

     — _____

2. — _____

     — Je suis désolé. Je n'ai pas de montre *(watch).*

3. — Pourriez-vous me dire où sont les toilettes?

     — _____

4. — _____

     — Avec plaisir, monsieur.

F. Have partners take turns requesting and accepting or refusing.

F. Des petits problèmes. Imaginez-vous dans les situations suivantes. Comment allez-vous demander poliment de l'aide ou des renseignements? Développez les scènes avec un(e) partenaire.

1. Vous êtes à l'hôtel El Mouradi à Sousse en Tunisie. Vous êtes en retard ce matin, et votre groupe est déjà parti pour faire le tour du port. Vous voulez prendre un taxi pour rattraper le groupe. Qu'est-ce que vous demandez au concierge?
2. Votre amie de Dakar arrive à l'aéroport de Marseille. Vous voulez la retrouver, mais vous ne savez pas l'heure ou le numéro du vol. Qu'est-ce que vous demandez à l'employé de la ligne aérienne?
3. Vous êtes touriste à Paris. Malheureusement, vous ne pouvez pas trouver votre passeport. Vous allez à l'ambassade pour demander de l'aide.
4. Vous avez un voyage d'affaires imprévu *(unexpected),* alors vous allez dans une agence de voyages pour avoir des renseignements au sujet des vols de Bruxelles à New York. Vous voulez partir demain matin le plus tôt possible.

Jeu de rôle

Think of an exciting trip you have taken or would like to take. Describe the trip to your partner, giving details about activities, hotels, and so on. Ask each other questions to make sure you have the whole story, then guess if the trip was real or **une pure invention!**

CULTURE ET RÉFLEXION

Internet

■ **Les vacances des Français.** Pour la majorité des Français, les «vraies vacances» restent celles de l'été, mais la tendance actuelle est d'étaler[1] ces vacances au cours de l'année. Quarante pour cent des Français partent en vacances d'hiver pour dix à quinze jours, et la durée moyenne[2] des vacances d'été est maintenant de quinze jours. La plage reste le lieu privilégié des vacances d'été, et l'on préfère rester dans un seul endroit plutôt que[3] de visiter une série de sites. La formule des week-ends prolongés

Sur la route des vacances: les bouchons du 1er juillet.

complète le profil des vacances des Français. Cette tendance au fractionnement s'explique par le désir de diversifier les expériences et par des facteurs économiques. Imaginez que vous avez cinq semaines de congés payés garanties par la loi. Est-ce que vous allez les prendre d'un seul coup[4] ou les étaler au cours de l'année?

Pourquoi? Qu'est-ce que vous allez faire? Si vous partez en vacances, allez-vous rester dans un seul endroit ou préférez-vous visiter une série de sites touristiques? Expliquez.

■ **Les Français en voiture.** Un écrivain satirique français, Pierre Daninos, compare ainsi les Anglais et les Français «au volant[5]»: «Les Anglais conduisent[6] plutôt mal, mais prudemment. Les Français conduisent plutôt bien, mais follement. La proportion des accidents est à peu près la même dans les deux pays», mais est-on «plus tranquille avec des gens qui font mal des choses bien» ou «avec ceux qui font bien de mauvaises choses»? (*Les Carnets du Major Thompson,* p. 198.) Voilà donc la réputation des Français! Il est vrai que la limite de vitesse[7] sur les autoroutes[8] françaises est de 130 km/h (81 miles/h), mais le permis de conduire[9] n'est pas facile à obtenir en France: il faut avoir dix-huit ans, investir environ 4.000 F ($650) en leçons d'auto-école

Une leçon d'auto-école.

(données non pas dans les écoles mais par des entreprises privées) et passer un examen de conduite très rigoureux. Par mesure de sécurité, les enfants de moins de dix ans ne peuvent pas s'asseoir à l'avant du véhicule. Que pensez-vous de tout cela? Est-ce une bonne idée d'avoir une limite de vitesse de 130 km/h sur les autoroutes? De passer le permis de conduire à dix-huit ans au lieu de seize? De ne pas permettre aux écoles secondaires de donner des leçons d'auto-école? De ne pas permettre aux jeunes enfants de s'asseoir à l'avant d'une voiture? Donnez votre opinion et proposez une réforme possible du code de la route dans votre pays—ou en France!

---

1. *spread out*   2. *average duration*   3. *stay in one place rather than*   4. *all at once*   5. *at the wheel*   6. *drive*
7. *speed*   8. *freeways*   9. *driver's license*

Troisième étape

À l'écoute: À la gare

This input section introduces students to train travel vocabulary and transactions.

Vous allez entendre deux petites conversations qui ont lieu dans une gare de Paris. Pour vous préparer, faites les activités 1 et 2, puis écoutez en suivant les instructions données.

Avant d'écouter

1 Voici un horaire des trains Paris–Marseille de 15 h à 18 h. Pour comprendre cet horaire, répondez aux questions page 258.

Numéro de train		54927	627	849	5640/1	6165/4	5001	877	827	835	54939	679	5642/3	5055	6132/3	5009	831	831	769	837
Notes à consulter			1	2	3	4	5	6	6	7	8	9	10	4	11	10	12	13	11	14
			TGV	TGV				TGV	TGV	TGV		TGV					TGV	TGV	TGV	TGV
Paris-Gare-de-Lyon	D		15.00	15.05				15.40	15.40	16.05		16.23				16.46	16.49	16.53	17.19	17.47
Dijon-Ville	D													16.45	16.57	19.14			19.03	
Macon-Ville	D					16.28								17.54	18.00	20.16				
Lyon-Part-Dieu	D		17.03	17.05		17.14	17.17					18.34		18.39	18.44	21.01	19.00	19.00		
Lyon-Perrache	D	16.22	17.10								17.49	18.42								
Vienne	A	16.46										18.13				21.21				
Valence Ville	A	17.40			17.55	18.08	18.12	18.33	18.33	19.03	19.11		19.27	19.33	19.39	21.58	19.53	19.53		20.40
Arles	A				19.24	19.32	19.38							20.55	21.03	23.30				
Marseille-St-Charles	A				20.10	20.17	20.21		20.25	21.09				21.25	21.41	21.49	00.15	21.44	21.44		22.36

Notes

1. Ne prend pas de voyageurs à Lyon-Part-Dieu- ♟- &.
2. Circule : du 18 juin au 28 août : tous les jours- ♟- &.
3. 🖴.
4. Circule : les ven- 🖴.
5. 🖴- &.
6. ♟- &.
7. Circule : jusqu'au 2 juil : les ven;les 3, 10, 17 et 24 sept- ♟- &.
8. Circule : tous les jours sauf les sam, dim et fêtes.
9. Circule : jusqu'au 2 juil : tous les jours sauf les sam, dim et fêtes;Circule du 9 juil au 27 août : les ven;à partir du 30 août : tous les jours sauf les sam et dim- Ne prend pas de voyageurs à Lyon-Part-Dieu- ♟- &.
10. Circule : les ven.
11. ♟.
12. Circule : les sam, dim et fêtes- ♟- &.
13. Circule : tous les jours sauf les sam, dim et fêtes- ♟- &.
14. 🍽1 re CL assuré certains jours- ♟- &.

Symboles

A Arrivée
D Départ
TGV Résa TGV : réservation obligatoire
🍽 Restauration à la place
♟ Bar
🖴 Vente ambulante
& Facilités handicapés

Remarque

Les trains circulant tous les jours ont leurs horaires indiqués en gras[1]
Tous les trains offrent des places assises en 1re et 2e classe sauf indication contraire dans les notes

Cue to Video Module 7 (00:32:13), where Élisabeth and Fatima discuss train schedules with a travel agent.

---

1. *boldface*

1 This activity is designed to familiarize students with French train schedules. Do the first couple of questions together, then students can work in pairs, with reports and comments after each question. This activity will be a good review of numbers as well!

To compare trip durations, students might look at trains 5009 and 831. ANSWERS: 1. La gare de Lyon 2. TGV: 627, 849, 877, 827, 835, 679, 831, 769, 837; réservation obligatoire; Paris–Marseille en TGV: 4 heures 45 minutes; en train ordinaire: 7 h 30 3. Facilités handicapés: 627, 849, 5001, 877, 827, 835, 679, 831, 837; Bar: 627, 849, 877, 827, 835, 679, 6132, 831, 837; Vente ambulante: 5640, 6165, 5001

5a. Non; circule seulement le vendredi jusqu'au 2 juillet, ou certains jours en septembre. 5b. Non; circule seulement le vendredi (ven). 5c. Trois possibilités: 16 h 46 → 21 h 58; 16 h 53 → 19 h 53; 17 h 47 → 20 h 40.

Cue to Video Module 7, street interviews (00:34:31), where people talk about their preferred means of travel.

1. Comment s'appelle la gare de Paris d'où partent les trains pour Marseille?
2. Quels trains sont des TGV (trains à grande vitesse)? Donnez le numéro de ces trains. Selon l'explication donnée sous «Symboles», qu'est-ce qui est obligatoire *(mandatory)* pour les TGV? Comparez la durée du voyage Paris–Marseille en TGV et en train ordinaire.
3. Regardez les notes. Quels trains ont des facilités pour handicapés? un bar? une vente ambulante, c'est-à-dire des employés qui circulent dans le train pour vendre *(sell)* des boissons et des sandwichs? Ici encore, donnez le numéro des trains.
4. Quels trains circulent tous les jours? (Voir «Remarque».)
5. Imaginez que...
   a. nous sommes au mois d'août; pouvez-vous prendre le train numéro 835?
   b. nous sommes un samedi; pouvez-vous prendre le train numéro 5009?
   c. vous voulez aller à Valence, avec départ de Paris un vendredi, entre 16 h 30 et 18 h. Quelles sont vos options? Donnez l'heure (les heures) du départ de Paris et de l'arrivée à Valence.

Note culturelle

Les trains en France. Trains are a very common mode of transportation in France and throughout Europe. The French railroad system, controlled by the **Société nationale des chemins de fer français (SNCF)** is one of the fastest and most reliable in the world. The **TGV (train à grande vitesse)** travels at speeds of 150 to 200 miles per hour. TGV lines are now expanding beyond the borders of France, from Paris to Madrid, to Amsterdam, and to other European cities.

Some tips for traveling by train in France:

- You can reserve your ticket by phone, by Minitel (computer terminal at home), or at the ticket window **(le guichet).**
- Your ticket must be validated **(composté)** by a machine at the railroad station just before you get on the train. You may be fined if you fail to do this.
- For overnight trips, you may reserve a berth **(une couchette)** in a sleeping compartment.
- On each platform, a diagram of the train indicates in advance where each car is going to be when the train stops. This allows you to get on the train in the precise spot where your reserved seat is located.

2 Les conversations que vous allez entendre incluent les mots suivants (en caractères gras). Pouvez-vous déduire leur sens par le contexte?

— Il est 10 h. Mon train est à 10 h 30. Alors je vais **attendre** 30 minutes.
— Il est 10 h 35. Mince! Mon train est déjà parti. J'**ai raté** mon train!

Audio CD

3 Écoutez les *deux* conversations une première fois pour déterminer qui fait les choses suivantes—Monsieur Godot ou Monsieur Estragon? Cochez la colonne appropriée.

	M. Godot	M. Estragon
Il attend le prochain train parce qu'il a raté le premier.	✔	
Il part en voyage d'affaires.		✔
Il a une petite maison à Cassis.	✔	
Il va retrouver sa femme et ses enfants qui sont déjà en vacances.	✔	
Il prend son billet.		✔
Il prend le train pour Marseille.	✔	
Il va à Lyon.		✔
Il va revenir demain soir.		✔

4 Écoutez encore, cette fois-ci en faisant attention aux expressions utilisées pour prendre un billet de train. Complétez et déduisez le sens des mots en caractères gras.

— Un billet <u>pour</u> Lyon, <u>s'il vous plaît</u> . Vous avez toujours des **places?**

— **Un aller-retour** ou un <u>aller</u> **simple?**

— <u>Première</u> ou <u>deuxième</u> **classe?**

— **Fumeurs** ou <u>non</u> **-fumeurs?**

Monsieur Estragon va être dans **le même** <u>train</u> que Monsieur Godot.

VOCABULAIRE ACTIF

À la gare
un aller simple
un aller-retour
l'arrivée (f.)
attendre
un billet
une couchette
le départ
le guichet
un horaire
le (la) même
Une place...
en première ou
    deuxième classe
fumeurs/non-fumeurs
le prochain train
rater le train
le TGV
un voyage d'affaires

ANSWER: 21 h 44, 19 h 00

5 Écoutez une dernière fois en faisant attention aux heures mentionnées.

Départ de Paris   Train raté: <u>15 h 40</u>

Prochain train pour Marseille: <u>16 h 53</u>

Retour de Lyon   Départ de Lyon: <u>18 h 47</u>

Arrivée à Paris: <u>20 h 49</u>

Maintenant consultez l'horaire, page 257, pour voir à quelle heure Monsieur Godot et Monsieur Estragon vont arriver à leur destination.

6 PRE-SPEAKING: Review with the whole class the questions/expressions needed for the role-play. If you wish, play the audio segment one last time as a model. Encourage students to add complications. FOLLOW-UP: Have a few groups perform their role-play. Other groups can report on the destination they chose and/or the train they took.

6 Imaginez que vous êtes à la gare de Lyon, à Paris. Jouez les rôles suivants avec un(e) partenaire: l'un de vous est le voyageur (la voyageuse) qui demande des renseignements et prend un billet, l'autre l'employé(e) de la SNCF. D'abord, sélectionnez ensemble une destination, puis jouez la situation au guichet.

Prononciation

La lettre l

■ The French [l] is fairly close to the [l] sound at the beginning of English words such as *list* or *love*. But it is never pronounced like the final [l] of English words, such as *pull* or *shell*. To say a French [l], remember to keep the tip of your tongue close to your top front teeth.

Quelle surprise!   Un aller-retour, s'il vous plaît.

■ The spelling **-ll-** is sometimes pronounced like the *y* in *yes*.

Marseille   un billet

Écoutez

Audio CD

Listen to the following phrases from the two **À l'écoute** conversations. When is the **-ll-** pronounced like a *y*? In the chart check the pronunciation you hear, then infer which vowel must precede the **-ll-** to create the *y* sound.

	l	*y*
Quelle surprise!	✔	
le prochain train pour Marseille		
un billet pour Lyon		
un aller-retour		

Vowel _____ + **ll** = *y* sound*

Essayez!

Audio CD

In the following sentences, underline each **-ill** that is pronounced like a *y*.

1. La famille Godot aime les villages tranquilles.
2. On a passé le mois de juillet à Deauville.
3. La fille dans le train mange une glace à la vanille.
4. Monsieur Estragon travaille à Versailles.
5. Quel train prenez-vous pour aller à Chantilly?

Now practice saying the sentences aloud, paying special attention to the **l**'s. Then listen to the sentences on the student audio CD to verify your pronunciation.

---

*Exceptions: **ville, mille, tranquille,** and their derivatives keep the [l] sound.

STRUCTURE: Talking about travel (II)

Les verbes en -re

Observez et déduisez

À Paris, gare de Lyon...

Monsieur Estragon attend depuis 15 minutes au guichet où on vend des billets.

Les gens au service d'accueil répondent poliment aux questions de la famille Paumé.

Thomas va au bureau des objets trouvés parce qu'il a perdu son billet pour Caen.

Hélène descend du train. Elle vient à Paris pour rendre visite à sa grand-mère.

Monsieur Godot n'a pas entendu l'annonce de son train parce qu'il dort. Il va rater son train.

- Read about the scene at the **gare de Lyon** in Paris and try to locate in the drawing above the people mentioned in the sentences. Can you infer the meaning of the verbs from context?
- Look at the verbs used in the sentences. Can you infer the **il/ils** forms for **perdre, rendre visite,** and **entendre?**
- Can you conjugate **répondre** in the passé composé?

To draw students' attention to the different oral and written forms, ask how many written forms they see in the chart. Now read the conjugation and ask how many forms they hear.

Point out that **attendre** is a false cognate.

Vérifiez *Les verbes en -re*

OPTIONAL DRILL: Transformez les phrases en remplaçant le sujet. CUES: 1. Monsieur Godot attend le prochain train. (je, mes amis, nous, tu) 2. Monsieur Godot descend du train. (vous, mon professeur, nous, les étudiants) 3. Monsieur Godot perd son temps. (je, mes amis, nous, tu) 4. Monsieur Godot n'a pas entendu l'annonce. (je, maman, tu, vous)

Le verbe attendre

j'attend**s**	nous attend**ons**
tu attend**s**	vous attend**ez**
il / elle / on attend	ils / elles attend**ent**

Passé composé: j'ai **attendu**

■ The following verbs are conjugated like **attendre:**

descendre	*to get off/out of; to go downstairs*
entendre	*to hear*
perdre	*to lose*
rendre visite (à)	*to visit (a person)*
répondre (à)	*to answer*
vendre	*to sell*

Point out that **rendre visite (à)** is used with people and **visiter** with places or things.

■ Verbs conjugated like **attendre** follow a regular pattern. The stem is formed by dropping the **-re** of the infinitive and adding the endings: **-s, -s, —, -ons, -ez, -ent.**

je **perd**-s
vous **vend**-ez

■ **Descendre*** is conjugated in the passé composé with **être.** The other **-re** verbs are conjugated in the passé composé with **avoir.**

Claudine **est descendue** du train à Paris.
Marie **a rendu visite à** son amie.
Elle **a entendu** des nouvelles *(news)* intéressantes.

ACTIVITÉS

A. Replay the CD if you feel students may not remember the story, then have students work in pairs/groups. ANSWERS: 1. Vrai 2. Faux (Marseille) 3. Faux (Ils l'ont toujours.) 4. Vrai (Possible; il a raté le train.) 5. Faux (Il fait un voyage d'affaires.) 6. Faux (Il va au guichet pour acheter son billet.) 7. Vrai

A. Vrai ou faux? Dites si les phrases suivantes sont vraies ou fausses selon l'histoire de Monsieur Godot et Monsieur Estragon.

1. Monsieur Godot attend le train.
2. Il descend à Lyon.
3. Monsieur et Madame Godot vendent leur petite maison à Cassis.
4. Monsieur Godot n'a probablement pas entendu l'annonce du train de 15 h 40.
5. Monsieur Estragon rend visite à son cousin à Lyon.
6. Il va au guichet parce qu'il a perdu son billet.
7. L'employée répond poliment à Monsieur Estragon.

Maintenant, corrigez les phrases fausses.

B. Review with students the **mots-liens** they have studied, such as **d'abord, ensuite, enfin.** (See p. 192.) Have students work in pairs, then read their stories. Ask several pairs to tell how they concluded the story.

B. Le "voyage" de Monsieur Ronfle. Employez les éléments indiqués pour raconter l'histoire de Monsieur Ronfle. Ajoutez des mots-liens et une phrase pour terminer l'histoire.

➡ Monsieur Ronfle / sortir de / maison / huit heures
Monsieur Ronfle sort de la maison à huit heures.

1. Il / rendre visite / petits-enfants
2. Il / aller / gare / pour prendre / train
3. Il / attendre / dix minutes / guichet
4. employé / répondre poliment / questions / Monsieur Ronfle / et / lui vendre / billet
5. train / partir / dans une heure
6. Monsieur Ronfle / dormir / pendant que / attendre

***Descendre à** can also be used to express the idea of staying at a hotel: Ils sont descendus à l'hôtel Dupleix.

7. Il / ne pas entendre / annonce
8. Il / rater / train
9. Il / perdre / patience*
10. ?

STRUCTURE: Avoiding repetition (III)
Le pronom **y**

Observez et déduisez

Une maison en Provence.

La famille Godot adore Cassis. Depuis qu'ils y ont acheté une petite maison, ils y passent toutes leurs vacances. Madame Godot et les enfants y vont début juillet en voiture. M. Godot y va en août, en train ou en avion. À Cassis, la famille trouve beaucoup de choses à faire: des promenades à pied, en vélo ou en bateau—et la plage, bien sûr, on peut y passer des heures!

Have students look at the first instance of the pronoun to find the antecedent. Then have them confirm by checking the other instances.

- Study examples of the pronoun **y** in the preceding paragraph. The first four times it is used, it refers to the same thing. What is it? What does it refer to in the last sentence?
- Where is **y** placed in relationship to a verb in the present tense? to a verb in the passé composé? Where is it placed when there is more than one verb, as in the last sentence?

*No article is required before the noun in the expression **perdre patience**.

Vérifiez   *Le pronom* **y**

■ The pronoun **y** can be used to avoid repeating the name of a place. It can substitute for a prepositional phrase beginning with **en, à, sur, dans,** or another preposition of location.

> Les Godot habitent **en France.**
> Ils **y** habitent depuis longtemps.
> Pendant les vacances, ils sont allés **à Cassis.**
> Ils **y** sont restés deux mois.

■ **Y** takes the same place in the sentence as do direct and indirect object pronouns: directly before the verb in the present; before the auxiliary verb in the passé composé; and before the infinitive in sentences with a verb followed by an infinitive.

> — Qui veut aller à la montagne?
> — Moi, je veux bien **y** aller. J'**y** vais le plus souvent possible.
> — Pas moi. J'**y** suis déjà allé(e) hier.

ACTIVITÉS

C. Mais où?   Dites où sont (où vont) Messieurs Godot et Estragon.

1. Messieurs Godot et Estragon y sont.
2. Monsieur Godot y va en train.
3. Monsieur Godot y a une petite maison.
4. Monsieur Estragon y fait un voyage d'affaires.
5. Monsieur Estragon y va pour acheter son billet.

Et vous? Où êtes-vous?

6. J'y étudie.
7. J'y habite.
8. J'y mange tous les jours.
9. J'y voyage en été.
10. J'y travaille.

D. Y ou lui?   Pour chaque question que le professeur vous pose, soulignez la bonne réponse.

1. Oui, il (y / lui) est.
2. Oui, il (y / lui) a une petite maison.
3. Oui, il (y / lui) téléphone.
4. Oui, il (y / lui) dit «bonjour».
5. Oui, il (y / lui) répond.
6. Oui, il (y / lui) prend son billet.
7. Oui, il (y / lui) voyage.
8. Oui, il (y / lui) rend visite.

E. Interviews.   Complétez les phrases suivantes avec le nom d'un endroit et la préposition qui convient.

1. Cet été je passe mes vacances _____ .

2. Mes parents vont _____ .

3. L'année prochaine je vais étudier _____ .

4. Mes copains et moi, nous allons voyager _____ .

5. Mon copain (ma copine) est allé(e) _____ pour faire un stage linguistique.

6. Ma sœur (Mon frère) a voyagé _____ .

Maintenant interviewez un(e) camarade de classe pour voir si vos réponses sont semblables.

➡ — *Tu passes tes vacances au Sénégal cet été?*
  — *Oui, j'y passe mes vacances.*
ou — *Non, je n'y passe pas mes vacances. Je vais passer mes vacances en Floride.*

F. Voyages. (1) Écrivez le nom de quatre endroits (destinations désirées) que vous voudriez visiter (villes ou pays). (2) Cherchez des camarades de classe qui ont déjà visité ces endroits. (3) Posez des questions pour compléter le tableau.

➡ — *Tu es allé à la Martinique?*
  — *Oui, j'y suis allé.*
  — *Comment est-ce que tu y es allé?*
  — *J'y suis allé en avion.*
  — *Qu'est-ce qu'on y trouve?*
  — *On y trouve de belles plages et du beau temps.*

ma destination désirée	camarade de classe	moyen de transport	ce qu'on y trouve

 **Jeu de rôle**

In groups of four or five, play the role of a family that has trouble deciding where to go on vacation. One of the children likes mountains and nature; another likes sports and the beach; the third wants to spend time shopping! One parent loves museums and tourist sites; the other simply wants some peace and quiet. Try to come up with a plan!

CD-ROM
Now that you have finished the Troisième étape of this chapter, do your Lab Manual activities with the audio program. Explore chapter topics further with the Mais oui! Video and CD-ROM. Viewing and comprehension activities are in the video section of your *Workbook/Lab Manual/Video Manual*.

Littérature: Le voyage du petit prince

Antoine de Saint-Exupéry, born in 1900, was a pilot by profession. He flew mail planes from France to Senegal and then pioneered air routes to Brazil and Chile. The trips he made in the early days of aviation inspired *Courrier-Sud* (1928), *Vol de nuit* (1931), and *Terre des hommes* (1939), three novels that tell of dangerous encounters with the elements, action and responsibility, solitary struggles and human bonds. During World War II, Saint-Exupéry was sent to New York to appeal for aid for the Free French. While in New York, he published *Pilote de guerre* (1942) and *Le Petit Prince* (1943). In 1943, he returned to combat and volunteered for a number of dangerous missions. In July 1944, his plane was shot down over the Alps, and he was presumed dead.

Les billets de banque français représentent souvent des artistes et des écrivains. Ce billet de 50 francs, sorti en 1994, fait honneur à Saint-Exupéry et au petit prince.

Le Petit Prince is a classic for both children and adults. The setting for most of the book is the Sahara Desert, where Saint-Exupéry himself almost died after a forced landing in 1935. In real life, Saint-Exupéry was rescued by some Bedouins. In *Le Petit Prince*, the pilot is rescued by an extraordinary little guy (**«un petit bonhomme tout à fait extraordinaire»**) who comes from another planet (**l'astéroïde B-612).** He lives alone on that planet until a beautiful rose appears, a rose who is really quite insecure and seeks attention in all the wrong ways. After a few misunderstandings with his rose, **le petit prince** decides to look for friends elsewhere. In the following excerpts, he travels to a number of small planets, each inhabited by a single person, and finally arrives on Earth.

Avant de lire

1 Le petit prince va visiter plusieurs petites planètes, chacune habitée par une seule personne. Il va rencontrer ainsi un buveur (une personne qui boit trop) et un businessman. Quelle personne pensez-vous que les expressions suivantes décrivent—le buveur ou le businessman?

1. un homme très occupé
2. un homme qui a honte *(is ashamed)*
3. un homme qui veut oublier quelque chose
4. un homme très sérieux

Enfin, le petit prince va arriver sur la Terre—dans le désert du Sahara, où il va parler avec un serpent. Puis il va traverser le désert et arriver dans une gare, où il va parler avec un aiguilleur, c'est-à-dire un homme qui contrôle la direction des trains. À votre avis, dans quel contexte—le désert ou la gare—le petit prince va-t-il dire les choses suivantes?

1. «Il n'y a donc personne *(no one)* sur la Terre?»
2. «On est un peu seul *(alone, lonely)* ici... »
3. «Ils sont bien pressés *(in a hurry)*. Que cherchent-ils?»

2 Dans ce texte, vous allez voir des verbes comme **il fit,** ou **il pensa.** Ces verbes sont au passé simple, qui est l'équivalent littéraire du passé composé.

il fit = il a fait   il pensa = il a pensé

Pouvez-vous donner le passé composé des verbes suivants?

il demanda   il répondit   il partit

En général

3 Parcourez le texte une première fois pour trouver les phrases données dans **Avant de lire.** Est-ce que vos prédictions étaient correctes?

1. Qui est très occupé?
2. Qui a honte de ce qu'il fait?
3. Qui veut oublier quelque chose?
4. Qui pense qu'il est sérieux?
5. Où est-ce que le petit prince demande: «Il n'y a donc personne sur la Terre?»
6. Où est-on «un peu seul»?
7. De qui parle le petit prince quand il dit, «Ils sont bien pressés»?

Le voyage du petit prince

La planète suivante était habitée par un buveur, installé en silence devant une collection de bouteilles.

— Que fais-tu là? dit le petit prince au buveur.
— Je bois, répondit le buveur.
— Pourquoi bois-tu? lui demanda le petit prince.
— Pour oublier, répondit le buveur.
— Pour oublier quoi?
— Pour oublier que j'ai honte, avoua le buveur.
— Honte de quoi? demanda le petit prince.
— Honte de boire!

Et le petit prince partit, perplexe.

Les grandes personnes sont décidément très très bizarres, se disait-il en lui-même durant le voyage.

La quatrième planète était celle du businessman. Cet homme était si occupé qu'il ne leva même pas la tête° à l'arrivée du petit prince.

— Bonjour, dit le petit prince.

— Trois et deux font cinq. Cinq et sept douze. Douze et trois quinze. Bonjour. Quinze et sept vingt-deux. Vingt-deux et six vingt-huit. Vingt-six et cinq trente et un. Ouf! Ça fait donc cinq cent un millions six cent vingt-deux mille sept cent trente et un.

— Cinq cent un millions de quoi?

— Hein? Tu es toujours là? Cinq cent un millions de... je ne sais plus... j'ai tellement de travail! Je suis sérieux, moi! Je disais donc cinq cent un millions...

— Millions de quoi?

— Millions de ces petites choses que l'on voit quelquefois dans le ciel.

— Des mouches°?

— Mais non, des petites choses qui brillent°.

— Ah! des étoiles?

— C'est bien ça. Des étoiles.

— Et que fais-tu de ces étoiles?

— Rien. Je les possède.

— Et à quoi cela te sert-il° de posséder les étoiles?

— Ça me sert à être riche.

— Et à quoi cela te sert-il d'être riche?

— À acheter d'autres étoiles.

Celui-là°, pensa le petit prince, il raisonne un peu comme le buveur. Les grandes personnes sont vraiment extraordinaires...

[En continuant son voyage, le petit prince arrive enfin sur la Terre, et voit un serpent.]

— Sur quelle planète suis-je tombé°? demanda le petit prince.

— Sur la Terre, en Afrique, répondit le serpent.

— Ah!... Il n'y a donc personne sur la Terre?

— Ici c'est le désert. Il n'y a personne dans les déserts. La Terre est grande, dit le serpent.

ne... didn't even look up

flies

shine

à quoi... what's the use

cet homme-là

suis... did I fall

— Où sont les hommes? demanda le petit prince. On est un peu seul dans le désert...

— On est seul aussi chez les hommes, dit le serpent.

[Le petit prince traverse le désert et arrive finalement dans une gare.]

— Bonjour, dit le petit prince.

— Bonjour, dit l'aiguilleur.

— Que fais-tu ici? dit le petit prince.

— J'expédie° les trains qui emportent° les voyageurs, tantôt vers la droite, tantôt vers la gauche, dit l'aiguilleur. *send / take away*

Et un rapide° illuminé, grondant comme le tonnerre°, fit trembler la cabine d'aiguillage°. *train / grondant... rumbling like thunder / de contrôle*

— Ils sont bien pressés, dit le petit prince. Que cherchent-ils?

— L'homme de la locomotive l'ignore lui-même, dit l'aiguilleur.

Et un second rapide illuminé gronda en sens inverse°. *en... dans la direction opposée*

— Ils reviennent déjà? demanda le petit prince.

— Ce ne sont pas les mêmes, dit l'aiguilleur.

— Ils n'étaient° pas contents, là où ils étaient? *were*

— On n'est jamais content là où l'on est, dit l'aiguilleur.

Et gronda le tonnerre d'un troisième rapide.

— Ils poursuivent° les premiers voyageurs? demanda le petit prince. *pursue*

— Ils ne poursuivent rien du tout, dit l'aiguilleur. Ils dorment là-dedans, ou bien ils bâillent°. Les enfants seuls écrasent leur nez contre les vitres°. *yawn / écrasent... press their noses to the windows*

— Les enfants seuls savent ce qu'ils cherchent, dit le petit prince. Ils perdent du temps pour une poupée de chiffons°, et elle devient très importante, et si on la leur enlève°, ils pleurent... *poupée... rag doll / take it away*

— Ils ont de la chance°, dit l'aiguilleur. *ont... are lucky*

Extrait et adapté de *Le Petit Prince* (Antoine de Saint-Exupéry)

En détail **4** **Les mots.** En utilisant les mots apparentés, le contexte et la logique, pouvez-vous déduire le sens des mots suivants?

1. Sur la planète du businessman:

— Et que fais-tu de ces étoiles?

— **Rien,** je les **possède.**

... il **raisonne** un peu comme le buveur.

2. Sur la Terre, à la gare:

J'expédie les trains ... **tantôt vers** la droite, **tantôt vers** la gauche...
Ils perdent du temps pour une poupée de chiffons, et elle **devient** très importante...

5 Le texte

A. Vrai ou faux?   Si les phrases suivantes sont vraies, expliquez-les. Si elles sont fausses, corrigez-les.

1. Le buveur veut sortir de sa situation.
2. Le businessman ne sait pas comment s'appellent les choses qu'il compte.
3. Le businessman est très matérialiste.
4. Selon le serpent, il y a des problèmes de communication et de solitude chez les hommes.
5. L'aiguilleur pense que les voyageurs savent ce qu'ils cherchent.
6. Les voyageurs du premier train reviennent déjà dans le second train.
7. Les voyageurs lisent et parlent dans les trains.
8. Les enfants savent regarder avec le cœur.

B. Répondez.

1. Pourquoi le petit prince pense-t-il que le businessman raisonne un peu comme le buveur?
2. Le buveur et le businessman sont seuls dans leur petit monde avec leurs problèmes ou leurs illusions. Est-ce que la situation des voyageurs dans les trains est différente? Expliquez.
3. Qu'est-ce que les enfants savent faire pour une poupée de chiffons?

Et vous?

Discutez avec un(e) partenaire.

1. Les petites planètes que le petit prince visite sont habitées par une seule personne. Puis quand il arrive sur la Terre, c'est dans un désert. Quel est le symbolisme commun?
2. «On n'est jamais content là où l'on est.» Une autre expression dit que «l'herbe (grass) est toujours plus verte de l'autre côté». Est-ce vrai? Pourquoi? Donnez des illustrations.
3. Imaginez que vous aussi, vous avez voyagé sur deux petites planètes, chacune habitée par une seule personne. Qui avez-vous vu sur chaque planète? Créez pour chaque personne une identité qui illustre un trait typiquement humain, et un petit dialogue avec cette personne.

Par écrit: Wish you were here!

Avant d'écrire

A. Strategy: Taking audience into account.   What you say when you write depends to a large extent on who your intended audience is. If you were developing brochures for tourists visiting your state, for example, the attractions you would emphasize to appeal to retirees would be different from the ones you would emphasize to entice young families with children. The adjectives you would use to describe your state might also vary.

Application.   Jot down two lists: (1) the types of leisure activities and amenities found in your state most likely to interest young families, and (2) those that would appeal to retirees. Remember, your lists need not be mutually exclusive!

B. Strategy: Using a telegraphic style. We sometimes encounter a telegraphic writing style used in advertising, and we often engage in it ourselves when we take notes in class, leave notes for friends, or send postcards. This highly informal style usually consists of incomplete sentences. Only the key words remain.

Application.   Look at the tourist brochure that follows and find several examples of telegraphic writing. Who do you think the intended audience is? Why?

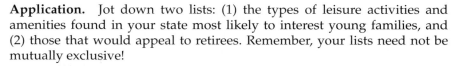

CASSIS

Petit port de pêche et de plaisance.

À 22 km de Marseille, situé entre le Massif des Calanques à l'ouest et la plus haute falaise d'Europe: le Cap Canaille (416 m) à l'est.

Station climatique et balnéaire.

Distractions et loisirs
- Casino municipal.
- Plongée sous-marine: 2 clubs.
- Voile et planche à voile: 2 clubs.
- Tennis: 2 clubs.

FESTIVITÉS - RENCONTRES SPORTIVES
Nombreuses festivités programmées par le Centre Culturel, Cassis Animation et l'Office Municipal de la Culture.

ITINÉRAIRES TOURISTIQUES
- Promenades - escalades dans le Massif des Calanques.
- Route des Crêtes dans le Massif du Cap Canaille.
- Route des vignobles de Cassis.
- Excursions organisées par l'Office Municipal du Tourisme.

Tous renseignements auprès de **OFFICE MUNICIPAL DU TOURISME** Place P. Baragnon 13260 CASSIS Tél. 42.01.71.17 Fax. 42.01.28.31

À voir
- Le Massif des Calanques.
- Le Cap Canaille.
- Le Vignoble Cassidain.
- Le Port.
- Promenades en mer dans les Calanques de Port-Miou, Port-Pin, En-Vau.
- Musée d'arts et traditions populaires de Cassis.

Hôtels
- 5 hôtels 3 étoiles: Les Jardins du Campanile - La Plage du Bestouan - La Rade - Les Roches Blanches - Le Royal Cottage.
- 7 hôtels 2 étoiles: Le Cassitel - Le Clos des Arômes - Le Grand Jardin - Le Golfe - Le Laurence - Le Liautaud - Le Provençal.
- 2 hôtels 1 étoile: Le Commerce - Le Joli Bois.
- 1 hôtel: Maguy.
- 1 résidence de tourisme: Eleis.

ÉCRIVEZ

Suggest students do some research in the library to learn more about the selected region if necessary.

1. Vous allez écrire une publicité touristique. Choisissez une région, par exemple, votre état ou une région francophone que vous avez visitée ou voudriez visiter. Avant de commencer, décidez quel groupe de touristes vous allez viser (*focus on*). Notez les sites touristiques et les agréments (*amenities*) qui vont intéresser ce groupe. Pensez à plusieurs titres intéressants, puis écrivez votre publicité en employant un style télégraphique.

2. Imaginez que vous êtes en vacances dans la région pour laquelle vous avez écrit une publicité. Écrivez une carte postale à un(e) ami(e), à un membre de votre famille ou à un(e) collègue. Il n'y a pas beaucoup de place sur une carte postale, alors il faut employer un style télégraphique. Qu'est-ce que vous avez vu? Qu'est-ce que vous avez fait? Comment allez-vous décrire la région?

3. Le petit prince, lui, a fait un voyage dans la solitude. Imaginez qu'après son voyage à la Terre, il écrit une carte à son amie, la rose. Qu'est-ce qu'il va lui dire?

➡ *Ma chère rose...*

VOCABULAIRE ACTIF

À l'hôtel

les bagages (m.) *luggage*
une baignoire *a bathtub*
une carte de crédit *a credit card*
(une chambre) libre *(a room) available*
un chien *a dog*
la clé *the key*
un garage *a garage, covered parking*

un jardin *a garden*
un lavabo *a bathroom sink*
la nuit *the night*
(petit déjeuner) compris *(breakfast) included*
une piscine *a swimming pool*
un(e) réceptionniste *a receptionist*

Les étages *(floors)*

un ascenseur *an elevator*
un escalier *the stairs*

le premier étage *the second floor*
le rez-de-chaussée *the ground floor*

Les vacances

acheter des souvenirs *to buy souvenirs*
une agence de voyages *a travel agency*
aller à la chasse *to go hunting*
aller à la pêche *to go fishing*
une cathédrale *a cathedral*
célèbre *famous*
un château *a castle*
faire du bateau *to go boating*
faire du camping *to go camping*

faire du ski nautique *to water-ski*
faire un séjour *to stay*
un lieu *a place*
un monument *a monument*
passer une semaine / ses vacances *to spend a week / one's vacation*
un séjour *a stay*
un vieux quartier *an old quarter / part of town*
visiter *to visit (a place)*
un voyage organisé *a tour*

La nature

le désert *the desert*
la forêt *the forest*
une île *an island*

un lac *a lake*
la mer *the sea*
la plage *the beach*

Les moyens de transport *(means of transportation)*

à pied *on foot*
en avion *by plane*
en bateau *by boat*

en train *by train*
en vélo *on bicycle*
en voiture *by car*

À la gare

un aller-retour *a round-trip ticket*
un aller simple *a one-way ticket*
l'arrivée (f.) *the arrival*
un billet *a ticket*
la consigne *baggage checkroom / locker*
une couchette *a couchette / berth*
le départ *the departure*
en première ou deuxième classe *first or second class*

fumeurs / non-fumeurs *smoking / nonsmoking*
le guichet *the ticket window*
un horaire *a schedule*
une place *a seat*
le prochain train *the next train*
le TGV *high-speed train*
une valise *a suitcase*
un voyage d'affaires *a business trip*

À l'aéroport

un avion *an airplane*   un vol *a flight*

Les pays
(Voir le tableau p. 251)
le monde *the world*

Verbes
attendre *to wait (for)*
descendre *to go down, to get off, to stay in a hotel*
dormir *to sleep*
entendre *to hear*
nager *to swim*
partir *to leave*
perdre *to lose*

rater (le train) *to miss (the train)*
rendre visite (à) *to visit (someone)*
répondre *to answer*
revenir *to come back*
servir *to serve*
sortir *to go out*
vendre *to sell*
venir *to come*

Expressions de temps
depuis *since*
depuis combien de temps? / depuis quand?
  how long? / since when?
il y a *ago*

pendant *for*
pendant combien de temps? *for how long?*
tout de suite *right away*

Pour demander et donner des renseignements / de l'aide
avec plaisir *with pleasure (my pleasure)*
un bureau de renseignements *an information bureau / desk*
Est-ce que vous pourriez... *Could you please . . .*
  me donner un coup de main *give me a hand*
  m'aider à... *help me . . .*
je regrette *I'm sorry*
Pourriez-vous m'indiquer... *Could you tell me . . .*

Divers
le (la) même *the same*   y *it, there*

Les relations humaines

Ces amies ont été jeunes, elles aussi, n'est-ce pas?

Qu'est-ce qu'elles faisaient ensemble quand elles étaient jeunes?

Quel était leur concept du bonheur?

Et vous?

Qu'est-ce que vous aimiez faire quand vous étiez enfant?

This chapter will enable you to

- **understand the gist of discussions on more abstract topics, such as the concept of happiness**
- **read an article on love and marriage in France, and a literary classic about friendship—as seen through the eyes of** *le petit prince*
- **relate how things used to be**
- **link ideas while describing people and things**
- **make suggestions and begin to state opinions**

Première étape

À l'écoute: L'amitié

This input section introduces students to the topic of friendship, with focus on *l'imparfait* and pronominal verbs.

Avant d'écouter

Cue to Video Module 8 (00:36:29), where Nicolas talks to his friends about his relationship with his *petite amie.*

Vous allez entendre un monsieur parler de l'amitié et de son meilleur ami.

1 Quand vous pensez à l'amitié, quelles sont les images qui vous viennent à l'esprit? Cochez les suggestions appropriées, puis complétez la liste selon votre expérience personnelle.

L'amitié, c'est...

_____ parler de tout

_____ communiquer sans parler

_____ savoir écouter

_____ rire* ensemble *(to laugh together)*

_____ s'amuser *(to have fun)* ensemble

_____ pleurer ensemble

_____ passer des heures au téléphone

_____ raconter des blagues *(to tell jokes)*

_____ prêter des vêtements *(to lend clothes),* des livres, des CD, etc.

_____ partager des idées, des secrets, etc.

_____ demander et donner des conseils *(advice)*

_____ faire des choses ensemble: sortir, aller en boîte *(to nightclubs),* au ciné (cinéma), à une soirée *(party),* etc.

_____ avoir les mêmes goûts *(same tastes)*

_____ ?

2 Les copains et les copines sont des camarades, c'est-à-dire des relations plus superficielles que les amis. Dans la liste qui précède, quelles sont les choses qu'on fait avec un(e) ami(e) mais pas avec un copain ou une copine?

3 Est-ce que vous voyez encore des ami(e)s d'enfance? Pensez à un(e) ami(e) d'enfance. Où et quand avez-vous fait sa connaissance *(did you meet)?*

---

*Rire se conjugue comme **dire** aux trois personnes du singulier **(je ris, tu ris, il/elle/on rit)** et comme **étudier** aux trois personnes du pluriel **(nous rions, vous riez, ils/elles rient).** Passé composé: **j'ai ri.**

Note culturelle

Ami? Copain? In French, different words indicate different kinds of friends. **Un(e) ami(e)** is a close friend; **un copain / une copine** is a pal, a buddy, a casual friend; **un petit ami** is a boyfriend and **une petite amie** is a girlfriend. In Canada, **un(e) chum** is the equivalent of **un copain / une copine**; **mon chum** is used for **mon petit ami;** and **ma blonde** or **ma chum** means **ma petite amie.**

Écoutons

4 ANSWER: parler de tout, raconter des blagues, rire, s'amuser, faire des choses ensemble, aller au ciné, en boîte

Audio CD

5 ANSWERS: 1. b 2. a 3. a 4. b 5. b 6. a

4 Écoutez une première fois les réflexions du monsieur en regardant la liste dans **Avant d'écouter.** Quelles activités de cette liste mentionne-t-il? Cochez-les une deuxième fois.

5 Écoutez encore pour trouver la bonne réponse à chacune des questions suivantes.

1. Quand le monsieur a-t-il fait la connaissance de son meilleur ami?
   a. au lycée
   b. dans son enfance

2. Où est-ce que son ami habitait?
   a. à côté de chez lui
   b. assez loin

3. Qu'est-ce qu'ils ne faisaient *pas* ensemble?
   a. jouer au basket
   b. jouer aux cow-boys et aux Indiens

4. Qu'est-ce qu'ils faisaient «quelquefois»?
   a. ils achetaient des glaces à la vanille
   b. ils avaient des petites disputes

5. Quand ils étaient étudiants, où allaient-ils le samedi soir?
   a. au café et au ciné
   b. en boîte

6. Qu'est-ce qui est différent maintenant?
   a. la vie les a séparés
   b. ils ne racontent plus de blagues

VOCABULAIRE ACTIF

l'amitié (f.)
s'amuser
une boîte (de nuit)
le ciné
communiquer
un conseil
ensemble
les goûts (m.)
pareil(le)
passer (des heures)
un(e) petit(e) ami(e)
pleurer
prêter
raconter des blagues (f.)
rire
un secret
une soirée
un tas de
de temps en temps
des vêtements (m.)
se voir

6 Écoutez encore la dernière partie du segment sonore, depuis «Plus tard... ». En utilisant le contexte et la logique, pouvez-vous déduire le sens des mots suivants? Reliez les mots en caractères gras à leurs synonymes.

1. on faisait **un tas** de choses...
2. ce n'est plus **pareil**
3. on continue à **se** voir **de temps en temps**

   a. quelquefois
   b. l'un l'autre
   c. beaucoup
   d. la même chose

Prononciation

*La lettre **g***

■ You have seen that sometimes the letter **g** is pronounced [ʒ] as in **partager;** sometimes it is pronounced [g] as in **regarder;** sometimes it is pronounced [ɲ] as in **baignoire.**

Écoutez

Audio CD

Look at the following words, which are all familiar to you, and listen to their pronunciation on the student audio CD. As you listen, try to infer when the letter **g** is pronounced [ʒ], [g], or [ɲ], checking the appropriate boxes in the chart.

1. gentil, énergique, gymnastique
2. garçon, golf, légume
3. renseignement, Allemagne
4. église, grand

	[ʒ]	[g]	[ɲ]
g + e, i, y	✓		
g + a, o, u		✓	
g + n			✓
g + other consonant		✓	

■ To retain the [ʒ] sound in some forms of verbs like **manger** or **partager,** a silent **e** is added after the **g** before an **o** or an **a.**

nous partag**e**ons   je partag**e**ais

■ To retain the [g] sound, a silent **u** is added after the **g** before an **e** or an **i.**

une blag**u**e   le g**u**ichet

Essayez!

Audio CD

Practice saying the following sentences aloud, then listen to them on the student audio CD to verify your pronunciation.

1. Mes amis aiment les voyages; après un séjour à la plage en Bretagne, ils veulent passer par la Bourgogne puis aller en montagne.
2. J'ai mis mes bagages à la consigne avant *(before)* d'aller voir un copain dans sa maison de campagne.
3. Georges et moi, nous avons les mêmes goûts—nous ne mangeons jamais d'oignons!

STRUCTURE: Talking about the way things used to be
L'imparfait

Observez et déduisez

Des amis d'enfance se retrouvent.

Patrick est mon meilleur ami d'enfance. Il habitait à côté de chez moi, et nous faisions tout ensemble. On allait à l'école ensemble; on racontait des blagues; on riait beaucoup. Quelquefois nous avions des disputes—quand il voulait jouer aux cow-boys et aux Indiens alors que moi, je voulais jouer au foot, par exemple—mais pas souvent.

> ■ In the preceding paragraph, a young man uses the imperfect tense to talk about his best friend and the things they used to do together. What forms of the imperfect can you identify?
>
> ■ Jot down the endings for the following forms: **je, on, nous.** Can you predict the endings for the **tu** and **vous** forms of the verb?

Vérifiez   *L'imparfait*

Point out that with the verbs **rire, oublier,** and **étudier,** the present tense stem ends in an **i** and the imperfect endings for **nous** and **vous** begin with an **i**, creating the uncommon **ii.**

OPTIONAL DRILL: Autrefois... 1. Je racontais des blagues. (nous, tu, mes copains, ma cousine, vous) 2. Nous buvions du lait. (tu, mes camarades, ma sœur, vous, je) 3. Tu lisais des bandes dessinées. (je, mon frère, mes parents, nous, vous)

■ The formation of the imperfect is regular for all verbs except **être.*** To form the imperfect, take the *nous* form of the present tense, drop the *-ons*, and add the endings **-ais, -ais, -ait, -ions, -iez, -aient.**

nous **parløns**
nous **sortøns**
nous **riøns**
nous **faisøns**

To draw students' attention to the different oral and written forms, ask how many written forms they see in the chart. Now read the paradigm and ask how many forms they hear. Point out that all forms except **nous** and **vous** sound alike and that **nous** and **vous** differ from the present tense only in the additional **i** of the ending.

L'imparfait			
je parlais	je sortais	je riais	je faisais
tu parlais	tu sortais	tu riais	tu faisais
il / elle / on parlait	il / elle / on sortait	il / elle / on riait	il / elle / on faisait
nous parlions	nous sortions	nous riions	nous faisions
vous parliez	vous sortiez	vous riiez	vous faisiez
ils / elles parlaient	ils / elles sortaient	ils / elles riaient	ils / elles faisaient

The use of the imperfect tense as background for verbs in the passé composé is discussed in Ch. 9, where the imperfect and passé composé are contrasted.

■ The stem for **être** is **ét-.** The endings are regular.

j'étais
nous étions

■ The imperfect is used to describe what things were like in the past, the way things used to be.

Autrefois, quand nous **étions** petits, nous **faisions** un tas de choses ensemble.
Nous **regardions** la télé; nous **jouions** avec notre chien et notre chat *(cat);* nous **riions** beaucoup.

VOCABULAIRE ACTIF
autrefois
un chat

---

*However, as you learned in Chapter 2, verbs ending in **-ger** add an **e** to the stem before endings beginning with **a.** Likewise, verbs ending in **-cer** add a cedilla to the **c** in the same cases:

je man**ge**ais BUT nous mangions   je commen**ç**ais BUT nous commencions

ACTIVITÉS

A. Une enfance française: comparaison.   Comparez votre enfance avec l'enfance de Chantal pendant les années 50. Est-ce que vos enfances étaient semblables?

	Moi aussi	Pas moi
1. J'avais une amie qui m'invitait souvent à manger le quatre-heures *(snack)* chez elle, en revenant de l'école.	——	——
2. Après ça, on jouait ensemble, ou on faisait nos devoirs ensemble.	——	——
3. J'aimais être la première de ma classe parce qu'à la fin de l'année, je recevais un prix qui était généralement un beau livre.	——	——
4. Je lisais beaucoup, surtout les aventures d'Alice, une jeune détective.	——	——
5. Je prenais des cours de danse et d'art dramatique au conservatoire municipal.	——	——
6. Pendant l'été, ma famille fermait la maison pendant deux mois, et on partait en vacances.	——	——
7. Quelquefois on louait une villa à la montagne ou au bord de la mer, ou on faisait du camping.	——	——
8. Chaque été, nous passions aussi deux ou trois semaines chez ma grand-mère.	——	——

Maintenant, comparez vos réponses avec celles de vos camarades de classe. Est-ce que l'enfance chez vous ressemble à l'enfance de Chantal?

B. Un enfant pas comme les autres!   Aviez-vous des goûts particuliers quand vous étiez petit(e)? D'abord, dans la colonne de gauche, complétez les phrases selon vos préférences *d'il y a dix ans.*

Il y a dix ans...	#1	#2	#3
je mangeais beaucoup de...			
j'allais souvent...			
je lisais...			
j'aimais...			
je détestais...			
j'avais...			
je...			

Maintenant, interviewez trois camarades de classe. Pouvez-vous trouver quelqu'un qui avait des goûts identiques?

➡ *Qu'est-ce que tu lisais il y a dix ans?*
   Est-ce que tu lisais... ?

C. For homework, have students write a paragraph using the information gathered in the interview. They may describe their partner's childhood or compare/contrast with their own.

C. Autrefois et aujourd'hui. Est-ce que la vie aujourd'hui ressemble à la vie d'autrefois? Comparez les deux en employant les expressions ci-dessous.

Autrefois je...   ma famille...   mes parents...   mon copain/ ma copine...

regarder souvent la télévision
aller au ciné le samedi après-midi
habiter avec mes (ses/leurs) parents
ne pas aimer faire la sieste
voyager en été
rire beaucoup

jouer au Monopoly
vouloir être pompier (*fireman*)
prêter des vêtements (des livres, des CD)
aimer mes (ses/leurs) professeurs
raconter des blagues
?

➡ *Autrefois je faisais beaucoup de sports; aujourd'hui j'étudie beaucoup. Autrefois mes parents... (ma copine...)*

Maintenant, interviewez un(e) partenaire et comparez vos souvenirs.

➡ *Est-ce que ta famille regardait souvent la télé? Et aujourd'hui?*

D. First have students brainstorm questions in groups, but tell the class you might not always respond truthfully. Then, as students ask you questions, have a volunteer write them on the board. Finally, have students decide which questions they believe you answered truthfully: «Vous aviez un chat, n'est-ce pas?»

D. De mon temps. Posez des questions à votre professeur pour savoir comment était sa vie quand il (elle) avait dix ans—mais ne soyez pas trop indiscret(-ète)! Écoutez ses réponses et devinez (*guess*) quelles réponses sont vraies et lesquelles sont fausses.

➡ *Est-ce que vous aviez un chat? Où est-ce que vous habitiez?*

E. You may want to assign this as homework so that students have time to think about their childhood friends. Allow time for students to share with the class and for other students to ask follow-up questions to get details.

E. Le portrait d'un(e) ami(e). Imaginez que vous êtes psychologue et que vous interrogez un(e) client(e) au sujet de son (sa) meilleur(e) ami(e) d'enfance. En travaillant avec un(e) partenaire, écrivez huit questions que vous allez lui poser.

➡ *Comment était votre meilleur(e) ami(e)? Qu'est-ce que vous faisiez ensemble?*

Ensuite, à tour de rôle, assumez l'identité du (de la) client(e), et décrivez votre meilleur(e) ami(e) d'enfance à votre partenaire, le (la) psychologue, en répondant aux questions que vous avez préparées.

STRUCTURE: Talking about friendships
Les verbes pronominaux (I)

Observez et déduisez   Mes meilleurs amis n'habitent plus à côté de chez moi, mais on continue à se voir de temps en temps, et chaque fois qu'on se retrouve, on s'amuse! Nous nous comprenons aussi bien aujourd'hui qu'auparavant—même si nous nous voyons rarement!

■ If **se voir** means *to see each other,* what would the following verbs mean?

se parler   se téléphoner   se comprendre   se disputer

■ Study the pronominal verbs in the paragraph on page 281, and fill in the following chart with the appropriate pronouns: **me (m'), te (t'), se (s'), vous.**

s'amuser	
je _____ amuse	nous nous amusons
tu _____ amuses	vous _____ amusez
il / elle / on s'amuse	ils / elles _____ amusent

Vérifiez   *Les verbes pronominaux*

Reflexive verbs are discussed in Ch. 10. Pronominal verbs are practiced more fully in Ch. 10, and their use in the futur proche and passé composé is discussed at that point.

Remind students that they used the pronominal verb **s'appeler** in the Chapitre préliminaire.

■ Pronominal verbs are conjugated like other verbs except that an extra pronoun is needed before the verb.

> **Le verbe se souvenir *(to remember)***
>
> je **me** souviens   nous **nous** souvenons
> tu **te** souviens   vous **vous** souvenez
> il / elle / on **se** souvient   ils / elles **se** souviennent

■ In the negative, **ne** precedes the pronoun.

Je **ne** me dispute jamais avec mes copains.

OPTIONAL DRILL: Changez le sujet de la phrase. CUES: 1. Je m'amuse! (on, tu, les étudiants, nous) 2. On ne s'ennuie pas! (tu, je, vous, le professeur) 3. Autrefois, les amis se parlaient souvent. (nous, on, vous, les étudiants)

■ Some pronominal verbs indicate a *reciprocal* action, an action two or more subjects do to or with one another.

se battre	*to fight with each other*
se disputer	*to argue with each other*
se retrouver	*to meet each other (to get together)*
se (re)voir	*to see each other (again)*
se parler	*to talk to each other*
se comprendre	*to understand each other*
se téléphoner	*to phone each other*
s'écrire	*to write each other*

Autrefois ma sœur et moi, **nous nous disputions** assez souvent, mais maintenant **nous nous comprenons** bien!

Point out that although reciprocal pronominals are logically plural, they may in some cases also be singular: «Je me parle» but not «Je me téléphone». The plural can also be replaced by **on**: On se parle.

■ Compare the pronominal and nonpronominal forms of these verbs:

Alexis et Marie-Pierre **se retrouvent** au café. *(They meet each other.)*
Alexis **retrouve** Marie-Pierre au café. *(He meets her.)*

■ Some pronominal verbs are used *idiomatically.*

s'entendre   *to get along (with each other)*
se souvenir   *to remember*

VOCABULAIRE ACTIF
Les verbes pronominaux
se comprendre, etc.

s'amuser   *to have fun*
s'ennuyer*   *to be bored*

Ma meilleure amie du lycée et moi, nous **nous entendions** bien. Je **me souviens** que nous **nous amusions** beaucoup tous les week-ends.

ACTIVITÉS

F. Nous deux.   Pensez à la relation que vous avez avec un frère, une sœur, un(e) autre parent ou un copain. Les phrases suivantes s'appliquent-elles *(apply)* à cette relation?

La personne: _____

	Oui	Non
1. Nous nous amusons ensemble.	_____	_____
2. Nous nous entendons bien.	_____	_____
3. Nous nous voyons assez souvent.	_____	_____
4. Nous ne nous parlons pas tous les jours.	_____	_____
5. Nous nous disputons rarement.	_____	_____
6. Nous nous comprenons bien.	_____	_____
7. Nous nous écrivons des messages électroniques.	_____	_____
8. Nous ne nous ennuyons jamais.	_____	_____

Maintenant, expliquez vos réponses à un(e) partenaire.

➡ *Ma sœur et moi, nous nous amusons ensemble. Nous jouons au tennis.*

G. Je me souviens que…   Hélène parle de ses souvenirs d'enfance en regardant son album de photos (ci-dessous et à la page 284). Imaginez ce qu'elle va dire en employant autant de verbes pronominaux que possible.

Je me souviens que…

1. … mes amis et moi, nous nous retrouvions souvent au café…

2. … Carole et Jean…

F. First have students choose the relationship that they will describe. Then have them discuss their answers with a partner before discussing as a whole class.

G. Do as a whole-class activity, or have the class brainstorm answers for #1, then have students work on #2–5 with a partner before reporting back. Remind them to use the imperfect tense and negative verbs also.

---

*Verbs ending in **-yer** are stem-changing verbs. Change **y** to **i** in all forms of the verb with silent endings: je m'ennui~~e~~, tu t'ennui~~es~~, il s'ennui~~e~~, ils s'ennui~~ent~~, BUT nous nous ennu<u>y</u>ons, vous vous ennu<u>y</u>ez.

3. ... mes cousins...

4. ... ma sœur et sa meilleure amie...

5. ... _____ et moi, nous...

An Information Gap activity **(LOTO: La vie d'autre-fois)** in the *Instructor's Resource Manual* gives students practice in using the imperfect to talk about "the way things used to be".

Jeu de rôle. Encourage students to use all active vocabulary as well as the pronominal verbs introduced in this section. Have volunteer pairs present skits as time allows. Ask other groups what kinds of memories the grandparent mentions in their skit.   ALTERNATIVE: Have students interview an older person they know about how life has changed over the past 30 years and report to the class.

W B

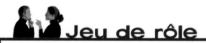

Jeu de rôle

It's the year 2050. You've aged and the world has changed a lot! With a part-ner, play the role of a grandparent and grandchild. The grandchild describes what his/her life is like "now"—in 2050—and asks if the grandparent did the same things as a young person. The grandparent talks about life fifty years ago, and explains what s/he did differently.

Deuxième étape

Lecture: L'amour et le mariage

This input section introduces vocabulary and serves as a springboard for discussion, with some elaboration, on the topic of love and marriage.

1 Vous allez lire un article sur l'amour et le mariage en France. À votre avis, quels sont les nombres qui vont s'appliquer aux catégories suivantes pour la France des années 90?

1. Pourcentage des jeunes entre 20 et 24 ans qui vivent (habitent) avec un(e) conjoint(e) (qui sont mariés):
   a. 20%   b. 30%   c. 40% ou plus

2. Nombre de mariages qui se terminent par un divorce:
   a. 1 sur *(out of)* 2   b. 1 sur 3   c. 1 sur 4

3. Pourcentage de couples qui vivent ensemble sans être mariés (l'union libre ou la cohabitation):
   a. 10–15%   b. 20–25%   c. 30% ou plus

4. Nombre de couples qui ont vécu (habité) ensemble avant le mariage:
   a. 40% ou moins   b. 50%   c. 60% ou plus

2 À votre avis, est-ce que le nombre de célibataires, c'est-à-dire de gens non mariés, a augmenté *(increased)* ou diminué dans les dernières années?

3 Où est-ce qu'on rencontre l'homme ou la femme de sa vie? Complétez la liste suivante, puis classez ces lieux de 1 (lieu le plus commun) à 8 (lieu le moins commun).

_____ au travail

_____ à la fac

_____ au lycée

_____ à un bal *(dance)*

_____ chez des amis

_____ dans son voisinage *(neighborhood)*

_____ dans une boîte de nuit

_____ ?

4 Parcourez le texte une première fois pour voir quels sujets sont traités dans l'article. Cochez-les.

_____ Les mariages mixtes (entre deux nationalités ou races différentes)

_____ Mariages religieux vs mariages civils

285

_____ ✓   Âge moyen des hommes et des femmes quand ils se marient

_____ ✓   Comparaison du nombre de divorces aujourd'hui et il y a vingt ans

_____   Comparaison de la proportion de célibataires chez les hommes et chez les femmes

_____ ✓   Relation éducation–mariage pour les femmes

_____ ✓   Évolution de la cohabitation

_____ ✓   Comparaison des circonstances de rencontre entre les années 1920 et aujourd'hui

_____ ✓   Saison privilégiée des rencontres

L'amour et le mariage en France

La vie en couple

Les mariés, une espèce en voie de disparition

Évolution du nombre annuel de mariages (en milliers) :

623   342   177   331   320   394   334   287   254

1920   1930   1940   1950   1960   1970   1980   1990   1995

INSEE

Depuis 1993, le nombre des mariages en France est le plus bas du siècle°, à l'exception des périodes des deux guerres mondiales°. Les 254 000 mariages enregistrés en 1995 représentent un mariage pour 228 habitants, le taux° le plus bas d'Europe après la Suède°. Et si l'on se marie moins, on se marie de plus en plus tard: l'âge moyen au premier mariage est de 27 ans pour les femmes (22 en 1970) et 29 ans pour les hommes (24 en 1970). On divorce aussi plus facilement: près d'un mariage sur deux se termine par un divorce, contre° un sur dix il y a vingt ans.

the lowest of the century
world wars

rate / Sweden

comparé à

Le célibat

Les célibataires sont de plus en plus nombreux: à peine° 20% des jeunes de 20–24 ans ont un(e) conjoint(e), contre 33% au début des années 80. La proportion de célibataires semble aussi liée° au niveau d'éducation: chez les hommes, il y a plus de célibataires dans les catégories sociales modestes; chez les femmes, au contraire, ce sont les femmes diplômées qui se marient le moins.

barely

linked

La cohabitation

Un couple concubin¹ sur dix

Évolution du nombre de couples non mariés en France et part dans le nombre total de couples:

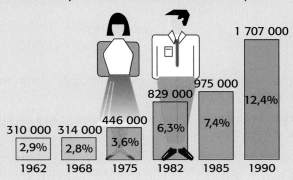

310 000	314 000	446 000	829 000	975 000	1 707 000
2,9%	2,8%	3,6%	6,3%	7,4%	12,4%
1962	1968	1975	1982	1985	1990

1. qui cohabite

Autre phénomène récent: le développement de l'union libre ou cohabitation. Apparue vers le milieu des années 70, la pratique de la cohabitation ou union libre concerne aujourd'hui plus de 12% de la population totale et dépasse° 20% chez les jeunes de 18 à 24 ans. Bien souvent, c'est l'arrivée attendue ou non d'un enfant qui motive l'officialisation de la cohabitation. Environ 60% des couples qui se marient aujourd'hui ont vécu ensemble avant le mariage, contre 8% pendant la période 1960–1969. L'union libre est considérée à la fois comme un «mariage à l'essai°» et une manière de conserver sa liberté.

exceeds

trial marriage

La rencontre

C'est seulement dans les contes de fées° que les princes épousent des bergères°. Dans la réalité, les princes épousent des princesses, et les bergères épousent des bergers. En effet, en France, on vit en général avec quelqu'un de son milieu social et de sa région. Mais le scénario des rencontres a évolué. Dans les années 1920, par exemple, quatre circonstances présidaient à la majorité des mariages: le voisinage, le travail, le bal et les rencontres chez des amis. Aujourd'hui on n'épouse plus son voisin (3% des mariages, contre 21% dans les années 1920) et le travail ou la fac ne produisent pas beaucoup de mariages. Les bals et les boîtes de nuit sont les lieux privilégiés des rencontres. Et la saison des amours, ce n'est pas le printemps, mais l'été, le temps des vacances où bals et sorties se multiplient.

comme Blanche Neige
shepherdess

Extrait de trois articles: «La famille française d'aujourd'hui», *Journal français d'Amérique*, 29 juin–26 juillet 1990; «La quête de l'âme sœur», *Ça m'intéresse*, août 1990; «Le couple», *Francoscopie* 1997.

Make sure students understand the difference between **se marier** (to get married) and **épouser (quelqu'un)** (to marry someone). Also, have students find in the last part of the text **(La rencontre)** another meaning for **le milieu**.

A. Point out that statistics in the U.S. are similar. For example, according to a 1987 U.S. study among women ages 20–29, 30% had cohabited at some time, and 12% were currently cohabiting. A 1980 study showed that 53% of people getting a marriage license had cohabited before marriage. The divorce rate is similar in the U.S.: one out of every two marriages ends in divorce.

B. ANSWERS: 1. F (hommes: 29 ans; femmes: 27 ans) 2. F (1 sur 10 vs. 1 sur 2) 3. F (20% contre 33%) 4. F (les femmes diplômées se marient moins) 5. V 6. F (même milieu) 7. F (bals et boîtes de nuit vs. voisinage, etc.) 8. F (l'été)

Discuss #1 and #2 of **Et vous?** with the whole class. As always, encourage students to keep their answers simple and to stick to vocabulary and structures they know. #3 and #4 are more concrete and can be discussed in small groups.

Et vous?

FOLLOW-UP: Compare answers from various groups and discuss further. For #3a, reward the group(s) who came up with the longest list.

VOCABULAIRE ACTIF

l'amour (m.)
un bal
célibataire
un couple
le divorce
épouser
le mariage
se marier
(l'âge) moyen
rencontrer/une rencontre

5 **Les mots.**   En utilisant le contexte et la logique, identifiez les mots qui ont la signification donnée.

partie du texte	français	anglais
La vie en couple	_____	*to get married*
Le célibat	_____	*the level*
La cohabitation	_____ _____	*the middle* *freedom*
La rencontre	_____ _____	*fairy tales* *to marry (someone)*

6 **Le texte**

A. **Les nombres.** Reprenez les nombres anticipés dans **Avant de lire.** Quelles sont les vraies réponses?

B. **Vrai ou faux?** Les phrases suivantes sont-elles vraies ou fausses? Si elles sont fausses, corrigez-les.

1. L'âge moyen du mariage est le même pour les hommes et les femmes.
2. Il y a vingt ans, le divorce était aussi commun qu'aujourd'hui.
3. Selon cet article, il y a plus de jeunes (20–24 ans) qui vivaient avec un(e) conjoint(e) en 1990 qu'au début (commencement) des années 80.
4. L'éducation et les diplômes encouragent le mariage chez les femmes.
5. La majorité des couples qui cohabitent ont moins de 24 ans.
6. On épouse souvent quelqu'un d'un milieu social différent.
7. Les lieux de rencontres n'ont pas changé depuis les années 1920.
8. Le printemps est la saison des amours par excellence.

1. À votre avis, pourquoi est-ce qu'il y a moins de jeunes de 20 à 24 ans qui ont un(e) conjoint(e) dans les années 90 que dans les années 80? Est-ce la peur du Sida *(fear of AIDS)?* la situation économique? d'autres facteurs? La situation est-elle la même aux États-Unis?
2. Pourquoi est-ce que les femmes diplômées se marient moins souvent que les femmes qui ont moins d'éducation? Est-ce parce qu'elles sont plus indépendantes? plus occupées? plus difficiles *(choosy)?* Est-ce la même chose aux États-Unis? Pensez à des femmes que vous connaissez—est-ce vrai pour elles?
3. «C'est seulement dans les contes de fées que les princes épousent des bergères. Dans la réalité, les princes épousent les princesses, et les bergères épousent des bergers.»
   a. Trouvez des exemples dans la littérature, le cinéma ou l'actualité où des «princes» ont épousé des «bergères». Préparez une liste de noms célèbres. Quel groupe va pouvoir faire la liste la plus longue?
   b. Est-ce vrai que dans la réalité, on épouse quelqu'un de son milieu social? Pourquoi? Donnez des exemples personnels (des membres de votre famille, des amis, etc.).

4. Réfléchissez aux lieux et saisons de rencontre en pensant aux membres de votre famille et à vos amis. Où ont-ils rencontré l'homme ou la femme de leur vie? En quelle saison? Préparez une liste, puis faites une synthèse des réponses que vous avez en commun avec vos partenaires.

STRUCTURE: Relating/linking ideas (I)
Les pronoms relatifs *qui* et *qu(e)*

Observez et déduisez   Si les attitudes envers le mariage ont changé, est-ce que la répartition des tâches domestiques dans les couples a changé elle aussi? Lisez le tableau suivant.

Répartition des tâches domestiques dans les couples (en %)				
	Hommes	Femmes	Les deux conjoints également	Autres
faire la lessive[1]	1,9	95,3	1,17	1,5
repasser[2]	2,2	89,3	0,9	7,6
laver la voiture	71,3	12,3	2,3	14,2
faire la cuisine	8,3	84,0	5,1	2,6
passer l'aspirateur[3]	13,5	77,9	2,1	6,3
faire la vaisselle[4]	16,4	73,7	6,8	3,11
faire les courses	19,9	67,4	10,6	2,2

1. *laundry*   2. *ironing*   3. *vacuuming*   4. *doing the dishes*

Selon le tableau, d'habitude c'est la femme qui fait la lessive. Quelles sont les tâches que les hommes font rarement? Et dans votre famille, quelles sont les tâches que vous faites?

> ■ In the preceding paragraph, what kind of word follows the pronoun **qui**: a subject or a verb? What kind of word follows the pronoun **que** (**qu'**)?

Rencontre dans une boîte.

Vérifiez   *Les pronoms relatifs* **qui** *et* **qu(e)**

Point out that in each sentence, the second noun or pronoun reference is deleted: **ils** and **tâche.**

■ Relative pronouns are used to relate (link) two sentences and to avoid repetition.

<blockquote>

Ce sont les enfants.   +   Ils font la vaisselle.

→ Ce sont les enfants **qui** font la vaisselle.

Ranger *(Straighten)* ma chambre est une tâche.   +   Je n'aime pas cette tâche.

→ Ranger ma chambre est une tâche **que** je n'aime pas.

</blockquote>

VOCABULAIRE ACTIF

faire la lessive
faire la vaisselle
laver la voiture
passer l'aspirateur
ranger
rarement
repasser
une tâche

■ Both **qui** and **que** can refer to either people or things, so the difference in these pronouns is their grammatical function. The pronoun **qui** is used as a *subject* and is usually followed directly by a verb. The pronoun **que** is an *object* and is followed by a subject *and* a verb.

Pronoms relatifs
qui + verb
Ce sont les enfants **qui** font la vaisselle. Il y a des tâches domestiques **qui** sont ennuyeuses.
que + subject + verb
Ranger ma chambre est la tâche **que** je n'aime pas. Les couples **que** tu connais sont-ils des couples «modernes»?

■ Although the words "that," "whom," or "which" may be omitted in English, **que** may *not* be omitted in French.

<blockquote>

les couples **que** je connais   *the couples I know*

</blockquote>

ACTIVITÉS

A. Have a volunteer elicit and record class data on the board, then compare with statistics in the table.
ALTERNATIVE: Have partners share answers and compare with those in the table.

A. Les tâches domestiques.   Complétez les phrases suivantes selon vos expériences personnelles, et partagez vos réponses avec la classe.

ma mère / mon père   les enfants   ?
mon/ma camarade de chambre   moi (je)

1. C'est (Ce sont) _____ qui passe(nt) l'aspirateur chez moi.

2. C'est (Ce sont) _____ qui fais (fait/font) les courses.

3. C'est (Ce sont) _____ qui repasse(nt) les vêtements.

4. C'est (Ce sont) _____ qui fais (fait/font) la vaisselle.

5. Faire la cuisine est une tâche que _____ déteste(nt).

6. Faire la lessive est une tâche que _____ déteste(nt).

7. Ranger la chambre est une tâche que _____ déteste(nt).

8. Laver la voiture est une tâche que _____ déteste(nt).

Maintenant, comparez le profil de la classe avec le tableau à la page 289.

B. FOLLOW-UP: Have the class correct #2 (sont plus souvent célibataires) and #4 (épouse souvent...), then ask students if the statements are true or false in their own country: «Est-ce que le mariage est une institution qu'on valorise de nouveau chez vous?»

B. L'amour et le mariage. Voici un résumé de la lecture aux pages 286–287. Complétez les phrases avec **qui** ou **que,** puis indiquez si les phrases sont vraies ou fausses *selon l'article.*

	Vrai	Faux
➡ Le mariage est une institution *qu*'on valorise de nouveau en France.	✓	_____

1. L'augmentation du divorce est un phénomène

   _____ les statistiques révèlent de façon inquiétante.   _____ _____

2. Les femmes _____ ont un diplôme et les hommes

   _____ sont dans les catégories sociales modestes vivent plus souvent en couple.   _____ _____

3. Pour ceux *(those)* _____ cohabitent, c'est bien

   souvent l'arrivée d'un enfant _____ motive le mariage.   _____ _____

4. En France, on épouse rarement quelqu'un _____ est de son milieu social.   _____ _____

5. Autrefois c'était souvent un voisin _____ on épousait.   _____ _____

6. Aujourd'hui, le Français typique épouse

   quelqu'un _____ il rencontre à un bal ou dans une boîte de nuit.   _____ _____

C. Encourage students to write in a fourth option for each statement. Before beginning interviews, elicit questions students need to ask: 1. Quels hommes... 2. Qui est-ce que... 3. Avec qui... 4. Comment est l'homme...

C. Préférences. Indiquez vos préférences en matière d'amour en cochant *toutes* les réponses qui sont vraies pour vous—ou ajoutez des réponses originales.

1. Je préfère les hommes (les femmes) qui/que...

   _____ comprennent mes problèmes.

   _____ je rencontre dans mes cours.

   _____ sont sérieux (sérieuses).

   ?

2. Je veux épouser quelqu'un qui/que...

_____ écoute bien.

_____ j'admire.

_____ mes parents aiment bien aussi.

?

3. Je ne sors pas avec les hommes (les femmes) qui/que...

_____ mes copains n'aiment pas.

_____ n'aiment pas rire.

_____ sont égoïstes.

?

4. Pour moi, l'homme (la femme) idéal(e) c'est quelqu'un qui/que...

_____ adore faire les tâches domestiques.

_____ je peux admirer.

_____ aime mon chien (mon chat).

?

Maintenant, interviewez plusieurs camarades de classe pour trouver la personne qui vous ressemble le plus.

➡ — _Quels hommes (Quelles femmes) est-ce que tu préfères?_
— _Je préfère les hommes (les femmes)_ **qui** _comprennent mes problèmes._
... **que** _je rencontre dans mes cours._

STRUCTURE: Avoiding repetition (IV)
Les pronoms d'objet direct et indirect: **_me, te, nous_** _et_ **_vous_**

Observez et déduisez

— Ah! il m'adorait; il m'écoutait; il me regardait toujours avec amour.
— Il t'attendait tous les soirs; il ne te demandait rien; il te comprenait.
— C'est vrai. Si seulement je pouvais trouver un homme aussi fidèle que mon chien!

■ In the preceding dialogue, which object pronoun corresponds to **je?** to **tu?**

■ Where are the pronouns **me (m')** and **te (t')** placed in relation to the verb?

■ If **il m'écoutait** means _he used to listen to me,_ how would you say _he used to talk to me? he used to love you?_

Vérifiez *Les pronoms d'objet direct et indirect:* **me, te, nous** *et* **vous**

Point out that **t'** and **m'** are used before a word beginning with a vowel.

■ You have already studied third-person direct object pronouns (**le, la, les**) and indirect object pronouns (**lui, leur**) in Chapter 6. **Me (m'), te (t'), nous,** and **vous** are first- and second-person direct *and* indirect object pronouns.

je → **me (m')**   nous → **nous**
tu → **te (t')**   vous → **vous**

Est-ce que tes amis **te** prêtent leur voiture?
Est-ce qu'ils **t'**écoutent?
Vos parents **vous** font souvent des cadeaux?
Est-ce qu'ils **vous** comprennent?

Have students read the example and articulate the rules for placement in the present tense, passé composé (and all simple tenses), and with an infinitive.

■ The placement of first- and second-person object pronouns is the same as for other object pronouns.

Mon ami **m'**a dit qu'il **m'**aime et qu'il veut **m'**épouser!

■ In the passé composé, the past participle will agree in number and gender with the preceding *direct* object pronoun (see page 213).

Tu **nous** as vus au bal, n'est-ce pas?

Résumé: Les pronoms		
pronoms sujets	pronoms d'objet direct	pronoms d'objet indirect
je	me	me
tu	te	te
il/elle/on	le, la, l'	lui
nous	nous	nous
vous	vous	vous
ils/elles	les	leur

ACTIVITÉS

D. First have students indicate all answers that apply, then have them compare responses with a classmate.

D. Quelle chance! Réfléchissez (pensez) à vos relations personnelles. À qui les phrases suivantes s'appliquent-elles, selon votre expérience?

mon père /   mon copain /   mon frère /   ?
ma mère   ma copine   ma sœur

1. Il/Elle me comprend.   3. Il/Elle m'aime.
2. Il/Elle m'écoute.   4. Il/Elle m'amuse.

mes camarades de classe   mes professeurs   mes parents   ?

5. Ils/Elles m'écrivent des messages électroniques.
6. Ils/Elles me racontent des histoires amusantes.
7. Ils/Elles me retrouvent au café de temps en temps.
8. Ils/Elles me font des cadeaux.

Est-ce que votre partenaire a des réponses identiques?

E. Un anxieux. Le petit ami de Juliette est très anxieux *(insecure)*. Elle veut le rassurer. Imaginez les questions qu'il lui pose et les réponses mélodramatiques de Juliette.

➡ téléphoner ce soir?   — *Tu me téléphones ce soir?*
                        — *Mais oui, je te téléphone ce soir.*

1. attendre après le cours?   4. écrire des lettres d'amour?
2. retrouver au cinéma?   5. aimer?
3. trouver irrésistible?   6. épouser?!

F. S'il vous plaît! Votre petit(e) ami(e) vient dîner chez vous, alors vous demandez à vos camarades de chambre de «libérer» l'appartement ce soir. Dites-leur tout ce que vous avez déjà fait pour eux ou elles *(them)*. Sont-ils (elles) d'accord ou non?

➡   préparer des repas
    — *Je vous ai préparé des repas.*
    — *C'est vrai. Tu nous as préparé des repas.*

    prêter de l'argent
    — *Je vous ai prêté de l'argent.*
    — *Mais non. Tu ne nous as pas prêté d'argent.*

1. servir le petit déjeuner au lit
2. acheter des cadeaux d'anniversaire
3. prêter mes CD
4. écouter à une heure du matin
5. aider à faire vos devoirs
6. ?

G. Un couple moderne. Pour un couple moderne, l'égalité absolue est importante. Jouez le rôle de l'homme ou de la femme en décrivant vos rapports selon l'exemple.

➡ adorer
  Mon époux (épouse) m'adore et je l'adore aussi!

1. écouter   4. admirer
2. téléphoner tous les jours du bureau   5. parler de tout
3. comprendre   6. dire la vérité

H. Les plaintes *(Complaints).* Les femmes ne comprennent pas toujours les hommes et vice versa. Composez deux listes avec des plaintes typiques des hommes et des femmes.

➡ (plaintes des femmes)   *Les hommes ne nous écoutent pas.*
  (plaintes des hommes)   *Les femmes nous demandent trop.*

 Jeu de rôle

You and a classmate will play the role of a matrimonial agency employee and a client looking for an ideal mate. The employee needs to know what kind of mate is sought (men you meet in nightclubs? women who are independent?). The client describes his/her ideal husband/wife. (I want a wife who buys me presents! I prefer a husband who likes to laugh.) Does this ideal mate exist?

CULTURE ET RÉFLEXION

■ **L'amitié.** On dit que les Français sont comme une bonne baguette: l'extérieur est parfois dur mais l'intérieur est souple et tendre! À l'extérieur,

Les Français sont comme une bonne baguette...

les Français semblent parfois distants, réservés, froids, mais quand ils s'ouvrent, quand ils offrent leur amitié, c'est pour la vie. Un(e) ami(e), pour un Français, c'est quelqu'un qui n'a pas peur d'intervenir. Dans son livre *Évidences invisibles,* l'ethnologue Raymonde Carroll donne l'exemple d'une Française vivant aux États-Unis, une jeune maman qui traverse une période difficile. Son «amie-voisine» américaine, à qui elle mentionne qu'elle est très fatiguée, dit tout simplement: «Let me know if there is anything I can do.» Une amie française, à qui elle mentionne la même chose, propose tout de suite de garder ses enfants pendant quelques heures, pour lui permettre de se reposer[1]. Selon Raymonde

Carroll, la différence de réaction est culturelle: pour l'amie américaine, prendre la situation en main[2], c'est prononcer un jugement moral et dire en quelque sorte: «Tu n'es pas capable de contrôler ta vie.» Pour l'amie française, prendre la situation en main est une obligation, une des responsabilités de l'amitié. L'amitié, pour un Français, c'est dire ce qu'on pense, même si ce n'est pas toujours gentil.

L'amitié, c'est s'engager[3], même si ce n'est pas toujours pratique. Les Français préfèrent avoir peu d'amis, mais de vrais amis, plutôt que beaucoup d'«amitiés» superficielles. Et vous? Préférez-vous avoir peu d'amis, mais de vrais amis? Quand un(e) ami(e) traverse une situation difficile, qu'est-ce que vous faites? Attendez-vous que votre ami(e) vous demande de l'aide, ou prenez-vous la situation en main? Est-ce que vous êtes toujours honnête avec vos amis? Expliquez.

■ **«Dating».** La France évoque toutes sortes d'images romantiques, n'est-ce pas? Ah, l'amour... Est-ce donc vrai qu'il n'y a pas de mot pour «dating» en français? Eh oui! Le concept de «dating» n'existe même pas. Un jeune homme ne vient jamais chercher une jeune fille chez elle pour l'amener au cinéma. Non, les jeunes sortent généralement en groupes, et ils se donnent rendez-vous devant le cinéma ou à la terrasse d'un café. Les couples se forment à l'intérieur du groupe. Un autre concept complètement étranger à la culture française est le concept des «proms» ou autres activités sociales organisées par les écoles. La vie sociale et l'école sont deux mondes totalement séparés en France. Comparez les coutumes d'interaction sociale pour les jeunes en France et dans votre culture. Quels sont les avantages et les désavantages de sortir en groupe? en couple? Est-ce le rôle des écoles d'organiser des activités sociales? Expliquez votre point de vue.

Les jeunes sortent généralement en groupes.

---

1. *rest*   2. *take charge*   3. *commit oneself*

Troisième étape

À l'écoute: Le bonheur

This input section introduces students to simple ways of discussing an abstract topic such as the concept of happiness. New vocabulary and cultural information will be acquired.

Cue to Video Module 8, street interviews (00:39:29), to hear different people talk about their concept of happiness.

Vous allez entendre deux personnes donner leur définition du bonheur. Est-ce que ces définitions vont correspondre à votre concept du bonheur?

Avant d'écouter

1 This activity can be done in groups; members will need to decide on elements and order of importance. Have various groups report, and summarize results on the board.

1 Qu'est-ce que c'est que le bonheur pour vous? Cochez les suggestions que vous trouvez appropriées, puis ajoutez d'autres possibilités selon votre expérience personnelle.

Le bonheur, c'est...

être / se sentir* *(to feel)*	avoir	pouvoir
_____ aimé(e)	_____ une famille	_____ s'accepter
_____ accepté(e)	_____ des ami(e)s	_____ trouver son identité
_____ apprécié(e)	_____ de l'argent	_____ aimer les autres
_____ libre *(free)*	_____ le confort matériel	_____ apprécier ce qu'on a
_____ indépendant(e)	_____ la santé *(health)*	_____ partager
_____ intelligent(e)	_____ un bon travail	_____ accumuler des choses matérielles
_____ beau (belle)	_____ confiance en soi *(self-confidence)*	_____ s'amuser
_____ ?	_____ ?	_____ arriver à ses objectifs *(reach one's goals)*
		_____ ?

* **(Se) sentir** se conjugue comme **partir**.

Maintenant choisissez dans ces listes les six éléments qui sont les plus importants pour vous et classez-les de 1 (le plus important) à 6 (le moins important).

Écoutons

Audio CD

2 Écoutez les conversations une première fois pour identifier le pays d'origine des deux personnes interviewées. Trouvez ces pays sur les cartes du monde francophone au début du livre.

1. Larmé vient de/du _____ .

2. Nayat est née *(was born)* en/au _____ , mais elle a grandi *(grew up)* en/au _____ .

3 ANSWER: Larmé—se sentir libre; arriver à ses objectifs. Nayat—trouver son identité, apprécier (ce qu'on a), être aimé(e), s'accepter, partager.

3 Écoutez encore en regardant le tableau page 296. Soulignez les définitions mentionnées par Larmé, et encerclez celles que Nayat suggère.

4 Écoutez encore pour compléter les extraits suivants des conversations avec les mots donnés. Conjuguez les verbes si c'est nécessaire et déduisez le sens des mots en caractères gras. Attention: chaque liste contient des mots supplémentaires; le même mot peut être utilisé plus d'une fois.

1. Larmé   [*Mots:* partager, **se passer, avoir besoin,** heureux, pareil, individualiste, **tout le monde,** sa famille, voisins, amis, le village, son pays]

   On _a besoin_____ des autres pour être _heureux_____ . En Europe et aux États-Unis c'est _pareil_____ , on est très _individualiste_____ , ou bien quand on _partage_____ , c'est avec _sa famille_____ ou quelques _amis_____ . En Afrique, quand quelque chose _se passe_____ , tout _le village_____ le sait, _tout le monde_____ participe.

2. Nayat   [*Mots:* **se développer,** s'accepter, **se sentir, isolé(e), déchiré(e),** libre, amour, identité, héritage, richesse, monde(s), culture(s)]

   Quand j'étais petite, je _me sentais_____ inférieure parce que j'étais _déchirée_____ entre deux _cultures_____ . Maintenant, pour moi le bonheur, c'est de trouver mon _identité_____ dans ces deux _cultures_____ , et d'apprécier la _richesse_____ d'un double _héritage_____ . Sans l'_amour_____ on est _isolé_____ et on ne peut pas vraiment _se développer_____ .

VOCABULAIRE ACTIF
apprécier
avoir besoin (de)
avoir confiance en soi
le bonheur
le confort matériel
(trouver) son identité
se passer (quelque chose
    se passe)
se sentir (libre)
la santé
tout le monde

Le bonheur c'est de se comprendre sans se parler.

5 This activity can be done in groups, and followed up with a discussion on both issues.

5 Écoutez une dernière fois et résumez...

  1. la différence entre les relations humaines en Afrique et en Europe ou aux États-Unis, selon Larmé.
  2. le problème de Nayat quand elle était petite.

Prononciation

This is the last **Prononciation** section of the text.

Les consonnes finales (suite)

■ You have learned that in French, most final consonants are silent unless they are followed by a mute **e.**

  peti~~t~~ / peti<u>t</u>e
  gran~~d~~ / gran<u>d</u>e
  françai~~s~~ / françai<u>s</u>e

■ Four consonants, however, are normally pronounced in final position—they are **c, r, f,** and **l,** all exemplified in the word CaReFuL.

  ave<u>c</u>   su<u>r</u>   neu<u>f</u>   i<u>l</u>

Exceptions:

  1. The **r** is silent in most **-er** endings.

  parle~~r~~   premie~~r~~   papie~~r~~

  2. Some words are individual exceptions. They are words in which a final **c, r, f,** or **l** is silent (**blan~~c~~, por~~c~~, genti~~l~~**), or words in which other final consonants are pronounced (tenni<u>s</u>, cin<u>q</u>, sep<u>t</u>, conce<u>pt</u>).

■ Whether or not they are the last letter in the word, final consonant sounds must be pronounced clearly and completely. In American English, final consonant sounds are not always fully enunciated. In French, they are completely "released." Contrast:

English	French
intelligen**t**	intelligen**te**
lam**p**	lam**pe**
sou**p**	sou**pe**
fil**m**	fil**m**

Écoutez

Quel, bonheur, pour, and **sentir** follow the CaReFuL rule; **sud, Tchad, concept, fait,** and **sens** are individual exceptions. The last sentence exemplifies the complete release of final consonant sounds (**monde, participe,** etc.).

Audio CD

On the student audio CD, listen to the following excerpts from the conversation with Larmé, and underline all the final consonants that are pronounced. Which ones follow the CaReFuL rule? Which are individual exceptions?

1. Je viens de Pala, un petit village au sud du Tchad.
2. Quel est votre concept du bonheur?
3. Le bonheur, ça dépend de l'individu. Pour moi, le bonheur c'est le fait de se sentir libre.
4. Dans quel sens?
5. En Afrique, quand quelque chose se passe, tout le village le sait, tout le monde participe.

Musique au Congo: une image du bonheur?

For additional practice with final consonants, give students three minutes to look through the **Vocabulaire** sections for Ch. 5, 6, and 7. How many words can they find that end in a pronounced **c, r, f,** or **l?**

Essayez!

Audio CD

Practice saying the sentences in **Écoutez** aloud, making sure you release all final consonant sounds clearly and completely. Then listen to the sentences again to verify your pronunciation.

STRUCTURE: Expressing obligation/necessity

*Le verbe **devoir***

Observez et déduisez

Je pense que pour être vraiment heureux, les jeunes doivent se sentir libres. On doit pouvoir décider ce qu'on veut faire dans la vie.

Moi, personnellement, je dois mon bonheur à la richesse d'un double héritage—français et algérien. Je dois beaucoup à ma famille.

> ■ What forms of the verb **devoir** do you see in the preceding sentences?
>
> ■ In which sentences does the verb mean *to owe*? In which sentences does it mean *must* or *to have to*?

Vérifiez   *Le verbe **devoir***

■ The verb **devoir** is irregular.

Le verbe devoir	
je dois	nous devons
tu dois	vous devez
il / elle / on doit	ils / elles doivent

passé composé: j'ai dû

■ **Devoir** can be followed by a noun or an infinitive. When followed by a noun, it means *to owe*.

> Nayat **doit** son identité à son double héritage.
> Mon camarade de chambre me **doit** de l'argent!

■ When used with an infinitive, **devoir** expresses obligation or necessity, and its meaning varies according to the tense.

présent: *have to (must)*
Pour être heureux, on **doit** se sentir accepté.

passé composé: *had to*
Pour arriver à mes objectifs, j'**ai dû** beaucoup travailler.

imparfait: *was supposed to*
Claire **devait** arriver à ses objectifs aussi, mais elle n'a pas travaillé.

Point out that the imperfect of **devoir** implies the activity was *not* done.

ACTIVITÉS

A. Have students share their opinions about the statements with a partner or in groups.

A. Le bonheur. Lisez les phrases suivantes, et indiquez si ce sont les opinions de Larmé ou de Nayat. (Écoutez encore **À l'écoute** si vous voulez.)

	Larmé	Nayat
Pour être heureux…		
1. On doit s'accepter.		✓
2. On doit se sentir libre.	✓	
3. On doit arriver à ses objectifs.	✓	
4. On doit partager avec les autres.		✓
5. On doit choisir ce qu'on veut faire dans la vie.	✓	
6. On doit trouver son identité.		✓
7. On doit apprécier son héritage.		✓
8. On doit se sentir aimé.		✓

Êtes-vous d'accord avec ces opinions? Lesquelles?

B. Obligations familiales. Pour que le bonheur règne dans la famille, chacun doit s'occuper de ses obligations, n'est-ce pas? Parlez des obligations dans votre famille.

➡ *Tout le monde doit ranger sa chambre.*

Je		faire la lessive
Ma sœur / Mon frère		travailler beaucoup
Mes parents		faire les devoirs
Tout le monde	devoir	faire les courses
?		passer l'aspirateur
		laver la voiture
		ranger sa (leur) chambre

C. First have students mark and total all their obligations from the preceding week, adding other activities if desired. Then have them circulate in the class, finding out what and how much other students had to do. FOLLOW-UP: Ask students what additional obligations they listed. Find out who had the highest/lowest number of obligations.

C. La semaine dernière. Indiquez vos obligations de la semaine dernière.

J'ai dû... / Je n'ai pas dû...

_____ aller au supermarché

_____ ranger ma chambre

_____ écrire un rapport

_____ laver ma voiture

_____ préparer un examen

_____ passer des heures à la bibliothèque

_____ parler français

_____ ?

_____ faire mes devoirs

_____ demander de l'argent à mes parents

_____ répondre aux questions du professeur

_____ travailler

_____ lire un roman

_____ prêter de l'argent à mon (ma) camarade de chambre

_____ ?

Maintenant, cherchez un(e) camarade de classe qui avait autant d'obligations que vous.

➡ *Tu as dû ranger ta chambre?*

D. Give students time to jot down as many items as possible before having volunteers share answers. Which activities are most commonly forgotten?

D. Zut alors! Votre mémoire n'est pas trop bonne. Dites ce que vous deviez faire récemment que vous avez oublié de faire.

➡ *Zut alors! Je devais téléphoner à ma sœur!*

STRATÉGIE DE COMMUNICATION
Making suggestions/Giving advice

Cue to Video Module 8 (00:37:49), where Élisabeth and Fatima give Nicolas some advice on making up with his girlfriend.

When friends and family complain to you about personal problems or difficulties, you may feel compelled to offer advice—whether it is requested or not! Look at the following dialogue, and identify some expressions in French used for giving advice or making suggestions.

— Tu as l'air triste, Patrick. Ça ne va pas?

— Ben, pas trop... Mes parents et moi, nous ne nous entendons pas très bien en ce moment. Et puis mes camarades de chambre sont toujours en train de se disputer. Et en plus, Béatrice ne veut plus sortir avec moi!

— Oh là là, pauvre Patrick! Il faut te changer les idées. Tu as besoin de sortir; tu devrais t'amuser un peu pour ne pas penser* à tes problèmes. Si *(What if)* tu venais au cinéma avec Josée et moi ce soir?

Expressions pour donner des conseils	
Tu as besoin de... (Vous avez besoin de...)	+ infinitif
Tu dois... (Vous devez...)	+ infinitif
Tu devrais*... (Vous devriez*...)	+ infinitif
Il faut...	+ infinitif
Si tu... (Si vous...)	+ verbe à l'imparfait

* You should . . .

****Ne** and **pas** are placed together before the verb when negating an infinitive.

ACTIVITÉS

E. Have students work in groups, brainstorming several answers for each expression.

E. Le bonheur. Quels conseils avez-vous pour une personne qui cherche le bonheur dans la vie?

1. Pour trouver le bonheur, il faut...
2. Pour trouver le bonheur, vous devriez...
3. Pour trouver le bonheur, vous avez besoin de...
4. Si vous...

G. Be sure that some students are preparing a response to each letter. Have volunteers share their responses to Patrick's letter. Ask the other students how they feel about the advice. «Ce sont de bonnes suggestions? Vous êtes d'accord, oui ou non? Quels conseils avez-vous pour Patrick?» Repeat with letters to Micheline.

If your institution is so equipped, you may want to set up an electronic bulletin board where students can leave messages anonymously, asking for advice about real or imaginary problems and responding to the problems of other classmates.

F. Soucis. Votre camarade de chambre a beaucoup de soucis (de problèmes). Qu'est-ce que vous lui conseillez dans les situations suivantes?

«Je ne m'entends pas bien avec mon (ma) petit(e) ami(e).»
«Mes parents ne me comprennent pas.»
«Mes copains ne me parlent plus.»
«J'ai de mauvaises notes.»
«Je veux perdre du poids (lose weight).»
«Je veux être riche.»

G. Le courrier du cœur. Il y a des gens qui envoient des lettres aux journaux pour demander des conseils—à Ann Landers, par exemple. Patrick et Micheline sont deux jeunes Français qui ont écrit des lettres à «Chère Chantal». Lisez leurs lettres, et préparez une réponse écrite à *une* de ces lettres avec un(e) partenaire.

Chère Chantal,
J'ai 18 ans et j'habite chez mes parents. Je ne m'entends pas bien du tout avec eux. Ils détestent mon petit ami, Gérard, et ils ne me permettent plus de sortir avec lui. Par conséquent, nous nous disputons souvent à la maison, et je me sens déchirée entre ma famille et mon ami. En fait, Gérard et moi, nous pensons que le mariage est peut-être une solution à notre problème. Qu'est-ce que vous nous conseillez? Nous avons tous les deux 18 ans.

Micheline

Chère Chantal,
J'ai un camarade de chambre vraiment embêtant! Nos goûts sont très différents. Lui, il aime le rock et moi, je préfère la musique country. Lui, il étudie le matin; moi, j'étudie le soir. Il est paresseux. Il passe des heures au téléphone, mais il n'a jamais le temps de ranger la chambre. En plus, il a un chat désagréable. Je suis allergique aux chats! À votre avis, qu'est-ce que je dois faire?

Patrick

Jeu de rôle

You and a couple of your childhood friends are reunited for the first time in many years. You reminisce about the way things used to be and share what is new in your lives, asking and giving advice, much as you did in the "good ol' days."

CD-ROM

Now that you have finished the Troisième étape of this chapter, do your Lab Manual activities with the audio program. Explore chapter topics further with the Mais oui! Video and CD-ROM. Viewing and comprehension activities are in the video section of your Workbook/Lab Manual/Video Manual.

Intégration

Littérature: Qu'est-ce que signifie «apprivoiser»?

We have seen **le petit prince** travel through the desert of loneliness. Here, he finds a road that leads him to a beautiful garden where, to his great surprise, he sees thousands of roses that look exactly like his rose—the rose back on his little planet, the one who had told him she was **«unique au monde».** So, she had lied! She was just an ordinary flower! **«Je me croyais riche d'une fleur unique... »**

Feeling betrayed, **le petit prince** starts to cry. That's when a fox **(un renard)** appears. He is going to mention the word **apprivoiser.** What do you think it means? **Qu'est-ce que signifie «apprivoiser»?**

Avant de lire

1 Les mots suivants en caractères gras sont importants dans le texte que vous allez lire. D'après le contexte de chaque phrase, déduisez le sens de ces mots et trouvez l'équivalent anglais dans la liste donnée.

1. Je ne suis pas très populaire; je **n'**ai **que** deux copains.
2. Un homme qui chasse les animaux est un **chasseur.**
3. Les chasseurs chassent avec des **fusils.**
4. Une **poule** produit des œufs.
5. Un **lien,** c'est ce qui attache des choses ou des personnes.
6. Le **blé** est une céréale.
7. À la campagne, il y a des **champs** de blé.
8. Le blé est couleur d'**or,** ou **doré.**

a. fields
b. chicken/hen
c. wheat
d. only
e. gold/golden
f. bond
g. guns
h. hunter

2 Dans ce texte, vous allez encore voir des verbes au passé simple, mais vous allez voir aussi des verbes au futur. **Je pleurerai,** par exemple, signifie *I will cry.* Utilisez le contexte et la logique pour identifier l'infinitif qui correspond à chaque verbe en caractères gras.

1. Nous **aurons** besoin l'un de l'autre.
2. Tu **seras** pour moi unique au monde, je **serai** pour toi unique au monde.
3. Tu **reviendras** me dire adieu.
4. Je te **ferai** cadeau d'un secret.

a. être
b. revenir
c. faire
d. avoir

3 Qu'est-ce qu'il faut faire pour commencer une amitié? Cochez les sugges-tions qui vous semblent appropriées et ajoutez d'autres possibilités, selon votre expérience personnelle.

Il faut...

_____ parler

_____ s'observer sans parler d'abord

_____ s'ouvrir *(open oneself up)* immédiatement à l'autre personne

_____ s'ouvrir progressivement

_____ donner son temps

_____ faire des cadeaux

_____ savoir écouter

_____ faire des choses ensemble

_____ ?

En général **4** Parcourez le texte une première fois. Dans quel ordre les idées générales suivantes sont-elles présentées? Classez-les de 1 à 8.

<u>2</u>_____ Le renard donne la définition du mot «apprivoiser».

<u>4</u>_____ Le renard pose des questions sur la planète du petit prince.

<u>1</u>_____ Le renard explique pourquoi il ne peut pas jouer avec le petit prince.

<u>6</u>_____ Le renard explique pourquoi les hommes n'ont pas d'amis.

<u>3</u>_____ Le renard explique comment on devient *(becomes)* unique au monde.

<u>8</u>_____ Le renard donne au petit prince son secret et des conseils très importants.

<u>5</u>_____ Le renard compare les cheveux du petit prince et les champs de blé.

<u>7</u>_____ Le renard explique qu'il va être triste quand le petit prince va partir.

Qu'est-ce que signifie «apprivoiser»?

— Bonjour, dit le renard.

— Bonjour, répondit poliment le petit prince. Qui es-tu?

— Je suis un renard, dit le renard.

— Viens jouer avec moi, lui proposa le petit prince. Je suis tellement° *so*
5 triste...

— Je ne peux pas jouer avec toi, dit le renard. Je ne suis pas apprivoisé.

— Ah! pardon, fit le petit prince.

Mais après réflexion, il ajouta:

— Qu'est-ce que signifie «apprivoiser»?

10   — Tu n'es pas d'ici, dit le renard, que cherches-tu?

— Je cherche les hommes, dit le petit prince. Qu'est-ce que signifie «apprivoiser»?

— Les hommes, dit le renard, ils ont des fusils et ils chassent. C'est bien gênant. Ils élèvent° aussi des poules. C'est leur seul intérêt. Tu cherches des   *raise*
15 poules?

— Non, dit le petit prince. Je cherche des amis. Qu'est-ce que signifie «apprivoiser»?

— C'est une chose trop oubliée, dit le renard. Ça signifie «créer des liens». Tu n'es encore pour moi qu'un petit garçon tout semblable à cent mille petits
20 garçons. Et je n'ai pas besoin de toi. Et tu n'as pas besoin de moi non plus. Mais si tu m'apprivoises, nous aurons besoin l'un de l'autre. Tu seras pour moi unique au monde. Je serai pour toi unique au monde.

— Je commence à comprendre, dit le petit prince. Il y a une fleur, je crois qu'elle m'a apprivoisé...

25   — C'est possible, dit le renard. On voit sur la Terre toutes sortes de choses...

— Oh, ce n'est pas sur la Terre, dit le petit prince.

Le renard parut intrigué.

— Sur une autre planète?

— Oui.

30   — Il y a des chasseurs sur cette planète?

— Non.

— Ça, c'est intéressant! Et des poules?

— Non.

— Rien n'est parfait, soupira° le renard.   *sighed*

35 Mais le renard revint à son idée.

    — Ma vie est monotone. Je chasse les poules, les hommes me chassent. Toutes les poules se ressemblent, et tous les hommes se ressemblent. Je m'en-nuie donc un peu. Mais si tu m'apprivoises, ma vie sera comme ensoleillée. Et puis, regarde! Tu vois, là-bas, les champs de blé? Je ne mange pas de pain. Le
40 blé pour moi est inutile°. Les champs de blé ne me rappellent rien. Et ça, c'est *useless* triste! Mais tu as des cheveux couleur d'or. Alors ce sera merveilleux quand tu m'auras apprivoisé! le blé, qui est doré, me fera penser à toi. S'il te plaît... apprivoise-moi!

    — Je veux bien, répondit le petit prince. Mais je n'ai pas beaucoup de
45 temps. J'ai des amis à découvrir° et beaucoup de choses à connaître. *trouver*

    — On ne connaît que les choses que l'on apprivoise, dit le renard. Les hommes n'ont plus le temps de rien connaître. Ils achètent des choses toutes faites chez les marchands. Mais comme il n'existe pas de marchands d'amis, les hommes n'ont plus d'amis. Si tu veux un ami, apprivoise-moi!

50   — Que faut-il faire? dit le petit prince.

    — Il faut être très patient, répondit le renard.

[Le renard explique qu'il faut s'asseoir chaque jour un peu plus près, ne pas parler quelquefois parce que «le langage est source de malentendus°». Il faut *misunderstanding* s'ouvrir progressivement, et venir toujours à la même heure pour avoir le
55 temps de se préparer le cœur, car l'anticipation est nécessaire au bonheur.]

    Ainsi le petit prince apprivoisa le renard. Et quand l'heure du départ arriva:

    — Ah, dit le renard... Je pleurerai.

    — C'est ta faute, dit le petit prince. Tu as voulu que je t'apprivoise.

60   — Bien sûr, dit le renard.

    — Mais tu vas pleurer! dit le petit prince.

    — Bien sûr, dit le renard.

    — Alors tu n'y gagnes rien°! *gain nothing*

    — J'y gagne, dit le renard, à cause de la couleur du blé.

65   Puis il ajouta:

    — Va revoir les roses. Tu comprendras que ta rose est unique au monde. Tu reviendras me dire adieu, et je te ferai cadeau d'un secret.

[Le petit prince va revoir les roses, comprend qu'elles ne sont pas du tout comme sa rose parce qu'elles ne sont pas apprivoisées. Sa rose est unique au
70 monde parce que c'est pour elle qu'il a sacrifié son temps, c'est elle qu'il a servie, c'est elle qu'il a écoutée, c'est elle qu'il a aimée—c'est elle qu'il aime.]

    Et il revint vers le renard.
    — Adieu, dit-il...
    — Adieu, dit le renard. Voici mon secret. Il est très simple. On ne voit bien
75 qu'avec le cœur. L'essentiel est invisible pour les yeux.
    — L'essentiel est invisible pour les yeux, répéta le petit prince, pour se souvenir.
    — C'est le temps que tu as perdu pour ta rose qui fait ta rose si importante...
80   — C'est le temps que j'ai perdu pour ma rose... fit le petit prince, pour se souvenir.
    — Les hommes ont oublié cette vérité°, dit le renard. Mais tu ne dois pas   *truth* l'oublier. Tu es responsable pour toujours de ce que tu as apprivoisé. Tu es responsable de ta rose...
85   — Je suis responsable de ma rose... répéta le petit prince, pour se souvenir.

Extrait et adapté de *Le Petit Prince* (Antoine de Saint-Exupéry)

En détail   **5** **Les mots.** En utilisant le contexte et la logique, pouvez-vous déduire ce que signifient les mots en caractères gras? Trouvez les synonymes.

  1. (Page 307, line 13) C'est bien **gênant.**
  2. (Page 307, line 18) Ça signifie **créer** des liens...
  3. (Page 307, line 19) Tu n'es encore pour moi qu'un petit garçon tout **semblable** à cent mille petits garçons.
  4. (Page 308, line 40) Les champs de blé ne me **rappellent** rien.
  5. (Page 308, line 64) J'y gagne, **à cause de** la couleur du blé.

  a. pareil
  b. parce qu'il y a
  c. faire, fabriquer
  d. problématique
  e. font penser à

6 **Le texte.** Répondez aux questions suivantes, selon le texte.

1. Pourquoi le renard ne peut-il pas jouer avec le petit prince?
2. Quel est le seul intérêt des hommes, selon le renard?
3. Qu'est-ce que signifie «apprivoiser»?
4. Pourquoi le renard dit-il que «rien n'est parfait» quand il parle de la planète du petit prince?
5. Pourquoi le renard veut-il que le petit prince l'apprivoise?
6. Pourquoi le petit prince n'a-t-il pas beaucoup de temps pour apprivoiser le renard? Est-ce ironique?
7. Pourquoi les champs de blé vont-ils être une consolation pour le renard après le départ du petit prince?
8. Qu'est-ce que le petit prince comprend quand il revoit les roses?
9. Quel est le secret du renard? Comment est-ce que l'expérience du petit prince avec les roses l'a préparé à comprendre ce secret?
10. Quelle vérité est-ce que les hommes ont oubliée, selon le renard?

Et vous?

1. Est-ce que vous êtes d'accord avec le renard quand il dit que «les hommes n'ont plus le temps de rien connaître» et «n'ont plus d'amis»? Avec un(e) camarade de classe, faites une liste des obstacles aux relations humaines dans la société moderne, puis comparez votre liste avec celles des autres groupes.
2. Qu'est-ce qu'il faut faire pour apprivoiser quelqu'un? En groupes de deux ou trois, comparez la liste du renard et votre liste à vous, selon vos expériences personnelles. Ensuite présentez vos conclusions à la classe.

Selon le renard **Selon nous**

FOLLOW-UP: (for #3 and #4) Have a few groups report, then compare and discuss answers.

3. Est-ce que vous avez «des champs de blé» dans votre vie—des objets, des chansons *(songs)*, des parfums ou d'autres choses—qui vous rappellent des personnes que vous aimez? En groupes de deux ou trois, comparez vos «champs de blé».
4. «On ne voit bien qu'avec le cœur. L'essentiel est invisible pour les yeux.» Pensez à deux personnes que vous aimez. Qu'est-ce qu'on voit avec les yeux quand on regarde ces personnes? Et avec le cœur? Individuellement d'abord, complétez le tableau suivant, puis partagez vos observations avec un(e) partenaire.

Nom ou initiale	Avec les yeux	Avec le cœur

Post scriptum

After realizing that he is responsible for his rose, **le petit prince** decides to return to his planet to take care of her. The return will not be easy. **Le petit prince** will have to leave his body on earth, because it will be too heavy to carry on the way up. The snake that he met when he arrived on Earth will help him make his ultimate sacrifice. The prince's death will be the supreme illustration of the fox's secret: it is only with the heart that one can truly see; what is essential is invisible to the eyes. The body is just a shell; the essential lives on. **On ne voit bien qu'avec le cœur. L'essentiel est invisible pour les yeux...**

Par écrit: The way we were

Avant d'écrire

A. Strategy: Using reporters' questions. The standard questions asked by reporters—who? what? where? when? why? and how?—can be used as an effective pre-writing tool to help generate ideas. The answers to some questions will, of course, be more important than others depending upon the topic, but the process of *asking* questions will help clarify which items are most relevant.

Application. What questions would you ask a friend you hadn't seen in a long time? What would you ask someone who has lived a long time? List as many questions as you can in each category.

VOCABULAIRE ACTIF
à cette époque-là
en ce temps-là

B. Strategy: Talking about the way things were. These expressions can be used to introduce a discussion of the way things were in the past.

autrefois   *back then*
à cette époque-là ⎫
en ce temps-là   ⎭   *at that time*

Application. Use the preceding expressions to introduce three sentences about what life was like when you were ten years old.

ÉCRIVEZ

Students who choose this task may also want to review the discussion between the little prince and the serpent and switchman in Ch. 7, **Intégration**.

1. Le petit prince se prépare à retourner sur sa planète. Il anticipe les questions que sa rose va lui poser et, dans son journal de voyage, prépare les réponses qu'il va donner, décrivant au passé ses impressions de la Terre. Qu'est-ce que le petit prince écrit dans son journal?

   Questions de la rose   **Réponses du petit prince**

Tell students that to answer the last two questions, they must also imagine what life is like in 2080.

2. C'est l'an 2080. Vous fêtez votre centième anniversaire, et un journaliste vous pose des questions pour un article qui va paraître dans le journal local. Comment allez-vous répondre à ses questions?

   Vous aviez une grande famille?
   Qu'est-ce que vous faisiez pour vous amuser quand vous étiez petit(e)?
   Vous aviez un(e) meilleur(e) ami(e) à cette époque-là? Comment était-il/elle?
   Est-ce que l'institution du mariage était différente autrefois?
   Et le concept du bonheur?

VOCABULAIRE ACTIF

Verbes et expressions verbales

apprécier *to appreciate*

avoir besoin (de) *to need*

avoir confiance en soi *to be self-confident*

communiquer *to communicate*

devoir *to have to, to owe*

épouser *to marry (someone)*

passer (des heures) *to spend hours*

pleurer *to cry*

prêter *to lend, to loan*

raconter *to tell (a story)*

rencontrer *to meet*

rire *to laugh*

Verbes pronominaux

s'amuser *to have fun*

se battre *to fight*

se comprendre *to understand one another*

se disputer *to fight, to argue*

s'écrire *to write one another*

s'ennuyer *to be bored*

s'entendre (bien ou mal) *to get along*

se marier *to get married*

se parler *to talk to one another*

se passer (quelque chose se passe) *to happen, to take place*

se retrouver *to meet (by previous arrangement)*

se (re)voir *to see each other (again)*

se sentir (apprécié, libre) *to feel (appreciated, free)*

se souvenir *to remember*

se téléphoner *to phone one another*

L'amour

un couple *a couple*

le divorce *divorce*

le mariage *marriage*

un(e) petit(e) ami(e) *a boyfriend / a girlfriend*

un rencontre *a (chance) meeting*

Les sorties

un bal *a dance*

une boîte (de nuit) *a nightclub*

le ciné (le cinéma)

une soirée *a party*

Les tâches domestiques *(domestic chores)*

faire la lessive *to do the laundry*

faire la vaisselle *to do the dishes*

laver la voiture *to wash the car*

passer l'aspirateur *to vacuum*

ranger (sa chambre) *to tidy up*

repasser *to iron*

Ce qu'on donne ou ce qu'on a

l'amitié *friendship*

le bonheur *happiness*

un chat *a cat*

le confort matériel *material comfort*

son identité (f.) *one's identity*

les (mêmes) goûts (m.) *(the same) tastes*

la santé *health*

les vêtements (m.) *clothes*

Ce qu'on dit ou ne dit pas

une blague *a joke*

un conseil *a piece of advice*

un secret *a secret*

Expressions pour donner des conseils

Il faut... *It is necessary . . .*

Si tu / Si vous (+ imparfait)... *What if you . . .*

Tu as / Vous avez besoin de... *You need to . . .*

Tu dois / Vous devez... *You must . . . / have to . . .*

Tu devrais / Vous devriez... *You should . . .*

Divers

(l'âge) moyen *the average (age)*
célibataire *single*
ensemble *together*

pareil(le) *the same*
un tas de *lots of*
tout le monde *everyone*

Adverbes de temps

à cette époque-là, en ce temps-là *at that time, in those days*
autrefois *in the past*
rarement *rarely*
de temps en temps *from time to time*

9 Les souvenirs

Qu'est-ce que ces enfants ont fait aujourd'hui?

Et vous?

Est-ce que vous vous souvenez de votre premier jour d'école?

Connaissiez-vous les autres enfants?

This chapter will enable you to

- **understand extended past narrations and descriptions**
- **read texts about French holidays and traditions, and a literary passage by a Moroccan author about a young immigrant's struggles with French past tenses**
- **distinguish between *the way things used to be* and *what happened* in the past**
- **handle social situations related to holidays and gift giving**
- **state thoughts and opinions at a simple level**
- **make comparisons**

À l'écoute: Un souvenir d'école

This input section introduces students to the difference between the passé composé and the imparfait.

Tout le monde a des souvenirs associés à l'école. Ici une dame va vous raconter quelque chose qui s'est passé quand elle était à l'école maternelle.

Avant d'écouter

1 Étudiez les phrases suivantes pour déduire le sens des mots en caractères gras. Complétez ensuite le tableau donné.

L'idée	La façon de le dire en français
To call on someone for an answer	interroger
To raise one's hand/finger	lever le doigt
To be mad or angry	être fâché(e)
To be ashamed	avoir honte
To be punished	être puni(e)
To beat	battre
Pictures	des images
To remain standing	rester debout
To be seated	être assis
To stop	arrêter (de)
To whisper	murmurer

1. Quand il n'y a pas assez de chaises, certaines personnes **sont assises,** mais d'autres **restent debout.**
2. En France, quand on veut répondre en classe, on **lève le doigt** (eh non, ce n'est pas la main, mais seulement l'index!) en espérant que le professeur va nous **interroger.**
3. Dans les livres d'enfants, il y a beaucoup d'**images** ou d'illustrations.
4. Quand on est fatigué de faire quelque chose, on **arrête** de le faire; c'est le contraire de commencer.
5. Si on ne veut pas que les autres entendent, on parle très doucement, on **murmure.**

6. Quand un enfant fait quelque chose de mal, il risque d'**être puni.** L'interdiction de regarder la télé est une forme de punition; **battre** quelqu'un est une punition corporelle. Si l'enfant regrette et se sent embarrassé, il **a honte** de sa mauvaise action.

7. Quand on **est fâché,** ou irrité, on perd quelquefois le contrôle de ses émotions.

2 Have students brainstorm in pairs for a couple of minutes; compare stories.

2 L'école maternelle, la maîtresse (l'institutrice), une petite fille, interroger, lever le doigt, une réponse, une image, fâché, battre, puni, la honte... Tous ces mots sont des mots-clés dans le «souvenir d'école» que vous allez entendre. Quelle sorte d'histoire anticipez-vous?

Écoutons

Audio CD

3 Écoutez d'abord pour comprendre la progression des idées dans cette histoire. Classez les images suivantes dans l'ordre chronologique, de 1 à 4.

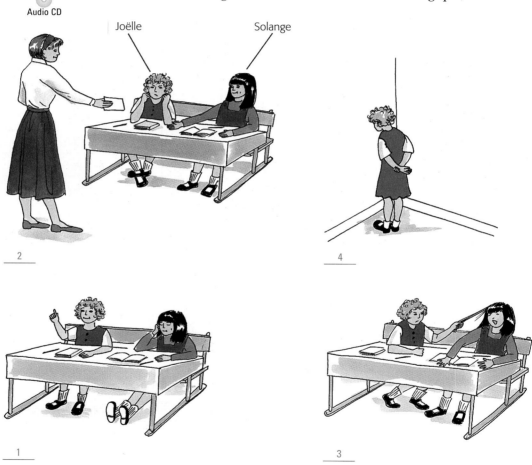

Joëlle   Solange

2   4

1   3

4 ANSWERS: 1. F (Elle ne travaillait pas trop bien.) 2. V 3. V 4. F (Non! Elle voulait les images pour sa collection.) 5. V 6. V 7. V 8. F (la maîtresse) 9. F (debout) 10. V

4 Écoutez encore et indiquez si les phrases suivantes sont vraies ou fausses. Si elles sont fausses, corrigez-les.

1. Solange était une bonne élève.
2. Joëlle faisait la collection d'images.
3. Un jour, la maîtresse a arrêté d'interroger Joëlle pour donner l'occasion aux autres de répondre.

4. Joëlle voulait aider Solange à avoir des images.
5. Chaque fois que Joëlle n'a pas été interrogée, elle a murmuré les réponses et sa voisine a entendu.
6. Joëlle a pensé qu'elle était victime d'une injustice.
7. Joëlle a battu* Solange.
8. Les autres élèves ont séparé Joëlle et Solange.
9. La punition de Joëlle a été de rester assise au coin de la classe pendant plus de deux heures.
10. Joëlle n'a plus jamais attaqué personne en classe!

VOCABULAIRE ACTIF

arrêter
avoir honte
battre
être assis(e)
être fâché(e)
être puni(e)
une image
interroger
lever le doigt
la maîtresse
murmurer
rester debout

5 Écoutez encore et complétez les extraits suivants du segment sonore avec la forme appropriée des verbes au passé composé ou à l'imparfait.

1. Je crois que j' _avais_____ cinq ans à l'époque, j' _étais_____ donc à l'école maternelle.

2. Quand on _répondait_____ bien, la maîtresse nous _donnait_____ des images.

3. Cinq ou six fois de suite, Solange _a levé_____ le doigt, la maîtresse _a interrogé_____ Solange, et Solange _a eu_____ des images, avec mes réponses.

4. J' _étais_____ tellement fâchée que j' _ai commencé_____ à battre Solange.

5. Je n' _ai jamais oublié_____ la honte et l'humiliation... mais ça m' _a appris_____ quelque chose.

STRUCTURE: Talking about the past (I)
L'imparfait et le passé composé

Observez et déduisez　J'aimais bien répondre aux questions de la maîtresse parce que, quand je répondais bien, elle me donnait des images.

Solange a levé le doigt, la maîtresse a interrogé Solange, et Solange a eu des images avec *mes* réponses. Quelle injustice!

■ In both of the preceding sentences, Joëlle is talking about the past. What verb tense is used in each sentence? Which sentence answers the question *What happened?* Which sentence answers the question *What were things like?*

***Battre** est un verbe irrégulier.

Présent:	je bats	nous battons
	tu bats	vous battez
	il/elle/on bat	ils/elles battent

Participe passé: battu

Vérifiez   *L'imparfait et le passé composé*

■ Any occurrence in the past can be viewed from different perspectives. Two of these perspectives are expressed in French through the imparfait and the passé composé. The imperfect tense is used to say what was going on in the past. The imperfect tense answers the questions *What was it like? What were the circumstances?* **(Quelles étaient les circonstances?)** There are two main instances in which you will use the imperfect tense:

1. As you learned in Chapter 8, the imperfect is used to tell *what it was like* in the past, *the way things used to be* (page 279).

   Quand j'**étais** petite, j'**adorais** l'école.

2. The imperfect is also used to "set the stage," to create a mood, to reveal the background conditions.

   Je crois que j'**avais** cinq ans à l'époque; j'**étais** donc à l'école maternelle.

   J'**étais** assise à côté d'une petite fille qui s'**appelait** Solange. Elle n'**aimait** pas l'école et elle ne **travaillait** pas trop bien.

   Conditions include all *physical* description.

   Moi, j'**avais** les cheveux courts *(short)* et bouclés *(curly)* tandis que Solange **avait** les cheveux longs et noirs.

■ Verbs in the passé composé answer the questions *What happened? What happened next?* **(Qu'est-ce qui s'est passé?)**

   La maîtresse **a arrêté** de m'interroger, mais j'**ai murmuré** les réponses et Solange les **a entendues.**

■ Since the imperfect sets the stage (describes the circumstances) and the passé composé tells what happened, it is not uncommon to see the two tenses used together.

   J'**étais** tellement fâchée ce jour-là que j'**ai attrapé** *(grabbed)* Solange par les cheveux, et j'**ai commencé** à la battre.

■ The choice between the imparfait and passé composé must be made *in context.* If you are unsure about your choice, ask yourself if—*in this context*—the verb answers the question *What were the circumstances?* (→ imperfect) or the question *What happened?* (→ passé composé).

   Joelle **était** fâchée et elle **a attaqué** Solange. Par conséquent, elle **a été** punie.

L'imparfait	Le passé composé
What were the circumstances?	What happened?
What was it like?	What happened next?

ACTIVITÉS

A. Un autre point de vue. (1) Écoutez le professeur lire l'histoire selon Solange. Décidez si les phrases indiquent *les circonstances* ou *ce qui s'est passé*.

➡ (Joëlle était la meilleure élève de la classe.)   *les circonstances*

(2) Écoutez l'histoire encore une fois. Trouvez au moins une différence entre l'histoire de Solange et l'histoire de Joëlle.

B. Conclusions. Quelles conclusions peut-on tirer de l'histoire de Joëlle? Complétez les phrases de la colonne de gauche avec une expression logique de la colonne de droite.

1. Solange était jalouse...
2. Joëlle était frustrée...
3. La maîtresse a été surprise...
4. Les élèves ont ri...
5. Joëlle était humiliée...
6. Les parents de Joëlle n'étaient pas contents...

a. quand les filles se sont battues.
b. parce qu'elle a dû rester au coin.
c. quand la maîtresse leur a raconté l'incident.
d. parce que Joëlle recevait toujours des images.
e. parce que la maîtresse ne l'interrogeait plus.
f. quand Joëlle a «attaqué» Solange.

C. Quels élèves! La maîtresse a quitté (*left*) la classe pendant quelques minutes. Décrivez la scène dans la salle quand elle est revenue.

➡ Quand la maîtresse est revenue...
(ne pas être contente)   *elle n'était pas contente*

avoir honte

ne pas être contente

rire/ murmurer

se battre

se disputer

travailler

D. Have students discuss in small groups. Remind them to consider whether each verb refers to circumstances (including physical descriptions) or to what happened (next).

D. Rêve ou cauchemar? *(Dream or nightmare?)* Solange est très troublée. Elle parle à une amie du rêve qu'elle a fait hier soir. Racontez le rêve en employant le passé composé et l'imparfait.

> Je suis à l'école. J'ai peur et j'ai froid. La maîtresse est très grande. Elle a les cheveux bleus. Je parle à mon amie quand la maîtresse commence à nous interroger. Je lève le doigt et je réponds à sa question, mais la réponse est fausse. J'ai honte. Les autres élèves rient et moi, je pleure. Puis ils me battent, mais la maîtresse, elle ne regarde pas. Elle mange une pomme noire!

E. Circulate as students fill in the columns, guiding the correct use of tenses as needed. For #3, have students write out a paragraph for homework before telling their stories orally in class. For large classes, have students relate stories in groups and choose the best one to share with the whole class.

E. Un souvenir d'école. Pensez à votre premier jour d'école. Comment était-il?

1. Complétez la colonne de gauche dans le tableau ci-dessous.

Quelles étaient les circonstances?	Qu'est-ce qui s'est passé?
La maîtresse (le maître) était...	
J'aimais (n'aimais pas)...	
Je voulais (ne voulais pas)...	
Les élèves étaient...	
Je pouvais (ne pouvais pas)...	
?	

See the *Instructor's Resource Manual* for the activity **Un voleur à l'école,** in which students practice narrating and describing in the past as they play the role of a crime witness or a police inspector.

2. Maintenant, pensez à *ce qui s'est passé* ce jour-là. Écrivez ce que vous avez fait—ou n'avez pas fait—dans la colonne de droite. (Par exemple: lever le doigt, répondre aux questions, avoir des images, apprendre beaucoup, s'amuser, rester debout, être puni(e), murmurer, se battre, etc.)
3. Finalement, organisez les phrases dans l'ordre logique (ajoutez des détails si vous le désirez!) et racontez votre expérience aux autres étudiants.

STRUCTURE: Talking about the past (II)
Quelques verbes à sens multiples

Observez et déduisez Solange devait écrire un rapport hier soir, mais elle a décidé de regarder la télé! Les étudiants qui voulaient avoir une bonne note ont dû travailler toute la nuit.

> ■ Some verbs have different meanings in the passé composé and the imparfait. Study the examples of the verb **devoir** in the preceding sentences. Based on those examples and what you remember from Chapter 8, in which tense does **devoir** mean *was supposed to*? In which tense does it mean *had to*?

Vérifiez *Quelques verbes à sens multiples*

We suggest you not complicate matters by introducing the use of **devoir** to suggest probability *(must have)* at this point.

■ As you saw with **devoir** in Chapter 8, some verbs have a special meaning when used in the passé composé or the imperfect.

> **devoir** ils devaient: *they were supposed to*
> ils ont dû: *they had to*

Les élèves **ont dû** travailler tard hier soir. Solange **devait** écrire un rapport aussi, mais elle ne l'a pas fait!

> **pouvoir** elle pouvait: *she could*
> elle a pu: *she succeeded in*
> elle n'a pas pu: *she failed to*

Joëlle ne **pouvait** pas comprendre pourquoi la maîtresse ne l'interrogeait pas. Plusieurs fois elle a levé le doigt, mais elle **n'a pas pu** attirer *(attract)* l'attention de la maîtresse. Solange, par contre, **a pu** répondre aux questions.

> **vouloir** elle voulait: *she wanted*
> elle a voulu: *she tried*
> elle n'a pas voulu: *she refused*

Joëlle **voulait** répondre à *toutes* les questions! Ce jour-là, quand elle **a voulu** répondre, la maîtresse **n'a pas voulu** l'interroger.

■ The verbs **être** and **avoir** usually occur in the imperfect because they are used most often to express conditions. When used in the passé composé, they reflect a *change* in that condition or a *reaction*.

condition

Joëlle **avait** une sœur et un frère.
Joëlle **était** fâchée contre Solange.

action/reaction

Quand elle a répondu à la question, elle **a eu** une image.
Quand Joëlle a attaqué Solange, la maîtresse **a été** fâchée.

Participes passés irréguliers	
pouvoir	j'ai **pu**
devoir	j'ai **dû**
vouloir	j'ai **voulu**
avoir	j'ai **eu**
être	j'ai **été**

F. Have students work in pairs to match sentences and pictures, then ask a volunteer to read the story. Ask questions to elicit similar experiences.

ACTIVITÉS

F. Un mauvais souvenir. Il y a des histoires qu'on préfère oublier, comme l'histoire suivante. Trouvez la phrase qui correspond à chaque image.

5

3

1

7

4

2

6

1. Mon camarade de chambre a voulu m'aider, mais il ne parle pas français.
2. Quand elle a vu que je voulais vraiment réussir, elle a été gentille.
3. Je devais travailler à la bibli avec des camarades, mais je n'ai pas pu les trouver.
4. Après la classe, j'ai dû parler au professeur.
5. Il faisait très beau, et je ne voulais pas vraiment préparer l'examen.
6. Elle a dit que je pouvais repasser l'examen. Croyez-moi, j'étais bien content!
7. Je n'ai pas eu une bonne note à l'examen, et quand j'ai vu ma note, j'ai eu honte.

Maintenant, racontez l'histoire dans l'ordre indiqué. Avez-vous eu une expérience semblable? Expliquez!

G. **Malentendu** *(Misunderstanding).*   Lisez l'histoire d'Hervé et son malentendu avec un agent de voyage. Mettez les verbes au passé composé ou à l'imparfait.

Hervé (vouloir) partir en vacances le 10 mai; malheureusement il (devoir) passer un examen final ce jour-là. Il a parlé au professeur, mais le professeur (ne pas vouloir) changer la date prévue. Quand Hervé a téléphoné à l'agence de voyage, il (savoir) que son vol (devoir) partir à neuf heures *du soir,* pas à neuf heures du matin. Hervé (avoir) donc assez de temps, et il (pouvoir) passer l'examen *et* partir en vacances le même jour! À l'examen, Hervé (savoir) toutes les réponses, alors il (avoir) une bonne note. Le professeur (être) content.

Jeu de rôle

Lately you and a classmate have not met certain obligations or been able to do the things you wanted. For one of you, unexpected circumstances have kept you from your assigned task (the library was closed? the computer "ate" your paper?). For the other, it's been other people who have hindered your plans (a classmate who borrowed a book? a boss who had you work overtime?). Role-play a scene with a partner in which you both commiserate on your fate and your frustration.

Brainstorm useful expressions with the class: Je devais... mais je n'ai pas pu... parce que... / Je ne pouvais pas... parce que j'ai dû... / Je voulais... mais mes copains n'ont pas voulu... parce que..., etc.

Deuxième étape

Lecture: Fêtes et traditions

Avant de lire

Cue to Video Module 9 (00:42:34), where Élisabeth and Fatima talk about family feasts in their countries of origin. Cue also to street interviews (00:45:20), where some French people talk about the feast days they celebrate and how.

1 Les jours de fête sont d'autres occasions riches en souvenirs. Ce sont des jours de congé (vacances), des occasions de s'amuser, de manger, d'offrir ou de recevoir des cadeaux, etc. Quelles sont les fêtes que vous célébrez dans votre famille? Noël? le Ramadan? Hanoukka? le Jour d'action de grâces (fête américaine, le quatrième jeudi de novembre)? Comment est-ce que vous fêtez votre anniversaire? la fête nationale de votre pays?

This input section introduces students to much cultural information/vocabulary about holidays, and the superlative.

Les Fêtes de la vigne à Dijon en Bourgogne.

2 Avec quelles fêtes est-ce que vous associez les choses suivantes?

1. une dinde

2. un sapin

3. une bougie

4. des jouets: un ours en peluche   une poupée   un ballon   un jeu électronique

5. un défilé militaire

6. un bouquet de fleurs

7. un pique-nique

3 ANSWERS: 1. A 2. A 3. B
4. B 5. A 6. B

3 Parcourez rapidement les deux textes et indiquez dans quel texte **(A. L'an-née des Français,** ou **B. Les Français et les fêtes de fin d'année)** on peut trouver des renseignements sur...

1. les fêtes civiles et religieuses en France.
2. les fêtes qui n'ont pas de date fixe.
3. les cadeaux qu'on fait le plus souvent aux enfants.
4. ce qu'on mange aux repas traditionnels de fin d'année.
5. ce qu'on mange le jour des Rois *(kings)*.
6. des traditions particulières à une région du sud de la France, la Provence.

A. L'année des Français: leurs jours de fête

Le 1er janvier, ou Jour de l'An (CF°): on se souhaite les uns aux autres une «bonne et heureuse année». On s'offre des petits cadeaux appelés «étrennes».

R: Fête religieuse C: Fête non religieuse, dite «civile» F: fixe, à la même date tous les ans M: mobile

Carnaval (RM°): période qui commence «le jour des Rois» (6 janvier). On mange en famille un gâteau plat appelé galette des Rois. Celui ou celle qui y trouve la fève° devient «roi» ou «reine» de la fête. Le carnaval même a lieu le Mardi gras (généralement en février). Certaines villes organisent des défilés dans les rues et des bals costumés.

hard token

Les dimanche et lundi de Pâques (RM): c'est la grande fête du printemps. On offre aux enfants des œufs en sucre ou en chocolat.

Le 1er mai (CF): fête du travail. Les «travailleurs» défilent dans les rues.

Le 8 mai (CF): anniversaire de la victoire des Alliés en 1945. Cérémonie du Souvenir.

L'Ascension (RM): le 6e jeudi après Pâques.

Les dimanche et lundi de Pentecôte (RM): dix jours plus tard, beaucoup de gens des villes vont passer «le congé de Pentecôte» à la campagne.

Le 14 juillet (CF): fête nationale, anniversaire du 14 juillet 1789. On danse dans les rues. À Paris, on va voir passer le défilé militaire sur les Champs-Élysées.

L'Assomption: le 15 août (RF). Fête de la Sainte-Vierge° et de toutes les Marie, la grande fête de l'été.

Marie, mère de Jésus

La Toussaint: le 1er novembre (RF). Fête de tous les saints. Le lendemain c'est «le jour des Morts°»: on va fleurir leurs tombes dans les cimetières.

dead

Le 11 novembre (CF): anniversaire de l'Armistice de 1918. Les anciens combattants° se souviennent...

veterans

Noël: le 25 décembre (RF). Anniversaire de la naissance du Christ. Dans la nuit du 24 au 25 beaucoup se réunissent pour partager le repas du «réveillon°» et/ou aller à la messe de minuit. Tous ceux, jeunes et moins jeunes, qui croient encore au «Père Noël» attendent les cadeaux.

célébration du soir avant Noël

La plupart° de ces jours de fête, quand ils ne tombent pas un dimanche, sont des jours fériés ou chômés: on ne travaille pas.

majorité

Extrait de *La France, j'aime!*

Cue to Video Module 9 (00:46:29), where Vincenti describes how his family observes the Provence traditions mentioned in this reading.

B.   Les Français et les fêtes de fin d'année

La plupart des Français établissent d'avance un budget spécial pour les fêtes de fin d'année. Les plus grandes dépenses sont représentées par les achats de jouets ou de nourriture.

Les peluches (ours, lapins° et autres animaux) restent le jouet privilégié, le cadeau le plus souvent offert aux enfants en saison de fête, devant les poupées et les jeux électroniques ou vidéo.

rabbits

Pendant longtemps, le repas traditionnel de Noël comprenait une oie°. De nos jours, la dinde farcie aux marrons° est devenue la reine incontestée des repas des fêtes. Les huîtres, le foie gras°, et la bûche° figurent aussi au menu classique de ces repas ou réveillons.

goose
farcie... stuffed with chestnuts
goose liver pâté / yule log cake

En Provence, où les vieilles traditions ont longtemps revêtu° un caractère particulier, le repas de Noël s'appelait «le gros souper». Le menu comprenait des poissons, des légumes, et toujours un plat de lasagnes au beurre et au fromage, car les lasagnes, à l'origine, symbolisaient les langes° de l'enfant Jésus. Le repas se terminait par treize desserts (des fruits secs ou confits° et des gâteaux), symboliques du Christ et de ses douze apôtres°. La tradition des treize desserts continue à être observée de nos jours.

pris

swaddling clothes

dried or candied / apostles

Extrait du *Journal français d'Amérique* (13–26 décembre 1991) et de *Noël en Provence*

En détail

4   Encourage students to find ways to explain as many words as they can in French, thus practicing circumlocution (for example, **reine:** c'est le féminin de **roi;** Elizabeth II est la reine d'Angleterre). If circumlocution is not possible with the vocabulary they have already had, allow English. Students can do this task in pairs first, then check/compare definitions/circumlocutions.

4 **Les mots.**   En utilisant le contexte et la logique, pouvez-vous déduire le sens des mots en caractères gras? Ils se trouvent tous dans le texte **A, L'année des Français.**

1. (1ᵉʳ janvier) On se **souhaite** une «bonne et heureuse année». On s'**offre** des petits cadeaux.
2. (6 janvier) ... devient roi ou **reine** de la fête.
3. (8 mai) anniversaire de la **victoire** des Alliés en 1945.
4. (1ᵉʳ novembre) On va **fleurir** les **tombes** (des morts) dans les **cimetières.**
5. (24 décembre) ... aller à la **messe** de minuit. Tous ceux qui croient encore au «**Père Noël**» attendent les cadeaux.

5 **Les textes**

A. **L'année des Français.**   Complétez le tableau suivant selon le texte.

Date	Nom de la fête	(C) Civile ou (R) religieuse	Ce qu'on fait
1er janv.	Jour de l'An	C	On s'offre des étrennes (des cadeaux de bonne année—argent ou bonbons).
(date mobile)	Pâques	R	On offre aux enfants des œufs en sucre ou en chocolat.
6 janvier	Jour des Rois	R	On mange la galette des rois.
un mardi de février	le Carnaval	R	Il y a des défilés et des bals costumés (avec des masques et des costumes historiques ou exotiques).
14 juillet	Fête nationale	C	On danse dans les rues. Défilé militaire.
11 nov.	l'Armistice	C	On se souvient de l'Armistice de la Première Guerre mondiale (WWI).
1er novembre	la Toussaint	R	On va fleurir les tombes.
24–25 déc.	Noël	R	Les catholiques (80% des Français) vont à la messe de minuit.

B. Les Français et les fêtes de fin d'année.   Répondez aux questions suivantes selon le texte.

1. Quelles sont les plus grandes dépenses dans le budget des fêtes de fin d'année?
2. Quel est le jouet le plus populaire qu'on offre comme cadeau?
3. Donnez quatre plats qui figurent au menu traditionnel du repas de Noël.

dans l'ensemble de la France	**en Provence**
la dinde farcie aux marrons	des poissons
les huîtres	des légumes
le foie gras	des lasagnes
la bûche	13 desserts

4. Quel est le symbolisme de deux des parties du repas traditionnel de Noël en Provence?

Et vous?

1. Avec un(e) partenaire, préparez un calendrier des jours de fête aux États-Unis, au Canada ou dans un autre pays que vous connaissez bien. Donnez la date, le nom de la fête, et une petite description de la façon de célébrer cette fête, sur le modèle de **L'année des Français.** Ensuite, comparez votre liste avec celles des autres groupes.

VOCABULAIRE ACTIF

un ballon
une bougie
un bouquet de fleurs
un défilé
une dinde
un jeu électronique
un jouet
un jour de congé
mort(e)
offrir (inf.)
une peluche
le Père Noël
un pique-nique
la plupart
une poupée
un roi/une reine
souhaiter
une tradition/
  traditionnel(le)

2. Répondez aux questions suivantes concernant les jouets.
   a. À votre avis, quels sont les jouets le plus souvent offerts aux enfants dans votre pays? Quels étaient vos jouets préférés quand vous étiez enfant?
   b. Racontez un souvenir particulier associé à un jouet. Pour vous aider à distinguer entre le passé composé et l'imparfait, organisez d'abord vos pensées dans le tableau suivant, puis comparez vos souvenirs.

Quelles étaient les circonstances? (conditions ou descriptions → imparfait)	Qu'est-ce qui s'est passé? (actions ou réactions → passé composé)
Comment était ce jouet?	Qui vous l'a donné? À quelle occasion?
	Quelle a été votre réaction? Avez-vous été surpris(e)?
Est-ce que vous saviez à l'avance?	
Est-ce que vous jouiez souvent avec ce jouet?	Quand avez-vous arrêté de jouer avec ce jouet?
Est-ce que vous le prêtiez?	Est-ce que ce jouet a causé une dispute un jour?
?	?

3. Changez de partenaire et racontez un souvenir particulier associé à un repas de fête.

Quelles étaient les circonstances? (imparfait)	Qu'est-ce qui s'est passé? (passé composé)
Qui était là?	Qu'est-ce que vous avez fait avant le repas?
Où est-ce que c'était? (Chez vous? Au restaurant?)	Qui a fait la cuisine?
	Qu'est-ce que vous avez mangé?
Comment étaient les plats?	
Comment étaient les gens?	De quoi est-ce que vous avez parlé?
?	?

Note culturelle

Le Ramadan. Ramadan, a religious observance practiced by the Muslim community throughout the world, occurs in the ninth month of the Islamic calendar. It is a time in which Muslims refrain from food, drink, tobacco, and sexual relations between sunrise and sunset. **Le Ramadan** is an important holiday in France because Islam is its second largest religion, with well over three and a half million followers.

STRATÉGIE DE COMMUNICATION

Expressing thanks, congratulations, and good wishes

Cue to Video Module 9 (00:44:29), where Élisabeth and Fatima celebrate Nicolas's birthday.

Birthdays, holidays, and other special events are often occasions for expressing good wishes or thanks to others and for acknowledging those wishes. Read the exchanges below and identify the expressions

- for wishing someone well
- for thanking
- for acknowledging

— Voici un petit cadeau d'anniversaire pour toi.
— Oh là là. Tu es trop gentil! Merci mille fois!
— Mais, ce n'est rien.

— Joyeux Noël, Monsieur Tournier.
— Et bonne année, Madame Robert!

— Vous avez terminé vos études?! Félicitations!
— Merci. Je suis très content.

— Une bonne note en français? Chapeau, Nancy, bravo!
— Merci, c'est gentil. J'ai eu de la chance.

Now check your answers in the chart that follows.

Pour remercier, féliciter, souhaiter	
remercier	**accepter des remerciements**
Merci beaucoup / mille fois.	Je vous en prie. / Je t'en prie.
C'est trop gentil / bien aimable.	Ce n'est rien.
Tu es trop gentil(le) / bien aimable.	De rien.
Vous êtes trop gentil(le) / bien aimable.	Il n'y a pas de quoi.
féliciter	**accepter des félicitations**
Félicitations!	Merci. C'est gentil.
Bravo!	
Chapeau!	
souhaiter	
Joyeux Noël! Joyeuses fêtes!	
Bonne année! Bon anniversaire!	
Bonne chance! Bon courage! Bon voyage! Bonnes vacances!	

ACTIVITÉS

A. Answers may vary. FOLLOW-UP or ALTERNATIVE: Have students make personal statements to which classmates can respond with expressions of thanks, congratulations, etc.

A. À vous! Complétez les dialogues avec des expressions convenables pour remercier, féliciter ou souhaiter.

1. — Je peux t'aider à préparer l'examen si tu veux.

— _____

— _____

2. — Vous avez acheté une nouvelle maison? _____!

— _____

3. — Enfin, c'est le dernier jour de classe!

— _____

4. — Que je suis nerveux! Aujourd'hui j'ai un examen vachement important.

— _____

B. Félicitations! Remerciements! Souhaits! Jouez le rôle des deux person-nes dans les situations suivantes avec un(e) camarade de classe. Une per-sonne va expliquer la situation; l'autre va réagir avec une expression appropriée.

➡ Vous avez eu la meilleure note de la classe à l'examen.
— *Quelle chance! J'ai eu une bonne note à l'examen!*
— *Chapeau!*

1. Vos amis ont un cadeau d'anniversaire pour vous.
2. Votre professeur va avoir 29 ans demain—encore!
3. Votre copain vous prête sa voiture.
4. Un ami de la famille vous invite à un concert de jazz.
5. Vos copains partent demain pour la France.
6. Votre cousine va se marier.

STRUCTURE: Making comparisons (II)
Le superlatif

Observez et déduisez   Chez nous, les plus grandes dépenses pour les fêtes de fin d'année sont pour les achats de jouets et de nourriture. Les peluches et les jeux vidéo sont les cadeaux les plus populaires, même s'ils ne sont pas les moins chers. La dinde farcie aux marrons est le repas de fête que l'on sert le plus souvent.

> ■ Find four examples of the superlative (e.g.: the most fun, the least expensive) in the preceding paragraph. What can you infer about the formation of the superlative?

Vérifiez   *Le superlatif*

■ The superlative is used to express extremes (negative and positive) in quality or quantity: the most, the least, the best, the worst, etc.

■ To form the superlative of an *adjective,* place a definite article and **plus** or **moins** before the adjective.

les moins chers

$$
\begin{array}{l} \text{le/l'} \\ \text{la/l'} \\ \text{les} \end{array} + \begin{array}{l} \text{plus} \\ \text{moins} \end{array} + \text{adjective}
$$

■ Adjectives in the superlative maintain their normal position before or after the noun. Note that when the adjective *follows* the noun, *two* definite articles are required.

Adjectives *following* the noun: **le**   cadeau **le**   plus populaire
(art. + noun + art. + plus + adj.)

Adjectives *preceding* the noun: **les**   plus   grandes dépenses
(art. + plus + adj. + noun)

■ Remember that both the article and the adjective agree in number and gender with the noun.

le meilleur gâteau   **la** meilleure fête

■ A phrase beginning with **de** may be used to qualify the superlative.

le cadeau le plus populaire de la liste
de tous
de la famille, etc.

■ To form the superlative of *adverbs,* simply insert **le** before the comparative. **Le** is invariable.

comparatif: Les repas français durent *(last)* **plus longtemps** que les repas américains.
superlatif: Le repas de Noël dure **le plus longtemps** de tous.

■ As in the comparative, **bon** and **bien** have irregular superlative forms:

Ce que j'aime **le mieux** comme chocolat? Les chocolats belges! Ce sont **les meilleurs** de tous!

ACTIVITÉS

C. Traditions.   Complétez les phrases selon vos traditions et vos préférences.

1. Dans notre famille, la fête la plus importante c'est...

_____ Noël   _____ Hanoukka   _____ le Ramadan

_____ le Jour d'action de grâces   _____ ?

2. Le plat le plus traditionnel pour les repas de fête chez nous c'est...

_____ la dinde   _____ le jambon   _____ l'oie   _____ le lapin

_____ ?

3. Le cadeau qu'on fait le plus souvent aux enfants c'est...

_____ une peluche   _____ un ballon   _____ un jeu électronique

_____ une poupée   _____ ?

4. Pour moi, le meilleur cadeau c'est...

_____ de l'argent   _____ des vêtements   _____ des CD

_____ des livres   _____ ?

5. La _moins_ grande dépense dans le budget des fêtes de fin d'année c'est pour...

_____ les cadeaux   _____ l'alimentation   _____ les voyages

_____ les décorations

6. Pour la fête nationale, l'activité la plus commune de la famille c'est...

_____ un pique-nique   _____ un défilé   _____ un bal costumé

_____ ?

Maintenant, pour chaque phrase, trouvez un(e) camarade de classe qui a répondu comme vous.

➡ _Quelle est la fête la plus importante de ta famille?_

Quelles sont les réponses les plus communes de la classe?

D. Students can share their answers with a partner or in small groups.

D. Insistez!   Les opinions suivantes sur les fêtes et les traditions ne sont pas très «passionnées». Exprimez votre propre opinion d'une manière plus enthousiaste selon l'exemple, ou changez l'adjectif si vous préférez.

➡ Halloween? C'est une tradition bizarre.
Pour moi, c'est la tradition la plus (la moins) bizarre!
ou: _Pour moi, c'est la tradition la plus amusante!_

Noël? C'est une fête importante.
Un CD? C'est un bon cadeau.
Le Père Noël? C'est un homme généreux.
La dinde farcie aux marrons? C'est un bon plat.
L'oie? C'est un plat élégant.
Un défilé militaire? C'est une tradition patriotique.

Est-ce que vos camarades de classe partagent vos opinions?

 Jeu de rôle

You and three classmates play the role of siblings who are organizing a family reunion. You discuss meals, activities, who you hope will attend—and who you hope won't! To no one's surprise, it is not easy to reach a consensus because no two siblings can agree on the best, the worst, the most, the least—about anything!

CULTURE ET RÉFLEXION

■ **Les griots.** Dans les sociétés africaines traditionnelles, les griots jouent un rôle très important: ils assurent le lien entre le passé et le présent. Spécialistes de généalogie, conteurs[1], poètes, musiciens, les griots sont présents à toutes les cérémonies familiales et communautaires. Par leurs paroles flatteuses, ils font revivre[2] les ancêtres et leurs légendes. Ils chantent le triomphe du bien sur le mal. Ils transmettent, de génération

Un village du Mali écoute sa griote.

en génération, l'histoire, la morale et la culture du peuple. Dans les sociétés occidentales, la tradition orale existe-t-elle toujours? Est-ce important de connaître ses ancêtres? Pourquoi ou pourquoi pas? Comment la morale se transmet-elle de génération en génération? Avons-nous des équivalents des griots? Expliquez.

■ **«Je me souviens».** La présence du passé se manifeste certainement dans la devise[3] officielle du Québec, «Je me souviens». De quoi les Québécois se souviennent-ils? De leurs origines françaises, d'un pays qui de 1535 à 1763 s'appelait la Nouvelle-France, de la domination anglaise (1763–1867), puis de la création de la Fédération du Canada permettant aux «Canadiens français» une certaine autonomie. Depuis 1974, la seule langue officielle du Québec est le français, mais les tensions linguistiques et culturelles entre les francophones et les anglophones continuent. Comment la devise «Je me souviens» peut-elle aider les Québécois à préparer leur avenir?

■ **«C'est pur, c'est français!»** Savez-vous qu'il existe en France une institution nationale chargée de protéger la pureté de la langue française? Eh oui, c'est le rôle de l'Académie française! Fondée en 1634, cette institution se compose de 40 membres, élus à vie[4], presque tous des écrivains illustres. Ses fonctions incluent la rédaction d'un *Dictionnaire de la langue française* (1ère édition en 1694, 9e édition en 1986) et d'une *Grammaire de la langue française* (publiée en 1933), l'attribution annuelle de prix littéraires, et la *Défense de la langue française,* une association officielle qui contrôle l'évolution de la langue et lutte contre l'invasion des mots étrangers, en particulier anglais. S'il existe un terme français pour désigner une nouvelle invention technologique, par exemple, défense[5] à tout document officiel d'utiliser le terme anglais. Exemple: «le courrier électronique» pour *e-mail*. Problème: beaucoup de jeunes Français disent «un e-mail»... À votre avis, est-il important de parler *correctement* sa langue maternelle? Donnez des exemples de «fautes[6]» qui sont maintenant acceptées dans l'anglais parlé.

Les membres de l'Académie française.

Qu'est-ce que vous considérez comme une «corruption» de votre langue? Est-ce du snobisme de résister à cette corruption?

---

1. *storytellers*   2. *bring to life*   3. *motto*   4. *elected for life*   5. *it is forbidden*   6. erreurs

Troisième étape

À l'écoute: Un souvenir de voyage

Ici, quelqu'un va vous raconter un souvenir de voyage—à Tahiti!

Avant d'écouter

This input section recycles narration and description in the past, and introduces students to cultural information about Tahiti, new vocabulary, and the use of **savoir** vs. **connaître**.

1 Quand vous pensez à la Polynésie, qu'est-ce que vous imaginez? Cochez les images qui vous semblent appropriées et complétez la liste selon votre imagination.

_____ des plages magnifiques   _____ des tableaux de Gauguin

_____ des fleurs exotiques   _____ ?

_____ des arbres exotiques:
des palmiers, des cocotiers
(*coconut trees*), etc.

2 Maintenant imaginez un repas tahitien. Cochez les plats qui, selon vous, vont figurer au menu, puis complétez la liste selon votre imagination.

_____ des poissons cuits (*cooked*)   _____ du taro (ou «fruit de la terre», comme une pomme de terre)

_____ des poissons crus (*raw*)

_____ des fruits cuits   _____ de la viande

_____ des fruits crus   _____ ?

Les délices de la cuisine tahitienne.

Écoutons

Audio CD

3 Écoutez d'abord pour identifier au moins six choses que vous avez anticipées dans **Avant d'écouter** et qui sont mentionnées dans le passage (nature, aliments typiques, etc.). Cochez-les une deuxième fois.

4 Have students work on this task in pairs, then list responses on the board. ANSWERS: 1. V 2. F (La végétation était comme un décor de film.) 3. V 4. F (pas de portes) 5. V 6. V 7. V 8. F (Ils les ont regardés manger.) 9. V 10. V

4 Écoutez encore et indiquez si les phrases suivantes sont vraies ou fausses. Si elles sont fausses, corrigez-les.

1. Quand Édith est arrivée à Papeete, elle a pensé qu'il faisait chaud et humide.
2. En sortant de l'aéroport, elle est allée au cinéma.
3. Quand elle a fait le tour de la ville, elle a vu que les maisons des Tahitiens étaient généralement très modestes.
4. Il n'y avait pas de fenêtres aux maisons.
5. Le tama'ara'a est un repas tahitien.
6. Quand elle a été invitée dans une famille tahitienne, elle a dû retirer ses chaussures *(take off her shoes)* avant d'entrer dans la maison.
7. Édith ne savait pas identifier certains plats qu'il y avait sur la table.
8. Les hôtes *(hosts)* ont mangé avec les invités.
9. Il n'y avait pas d'assiettes pour les hôtes sur la table.
10. Un repas traditionnel tahitien se mange avec les doigts.

VOCABULAIRE ACTIF

cru(e) ≠ cuit(e)
frapper (ce qui m'a frappé[e])
magnifique
montrer
ouvert(e)
reconnaître
tahitien(ne)

5 Lisez le passage suivant, en écoutant la conversation. Écoutez encore la conversation pour pouvoir compléter le résumé suivant avec les verbes donnés, au passé composé ou à l'imparfait. (Pour les nouveaux verbes, une forme du passé composé et de l'imparfait vous est donnée.) Ensuite écoutez la conversation une dernière fois pour vérifier vos réponses (choix du verbe et temps). Pouvez-vous déduire le sens des mots en caractères gras?

avoir l'impression	manger (2 fois)
reconnaître (a reconnu/reconnaissait)	descendre
être	s'asseoir (s'est assis/
frapper	s'asseyait)

Quand elle <u>est descendue</u> de l'avion, ce qui l' <u>a frappée</u> ,

c'était la chaleur et l'humidité. Elle <u>avait l'impression</u> d'être dans un

sauna. Les portes <u>étaient</u> **ouvertes** en permanence.

Sur la table, il y avait des œufs de **tortue** et d'autres choses qu'elle

(ne... pas) <u>ne reconnaissait pas</u> . Seuls les parents

<u>se sont assis</u> à table avec les invités. **Plus** les invités

<u>mangeaient</u> , **plus** les hôtes étaient contents. Les hôtes (ne... pas)

<u>n'ont pas mangé</u> devant les invités, pour **montrer** leur respect.

6 Imaginez que vous êtes parmi les invités à ce repas tahitien. Préparez trois ou quatre questions que vous aimeriez poser à vos hôtes.

STRUCTURE: Saying you know someone or something
Les verbes savoir et connaître

Observez et déduisez

Édith connaît une famille tahitienne et, depuis son voyage là-bas, elle connaît un peu Tahiti aussi. Maintenant elle sait préparer quelques plats tahitiens et a appris quelques coutumes du pays. Par exemple, elle sait que dans la famille traditionnelle on mange avec les doigts, et elle sait pourquoi la famille ne mange pas avec les invités.

> ■ French has two verbs that mean *to know,* **savoir** and **connaître.** Study the use of the two verbs in the paragraph above. Which verb means *to know* a person? Which one means *to know* a fact or piece of information? Which one means *to know of* or *to be familiar with* a place? Which one means *to know how to do something?*

Le verbe *savoir*

Le verbe **savoir**	
je sais	nous savons
tu sais	vous savez
il / elle / on sait	ils / elles savent
Passé composé: j'ai su	

■ When followed by an infinitive, **savoir** means *to know how to do something.*

Édith sait faire la cuisine tahitienne.

■ **Savoir** is used to say one does or doesn't know how to speak a language.

Elle ne sait pas le tahitien; elle sait le français et l'anglais.

Give several examples, then have volunteers complete the sentence: Je sais que... (où... pourquoi...)

■ **Savoir** is used to say one knows facts (things learned or memorized).

Elle sait les noms des plats traditionnels.

■ **Savoir** can also be followed by a clause beginning with **que, où, pourquoi,** etc.

Elle sait pourquoi la famille ne mange pas avec les invités.

*Le verbe **connaître***

VOCABULAIRE ACTIF
connaître
se connaître
savoir

Le verbe connaître	
je connais	nous connaissons
tu connais	vous connaissez
il / elle / on connaît	ils / elles connaissent

Passé composé: j'ai connu

Remind students they learned «Tu connais Nicolas?» in Ch. 1.

Ask students, «Quelles villes (quels pays) est-ce que vous connaissez bien?»

Tell students if you have met a famous person and/or ask them who they have met: «Vous avez connu quelqu'un de célèbre?»

■ To express the idea of knowing *people,* use **connaître.**

Édith connaît une famille tahitienne.

■ **Connaître** also means *to know of* or *be familiar with* a place or a topic.

Elle connaît bien Tahiti et son histoire.

■ In the passé composé, **connaître** can also mean *met* (as well as *knew*).

Édith **a connu** beaucoup d'amis de la famille tahitienne.

■ **Se connaître** means *to know each other.*

Édith et la famille se connaissent depuis longtemps.

■ **Reconnaître** means *to recognize.*

Il y avait des plats qu'Édith ne reconnaissait pas.

ACTIVITÉS

A. Have volunteers read a sentence and then call on a classmate who responds, «Moi aussi, je sais/ connais... » or «Pas moi. Je ne sais/connais pas... »

A. Connaître ou savoir?   Reliez les expressions de gauche avec des expressions logiques à droite (ci-dessous et à la page 339). Ensuite indiquez si les phrases sont vraies pour vous aussi.

		Moi aussi	Pas moi
Je sais...	le tahitien	_____	_____
Je connais...	Papeete	_____	_____
	un restaurant tahitien	_____	_____
	préparer le taro	_____	_____
	où est Tahiti	_____	_____
	des tableaux de Gauguin	_____	_____

une famille tahitienne   _____   _____

pourquoi Édith est allée à Papeete   _____   _____

les noms des amis d'Édith   _____   _____

B. Interviews. Demandez à votre partenaire si les personnes indiquées connaissent ou savent les choses suivantes.

➡ Tu... (Tahiti, le tahitien)
— _Tu connais Tahiti?_
— _Oui, je connais Tahiti._
— _Tu sais le tahitien?_
— _Non, je ne sais pas le tahitien._

1. (des Français, le français, un bon restaurant français)
   Est-ce que tes amis...
2. (dessiner, les tableaux impressionnistes, un grand musée)
   Est-ce que tu...
3. (s'amuser en vacances, les coutumes d'un autre pays, où aller en vacances)
   Est-ce que ta famille et toi, vous...
4. (pourquoi tu apprends le français, parler français, ton professeur de français)
   Est-ce que ton copain (ta copine)...

C. To determine the collective knowledge of the class on each topic, ask groups to read their statements aloud. Then have each group come up with an original topic and repeat the activity.

C. Que sait-on? Partagez vos connaissances avec vos camarades de classe en groupes de trois ou quatre. Qu'est-ce que vous savez ou connaissez sur les sujets mentionnés?

➡ Tahiti
Je connais un bon hôtel à Tahiti.
Moi, je sais où se trouve une plage magnifique.
Et moi, je connais des gens qui habitent à Papeete.

A **Loto** game in the _Instructor's Resource Manual_ helps students practice the use of **savoir** and **connaître**.

1. les repas traditionnels tahitiens
2. le climat et la végétation à Tahiti
3. les coutumes dans un autre pays
4. ?

STRUCTURE: Negating
Les expressions _ne ... rien, ne ... personne_

Observez et déduisez   Quel cauchemar! Thomas a participé à un dîner traditionnel tahitien chez les amis d'un ami, mais il ne connaissait pas les traditions du pays. Il ne connaissait personne à côté de lui, et il ne reconnaissait rien sur son assiette. Il n'y avait pas de fourchette ou de couteau, et les hôtes n'ont rien mangé—ils l'ont regardé manger! Pauvre Thomas. Personne ne lui a expliqué les coutumes tahitiennes!

> ■ Find two new negative expressions in **Observez et déduisez**. Which expression means _nothing_? Which one means _no one_?

Vérifiez *Les expressions **ne ... rien**, **ne ... personne***

■ You have seen the negative expressions **ne ... rien** *(nothing)* and **ne ... personne** *(no one)* in activities throughout the book. They correspond to the affirmative expressions **quelque chose** and **quelqu'un.**

ne ... rien ≠ quelque chose
ne ... personne ≠ quelqu'un

Notice in the chart below that **ne ... rien** follows the same placement rules as the other negative expressions you've studied: **ne ... pas, ne ... plus, ne ... jamais.** However, note the placement for **personne** in the passé composé and the futur proche.

	temps simples (présent, imparfait)	temps composé (passé composé)	futur proche
rien	Il **ne** reconnaissait **rien** sur l'assiette.	Il n'a **rien** compris.	Il **ne** va **rien** dire.
personne	Il **ne** connaissait **personne.**	Il n'a compris **personne.**	Il **ne** va regarder **personne.**

■ Both **personne** and **rien** follow the preposition of verbs requiring a preposition.

Parce qu'il était un peu timide, Thomas **n'**a parlé à **personne;** il **n'**a parlé de **rien.**

■ **Rien** and **personne** may both be used as the subject of a sentence. In this case, both parts of the expression precede the verb.

Personne ne lui a expliqué les coutumes.
Rien ne lui était familier.

The use of **personne** and **rien** as subjects is presented for recognition only.

■ Like **jamais,** both **rien** and **personne** can be used alone to answer a question.

— Qu'est-ce qu'il a dit?
— **Rien!**

— Qui est-ce qu'il connaissait?
— **Personne!**

ACTIVITÉS

D. Vrai ou faux? Écoutez encore **À l'écoute,** puis lisez les phrases suivantes et indiquez si elles sont vraies ou fausses selon Édith.

Son voyage

1. Édith ne connaît personne à Tahiti.
2. Rien à Tahiti ne lui plaît.
3. Personne n'invite Édith à la maison.
4. Elle n'apprend rien d'intéressant au sujet de Tahiti.

Les traditions tahitiennes

5. Personne ne porte de chaussures *(shoes)* dans la maison.
6. Personne ne ferme la porte de la maison.
7. À un dîner traditionnel tahitien, on ne boit rien.
8. Les hôtes ne mangent rien.

E. Pauvre Thomas.   Après un voyage à Tahiti, les copains de Thomas lui ont posé beaucoup de questions. Jouez le rôle de Thomas, et répondez à leurs questions en employant **ne ... rien** et **ne ... personne.**

➡ Qu'est-ce que tu as appris sur les coutumes tahitiennes avant d'y aller?
Malheureusement, je n'ai rien appris.

1. Alors une fois arrivé, qui t'a parlé des coutumes?
2. Qui est-ce que tu connaissais au dîner?
3. Qu'est-ce que tu as dit aux autres invités?
4. Qu'est-ce que tu as reconnu sur ton assiette?
5. Qu'est-ce que les hôtes ont mangé?
6. Qu'est-ce qu'ils ont bu?

F. Moi, non.   Faites une liste de tout ce que vous ne faites *pas* quand vous êtes en vacances. Employez les expressions **ne ... rien** et **ne ... personne.**

➡ *Je ne lis rien...   Je ne téléphone à personne...*

Jeu de rôle

With a partner, play the role of two complaining friends. One of you has returned from a vacation in which everything seemed to go wrong (bad weather, missed flights, closed museums, etc.). The other had to stay home and is unhappy about not having a vacation. Each describes the circumstances and events of their "miserable" experience.

Remind students about appropriate uses of the passé composé and the imperfect, and encourage them to use all the negative expressions they have learned: **ne ... pas/jamais/plus/rien/personne.**

Now that you have finished the Troisième étape of this chapter, do your Lab Manual activities with the audio program. Explore chapter topics further with the Mais Oui! Video and CD-ROM. Viewing and comprehension activities are in the video section of your *Workbook/Lab Manual/Video Manual.*

Littérature: La concordance des temps

Born in Fès, Morocco, in 1944, Tahar Ben Jelloun has become an important spokesman for French-speaking Arabs. Through his poems, his short stories, and most of all his novels, he has exposed the wounds and the scars of a people torn between past and present and between two cultures. In *Les yeux baissés (With Lowered Eyes)*, a novel published in 1991, he shows the boring and oppressed life of a young shepherd girl who grows up in a very poor village in southern Morocco. When she is about eleven years old, she moves to Paris with her family and discovers a new world, one that seems to require a new identity, a new birth. If she is to survive in this world, she must learn the language. For her, the biggest problem with the French language is **la concordance des temps**—knowing which tense to use in the past! In the following excerpt, we learn that her struggle with past tenses is actually symbolic of the identity crisis she faces as she tries to adjust to a new and totally different culture. One day, she enters a church in Paris to sort out her frustrations.

Avant de lire | **1** | Voici quelques expressions que vous allez voir dans la lecture qui suit. Analysez d'abord le sens des mots en caractères gras, puis complétez les phrases en choisissant parmi ces mots.

une corde, un nœud

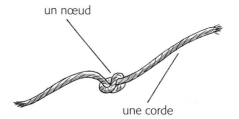

un nœud

une corde

vide, plein

un verre vide   un verre plein

une faute, se tromper	Quand on écrit quelque chose qui n'est pas correct, c'est une erreur ou **une faute. Se tromper,** c'est faire des fautes.
par cœur	Apprendre **par cœur,** c'est mémoriser.
sentir, une odeur	Les parfums **sentent** bon; ils ont une bonne **odeur.** On **sent** les **odeurs;** on entend les
un bruit **l'essence**	**bruits.** Dans les villes on entend **le bruit** des voitures et on sent **l'odeur** de **l'essence. L'essence** est une forme de pétrole utilisée par les voitures.

1. Quand rien ne se passe, les journées sont <u>vides</u> et ennuyeuses. Quand les activités sont nombreuses, au contraire, les journées sont bien <u>pleines</u> .

2. Le temps peut être comparé à une <u>corde</u> avec des <u>nœuds</u> pour représenter les événements importants.

3. Quand je pense au village de mon enfance, je peux encore <u>sentir</u> les <u>odeurs</u> des arbres, des fleurs, des rues...

4. Les enfants dorment—ne faites pas trop de <u>bruit</u> , s'il vous plaît.

5. J'ai besoin de prendre de <u>l'essence</u> à la station-service.

6. J'ai appris <u>par cœur</u> mes conjugaisons, mais j'ai fait plusieurs <u>fautes</u> à l'examen; je <u>me suis trompé</u> de temps—j'ai utilisé le passé composé au lieu de l'imparfait!

2 Have students speculate in French in small groups, then compare stories.

2 Voici des phrases-clés dans le texte que vous allez lire:

> Je continuais à faire des fautes...
> Je repensais alors au village...
> Mon passé était vraiment simple...
> J'ai compris qu'il fallait [était nécessaire de] se détacher complètement du pays natal.
> ... j'ai pu maîtriser [contrôler] la concordance des temps

D'après ces phrases-clés, quelle sorte d'histoire est-ce que vous anticipez pour cette petite bergère marocaine qui essaie de s'adapter à la vie à Paris?

En général

3 Have students do this task in pairs first, then discuss answers.

3 Parcourez le texte une première fois puis classez (de 1 à 6) les idées générales suivantes dans l'ordre où elles sont présentées dans l'histoire.

<u>2</u> Le concept du temps dans le village de la jeune bergère

<u>3</u> Le concept du temps en France

<u>1</u> Le problème principal de la langue française

La concordance des temps

1 Je continuais à faire des fautes en écrivant mais je lisais correctement. Mon handicap majeur était l'utilisation des temps. J'étais fâchée avec la concordance des temps. Je n'arrivais pas à distinguer toutes ces nuances du passé dans une langue que j'aimais mais qui ne m'aimait pas. Je butais contre° l'imparfait, le passé simple—simplicité toute illusoire—et le passé composé. Pour tout simplifier, je réduisais° l'ensemble au présent, ce qui était absurde.

butais... *stumbled against*

reduced

2 Je repensais alors au village, aux journées identiques où il ne se passait rien. Ces journées vides, s'étiraient° comme une corde entre deux arbres. Le temps, c'était cette ligne droite°, marquée au début, au milieu et à l'autre bout par trois nœuds, trois moments où il se passait quelque chose: les états° du soleil. La vie était ces trois moments où il fallait penser à sortir les bêtes°, manger au moment où le soleil est au-dessus de la tête, rentrer les bêtes quand il se couchait°.

stretched

ligne... *straight line*

positions

animaux

quand... le soir

3 Mon passé était vraiment simple, fait de répétition, sans surprise. En arrivant en France j'ai su que la fameuse corde était une suite° de nœuds serrés° les uns aux autres, et que peu de gens avaient le loisir de s'arrêter sous l'arbre.

série / *close together*

4 Je connaissais par cœur les conjugaisons des verbes «être» et «avoir», mais je me trompais tout le temps quand il s'agissait de les utiliser dans une longue phrase. J'ai compris qu'il fallait se détacher complètement du pays natal. Mais le village était toujours là; il rôdait autour° de moi. Je résistais. Je niais° cette présence. Je suis entrée un jour dans une église pour ne plus sentir les odeurs du village. Mais j'étais ramenée au village par une main magique et je revoyais la même corde avec les trois nœuds, et moi assise sous l'arbre, attendant... Dans cette église obscure, j'entendais la litanie° des enfants de l'école coranique°, et je voyais, par moments, la tête du vieux fqih° qui dormait. Sa bouche entrouverte° laissait passer un filet de salive° transparent.

rôdait... *prowled around* / *denied*

récitation / religieuse arabe

professeur du Coran

un peu ouverte / filet... *string of saliva* / *shiver*

5 Cette image venue de si loin m'a donné un frisson°: ç'a été le coup de fouet° dont j'avais besoin pour arrêter de perpétuer la présence du village.

coup... *whiplash*

6 Dehors, j'ai apprécié l'agitation de la ville, l'odeur de l'essence, le bruit du métro°, et tout ce qui annulait° en moi le souvenir du village.

subway / canceled

7 À partir de là, j'ai pu maîtriser la concordance des temps. J'ai fait des exercices et je n'ai plus utilisé le présent. Cela m'amusait, car je savais que le jour où je ne mélangerais plus° les temps, j'aurais réellement quitté° le village.

ne... *would no longer mix* / aurais quitté: *would have left*

Extrait de *Les yeux baissés* (Tahar Ben Jelloun)

En détail

4   ANSWERS: 1. identiques
2. bout   3. tout le temps, il s'agissait
de   4. ramenée

4 **Les mots.**   Trouvez dans le texte des synonymes pour les mots en caractères gras et substituez-les dans les phrases suivantes, qui sont des paraphrases du texte.

1. (¶2)   Au village, les journées étaient toutes **pareilles.**
2. (¶2)   Le temps était comme une corde, ou une ligne droite, marquée au début, au milieu et à l'autre **extrémité** par trois nœuds.

3. (¶4) La narratrice se trompait **constamment** quand **il était question d'**utiliser les verbes au passé dans des phrases.

4. (¶4) Elle voulait refuser la présence de son village, mais elle était toujours **transportée** dans son village par une force magique.

5 **Le texte.** Répondez aux questions du tableau, selon le texte.

Quelles étaient les circonstances?	Qu'est-ce qui s'est passé?
1. Quel était le handicap majeur de la narratrice?	
2. Combien de nœuds y avait-il dans la corde du temps de son village? Quels étaient ces nœuds?	
3. Comment était la corde du temps en France?	4. Qu'est-ce qu'elle a fait un jour pour essayer d'oublier son village?
5. Comment était l'image «venue de si loin»? Qu'est-ce qu'elle «entendait» dans sa mémoire? Qu'est-ce qu'elle «voyait»?	6. Quelle a été la réaction de la jeune Marocaine à cette image?
	7. Qu'est-ce qu'elle a pu apprécier en sortant de l'église?
	8. Qu'est-ce qui a changé pour elle dans la langue française?

Et vous?

1. L'auteur présente le temps comme une corde avec des nœuds. Avec un(e) partenaire, comparez la corde du temps à différentes périodes de votre vie. Combien y avait-il de nœuds, c'est-à-dire de moments importants, dans chacune de ces cordes, et quels étaient ces nœuds? (Le petit déjeuner? Le départ pour l'école? Une activité particulière? Une émission de télévision? Le repas du soir? etc.)
   a. Quand vous étiez à l'école primaire.
   b. Quand vous étiez au lycée.
   c. Aujourd'hui.

2. Considérez les problèmes de séparation et d'adaptation de la narratrice.
   a. Pourquoi la jeune Marocaine devait-elle arrêter de vivre mentalement dans son village pour pouvoir s'adapter à son nouveau monde?
   b. Pensez à un moment où vous avez dû vous adapter à une nouvelle situation (par exemple, quand vous avez quitté votre famille pour la première fois, ou la première semaine dans une nouvelle école). Organisez d'abord vos pensées selon le tableau à la page 346, puis discutez avec un(e) camarade de classe.

Quelles étaient les circonstances?	Qu'est-ce qui s'est passé?
Où étiez-vous?	Qu'est-ce que quelqu'un a dit ou fait?
Avec qui étiez-vous?	
À quoi pensiez-vous?	Quelle a été votre réaction?
Qu'est-ce qui était familier/ différent?	Qu'est-ce que vous avez fait pour vous adapter à la nouvelle situation?
Qu'est-ce qui était facile/difficile?	Qu'est-ce que vous avez appris?
Pourquoi?	Qu'est-ce qui n'a pas changé?
?	?

Par écrit: I had *so* much fun!

Avant d'écrire

A. **Strategy: Using sentence cues.** Sometimes getting an idea to write about is the most difficult aspect of a writing assignment. Sentence completions can serve as a stimulant to generate ideas. Completing a sentence that begins, "Last year while Christmas shopping . . . ," for example, could trigger memories about the sights, sounds, smells, and people associated with this moment in the past.

Application. What thoughts/impressions are brought to mind by the following topics? Jot down as many ideas as you can for each cue.

a. L'année dernière pendant les fêtes de fin d'année...
b. Une fois à l'école quand j'avais 8 (12, 16) ans...
c. Je me souviens bien de nos vacances en...

B. **Strategy: Organizing a story in the past.** In this chapter you learned that in French, you need to distinguish between two past tenses when relating a memory from your past. You may want to use a diagram to visualize the relationship between what happened and what the conditions were.

Application. Choose a memorable moment from those you listed above and construct a diagram related to it using the example below. First write a name for the memory in the center of the page. In a column to the right, develop a list of verbs telling what happened. To the left, develop a list of circumstances, e.g., how you felt, what your attitude was, what the weather was like, who was there, and so on. You may have a "circumstance" for each "event"—or you may not. In order to make the story come alive as you tell it, however, it is important to balance the story narrative—what happened—with descriptive detail relating what it was like for you. Now draw the diagram showing the relationship between the circumstances (C) and the events (É).

circonstances	*un souvenir*	événements
C, C	⟷	É
	⟷	É
C	⟷	É
	⟷	É, É, É
C, C	⟷	É

ÉCRIVEZ

1. C'est le Jour de l'An et vous écrivez une carte à votre cousine que vous n'avez pas vue depuis des mois. Souhaitez-lui une bonne année et racontez-lui ce que vous avez fait pendant les fêtes de fin d'année.

2. Vous avez un souvenir amusant que vous voulez publier dans le *Journal français d'Amérique*. Alors, il faut, bien sûr, être précis et bref— mais intéressant aussi. Vous devez raconter votre histoire en moins de 100 mots. Choisissez votre titre (par exemple, «Humour à l'école»? «Rire en famille»? «S'amuser en voyage»?) et écrivez l'essentiel de ce qui s'est passé et quelles étaient les circonstances.

VOCABULAIRE ACTIF

Verbes

arrêter *to stop*
avoir honte (de) *to be ashamed (of)*
battre *to beat*
connaître *to know (someone)*
se connaître *to know one another, to meet*
être assis(e) *to be seated*
être fâché(e) *to be mad, angry*
être puni(e) *to be punished*
féliciter *to congratulate*
frapper (Ce qui m'a frappé(e)...)
   to strike (What struck me . . .)

interroger (quelqu'un) *to call on / to question (someone)*
lever le doigt *to raise one's hand*
montrer *to show*
murmurer *to whisper*
offrir (inf.) *to offer, give (a gift)*
reconnaître *to recognize*
remercier *to thank*
rester debout *to remain standing*
savoir *to know (something)*
souhaiter *to wish*

Verbes à sens multiples

j'ai dû *I had to*
j'ai pu / je n'ai pas pu *I was able (I succeeded in) / I couldn't (I failed to)*

j'ai su *I found out*
j'ai voulu / je n'ai pas voulu *I tried / I refused*

Adjectifs

cuit(e) ≠ cru(e) *cooked ≠ raw*
magnifique *magnificent*
mort(e) *dead*

ouvert(e) *open*
tahitien(ne) *Tahitian*
traditionnel(le) *traditional*

Noms

un ballon *a ball*
une bougie *a candle*
un bouquet de fleurs *a bouquet of flowers*
un coutume *a custom*
un défilé *a parade*
une dinde *a turkey*
une image *a picture*
un jeu électronique *an electronic game*
un jouet *a toy*

un jour de congé *a holiday, a day off*
la maîtresse *the (elementary school) teacher*
une peluche *a stuffed animal*
le Père Noël *Santa Claus*
un pique-nique *a picnic*
une poupée *a doll*
une reine *a queen*
un roi *a king*
une tradition *a tradition*

Expressions pour remercier, féliciter, souhaiter
Bon anniversaire! *Happy birthday!*
Bonne année! *Happy New Year!*
Bonne chance! *Good luck!*
Bon courage! *Hang in there!*
Bonnes vacances! *Have a good vacation!*
Bon voyage! *Have a nice trip!*
Bravo! / Chapeau! / Félicitations! *Congratulations!*
CE n'est rien *think nothing of it*
Joyeux Noël *Merry Christmas*

Le superlatif
le moins... *the least . . .*   le (la) meilleur(e) *the best (adj.)*
le plus... *the most . . .*   le mieux *the best (adv.)*

Divers
longtemps *a long time*   la plupart (des gens) *most (people)*
personne *nobody*   rien *nothing*

La vie de tous les jours

EPP 6005

EPP 6005

Quelle est la routine quotidienne de cette jeune maman? Imaginez! Et vous?

Quelles sont les activités de votre routine quotidienne?

This chapter will enable you to
- **understand longer conversations about daily life and exercise**
- **read some fashion tips from a popular French magazine and a French-Canadian short story about a sweater—and hockey**

- **talk about your daily routine**
- **describe the clothes you wear**
- **respond to compliments in a French manner**
- **discuss choices related to health and exercise**

349

Première étape

À l'écoute: La routine quotidienne

This input introduces cultural information about daily life in an African village; it also presents reflexive verbs.

Est-ce que vous vous souvenez de Larmé, le jeune homme du Tchad qui nous a parlé du bonheur (Chapitre 8)? Cette fois, il va vous parler de la vie de tous les jours dans son village. Avant de l'écouter, pensez à votre routine quotidienne (de tous les jours).

Avant d'écouter

1 Regardez les illustrations et les verbes donnés, et dites quand et dans quel ordre vous faites les actions suivantes le matin.

➡ *Je me réveille à / vers sept heures; je..., puis..., après ça je...*

se réveiller

se lever*

se laver / prendre une douche

se brosser les dents

se peigner / se coiffer

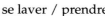
se maquiller

---

*Se lever se conjugue comme **acheter** (avec un accent grave devant une syllabe muette): je me lève, mais nous nous levons.

se raser   s'habiller   prendre le petit déjeuner

2 Write **se reposer / se coucher** on the board; have students infer the meaning of both verbs.

2 Parlez de votre routine du soir. Qu'est-ce que vous faites pour **vous reposer?** Vous regardez la télé? Vous faites de l'exercice physique? Vous lisez? À quelle heure est-ce que **vous vous couchez** (allez au lit)?

3 Maintenant imaginez la vie dans un village africain. À quelle heure pensez-vous que la journée commence? Quelles sont les actions déjà mentionnées qui vont / ne vont pas faire partie de la routine quotidienne?

Les femmes font la cuisine dans un village du Burkina Faso.

Écoutons

Audio CD

4 Écoutez d'abord pour identifier les idées générales de la conversation. Cochez parmi les sujets ci-dessous et à la page 352 ceux qui sont traités.

_____ ✓ la routine du matin

_____ ✓ la routine du soir

_____✓_____ les responsabilités des hommes

_____✓_____ les responsabilités des femmes

_____ les activités des enfants pendant la journée

_____✓_____ ce qu'on mange le matin

_____ ce qu'on mange le soir

_____✓_____ avec qui on mange le repas du soir

5 ANSWERS: se lever, se laver, s'habiller, (prendre) le petit déjeuner, se reposer, se coucher

6 ANSWERS: 1. F (vers 5 ou 6 h) 2. F (Les femmes apportent le petit déjeuner aux champs.) 3. F (Si!) 4. F (Ils se reposent pendant que les femmes travaillent.) 5. V 6. V 7. F (Les garçons...) 8. V

5 Écoutez encore en regardant les verbes donnés dans **Avant d'écouter.** Quelles sont les actions qui sont mentionnées dans la conversation?

6 Écoutez encore et indiquez si les phrases suivantes sont vraies ou fausses. Si elles sont fausses, corrigez-les.

1. Dans ce village du sud du Tchad, on se lève vers sept ou huit heures.
2. On mange avant d'aller aux champs.
3. Les femmes ne travaillent pas aux champs.
4. Après le travail aux champs, les hommes aident les femmes à préparer le repas du soir.
5. Les hommes ne mangent pas avec les femmes.
6. Les hommes et les femmes ont des causeries (conversations) différentes.
7. Les filles de plus de dix ou douze ans mangent séparément.
8. On se couche vers dix heures du soir.

7 Écoutez une dernière fois et complétez les phrases avec les mots suivants. Pouvez-vous déduire le sens de ces mots?

noir   dur   le feu   la lune   du bois

1. Larmé dit que les femmes travaillent plus _dur_____ que les hommes. Après le travail des champs, et avant de pouvoir préparer à manger, elles vont chercher _du bois_____ pour _le feu_____ .

2. Quand est-ce qu'on se couche? Ça dépend de _la lune_____ . Comme il n'y a pas d'électricité, on se couche quand il fait trop _noir_____ pour y voir.

VOCABULAIRE ACTIF

le bois
le feu
la lune
La routine quotidienne
  se réveiller
  se lever
  se laver, prendre une
    douche
  se brosser les dents
  se peigner
  se coiffer
  se maquiller
  se raser
  s'habiller
  se reposer
  se coucher
(travailler) dur

STRUCTURE: Talking about daily routines (I)
Les verbes pronominaux (II)

Observez et déduisez

Help students use logic and context to discover meaning (e.g., to help them understand **se fâcher,** reason that if Larmé's father's not happy _either,_ his mother must be . . . ? For **se dépêcher,** ask "When you get up late, do you usually dawdle or . . . ?").

Aujourd'hui la maman de Larmé se fâche parce qu'il se réveille tard, et il ne veut pas se lever tout de suite. Son papa n'est pas content non plus parce qu'il ne se dépêche pas. «Larmé! Quand vas-tu t'habiller?»

■ From the context, which verb in the preceding paragraph means _to hurry up?_ Which one means _to get mad?_

■ What happens to the pronoun when the pronominal verb is an infinitive?

Vérifiez *Les verbes pronominaux*

This section briefly recycles the present tense of pronominal verbs and introduces pronominal infinitives. The passé composé of pronominal verbs is introduced in the next section.

■ Some pronominal verbs indicate a *reflexive* action, that is, an action that reflects back on the subject of the verb. The reflexive pronoun is often *not* expressed in English.

> Je me lève tôt le matin, et je me douche tout de suite.
> *I get (myself) up   I shower (myself)*

■ Just as with the pronominal verbs you saw in Chapter 8, the reflexive pronoun always precedes the verb directly, even in the interrogative and the negative.

> **Vous** couchez-vous tôt ou tard?
> Nous nous couchons vers dix heures, mais nous **ne nous** endormons **pas** tout de suite.

■ The pronoun agrees with the subject when an infinitive is used.

> **Je** ne passe pas beaucoup de temps à **me** peigner.

■ Remember that some verbs have a pronominal *and* a nonpronominal form.

> D'abord le papa **se réveille** puis il **réveille** les enfants.

VOCABULAIRE ACTIF
se dépêcher
se doucher
s'endormir
se fâcher

ACTIVITÉS

A. Have students mark their own answers, then elicit possible questions for each cue before they begin interviewing a partner. FOLLOW-UP: Ask volunteers to compare their routine with their partner's.

A. Typique? Lisez la description d'une routine quotidienne. Indiquez si votre routine est pareille (*«Moi aussi»*) ou différente (d'autres choix).

1. Je me réveille *assez tôt*. _____ Moi aussi

   _____ vers __?__ heures   _____ aussi tard que possible   _____ ?

2. Une fois réveillé, je me lève *tout de suite*. _____ Moi aussi

   _____ après quelques minutes   _____ au dernier moment   _____ ?

3. Je me brosse les dents *avant de prendre le petit déjeuner*. _____ Moi aussi

   _____ après le petit déjeuner   _____ si je m'en souviens   _____ ?

4. Je passe *très peu de temps* à me coiffer. _____ Moi aussi

   _____ __?__ minutes   _____ des heures   _____ ?

5. Je m'habille *selon le temps qu'il fait*. _____ Moi aussi

   _____ selon la mode   _____ selon mon humeur   _____ ?

6. Je me douche *le matin*. _____ Moi aussi

   _____ le soir   _____ le week-end   _____ ?

7. Quand je me couche, je m'endors *tout de suite*. _____ Moi aussi

   _____ difficilement   _____ avec une peluche   _____ ?

Maintenant, comparez vos réponses avec celles d'un(e) partenaire.

➡ *Quand est-ce que tu te réveilles? Est-ce que tu t'habilles selon la mode?*

B. Have students decide in groups or with a partner what they think a typical young man will or won't do, then share their answers with the class. Remind them to use the *futur proche.* Begin the second task by giving your own examples: «Mes parents vont se lever tôt ce week-end. Et vos parents?»

B. **Stéréotypes.**   Larmé est un jeune homme typique du Tchad. Imaginez un jeune homme typique de chez vous. Que va-t-il faire ce week-end à votre avis?

➡ se réveiller à midi?
> *Oui, il va se réveiller à midi.*

ou: *Non, il ne va pas se réveiller à midi. Il va se réveiller à deux heures!*

1. se lever tôt?
2. passer des heures à se coiffer?
3. se raser?
4. se dépêcher?
5. s'amuser?
6. s'endormir tard?

Maintenant, dites si les personnes suivantes vont faire ces mêmes activités ou pas.

Mes parents...
Mes copains et moi, nous...
Le professeur (Vous...)
Moi (Je...)

STRUCTURE: Talking about daily routines (II)
Les verbes pronominaux (III)

Observez et déduisez   J'habite au Texas, pas au Tchad, mais ma routine n'est pas très différente de celle de Larmé. Ce matin, je me suis levée assez tôt; je me suis brossé les dents; j'ai pris mon petit déjeuner; je me suis dépêchée d'aller au travail. Et vous? Vous vous êtes réveillés de bonne heure? Vous vous êtes lavé les cheveux?

> ■ Which auxiliary is used in the passé composé of pronominal verbs?
>
> ■ Is the author of the paragraph male or female? How do you know?
>
> ■ Compare the past participles of the verbs in the preceding paragraph. Can you think of any reason why the past participles of **se brosser les dents** and **se laver les cheveux** are different from the others?

Vérifiez   *Les verbes pronominaux*

■ All pronominal verbs require **être** as the auxiliary in the passé composé.

> Mon frère s'**est** levé à neuf heures aujourd'hui.

■ As with object pronouns, the reflexive pronoun always comes directly before the auxiliary in the passé composé.

> Moi non plus, je ne **me** suis pas dépêché ce matin. Je **me** suis promené dans le parc.
>
> Et vous? **Vous** êtes-vous reposés aussi?

Rules for participle agreement can be presented for recognition only.

■ The past participle usually agrees in number and gender with the reflexive pronoun (and the subject).

> Ma sœur? **Elle** ne s'**est** pas peign**ée** ce matin.

However, the past participle does *not* agree if the verb is *followed* by a direct object.

> Elle ne s'est pas bross**é** **les cheveux.** En plus, elle ne s'est pas bross**é** **les dents!**

It also does *not* agree if the reflexive pronoun serves as an *indirect* object, as is the case with verbs like **se parler** and **se téléphoner.** (On parle **à** quelqu'un. On téléphone **à** quelqu'un.)

> Mes copains et moi, nous nous sommes téléphon**é.**
> Vos copines et vous, vous vous êtes parl**é** aujourd'hui?

VOCABULAIRE ACTIF
se promener

ACTIVITÉS

C. For the first task (pp. 355–356), students write the number of each cue under the corresponding picture. CUES: 1. Il s'est disputé avec quelqu'un. 2. Il s'est dépêché. 3. Il s'est promené avec quelqu'un. 4. Il s'est réveillé. 5. Il s'est ennuyé. 6. Il s'est bien entendu avec sa copine. 7. Il s'est peigné. 8. Il s'est brossé les dents.

For the second task (p. 356), students can compare answers with a partner or in small groups.

C. Aujourd'hui. (1) Regardez les images suivantes et à la page 356. Qu'est-ce que ce petit garçon a fait aujourd'hui? Écoutez votre professeur, et numérotez les images selon les descriptions que vous entendez.

7   8

1   4   6

_____5_____   _____2_____   _____3_____

(2) Maintenant, dites si vous avez fait les mêmes choses aujourd'hui.

➡ *Je me suis peigné. Je ne me suis pas ennuyé.*

D. Les esprits curieux.   Travaillez en petits groupes, et imaginez ce que le professeur a fait hier en employant les verbes ci-dessous. Cochez votre choix.

➡ se réveiller   ✓ tôt / _____ tard

1. se lever   _____ tout de suite / _____ dix minutes plus tard

2. se laver   _____ hier matin / _____ hier soir

3. s'habiller avant de se brosser les dents   _____ oui / _____ non

4. _____ prendre / _____ ne pas prendre le petit déjeuner

5. lire le journal   _____ hier matin / _____ hier soir

6. _____ se dépêcher / _____ ne pas se dépêcher hier matin

7. se promener   _____ après / _____ avant le travail

8. _____ se reposer / _____ travailler après le dîner

9. se coucher   _____ tard / _____ tôt

Maintenant, lisez vos listes au professeur, qui va vous dire si vous avez raison.

➡ (groupe 1)   *Nous pensons que vous vous êtes réveillé(e) tôt.*
    (groupe 2)   *Nous ne sommes pas d'accord. Nous pensons que...*
    (professeur)   *Vous avez raison. Je me suis réveillé tôt.*
        ou: *Mais non! Je me suis réveillé à midi, hier!*

E. Trouvez quelqu'un...   Qu'est-ce que vos camarades de classe ont fait hier? Pour chaque question que vous posez, trouvez une personne différente qui répond «oui». Écrivez le nom de la personne.

➡ — *Tu t'es couché(e) avant neuf heures?*
    — *Non, je me suis couché(e) à une heure et demie du matin!*

Trouvez quelqu'un qui... **Camarade de classe**

1. s'est couché avant neuf heures. _____

2. s'est fâché contre un copain (une copine). _____

3. s'est reposé sous un arbre. _____

4. s'est réveillé avant six heures (du matin!). _____

5. a pris une douche après minuit. _____

6. s'est promené avec un(e) ami(e). _____

7. ne s'est pas brossé les dents. _____

8. s'est amusé en classe. _____

Quelles sont les activités les plus communes de la classe? les moins communes?

F. First give students time to make a list of their activities. Have them make their excuses to a partner, referring to the pictures in task 1 and in Activity C if needed. Then call on volunteers to give their excuses to the class (remind them to use sequencing expressions), who can decide which student had the best reasons for not helping out his/her roommate.

F. Des excuses. Vous avez promis d'aider votre camarade de chambre hier, mais vous ne l'avez pas fait. Maintenant, faites vos excuses et expliquez tout ce que vous avez fait hier—du matin au soir.

➡ *J'étais vraiment occupé(e) hier. D'abord, je me suis réveillé(e) à six heures et demie...*

 Jeu de rôle

It's near the end of the semester, and you and your roommate are suffering from burnout. You've decided to change your routine as soon as the semester ends. Role-play a scene in which you discuss what you're going to do differently.

W B

Deuxième étape

Lecture: Arithmétique de la mode

This input section introduces the topic of clothes and much new vocabulary.

Le texte suivant est extrait de *Biba,* un magazine semblable à *Elle* ou *Vogue,* mais destiné principalement aux jeunes. L'article en question s'intitule **Système b,** c'est-à-dire Système (ou Suggestions ingénieuses)–Biba pour la vie quotidienne. Ici, le «système vestiaire» donne des conseils de mode *(fashion).*

Avant de lire

1 ANSWER: b

1 Regardez d'abord le titre et les illustrations qui accompagnent le texte. À votre avis, de quoi s'agit-il dans cet article?

    a. Des vêtements et accessoires qu'on peut porter *(wear)* pour faire du jogging.

    b. Des vêtements et accessoires qui peuvent accompagner un jogging ou pantalon de survêtement *(sweatpants)* pour diverses activités.

    c. Trois options d'articles qu'on peut acheter pour le prix d'un jogging de luxe.

En général

2 Parcourez le texte une première fois pour confirmer votre hypothèse. Quelle est la bonne réponse à l'activité 1 ci-dessus?

3 Parcourez le texte une deuxième fois pour identifier l'ordre des renseignements donnés pour chaque vêtement ou accessoire. Numérotez de 1 à 5.

    <u>1</u> la description de l'article

    <u>4</u> le prix

    <u>3</u> la marque (Christian Dior, Ralph Lauren, etc.)

    <u>5</u> le nombre de coloris ou couleurs possibles

    <u>2</u> la matière ou le tissu (polyester, coton, etc.)

Système vestiaire

(arithmétique de la mode)

Le jogging en ville

AVEC LUI, DÉSORMAIS, ON COURT AUSSI LES RENDEZ-VOUS, LES BOUTIQUES ET LES VERNISSAGES. RECYCLEZ LE VÔTRE OU CHOISISSEZ-EN UN URBAIN.

PANTALON DE SURVÊTEMENT ANTHRACITE, EN COTON ET POLYESTER, CHEVIGNON GIRL, 295 F. EXISTE EN GRIS CLAIR CHINÉ ET MARINE.

Version night-bar

Lunettes de soleil à monture acétate, Scooter, 595 F. 3 coloris.
+ Tunique près du corps, col chinois, en soie rebrodée de fleurs, Paul & Joe, 875 F, existe en noir.
+ Mini-pochette zippée en velours bordeaux, Claudie Pierlot, 110 F, 3 coloris.
+ Sandales hautes à plateau en crêpe de Chine irisé, Nine West, 595 F, 3 coloris.

Version shopping

Capeline en flanelle, Printemps, 249 F, 3 coloris.
+ Chemise en satin de polyester, Unanyme de Georges Rech, 660 F, 6 coloris.
+ Veste ceinturée en maille acrylique chinée, Kookaï, 329 F, 3 coloris.
+ Bottines lacées en veau velours, semelle crêpe, Sequoïa, 495 F env., 10 coloris.

Version concert de rap

Lunettes bandeau profilées, verres polycarbonate, Diesel by Safilo, 540 F.
+ T. shirt col montant zippé à inscription argentée, en polyamide, Marithé et François Girbaud, 500 F, 3 coloris.
+ Cabas zippé 4 poches en nylon et cuir, existe aussi en marron, Y'Saccs Tokyo au Printemps, 595 F.
+ Bottines en cuir souple, semelle en microfibre, Ligne basket Nimasc de Nimal, 630 F, 4 coloris.

Version night-bar   **Version shopping**   **Version concert de rap**

Page réalisée par Christine Lerche assistée de Sylvie Poidevin.

---

désormais = maintenant   on court = *one runs*   vernissages = *art exhibit previews*   rebrodée = *embroidered*
Printemps = chaîne de grands magasins en France   veau = *calf*

VOCABULAIRE ACTIF

la mode
porter
la marque
Les vêtements
  une chemise
  un col
  un jean
  un jogging
  un pantalon
  une poche
  un polo
  un pull
  un T-shirt à manches
    courtes/longues
  une veste
Les accessoires (m.)
  une casquette
  une ceinture
  un chapeau
  des lunettes (f.) de
    soleil
Les chaussures (f.)
  des baskets (f.)
  des tennis (f.)
  des mocassins
  des sandales (f.)
  des bottines (f.)
Les matières et les
  tissus
  en coton (m.)
  en cuir (m.)
  en flanelle (f.)
  en laine (f.)
  en nylon (m.)
  en polyester (m.)
  en soie (f.)
  en velours (m.)
Les couleurs
  gris clair/foncé, bleu
    clair/bleu marine,
    bordeaux, marron
une fleur
haut(e)

Identifiez le nom des vêtements ou accessoires mentionnés. Écrivez le numéro correspondant à côté de l'illustration (ou *des* illustrations selon le cas).

1. des lunettes de soleil
2. des chaussures (sandales ou bottines)
3. une chemise
4. une tunique
5. une veste
6. un T-shirt
7. un chapeau (une capeline)
8. un cabas
9. une pochette

5 **La matière.**   Identifiez les articles qui sont faits des matières suivantes.

→ en coton et polyester   *Le pantalon de survêtement (le jogging)*

1. en soie *(silk)*
2. en velours *(velvet)*
3. en satin de polyester
4. en flanelle
5. en cuir souple *(soft leather)*
6. en nylon et cuir
7. en polyamide *(tissu synthétique)*
8. en maille *(knit)* acrylique

5 ANSWERS: 1. La tunique
2. La mini-pochette   3. La chemise
4. La capeline   5. Les bottines de la
version concert de rap   6. Le cabas
(sac) 7. Le T-shirt   8. La veste

6 En utilisant le contexte et la logique, déduisez le sens des mots suivants. Attention, il y a un choix de trop dans chaque section!

Le jogging

1. anthracite (gris foncé)
2. gris clair
3. marine

  a. *navy blue*
  b. *light blue*
  c. *dark gray*
  d. *light gray*

Version night-bar

1. un col
2. une fleur
3. bordeaux
4. haut(e)
5. à plateau

  a. *high*
  b. *low*
  c. *a collar*
  d. *platform*
  e. *burgundy*
  f. *a flower*

Version shopping

1. une ceinture
2. une semelle

  a. *a belt*
  b. *a sole*
  c. *a hood*

Version concert de rap

1. des verres (m.)   *a. lenses*
2. argenté   *b. brown*
3. des poches (f.)   *c. silver*
4. marron   *d. zipper*
       e. pockets

7   This activity, which reviews the vocabulary, can be done as a game; whoever comes up with the right answer in 5 seconds or less (orally or in writing) gets a point.

7   **Qu'est-ce que c'est?**   Pouvez-vous identifier les articles ci-dessous?

1. Cet article de Marithé et François Girbaud coûte 500F. (le T-shirt)
2. Cet article est la base des trois versions. (le pantalon de survêtement/le jogging)
3. Cet article a un col chinois et des fleurs. (la tunique)
4. Cet article existe en 6 coloris. (la chemise)
5. Cet article a des semelles à plateau. (les sandales)
6. Cet article se porte sur les yeux. (les lunettes de soleil)
7. Cet article a une ceinture. (la veste)
8. Cette version inclut un chapeau. (la version shopping)

8   **L'arithmétique de la mode...**   Faites le total des prix—en français, bien sûr. Combien coûte chaque version, pantalon inclus? Laquelle des trois versions est la meilleure affaire *(deal)?* Comparez les prix en France et chez vous.

Et vous?

Model new vocabulary before students start working in pairs. Have students infer the meaning of **en laine, à manches courtes/ longues.** Encourage students to mention fabrics, colors, and name brands as appropriate.   FOLLOW-UP: Have several groups report, then compare answers.

Avez-vous une garde-robe *(wardrobe)* versatile? Avec les articles mentionnés dans le texte et les articles supplémentaires suivants, créez votre version école, votre version cinéma et votre version shopping. Votre base: le pantalon universel des jeunes—le jean!

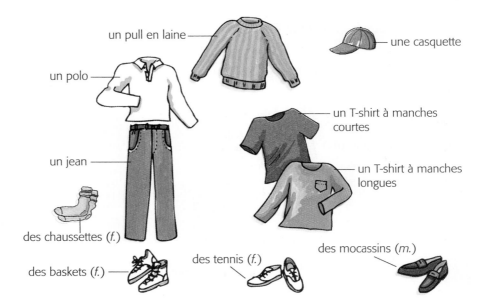

un pull en laine

une casquette

un polo

un T-shirt à manches courtes

un T-shirt à manches longues

un jean

des chaussettes (f.)

des mocassins (m.)

des baskets (f.)

des tennis (f.)

VOCABULAIRE
Les vêtements

Cue to Video Module 10 (00:47:46), where Élisabeth and Fatima go shopping for clothes.

Pour sortir

un smoking   un costume   une cravate   une robe   un tailleur

une robe du soir

un chemisier

une jupe

des chaussures (*f.*) habillées

Pour la pluie et le froid

un manteau   un blouson   un imperméable   un parapluie

des gants (*m.*)

une écharpe

un cardigan   des bottes (*f.*)   un anorak

Pour la nuit

une robe de chambre   un pyjama   une chemise de nuit

des pantoufles (*f.*)

Pour le beau temps

une chemise à fleurs

un short uni

un maillot de bain à rayures

un maillot de bain à pois

un short à carreaux

Portez-vous un jogging en ville? Qu'est-ce que vous portez pour faire du shopping? pour vous reposer à la maison? pour aller dans une discothèque?

ACTIVITÉS

A. CUES: 1. un pantalon 2. un chemisier 3. des sandales 4. une veste 5. une chemise 6. un maillot de bain 7. un short 8. un tailleur 9. un pull 10. une cravate 11. une robe 12. un costume

A. Masculin, féminin, unisexe? Classez les mots que vous entendez. Est-ce que ce sont des vêtements pour hommes? pour femmes? ou des vêtements unisexe?

➡ **pour hommes**   **pour femmes**   **unisexe**
    une cravate   *une jupe*   *des gants*

Maintenant, écoutez encore une fois et levez la main si vous portez le vêtement mentionné.

B. Students may come up with other reasonable responses.

B. Chassez l'intrus. Dans chaque groupe ci-dessous et à la page 364, trouvez le mot qui ne va pas, et expliquez pourquoi.

1. un costume, une robe, un tailleur, un chemisier
2. des tennis, des sandales, des bottes, des gants
3. un pull, un chemisier, un blouson, un jean

4. un short, des tennis, un jogging, ~~une jupe~~
5. un manteau, une veste, un pull, ~~un maillot de bain~~
6. un pantalon, une chemise, ~~un pyjama,~~ une cravate

C. Have students first devise descriptions with a partner, then share with the whole class.

C. Que porte-on?   À votre avis, qu'est-ce que les gens suivants portent pour aller aux endroits mentionnés? (Si vous ne savez pas, imaginez!)

➡ Céline Dion / pour chanter à la Maison-Blanche
Elle porte une longue robe du soir en soie bleu marine avec des chaussures habillées.

le (la) président(e) de votre institution / pour travailler
votre camarade de chambre / pour aller en ville
vos professeurs / pour sortir le week-end
vous / pour voyager en avion
Madonna / pour se reposer à la maison
Dennis Rodman / pour aller dans une discothèque

A game of **Concentration** in the *Instructor's Resource Manual* helps students practice clothing vocabulary.

D. Quelle chance!   Vous avez gagné 500 dollars à la loterie! Décrivez à un(e) partenaire les vêtements que vous voudriez acheter avec cet argent. Mentionnez l'occasion pour laquelle vous achetez les vêtements, la couleur, le tissu, etc. Il/Elle va essayer d'en faire un sketch!

➡ *D'abord, je vais m'acheter une robe imprimée en coton et des sandales noires pour sortir le week-end quand il fait chaud…*

STRUCTURES: Talking about what you wear and when
*Le verbe **mettre** • Les pronoms avec l'impératif*

Observez et déduisez

Cue to Video Module 10, street interviews (00:50:28), where people explain what they wear and when.

— Papa, qu'est-ce qu'on met pour aller faire du vélo cet après-midi?
— Selon la météo, il va faire beau. Mettez des shorts et des T-shirts… Mais prenons nos blousons aussi. Au moins mettez-les dans la voiture—en cas de vent.

> ■ **Mettre** is an irregular verb. Using the examples and what you already know about verbs, can you fill in the chart with the forms of **mettre**?
>
> | je mets | nous _____ |
> |---|---|
> | tu _____ | vous _____ |
> | il / elle / on _____ | ils / elles _____ |
>
> ■ What do you notice about the placement of the pronoun **les** in the preceding dialogue?

Draw students' attention to the different oral and written forms. Ask how many forms they see, then read the conjugation and ask how many forms they hear.

Vérifiez *Le verbe mettre*

■ **Mettre*** *(to put, to put on)* is conjugated in the passé composé with **avoir**.

   j'**ai mis**   ils **ont mis**

Les pronoms avec l'impératif

■ Object pronouns follow a verb in the imperative if the sentence is affirmative. Join the verb and pronoun with a hyphen.

   — Qu'est-ce que je fais de nos pulls?
   — Donne-**les** à maman.

If the sentence is negative, the pronoun maintains its regular position in front of the verb.

   — Ne **les** mets pas dans la valise.

■ The pronouns **me** and **te** become **moi** and **toi** when they follow the verb.

   Claire! Donne-**moi** ta valise… et dépêche-**toi**. Nous sommes en retard!

VOCABULAIRE ACTIF
mettre
une valise

ACTIVITÉS

E. Have all students discuss with a partner before calling on volunteers to share answers with the class.

E. Ce qu'on met. Est-ce que les phrases suivantes sont vraies ou fausses selon votre expérience personnelle? Discutez avec un(e) partenaire et corrigez les phrases qui sont fausses.

	Vrai	Faux
➡ Quand j'ai froid, je mets des vêtements en laine. *Je mets des vêtements en coton. Je n'aime pas la laine.*	____	✓
1. Quand j'ai chaud, je mets un jean et un T-shirt.	____	____
2. Je mets souvent des vêtements à rayures.	____	____

*****Permettre** *(to permit, allow)* and **promettre** *(to promise)* are conjugated like **mettre**.

	Vrai	Faux
3. Quand j'étais petit(e), mes ami(e)s et moi, nous mettions toujours un short pour jouer dehors.	_____	_____
4. Pour aller à la plage, nous mettions un maillot de bain et des bottes.	_____	_____
5. Mes copains ont mis des chaussures habillées hier pour aller en cours.	_____	_____
6. Ils ne mettent jamais de costume pour aller en cours.	_____	_____
7. Le professeur a mis des vêtements à carreaux la semaine dernière.	_____	_____
8. Il/Elle ne met jamais de sandales.	_____	_____

F. ALTERNATIVE: Have partners describe what each person(s) would pack for the same trip. For example, would everyone pack the same things to go to New York?

F. Dans ma valise...   Reliez les personnes de la colonne de droite avec une situation de la colonne de gauche, et dites ce qu'elles mettent dans leurs valises pour faire le voyage indiqué.

➡ Pour aller en Floride, je...
... je mets des shorts, des chaussettes, des T-shirts, des tennis, une robe, des sandales et un maillot de bain.

Pour passer le week-end chez un copain	moi, je...
Pour passer une semaine à la montagne	mes copains et moi, nous...
Pour voyager au Sénégal en été	le professeur...
Pour aller en Alaska en hiver	mes parents...
Pour aller à New York	mon (ma) camarade de chambre...

G. Des cadeaux. Votre copain vous demande conseil pour ses achats de Noël. Dites-lui quels vêtements il devrait acheter pour les personnes suivantes.

➡ ses camarades de chambre qui préfèrent les vêtements habillés
Donne-leur des cravates!

1. son oncle Bernard qui aime le jogging
2. ses petites sœurs qui aiment nager
3. ses cousins qui vont faire un voyage en Alaska

4. sa petite amie
5. vous!

Cue to Video Module 10 (00:48:44), where Élisabeth responds to Fatima's compliments.

Note culturelle

Les compliments.   Appropriate social responses do not always "translate" well from one culture to another. Whereas in North America you are expected to say "thank you" when someone compliments you on something you have done, what you are wearing, or how you look, in France you should not respond with **merci.** That would suggest that you agree with the compliment and are boasting. Instead, you should try to minimize the compliment by disclaiming responsibility or expressing doubt that you deserve it. You may also deflect it by commenting on the other person's kindness.

STRATÉGIE DE COMMUNICATION
Giving and responding to compliments

Study the mini-dialogues below and find some examples of
- how compliments are given
- how compliments are minimized

— J'aime beaucoup ta robe! Elle est très jolie.
— Tu trouves? Je l'ai depuis longtemps.

— Quelle belle cravate!
— C'est ma femme qui me l'a achetée. Elle a bon goût, n'est-ce pas?

— Il est vraiment chic, votre costume.
— Vraiment? Vous pensez que ça me va *(fits me)*?
— Ah oui. Et cette couleur vous va vraiment bien.
— Vous êtes bien gentil.

— Tu as vraiment fait du bon travail!
— Tu trouves? Ce n'était pas si difficile que ça.

Pour faire ou répondre à un compliment

Pour faire un compliment

C'est vraiment chic, votre... (costume, etc.)
Quelle belle cravate (Quel beau pantalon, etc.)
Cette couleur (Ce jogging) vous va bien.

Pour répondre à un compliment

Vous trouvez? / Tu trouves?
Vous pensez que ça me va? / Tu penses que ça me va?
Vous êtes bien gentil(le).
Vraiment? Je ne sais pas.
C'est ma femme (mon père) qui...
Je l'ai depuis longtemps.

ACTIVITÉS

H. Des compliments.   Avec un(e) partenaire, jouez les scénarios suivants et à la page 368. À tour de rôle, faites un compliment ou acceptez le compliment «à la française».

1. Vous aimez beaucoup la coiffure d'une copine.
2. Vous admirez le pantalon de votre professeur.
3. Vous aimez les nouvelles chaussures d'un(e) camarade de classe.
4. Votre petite sœur vous fait un compliment sur votre nouveau pull (et non, vous ne voulez pas le lui prêter).

5. Vous complimentez votre camarade de chambre sur le dîner qu'il (elle) a préparé.
6. Vous pensez que la veste de votre meilleur(e) ami(e) lui va très bien.

Jeu de rôle

Prepare a fashion show with your classmates. Each student takes a turn as the announcer, describing and complimenting the clothes of another student. In addition, each student plays the role of the fashion model on the runway as the announcer describes the clothes.

CULTURE ET RÉFLEXION

■ La haute couture. C'est au grand Louis XIV que nous devons la tradition française de haute couture. Roi de France de 1643 à 1715, le «Roi-Soleil»

La haute couture—pas tout à fait du prêt-à-porter!

installe sa cour[1] à Versailles, qui devient le centre de la vie politique, sociale et artistique de l'époque. C'est Louis XIV qui établit «l'étiquette», c'est-à-dire les conventions dictant comment les gens se comportent[2] et s'habillent. Que porte-t-on pour aller au théâtre? à la chasse? aux «salons» sociaux? La cour de Versailles devient le modèle de la mode pour toute l'Europe. Les styles ont beaucoup changé depuis l'époque de Louis XIV, mais le règne de la haute couture française

continue dans les boutiques de l'Avenue Montaigne à Paris, avec des noms comme Christian Dior, Coco Chanel, Yves Saint-Laurent, Givenchy, Hermès, etc. Évidemment, la haute couture a une clientèle assez limitée, mais son influence se fait sentir dans le prêt-à-porter[3], accessible à tous. Qu'est-ce qui influence le plus votre choix quand vous achetez des vêtements: le style? le prix? la marque?

Un costume bien breton de la région de Pont L'Abbé, dans le Finistère. Pas très pratique pour monter en voiture!

Quelles sont vos marques préférées? Pourquoi? Est-ce qu'une grande marque assure la qualité du vêtement? Pourquoi les gens suivent-ils la mode, à votre avis? Est-ce du snobisme ou autre chose? Expliquez.

■ Les costumes régionaux. La coiffe[4] bretonne, la jupe provençale, le boubou africain—ces costumes sont depuis des siècles une façon d'indiquer sa région d'origine. On porte, littéralement, son identité culturelle. Si ces traditions restent fortes dans certaines régions, beaucoup de costumes régionaux sont maintenant réservés aux jours de fêtes, ou disparaissent complètement. Les vêtements se standardisent, comme les modes de vie. À votre avis, est-ce une bonne chose de remplacer l'identité régionale par une identité globale? Y a-t-il un style de vêtements particulier à votre région? Décrivez-le.

Le boubou africain—ample et confortable.

---

1. *court*   2. *behave*   3. *ready-to-wear*   4. *headdress*

Troisième étape

À l'écoute: La forme

This input introduces vocabulary having to do with the body and exercise—with a touch of French humor!

Pour être en forme *(in shape)*, il faut faire de l'exercice physique, n'est-ce pas? Avant d'écouter la conversation, une préparation linguistique et psychologique s'impose...

Avant d'écouter

1 Voici, extraits du magazine français *Vital*, deux exercices très simples: des pompes et un exercice de raffermissement du haut du corps *(upper body firming)*. Lisez la description de ces exercices—et essayez-les à la maison si vous le désirez!

Exercice A

Exercice B

Effectuez des pompes à plat ventre (1), les mains (2) placées sous les épaules (3). Les genoux (4) sont pliés *(bent)*, les pieds (5) en l'air pour assurer une bonne position du dos (6). Tendez *(Straighten)* les bras (7), puis repliez-les alternativement.

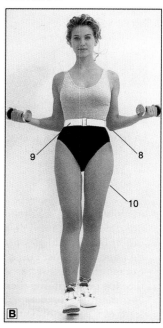

Debout, les coudes (8) contre la taille (9), une haltère dans chaque main. Levez (↑) et abaissez (↓) les haltères sans bouger les coudes. En même temps, montez et descendez sur les demi-pointes *(balls)* des pieds, sans plier les jambes (10).

2 Maintenant un autre genre d'exercice—un petit exercice de mémoire! Sans regarder le texte, est-ce que vous pouvez nommer toutes les parties du corps indiquées par des numéros sur les photos?

3 Quel genre d'exercice physique est-ce que vous faites? Du tennis? Du vélo? Du jogging? De l'aérobic? De la musculation *(weight lifting)?* Combien de fois par semaine faites-vous de l'exercice?

4 **Une devinette!** Pour bien comprendre la conversation que vous allez entendre, il faut comprendre le mot «paupières». Si l'on vous dit que les paupières sont les «portes» des yeux, pouvez-vous deviner ce que c'est? Montrez vos paupières!

Écoutons

Audio CD

5 Écoutez une première fois pour répondre aux questions suivantes.

1. Pourquoi le monsieur pose-t-il ces questions à la dame?
2. Est-ce que la dame a un programme régulier d'exercice physique?

6 Écoutez encore. Quel est son programme régulier d'exercice physique? Quand est-ce qu'elle le fait?

7 Écoutez une dernière fois pour compléter les phrases suivantes avec les parties du corps qui sont mentionnées. Ensuite, déduisez le sens des mots en caractères gras.

1. La dame n'aime pas l'aérobic parce que **ça fait mal** <u>aux jambes</u> , <u>au dos</u> , <u>aux bras</u> , etc.

2. La dame n'aime pas le jogging parce que c'est très mauvais pour <u>les genoux</u> .

3. Elle n'aime pas la marche parce qu'elle a les <u>pieds</u> **sensibles.** As students infer the meaning of **sensibles**, point out it is a false cognate.

4. Elle n'aime pas les abdominaux parce que ça fait mal <u>au ventre</u> , <u>au dos</u> , ça fait mal **partout!**

8 Est-ce que vous aimez le programme d'exercice physique de cette dame? Est-ce que vous êtes d'accord avec ce qu'elle dit sur l'aérobic? le jogging? la marche? la musculation?

VOCABULAIRE ACTIF

Le corps
les bras (m.)
les coudes (m.)
le dos
les épaules (f.)
les genoux (m.)
les jambes (f.)
les mains (f.)
les paupières (f.)
les pieds (m.)
la taille
le ventre

L'exercice physique
l'aérobic
baisser
lever
la musculation
les pompes (f.)

Divers
être en forme
faire mal (à)
partout

VOCABULAIRE

La tête

If you wish, present: le menton, les cils, les sourcils.

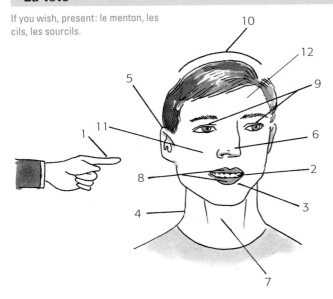

Selon les descriptions suivantes, écrivez les numéros qui correspondent à l'image.

<u>1</u> On peut montrer avec le **doigt.**

<u>5</u> On entend avec les **oreilles.**

<u>8</u> On fait la bise avec les **lèvres.**

<u>11</u> On a les **joues** rouges quand on est embarrassé.

<u>2</u> On va chez le dentiste pour soigner ses **dents.**

<u>6</u> On sent les odeurs et les parfums avec le **nez.**

<u>9</u> On voit avec les **yeux (un œil).**

<u>3</u> La nourriture entre par la **bouche** et passe par...

<u>7</u> ... la **gorge** en route vers l'estomac.

<u>10</u> La **tête** est la partie supérieure du corps.

<u>4</u> Le **cou** est entre la tête et le corps.

<u>12</u> Le **front** est entre les yeux et les cheveux.

ACTIVITÉS

A. Begin by pointing to each body part yourself as you give the cues so that students can follow you. After you have given all the cues, repeat the cues in a different order, but do not point. As students gradually begin to learn the vocabulary, ask for volunteers to lead the group.   CUES: ventre, main, épaule, genoux, pied, dos, bras, coude, taille, jambe, paupière, tête, œil, nez, bouche, dent, gorge, oreille, lèvre, joue, front

B. If your class likes competition, see which pair can come up with the longest lists within one minute.

C. Students may suggest several possibilities for some cues.

See the *Instructor's Resource Manual* for a game using vocabulary for body parts and the imperative.

A. Montrez *(Point to)...*   Écoutez le professeur. Montrez la partie du corps que vous entendez.

➡ Montrez la tête!   *(Point to your head.)*

B. Avez-vous une bonne mémoire?   Composez trois listes des parties du corps sans regarder votre manuel en travaillant avec un(e) partenaire.

On a une... ; on a deux... ; on a plusieurs...

C. Où est-ce que ça fait mal?   Dites où on a mal selon la situation indiquée.

➡ Quand on fait trop de musculation... *on a mal aux bras, au dos...*

1. Quand on mange trop...
2. Quand on fait trop de pompes...
3. Quand on met des chaussures qui sont trop petites...
4. Quand on fait du jogging pendant des heures...
5. Quand on regarde trop de télévision...
6. Quand on écoute la radio avec le son trop fort...
7. ?

Maintenant dites *dans quelles circonstances* on a mal aux autres parties du corps.

➡ *On a mal aux dents quand on mange trop de sucre.*

STRUCTURE: Talking about choices
Les verbes comme *choisir*

Observez et déduisez

— J'ai grossi pendant les vacances de Noël, et maintenant je ne réussis pas à maigrir.
— Et qu'est-ce que tu fais pour maigrir, Thomas? Tu n'es pas discipliné! Tu ne fais jamais d'exercice!
— Mais tu vois bien que je choisis des plats sains: des légumes, du poisson au lieu *(instead of)* de viande...
— Oui, mais regarde, Thomas, tu finis par un gros morceau de gâteau au chocolat!

■ Several new verbs are introduced in the preceding conversation. Using the context and your knowledge of cognates, can you match the verbs with their meaning?

1. grossir   a. to lose weight
2. réussir à   b. to finish
3. maigrir   c. to gain weight
4. finir   d. to choose
5. choisir   e. to succeed in

■ Can you infer the **je** and **tu** forms of **grossir** and **maigrir?**

■ Based on the example of **grossir** in the conversation, how would you form the passé composé of the other new verbs?

VOCABULAIRE ACTIF
choisir
discipliné
finir
grossir
maigrir
réussir

Vérifiez   *Les verbes comme **choisir***

■ Verbs conjugated like **choisir** are known as regular **-ir** verbs. (Verbs like **sortir,** page 238, are *not* regular **-ir** verbs.)

■ The stem of **choisir** in the present is **chois-**. To this stem, add the endings shown in the following chart. Add **i** to the singular stem to form the past participle.

Le verbe **choisir**	
je chois**is**	nous chois**issons**
tu chois**is**	vous chois**issez**
il / elle / on chois**it**	ils / elles chois**issent**
Passé composé j'ai chois**i**	
Imparfait je chois**issais**	

■ Some of these **-ir** verbs require a preposition when followed by an infinitive.

Thomas a fini **de** manger.
Il a choisi **d'**oublier son régime.
Bien sûr, il ne réussit* pas **à** maigrir.

ACTIVITÉS

D. L'étudiant typique.   D'abord, lisez les phrases ci-dessous et à la page 374 et indiquez si elles sont vraies ou fausses pour vous.

	moi		mon partenaire	
	vrai	faux	vrai	faux
1. Je maigris facilement.	_____	_____	_____	_____
2. D'habitude je grossis pendant les vacances de fin d'année.	_____	_____	_____	_____

*Réussir à un examen** means *to pass an exam.* (Remember that **passer un examen** means *to take an exam.*)

Draw students' attention to the different oral and written forms. Ask how many forms they see, then read the conjugation and ask how many forms they hear.

DISCRIMINATION DRILL: Have students indicate whether the verb they hear is singular or plural. CUES: 1. Ils finissent leur repas. 2. Il choisit du poisson. 3. Elles ne maigrissent pas. 4. Elles grossissent. 5. Ils ne réussissent pas à maigrir non plus. 6. Il finit le dîner par un dessert. 7. Elle réussit à faire de l'exercice tous les jours. 8. Elle choisit l'aérobic.

OPTIONAL DRILL: 1. Je choisis des plats sains. (nous, le professeur, les médecins, tu) 2. Tu as fini ton dessert. (maman, mes amis, vous, je) 3. Thomas réussissait toujours aux examens. (nous, je, vous, la fille)

D. Have students mark their own answers, then interview a partner and record his/her responses. Finally, get reports from each pair, then have the class summarize by describing the "typical" student based on those reports.

	moi		mon partenaire	
	vrai	faux	vrai	faux
3. Je choisis des plats sains au restaurant.	_____	_____	_____	_____
4. Je finis mon dîner avant de goûter *(taste)* le dessert.	_____	_____	_____	_____
5. Je finis mes devoirs avant de m'amuser.	_____	_____	_____	_____
6. Je choisis de faire de l'exercice tous les jours.	_____	_____	_____	_____
7. Je réussis toujours à me réveiller à l'heure.	_____	_____	_____	_____
8. Normalement, je réussis à me coucher avant minuit.	_____	_____	_____	_____

Maintenant, interviewez un(e) camarade de classe et notez ses réponses.

➡ *Tu maigris facilement?*

Partagez les résultats avec la classe. Comment est l'étudiant(e) «typique»? Est-il (elle) en bonne forme? discipliné(e)?

E. Un test psychologique.   Quel genre de personne êtes-vous? Complétez les phrases suivantes. Est-ce que vos réponses sont révélatrices? Êtes-vous discipliné(e)? optimiste? bavard(e)? calme?

1. Hier, j'ai (je n'ai pas) fini (de)...
2. Autrefois, mes copains et moi, nous réussissions toujours (ne réussissions jamais) à... mais maintenant...
3. Je choisis souvent (de)... alors que mes parents...
4. J'ai maigri (grossi) parce que... Quand je (maigris) grossis...

Jeu de rôle

Choose one of the pictures below and play the role of that person. Imagine and explain to the class (or a partner) what's going on in your life at the moment, what happened earlier, what's going to happen later. Use as many **-ir** verbs as possible to explain the situation. (You didn't finish . . . ; your parents chose to . . . ; your friend didn't succeed in . . . ; etc.)

Now that you have finished the Troisième étape of this chapter, do your Lab Manual activities with the audio program. Explore chapter topics further with the Mais oui! Video and CD-ROM. Viewing and comprehension activities are in the video section of your *Workbook/Lab Manual/Video Manual*.

Intégration

Littérature: Une abominable feuille d'érable sur la glace

Born near Montreal in 1937, Roch Carrier belongs to the generation of Quebecois writers who have sought to express the unique identity of the French-Canadian people, their intense attachment to their native land, and their rejection of the political and cultural domination by the English-speaking minority in the predominantly French-speaking province of Quebec. In the 1960s and '70s, a growing secessionist movement formed **le Parti québécois,** a political party that won a large majority in the provincial assembly in the 1976 elections. In 1980, Quebec's voters turned down a referendum to secede from Canada, but French separatism remained strong. It was right at that time—1979—that Roch Carrier published *Les enfants du Bonhomme dans la lune,* a collection of tales that received **le Grand Prix littéraire de la ville de Montréal** in 1980. In that collection, *Une abominable feuille d'érable sur la glace (An abominable maple leaf on the ice)* is about a boy, hockey, a sweater, and a very symbolic maple leaf.

Avant de lire

1 Que faut-il pour jouer au hockey?

un arbitre   une patinoire   un bâton

les patins

deux équipes

2 Vous avez déjà vu dans vos lectures des verbes au passé simple. Pouvez-vous reconnaître les verbes suivants? Trouvez l'équivalent au passé composé.

il/elle fit	a pris
commença	a eu
prit	est venu
écrivit	a fait
eut	a commencé
vint	a sauté
sauta (*jumped*)	a écrit

3 Voici quelques expressions-clés du texte:

... le chandail bleu, blanc, rouge des Canadiens de Montréal...

... un chandail bleu et blanc, avec la feuille d'érable au devant, le chandail des Maple Leafs de Toronto.

... une des plus grandes déceptions (*disappointments*) de ma vie!

À la troisième période, je n'avais pas encore joué (*I hadn't played yet*)... C'est de la persécution!

D'après ces expressions, quelle sorte d'histoire est-ce que vous anticipez?

En général

4 Parcourez le texte une première fois, simplement pour identifier l'idée générale. Ce texte est l'histoire d'un garçon qui

4   ANSWER: c

a. est fatigué de porter toujours le même uniforme de hockey et demande à sa mère de lui acheter un chandail complètement différent.

b. est invité à jouer pour l'équipe des Maple Leafs de Toronto.

c. fait partie d'une équipe de jeunes fanatiques des Canadiens de Montréal mais est obligé de porter le chandail des Maple Leafs de Toronto.

Une abominable feuille d'érable sur la glace

Les hivers de mon enfance étaient des saisons longues, longues. Nous vivions en trois lieux: l'école, l'église et la patinoire; mais la vraie vie était sur la patinoire.

Tous, nous portions le même costume que Maurice Richard, notre héros, ce costume rouge, blanc, bleu des Canadiens de Montréal, la meilleure équipe de hockey au monde; tous, nous peignions nos cheveux à la manière de Maurice Richard. Nous lacions° nos patins à la manière de Maurice Richard. Nous découpions° dans les journaux toutes ses photographies. Sur la glace, nous étions cinq Maurice Richard contre cinq autres Maurice Richard; nous étions dix joueurs qui portions, avec le même enthousiasme, l'uniforme des Canadiens de Montréal. Tous nous avions au dos le très célèbre numéro 9.

laced
cut out

Un jour, mon chandail des Canadiens de Montréal était devenu trop petit; puis il était déchiré° ici et là. Ma mère me dit: «Avec ce vieux chandail, tu vas nous faire passer pour pauvres!» Elle fit ce qu'elle faisait chaque fois que nous

torn

avions besoin de vêtements. Elle commença de feuilleter° le catalogue que la compagnie Eaton° nous envoyait par la poste chaque année. Ma mère était fière°. Elle n'a jamais voulu nous habiller au magasin général; seule la dernière mode du catalogue Eaton était acceptable. Pour commander mon chandail de hockey, elle prit son papier à lettres et elle écrivit: «Cher Monsieur Eaton, auriez-vous l'amabilité de m'envoyer un chandail de hockey des Canadiens pour mon garçon qui a dix ans et qui est un peu trop grand pour son âge, et que le docteur Robitaille trouve un peu trop mince? Je vous envoie trois piastres° et retournez-moi le reste s'il en reste.»

    Monsieur Eaton répondit rapidement à la lettre de ma mère. Deux semaines plus tard, nous recevions le chandail. Ce jour-là, j'eus l'une des plus grandes déceptions de ma vie! Au lieu du° chandail bleu, blanc, rouge des Canadiens de Montréal, M. Eaton nous avait envoyé un chandail bleu et blanc, avec la feuille d'érable au devant, le chandail des Maple Leafs de Toronto. J'avais toujours porté le chandail bleu, blanc, rouge des Canadiens de Montréal; tous mes amis portaient le chandail bleu, blanc, rouge; jamais dans mon village on n'avait vu un chandail des Maple Leafs de Toronto. De plus, l'équipe de Toronto se faisait battre régulièrement par les triomphants Canadiens. Les larmes° aux yeux, je trouvai assez de force pour dire:

    — J'porterai° jamais cet uniforme-là.

    — Mon garçon, tu vas d'abord l'essayer! Si tu te fais une idée sur les choses avant de les essayer, mon garçon, tu n'iras° pas loin dans la vie...

    Elle tira° le chandail sur moi. Je pleurais.

    — J'pourrai jamais porter ça.

    — Pourquoi? Ce chandail te va très bien... Comme un gant...

    — Maurice Richard se mettrait jamais ça sur le dos...

    — T'es° pas Maurice Richard. Puis, c'est pas ce qu'on se met sur le dos qui compte, c'est ce qu'on se met dans la tête... Si tu gardes pas ce chandail, il va falloir écrire à M. Eaton pour lui expliquer que tu veux pas porter le chandail de Toronto. M. Eaton, c'est un Anglais; il va être insulté parce que lui, il aime les Maple Leafs de Toronto. S'il est insulté, penses-tu qu'il va nous répondre très vite? Le printemps va arriver et tu auras pas joué° une seule partie° parce que tu auras pas voulu porter le beau chandail bleu que tu as sur le dos.

    Je fus donc obligé de porter le chandail des Maple Leafs. Quand j'arrivai à la patinoire, tous les Maurice Richard en bleu, blanc, rouge s'approchèrent° un à un pour regarder ça. Au coup de sifflet° de l'arbitre, je partis prendre mon poste habituel. Le chandail des Maple Leafs pesait° sur mes épaules comme une montagne. Le chef d'équipe vint me dire d'attendre. Il aurait besoin de moi à la défense, plus tard. À la troisième période, je n'avais pas encore joué; un des joueurs de défense reçut un coup de bâton° sur le nez, il saignait°; je sautai sur la glace: mon heure était venue! L'arbitre m'arrêta. Il prétendait° que j'avais sauté sur la glace quand il y avait encore cinq joueurs. C'était trop injuste!

    C'est de la persécution! C'est à cause de mon chandail bleu! Je frappai mon bâton sur la glace si fort qu'il se brisa°. Le vicaire°, en patins, vint tout de suite vers moi.

    — Mon enfant, un bon jeune homme ne se fâche pas comme ça. Enlève tes patins et va à l'église demander pardon à Dieu.

    Avec mon chandail des Maple Leafs de Toronto, j'allai à l'église, je priai Dieu; je lui demandai qu'il envoie au plus vite des mites° qui viendraient dévorer mon chandail des Maple Leafs de Toronto.

Extrait de Une abominable feuille d'érable sur la glace *(Roch Carrier)*

Marginal glosses:

regarder
grand magasin canadien
proud

vieille monnaie québécoise

instead of

tears / (Je) / futur de **porter**
futur d'**aller**
a mis

tu n'es

won't have played / un match

sont venus
whistle
weighed

was hit / *was bleeding*
claimed

broke / *priest*

moths

5 **Le texte.** Lisez plus attentivement et indiquez si les phrases suivantes sont vraies ou fausses. Si elles sont fausses, corrigez-les.

1. Maurice Richard était un des garçons qui jouaient dans l'équipe du narrateur.
2. Les joueurs des deux équipes portaient tous le même uniforme, et tous les joueurs avaient le même numéro sur le dos.
3. La mère du narrateur pensait que le magasin général de la ville n'était pas assez bien pour acheter les vêtements de la famille.
4. La mère du narrateur faisait confiance *(trusted)* au catalogue de la compagnie Eaton.
5. Dans sa lettre à M. Eaton, la mère du narrateur a oublié de spécifier le nom de l'équipe (les Canadiens).
6. Elle a mis de l'argent dans la lettre à M. Eaton.
7. L'équipe des Maple Leafs de Toronto était la meilleure équipe du Canada.
8. Quand le narrateur a vu le chandail des Maple Leafs, il a pleuré.
9. La maman a expliqué que pour réussir dans la vie, il faut essayer les choses avant de les juger.
10. Elle a aussi expliqué que ce qu'on pense est plus important que les vêtements qu'on porte.
11. La maman pense que si elle demande à M. Eaton d'échanger *(exchange)* le chandail, M. Eaton va le faire très vite.
12. Quand le narrateur est arrivé à la patinoire avec son nouveau chandail, les autres joueurs sont tous venus lui faire des compliments.
13. Le chef d'équipe n'a pas voulu donner au narrateur son poste habituel.
14. Le narrateur a utilisé son bâton pour frapper *(hit)* l'arbitre.
15. Le vicaire a demandé au narrateur d'aller prier *(pray)* à l'église.
16. La prière du narrateur montrait une vraie repentance!

6 **Les mots.** En utilisant le contexte et la logique, pouvez-vous déduire le sens des mots suivants?

1. **envoyer** («... le catalogue que la compagnie Eaton nous **envoyait** par la poste... »)
2. **recevoir** («Deux semaines plus tard, nous **recevions** le chandail.»)
3. **enlever** («**Enlève** tes patins et va à l'église... »)
4. **dévorer** («... des mites qui viendraient **dévorer** mon chandail... »)

1. En groupes de deux, préparez un résumé de l'histoire du chandail. L'un(e) de vous va être responsable des circonstances/conditions (comment étaient les choses?); l'autre va donner les actions (qu'est-ce qui s'est passé?). Sur une feuille de papier, faites deux colonnes comme dans le tableau suivant, puis remplissez chaque colonne avec les détails importants. Ensuite, soyez prêt(e)s à lire votre résumé à la classe.

Étudiant(e) A Comment étaient les choses?	Étudiant(e) B Qu'est-ce qui s'est passé?
Quand le narrateur avait 10 ans... Etc.	 Un jour, sa mère a décidé de lui acheter un nouveau chandail... Etc.

Start this activity with the whole class to model types of answers (le chandail bleu, blanc, rouge: symbole du Canada français, l'identité québécoise, etc.; chandail bleu et blanc: uniforme des Maple Leafs de Toronto, symbole du Canada anglais). Show that several interpretations are possible (l'erreur de M. Eaton: les anglophones veulent dominer les francophones?/les anglophones et les francophones ne se comprennent pas? Maurice Richard: symbole du Parti québécois? etc.). Encourage students to find other symbols (la réaction de la mère; la réaction des autres joueurs et de l'arbitre). Remind students to use words and structures that they already know; keep the discussion simple.

2. On peut lire cette histoire à un niveau littéral, mais on peut aussi y voir des symboles. Complétez le tableau suivant selon votre interprétation. Relisez l'introduction sur Roch Carrier au besoin.

	Littéralement	Figurativement
le chandail bleu, blanc, rouge	uniforme des Canadiens de Montréal	
le chandail bleu et blanc avec la feuille d'érable		
Monsieur Eaton		les «Anglais»
L'erreur de M. Eaton	une simple erreur?	les anglophones...
Maurice Richard		

Par écrit: Close encounters

Avant d'écrire

A. Strategy: Viewing different facets of an object.   To use this strategy, you are going to answer a series of questions that will lead you to examine a topic from a variety of viewpoints before you begin writing. When you do begin to write, you do *not* need to describe your topic from all perspectives. You can focus on only one or blend two or more together. Choose the ones that best spark your imagination.

Application.   Imagine you wish to describe an article of clothing that has some special significance for you. The garment may be new or old, elegant or ugly, yours or someone else's. It may evoke memories of pleasant or unpleasant circumstances, or it may remind you of someone else. What-ever the case, think about the article of clothing as you try to answer the following questions.

How would you describe the garment to someone who is not in the room?
Does it remind you of someone, something, or some event?
What can you do with the article besides wear it?
How would you divide the garment into its constituent parts?
What other garment is similar? different? Explain.
Do you like the article of clothing? Why or why not?

B. Strategy: Making descriptions vivid. Descriptions become memorable when details appeal to the senses and sharp images are produced. Study the following example from *Une abominable feuille d'érable sur la glace:*

> ... un chandail bleu et blanc, avec la feuille d'érable au devant, le chandail des Maple Leafs de Toronto.

Application. Now try completing the following sentence in a way that depicts an old sweater in an evocative and vivid manner.

> J'ai un vieux chandail...

ÉCRIVEZ

Choisissez un des sujets suivants.

1. Le narrateur dans le conte de Carrier raconte un souvenir de sa jeunesse associé à un chandail. Vous souvenez-vous d'un vêtement particulier de votre passé? Votre premier costume, par exemple, ou votre première robe du soir? Ou, vous souvenez-vous du jour où votre tante vous a acheté ce grand manteau à carreaux (orange!)? Écrivez un paragraphe où vous décrivez le vêtement. Pourquoi est-ce que vous vous souvenez de ce vêtement? Pourquoi est-il mémorable?

2. Quelle chance! En vous promenant hier soir, vous avez rencontré un extraterrestre avec qui vous avez parlé! Maintenant vos copains pensent que vous avez perdu la boule *(your marbles)*. Alors il faut décrire le bonhomme en détail. Comment était-il (description physique, portrait moral)? À quoi ressemblait-il? Vous a-t-il fait une bonne impression? Pourquoi? / pourquoi pas?

VOCABULAIRE ACTIF

Les vêtements (m.)

un anorak *ski jacket, parka*
un blouson *a short jacket*
un cardigan *a button-up sweater*
des chaussettes (f.) *socks*
une chemise *a man's shirt*
une chemise de nuit *a nightgown*
un chemisier *a blouse*
un col *a collar*
un costume *a man's suit*
une cravate *a tie*
un imperméable *a raincoat*

un jean *jeans*
un jogging *a jogging suit*
une jupe *a skirt*
un maillot de bain *a swimsuit*
un manteau *a coat*
une marque *a brand*
la mode *fashion*
un pantalon *(a pair of) pants*
une poche *a pocket*
un polo *a polo shirt*

un pull *a sweater (generic term)*
un pyjama *pajamas*
une robe *a dress*
une robe de chambre *a bathrobe*
une robe du soir *an evening gown*
un short *shorts*
un smoking *a tuxedo*
un tailleur *a woman's suit*
un T-shirt *a T-shirt*
une veste *a jacket (generic)*

Les chaussures (f.)

des baskets (f.) *basketball shoes*
des bottes (f.) *boots*
des bottines (f.) *ankle-boots*
des chaussures habillées *dress shoes*

des mocassins (m.) *moccasins*
des pantoufles (f.) *slippers*
des sandales (f.) *sandals*
des tennis (f.) *tennis shoes*

Les accessoires (m.)

une ceinture *a belt*
un chapeau *a hat*
une écharpe *a winter scarf*

des gants (m.) *gloves*
des lunettes (f.) de soleil *sunglasses*

Les matières (f.) et les tissus (m.)

en coton (m.) *cotton*
en cuir (m.) *leather*
en flanelle (f.) *flannel*
en laine (f.) *wool*
en nylon (m.) *nylon*
en polyester (m.) *polyester*
en soie (f.) *silk*

en velours (m.) *velvet*
à carreaux *plaid*
à fleurs *flowered*
à pois *polka dot*
à rayures *striped*
uni *solid (color)*
(gris) clair *light (gray)*

(gris) foncé *dark (gray)*
bleu marine *navy blue*
bordeaux *burgundy*
marron *brown*
à manches courtes / longues
 short-sleeved / long-sleeved
haut(e) *high*

La tête

la bouche *mouth*
le cou *neck*
les dents (f.) *teeth*
le front *forehead*

la gorge *throat*
la joue *cheek*
les lèvres (f.) *lips*
le nez *nose*

un œil / des yeux (m.) *eye / eyes*
les oreilles (f.) *ears*
les paupières (f.) *eyelids*

Le corps

le bras *arm*
le coude *elbow*
le doigt *finger*
le dos *back*

l'épaule (f.) *shoulder*
le genou *knee*
la jambe *leg*
la main *hand*

le pied *foot*
la taille *waist*
le ventre *stomach*

La forme

l'aérobic (m.)
discipliné(e) *disciplined*
être en bonne forme *to be in good shape*

l'exercice physique (m.) *exercise*
la musculation *weight training*
des pompes (f.) *pushups*

Verbes

aller bien / mal *to fit well / poorly*
baisser *to lower*
se brosser les dents / les cheveux
 to brush one's teeth / hair
choisir (de) *to choose (to)*
se coiffer *to do one's hair*
se coucher *to go to bed*
se dépêcher *to hurry*
se doucher *to shower*
s'endormir *to fall asleep*

se fâcher *to get mad*
faire mal (à) *to hurt*
finir (de) *to finish*
grossir *to gain weight*
s'habiller *to get dressed*
se laver *to wash (oneself)*
lever *to raise*
se lever *to get up*
maigrir *to lose weight*
se maquiller *to put on makeup*

mettre *to put (on)*
se peigner *to comb one's hair*
porter *to wear*
prendre une douche *to take a
 shower*
se promener *to go for a walk*
se raser *to shave*
se reposer *to rest*
réussir (à) *to succeed (in)*
se réveiller *to wake up*

Adverbes

(travailler) dur *(to work) hard*
partout *everywhere*

Divers

le bois *wood*
le feu *fire*
une valise *a suitcase*

la lune *the moon*
la routine quotidienne *the daily routine*

Qu'est-ce que ces étudiants feront dans l'avenir?

Quelle profession choisiront-ils?

Seront-ils heureux?

Se marieront-ils?

Auront-ils des enfants?

Et vous?

Qu'est-ce que vous ferez dans vingt ans?

Où serez-vous?

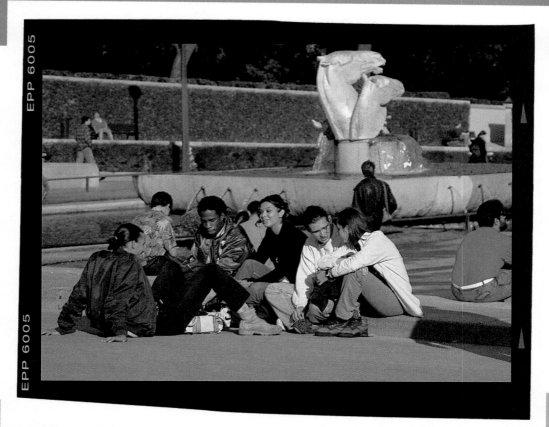

This chapter will enable you to

• model a conversation between a job applicant and a prospective employer; understand an excerpt from a radio interview between two political figures in France

• read an article on people's perceptions of work and a literary text from Senegal about the condition of women in an African society

• talk about the future

• discuss jobs, careers, and other issues related to the professional world

• interrupt in a conversation

Première étape

À l'écoute: Le monde du travail

This input section introduces vocabulary about professions and the future tense.

Comment se passe une conversation téléphonique entre quelqu'un qui cherche du travail et un employeur en France? Cette étape vous propose un exemple d'une telle conversation.

Avant d'écouter

1 If your class likes competition, have groups compete to see who can finish the fastest. Discuss answers and clues that led to the answers. Explain that **D.É.** means **Diplômé d'État;** have students infer that **Référ.** means **références;** point out that **gagner** means *to earn* or *to win.*

Imaginez que vous cherchez du travail dans la région parisienne. En consultant le journal, vous voyez les petites annonces page 384.

1 Avec un(e) camarade de classe, trouvez dans les annonces les mots donnés dans la colonne de gauche. En utilisant le contexte et la logique, pouvez-vous relier ces mots à leur définition (à droite)?

1. un comptable
2. un(e) débutant(e)
3. un gagneur
4. un vendeur / une vendeuse
5. le salaire
6. de haut niveau
7. exigé
8. juridique
9. un infirmier / une infirmière
10. le bloc opératoire

a. quelqu'un qui vend quelque chose dans un magasin
b. quelqu'un qui travaille avec les nombres, les budgets, etc.
c. quelqu'un qui assiste un médecin dans un hôpital
d. quelqu'un qui aime la compétition et être le premier
e. quelqu'un qui commence (dans le monde du travail ou autre chose)
f. un synonyme de «nécessaire» ou «obligatoire»
g. un adjectif qui se rapporte à la justice
h. la partie d'un hôpital où on fait les opérations
i. l'argent qu'on gagne par mois ou de l'heure quand on travaille
j. compliqué, sophistiqué

2 Maintenant avec votre partenaire, discutez chaque petite annonce; dites pourquoi ces postes vous intéressent ou non, soit comme emplois temporaires ou comme carrières. Comparez-les avec des emplois que vous avez déjà eus et la profession que vous voulez exercer.

CARRIÈRES ET EMPLOIS

CENTRE HOSPITALIER recherche **INFIRMIÈRS[ES]** D.É. BLOC OPÉRATOIRE salaire intéressant Tél: (1) 49.11.60.53	IMPORTANT GROUPE DE PRESSE recrute **SUPERVISEURS** POUR GRANDE CAMPAGNE DE TÉLÉMARKETING Vous avez 20 à 30 ans. Vous avez le sens de l'animation et l'expérience du télémarketing. Appelez dès maintenant de 9 heures à 18 heures. Tél: 43.87.03.00
HÔTEL *** cherche **ASSISTANT[E]** **DE DIRECTION** Bilingue anglais Formation hôtelière Référ. exigées Tél: (1) 42.56.88.44	
AGENCE DE PUBLICITÉ FINANCIÈRE recherche **COMPTABLE** connaissance informatique Tél: 40.26.55.50	SOCIÉTÉ COMMUNICATION recherche **CONSEILLERS** **COMMERCIAUX** • débutant(es) accepté(es) • tempérament de gagneur • capables négociations de haut niveau • formation assurée • promotion rapide possible Tél: 48.98.55.00
SECRÉTAIRE **BILINGUE ANGLAIS** Expérience service juridique. Très bon salaire. Poste stable. Tél: 43.71.89.89	
VENDEUSE vêtements femmes. Qualifiée, bonne présentation, anglais si possible. Âge min, 25 ans Référ. récentes. Tél: 40.06.57.52	ÉCOLE INTERNATIONALE recrute **RESPONSABLE** **DÉPARTEMENT** **BILINGUE ANGLAIS** Expérience pédagogique obligatoire universitaire ou secondaire. 39 h minimum par semaine. Logement. Tél: 43.07.86.06

Écoutons

3   ANSWER:
1. L'annonce du Centre hospitalier

Audio CD

3 Écoutez une première fois pour identifier

1. la petite annonce qui a occasionné cette conversation.
2. l'expérience professionnelle de la jeune fille. Quelles sont les phrases qui décrivent sa situation?

_____ Elle n'a pas encore fini ses études.

✓_____ Elle a déjà son diplôme.

✓_____ Elle a travaillé pendant trois mois.

_____ Elle a trois ans d'expérience professionnelle.

4 Écoutez encore pour déduire d'après le contexte le sens des mots dans la colonne de gauche. Reliez-les à leur définition dans la colonne de droite. (Attention, il y a deux définitions supplémentaires.)

1. un stage	a. 39–40 heures par semaine
2. un poste	b. une position
3. à plein temps	c. une période de vacances
4. à mi-temps	d. un résumé de ses qualifications
5. un curriculum vitae	e. une conversation officielle
6. prendre rendez-vous	f. une période de travail pratique dans un programme d'études
7. un entretien	g. à temps partiel
8. remplir une demande d'emploi	h. perdre son travail
9. être embauché(e)	i. être choisi(e) comme employé(e)
	j. décider d'une heure spécifique pour voir quelqu'un
	k. compléter un formulaire *(form)* pour essayer d'avoir un travail

VOCABULAIRE ACTIF

un(e) comptable
un curriculum vitae
un(e) débutant(e)
embaucher /
    être embauché(e)
un emploi
un(e) employé(e)
un employeur
un entretien
(faire) une demande
    d'emploi
un infirmier /
    une infirmière
un poste à mi-temps /
    à plein temps
prendre rendez-vous
remplir un formulaire
le salaire
un stage
un vendeur /
    une vendeuse
venir de

5 Écoutez encore en faisant particulièrement attention aux verbes.

1. D'après le contexte, quel est le sens de **je viens de...** (...sortir, etc.)?
   a. I've come to   b. I have just

2. Plusieurs verbes dans cette conversation sont au futur. Cochez dans la liste suivante les formes que vous entendez.

   _____ vous chercherez

   ✓_____ vous prendrez

   ✓_____ vous viendrez

   _____ vous remplirez

   _____ il fera

   ✓_____ il faudra

   _____ je commencerai

   ✓_____ je pourrai

Maintenant pouvez-vous identifier l'infinitif ou la forme correspondante du présent pour chacun des verbes de la liste ci-dessus? Quel est le futur de l'expression **il faut?** Quel est le futur du verbe **faire? pouvoir? venir?**

6 ANSWERS: 1. Elle veut savoir (a) si elle est diplômée; (b) quel genre d'expérience elle a; (c) si elle cherche un poste à plein temps ou à mi-temps. 2. Envoyer un CV; prendre rendez-vous pour un entretien; remplir une demande d'emploi. 3. Si elle est embauchée, quand elle va pouvoir (pourra) commencer; le premier du mois.

6 Écoutez la conversation une dernière fois pour répondre aux questions suivantes.

1. Quelles sont les trois choses que l'employeur veut savoir?
2. Quelles sont les trois choses que l'employeur dit à la jeune fille de faire?
3. La jeune fille ne pose qu'une seule question. Quelle est cette question, et quelle est la réponse?

Cue to Video Module 11 (00:53:23) for an example of a job interview.

7 Avec un(e) partenaire, choisissez une petite annonce qui vous intéresse et jouez le rôle d'un(e) postulant(e) (une personne qui fait une demande d'emploi) et de l'employeur. Dans une conversation téléphonique semblable à celle que vous venez d'entendre, posez les questions appropriées—et improvisez les réponses!

VOCABULAIRE
Pour parler du travail

Mes amis ont des rêves grandioses. Par exemple, Gilles ne veut pas être ouvrier chez Renault; il veut être chef d'entreprise ou homme d'affaires. Nadia ne veut pas être journaliste; elle veut avoir un poste de direction au *Nouvel Observateur*. Karim ne veut pas être un simple cuisinier; il veut être le patron de son propre restaurant. Didier veut être non seulement banquier, mais cadre à la Banque de France. José veut exercer une profession libérale comme médecin ou avocat, ou peut-être enseignant dans une école supérieure. Moi, je veux être fonctionnaire; j'aime la sécurité de travailler pour le gouvernement.

■ En choisissant parmi le nouveau vocabulaire de cette étape, complétez les phrases suivantes d'une façon personnelle en parlant de vos «rêves grandioses».

Je ne veux pas être...
Je voudrais...

Cue to Video Module 11, street interviews (00:55:25), for examples or descriptions of other types of jobs; also to Module 4, street interviews (00:20:21), to hear students talk about their professional future.

ACTIVITÉS

A. Have students work in small groups. Encourage creativity. Students may use words from the list as titles for the categories. If groups need help, suggest a category called **«divers»**.

A. Quelles catégories? Classez le vocabulaire suivant selon quatre catégories que vous développez avec des camarades de classe.

curriculum vitae   poste   cadre   ouvrier
   entreprise   salaire   emploi
exercer   poste de direction   banquier
   fonctionnaire   formation   carrière
gagner   patron   enseignant
   profession libérale   expérience   embaucher
chef d'entreprise   journaliste   stage
   remplir   employé(e)   homme/femme d'affaires
promotion   employeur   vendeur
   rendez-vous   débutant   comptable
entretien   infirmier   demande d'emploi

B. Préférences. Cochez les professions que les personnes suivantes voudraient exercer, à votre avis. Interviewez un(e) partenaire pour compléter la colonne de droite.

	moi	mon copain/ ma copine	mon frère/ ma sœur	mon/ma camarade de chambre	mon/ma partenaire
comptable					
journaliste					
infirmier/-ère					
vendeur/ vendeuse					
banquier/-ère					
enseignant(e)					
homme/ femme d'affaires					
?					

Maintenant, expliquez vos réponses. Par exemple, est-ce une profession où on gagne beaucoup d'argent? où il y a beaucoup de temps libre? où il y a très peu de stress? etc.

➡ *Ma copine voudrait être comptable parce qu'elle aime les mathématiques et la sécurité d'un bon travail.*

STRUCTURE: Talking about the future (I)
L'infinitif

Observez et déduisez

Qu'est-ce que l'avenir réserve à ces jeunes gens? Sandrine espère être cadre. Didier a l'intention d'être banquier. Christelle compte devenir* journaliste. Julien veut devenir comptable. Isa a envie d'être infirmière.

Sandrine   Didier   Christelle   Julien   Isa

■ Study the examples above. Can you find five different verbs or expressions to talk about the future?

*Devenir is conjugated like venir.

Vérifiez   *L'infinitif*

■ There are many ways to speak about the future in French without using the future tense. You have already learned the immediate future *(futur proche)* in Chapter 3 (page 106).

Je **vais parler** à mon patron.

VOCABULAIRE ACTIF
l'avenir
avoir envie de
avoir l'intention de
compter
devenir
espérer

■ The following expressions, followed by an infinitive, can also be used to speak about the future.

espérer* *(to hope to)*
vouloir
compter *(to plan to)*   } +   infinitive
avoir l'intention de *(to intend to)*
avoir envie de *(to want to)*

ACTIVITÉS

C. Be sure students vary the expressions used.

C. L'avenir et le travail.   Voici les résultats d'un sondage effectué auprès de jeunes Français de 15 à 24 ans. Récapitulez leurs réponses en utilisant les expressions données dans **Vérifiez**.

➡ *Vingt pour cent des jeunes Français* **comptent travailler** *dans la fonction publique.*

	L'avenir		
Vous préférez travailler dans		**Dans dix ans, professionnellement, pensez-vous être**	
une grande entreprise	31%	ouvrier	3%
une PME[1]	12%	employé	15%
la fonction publique	20%	cadre moyen	18%
une profession libérale	34%	cadre supérieur	18%
ne sait pas	3%	pratiquant une profession libérale	23%
		enseignant (professeur)	8%
		chef d'entreprise	9%

1. petite ou moyenne entreprise

Le Français dans le monde, N° 246

Et vous? Quelles sont vos réponses personnelles à ce sondage? Faites un sondage de votre classe.

➡ *J'espère travailler dans la fonction publique. Je n'ai pas envie de travailler dans une grande entreprise.*

***Espérer** has a stem-changing conjugation like **préférer:** j'espère, tu espères, on espère, nous espérons, vous espérez, ils espèrent.

D. L'avenir. Comment voyez-vous l'avenir? Complétez les phrases suivantes en ajoutant un infinitif.

Dans 10 ans...

1. je / vouloir...
2. mon (ma) camarade de chambre / compter...
3. mes parents / espérer...
4. mes amis / avoir l'intention de...
5. les étudiants d'aujourd'hui / aller...

STRUCTURE: Talking about the future (II)
Le futur simple

Observez et déduisez

> J'espère que le patron m'embauchera.

> J'espère que les postulants seront qualifiés.

> J'espère que j'aurai du succès dans ma carrière.

> J'espère que nous trouverons des postes dans un hôpital.

- Match the hopes expressed above with the person most likely to have voiced each:

  une débutante / un postulant / des infirmiers / un patron

  Write the name under the appropriate bubble.
- Can you infer the infinitive of the verb **aurai? seront?**
- The verbs in the preceding examples are in the *futur simple.* Based on the examples given and previous knowledge, can you infer the rest of the *futur simple* conjugation?

je _____	nous _____
tu chercheras	vous _____
il / elle / on _____	ils / elles chercheront

Vérifiez   *Le futur simple*

- The simple future in French, as in English, is used to say what *will take place* or what one *will do.*

  Les nouveaux diplômés **chercheront** un poste.

■ The future tense is formed by adding the following endings to the infinitive: **-ai, -as, -a, -ons, -ez, -ont.**

Le futur simple	
je travaillerai	nous travaillerons
tu travailleras	vous travaillerez
il / elle / on travaillera	ils / elles travailleront

■ For infinitives ending in **-e,** drop the **-e** before adding the future ending.

Le postulant **prendra** rendez-vous avec la patronne.

■ Certain irregular verbs have irregular stems to which the future endings are added.

être	**ser-**	vouloir	**voudr-**
avoir	**aur-**	devoir	**devr-**
faire	**fer-**	falloir	**faudr-**
aller	**ir-**	venir	**viendr-**
pouvoir	**pourr-**	savoir	**saur-**

Pour parler de l'avenir

- Le futur proche (**aller** + infinitif)

  Je **vais chercher** un poste.

- Autres expressions verbales + infinitif

  J'**ai envie de travailler** comme infirmier.

  Je **compte travailler...**

- Le futur simple

  J'**aurai** une profession intéressante.

ACTIVITÉS

E. Cherchons un travail! Normalement, on ne trouve pas de poste au hasard *(by chance);* il y a une certaine progression. Mettez les activités suivantes dans l'ordre logique.

_____ faire une demande d'emploi   _____ parler au patron

_____ pouvoir gagner sa vie   _____ demander un entretien

_____ choisir une profession   _____ lire les petites annonces

_____ travailler dur   _____ prendre rendez-vous

_____ être embauché(e)   __1__ finir ses études

Maintenant, dites à un(e) partenaire ce que vous ferez pour chercher un travail. Comparez votre progression à celle de votre partenaire.

➡ *Bon, d'abord je finirai mes études...*

F. Allow students time to prepare answers and practice with a partner or small group before sharing comments with the class. Encourage students to be creative (even fanciful) for #5.

F. Clairvoyant(e). En employant le futur simple, dites ce que les personnes suivantes feront dans les circonstances indiquées... selon votre «boule de cristal»!

➡ vous / dans cinq ans (avoir, trouver, ?)
Dans cinq ans j'aurai un appartement à New York. Je trouverai un bon poste. Je serai reporter pour le New York Times...

1. vous / dans cinq ans (vouloir, aller, ?)
2. vos copains (copines) / après leurs études (savoir, ne plus devoir, ?)
3. votre famille / ce week-end (faire, devoir, ?)
4. le professeur / pendant les vacances (être, ne pas venir, ?)
5. ? / ?

G. Give students sufficient time to come up with answers or assign as homework. Ask volunteers to share responses.

G. Un monde idéal. Qu'est-ce que vous espérez pour l'avenir? Complétez les phrases suivantes, puis partagez vos réponses avec la classe.

J'espère que ma famille...
      mes copains (copines)...
      les gens...
      le gouvernement...
      ?

 Jeu de rôle

Imagine that you are a famous figure from the past or a modern-day celebrity. Now, with that identity in mind, imagine you're still in high school, and you're writing a paper called *«Mon avenir»* for your French class. Share your aspirations of future accomplishments with your classmates! Will you be Picasso? Queen Victoria? Napoleon? Mother Teresa? Someone else?

Give students an example, and ask them to guess the person (such as the following description of Ernest Hemingway: «Je serai écrivain. J'écrirai des contes et des romans. Je gagnerai le prix Nobel. J'irai souvent à la pêche. J'irai aussi en Espagne. J'aurai de belles petites-filles qui seront actrices.»).

W
B

Deuxième étape

Lecture: L'image du travail

This input introduces cultural information and vocabulary on the professional world.

Le travail et la réussite professionnelle (le succès) ont un sens différent pour différentes personnes. Le texte que vous allez lire dans cette étape analyse l'image du travail chez les Français d'aujourd'hui.

Avant de lire

🖥 Cue to Video Module 11, street interviews (00:56:16), to hear what some people think is necessary for success.

1 Quelle est votre image du travail? Cochez les réponses qui expriment votre opinion et ajoutez d'autres réponses au besoin.

Pour moi, le travail (une carrière), c'est...

_____ un mal nécessaire

_____ un moyen de gagner sa vie (*earn a living*)

_____ un moyen de faire fortune (devenir riche)

_____ un moyen de s'épanouir (développer ses talents et sa personnalité)

_____ un moyen d'acquérir un statut social

_____ un moyen de monter dans la société

_____ un moyen d'établir des contacts sociaux (collègues, amis)

_____ un moyen d'avoir la sécurité, sans la peur du chômage (*unemployment*)

_____ un moyen d'être utile (*useful*) à la société

_____ un moyen d'éviter l'ennui (*avoid boredom*)

_____ ?

2 L'illustration qui accompagne le texte est un peu insolite (bizarre), n'est-ce pas? Quelle est la conception du travail de ce jeune homme, à votre avis? Est-il ambitieux? conformiste? Qu'est-ce que ses vêtements révèlent? et ses patins à roulettes (*roller skates*)? Imaginez sa profession, sa personnalité et ses projets d'avenir.

En général

3 ANSWER: sécuritaire, financière, affective, libertaire

3 Parcourez le texte une première fois pour identifier les idées générales.

Quatre conceptions nouvelles du travail

Quels sont les quatre adjectifs qui définissent ces conceptions?

La régression du carriérisme

1. Cochez les idées qui sont mentionnées dans cette partie du texte.

   ✓_____ La mentalité des jeunes cadres dans les années 80.

   ✓_____ Les attentes (*expectations*) des jeunes cadres dans les années 90.

_____ Les professions préférées des jeunes des années 80.

✓_____ Les professions préférées des jeunes des années 90.

_____ Les prédictions d'un sociologue pour le vingt et unième siècle.

✓_____ Une analyse de la situation actuelle par un sociologue.

2. Answers may vary!

2. Quelle génération de jeunes cadres le jeune homme de l'illustration représente-t-il? Pourquoi?

L'image du travail

Quatre conceptions nouvelles du travail

Quelle est l'attitude des Français vis-à-vis du travail? Une vieille chanson populaire dit que «le travail c'est la santé, rien faire c'est la conserver!... » Peu de Français sont assez naïfs pour imaginer qu'on puisse se soustraire° à l'obligation de travailler, mais avec la crise économique et la peur croissante du chômage, quatre conceptions nouvelles du travail sont apparues°.

Une conception «sécuritaire» s'est développée dans les catégories les plus vulnérables de la population. Elle est particulièrement forte chez tous ceux qui se sentent menacés dans leur vie professionnelle pour des raisons diverses: manque de formation, charges de famille, une entreprise ou une profession vulnérable.

On rencontre aussi chez les personnes les plus attachées à la consommation une conception «financière». Leur vision du travail est simple et concrète. Il s'agit avant tout de bien gagner sa vie, afin de pouvoir dépenser sans trop compter.

La conception «affective» est répandue° chez ceux qui accordent une importance prioritaire aux relations humaines dans le travail et qui cherchent à s'épanouir. Elle concerne beaucoup de jeunes et d'adultes des classes moyennes pour qui la nature de l'activité professionnelle revêt° une importance particulière, ainsi que son environnement (les collègues, la hiérarchie, le cadre° de travail...).

Enfin, la conception «libertaire» représente une façon d'envisager° le travail comme une aventure professionnelle. Ses adeptes sont attirés surtout par la liberté, propice° à la création et à la réalisation de soi-même. Ils sont ouverts à toutes les formes nouvelles de travail (temps partiel, interim°) ainsi qu'à l'utilisation des technologies dans l'entreprise. Ils sont par principe très mobiles et considèrent tout changement de travail, d'entreprise ou de région comme une opportunité.

La régression du carriérisme

Les années 80 étaient l'ère du *golden boy*, le jeune cadre dynamique pour qui réussite professionnelle et argent étaient synonymes. L'ambition des «jeunes loups°» était de faire fortune. Aujourd'hui, le désir de s'épanouir en occupant un emploi intéressant leur paraît de plus en plus légitime. Pour beaucoup, le travail idéal, c'est celui que

éviter

arrivées

commune

prend

environnement
considérer

favorable

travail temporaire

wolves

l'on accomplit sans avoir l'impression de travailler. De plus, le désir de gagner le plus d'argent possible en travaillant, ou d'accélérer son ascension dans l'entreprise, semble s'essouffler° depuis quelques années. Ainsi, les métiers qui, dans l'absolu, ont aujourd'hui les faveurs des jeunes (chercheur, médecin, journaliste, professeur...) ne sont pas systématiquement ceux qui permettent de gagner le plus d'argent ou d'acquérir du pouvoir. Les attentes qualitatives tendent à s'accroître°: être utile; exercer des responsabilités; participer à un projet collectif; apprendre et se développer sur le plan personnel; avoir des contacts enrichissants; créer. Le sociologue Gilles Lipovetsky, auteur de *L'Ère du vide* (éd. Gallimard) confirme: «Désormais°, penser l'ambition uniquement en termes de progression sociale est dépassé°. Les gens veulent toujours gagner de l'argent mais se demandent pour quoi faire? L'argent doit être utile à réaliser de nouveaux luxes: ceux d'aider les autres, de prendre son temps, de réaliser ses désirs.»

diminuer

augmenter

from now on
outdated

Gérard Mermet, *Francoscopie 1997,* pp. 261–263

En détail

4 Les mots. En utilisant le contexte et la logique, déduisez le sens des mots suivants.

Quatre conceptions nouvelles du travail, ¶2

1. **menacé** («... ceux qui se sentent menacés dans leur vie professionnelle»)
   a. en situation de risque b. en situation de sécurité
2. **(le) manque de formation**
   a. l'absence d'organisation b. l'absence de préparation académique
3. **les charges** (de famille)
   a. les accusations b. les obligations financières
4. **une entreprise** («une entreprise ou une profession vulnérable»)
   a. une compagnie b. un projet

La régression du carriérisme

5. **un métier** («les métiers qui ont aujourd'hui les faveurs des jeunes»)
   a. un domaine d'études b. une profession
6. **le pouvoir** («qui permettent d'acquérir du pouvoir»)
   a. l'autorité, la capacité de dominer b. l'aptitude, la capacité d'essayer
7. **réaliser** («L'argent doit être utile à réaliser de nouveaux luxes»)
   a. comprendre b. obtenir

5 Le texte. Lisez plus attentivement pour voir si les phrases suivantes sont vraies ou fausses. Si elles sont fausses, corrigez-les.

Quatre conceptions nouvelles du travail

1. Selon une vieille chanson populaire, «le travail, c'est la santé» et donc la meilleure façon de conserver sa santé, c'est de travailler constamment.
2. Les quatre conceptions nouvelles du travail sont dues à la crise économique.
3. La première conception est celle des gens qui ont particulièrement peur du chômage.

5 ANSWERS: 1. F («Rien faire» c'est conserver la santé!) 2. V 3. V 4. V 5. F (... les jeunes et adultes des classes moyennes.) 6. F (... des gens qui aiment le changement, qui sont ouverts aux formes nouvelles de travail, etc.) 7. V 8. F (... un travail que l'on accomplit sans avoir l'impression de travailler.) 9. F («ne sont pas systématiquement ceux qui permettent de gagner le plus d'argent ou d'acquérir du pouvoir») 10. V 11. F (Ce concept est dépassé.) 12. V

4. La deuxième conception est une vision tout à fait matérialiste.
5. La troisième conception concerne principalement les riches qui ont moins de préoccupations financières.
6. La quatrième conception est celle des gens qui aiment la routine.

La régression du carriérisme

7. Les «jeunes loups» des années 80 préféraient un emploi qui paye bien à un emploi intéressant.
8. Le travail idéal d'aujourd'hui est défini comme un travail où l'on peut être son propre (own) patron.
9. Les métiers préférés des jeunes d'aujourd'hui sont des métiers qui permettent une ascension sociale rapide.
10. Le désir de s'épanouir est une attente qualitative.
11. Selon le sociologue cité, l'ambition est toujours une question de progression sociale.
12. Prendre son temps et épanouir sa personnalité sont des luxes dans la société d'aujourd'hui.

6 **Récapitulation.**   En utilisant vos propres mots, définissez

1. les quatre conceptions du travail présentées dans le texte.
2. le *golden boy* des années 80.
3. l'ambition des jeunes cadres d'aujourd'hui.

Et vous?

Discutez les sujets suivants en groupes de deux ou trois, puis comparez vos réponses avec celles des autres groupes.

1. Est-ce que votre conception du travail correspond à l'une des quatre catégories présentées dans le texte? Laquelle? Pourquoi?
2. Est-ce que ce texte reflète les valeurs de la société américaine pour les années 80? pour les années 90? Est-ce que le *golden boy* existe toujours? Où?
3. Quelle est votre définition du luxe? Quels luxes voulez-vous réaliser dans votre vie?
4. Le texte parle à plusieurs reprises d'épanouissement. Comment peut-on «s'épanouir» dans sa vie professionnelle, personnelle et familiale? Donnez des idées pour chaque domaine.
5. À votre avis, les conceptions du travail et de la réussite professionnelle seront-elles différentes dans 20 ans? Imaginez les définitions de l'avenir.

VOCABULAIRE ACTIF

l'ambition (f.)
les attentes (f.)
une carrière
le chômage
une crise
l'ennui (m.)
une entreprise
éviter
la formation
gagner (sa vie, de l'argent)
un manque (de)
un métier
le pouvoir
réaliser (ses rêves, ses désirs)
la retraite
la réussite
la société
le succès
utile

Note culturelle

Le chômage.   1996 figures indicate that unemployment in France reached an all-time high of 12.4% (9.8 in Belgium, 9.5 in Canada, 5.4 in the U.S., 3.3 in Switzerland). Unemployment is highest among the youth and among women: 22.1% of men 24 years of age or under, and 31.9% of women in the same age group are unemployed. These figures drop to 9.6% for men and 13.6% for women in the 25–49 age category. To fight unemployment, the French government has instituted or is considering a number of measures: **les stages d'insertion** (through which private companies receive subsidies to hire young people right out of school for a few months), **la semaine de 35 heures** (passed in 1998), **la retraite à 55 ans** (retirement), etc.

STRUCTURE: Talking about the future (III)
Le futur simple après certaines locutions

Observez et déduisez   Quelle est votre définition de la réussite?

Si je deviens riche, j'achèterai une voiture de luxe.

Moi, dès que j'aurai assez d'argent, je voyagerai.

Et moi, quand je pourrai, j'aiderai les autres.

> ■ Study the sentences in the preceding dialogue. What tense is used after the conjunctions **quand** and **dès que** *(as soon as)?* What tense is used after **si?**

Vérifiez   *Le futur simple après certaines locutions*

VOCABULAIRE ACTIF

dès que

■ In French, the future tense—*not* the present—is required after the expressions **quand** and **dès que** if one is speaking about the future.

> **Dès qu**'il **aura** la sécurité d'un travail sûr, il n'**aura** plus peur du chômage.

■ The future tense is also used to indicate what will happen if certain conditions are met. Use **si** and a verb in the *present* tense to express the *conditions.* Use the *future* tense to explain the *consequences.*

> **Si** tu **es** au bon endroit au bon moment, tu **feras** fortune!

ACTIVITÉS

A. Choisissez!   Qu'est-ce qu'une carrière représente pour vous? Complétez les phrases suivantes, en soulignant la phrase qui exprime ce qui compte le plus pour vous.

1. Dès que j'aurai un bon poste...
   a. je serai utile à la société.
   b. je me développerai sur le plan professionnel.
2. Quand je finirai mes études...
   a. je ferai fortune.
   b. je gagnerai ma vie.

3. Quand je commencerai ma carrière...
   a. je monterai vite dans l'entreprise.
   b. j'aurai des collègues sympathiques.
4. Dès que j'aurai mon diplôme...
   a. je chercherai un travail intéressant.
   b. je n'aurai plus peur du chômage.
5. Quand j'aurai un travail...
   a. je chercherai à acquérir du pouvoir.
   b. j'exercerai des responsabilités importantes.

Maintenant, comparez vos réponses en groupes de trois ou quatre. Quels concepts sont les plus importants pour votre groupe? Faire fortune ou gagner sa vie? etc. Faites un résumé de vos réponses pour la classe.

B. Students should mix and match items from the two columns. Before beginning, remind them of the tense sequence: **si** + present + future. ALTERNATIVE: Have students work in pairs to come up with several consequences for each condition.

B. Des conseils. Lisez les conditions et les conséquences suivantes et formulez des conseils logiques pour quelqu'un qui cherche un travail.

➡ avoir ton diplôme / pouvoir trouver un bon poste
Si tu as ton diplôme, tu pourras trouver un bon poste.

conditions	conséquences
être au bon endroit au bon moment	réussir ta vie
	être heureux (heureuse)
avoir de l'ambition	avoir un bon emploi
étudier	choisir une carrière qui te plaît
penser aux autres	devoir travailler dur
vouloir être heureux	apprendre (à)
se réveiller tôt	avoir besoin d'argent
être responsable	faire fortune
avoir un diplôme universitaire	t'amuser
?	donner un sens à ta vie
	?

See the *Instructor's Resource Manual* for an information gap activity, **La boule de cristal**, in which students practice using the *futur simple*.

C. Mon avenir. Complétez les phrases pour parler de vos projets d'avenir.

1. Dès que j'aurai mon diplôme...
2. Quand je trouverai un bon emploi...
3. Dès que je ferai fortune...
4. Quand je me marierai...
5. Quand j'aurai 40 ans (65 ans)...
6. Quand je serai prêt(e) à acheter une maison...

STRUCTURE: Adding emphasis
Les pronoms toniques

Observez et déduisez

— Qu'est-ce que la réussite pour toi, Nadine?
— Pour moi, la réussite c'est exercer des responsabilités, participer à des projets collectifs...
— Et pour toi, Patrick?
— Eh bien, moi, je pense que la réussite c'est avoir un travail intéressant et avoir du temps libre aussi.

- What two pronouns do you find after the preposition **pour** in the preceding conversation? Can you infer the subject pronouns to which they correspond?

- Fill in the following stress pronouns next to the corresponding subject pronouns in the chart below:

  elles, nous, vous, lui, eux, elle, soi

subject pronoun	stress pronoun	subject pronoun	stress pronoun
je	*moi*	nous	
tu	*toi*	vous	
il		ils	
elle		elles	
on			

- In the last sentence of the dialogue, you see «Moi, je... ». You have seen this use of **Moi, je...** many times throughout this text. Can you infer its function from the context?

Vérifiez   *Les pronoms toniques*

- Stress, or tonic, pronouns are used after prepositions:

    Réussir?
    C'est avoir de bons collègues; c'est participer à des projets avec **eux**.
    C'est retrouver ma copine; c'est aller chez **elle**.
    Et pour **toi?** Qu'est-ce que «réussir»?

- for emphasis:

    Moi, je veux un travail sûr. **Lui,** il veut se sentir libre.

- after **c'est/ce sont:**

    C'est **nous** qui cherchons une «aventure» professionnelle.
    Ce sont **eux** qui veulent faire fortune.

  (Use **ce sont** only with the third-person plural, **eux/elles.**)

- and alone as a question or as an answer to a question:

    — Qui veut réussir?
    — **Moi!**
    — **Vous** aussi?

ACTIVITÉS

D. Qu'est-ce qu'une vie réussie? Écoutez les activités mentionnées et indiquez si elles jouent un rôle important dans le concept d'une vie réussie pour vous, pour votre meilleur(e) ami(e), ou pour vous deux.

➡ (se marier?)   pour moi   pour elle/lui   pour nous deux

              _____   ✓   _____

Maintenant réfléchissez à vos réponses. Est-ce que vous ressemblez beaucoup à votre ami(e)?

E. La réussite. Regardez les photos ci-dessous, puis lisez les phrases suivantes. Décidez qui a dit chacune de ces phrases: l'homme? le couple? la femme? Est-ce que les phrases pourraient s'appliquer à différentes personnes?

➡ «La réussite, c'est arriver à ses objectifs.»
C'est lui qui l'a dit.

«La réussite, c'est s'accepter.»

«La réussite, c'est avoir confiance en soi.»

«La réussite, c'est être libre.»

«La réussite, c'est avoir le confort matériel.»

«La réussite, c'est avoir la tranquillité.»

«La réussite, c'est avoir du temps libre.»

«La réussite, c'est avoir de l'argent.»

«La réussite, c'est pouvoir voyager.»

F. Moi, je... et toi?   (1) Parmi les descriptions suivantes, cochez dans la 1ère colonne celles qui s'appliquent à vous.

	s'applique à moi	s'applique à...
1. être ambitieux (-euse)	____	_____
2. être attiré(e) par la créativité	____	_____
3. se sentir menacé(e) par le chômage	____	_____
4. être attaché(e) à la consommation	____	_____
5. accorder une importance prioritaire aux relations humaines	____	_____
6. chercher l'aventure professionnelle	____	_____
7. ?	____	_____

(2) Interviewez quatre camarades de classe pour voir si vous vous ressemblez. Écrivez les noms des camarades qui vous ressemblent.

➡ s'ennuyer quelquefois
— *Moi, je m'ennuie quelquefois. Et toi?*
— *Moi aussi, je...*   ou: — *Moi, je ne m'ennuie jamais!*

 **Jeu de rôle**

Role-play a scene with three classmates in which each of you is a proponent of a different «conception du travail». Defend your «conception», and ask your classmates questions to force them to defend their opinions.

CULTURE ET RÉFLEXION

■ **Le monde des affaires.**
Comme le dit Polly Platt dans son livre *French or Foe?,* les affaires en France sont «un tango» et il faut connaître les pas[1] pour pouvoir danser.

Un petit brin de conversation avant la transaction.

Tout d'abord, il faut savoir que si vous voulez le pain le plus frais chez le boulanger du coin ou des échantillons gratuits[2] à la parfumerie, il faut établir un rapport personnel avec les commerçants. Un brin[3] de conversation («Votre maman est sortie de l'hôpital? À cet âge-là, évidemment, on devient fragile... ») avant la transaction assure un meilleur service. Il est vrai que cela prend du temps, mais c'est un investissement qui rapporte[4], que ce soit[5] à la banque, chez l'avocat, chez le médecin ou dans un magasin, le client le mieux servi ne sera pas nécessairement celui qui dépense le plus d'argent, mais celui qui prend le temps d'établir un rapport personnel avec son interlocuteur. Pensez au monde des affaires dans votre pays: les transactions sont-elles personnalisées? Si oui, comment? Si non, pourquoi pas, à votre avis?

Préférez-vous une culture où «le temps, c'est de l'argent», ou une culture où les relations humaines sont plus valorisées? Peut-on avoir les deux?

■ **La femme au Sénégal.**
L'article 154 du Code de la Famille stipule: «La femme peut exercer une profession, à moins que[6] son mari ne s'y oppose.» L'article 134 de ce même code stipule que «la femme peut demander à son mari, à l'occasion du mariage ou postérieurement, d'opter pour le régime de la monogamie ou de la limitation de la polygamie». Si le mari s'y oppose, le mariage est automatiquement placé sous le régime de la polygamie, qui autorise l'homme à avoir jusqu'à quatre femmes. Ces lois semblent rétrogrades aux Occidentaux. Cependant, l'écrivain sénégalais Cheik Aliou Ndao fait remarquer que «il serait dangereux de juger l'Afrique comme s'il s'agissait d'un pays européen, sous le prétexte d'une universalité qui, en fait, n'est que la généralisation de la réflexion européenne». Ndao explique que la société africaine traditionnelle est basée sur l'harmonie entre l'homme et la femme et que la femme devient l'inférieure de l'homme seulement s'il devient un «rival» —un concept occidental.

La femme africaine dans un monde en transition.

Quels sont les dangers de juger une société non-occidentale selon les valeurs occidentales? Donnez des exemples de tels jugements et leurs conséquences.

---

1. *steps*   2. *free samples*   3. peu   4. *pays off*   5. *be it*   6. *unless*

Troisième étape

À l'écoute: Hommes et femmes—l'égalité?

This input introduces thought-provoking cultural information, a few adverbs, and conversation strategies.

Vous allez entendre deux députés (ou représentants) à l'Assemblée nationale, dans le Parlement français, discuter la question de l'égalité *(equality)* des hommes et des femmes en France.

Avant d'écouter

1 À votre avis, l'égalité des sexes est-elle un mythe ou une réalité de nos jours? Est-ce que l'égalité des droits *(rights)* garantit l'égalité des chances? Pensez à la société nord-américaine. En groupes de deux ou trois, décidez si les femmes sont les égales des hommes dans les domaines suivants. Donnez des explications ou des exemples pour justifier vos réponses, puis, si vous le désirez, ajoutez d'autres catégories où la question d'égalité se pose.

1. dans les écoles et les universités
2. dans le monde professionnel
   a. embauche
   b. promotions
   c. postes de direction
   d. salaires
3. dans le monde politique
4. ?

The audio segment on the student CD is adapted from an actual interview; the names have been changed.

2 Selon vous, qu'est-ce qui est plus difficile pour les femmes: entrer ou monter (avoir des promotions) dans les domaines traditionnellement masculins? Expliquez.

L'Assemblée nationale—quelques femmes?

3 Écoutez d'abord pour identifier le point de vue de Françoise Brasseur et de Philippe Aubry sur l'égalité entre les hommes et les femmes. Est-ce un mythe ou une réalité pour elle? pour lui?

4 Écoutez encore en faisant attention aux chiffres. Complétez.

1. Les femmes constituent _____46_____ pour cent de la population active (qui travaille).

2. À profession égale, les femmes gagnent en moyenne (*average*) _____25_____ pour cent de moins que les hommes.

3. Il y a _____6_____ pour cent de représentation féminine au Parlement.

4. Les femmes ont le droit de voter depuis _____50_____ ans.

5. Dans _____50_____ ans, la situation sera très différente.

Notes culturelles

Le gouvernement français. The French government is divided into two branches. In the executive branch, **le président de la République,** elected for seven years, is assisted by **le Premier ministre** and **le Conseil des ministres.** In the legislative branch, **le Parlement** consists of **l'Assemblée nationale,** with approximately 500 **députés** who are elected for five years, and **le Sénat,** with approximately 300 **sénateurs** elected for nine years.

Le droit de vote. Women in France and Belgium gained the right to vote in 1944; in Switzerland, it was not until 1971 that women were able to vote in national elections.

5 Écoutez encore ce que dit Françoise Brasseur pour trouver le contexte des mots suivants et déduire leur sens. Donnez un synonyme, un antonyme ou une définition.

➡ en théorie
   Contexte: «*On peut en parler, oui, en théorie!*»
   Sens: *Le contraire de la pratique.*   ou: *C'est ce qu'on dit mais pas ce qu'on fait.*

1. réservé (à)   2. évidemment   3. franchement

6 Écoutez une dernière fois et reconstituez les arguments des deux députés.

1. Deux «preuves» que l'égalité est plus qu'une théorie.
2. Trois «preuves» que l'égalité est seulement une théorie.
3. Une raison pour laquelle l'égalité est difficile à réaliser.

VOCABULAIRE ACTIF
l'égalité (f.)
évidemment
franchement
une promotion
la réalité
réservé(e) à
seulement
traditionnellement

7 Before the activity, discuss or estimate together current corresponding statistics for the U.S. FOLLOW-UP: Have a couple of groups perform their interview in front of the whole class. Ask other groups to report on additional points they discussed.

7 Discutez les sujets suivants.

1. Imaginez une discussion semblable entre des démocrates et des républicains aux États-Unis. Est-ce que les arguments seront les mêmes? En groupes de trois, adaptez l'interview au contexte américain. Discutez d'abord les différences et les ressemblances que vous voyez, puis jouez l'interview.

2. Philippe Aubry pense que dans cinquante ans, la situation sera très différente. Êtes-vous aussi optimiste? À votre avis, qu'est-ce qui sera différent? Qu'est-ce qui ne changera pas dans la condition des femmes—et des hommes? Faites une liste de vos prédictions.

STRUCTURE: Qualifying an action

Les adverbes

Observez et déduisez

Evidemment, les femmes peuvent entrer dans toutes les professions aujour-d'hui. Malheureusement elles montent difficilement aux postes de direction, et elles gagnent rarement autant que les hommes à profession égale.

If this task is completed in class, ask leading questions to help students infer rules: "What seems to be happening with the first set of adjectives? How is the second set different from the first? What do the last two adjectives have in common?"

- Adverbs frequently describe how something is done. Study the preceding examples, and infer two rules for the placement of adverbs in a sentence.
- Study the following examples and complete the chart showing how adverbs are formed.

certain	→	certaine	→	certain**ement**
traditionnel	→	traditionnel**le**	→	traditionnel**lement**
actif	→	_____	→	_____
poli		→		poli**ment**
absolu		→		_____
impati**ent**		→		impati**emment**
récent		→		_____

Vérifiez *Les adverbes*

- The suffix **-ment** corresponds to *-ly* in English. Many adverbs of manner are formed by adding **-ment** to the feminine form of an adjective.

  heureuse → heureusement   seule → seulement

The **-ment** suffix is added directly to the masculine form if it ends in a vowel.

  rapide → rapidement   vrai → vraiment

If the adjective ends in **-ent** or **-ant,** change the ending as follows:*

constant → const**amment**   fréquent → fréqu**emment**

■ In a simple tense (present, imperfect, future), most adverbs follow the verb.

> Aujourd'hui, les femmes entrent **facilement** dans le monde professionnel...

In the negative, they follow **pas.**

> ... mais elles ne montent pas **rapidement.**

■ Adverbs of time (like **aujourd'hui**) and those that modify the entire idea are placed at the beginning or the end of the sentence.

> **Malheureusement,** les femmes gagnent 25 pour cent de moins que les hommes.
> Et il y a très peu de femmes au Parlement, **évidemment.**

■ In the passé composé, adverbs ending in **-ment** usually follow the past participle.

> Elle a attendu **patiemment** une promotion.

Short, common adverbs like many you have already learned (**bien, mal, déjà, encore, souvent, quelquefois, beaucoup, assez, trop, jamais, rien,** etc.) come *between* the auxiliary and the past participle.

> Elle a **beaucoup** travaillé, mais elle n'a **jamais** eu de promotion.

■ Below is a chart of some common adverbs and their uses.

VOCABULAIRE ACTIF

absolument
activement
certainement
constamment
difficilement
facilement
fréquemment
généralement
heureusement
lentement
malheureusement
patiemment /
  impatiemment
poliment
rapidement
rarement
récemment
sérieusement

Résumé: les adverbes		
interrogation	**fréquence**	**quantité**
où?	encore	trop
comment?	souvent	beaucoup / peu
combien?	rarement	assez
quand?	quelquefois	plus / moins
pourquoi?	déjà	autant
négation	**temps**	**manière**
ne ... plus	hier	bien / mal
ne ... jamais	demain	rapidement
ne ... pas (du tout)	aujourd'hui	seulement
	autrefois	sérieusement
		vraiment
		etc.

*The adverb **lentement** (*slowly*) does not follow this rule.

ACTIVITÉS

A. Égalité entre hommes et femmes? Écoutez le professeur et cochez l'adverbe qui exprime (expresses) le mieux votre opinion sur l'égalité dans le monde professionnel.

➡ (1. Les femmes sont les égales des hommes dans le monde professionnel.)

1. _____ absolument   ✓ rarement   _____ heureusement
2. _____ évidemment   _____ récemment   _____ seulement
3. _____ facilement   _____ fréquemment   _____ traditionnellement
4. _____ vraiment   _____ rapidement   _____ lentement
5. _____ généralement   _____ souvent   _____ certainement
6. _____ sérieusement   _____ beaucoup   _____ peu
7. _____ constamment   _____ quelquefois   _____ lentement
8. _____ ne ... plus   _____ impatiemment _____ malheureusement

Est-ce que vos camarades de classe sont d'accord avec vous?

B. Comparaisons. Comparez les femmes modernes et les femmes traditionnelles à l'aide des suggestions suivantes (ou choisissez un autre adverbe si vous le voulez).

➡ parler (franchement?) *Les femmes modernes parlent plus franchement (moins poliment / aussi raisonnablement) que les femmes traditionnelles.*

1. entrer dans le monde professionnel (facilement?)
2. travailler (sérieusement?)
3. discuter l'égalité (timidement?)
4. monter dans leur carrière (rapidement?)
5. attendre l'égalité (patiemment?)
6. diriger des entreprises (rarement?)
7. choisir une carrière (difficilement?)
8. avoir des promotions (fréquemment?)

C. Dans un monde idéal... Décrivez le patron (la patronne) idéal(e). Complétez les phrases suivantes en employant des adverbes de manière, de fréquence ou de temps.

➡ Le patron (La patronne) idéal(e) remerciera *constamment les employés.* Il (Elle) se fâchera *rarement.*

1. Il (Elle) travaillera...
2. Il (Elle) dirigera...
3. Il (Elle) écoutera...
4. Il (Elle) comprendra...
5. Il (Elle) répondra...
6. Il (Elle) parlera...
7. ?

STRATÉGIES DE COMMUNICATION
Taking part in a conversation • Interrupting

There are times in conversation when you'll want to interrupt the speaker, for example, in a lively discussion on a controversial topic. Study the following example, and identify the expressions used to interrupt.

— Est-ce qu'on peut parler d'égalité entre les hommes et les femmes? Eh bien, oui, en théorie...

— Excusez-moi, mais c'est plus que de la théorie! Les femmes aujourd'hui peuvent entrer dans toutes les professions...

— Attendez! Entrer, peut-être, mais pas *monter*. Le pouvoir économique et politique est encore réservé aux hommes, et...

— Oui, mais il faut du temps pour changer les institutions et la mentalité de la société...

— Franchement, il faut *trop* de temps!

Expressions pour prendre la parole ou interrompre	
Oui/Non, mais...	Excusez-moi, mais...
Écoute/Écoutez...	Au contraire!
Attends!/Attendez!	Franchement...

Note culturelle

Les interruptions. According to cultural ethnographer Raymonde Carroll, misunderstandings often occur during conversations among French and Americans because their respective conversational styles are so different. Americans claim the French are "rude" and "interrupt constantly," while the French think Americans are "boring" and tend to "lecture." According to Carroll, the French save "long, uninterrupted responses, attentively listened to" for the kind of serious conversations that don't usually occur at social gatherings. And they use interruptions to react, to "punctuate" a conversation and keep it animated, *not* to cut someone off in mid thought or change the subject.

ACTIVITÉS

D. Une conversation animée. Avec un(e) partenaire jouez le rôle de deux député(e)s au Parlement en utilisant les éléments suivants. Vous voulez expliquer votre position; votre partenaire veut vous interrompre. Employez des expressions pour hésiter (page 61) et pour interrompre (page 407).

Député républicain

Les femmes constituent aujourd'hui 46 pour cent de la population active.
Elles peuvent entrer dans toutes les professions.
Elles ont le droit de voter seulement depuis cinquante ans.
Cinquante ans, ce n'est pas beaucoup.
Les institutions et les mentalités changent lentement.
Dans cinquante ans, la situation des femmes sera différente.

Député socialiste

Les femmes ne montent pas facilement dans le monde professionnel.
Une femme dans un poste de direction est l'exception.
Le pouvoir économique et politique est réservé aux hommes.
Les hommes dirigent toutes les grandes entreprises.
Les femmes gagnent en général 25 pour cent de moins que les hommes.
Seulement 6 pour cent des membres du Parlement sont des femmes.

Jeu de rôle

How have the relationships and responsibilities of men and women changed in the last thirty years? What will they be like in 2020? In groups of three, play the roles of colleagues who have different opinions on the answers to these questions. One thinks that the relationship between men and women was better in the past; another prefers today's situation; the third is impatiently awaiting a brighter future. Try to convince your partners of your point of view.

   CD-ROM **Now that you have finished the Troisième étape of this chapter, do your Lab Manual activities with the audio program. Explore chapter topics further with the Mais oui! Video and CD-ROM. Viewing and comprehension activities are in the video section of your *Workbook/Lab Manual/Video Manual.***

Intégration

Littérature: Une si longue lettre

Mariama Bâ (1929–1981), a writer from Senegal, was one of the pioneers of women's literature in Africa. *Une si longue lettre,* published in 1979, is a 130-page letter from Ramatoulaye, a Senegalese woman, to her best friend, Aïssatou. Ramatoulaye and Aïssatou were among the first girls in Senegal to receive an advanced degree from **«l'école des Blancs»,** and both have become schoolteachers. Aïssatou married Mawdo Bâ, a doctor, and Ramatoulaye married Modou Fall, an intellectual who has become an administrator and politician. Both couples are **«résolument progressistes»,** but they also live in a very traditional society, deeply rooted in the practice of polygamy. After twenty years of marriage, and under much pressure from his family, Mawdo Bâ takes a second wife **(une co-épouse).** A few years later, Modou Fall also takes a **co-épouse**—his daughter's best friend—and abandons Ramatoulaye and their twelve children. In *Une si longue lettre,* Ramatoulaye shares her distress with Aïssatou—Aïssatou who has gone through the same ordeal, who understands, who has asked herself the same painful questions on women's condition in an African Muslim society. In the excerpt, Ramatoulaye remembers what it was like when her friend lost her husband.

Avant de lire

1 Le texte que vous allez lire contient des mots illustrés dans le paragraphe suivant. Lisez ce paragraphe sur le cycle de la vie, puis, en utilisant le contexte et la logique, associez chaque mot en caractères gras avec son équivalent anglais, dans la liste donnée.

> Quand on arrive dans ce monde, c'est la naissance; les **sages-femmes** ou les médecins aident les bébés à **naître.** Puis les parents **élèvent** leurs enfants et leur **enseignent** des principes, des valeurs. Plus tard, les jeunes choisissent de **garder** ou de **rejeter** ces valeurs, d'obéir aux **lois** ou de **mépriser** les traditions. **Mûrir,** pour beaucoup, c'est apprendre à **faire son devoir, gagner sa vie,** assumer des responsabilités. Petit à petit, on **vieillit,** et finalement on meurt; on peut **mourir** de causes naturelles ou être victime d'une **maladie** qui **tue,** comme certaines formes de cancer.

Équivalents anglais: *to be born; to die; to kill; to keep; to reject; to despise; to raise; to teach; laws; midwives; disease / sickness; to earn a living; to do one's duty; to mature; to grow old*

2 Dans l'extrait que vous allez lire, il est question de «Tante Nabou» et de «la petite Nabou». Tante Nabou, mère de Mawdo Bâ, vient d'une famille royale et n'a jamais approuvé le mariage de son fils avec Aïssatou, fille

2 To help students keep names straight, recap relationships on the board. Qui est le mari d'Aïssatou? (Mawdo Bâ). Comment appelle-t-on la mère de Mawdo? (Tante Nabou). Qui est «la petite Nabou»? (nièce de Tante Nabou; cousine et co-épouse de Mawdo). Have students speculate and elaborate on possible plots in small groups for a minute or two, then compare guesses/stories.

409

d'un simple bijoutier *(jeweler)*. Pour perpétuer le sang royal *(royal blood)*, Tante Nabou prépare une jeune nièce, qui s'appelle aussi Nabou—«la petite Nabou»—à devenir la co-épouse de Mawdo. Sous la pression de la famille et de la tradition, quelle va être la réaction de Mawdo? Et quelle va être la réaction d'Aïssatou, la première épouse? Va-t-elle accepter de partager l'homme qu'elle aime? Choisira-t-elle le compromis (c'est-à-dire rester, accepter la situation) ou la rupture (c'est-à-dire partir, divorcer)? Discutez vos prédictions en groupes.

En général

Remind students that this is a letter to Aïssatou; Ramatoulaye addresses Aïssatou as **toi**.

3 ANSWERS: 1. d 2. e 3. a
4. g 5. b 6. h 7. f 8. c

3 Parcourez le texte une première fois pour identifier les paragraphes qui contiennent les idées générales suivantes.

paragraphes

1. «La petite Nabou est entrée... »
2. «Après son certificat d'études... »
3. «La petite Nabou est donc... »
4. «Je savais. La ville savait... »
5. «C'est pour ne pas voir... »
6. «Alors, tu n'as plus compté... »
7. «Mawdo ne te chassait pas... »
8. «Tu as choisi la rupture... »

idées générales

a. Tante Nabou annonce à Mawdo qu'il doit épouser la petite Nabou.
b. Raisons pour lesquelles Mawdo obéit à sa mère
c. Réaction d'Aïssatou
d. Formation domestique de la petite Nabou
e. Formation scolaire et professionnelle de la petite Nabou
f. Mawdo parle à Aïssatou d'amour et de devoir.
g. Mawdo explique à Aïssatou pourquoi il doit épouser la petite Nabou.
h. Les enfants d'Aïssatou sont inférieurs.

Une si longue lettre

1 La petite Nabou est entrée à l'école française. Mûrissant sous la protection de sa tante, elle apprenait le secret des sauces délicieuses, à manier fer à repasser et pilon°. Sa tante ne manquait jamais l'occasion de lui rappeler son origine royale et lui enseignait que la qualité première d'une femme est la docilité.

à... les tâches domestiques

2 Après son certificat d'études° et quelques années au lycée, Tante Nabou a conseillé à sa nièce de passer le concours° d'entrée à l'École des Sages-Femmes d'État°: «Cette école est bien. Là, on éduque. Des jeunes filles sobres, sans boucles d'oreilles°, vêtues de blanc, couleur de la pureté. Le métier que tu y apprendras est beau; tu gagneras ta vie et tu aideras à naître des serviteurs° de Mahomet°. En vérité, l'instruction d'une femme n'est pas à pousser. Et puis, je me demande comment une femme peut gagner sa vie en parlant matin et soir°.»

diplôme d'études primaires
examen
State
earrings
servants
prophète des musulmans
allusion au métier d'institutrice

3 La petite Nabou est donc devenue sage-femme. Un beau jour, Tante Nabou a convoqué Mawdo et lui a dit: «Mon frère te donne la petite Nabou comme femme pour me remercier de la façon digne° dont je l'ai élevée. Si tu ne la gardes pas comme épouse, je ne m'en relèverai jamais°. La honte tue plus vite que la maladie.»

honorable
je... I'll never get over it

4   Je savais. La ville savait. Toi, Aïssatou, tu ne soupçonnais° rien. Et parce *suspected*
que sa mère avait pris date pour la nuit nuptiale, Mawdo a enfin eu le courage
de te dire ce que chaque femme chuchotait°: tu avais une co-épouse. «Ma mère *was whispering*
est vieille. Les chocs et les déceptions° ont rendu son cœur fragile. Si je méprise *disappointments*
cette enfant, elle mourra. C'est le médecin qui parle, non le fils. Pense donc, la
fille de son frère, élevée par ses soins°, rejetée par son fils. Quelle honte devant *ses... elle (Tante Nabou)*
la société!»

5   C'est «pour ne pas voir sa mère mourir de honte et de chagrin» que
Mawdo était décidé à aller au rendez-vous de la nuit nuptiale. Devant cette
mère rigide, pétrie° de morale ancienne, brûlée intérieurement par° les féroces *formée / brûlée... burnt inside by*
lois antiques, que pouvait Mawdo Bâ? Il vieillissait et puis, voulait-il seulement
résister? La petite Nabou était bien jolie...

6   Alors, tu n'as plus compté, Aïssatou, pas plus que tes quatre fils: ceux-ci ne
seront jamais les égaux° des fils de la petite Nabou. Les enfants de la petite *equals*
Nabou seront de sang royal. La mère de Mawdo, princesse, ne pouvait pas se
reconnaître dans les fils d'une simple bijoutière. Et puis une bijoutière peut-elle
avoir de la dignité, de l'honneur?

7   Mawdo ne te chassait pas°. Il allait à son devoir et souhaitait que tu restes. *ne... wasn't kicking you out*
La petite Nabou habiterait° toujours chez sa mère; c'est toi qu'il aimait. Tous les *would live*
jours, il irait°, la nuit, voir l'autre épouse, pour «accomplir un devoir». *would go*

8   Tu as choisi la rupture, un aller sans retour avec tes quatre fils. Tu as eu le
courage de t'assumer. Tu as loué une maison et, au lieu de regarder en arrière°, *backwards*
tu as fixé l'avenir obstinément.

Extrait de *Une si longue lettre* (Mariama Bâ)

4 **Les mots.** En utilisant le contexte et la logique, pouvez-vous déduire le sens des expressions en caractères gras?

1. «Sa tante **ne manquait jamais l'occasion de** lui rappeler son origine royale... »
2. «En vérité, l'instruction d'une femme **n'est pas à pousser.**»
3. «Tu as eu le courage de **t'assumer.**»
4. «... tu **as fixé** l'avenir **obstinément.**»

5 **Le texte.** Répondez aux questions suivantes.

1. Quelle est la qualité la plus importante d'une femme, selon Tante Nabou?
2. Pourquoi Tante Nabou a-t-elle voulu que sa nièce entre à l'École des Sages-Femmes?
3. Si Mawdo refuse de prendre la petite Nabou comme épouse, quelle sera la réaction de sa mère?
4. Quelle explication Mawdo a-t-il donnée à Aïssatou pour justifier son mariage à la petite Nabou?
5. Mawdo Bâ voulait-il vraiment résister à ce mariage? Donnez deux indications du contraire.
6. Quel était le problème d'Aïssatou, selon la mère de Mawdo? Pourquoi les fils d'Aïssatou ne seront-ils jamais les égaux des fils de la petite Nabou?
7. Quel arrangement Mawdo a-t-il proposé à Aïssatou?
8. Quelle a été la réaction d'Aïssatou?

Et vous?

Before group discussion on question 2, brainstorm together on situations that could be used and the vocabulary needed to discuss them. Possibilities in **literature**: the excerpts from *Du camembert, chéri...* (Ch. 5), *Les yeux baissés* (Ch. 9), or *Une abominable feuille d'érable sur la glace* (Ch. 10); Chaim Potok's novels (*My Name Is Asher Lev* and others); in **movies**: *Dead Poets Society* and many others. After group work, have students report on some of the examples they discussed. Before group work on question 3, you may wish to model the activity with the whole class. Pick traditions concerning marriage, for example, and compare together how it was viewed 50 years ago vs. today, then predict how it will be 50 years from now. After group work, have each group report on one tradition they discussed. Compare/ Discuss opinions in a nonjudgmental manner.

1. Quelques pages plus tard, Ramatoulaye dira qu'Aïssatou était la «victime innocente d'une injuste cause». À votre avis, de quoi exactement Aïssatou était-elle la victime?

2. Mawdo Bâ et Aïssatou se disaient «progressistes», mais c'est la tradition qui a été la plus forte pour Mawdo. À votre avis, la tradition et le progrès sont-ils compatibles? En groupes de deux ou trois, trouvez des situations, dans l'histoire, l'actualité, la littérature, le cinéma ou même dans votre expérience personnelle, qui illustrent ce conflit entre la tradition et le changement.

3. Chaque culture a ses traditions et ses valeurs concernant le mariage, la famille, la religion, la notion du bien et du mal, le concept du devoir, l'attitude vis-à-vis de la nature, et bien d'autres choses. Prenez deux ou trois traditions de votre culture et comparez ces traditions il y a 50 ans et aujourd'hui. Ont-elles changé? Comment voyez-vous l'avenir de ces traditions ou valeurs? Organisez vos idées en quatre colonnes: **Traditions, Il y a 50 ans, Aujourd'hui, Dans 50 ans.**

Par écrit: In my crystal ball . . .

Avant d'écrire

A. Strategy: Webbing. Webbing allows a writer to draw on both sides of the brain, the analytical and the intuitive, making visible the processes of association, imagination, and feeling. You begin by writing your topic in the center of a circle. Lines radiating from the circle lead to other words brought to mind through free association. Some of the associations are "logical," i.e., they can be analyzed:

emploi → travailler

Others are on an intuitive or feeling level drawn from personal experience:

avenir → incertain

Application. Try webbing as a prewriting technique using the terms **avenir** and **emploi** as centers of thought. Spend five to ten minutes on each web before beginning the writing activities.

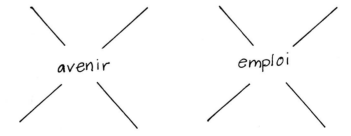

avenir   emploi

B. Strategy: Adding variety to sentence beginnings. Your writing will be monotonous if you begin each sentence with the same word or type of word. To see how well you do at varying sentence beginnings, take one of your previous creative writing efforts and circle the first word in each sentence. Did your sentences begin in different ways or did most of your sentences begin with a subject pronoun (je, il...)?

Application. Study the examples that follow, then try to rewrite four or five sentences from your previous writing effort, using each of the following types of sentence beginnings.

noun:	Mawdo ne te chassait pas.
pronoun:	Je savais.
article:	La petite Nabou entra...
preposition:	Après son certificat d'études...
	Devant cette mère rigide...
adjective:	Quelle honte devant la société!
	Cette école est bien.
verb:	Pense donc,...
	Mûrir, pour beaucoup, c'est apprendre...
conjunction:	Si tu ne la gardes pas comme épouse,...
	Et puis, je me demande...

ÉCRIVEZ

Have students follow the procedure suggested in **Avant d'écrire B,** circling the first word in each sentence of the first draft, then revising to add variety. After students have written their ending to Aïssatou's story, you may want to tell them that, according to Bâ's novel, Aïssatou's love of books leads her to finish school and to go to France where she becomes an interpreter, eventually traveling to the United States to work in the Senegalese embassy.

1. L'extrait d'*Une si longue lettre* se termine par la phrase «au lieu de regarder en arrière, tu as fixé l'avenir obstinément.» Mais, ce n'est pas vraiment la fin de la lettre. À vous maintenant de terminer l'histoire d'Aïssatou. Écrivez un paragraphe sur ce qui arrivera à la jeune femme et ses quatre fils. Qu'est-ce qu'elle fera? Est-ce qu'elle trouvera un emploi? Où est-ce qu'elle habitera? etc. N'oubliez pas de varier les débuts des phrases.

2. Quelle chance! Vous vouliez passer l'été au Québec et vous allez pouvoir le faire! Vous venez d'être embauché(e) pour le poste décrit dans une des annonces ci-dessous et à la page 414. Maintenant il faut expliquer à votre camarade de chambre que vous ne pourrez pas venir lui rendre visite comme prévu *(planned)*. Envoyez-lui une lettre pour expliquer la situation. Dites-lui où vous passerez l'été, où vous travaillerez, ce que vous ferez et ce que vous espérez voir pendant votre séjour.

TÉLÉPHONISTES-RÉCEPTIONNISTES
(liste de rappel)

Le CENTRE HOSPITALIER DES CONVALESCENTS DE MONTRÉAL désire s'adjoindre des téléphonistes-réceptionnistes pour travailler sur appel. Les exigences du poste sont les suivantes: horaire flexible, incluant quarts de travail de soir et de fin de semaine, bilinguisme à l'oral et à l'écrit, connaissance d'une console téléphonique, expérience d'au moins une année dans un milieu de travail semblable.

Les candidat(e)s intéressé(e)s sont prié(e)s de faire parvenir leur curriculum vitae au plus tard le 30 septembre à:

    Mme S. Marcil
    Dossier 4521
    Direction des ressources humaines
    Centre hospitalier
    des Convalescents de Montréal
    6363, chemin Hudson
    Montréal (Québec) H3S 1M9

Journaliste

LE DEVOIR est à la recherche de deux jeunes journalistes à titre de surnuméraires d'été pour travailler au sein de la section des informations générales.

Un diplôme universitaire de premier cycle (en journalisme, en communication et/ou dans un autre domaine), une connaissance de la presse écrite et la maîtrise d'autres langues que le français seront des atouts.

Durée de l'emploi: 10 semaines

Rémunération: selon la convention collective en vigueur.

Envoyez vos candidatures avant le 15 mai à:

Bernard Descôteaux,
rédacteur en chef
LE DEVOIR
2050 de Bleury, 9e étage
Montréal (Québec)
H3A 3M9

Rabais Campus
Journaux et magazines

Nous recherchons des représentant(e)s pour nos promotions de ventes d'abonnements par kiosques du **DEVOIR** pour les campus étudiants de Montréal, Québec, Ottawa, Sherbrooke, Trois-Rivières et Chicoutimi.

Exigences: Dynamisme, aptitudes à la vente, disponibilité et bonne présentation

Salaire: de 8 $ à 9 $/hre;
de 1 à 5 semaines

Pour informations:

Hélène Génier (514) 982-0637
Monique Lévesque (418) 529-4250
Entre 9 h 00 et midi

VOCABULAIRE ACTIF

Le monde du travail

l'ambition (f.) *ambition*
les attentes (f.) *expectations*
l'avenir (m.) *the future*
un banquier *a banker*
un cadre *a professional (manager, executive, etc.)*
une carrière *a career*
un chef d'entreprise *a CEO*
le chômage *unemployment*
un(e) comptable *an accountant*
un(e) cuisinier (-ière) *a cook*
un curriculum vitae (un CV) *a résumé*
un(e) débutant(e) *a beginner*
l'égalité (f.) *equality*
un emploi *a job*

un(e) employé(e) *an employee*
un employeur *an employer*
l'ennui (m.) *boredom*
un(e) enseignant(e) *a teacher*
une entreprise *a company*
un entretien *an interview*
un(e) fonctionnaire *a government employee, a civil servant*
la formation *education, training*
un homme / une femme d'affaires *a businessman / -woman*
un(e) infirmier (-ière) *a nurse*
un manque (de) *a lack (of)*
un métier *a job, career*
un(e) ouvrier (-ière) *a factory worker*

le patron / la patronne *the boss*
un poste à mi-temps / à plein temps *a half-time / full-time position*
le pouvoir *power*
une profession (libérale) *a profession*
un poste de direction *a management position*
une promotion *a promotion*
la réalité *reality*
la retraite *retirement*
la réussite, le succès *success*
le salaire *salary*
la société *society*
un stage *an internship*
un(e) vendeur (-euse) *a salesperson*

Verbes et expressions verbales

avoir l'intention de *to intend to*
compter (+ infinitif) *to plan to, to count on*
devenir *to become*

embaucher / être embauché(e) *to hire / to be hired*
espérer *to hope*
éviter *to avoid*

faire une demande d'emploi *to apply for a job*
gagner (sa vie, de l'argent) *to earn (a living, money)*
prendre rendez-vous *to make an appointment*
réaliser (ses désirs, un projet) *to fulfill, to achieve,*
  to accomplish

remplir un formulaire *to fill out a form*
venir de (faire quelque chose) *to have just (done*
  something)

Adjectifs
professionnel(le) *professional*
réservé(e) à *reserved (for)*
utile *useful*

Adverbes
absolument *absolutely*
activement *actively*
certainement *certainly*
constamment *constantly*
difficilement *with difficulty*
évidemment *obviously*
facilement *easily*

fréquemment *frequently*
généralement *generally*
heureusement *fortunately*
lentement *slowly*
patiemment / impatiemment
  patiently / impatiently
poliment *politely*

rapidement *fast*
rarement *rarely*
récemment *recently*
sérieusement *seriously*
seulement *only*
traditionnellement *traditionally*

Expressions communicatives
attends / attendez *wait*
au contraire *on the contrary*
écoute / écoutez *listen*
Excuse-moi / Excusez-moi, mais... *Excuse me, but . . .*
franchement *frankly*

Pronoms toniques
moi, toi, lui, elle, soi, nous, vous, eux, elles *me, you, him, her, oneself, us, you, them*

Divers
dès que *as soon as*

12 Soucis et rêves

EPP 6005

EPP 6005

Quels sont les soucis de cette dame?

Imaginez ses problèmes.

Et vous?

Si vous étiez à sa place, qu'est-ce que vous feriez?

This chapter will enable you to
- **understand conversations about health and fears**
- **read an article and a literary passage about dreams**
- **discuss physical and mental health**
- **say what you would do if . . .**
- **express regrets and give advice**

Première étape

À l'écoute: Ça ne va pas du tout

This input introduces vocabulary about health and sickness, and hypothesis.

Quand vous êtes malade, êtes-vous optimiste («Ce n'est rien... ») ou êtes-vous pessimiste («Ça ne va pas du tout... »)? Est-ce que vous vous inquiétez *(worry)* facilement? La conversation que vous allez entendre traite des maladies et des inquiétudes (ou soucis) de certaines personnes.

Avant d'écouter

1 Students may work in groups of 4 or 5, compare their answers, then report on who is prone to what.

1 Quand est-ce que vous attrapez les maladies suivantes? Souvent? De temps en temps? Rarement? Jamais?

> un rhume *(a cold)*
> la grippe *(the flu)*
> une indigestion
> le rhume des foins (allergie aux pollens, etc.)

2 Pour chaque maladie, où est-ce qu'on a mal? Reliez la maladie au(x) symptôme(s).

Quand on a...	**On a mal...**
1. un rhume	a. au ventre
2. la grippe	b. à la tête et à la gorge
3. une indigestion	c. partout!

Écoutons

Cue to Video Module 12 (00:59:15), in which Fatima goes to see the doctor and tells him her symptoms.

Audio CD

3 Écoutez d'abord pour identifier

1. qui parle.
   a. deux personnes optimistes
   b. deux hypocondriaques
   c. une hypocondriaque et une personne optimiste

2. les maladies mentionnées. (Cochez-les.)

   ✓____ un rhume

   ✓____ la grippe

   ____ le rhume des foins

   ____ une indigestion

   ✓____ une bronchite

   ____ une pneumonie

4 After students check symptoms mentioned, have volunteers demonstrate the meaning of the expressions in bold, or you may act them out and have students say what you are doing, using the expressions in bold with proper agreement (i.e., **vous toussez,** etc.). Make sure students notice that when you sneeze in French, you go **Atchoum!**

4 Écoutez encore. Quels sont les symptômes mentionnés? Cochez toutes les réponses appropriées, puis déduisez le sens des mots en caractères gras.

1. Odile a mal

    ✓_____ à la tête.

    _____ au ventre.

    ✓_____ à la gorge.

    ✓_____ partout.

2. Elle

    ✓_____ a **le nez bouché** (congestionné).

    ✓_____ **éternue.**

    ✓_____ **tousse.**

    _____ a **la nausée.**

    ✓_____ a **de la fièvre.**

5 Écoutez encore la conversation et cochez toutes les réponses qui sont correctes.

1. Pour savoir si elle a de la fièvre, Odile demande à son amie de

    _____ prendre sa température avec un thermomètre.

    ✓_____ toucher son front.

    _____ toucher ses joues.

2. Odile pense que sa toux est

    ✓_____ étrange.

    _____ normale.

    _____ contagieuse.

3. Son amie dit que si elle appelle le médecin,

    ✓_____ il lui prescrira des médicaments (du sirop, un antibiotique, etc.).

    ✓_____ elle sera plus tranquille.

    ✓_____ les autres auront la paix (*peace*)!

6 Écoutez une dernière fois en faisant attention aux verbes au conditionnel (*actions that **would** happen*). Quelles sont les formes du conditionnel? Encerclez les réponses selon ce que vous entendez.

1. À ta place, je ne _____ pas.
    a. m'inquiétais
    (b.) m'inquiéterais

2. À ta place, j'_____ un médecin.
    (a.) appellerais
    b. appelais

VOCABULAIRE ACTIF

un antibiotique
appeler le médecin
avoir de la fièvre
avoir mal à (la tête, la gorge, etc.)
avoir la nausée
avoir le nez bouché
une bronchite
contagieux
éternuer
étrange
la grippe
une indigestion
s'inquiéter
un médicament
un pharmacien
une pneumonie
prendre sa température
prescrire
un rhume
le rhume des foins
du sirop
un souci
tousser; la toux
tranquille

3. Il te _____ des médicaments.
   a. prescrirait
   b. prescrira

4. Et surtout, tu _____ plus tranquille.
   a. seras
   b. serais

Cue to Video Module 12, street interviews (01:01:40), in which people mention the role of **la sécurité sociale** in health care.

Note culturelle

La médecine en France. Medical care in France is socialized, with both employers and employees paying into a common fund. Most medical expenses, including the cost of medications, are reimbursed by **la sécurité sociale.** Individuals are free to choose their own doctors as long as the charges are in line with governmental norms. Doctors still make house calls; no one suffering from a serious case of the flu, for example, would dream of getting out of bed to get medical attention. For minor ailments, the French will often consult their local pharmacist instead of their doctor. **Les pharmaciens** give advice, dispense nonprescription medicine, and apply some first aid.

VOCABULAIRE
Pour parler de la santé

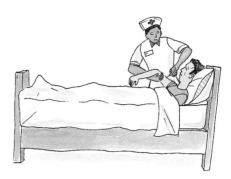

Le garçon est tombé et il s'est blessé. Il a une blessure. / Son père met un pansement sur sa blessure.

Odile ne se sent pas bien. Elle a mal à la tête. Le pharmacien a recommandé des comprimés.

Ce monsieur est tombé malade. Le médecin a prescrit* une piqûre.

POSSIBLE RESPONSES: me sens bien; me sens mal; me prescrit des piqûres; j'ai mal au dos; me suis blessé

■ Complétez les phrases suivantes en employant les verbes **prescrire, se blesser, avoir mal à** et **se sentir bien/mal.**

En général, je...
Quand je tombe malade, je...
Le médecin...
Quand je fais trop d'exercice physique, j(e)...
Quand je suis tombé(e) dans la rue, j(e)...

---

*Prescrire** se conjugue comme **écrire.**

Allow students a few minutes to work individually or in groups on the categories before comparing responses. If answers vary, ask students to justify their categorization: «Ce sont des professionnels de la santé qui prescrivent.» «On prescrit un médicament.»

■ Odile connaît bien le vocabulaire de la santé! Vous aussi? Classez le vocabulaire suivant selon les catégories indiquées. Devinez le sens des nouveaux mots apparentés.

un rhume   un pansement   un(e) dentiste
la température   tousser   un antibiotique
le cancer   une migraine   éternuer
la nausée   le sida (AIDS)   une indigestion
le nez qui coule   une crise cardiaque   examiner
une piqûre   de l'aspirine   une toux
un médecin   le rhume des foins   un(e) spécialiste
de la fièvre   la grippe   un(e) pharmacien(ne)
un médicament   un(e) infirmier (-ère)   du sirop
la bronchite   contagieux (-euse)   une attaque cérébrale
un comprimé   le nez bouché   une pneumonie

les maladies	les symptômes	les traitements	les professionnels de la santé

ACTIVITÉS

A. Associations. À votre avis, quels mots (symptômes, traitements, etc.) associez-vous avec les maladies suivantes? Cochez toutes les réponses logiques.

1. un rhume

   _____ le dentiste   _____ éternuer

   _____ le nez bouché   _____ la nausée

2. une crise cardiaque

   _____ un(e) pharmacien(ne) _____ du sirop

   _____ un(e) spécialiste   _____ de l'aspirine

3. une migraine

   _____ mal à la tête   _____ la nausée

   _____ contagieuse   _____ une piqûre

4. une indigestion

   _____ un comprimé   _____ de la température

   _____ un pansement   _____ mal à l'estomac

5. le rhume des foins

_____ tousser   _____ le nez qui coule

_____ de la fièvre   _____ du sirop

Cue to Video Module 12, street interviews (01:01:40), in which people say what they do when they get sick.

B. Maladies et traitements.   Indiquez ce qu'on fait normalement (ou ne fait *pas*) quand on souffre des maladies suivantes:

une pneumonie, une migraine, mal aux dents, le rhume des foins

➡ *Quand on a une indigestion, on n'appelle pas le médecin; on prend des comprimés et on mange moins!*

appeler le médecin (dentiste)?   se coucher?

  prendre des médicaments?   aller à l'hôpital?

faire une piqûre?   parler au pharmacien?   mettre un pansement?

  prendre un antibiotique?   aller voir un spécialiste?

boire beaucoup de jus de fruits?   rester au lit?

See the *Instructor's Resource Manual* for an information gap activity, **Tant de malades,** practicing health-related vocabulary.

C. Le malade imaginaire.   Choisissez votre maladie «favorite», puis jouez le rôle d'un(e) malade en décrivant tous vos symptômes à un(e) camarade de classe. Il (Elle) va faire un diagnostic et recommander un traitement. Ensuite, changez de rôle et répétez.

—J'ai mal partout. Je tousse et j'éternue. Je n'ai pas de fièvre.
—Vous avez un rhume. Il faut prendre du sirop...

STRUCTURE: Saying what you would do
Le conditionnel (I)

Observez et déduisez

VOCABULAIRE ACTIF
mort(e)
mourir

— Quel malheur! J'ai le nez bouché, j'ai mal aux oreilles, je tousse, j'éternue constamment... Je vais mourir* *(die)!*
— Pauvre Odile. À ta place, j'appellerais le médecin. Il te prescrirait des médicaments et tu serais plus tranquille.
— Alors, tu voudrais bien lui téléphoner pour moi? S'il te plaît... ?
— Bien sûr! Et je pourrais passer par la pharmacie aussi.
— Tu es gentille!

Point out that **boire** ends in **-re,** as does **prescrire.**

■ What does Odile's friend say she *would* do if she were Odile? What does she say the doctor *would* do? Study those examples, then imagine you are Odile's friend and say how you would express the following:

I would sleep. I would drink juice.

■ Do you recognize the last three conditional verbs in the preceding dialogue? What are the infinitives? Based on those examples, how would you express the following:

I would not go to class. I would not do my homework. I would need medicine.

Help students recognize the future stems by asking, «Où est-ce que nous avons déjà vu **ser-**?»

---

*__Mourir__ is an irregular verb that is used most often in the passé composé.

Il **est mort.** / Elle **est morte.**

Vérifiez *Le conditionnel*

■ In French, the conditional is used to state what someone *would* or *would not* do under certain conditions. It is a simple tense formed by adding the imperfect endings to the infinitive: **-ais, -ais, -ait, -ions, -iez, -aient.**

Le conditionnel	
je me coucher**ais**	nous nous coucher**ions**
tu te coucher**ais**	vous vous coucher**iez**
il / elle / on se coucher**ait**	ils / elles se coucher**aient**
je prendr**ais**	nous prendr**ions**
tu prendr**ais**	vous prendr**iez**
il / elle / on prendr**ait**	ils / elles prendr**aient**

DISCRIMINATION DRILL: As you read the cues, have students indicate if the sentences are in the **imparfait** or the **conditionnel.** CUES: 1. Les enfants se sentaient mal. 2. Ils n'iraient pas chez le médecin. 3. Son père lui téléphonerait. 4. Le médecin disait «Ce n'est pas sérieux.» 5. Il prescrirait des comprimés. 6. Les enfants n'étaient pas contents. 7. Ils préféreraient prendre du sirop. 8. Ils seraient en bonne santé.

■ Although they have the same endings, be sure not to confuse the imperfect tense of the verb with the conditional.

Imparfait: Elle **s'inquiétait** facilement.
Conditionnel: Elle **s'inquiéterait** encore.

■ Verbs that have an irregular stem in the future (see page 390) have the same irregular stem in the conditional.

Tu **ser**ais plus tranquille.
Tu n'**aur**ais plus mal à la tête.

-re verbs drop the **-e** before adding the ending.

Le médecin te **prescrir**ait des médicaments.

■ Use the conditional of **pouvoir** to suggest what someone *could* do.

Tu **pourrais** appeler le médecin.

Use the conditional of **devoir** to say what someone *should* do.

Tu **devrais** te coucher tout de suite.

■ Remember that the conditional tense is used most frequently to express wishes and requests politely (see page 84).

Je **voudrais** parler au médecin, s'il vous plaît.
Auriez-vous le numéro de téléphone de la pharmacie?

ACTIVITÉS

D. Poll the class to discover the most common response for each cue. Ask volunteers to share any original answers they added.

D. Que feraient-ils? Indiquez ce que les personnes suivantes feraient (✓) et ne feraient pas (X) si vous aviez la pneumonie.

➡ Ma grand-mère... _✓_ *me préparerait de la soupe au poulet*

_X_ *aurait peur*

1. Je...

_____ me coucherais   _____ serais anxieux (-euse)

_____ pleurerais   _____ ?

2. Mes parents...

_____ viendraient me voir   _____ prendraient ma température

_____ appelleraient le médecin   _____ ?

3. Le médecin...

_____ m'examinerait   _____ prescrirait des médicaments

_____ me conseillerait de faire   _____ ?
de l'exercice

4. Mes copains...

_____ feraient mes devoirs   _____ seraient tristes

_____ sortiraient sans moi   _____ ?

5. Mon professeur...

_____ comprendrait   _____ demanderait un certificat du
                                        médecin

_____ serait triste   _____ ?

Quelles sont les réponses les plus communes de la classe?

E. For #6, have pairs brainstorm other requests they might make in this situation.

E. Vous êtes vraiment malade! Parce que vous devez rester au lit, vous appelez souvent pour demander des petits services à votre famille. Pour être plus poli(e), refaites les phrases en employant le conditionnel de **vouloir** et de **pouvoir**.

➡ Nicolas, j'ai soif. Va me chercher du jus d'orange.
Nicolas, tu voudrais m'apporter du jus d'orange, s'il te plaît?
ou: _Nicolas, est-ce que tu pourrais m'apporter du jus d'orange, s'il te plaît?_

1. Papa, apporte-moi de l'aspirine.
2. Maman, j'ai faim. Prépare mon déjeuner.
3. Nathalie, Andrée! Je m'ennuie. Apportez-moi le journal.
4. Maman, papa, j'ai mal partout. Téléphonez au médecin.
5. Andrée, je tousse. Donne-moi le sirop.
6. ?

F. À ta place. Odile veut votre opinion sur tous ses problèmes. Quelles suggestions avez-vous pour elle? (Commencez vos suggestions par **À ta place...**)

➡ Mon copain est à l'hôpital.
À ta place, je lui rendrais visite. Je choisirais des magazines intéressants, et je lui apporterais des fruits aussi!

1. J'ai une migraine.
2. Je me suis blessée en faisant de la gymnastique.
3. Je veux être en bonne forme.
4. Je veux perdre du poids.

Jeu de rôle

Read the following notes in the medical files of three patients, then imagine you are the doctor of one of them. What would you say to your patient, played by a classmate? Say what s/he can do to improve his/her condition. Your partner will ask questions about what habits s/he should change and may present some excuses for bad habits. Present your recommendations using your best bedside manner.

Hôpital St-Pierre

Nom: MÉGOT, Michel   Age: 47   Poids: 100 kilos

Remarques:

Père et 2 oncles morts d'une crise cardiaque

Fumeur

Hôpital St-Pierre

Nom: BOUFFETOUT, Jean-Paul   Age: 8 ans   Poids: 60 kilos

Remarques:

Déteste l'exercice physique; régime malsain

Parents trop tolérants

Hôpital St-Pierre

Nom: LAFOLIE, Patricia   Age: 28 ans   Poids: 57 kilos

Remarques:

Histoire médicale chargée: bronchite, 1992; pneumonie, 1993; migraines, 1993→présent; indigestions fréquentes; rhume des foins chronique. Hypocondriaque?

Deuxième étape

Lecture: Les fantasmes des Français

This input introduces cultural information and vocabulary about personal dreams; it also recycles the conditional and expands on hypotheses.

Un fantasme est un rêve, conscient ou inconscient. Quels sont vos fantasmes? Quels sont les fantasmes des Français?

Avant de lire

1 Parlons d'abord de vos fantasmes. Est-ce que vous rêvez d'être célèbre? d'être riche? de voyager? Complétez l'étoile de vos rêves personnels et comparez-les avec ceux d'un(e) camarade de classe.

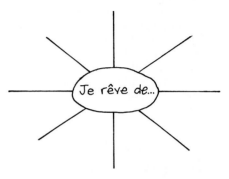

Je rêve de...

En général

2 Regardez l'article sur **Les fantasmes des Français.** Est-ce que vous reconnaissez dans le texte ou dans les résultats du sondage des rêves mentionnés dans votre étoile personnelle? Lesquels?

3 Parcourez l'article. Les sujets suivants sont-ils traités dans le texte, dans les résultats du sondage, ou dans les deux? Complétez le tableau.

sujets	texte	sondage	les deux
le «plus grand fantasme»		✓	
les sept pôles de l'imagination	✓		
les professions de rêve			✓
les cadeaux		✓	
les voyages			✓
la maison			✓
les actes extraordinaires (exploits)		✓	
le bonheur affectif	✓		
la sexualité	✓		
un quart d'heure à la télévision		✓	
l'éternité	✓		

A. Les fantasmes des Français

Le fantasme n° 1 des Français, c'est partir. Tous ne rêvent pas de traverser les continents. Il y a mille et une manières de partir, de rompre° avec la routine, avec soi-même. Pour savoir quels rêves cachés caressent les Français, *L'Express* a demandé à l'institut Louis Harris de sonder leurs fantasmes. Le résultat est surprenant.

break

En fait, les fantasmes des Français sont, comme eux, multicolores et multiformes. L'imagination ne s'empare° pas des mêmes images selon que l'on est jeune ou vieux, homme ou femme, riche ou pauvre. Mais pour la plupart, l'imagination est attirée° par sept grands pôles. Dans l'ordre: 1. les voyages; 2. l'argent, tombé du ciel, grâce à saint Loto°; 3. le travail: la profession qu'on aurait rêvé d'exercer; 4. la maison, «neuve», «jolie», «grande», à la campagne ou au bord de la mer, «à soi»; 5. le bonheur affectif, en famille, en couple, ou dans une société qu'on rêve plus juste, plus démocratique et pacifique; 6. la sexualité, qui fait surtout rêver les plus jeunes; 7. enfin, l'éternité: tout est bon pour défier ou éviter la mort°—devenir célèbre, vivre cent ans, mille ans.

prend

attracted

grâce à... thanks to Saint Lottery

défier... challenge or avoid death

Les fantasmes des Français sont effectivement plutôt «réalistes». Un réalisme teinté d'humanitarisme, un rêve de retour à la vraie vie, odorante° comme une miche° de pain.

qui sent bon
loaf

B. Sondage

Quel est votre plus grand fantasme?

Être le (la) plus compétent(e)	39%
Être le (la) plus aimé(e)	23
Être le (la) plus drôle	14
Être le (la) plus intelligent(e)	12
Être le (la) plus célèbre	3
Être le (la) plus sexy	2
Être le (la) plus grand(e)	1
Être le (la) plus beau (belle)	1
Sans opinion	5

Quelle profession auriez-vous rêvé exercer?

Médecin sans frontières[1]	32%
Berger[2]	11
Cosmonaute	9
Navigateur solitaire	8
Prince ou princesse	8
Chanteur à succès	7
Ambassadeur de France	6
Chef de la brigade antigang	5
Président de la République	3
Raider en Bourse[3]	2
Prostituée de luxe	1
Évêque[4]	1
Sans opinion	7

1. volontaires dans les pays pauvres ou situations de crise
2. *shepherd*   3. *stock market*   4. *bishop*

L'exploit de vos fantasmes?

Sauver un enfant de la noyade[1]	46%
Faire le tour du monde à la voile[2]	16
Recevoir le prix Nobel	10
Écrire un best-seller	9
Escalader l'Himalaya	8
Marquer le but de la victoire[3] en coupe du monde	6
Commettre le crime parfait	4
Sans opinion	1

1. *drowning*   2. *in a sailboat*   3. *score the winning goal*

Si vous gagniez 10 millions de francs au Loto, comment rêveriez-vous de les dépenser?

En arrêtant de travailler pour vivre en rentier[1]	25%
En créant une entreprise	24
En donnant tout aux déshérités[2]	18
En quittant tout pour refaire votre vie au bout du monde[3]	11
En dépensant tout votre argent n'importe comment[4]	7
En achetant un château et une Rolls	7
Sans opinion	8

1. *person of independent means*   2. pauvres   3. loin
4. impulsivement

Le cadeau de vos fantasmes?

Une Ferrari	**22%**
Un bijou de chez Cartier	18
Une place dans la prochaine navette spatiale[1]	17
Une caisse de vin de pommard de 1929	16
Un tableau de Matisse	12
Un costume ou une robe de chez Christian Dior	8
Un tuyau d'initié[2] en Bourse	4
Sans opinion	3

1. *space shuttle*   2. *an insider's tip*

Le week-end de vos fantasmes?

Sur une île déserte	**52%**
Dans un palace[1]	36
Au lit	8
Sans opinion	4

1. hôtel de grand luxe

La contrée de vos fantasmes?

Tahiti	**25%**
Australie	17
Californie	14
Brésil	12
Japon	11
Tibet	7
Sahara	5
Grand Nord	4
Sans opinion	5

Si on vous offrait un quart d'heure d'antenne[1] à la télévision, qu'en feriez-vous?

Vous défendriez une grande cause humanitaire	**48%**
Vous feriez la morale aux hommes politiques	22
Vous feriez une déclaration d'amour	12
Vous feriez votre propre publicité	7
Vous raconteriez votre vie	5
Vous diriez du mal de votre pire ennemi[2]	1
Sans opinion	5

1. *air time*   2. parleriez négativement de votre plus grand ennemi

La maison de vos fantasmes?

Une cabane au Canada	**25%**
Un bungalow aux Seychelles[1]	24
Un château dans le Périgord[2]	17
Une villa hollywoodienne à Saint-Tropez[3]	13
Un hôtel particulier à Paris	8
Un palais à Marrakech[4]	7
Un loft à New York	3
Sans opinion	3

1. îles de l'océan Indien   2. région de France   3. ville touristique de la Côte d'Azur *(Riviera)*   4. résidence royale au Maroc

Extrait de *L'Express,* 24 mars 1989, pp. 24–31.

A. ANSWERS: 1. Partir, rompre avec la routine   2. Âge, sexe, argent 3. Voyages, argent, travail, maison, bonheur affectif, sexualité, éternité 4. Plus juste, plus démocratique, plus pacifique   5. Devenir célèbre, vivre cent ans   6. Odorante comme une miche de pain

4 Le texte

A. Le texte même.

1. Quel est le fantasme n° 1 des Français?
2. Quels sont les facteurs qui font varier les «images» de l'imagination?
3. Quels sont les sept pôles principaux de l'imagination des Français?
4. Comment les Français rêvent-ils la société?
5. Comment peut-on défier la mort? Donnez deux «solutions» mentionnées dans l'article.
6. Quelle comparaison l'auteur de l'article utilise-t-il pour décrire «la vraie vie»?

B. Le sondage. Quel est l'ordre de préférence des fantasmes suivants? Complétez le tableau. Suivez l'exemple du numéro 1.

fantasme	ordre	derrière	devant
1. être le (la) plus drôle (comique)	3ᵉ	le (la) plus aimé(e)	le (la) plus intelligent(e)
2. être cosmonaute (astronaute)	3ᵉ	berger	navigateur solitaire
3. sauver un enfant de la noyade	1ᵉʳ		faire le tour du monde à la voile
4. créer une entreprise	2ᵉ	vivre en rentier	donner tout aux déshérités
5. avoir un vêtement de chez Christian Dior	6ᵉ	un tableau de Matisse	un tuyau d'initié en Bourse
6. passer le week-end dans un palace	2ᵉ	sur une île déserte	au lit
7. aller en Californie	3ᵉ	Australie	Brésil
8. faire la morale (donner une leçon) aux hommes politiques	2ᵉ	défendre une grande cause	faire une déclaration d'amour
9. vivre dans un hôtel particulier (une maison de luxe) à Paris	5ᵉ	une villa à St Tropez	un palais à Marrakech

VOCABULAIRE ACTIF

un bijou
caché(e)
dépenser
en fait
une étoile
faire le tour du monde
un fantasme, un rêve
quitter
rêver
soi-même
surprenant(e)
un tableau

5 ANSWERS: 1. soi-même; caché; surprenant 2. tombé du ciel; on aurait rêvé; à soi 3. effectivement; en fait 4. la coupe du monde 5. quitter; dépenser (de l'argent) 6. un bijou; une caisse (de vin); un tableau 7. votre propre publicité

5 **Les mots.** Utilisez le contexte et la logique pour trouver dans l'article les mots qui ont le sens suivant. Vous avez déjà vu certains de ces mots.

1. Premier paragraphe: *oneself; hidden; surprising*
2. Deuxième paragraphe: *heaven-sent; one would have dreamed; one's own*
3. Troisième paragraphe: *actually* (Trouvez un synonyme dans le deuxième paragraphe.)
4. Sondage «L'exploit... »: *the World Cup*
5. Sondage «Si vous gagniez... »: *leaving (someone or something); to spend money*
6. Sondage «Le cadeau... »: *a jewel; a case (of wine); a painting*
7. Sondage «Si on vous offrait... »: *your own advertisement*

Et vous?

FOLLOW-UP: For #2 (if time allows): Have each group choose one section of their new survey and poll their classmates.

1. L'article donne les sept grands pôles de l'imagination des Français. À votre avis, est-ce que ces pôles seraient les mêmes pour les Américains? Dans le même ordre? En groupes de quatre ou cinq personnes, discutez les différences possibles et préparez un rapport pour la classe.
2. Si ce sondage s'adressait au public américain, est-ce que les questions seraient les mêmes? Par exemple, pour les professions, est-ce que «médecin volontaire» ou «berger» seraient mentionnés? Avec vos partenaires, reprenez chaque partie du sondage et faites les changements que vous jugez nécessaires.

3. L'auteur de l'article dit que les Français rêvent de retourner à «la vraie vie, odorante comme une miche de pain». Que pensez-vous de cette image? Quelles sont les autres images qui vous viennent à l'esprit quand vous pensez à «la vraie vie»? Avec un(e) partenaire, faites une liste de huit à dix images, puis comparez votre liste avec celles de vos camarades de classe.

STRUCTURE: Hypothesizing
Le conditionnel (II)

Observez et déduisez

Des vacances de rêve sur une île déserte.

Fantasmes et rêves...

— Si je gagnais 10 millions de francs à la loterie, je dépenserais tout mon argent. Je m'achèterais une Ferrari et...
— Si j'avais le temps, j'arrêterais de travailler et je ferais le tour du monde.
— Si j'étais riche et célèbre, je serais sûrement heureux.

> ■ To hypothesize is to predict consequences based on conditions that have not yet occurred. You have already learned (page 396) to hypothesize about probable future events using the following tense sequence:
>
> **si** + **present** + **future**
>
> Si j'ai le temps, j'irai au cinéma ce soir.
>
> ■ When you hypothesize about events that are *less* likely to occur, a different combination of verb tenses is used. Study the preceding examples and complete the following sentences, using the new tense sequence.
>
> Si je gagnais à la loterie, _____ .
> Je serais heureux (-euse) si _____ .
>
> Write the tense sequence below.
>
> **si** + _____ + _____

Vérifiez *Le conditionnel*

■ To hypothesize about imaginary circumstances and consequences, use **si** and the *imperfect* to express the circumstances and the *conditional* to express the consequences.

> Si j'**étais** plus âgé, je **comprendrais** tout!
> *(condition)* → *(consequence)*

■ Either the condition or the consequence clause may come first, but the conditional tense is never used in the **si** clause.

> — **Si** j'avais le temps, je ferais mes devoirs.
> — Et moi, j'irais à la plage **si** j'avais le temps!

ACTIVITÉS

A. Mes rêves. Complétez les phrases suivantes selon vos rêves personnels.

1. Si je gagnais 10 millions de francs à la loterie,

   j'achèterais _____ , et j'irais

   _____ .

2. Si on m'offrait le cadeau de mes rêves,

   je demanderais _____ , et je voudrais aussi

   _____ .

3. Si j'avais la maison de mes rêves,

   j'aurais _____ , et j'habiterais à (en, au, aux)

   _____ .

4. Si j'exerçais la profession de mes rêves,

   je serais _____ , et je travaillerais

   _____ .

5. Si je pouvais réaliser mon plus grand rêve,

   j(e) _____ , et j(e)

   _____ .

Maintenant, interviewez un(e) partenaire et comparez vos réponses. Vos rêves sont-ils semblables ou non? Qui a les rêves les plus grandioses?

➡ *Si tu gagnais 10 millions de francs à la loterie, qu'est-ce que tu achèterais?*

B. Students may use any of the cues as conditions or consequences. Encourage them to improvise.

B. Hypothèses. Parlez de vous et de vos copains (copines) en employant les expressions suivantes. Montrez un rapport logique entre les conditions et les conséquences selon l'exemple.

➡ *Si j'avais le temps et l'argent, je voyagerais dans un pays francophone. Mes copains eux, ils iraient sur une île déserte.*

Si...

être le prof	être célèbre (riche, etc.)
avoir un million de dollars	arrêter de travailler

habiter une île déserte
exercer la profession de
   mes rêves
avoir 35 ans

parler parfaitement le français
voyager dans un pays francophone
avoir le temps
?

C. Gagnants! Pour fêter son ouverture (*grand opening*), une agence de voyage offre un séjour au Québec—tous frais payés, bien sûr! Lisez les renseignements suivants, puis dites ce que les personnes suivantes feraient ou ne feraient pas si elles gagnaient le prix.

➡ *Si j'allais à Québec, je mangerais au restaurant Aux Anciens Canadiens.*

1. vous
2. vos parents
3. votre professeur de français
4. votre camarade de chambre ou un(e) ami(e)

Québec et sa région—sites à visiter

Palais Montcalm On y présente du théâtre, des concerts de musique classique et des spectacles de variétés.

Colisée de Québec Club de hockey Les Nordiques. Les Nordiques représentent la ville de Québec au sein de la Ligue nationale de hockey.

Le vieux quartier

Hôtel du Parlement Premier site historique national du Québec, l'Hôtel du Parlement est un édifice imposant.

Quartier du Petit-Champlain Aujourd'hui, suite à une restauration générale, le quartier du Petit-Champlain rappelle un coquet village au bord du fleuve. Ses rues étroites d'antan sont animées par des musiciens, des clowns et des jongleurs.

Parc des Champs-de-Bataille Créé en 1908, le parc a été le théâtre de la bataille entre les armées anglaise et française dirigées par Wolfe et Montcalm (1759).

D. After groups prepare their lists, have a volunteer elicit responses and compile them on the board. Ask students to predict the changes to which they think you'd agree. ALTERNATIVE: Prepare your own list of statements you predict students will make, and compare your predictions with their actual responses.

D. Remue-méninges. La profession de vos rêves: *professeur de français?!* Peut-être pas... mais imaginez de toute façon. Si vous étiez le professeur pendant une semaine, qu'est-ce que vous feriez? Qu'est-ce que vous ne feriez pas? Qu'est-ce que vous changeriez? Préparez une liste avec des camarades de classe.

➡ *Si nous étions le professeur, nous regarderions des films français tous les jours.*

STRATÉGIE DE COMMUNICATION
Expressing obligation, regret, disapproval, and empathy

Neglecting obligations can lead to regret (our own) and the disapproval of others—or occasionally their reassurances! Read the following conversation and identify the expressions used

- to describe obligations
- to express regret
- to show disapproval
- to empathize

Deux amies se retrouvent après des années sans s'être vues. Elles parlent de leurs ambitions, de leurs rêves et de leurs efforts pour les réaliser.

For **Si j'avais su,** ask students to identify the infinitive, then infer the meaning of the expression. It is presented here as a lexical item.

— Je me souviens que tu voulais devenir chef d'entreprise et gagner beaucoup d'argent!
— C'est vrai, mais pour cela j'aurais dû finir mes études. Je me suis mariée très jeune et j'ai abandonné mes études. Comme j'ai été bête! Si j'avais su alors ce que je sais maintenant!
— Bof! Ne t'en fais pas! Ça arrive à tout le monde de faire des bêtises quand on est jeune. Tu vas voir: tout va s'arranger. Tu as encore le temps...
— Tu as raison, mais ma mère n'arrête pas de me dire: «Tu aurais dû finir tes études. Tu as eu tort de croire que ton avenir était assuré une fois mariée.» Maintenant je dois recommencer à zéro; tu crois que je devrais reprendre mes études?

Pour exprimer l'obligation, le regret, la désapprobation, le réconfort

L'obligation	Le réconfort
Je dois...	Ne t'inquiète pas.
Je devais...	Ne t'en fais pas.
Je devrais...	Ce n'est pas grave.
	Ça arrive à tout le monde.
	Tout va s'arranger.

Le regret	La désapprobation
Comme j'ai été bête!	Quelle bêtise!
Que je suis bête!	Tu as (eu) tort de...
J'ai eu tort de...	Tu aurais dû... / Tu n'aurais pas dû...
J'aurais dû... / Je n'aurais pas dû...	
Si j'avais su...	

ACTIVITÉS

E. De quoi parle-t-on? Complétez les conversations suivantes d'une façon logique. Travaillez avec un(e) camarade de classe.

1. — Oh, là, là. Quelle mauvaise note! J'aurais dû

    _____ .

    — Mais ça arrive à tout le monde de temps en temps.

2. — Je devrais _____ , mais je n'ai pas le

    temps. Zut!

    — Ce n'est pas grave. Je peux le faire pour toi.

3. — Comme j'ai été bête! Je devais _____ ,

    mais _____ .

    — Ne t'inquiète pas! Tout va s'arranger.

4. — Quelle bêtise! Tu as eu tort de _____ . Tu

    aurais dû _____ .

    — C'est vrai. Si j'avais su...

F. Excuses. Essayez d'expliquer les situations suivantes de manière à solliciter la sympathie.

➡ Vous dépensez trop d'argent pour vous amuser, et maintenant vous n'avez pas assez d'argent pour payer le loyer.
C'est vrai que je n'ai pas l'argent pour le loyer, mais j'ai dû acheter beaucoup de manuels de classe ce semestre.

1. Vous n'êtes pas diligent(e) au travail, et maintenant on pense vous renvoyer *(fire you)*.
2. Vous ne faites jamais vos devoirs, et vous avez raté vos examens.
3. Vous n'avez jamais le temps de sortir avec vos copains, et maintenant ils ne vous téléphonent plus.
4. Vous mangez mal et vous ne faites jamais d'exercice; maintenant, vous êtes vraiment malade.

Maintenant, mettez vos «excuses» à l'essai avec vos camarades de classe. Vont-ils réagir avec désapprobation *(Tu as eu tort de...)* ou réconfort *(Ne t'en fais pas)*?

 Jeu de rôle

Everyone has regrets in life. With a classmate, role-play a scene between old friends who are commiserating over missed opportunities. One has a profession s/he no longer enjoys and regrets not having pursued a different major in college. The other regrets a relationship that didn't work out and wishes s/he had done things differently.

W
B

CULTURE ET RÉFLEXION

Aminata Sow Fall est considérée comme la femme écrivain la plus éminente de l'Afrique franco-phone actuelle. Auteur de *La Grève des Bàttu* (*The Beg-gars' Strike,* 1979) et *L'Appel des Arènes* (*The Call of the Ring,* 1982), qui ont reçu de grands prix litté-raires internationaux, Aminata Sow Fall vient de publier son sixième roman, *Douceurs du Bercail* (*Sweetness of Home,* 1998), qui a déjà été traduit en plusieurs langues. Ses autres activités incluent la direction du Centre pour l'étude des civilisations au Ministère de la culture du Sénégal, la fonda-tion du Bureau africain pour la défense des libertés des écrivains, des conférences aux quatre coins du monde, et une intervention comme invitée d'honneur aux Nations Unies (janvier 1999). Ici, elle écrit, expressément pour *Mais oui!,* ses pensées sur les soucis et rêves de l'Afrique.

Internet

■ Soucis et rêves de l'Afrique
L'Afrique: on serait tenté de dire «la Terre des soucis». Le continent est en effet rongé[1] par mille et un fléaux[2] qui sont autant de facteurs d'anéantissement[3]. Et chaque jour apporte son lot[4] de calamités naturelles ou d'incendies attisés[5] par l'ambition et la déraison. Les champs de mort au Rwanda sont encore fumants[6] sous la clameur désespérée des rescapés[7] du génocide et voici que les armes tonnent encore[8] en République du Congo, à Brazzaville, en Guinée-Bissau, au Lesotho, faisant écho aux bombes qui sèment[9] l'horreur en Algérie. Le tout sur fond de misère, d'analphabétisme, de dictature[10] (Eh oui, en cette ère de démocratie!).

Mais je veux rêver. Quel-que chose au fond de moi me dit que ce géant blessé va se relever[11]; que ce grand malade va se secouer pour se débarrasser[12] de tous ses complexes et pesanteurs[13] pour mieux capter ses éner-gies morales et spirituelles dangereusement diluées dans l'attentisme qui a généré une mentalité d'assisté[14]. Mes rêves de l'Afrique: un continent debout avec un mental de gagneur[15], avec une voix[16] réelle au concert des Nations, avec la volonté[17] réelle d'exister. Et je sais que le rêve n'est pas utopie: il y a le soleil, les rires, le bleu du ciel, une faune et une flore magnifiques. Et il y a des hommes et des femmes qui savent écouter et aimer, qui croient en la culture, donc à l'Humain.

Aminata Sow Fall

Aminata Sow Fall (Dakar, octobre 1998)

D'après ce texte, quels sont les soucis de l'Afrique? Quelles sont les calamités politiques et sociales mentionnées? Qu'est-ce que «ce géant blessé», «ce grand malade» doit faire pour «se relever» et chanter «avec une voix réelle au concert des Nations»? Qu'est-ce qu'il y a en Afrique qui indique que le rêve n'est pas une utopie? Et vous, comment voyez-vous l'avenir de l'Afrique? Si l'on vous demandait d'écrire un paragraphe ou deux sur les soucis et les rêves de votre pays, que diriez-vous? Essayez...

---

1. attaqué   2. *plagues*   3. destruction   4. sa dose   5. *fires fed by*   6. *still smoking*   7. survivants   8. *the thunder of gunfire is still heard up*   12. *is going to shake off*   13. inertie   14. *diluted in the wait-and-see attitude of welfare recipients*   15. *a winning attitude*   16. *voice*   17. le désir   9. *sow*   10. *All these on a background of misery, illiteracy, and dictatorship*   11. *get back*

Troisième étape

À l'écoute: Peurs et phobies

This input introduces vocabulary about fears and phobias, and some new pronouns to link ideas together or avoid repetition.

Dans cette étape, vous allez entendre plusieurs personnes répondre à la question «Qu'est-ce qui vous fait peur?»

Avant d'écouter

1 Qu'est-ce qui vous fait peur? Le noir (l'obscurité)? La solitude? La foule (une multitude de gens)? Certains animaux? Les examens? L'avenir? Le chômage? La mort? En groupes de quatre ou cinq, faites une liste des peurs communes pour les catégories de personnes dans le tableau, puis indiquez vos peurs personnelles.

les jeunes enfants	les adolescents	les étudiants	les gens qui commencent carrière et/ou famille	les gens âgés	vous

Écoutons

2 ANSWER: une personne âgée, une étudiante, un adolescent, une petite fille

Audio CD

2 Écoutez d'abord pour identifier à quelles catégories du tableau d'**Avant d'écouter** les personnes interviewées appartiennent (si on le sait) et cochez-les dans le tableau. Est-ce que vous reconnaissez certaines peurs que vos camarades de classe et vous avez mentionnées dans le même tableau? Si oui, cochez-les aussi.

3 Qui a peur de quoi? Écoutez encore et complétez le tableau suivant.

Qui...	... a peur de quoi?
l'étudiante	du chômage
la 1re personne	des maladies
le copain de la 3e personne	de tout
le copain de la 3e personne	des araignées (*spiders*), des chiens
la petite fille	des ascenseurs
le copain de la 3e personne	des espaces clos (fermés)
la 3e personne	de rien

VOCABULAIRE ACTIF

un animal / des animaux
une araignée
faire peur (à)
la foule
l'obscurité (f.)
la solitude
supporter (je ne peux pas supporter...)

4 Écoutez une dernière fois, complétez les phrases suivantes, puis déduisez le sens des expressions en caractères gras.

1. Les maladies dont le monsieur âgé a peur sont <u>le cancer</u> ou les **attaques cérébrales.** Il a peur de <u>perdre</u> ses facultés et donc de devenir **un fardeau** pour les autres.

2. La jeune fille dit qu'il y a <u>10</u> pour cent de **chômeurs** dans l'ensemble de la population active, mais que <u>20</u> pour cent des jeunes de moins de <u>25</u> ans cherchent un emploi.

3. La personne **claustrophobe** ne peut pas **supporter** les <u>portes</u> fermées, les pièces dont les <u>fenêtres</u> ne s'ouvrent pas, les <u>avions</u> , etc.

5 Racontez l'histoire de la petite fille!

Note culturelle

Promotion de l'emploi des jeunes.   To try to alleviate unemployment among the youth, in the last few years the French government has instituted some programs to encourage employers to hire young people. One such program, the SIVP (Stages d'insertion dans la vie professionnelle), allows newcomers to the job market to get practical experience in private companies for three to six months through government subsidies.

STRUCTURE: Avoiding repetition (V)
*Le pronom **en***

Observez et déduisez

Le chômage? Mais bien sûr que j'en ai peur.
De l'argent? J'en ai besoin, comme tout le monde. J'ai des enfants à nourrir—en fait, j'en ai trois. Et des soucis, j'en ai trop.

> ■ The pronoun **en** is used several times in the preceding paragraph. To what or whom does it refer in each case? What can you infer about the placement of this pronoun in relation to the verbs in the sentences?

Vérifiez *Le pronom **en***

■ The pronoun **en** is used with verbal expressions requiring the preposition **de** such as **avoir peur (honte, besoin, envie) de** and **parler de.***

> Vous avez peur **du chômage?**   Bien sûr que j'**en** ai peur.

■ Use **en** to replace a noun preceded by the following:

an indefinite or a partitive article (see page 163),

> Vous cherchez **du travail?**   Bien sûr que j'**en** cherche. Je suis au chômage.

a number,

> Vous avez **deux enfants?**   Non, j'**en** ai trois.

or an expression of quantity.

> Vous avez **beaucoup de soucis?**   J'**en** ai trop.

■ The pronoun **en** takes the same position in the sentence as other object pronouns, that is, before the verb of which it is the object.

> Des interviews? J'**en** ai déjà eu plusieurs—sans résultats positifs.

ACTIVITÉS

A. All students need do in this activity is recognize and underline the complements that could be replaced by the pronoun.

A. Premier brouillon (*First draft*).   Un étudiant de français fait ses devoirs; il écrit un paragraphe qui s'intitule *Un copain peureux*. Aidez-le à compléter son premier brouillon en soulignant tous les compléments qui sont répétés.

> Martin a vraiment peur de tout. Par exemple, il est claustrophobe, alors il a peur des espaces clos. Il parle des espaces clos tout le temps parce qu'il y a beaucoup d'espaces clos là où il travaille: l'ascenseur, le cabinet de toilette, son bureau! Il a besoin de fenêtres, mais son bureau n'a pas de fenêtre. En plus, Martin a peur des chiens. Malheureusement, sa petite amie a trois chiens. Euh, les espaces clos, les chiens, quoi d'autre? L'eau? Oui, il a peur de l'eau. Les insectes? Oui, il a peur des insectes. La maladie et la mort? Bien sûr qu'il a peur de la maladie et la mort. Je te dis, il a peur de tout!

B. Do this activity as a class, calling on volunteers to read the sentences aloud using the pronouns.

B. Deuxième brouillon.   Regardez encore le paragraphe de l'activité A. Cette fois-ci, aidez l'étudiant à mieux rédiger son paragraphe en remplaçant les compléments que vous avez soulignés par le pronom **en.** Attention au placement du pronom.

---

*But remember to use a stress pronoun to replace a person:

Tu as peur du professeur? Mais non, je n'ai pas peur de **lui.**

The goal of activities C and D is to help students develop an automatic association between the pronoun **en** and certain verbal expressions.

C. Read the cues as students underline their reactions. As you read the cues a second time, have students raise their hands for each option to determine the most common responses. CUES: 1. la maladie 2. l'argent 3. mes notes en français 4. une Ferrari 5. la politique 6. des amis 7. des petit(e)s ami(e)s 8. du chocolat

C. Moi? Écoutez le professeur et soulignez la réponse qui exprime le mieux votre réaction personnelle.

➡ (la maladie) J'en ai peur. ou: Je n'en ai pas peur.

1. J'en ai peur. / Je n'en ai pas peur.
2. J'en ai besoin. / Je n'en ai pas besoin.
3. J'en ai honte. / Je n'en ai pas honte.
4. J'en ai envie. / Je n'en ai pas envie.
5. J'en parle souvent. / Je n'en parle pas souvent.
6. J'en ai beaucoup. / Je n'en ai pas beaucoup.
7. J'en ai deux. / Je n'en ai pas.
8. J'en voudrais. / Je n'en veux pas.

Quelles sont les réactions les plus communes de la classe?

D. Begin by eliciting possible complements: «De quoi a-t-on besoin?» Have partners/groups develop the survey questions, then conduct the surveys.

D. Sondage. Pensez à quatre compléments logiques pour les expressions verbales suivantes. Employez-les pour préparer un sondage avec un(e) camarade de classe.

➡ avoir peur de (le cancer, les ascenseurs, rater les cours, etc.)
Tu as peur des ascenseurs? (du cancer? de rater tes cours?...)

avoir peur de
avoir besoin de
avoir envie de
vouloir
avoir honte de
en parler de

Ensuite, faites le sondage et répondez aux questions des autres, en employant **en,** bien sûr!

➡ — *Tu as peur des ascenseurs?*
— *Non, je n'en ai pas peur.*

Maintenant, présentez les résultats de votre sondage à la classe.

➡ *Six personnes ont peur des ascenseurs...*

E. First ask students whether or not they discuss certain topics (chosen from the survey) with their parents or friends (Parlez-vous de vos études avec vos parents? Oui, nous **en** parlons, etc.). Next, ask students to look at the survey results and say how many young French people discuss certain topics with their parents or friends (Est-ce que beaucoup de jeunes Français parlent du cinéma avec leurs copains? Il y **en** a beaucoup / Il y **en** a 67% qui **en** parlent, etc.).

E. Peur de parler? Avez-vous peur de parler de certains sujets avec votre famille ou est-ce qu'il y a simplement certaines choses que vous préférez discuter avec vos copains/copines? D'abord, répondez aux questions du professeur selon votre expérience personnelle. Ensuite, lisez les résultats du sondage suivant et discutez-en.

Ils en parlent

Les sujets dont les 15–24 ans parlent le plus fréquemment avec leurs parents sont: le travail (61%), l'argent (51%), l'avenir (51%), la vie de famille (46%), les études (46%), l'actualité (45%). Les sujets dont ils parlent le plus fréquemment avec leurs amis sont: les vacances ou les week-ends (78%), le cinéma (67%), la musique (59%), la prochaine sortie (57%), le travail (49%), l'avenir (46%), les sports (43%), l'actualité (42%), les études (41%), les vêtements (40%).

Le Français dans le monde, N° 246

STRUCTURE: Relating / linking ideas (II)
*Les pronoms relatifs **dont** et **où***

Observez et déduisez   Alexis Duhamel, 76 ans: «C'est la maladie qui me fait peur. Perdre mon indépendance, être un fardeau pour mes enfants, voilà des situations que je veux absolument éviter.»

Rémi Wéry, 27 ans: «Moi, je suis claustrophobe. Ce sont les espaces clos dont j'ai peur.»

Claudine Garnier, 8 ans: «J'ai peur des ascenseurs. Je me souviens bien du jour où l'ascenseur est parti sans maman... »

- In Chapter 8 (page 290), you learned that the relative pronouns **qui** and **que** are used to combine two sentences. They refer back to a noun (the antecedent) in the first clause. In the first example above, to which nouns do **qui** and **que** refer?

- **Où** and **dont** are also relative pronouns. In the last two examples, to which nouns do **où** and **dont** refer?

Vérifiez   *Les pronoms relatifs **dont** et **où***

VOCABULAIRE ACTIF

Les pronoms relatifs
dont
où

- Remember that the relative pronouns **qui** and **que** introduce a relative clause and that both can refer to people or things.

- The pronoun **dont** also introduces a relative clause and is used for both people and things. Use **dont** to say *whose.*

> Madame Wéry est la femme **dont** le mari est claustrophobe.
> Il ne supporte pas les pièces **dont** les fenêtres ne s'ouvrent pas.

- **Dont** is also used to replace a noun preceded by the preposition **de.**

> Voilà l'espace clos.   +   Il a peur de l'espace clos.
> Voilà l'espace clos **dont** il a peur.

> Voilà le psychiatre.   +   Il a besoin d'un psychiatre.
> Voilà le psychiatre **dont** il a besoin.

■ The pronoun **où** introduces a relative clause referring to a place *(where)* or a time *(when)*.

> C'est l'ascenseur **où** la petite fille a eu peur.
> Elle se souvient bien du jour **où** elle a perdu sa mère.

ACTIVITÉS

F. Réponses révélatrices. Qu'est-ce que les réponses aux phrases suivantes révèlent sur votre personnalité? Écrivez une réponse personnelle qui convient à chaque phrase.

➡ C'est la chose dont j'ai le plus besoin. *Plus de temps! (De l'argent...)*
C'est le mois où je suis le (la) plus occupé(e). *Novembre (Mai...)*

1. C'est le sujet dont je parle le plus avec mes copains.
2. C'est le talent dont j'ai le plus envie.
3. C'est le défaut personnel dont j'ai le plus honte.
4. C'est une qualité dont je suis fier (-ère) *(proud)*.
5. C'est le cours où j'ai le plus de confiance en moi.
6. C'est le jour de fête où je m'amuse le plus.
7. C'est l'endroit où je me sens le (la) plus libre.
8. C'est le moment de la journée où je peux vraiment me reposer.

Maintenant, comparez vos réponses avec celles d'un(e) partenaire. Quelles sont les réponses les plus amusantes? les plus bizarres?

G. Il n'a plus peur. Un copain vous montre plusieurs photos d'Antoine, un petit garçon qu'il connaissait autrefois. Racontez son histoire en employant **où** et **dont** pour relier les phrases suivantes.

➡ Je vais te montrer l'album. Je mets mes photos dans cet album.
Je vais te montrer l'album où je mets mes photos.

1. Voici le petit Antoine. Je t'ai parlé d'Antoine l'autre jour.
2. Voici la petite maison. Il habitait dans cette maison.
3. Et voilà le chien. Il avait peur de ce chien.
4. Voici le jardin. Le chien l'a chassé *(chased)* dans ce jardin.
5. C'était un jour de fête. Je me souviens bien de ce jour.
6. Voilà la piscine du quartier. Antoine est tombé dans la piscine.
7. Voici Monsieur Fido. Le chien de Monsieur Fido a sauvé Antoine de la noyade *(drowning)*.
8. Voilà Antoine avec le chien. Il n'avait plus peur du chien.

H. Begin by having students recall cues for the different pronouns: **de** for **dont**; place/time for **où**; **qui** + verb; **que** + subject/verb.

H. Aucune crainte! Valérie n'a peur de rien. Dans les phrases suivantes, elle exprime son opinion sur des phobies ordinaires. Complétez les phrases avec le pronom correct: **qui, que, où, dont.**

1. Les chiens?! Mais, un chien est un animal <u>que</u> tout le monde adore.

2. Les ascenseurs?! Mais un ascenseur est simplement un endroit <u>où</u> on entre pour monter et descendre.

3. La foule?! Mais la foule est un groupe de gens <u>qui</u> sont comme vous.

4. Le chômage?! Le chômage est une situation économique <u>dont</u>
personne n'est content, mais <u>qui</u> est temporaire.

5. L'eau?! L'eau est une substance <u>dont</u> tout le monde a besoin.

6. Les cimetières *(cemeteries)*?! Mais un cimetière est un endroit
<u>où</u> on n'a plus peur de rien!

7. Les araignées?! Les araignées sont des animaux <u>que</u> beaucoup
de gens n'aiment pas mais <u>qui</u> ont une fonction importante
dans la nature et <u>dont</u> le monde a vraiment besoin.

8. Le vendredi treize?! Mais le vendredi treize est le jour <u>où</u> on
s'amuse le plus!

9. La mort?! Eh bien, la mort est un phénomène <u>dont</u> tout le
monde a peur!

Êtes-vous d'accord avec les opinions exprimées? Discutez en petits groupes,
et changez les phrases avec lesquelles le groupe n'est pas d'accord.

➡ *Les araignées sont importantes à la nature, mais quelquefois elles sont
dangereuses aussi.*

Finalement, présentez vos idées aux autres groupes.

 Jeu de rôle

Role-play a scene between the French student in activity A (page 437) and
his fearful friend Martin. Martin expresses his many fears and phobias while
his friend tries to encourage him by explaining what he would do in each
case. (If I couldn't find work in my field, I'd . . . , If I were claustrophobic . . . , If
I were stuck in an elevator . . . , etc.)

   **Now that you have finished the Troisième étape of this chapter, do your Lab Man-
ual activities with the audio program. Explore chapter topics further with the
Mais oui! Video and CD-ROM. Viewing and comprehension activities are in the
video section of your *Workbook/Lab Manual/Video Manual*.**

Intégration

Littérature: Les Choses

Born in Paris in 1936, Georges Perec was the only child of a Jewish couple who had emigrated from Poland. His father was killed in World War II in 1940, and his mother died at the Auschwitz concentration camp in 1943. Left orphaned at age 7, Georges was raised by an aunt and uncle, and soon found refuge in what would be his life's passion: writing. From about 1960 until 1982, when he died of cancer, he devoted himself to being a novelist, essayist, and poet.

Known as **«un virtuose de la langue»,** Perec challenged himself with all kinds of language experiments. For example, he wrote a whole novel, *La Disparition,* without the most common vowel in French, the letter *e!* He also wrote a puzzle-novel, *La Vie, mode d'emploi (Life, Operating Instructions),* in which the reader is expected to piece the different parts of the novel together. *Les Choses,* Perec's first published novel (1965), was an instant success. It is the story of a young middle-class couple, Jérôme and Sylvie, whose quest for happiness in material possessions, **«les choses»,** ends in broken dreams and a sense of emptiness. The novel also experiments with moods and tenses: the story starts out in the conditional, then moves to the past, and ends in the future. In the opening chapter, Jérôme and Sylvie depict in great detail each room of their would-be apartment—the perfect setting for the perfect life.

Avant de lire

1 Read questions aloud for the whole class, then have students discuss in small groups and report.

1 Décrivez votre maison ou votre appartement idéal.

1. Quelles choses est-ce qu'il y aurait sur les murs? (des livres? des objets d'art? des photos?)
2. Est-ce que vous préféreriez les couleurs vives *(bright)* ou les couleurs douces? La lumière *(light)* et les choses lumineuses, ou l'obscurité et les choses sombres?
3. Est-ce que les pièces seraient en ordre ou en désordre? Est-ce que vous auriez une femme de ménage (une employée) pour nettoyer la maison et y mettre de l'ordre?

En général

2 ANSWER: 1. une cuisine

2 Parcourez le texte une première fois en pensant aux questions suivantes.

1. Quelle pièce est décrite dans cet extrait?
2. Les goûts de Jérôme et de Sylvie sont-ils semblables aux vôtres? Reprenez les questions d'**Avant de lire** et trouvez les points que vous avez en commun.

3 Dans quel paragraphe trouve-t-on les idées suivantes? Reliez les paragraphes et les idées.

¶1 «La vie, là,... »   a. L'harmonie des choses et de la vie
¶2 «Ils ouvriraient... »   b. Le petit déjeuner
¶3 «Leur appartement... »   c. L'anticipation du bonheur
¶4 «Il leur semblerait... »   d. Les activités du matin, après le
¶5 «Ils savaient... »   petit déjeuner
                              e. Le charme de l'appartement

Les choses

1   La vie, là, serait facile, serait simple. Toutes les obligations, tous les problèmes qu'implique la vie matérielle trouveraient une solution naturelle. Une femme de ménage serait là chaque matin. Il y aurait une cuisine vaste et claire, avec des carreaux° bleus, trois assiettes de faïence° décorées d'arabesques jaunes, des placards° partout, une belle table de bois blanc au centre, des tabourets°, des bancs°. Il serait agréable de venir s'y asseoir, chaque matin, après une douche, à peine° habillé. Il y aurait sur la table des pots de marmelade, du beurre, des toasts, des pamplemousses° coupés en deux.

tiles / stoneware
cabinets
stools / benches
hardly
grapefruit

2   Ils ouvriraient les journaux. Ils sortiraient. Leur travail ne les retiendrait que quelques heures, le matin. Ils se retrouveraient pour déjeuner; ils prendraient un café à une terrasse, puis rentreraient chez eux, à pied, lentement.

3   Leur appartement serait rarement en ordre mais son désordre même serait son plus grand charme. Leur attention serait ailleurs: dans le livre qu'ils ouvriraient, dans le texte qu'ils écriraient, dans le disque qu'ils écouteraient, dans leur dialogue.

4   Il leur semblerait° parfois qu'une vie entière pourrait harmonieusement s'écouler° entre ces murs couverts de livres, entre ces choses belles et simples, douces, lumineuses.

Il... Ils penseraient
se passer

5   Ils savaient ce qu'ils voulaient; ils avaient des idées claires°. Ils savaient ce que seraient leur bonheur, leur liberté. Il leur arrivait d'avoir° peur. Mais le plus souvent, ils étaient seulement impatients: ils se sentaient prêts; ils étaient disponibles: ils attendaient de vivre, ils attendaient l'argent. Ils aimaient la richesse avant d'aimer la vie.

précises
Il... Parfois ils avaient

Extrait de *Les Choses* (Georges Perec)

En détail   **4** **Les mots.** Utilisez le contexte et la logique pour déduire le sens des expressions en caractères gras ci-dessous et à la page 444.

¶1 «... des pamplemousses **coupés en deux.**»
   a. two by two   b. cut in half

¶2 «Leur travail **ne les retiendrait que** quelques heures... »
   a. would only keep them   b. would not keep them

¶3 «Leur attention serait **ailleurs...** »
   a. elsewhere   b. nowhere

¶4 «... **couverts de livres**... »
a. book covers   b.) covered with books

¶5 «... ils se sentaient **prêts**; ils étaient **disponibles**... »
a.) ready / available   b. close / busy

5 **Le texte.**   Les phrases suivantes sont-elles vraies ou fausses? Justifiez vos réponses.

1. Jérôme et Sylvie n'auraient pas de soucis matériels.
2. Une femme de ménage viendrait une fois par semaine.
3. Les placards de la cuisine seraient décorés d'arabesques jaunes.
4. Ils prendraient une douche avant le petit déjeuner.
5. Ils prendraient le déjeuner ensemble.
6. Ils rentreraient chez eux en voiture.
7. Les livres, les disques, leurs activités et leur conversation seraient plus importants que l'ordre ou le désordre de leur appartement.
8. Ils seraient heureux de passer toute leur vie dans cet appartement.
9. Ils acceptaient le présent avec patience.
10. Ils aimaient la vie plus que l'argent.

Et vous?

1. La journée idéale—qu'est-ce que vous feriez? À la manière de Jérôme et Sylvie, décrivez ce que vous feriez du matin jusqu'au soir. Décrivez aussi les choses qui seraient autour de vous aux différents moments de cette journée.
2. Jérôme avait 24 ans et Sylvie en avait 22 quand ils ont tous les deux abandonné leurs études universitaires pour prendre des emplois temporaires, avec l'espoir de vite gagner beaucoup d'argent. Ont-ils eu raison? Imaginez que vous parlez à Jérôme ou à Sylvie au moment de leur décision. Divisez-vous en deux groupes: un groupe sera pour les études, et l'autre contre. Préparez d'abord une liste de conseils et d'arguments. Ensuite essayez vos conseils et arguments sur le professeur qui jouera le rôle de Jérôme ou de Sylvie. Qui aura les meilleurs arguments?

   ➡ *À ta place, je finirais / j'abandonnerais mes études parce que...*
   ou: *Tu devrais finir / abandonner tes études parce que...*
   Si tu finissais / abandonnais tes études, tu pourrais...

3. «Ils attendaient de vivre, ils attendaient l'argent.» Parfois, on «attend de vivre», comme un enfant avant de commencer l'école, par exemple, ou un(e) étudiant(e) avant de commencer «la vraie vie» du monde professionnel. En groupes de deux ou trois, faites une liste de situations où, parfois, on «attend de vivre». Pour chacune de ces situations, indiquez ce qu'on attend, et les dangers ou les avantages de cette anticipation.
4. «Ils aimaient la richesse avant d'aimer la vie.» En groupes de deux, contrastez l'attitude, les priorités et les actions des gens dans les deux catégories suivantes. Trouvez au moins cinq contrastes.

Les gens qui aiment la richesse avant d'aimer la vie	**Les gens qui aiment la vie avant d'aimer la richesse**

Par écrit: If only . . .

A. Strategy: Looping. Often one of the most difficult prewriting tasks is narrowing the focus of the topic. Looping, a technique involving several stages of prewriting, is designed to help you do just that: decide on which elements of a broad theme you will concentrate. Begin looping by freewriting (writing without stopping) for five to ten minutes on the assigned subject. Next, stop and read what you've written, consciously seeking out the "center of gravity," the feature that seems to prevail. Once you've identified this focal point of the first "loop," use it as the topic for the next five to ten minutes of freewriting, the second loop. The process can be repeated as often as necessary until you feel you have clearly identified the focus of the paper you wish to write.

Application. Practice looping using one of the following topics:

> Mon plus grand rêve
> La maison de mes rêves

B. Strategy: Adding variety through analogy. An analogy is an attempt to explain or describe something by comparing it to something else, often something that at first glance may seem totally unrelated. You are probably familiar with the use of similes and metaphors in literature to express analogies. In French, descriptions can also be enhanced through the use of these stylistic techniques, for example:

> Ma maison est vieille **comme** le monde,
> elle **ressemble à** une cabane,
> mais **c'est** une forteresse contre le temps.

Application. Now try creating three analogies of your own using the topic **Ma maison** and the preceding examples as models.

ÉCRIVEZ

Remind students to use the conditional tense in hypothesizing.

1. Dans l'extrait de *Les Choses*, Jérôme et Sylvie imaginent une maison parfaite, une vie idéale. À vous maintenant de décrire la maison de vos rêves. Comment serait-elle? Qu'est-ce qu'elle aurait? n'aurait pas? Qu'est-ce qui s'y passerait? Avant d'écrire, décidez quel sera le point de départ de votre description: les *choses*—ce qu'il y aurait (le décor et les objets matériels); les *activités*—ce que vous y feriez; ou *autres choses*—les rêves familiaux, les expériences partagées, les valeurs, les éléments immatériels. Limitez votre sujet en employant la technique décrite dans **Avant d'écrire** (A).
2. Si votre bonne fée *(fairy godmother)* vous accordait votre plus grand désir, qu'est-ce que ça serait? Décrivez ce qui se passerait si vous aviez cette bonne fortune. Est-ce que vous achèteriez quelque chose? Iriez-vous quelque part? Feriez-vous quelque chose d'extraordinaire? Donnez autant de détails que possible.

VOCABULAIRE ACTIF

La santé et les maladies (f.)

une attaque cérébrale *a stroke*
une bronchite *bronchitis*
le cancer *cancer*
une crise cardiaque *a heart attack*
la grippe *the flu*
une indigestion *indigestion*

une migraine *a migraine*
mort(e) *dead*
une pneumonie *pneumonia*
un rhume *a cold*
le rhume des foins *hay fever*
le sida *AIDS*

Les symptômes (m.)

avoir de la fièvre *to have a fever*
avoir la nausée *to be nauseated*
avoir le nez bouché *to be congested*
avoir le nez qui coule *to have a runny nose*
avoir mal à la tête / à la gorge *to have a
   headache / a sore throat*
se blesser *to get injured / to hurt oneself*
une blessure *a wound*

éternuer *to sneeze*
mourir *to die*
prendre sa température *to take (check) one's temperature*
se sentir mal / mieux / bien *to feel ill / better / well*
tomber malade *to get sick*
tousser *to cough*
la toux *a cough*

Les traitements (m.)

un antibiotique *an antibiotic*
appeler / aller voir le médecin *to call /
   to see the doctor*
de l'aspirine *aspirin*
un comprimé *a tablet*
examiner *to examine*
(faire) une piqûre *to give a shot*

un médicament *a medication*
un pansement *a bandage*
un(e) pharmacien(ne) *a pharmacist*
prescrire *to prescribe*
recommander *to recommend*
un(e) spécialiste *a specialist*
du sirop *syrup*

Les rêves (m.) et les peurs (f.)

un animal (des animaux)
une araignée *a spider*
un bijou (des bijoux) *a jewel*
dépenser (de l'argent) *to spend (money)*
une étoile *a star*
un fantasme *a fantasy*
faire peur à *to scare*
la foule *the crowd*
s'inquiéter *to worry*
la loterie *the lottery*

l'obscurité (f.) *the dark*
quitter (quelqu'un / un endroit)
   to leave (someone / a place)
rêver *to dream*
la solitude *solitude*
un souci *a worry*
supporter (je ne peux pas supporter...)
   to stand (I can't stand / tolerate)
un tableau *a painting*
le tour du monde *a trip around the world*

Adjectifs

caché(e) *hidden*
contagieux (-euse) *contagious*
étrange *strange*

surprenant(e) *surprising*
tranquille *calm*

Expressions communicatives

je dois *I must, have to*
je devais *I was supposed to*
je devrais *I should*
j'aurais dû / je n'aurais pas dû
  I should have / I shouldn't have
si j'avais su *if I had known*
Que je suis bête! / Comme j'ai été bête!
  How stupid of me!

Quelle bêtise! *How stupid!*
J'ai eu tort de... *I was wrong to . . .*
Tant pis pour toi! *Too bad for you!*
Ne t'inquiète pas / Ne t'en fais pas *Don't worry*
Ce n'est pas grave *It's not bad*
Ça arrive à tout le monde *It can happen to anyone*
Tout va s'arranger *Everything is going to be alright*

Pronoms relatifs

dont *whose, of which*
où *where, when*

Divers

en (pronom) *some / . . . of them*
en fait *actually*
soi-même *oneself*

Des questions d'actualité

Quelles sont
les revendications
de ces
manifestants?
Et vous?
À votre avis, quels
sont les problèmes
les plus graves du
monde actuel?
L'immigration et le
racisme? Les
sans-abri? Autre
chose?

This chapter will enable you to

- **read about immigration in France, and the effects of colonialism in Martinique**
- **understand the gist of an appeal by a famous French activist for the homeless (l'abbé Pierre)**
- **express your opinions about social issues**
- **learn the basics of developing an argument in French**

Lecture: L'immigration

Vous allez lire un article qui résume les problèmes de l'immigration en France.

1 L'immigration pose des problèmes sociaux, politiques, culturels et moraux. En groupes de deux ou trois, discutez les questions suivantes.

1. Est-ce qu'un pays «riche» devrait **accueillir les étrangers** (accepter les gens d'autres pays), ou **fermer ses frontières** (borders)? Considérez les circonstances suivantes et, pour chacune, indiquez ce que vous feriez—est-ce que vous accueilleriez les étrangers ou est-ce que vous fermeriez les frontières?
   a. L'économie du pays est bonne; il n'y a pas beaucoup de chômage.
   b. Le pays traverse une crise économique.
   c. Les étrangers sont des réfugiés politiques.
   d. Les étrangers ont des qualifications professionnelles et parlent la langue du pays d'adoption.
   e. Les étrangers n'ont pas de qualifications professionnelles et ne parlent pas la langue du pays d'adoption.
2. Qu'est-ce qu'il faut faire pour s'intégrer à un nouveau pays? (Apprendre la langue? Parler la langue du pays d'adoption à la maison? Abandonner sa culture d'origine? Ignorer les préjugés *[prejudices]?*) Faites une liste de quatre ou cinq éléments qui, selon vous, sont nécessaires à l'intégration.

2 Qui sont les étrangers dans votre pays ou région? Imaginez la situation en France: d'où viennent la plupart des étrangers? Des autres pays européens? D'Afrique? D'Asie? Devinez!

3 Parcourez le texte une première fois en faisant attention à son organisation. Dans quelle partie du texte—(1) **Les étrangers,** (2) **Un cercle vicieux** ou (3) **L'intégration**—se trouvent les renseignements suivants?

Renseignements/sujets	Étrangers	Cercle vicieux	Intégration
a. Handicaps des jeunes étrangers		✓	
b. Les différentes catégories d'étrangers	✓		
c. Conséquences de la crise économique de 1974 sur l'immigration	✓		
d. Comparaison des immigrés autrefois et aujourd'hui			✓
e. Problèmes d'assimilation des musulmans (religion de l'islam)			✓
f. Nouvelles lois (laws) de l'immigration	✓		
g. Raisons possibles pour les actes de délinquance		✓	

4 Maintenant regardez le tableau des pourcentages sur l'évolution de l'immigration. D'où viennent la plupart des étrangers résidant en France actuellement? Est-ce que vos prédictions étaient correctes?

L'immigration en France

Les étrangers

La politique française en matière d'immigration a connu une rupture spectaculaire en 1974: avec la crise économique, la France a fermé ses frontières aux étrangers. Cette crise économique a eu pour conséquence le développement, dans certaines couches° de la population, de sentiments xénophobes° à l'égard des étrangers, accusés de «prendre le travail des Français». Le Front national, le parti d'extrême droite de Jean-Marie le Pen, propose en effet de lutter contre le chômage en rendant «la France aux Français». Les lois Pasqua de 1993 ont ajouté aux mesures de contrôle de l'immigration en réformant le code de la nationalité. Elles stipulent, par exemple, que les enfants nés en France de parents étrangers ne recevront plus automatiquement la nationalité française et que le mariage à une citoyenne ou un citoyen français ne garantit pas la nationalité française. Ces lois sont jugées draconiennes par des organismes comme S.O.S.-Racisme, dont le slogan «Touche pas à mon pote°» prêche la tolérance.

couches : catégories
xénophobes : hostiles

pote : copain

Les étrangers représentent 6 à 8% de la population. Parmi eux, on distingue principalement trois catégories:

• les étrangers installés depuis longtemps, Italiens, Polonais et Espagnols, par exemple: ils sont souvent bien intégrés.

• «les immigrés», Portugais et Maghrébins (Algériens, Marocains ou Tunisiens), auxquels l'économie française a fait appel° à partir des années 60, quand elle était en période d'expansion.

auxquels... que l'économie française a invités

• les réfugiés qui sont venus d'Asie ou d'Europe de l'Est, par exemple, pour des raisons politiques.

Officiellement, la France n'accueille plus de nouveaux immigrants depuis 1974, sauf° pour des cas particuliers: regroupement de familles, personnes susceptibles d'obtenir le statut de réfugié politique, spécialistes dont le pays a besoin. Une immigration clandestine continue cependant.

sauf : excepté

Un cercle vicieux

Les statistiques tendent à montrer que les étrangers ou les Français d'origine étrangère sont plus fréquemment responsables d'actes de délinquance (vols, usage et vente de drogues, etc.). Elles montrent aussi que les jeunes Maghrébins réussissent moins bien leurs études que les Français de souche° ou que les étrangers d'autres origines. Mais ces chiffres°, qui servent à alimenter la xénophobie, sont rarement accompagnés des explications nécessaires. Ils n'indiquent pas, en particulier, que les conditions de vie des enfants d'étrangers sont souvent moins favorables que celles des autres enfants. Si moins de 25% des enfants nés de parents maghrébins obtiennent le baccalauréat, contre 40% en moyenne nationale, c'est parce qu'ils cumulent les handicaps et les retards dès° l'école primaire. Il n'est donc pas étonnant que le taux° de chômage des jeunes d'origine algérienne soit deux fois plus élevé° que celui des jeunes Français. De même, beaucoup de jeunes des cités° se sentent oubliés par la société et les institutions et font preuve d'indifférence ou de délinquance.

de souche : d'origine / *chiffres* : nombres

dès : depuis
taux : pourcentage
élevé : grand
cités : subsidized housing

L'intégration

Les principes révolutionnaires de 1789 défendaient l'idée de l'homme universel. La France considérait que l'intégration des étrangers sur son sol°   territoire
devait se faire par assimilation, c'est à dire par abandon des particularismes
culturels des pays d'origine.

   Autrefois, la plupart des étrangers qui s'installaient en France étaient
européens. Ils avaient les mêmes valeurs judéo-chrétiennes que les
Français, apprenaient la langue française et s'intégraient rapidement.

   Mais l'assimilation est moins facile pour les étrangers qui viennent
d'Afrique du Nord et d'Afrique noire. Les différences culturelles sont plus
marquées, et beaucoup de Français (49%) considèrent que les préceptes de
la religion islamique rendent° l'intégration des immigrés musulmans impos-   font
sible. Le débat sur «le droit° à la différence» ne fait que commencer°.   *the right* / ne... *has only begun*

Extrait de *La France d'aujourd'hui,* CLE International, 1991 (pp. 26–28) et *Francoscopie 1997*
(pp. 205–207).

Plus d'Africains, moins d'Européens

Évolution du nombre d'étrangers en provenance d'Europe, d'Afrique et
d'Asie résidant en France et répartition selon les nationalités aux recense-
ments (en %).

	1954	**1975**	**1982**	**1990**
Nationalités				
d'Europe	84,0%	62,0%	48,5%	41,3%
d'Afrique	13,5%	35,0%	43,5%	46,8%
d'Asie	2,5%	3,0%	8,0%	11,9%
Nombre d'étrangers (en millions)	1,7	3,4	3,6	3,6

▲ 76% des Français estiment qu'il y a trop d'Arabes en France, 46% trop de
Noirs, 40% trop d'Asiatiques, 34% trop d'Européens du Sud (Espagne,
Portugal).

▲ 41% des Français avouent avoir une tendance au racisme.

▲ 49% des étrangers vivant en France souhaitent s'intégrer à la société
française, 38% d'entre eux se sentent déjà intégrés.

INSEE

En détail

You may wish to have students infer
the difference between **immigré**
and **immigrant:** «Le texte mentionne les immigrés et les immigrants.
D'après le contexte et la logique, quel
est le mot qui décrit les étrangers qui
arrivent vs. les étrangers qui sont
déjà arrivés?»

5 **Les mots.**   Utilisez le contexte et la logique pour déduire le sens des mots
en caractères gras.

Les étrangers

1. La politique française en matière d'immigration a connu **une rupture**
   spectaculaire en 1974.
   a. un changement brutal   b. une augmentation
2. Le Front national [...] propose en effet de **lutter** contre le chômage...
   a. se battre   b. encourager

3. Les lois Pasqua stipulent, par exemple, [...] que le mariage à **une citoyenne ou un citoyen** français...
   a. quelqu'un qui habite dans une ville
   b. quelqu'un qui a la nationalité du pays

Un cercle vicieux

4. **Il n'est donc pas étonnant** que le taux de chômage...
   a. Ce n'est donc pas une surprise   b. Ce n'est donc pas logique
5. Beaucoup de jeunes des cités **font preuve** d'indifférence...
   a. regrettent   b. manifestent

6 **Le texte.**   Lisez le texte plus attentivement et répondez aux questions suivantes.

1. Quelles ont été les conséquences de la crise économique de 1974 sur l'immigration en France?
2. De quoi les étrangers sont-ils accusés?
3. Qu'est-ce que c'est que le Front national? Quel est son slogan?
4. Qu'est-ce que les lois Pasqua ont réformé? Donnez un exemple de réforme.
5. Que prêche l'organisme S.O.S.-Racisme? Quel est son slogan?
6. Quelles sont les trois catégories d'étrangers? Qui sont les Maghrébins?
7. Dans quels cas particuliers la France accueille-t-elle encore de nouveaux immigrants?
8. Qu'est-ce que les statistiques montrent? Qu'est-ce qu'elles n'indiquent pas?
9. Quel est le taux de jeunes Maghrébins qui obtiennent le baccalauréat par rapport à la moyenne nationale? Quelles sont les raisons et les conséquences de cette différence?
10. Pourquoi l'intégration des immigrés d'autrefois était-elle plus facile?
11. Pourquoi l'intégration des immigrés d'aujourd'hui est-elle plus difficile?
12. Quel est le pourcentage
    a. d'étrangers dans la population française?
    b. de Français qui disent qu'ils ont tendance à être racistes?
    c. d'étrangers qui étaient originaires d'Afrique en 1954 et en 1990?
    d. d'étrangers qui se sentent bien intégrés à la société française?

6 ANSWERS: 1. La France a fermé ses frontières; sentiments xénophobes 2. de prendre le travail des Français 3. Le parti d'extrême droite. «La France aux Français.» 4. Le code de la nationalité. Être né en France ou mariage avec un citoyen français ne garantissent pas la nationalité française. 5. La tolérance. «Touche pas à mon pote.» 6. Étrangers installés depuis longtemps, immigrés portugais et maghrébins, réfugiés politiques. Les Maghrébins sont les Algériens, les Marocains ou les Tunisiens. 7. Regroupement de familles, réfugiés politiques, spécialistes. 8. Que les étrangers sont plus fréquemment responsables d'actes de délinquance et qu'ils réussissent moins bien leurs études; que les conditions de vie sont souvent moins favorables. 9. 25% par rapport à 40%. Raisons: les jeunes Maghrébins cumulent les handicaps et les retards. Conséquences: chômage, indifférence, délinquance. 10. C'étaient des Européens, qui avaient les mêmes valeurs judéo-chrétiennes et apprenaient la langue. 11. Ce sont des Africains, souvent musulmans, et les différences culturelles sont plus marquées. 12. a. 6 à 8% b. 41% c. 13,5% vs. 46,8% d. 38%

Et vous?

1. Les États-Unis sont un pays d'immigration. Quelles sont les origines de votre famille? Comparez vos origines avec celles de quatre ou cinq camarades de classe.
2. Y a-t-il des «cercles vicieux» pour les gens qui immigrent dans votre pays? Expliquez.
3. Le texte définit l'assimilation comme «l'abandon des particularismes culturels des pays d'origine». Avec deux ou trois partenaires, considérez différents groupes ethniques dans votre pays/région.
   a. Quels sont les particularismes de ces groupes? (Langue, musique, nourriture, fêtes, religion, vêtements, etc.) Faites une liste.

b. Dans la liste que vous venez de faire, quels sont les particularismes qu'il faut «abandonner», selon vous, pour s'intégrer à la société américaine? Quels particularismes est-il bon de garder? Discutez puis comparez vos idées avec celles des autres groupes.

4. Que pensez-vous du «droit à la différence»? Considérez d'abord le cas des jeunes filles islamiques qui habitent en France et qui revendiquent le droit de porter le foulard *(scarf)* islamique dans les écoles publiques.

Le foulard islamique interdit à l'école?

Note that the first part of this activity is primarily a recognition activity—students simply agree or disagree. For the latter part, keep discussion simple, reminding students to use vocabulary and structures they already know, or to pattern answers after the arguments given as examples.

Parmi les arguments suivants, avec lesquels êtes-vous d'accord?

a. Les signes extérieurs de différence encouragent la division; le rôle des écoles publiques est de favoriser l'intégration et non la division; les écoles publiques doivent donc interdire le port *(forbid the wearing)* du foulard islamique.

b. La liberté d'expression garantit le droit de porter des signes religieux. Au nom de la liberté, les écoles publiques doivent donc permettre le port du foulard islamique.

c. Si le port du foulard islamique est un prétexte pour des manifestations nationalistes, il faut l'interdire.

Maintenant pensez aux groupes ethniques que vous connaissez. Quels «droits» veulent-ils? Qu'en pensez-vous?

STRUCTURE: Expressing opinions and desire
Le présent du subjonctif

Observez et déduisez

Des jeunes Français discutent des problèmes de l'intégration.

— À mon avis, il faut que tous les gens qui habitent en France apprennent le français.
— Tiens, que tu es intolérante. Tu es xénophobe? Tu veux que les immigrés abandonnent leur héritage culturel?
— Pas du tout! C'est bien que des gens de cultures différentes habitent en France. Je n'ai pas de préjugés. Mais il vaudrait mieux qu'ils apprennent à parler la langue du pays pour s'intégrer et réussir.

> ■ Find three expressions in the preceding dialogue that are used to indicate an opinion. What word follows each of those expressions?

Vérifiez   *Le présent du subjonctif*

The main purpose of this section is to introduce students to the subtle distinction between the subjunctive and indicative moods. Students may be expected to memorize verb paradigms and to recognize a few high-frequency expressions requiring the subjunctive but not to produce it spontaneously in speech. Thus, activities focus mainly on recognition of the subjunctive and familiarization with key vocabulary related to the input topics.

Tell students that other expressions may also require the subjunctive, but that they will focus on these high-frequency ones.

■ The tenses you have studied so far (past, present, future) have all been in the indicative mood. The indicative mood is used to indicate *facts;* it implies a sense of objectivity. Compare the following statements:

On apprend le français.   Il faut qu'on apprenne le français.

The second sentence is a *subjective* statement of opinion expressed in the *subjunctive* mood.   If students ask, explain that *tense* denotes time, whereas *mood* conveys the speaker's perspective, i.e., how s/he views the situation or topic.

■ The subjunctive occurs in a clause introduced by **que** following certain verbs and impersonal expressions. Use the subjunctive to indicate an *opinion* after **il faut, il vaut (vaudrait) mieux, il est temps,** and **c'est dommage/bien:**

Il vaudrait mieux qu'ils apprennent le français, mais **il ne faut pas** qu'ils abandonnent leur langue maternelle.

or to express *desire* after the verbs **vouloir** and **aimer:**

Je **voudrais que** la discrimination finisse.
J'**aimerais que** nous nous entendions.

The subjunctive is also used following the verbs **regretter** and **douter:**

Nous **regrettons que** notre pays ferme ses frontières.
Je **doute que** les immigrés contribuent aux problèmes économiques.

■ To form the present subjunctive, use the stem of the **ils** form of the present *indicative.*

> ils finiss—   ils parl—
> ils apprenn—   ils sort—

Point out that for the **-er** verbs, these forms are the same as the present of the indicative.

For **je, tu, il/elle/on** and **ils/elles,** add the following endings to the stem.

> que je finiss**e**   que tu apprenn**es**   qu'il parl**e**   qu'elles sort**ent**

The **nous** and **vous** forms are identical to the imperfect; add **-ions** and **-iez** respectively.

> que nous finiss**ions**   que nous parl**ions**
> que vous appren**iez**   que vous sort**iez**

VOCABULAIRE ACTIF
À mon avis
C'est bien/dommage
douter
il est temps
il vaut (vaudrait) mieux
intolérant(e)
regretter

Le présent du subjonctif

Il faut qu(e)...		Il est temps qu(e)...	
je parle	nous parlions	je finisse	nous finissions
tu parles	vous parliez	tu finisses	vous finissiez
il/elle/on parle	ils/elles parlent	il/elle/on finisse	ils/elles finissent

Il vaudrait mieux qu(e)...

j'apprenne	nous apprenions
tu apprennes	vous appreniez
il/elle/on apprenne	ils/elles apprennent

ACTIVITÉS

A. Front national/S.O.S.-Racisme.   Dans un débat entre partisans des deux groupes, attribuez les phrases suivantes au Front national (FN) ou au groupe S.O.S.-Racisme (R).

1. _____ Il vaut mieux que la France ferme ses frontières.

2. _____ Je voudrais qu'on accepte les étrangers.

3. _____ Il faut que les immigrés retournent dans leurs pays d'origine.

4. _____ Je doute que les étrangers contribuent aux problèmes économiques.

5. _____ Il est temps que nous respections les valeurs des autres cultures.

6. _____ J'aimerais que les immigrés se sentent les bienvenus dans notre pays.

7. _____ L'intolérance est le plus grand problème de nos jours.

8. _____ Le taux de chômage en France est dû au grand nombre d'immigrés.

Maintenant, «corrigez» les phrases avec lesquelles vous n'êtes pas d'accord.

B. In this activity, students are sensitized to the difference in moods. Tell students that although all the statements may be considered opinions, the form chosen to express them suggests the speaker's perspective. Complete as a whole-class activity.

B. Opinions? Quelques étudiants de l'université de Rennes discutent des problèmes de l'immigration dans un café. Est-ce que leurs déclarations signalent une réalité objective (O) ou un point de vue subjectif (S)?

1. _____ Les statistiques indiquent que le racisme est un problème sérieux dans les grandes villes.

2. _____ Il faut qu'on respecte tout le monde, mêmes si les gens sont différents.

3. _____ C'est vrai. Mais il ne faut pas que les particularismes culturels encouragent la division.

4. _____ Moi, j'aimerais que les immigrés s'intègrent mieux à la société française.

5. _____ C'est dommage que la crise économique rende la situation des immigrés plus difficile.

6. _____ C'est vrai. On accuse les étrangers de causer le chômage.

7. _____ Il est temps qu'on trouve une solution au problème de l'immigration.

Maintenant, parlez avec un(e) partenaire. Dites avec quelles déclarations vous êtes d'accord. Vos réponses se ressemblent-elles?

C. Point de vue. Complétez les phrases suivantes avec l'expression qui exprime le mieux votre opinion: **Il faut (ne faut pas) que** ou **je voudrais (ne voudrais pas) que.**

1. _____ mon pays ferme ses frontières aux étrangers.

2. _____ le gouvernement reconnaisse ses responsabilités envers les immigrés.

3. _____ on interdise la liberté d'expression religieuse.

4. _____ des gens de cultures différentes habitent parmi nous.

5. _____ qu'on apprécie les contributions des immigrés.

6. _____ les immigrés apprennent la langue du pays où ils habitent.

7. _____ les étrangers abandonnent totalement leur culture.

8. _____ tout le monde s'entend mieux.

D. Vos opinions. Comment peut-on se comprendre mieux? Discutez les questions suivantes en petits groupes et expliquez vos réponses par écrit.

1. À votre avis, vaut-il mieux que les immigrés abandonnent leurs particularismes culturels?
2. Faut-il qu'ils apprennent la langue du pays où ils habitent?
3. Faut-il que tout le monde se ressemble pour avoir une société stable?
4. Aimeriez-vous que votre pays accepte plus d'étrangers?
5. Voudriez-vous que le gouvernement aide les immigrés à s'intégrer dans votre pays? Comment?

W B

Maintenant, comparez vos réponses avec celles des autres groupes. Les groupes sont-ils d'accord sur certaines idées?

À l'écoute: L'appel de l'abbé Pierre

Vous allez entendre la voix *(voice)* de quelqu'un que tout le monde en France connaît, respecte et admire. Son nom: l'abbé Pierre. Depuis plus de cinquante ans, il est le défenseur des pauvres et surtout des gens qui n'ont pas de logement: les sans-abri *(homeless)*.

L'abbé Pierre est devenu célèbre en février 1954 quand, pendant un hiver glacial, il a lancé (fait) un appel à la radio en faveur des sans-abri et a provoqué dans la population française une mobilisation nationale immédiate. En février 1994, pendant un hiver de récession économique et de chômage, l'infatigable abbé Pierre, âgé de 81 ans, a lancé un autre appel à la radio et à la télévision. C'est cet appel que vous allez entendre.

 Attention!   Ne vous inquiétez pas si vous ne comprenez pas tout. C'est normal! Nous allons vous demander seulement de comprendre les idées principales et quelques détails. Faites l'activité préparatoire, puis écoutez en fonction des questions données.

L'abbé Pierre et les sans-abri.

Avant d'écouter

1   To help students recognize the expressions in the list as they listen to the segment, read each item aloud, modeling pronunciation.

1 Imaginez un discours d'une personnalité religieuse sur la pauvreté et les sans-abri. De quoi va-t-il parler? Cochez les sujets que vous anticipez et complétez la liste ci-dessous et à la page 458 avec vos idées personnelles.

1. _____ La guerre *(war)* contre la misère (la pauvreté)

2. _____ Le nombre de personnes qui vivent en-dessous du seuil de la pauvreté *(below poverty level)*

3. _____ Des statistiques qui comparent le nombre de sans-abri aux États-Unis et en Europe

4. _____ Des exemples de catastrophes qui ont causé la misère

5. _____ Une définition du public à qui cet appel, ou ce cri *(cry for help)* est adressé

6. _____ La responsabilité des municipalités (villes) et des citoyens français en général dans ces efforts pour détruire (éliminer) la misère

7. _____ La responsabilité des églises et des groupes religieux

8. _____ Des suggestions pour trouver ou bâtir *(build)* des logements pour les sans-abri

9. _____ ?

Écoutons

2 ANSWERS: 1, 2, 5, 6, 8, (9?)

Audio CD

3 To help students identify answers, preview all the questions, modeling pronunciation, before you play the segment again.

VOCABULAIRE ACTIF

un appel
bâtir
une catastrophe
détruire
la guerre
l'indifférence
la misère
la pauvreté
   un(e) pauvre
une pétition
respecter
un(e) sans-abri
se mobiliser
une solution

2 Écoutez une première fois pour vérifier vos prédictions. Parmi les sujets que vous avez anticipés, lesquels sont réellement mentionnés? Cochez-les une deuxième fois.

3 Écoutez encore et cochez les bonnes réponses.

1. L'abbé Pierre appelle son public
   (a.) «Mes amis».
   b. «Françaises, Français».
2. Dans la guerre contre la misère, l'ennemi est
   (a.) l'indifférence.
   b. l'argent.
3. La misère attaque
   a. les minorités ethniques.
   (b.) l'univers total des hommes.
4. Le nombre de personnes qui vivent en-dessous du seuil de la pauvreté en Europe est de
   (a.) 40 000 000.
   b. 40 000.
5. Quand il parle des gens qui sont laissés à l'abandon (abandonnés), sans espoir, dans les grandes villes, l'abbé Pierre mentionne
   a. les vieux.
   (b.) des générations de jeunes.
6. L'abbé Pierre dit que pour se mobiliser (pour faire quelque chose)
   (a.) il ne faut pas attendre des catastrophes bien visibles.
   b. il faut regarder des films sur les sans-abri.
7. L'appel de l'abbé Pierre s'adresse
   (a.) à tous les gens qui écoutent, et surtout les jeunes.
   b. aux organisations politiques.
8. Beaucoup de municipalités trahissent *(betray)* la cause parce qu'elles
   a. n'ont pas de gîtes *(shelters)* pour les pauvres.
   (b.) refusent (ferment) leurs gîtes aux plus faibles (vulnérables).
9. Selon l'abbé Pierre, il faut que la France
   (a.) utilise les logis vides (les logements non-occupés) et les bureaux vides pour les sans-abri.
   b. détruise (élimine) les mauvais logements.

10. Il dit aussi que la France
    (a.) a les ressources nécessaires (argent, technique, etc.) pour bâtir des logements immédiatement.
    b. doit choisir un nouveau gouvernement, plus favorable aux pauvres.
11. L'abbé Pierre demande aux citoyens français
    a. de voter aux élections du 15 mars.
    (b.) d'écrire à leurs maires (*mayors*) et de faire des pétitions.

4 Imaginez que vous êtes le maire d'une ville qui a beaucoup de sans-abri. Comment allez-vous les aider? (Est-ce que vous allez demander aux propriétaires de bureaux ou d'appartements vides de les ouvrir aux sans-abri? Qu'est-ce que vous allez faire pour aider les sans-abri à trouver un emploi ou pour trouver de l'argent pour bâtir de nouveaux logements? Allez-vous mobiliser le public par une campagne dans les médias? Demanderez-vous de l'aide aux groupes religieux?) Avec deux ou trois partenaires, faites une liste des solutions que vous proposez pour aider les victimes de la crise économique.

4   To help students, brainstorm other ideas together before students begin group work; allow students to express ideas in English, and together, find a way to say it in French. Provide a few words as needed. Again, remind students to keep the discussion simple.

4   After this activity, you may wish to tell students that l'abbé Pierre, one week before Christmas 1994, led a group of over one hundred **sans-abri** to occupy a large vacant building in the heart of Paris. His initiative was approved by most political figures in France.

STRUCTURES: Expressing personal viewpoints
Subjonctif ou infinitif? • *Le subjonctif irrégulier*

Observez et déduisez   L'abbé Pierre veut alerter le public. Il ne voudrait pas qu'on soit indifférent aux problèmes des sans-abri. À son avis, il ne faut pas attendre des catastrophes bien visibles. Il faut qu'on fasse quelque chose immédiatement; il faut se mobiliser!

VOCABULAIRE ACTIF
indifférent(e)

■ Based on the preceding paragraph, besides the subjunctive, what form of the verb can follow **vouloir** and **il faut?**

■ The preceding sentences contain examples of some irregular subjunctive verbs. Can you identify the subjunctive forms of **être** and **faire?**

Vérifiez   *Subjonctif ou infinitif?*

■ Expressions of opinion, desire, and emotion can also be made in French *without* using the subjunctive. If the subject of both clauses is the same or if the subject is not indicated, the expression or verb must be followed by an infinitive. Compare the following pairs of sentences.

L'abbé Pierre voudrait **aider** les sans-abri.
(one subject   →   infinitive)

L'abbé Pierre voudrait que *le gouvernement* **aide** les sans-abri.
(different subjects   →   subjunctive)

Il ne faut pas **attendre** une catastrophe.
(unspecified subject → infinitive)

Il ne faut pas que *nous* **attendions** une catastrophe.
(specified subject → subjunctive)

■ After the verb **regretter** and after expressions with **être,** use the preposition **de** before the infinitive.

L'abbé Pierre regrette **de** voir détruire des logements vides.
C'est dommage **de** détruire des logements vides.

Le subjonctif irrégulier

These irregular verb forms are taught primarily for recognition.

■ Several common verbs are irregular in the subjunctive.

Verbs with irregular stems and endings		
	être **soi- / soy-**	**avoir** **ai- / ay-**
que j(e)	sois	aie
que tu	sois	aies
qu'il / elle / on	soit	ait
que nous	soyons	ayons
que vous	soyez	ayez
qu'ils / elles	soient	aient

Verbs with a single stem and regular endings			
	faire **fass-**	**savoir** **sach-**	**pouvoir** **puiss-**
que je	fasse	sache	puisse
que tu	fasses	saches	puisses
qu'il / elle / on	fasse	sache	puisse
que nous	fassions	sachions	puissions
que vous	fassiez	sachiez	puissiez
qu'ils / elles	fassent	sachent	puissent

Verbs with two stems and regular endings		
	aller **aill- / all-**	**vouloir** **veuill- / voul-**
que j(e)	aille	veuille
que tu	ailles	veuilles
qu'il / elle / on	aille	veuille
que nous	allions	voulions
que vous	alliez	vouliez
qu'ils / elles	aillent	veuillent

ACTIVITÉS

E. Logique. Complétez les phrases en cochant toutes les possibilités logiques—et correctes! (Faites attention à la forme des verbes et à la syntaxe.)

1. Il faut que

   ✓_____ les citoyens fassent des pétitions.

   _____ bâtir des logements.

   ✓_____ nous nous mobilisions.

2. Il est temps

   ✓_____ d'aider les sans-abri.

   ✓_____ que nous allions à la mairie avec nos pétitions.

   _____ combattre la misère.

3. C'est dommage

   ✓_____ que tant de gens n'aient pas de logement.

   _____ refuser des gîtes aux plus faibles.

   ✓_____ que tant de citoyens soient indifférents à la misère.

4. Je ne voudrais pas

   ✓_____ être sans logement.

   ✓_____ vivre dans la rue.

   ✓_____ que le problème continue.

5. Il vaut mieux

   ✓_____ se mobiliser pour aider les pauvres.

   _____ de s'entendre.

   ✓_____ que le public soit éduqué.

6. Je doute

   ✓_____ que le maire comprenne les problèmes des sans-abri.

   _____ oublier les sans-abri.

   ✓_____ qu'il y ait assez de gîtes.

F. Have students study the example. Point out that the second subject is eliminated when the infinitive is used. Be sure students remember to use **de** before the infinitive where necessary.

F. L'appel. Trouvez ci-dessous quelques affirmations de l'abbé Pierre. Transformez-les en employant un infinitif selon l'exemple pour créer des phrases plus générales.

➡ Il faut que tout le monde fasse quelque chose.
   Il faut faire quelque chose.

1. C'est dommage que nous attendions une catastrophe bien visible.
2. Il ne faut pas que le gouvernement détruise des logis vides.
3. Il est temps que le gouvernement construise de nouveaux logements.

4. Il vaut mieux qu'on ait un plan d'action.
5. C'est bien que nous nous mobilisions.
6. Il est temps que nous écrivions aux maires.
7. Il faut que nous fassions des pétitions.

G. Mes préférences.   Formez six phrases pour exprimer vos propres idées. Utilisez des mots de chaque colonne, et employez le subjonctif ou un infinitif selon le cas.

➡ *Je voudrais que tout le monde fasse appel aux députés.*
Il est temps de construire des gîtes.
Je ne voudrais pas vivre dans la rue.

| Je voudrais (ne voudrais pas) Je regrette Il faut (ne faut pas) Il vaudrait mieux Il est (n'est pas) temps | que de — | le gouvernement tout le monde on — ? | aider les enfants sans-abri lancer des pétitions se mobiliser détruire des logis vides s'intéresser au problème construire des gîtes avoir un logement être indifférent faire quelque chose pour aider les pauvres vivre dans la rue arrêter la misère faire appel aux députés ? |

CD-ROM

You are now ready to do your Lab Manual activities with the audio program. Explore chapter topics further with the Mais oui! Video and CD-ROM. Viewing and comprehension activities are in the video section of your *Workbook/Lab Manual/Video Manual*. Go to the Mais oui! Web Site for Internet activities related to the topics discussed in this chapter.

Internet

Littérature: Chemin-d'école

Born in Martinique in 1952, Patrick Chamoiseau published his first novel, *Chronique des sept misères,* in 1986. In 1992, he received **le prix Goncourt,** one of the most distinguished literary prizes in France, for his novel *Texaco.* A disciple of Aimé Césaire, another writer from Martinique who, in the 1930s, launched in literature a black awareness movement called **la négritude,** Chamoiseau raises a more sarcastic voice against colonialism. Mixing Creole and French, tenderness and irony, he explores through his writings the contradictions between the white world of government and education, and the everyday realities of the Creole world. Chamoiseau gives these contradictions a very personal dimension in the two volumes of his autobiography. Calling himself **le négrillon** *(the little Negro boy),* he first portrays, in *Antan d'enfance* (1990), an inquisitive preschooler immersed in the traditions of his people. In *Chemin-d'école* (1994), **le négrillon** goes to school, a colonial school where he learns to read using books about **le petit Pierre,** a little boy with blond hair and blue eyes who makes snowmen in the winter.

> Pour nous, le petit Pierre des lectures faisait figure d'extraterrestre.
> Mais à mesure des lectures sacralisées *(made sacred),* c'est Petit-Pierre qui devenait normal.

Une école coloniale en Martinique, scène du film *Rue Cases-nègres.* Ce film décrit une situation semblable à celle du négrillon.

Little by little, **le négrillon** fills his head with images from another world that has become his new reality.

> Cet univers devenait la réalité. Il dessinait avec. Rêvait avec. Pensait avec. Mentait avec. Imaginait avec. Son corps, lui, allait en dérive *(adrift)* dans son monde créole inutile. *(Chemin-d'école,* p. 156)

In the following excerpt, **le négrillon** reflects on the "civilizing mission" of his schoolteacher, **le Maître.**

1 Imaginez que vous êtes dans une école coloniale des Caraïbes. Selon le point de vue des Européens (les colons), à quel monde s'appliquent les éléments suivants—le monde noir (N) ou le monde blanc (B)? Mettez l'initiale appropriée devant chaque élément, selon ce que vous anticipez.

_____ les mauvaises mœurs (*mores, customs*)	_____ une longue nuit de non-humanité, d'inexistence
_____ la Civilisation	_____ les races supérieures
_____ l'Histoire	_____ les races primitives
_____ une non-histoire cannibale	_____ les ténèbres (*darkness*)
_____ des millions de sauvages	_____ la lumière (*light*)

2 Les mots suivants sont des mots importants dans le texte que vous allez lire. D'après le contexte de chaque phrase, déduisez le sens de ces mots et trouvez le synonyme ou la définition dans la liste donnée.

1. L'animal est **la proie** du chasseur.
2. Il y a **un fantôme** qui hante ce château.
3. Cet instrument est en **fer.**
4. Une voiture a quatre **roues.**
5. Avant l'invention de la voiture, **le cheval** (*pl.* **les chevaux**) servait de moyen de transport.
6. **La canne-à-sucre** est une des ressources principales des Caraïbes.

a. un type de métal
b. une plante tropicale
c. un objet rond qui tourne
d. un animal domestique utilisé pour l'équitation
e. une apparition surnaturelle de quelqu'un qui est mort
f. une victime

3 Deux autres mots importants dans ce texte sont **le droit** et **le devoir** (*duty*). À votre avis, qui va utiliser ces mots—les colons (les Blancs) ou les Martiniquais (les Noirs)?

4 Parcourez le texte une première fois. Dans quel ordre les idées générales sont-elles présentées? Classez-les de 1 à 5.

_____ Rôle de l'Universel (les choses communes à tous) dans le concept de la civilisation

_____ Bénéfices (conséquences positives) de la colonisation

_____ Raison pour laquelle les enfants créoles doivent aller à l'école

_____ Origines de l'Histoire et de la Civilisation

_____ Réaction du négrillon

5 Relisez le texte pour vérifier vos réponses aux tâches 1 et 3.

Chemin-d'école

On allait à l'école pour perdre de mauvaises mœurs: mœurs d'énergumène°, mœurs nègres ou mœurs créoles—c'étaient les mêmes.
[...] Le souffle vibrant du savoir° et notre être créole semblaient en insurmontable contradiction. Le Maître devait nous affronter° mais aussi affronter le

personne possédée du démon
Le... les choses qu'on apprenait
confront

pays tout entier. Il était en mission de civilisation. [...] Chacun de ses mots, de ses gestes, chaque injonction, chaque murmure était donc bardé° d'Universel. L'Universel était un bouclier°, un désinfectant, une religion, un espoir, un acte de poésie suprême. L'Universel était un ordre.

    En ce temps-là, le Gaulois aux yeux bleus, à la chevelure blonde comme les blés, était l'ancêtre de tout le monde. En ce temps-là les Européens étaient les fondateurs° de l'Histoire. Le monde, proie initiale des ténèbres, commençait avec eux. Nos îles avaient été là, dans un brouillard d'inexistence, traversée par de vagues fantômes caraïbes, eux-mêmes pris dans l'obscurité d'une non-histoire cannibale. Et, avec l'arrivée des colons, la lumière fut.* La Civilisation. L'Histoire. L'humanisation de la Terre.

    Christophe Colomb avait découvert l'Amérique, et aspiré° au monde des millions de ces sauvages, qui durant une nuit immémoriale, soustraits à l'humanité°, l'avaient attendu.

    — Savez-vous, ostrogoths°, qu'ils portèrent au Nouveau Monde le fer, la roue, le bœuf, le porc, les chevaux, le blé, la canne-à-sucre... ?

    — Les races supérieures, il faut le dire ouvertement, ont, vis-à-vis des races primitives, le droit et le devoir de ci-vi-li-sa-tion!

    Le négrillon aimait entendre le Maître leur conter l'Histoire du monde. Tout semblait simple et juste.

plein

shield

founding fathers

mis

durant... pendant une longue nuit de non-humanité / sauvages

Extrait de *Chemin-d'école* (Patrick Chamoiseau)

En détail

6 ANSWERS: 1. F (de mauvaises mœurs) 2. V 3. V 4. V 5. F (l'ancêtre de tout le monde) 6. V 7. V 8. F (apportée par les colons) 9. V 10. F (Tout ce que le Maître disait lui semblait simple et juste.)

6 **Le texte.** Lisez plus attentivement et indiquez si, *selon le texte*, les phrases suivantes sont vraies ou fausses. Si elles sont fausses, corrigez-les.

1. À l'école, les mœurs nègres ou créoles étaient considérées comme un héritage précieux.
2. Il y avait une grande contradiction entre l'identité créole des enfants et ce qu'ils apprenaient à l'école.
3. Dans sa mission de civilisation, le Maître devait civiliser non seulement les enfants mais aussi leur famille et toute la Martinique.
4. Selon le Maître, la civilisation, commencée par les Européens, était quelque chose d'universel qui s'appliquait à toutes les races.
5. Le Gaulois aux yeux bleus et aux cheveux blonds était seulement l'ancêtre des Français.
6. Avant l'arrivée des Européens, le Nouveau Monde était habité par des fantômes, des cannibales et des sauvages.
7. Les Européens ont apporté la lumière et le progrès au Nouveau Monde.
8. La canne-à-sucre existait déjà dans les îles des Caraïbes quand Christophe Colomb est arrivé en Amérique.
9. Les races supérieures ont la responsabilité de civiliser les races primitives.
10. Le négrillon ne croyait pas ce que le Maître disait.

---

*Référence à la Bible: «Que la lumière soit, et la lumière fut» ("Let there be light, and there was light").

1. Pourquoi est-ce que «tout semblait simple et juste» au négrillon? Avec un(e) partenaire, faites une liste de raisons possibles, puis comparez vos réponses avec celles de vos camarades de classe.
2. À votre avis, est-ce que c'était «simple et juste» d'apprendre au négrillon que les mœurs créoles étaient mauvaises? Faites une liste des choses qui, selon vous, n'étaient pas «simples et justes» dans cette mission de civilisation. (Ce n'était pas juste de dire que...)
3. Maintenant pensez aux livres qui vous ont appris l'histoire. Est-ce que tout était «simple et juste»? Donnez un ou deux exemples qui peut-être ne l'étaient pas.

VOCABULAIRE ACTIF

Verbes et expressions verbales

abandonner *to abandon*
accueillir (infinitive only) *to welcome*
bâtir *to build*
détruire *to destroy*
douter *to doubt*
encourager *to encourage*

s'intégrer *to integrate (oneself)*
lutter (contre) *to fight (against)*
se mobiliser *to rally, mobilize*
regretter *to regret*
respecter *to respect*

Expressions pour donner son opinion

à mon avis *in my opinion*
c'est bien que *it's a good thing that*
c'est dommage que *it's too bad that*
il est temps que *it's (about) time that*

il faut que *it is necessary that*
il vaut mieux que *it is better / preferable that*
il vaudrait mieux que *it would be better*

Noms

un appel *an appeal*
une catastrophe *a catastrophe*
un(e) citoyen(ne) *a citizen*
une crise *a crisis*
la délinquance *delinquency*
un droit *a right*
un(e) étranger (-ère) *a foreigner*
un foulard *a scarf*
une frontière *a border*
la guerre *war*
un(e) immigré(e) *an immigrant*
l'indifférence (f.) *indifference*

l'intolérance (f.) *intolerance*
une loi *a law*
la misère *destitution, misery*
l'origine (f.) *origin, background*
    d'origine africaine *of African origin*
les pauvres *the poor*
la pauvreté *poverty*
une pétition *a petition*
un préjugé *a prejudice*
le racisme *racism*
les sans-abri *the homeless*
une solution *a solution*

Adjectifs

étonnant(e) *surprising*
indifférent(e) *indifferent*
intolérant(e) *intolerant*

Adverbe

donc *therefore*

Regular Verbs

Infinitif	Indicatif					Impératif	Subjonctif	Conditionnel
	Présent	Passé Composé	Imparfait	Futur				
-ER écouter								
je / j'	écoute	ai écouté	écoutais	écouterai			écoute	écouterais
tu	écoutes	as écouté	écoutais	écouteras		écoute	écoutes	écouterais
il / elle / on	écoute	a écouté	écoutait	écoutera			écoute	écouterait
nous	écoutons	avons écouté	écoutions	écouterons		écoutons	écoutions	écouterions
vous	écoutez	avez écouté	écoutiez	écouterez		écoutez	écoutiez	écouteriez
ils / elles	écoutent	ont écouté	écoutaient	écouteront			écoutent	écouteraient
-IR sortir								
je / j'	sors	suis sorti(e)	sortais	sortirai			sorte	sortirais
tu	sors	es sorti(e)	sortais	sortiras		sors	sortes	sortirais
il / elle / on	sort	est sorti(e)	sortait	sortira			sorte	sortirait
nous	sortons	sommes sorti(e)s	sortions	sortirons		sortons	sortions	sortirions
vous	sortez	êtes sorti(e)(s)	sortiez	sortirez		sortez	sortiez	sortiriez
ils / elles	sortent	sont sorti(e)s	sortaient	sortiront			sortent	sortiraient
-IR finir								
je / j'	finis	ai fini	finissais	finirai			finisse	finirais
tu	finis	as fini	finissais	finiras		finis	finisses	finirais
il / elle / on	finit	a fini	finissait	finira			finisse	finirait
nous	finissons	avons fini	finissions	finirons		finissons	finissions	finirions
vous	finissez	avez fini	finissiez	finirez		finissez	finissiez	finiriez
ils / elles	finissent	ont fini	finissaient	finiront			finissent	finiraient

Regular Verbs

Infinitif	Indicatif				Impératif	Subjonctif	Conditionnel
	Présent	Passé Composé	Imparfait	Futur			
-RE vendre							
je / j'	vends	ai vendu	vendais	vendrai		vende	vendrais
tu	vends	as vendu	vendais	vendras	vends	vendes	vendrais
il / elle / on	vend	a vendu	vendait	vendra		vende	vendrait
nous	vendons	avons vendu	vendions	vendrons	vendons	vendions	vendrions
vous	vendez	avez vendu	vendiez	vendrez	vendez	vendiez	vendriez
ils / elles	vendent	ont vendu	vendaient	vendront		vendent	vendraient
-IRE écrire							
j'	écris	ai écrit	écrivais	écrirai		écrive	écrirais
tu	écris	as écrit	écrivais	écriras	écris	écrives	écrirais
il / elle / on	écrit	a écrit	écrivait	écrira		écrive	écrirait
nous	écrivons	avons écrit	écrivions	écrirons	écrivons	écrivions	écririons
vous	écrivez	avez écrit	écriviez	écrirez	écrivez	écriviez	écririez
ils / elles	écrivent	ont écrit	écrivaient	écriront		écrivent	écriraient

Auxiliary Verbs

Infinitif	Indicatif				Impératif	Subjonctif	Conditionnel
	Présent	Passé Composé	Imparfait	Futur			
avoir							
j'	ai	ai eu	avais	aurai		aie	aurais
tu	as	as eu	avais	auras	aie	aies	aurais
il / elle / on	a	a eu	avait	aura		ait	aurait
nous	avons	avons eu	avions	aurons	ayons	ayons	aurions
vous	avez	avez eu	aviez	aurez	ayez	ayez	auriez
ils / elles	ont	ont eu	avaient	auront		aient	auraient
être							
je / j'	suis	ai été	étais	serai		sois	serais
tu	es	as été	étais	seras	sois	sois	serais
il / elle / on	est	a été	était	sera		soit	serait
nous	sommes	avons été	étions	serons	soyons	soyons	serions
vous	êtes	avez été	étiez	serez	soyez	soyez	seriez
ils / elles	sont	ont été	étaient	seront		soient	seraient

Reflexive Verb

Infinitif	Indicatif				Impératif	Subjonctif	Conditionnel
	Présent	Passé Composé	Imparfait	Futur			
se laver							
je	me lave	me suis lavé(e)	me lavais	me laverai		me lave	me laverais
tu	te laves	t'es lavé(e)	te lavais	te laveras	lave-toi	te laves	te laverais
il / elle / on	se lave	s'est lavé(e)	se lavait	se lavera		se lave	se laverait
nous	nous lavons	nous sommes lavé(e)s	nous lavions	nous laverons	lavons-nous	nous lavions	nous laverions
vous	vous lavez	vous êtes lavé(e)(s)	vous laviez	vous laverez	lavez-vous	vous laviez	vous laveriez
ils / elles	se lavent	se sont lavé(e)s	se lavaient	se laveront		se lavent	se laveraient

Verbs with Stem Changes

Infinitif		Présent	Passé Composé	Imparfait	Futur	Impératif	Subjonctif	Conditionnel
acheter								
	j'	achète	ai acheté	achetais	achèterai		achète	achèterais
	tu	achètes	as acheté	achetais	achèteras	achète	achètes	achèterais
	il / elle / on	achète	a acheté	achetait	achètera		achète	achèterait
	nous	achetons	avons acheté	achetions	achèterons	achetons	achetions	achèterions
	vous	achetez	avez acheté	achetiez	achèterez	achetez	achetiez	achèteriez
	ils / elles	achètent	ont acheté	achetaient	achèteront		achètent	achèteraient
appeler								
	j'	appelle	ai appelé	appelais	appellerai		appelle	appellerais
	tu	appelles	as appelé	appelais	appelleras	appelle	appelles	appellerais
	il / elle / on	appelle	a appelé	appelait	appellera		appelle	appellerait
	nous	appelons	avons appelé	appelions	appellerons	appelons	appelions	appellerions
	vous	appelez	avez appelé	appeliez	appellerez	appelez	appeliez	appelleriez
	ils / elles	appellent	ont appelé	appelaient	appelleront		appellent	appelleraient
préférer								
	je / j'	préfère	ai préféré	préférais	préférerai		préfère	préférerais
	tu	préfères	as préféré	préférais	préféreras	préfère	préfères	préférerais
	il / elle / on	préfère	a préféré	préférait	préférera		préfère	préférerait
	nous	préférons	avons préféré	préférions	préférerons	préférons	préférions	préférerions
	vous	préférez	avez préféré	préfériez	préférerez	préférez	préfériez	préféreriez
	ils / elles	préfèrent	ont préféré	préféraient	préféreront		préfèrent	préféreraient
payer								
	je / j'	paie	ai payé	payais	payerai		paie	payerais
	tu	paies	as payé	payais	payeras	paie	paies	payerais
	il / elle / on	paie	a payé	payait	payera		paie	payerait
	nous	payons	avons payé	payions	payerons	payons	payions	payerions
	vous	payez	avez payé	payiez	payerez	payez	payiez	payeriez
	ils / elles	paient	ont payé	payaient	payeront		paient	payeraient

Irregular Verbs

Infinitif	Présent	Passé Composé	Imparfait	Futur	Impératif	Subjonctif	Conditionnel
aller							
je / j'	vais	suis allé(e)	allais	irai		aille	irais
tu	vas	es allé(e)	allais	iras	va	ailles	irais
il / elle / on	va	est allé(e)	allait	ira		aille	irait
nous	allons	sommes allé(e)s	allions	irons	allons	allions	irions
vous	allez	êtes allé(e)(s)	alliez	irez	allez	alliez	iriez
ils / elles	vont	sont allé(e)s	allaient	iront		aillent	iraient
boire							
je / j'	bois	ai bu	buvais	boirai		boive	boirais
tu	bois	as bu	buvais	boiras	bois	boives	boirais
il / elle / on	boit	a bu	buvait	boira		boive	boirait
nous	buvons	avons bu	buvions	boirons	buvons	buvions	boirions
vous	buvez	avez bu	buviez	boirez	buvez	buviez	boiriez
ils / elles	boivent	ont bu	buvaient	boiront		boivent	boiraient
connaître							
je / j'	connais	ai connu	connaissais	connaîtrai		connaisse	connaîtrais
tu	connais	as connu	connaissais	connaîtras	connais	connaisses	connaîtrais
il / elle / on	connaît	a connu	connaissait	connaîtra		connaisse	connaîtrait
nous	connaissons	avons connu	connaissions	connaîtrons	connaissons	connaissions	connaîtrions
vous	connaissez	avez connu	connaissiez	connaîtrez	connaissez	connaissiez	connaîtriez
ils / elles	connaissent	ont connu	connaissaient	connaîtront		connaissent	connaîtraient

Irregular Verbs

Infinitif	Indicatif				Impératif	Subjonctif	Conditionnel
	Présent	Passé Composé	Imparfait	Futur			
devoir							
je / j'	dois	ai dû	devais	devrai		doive	devrais
tu	dois	as dû	devais	devras	dois	doives	devrais
il / elle / on	doit	a dû	devait	devra		doive	devrait
nous	devons	avons dû	devions	devrons	devons	devions	devrions
vous	devez	avez dû	deviez	devrez	devez	deviez	devriez
ils / elles	doivent	ont dû	devaient	devront		doivent	devraient
dire							
je / j'	dis	ai dit	disais	dirai		dise	dirais
tu	dis	as dit	disais	diras	dis	dises	dirais
il / elle / on	dit	a dit	disait	dira		dise	dirait
nous	disons	avons dit	disions	dirons	disons	disions	dirions
vous	dites	avez dit	disiez	direz	dites	disiez	diriez
ils / elles	disent	ont dit	disaient	diront		disent	diraient
faire							
je / j'	fais	ai fait	faisais	ferai		fasse	ferais
tu	fais	as fait	faisais	feras	fais	fasses	ferais
il / elle / on	fait	a fait	faisait	fera		fasse	ferait
nous	faisons	avons fait	faisions	ferons	faisons	fassions	ferions
vous	faites	avez fait	faisiez	ferez	faites	fassiez	feriez
ils / elles	font	ont fait	faisaient	feront		fassent	feraient

Irregular Verbs

Infinitif	Présent	Passé Composé	Imparfait	Futur	Impératif	Subjonctif	Conditionnel
		Indicatif					
mettre							
je / j'	mets	ai mis	mettais	mettrai		mette	mettrais
tu	mets	as mis	mettais	mettras	mets	mettes	mettrais
il / elle / on	met	a mis	mettait	mettra		mette	mettrait
nous	mettons	avons mis	mettions	mettrons	mettons	mettions	mettrions
vous	mettez	avez mis	mettiez	mettrez	mettez	mettiez	mettriez
ils / elles	mettent	ont mis	mettaient	mettront		mettent	mettraient
pouvoir							
je / j'	peux	ai pu	pouvais	pourrai		puisse	pourrais
tu	peux	as pu	pouvais	pourras		puisses	pourrais
il / elle / on	peut	a pu	pouvait	pourra		puisse	pourrait
nous	pouvons	avons pu	pouvions	pourrons		puissions	pourrions
vous	pouvez	avez pu	pouviez	pourrez		puissiez	pourriez
ils / elles	peuvent	ont pu	pouvaient	pourront		puissent	pourraient
prendre							
je / j'	prends	ai pris	prenais	prendrai		prenne	prendrais
tu	prends	as pris	prenais	prendras	prends	prennes	prendrais
il / elle / on	prend	a pris	prenait	prendra		prenne	prendrait
nous	prenons	avons pris	prenions	prendrons	prenons	prenions	prendrions
vous	prenez	avez pris	preniez	prendrez	prenez	preniez	prendriez
ils / elles	prennent	ont pris	prenaient	prendront		prennent	prendrait
savoir							
je / j'	sais	ai su	savais	saurai		sache	saurais
tu	sais	as su	savais	sauras	sache	saches	saurais
il / elle / on	sait	a su	savait	saura		sache	saurait
nous	savons	avons su	savions	saurons	sachons	sachions	saurions
vous	savez	avez su	saviez	saurez	sachez	sachiez	sauriez
ils / elles	savent	ont su	savaient	sauront		sachent	sauraient

Irregular Verbs

Infinitif		Indicatif				Impératif	Subjonctif	Conditionnel
	Présent	Passé Composé	Imparfait	Futur				
venir								
je	viens	suis venu(e)	venais	viendrai			vienne	viendrais
tu	viens	es venu(e)	venais	viendras		viens	viennes	viendrais
il / elle / on	vient	est venu(e)	venait	viendra			vienne	viendrait
nous	venons	sommes venu(e)s	venions	viendrons		venons	venions	viendrions
vous	venez	êtes venu(e)(s)	veniez	viendrez		venez	veniez	viendriez
ils / elles	viennent	sont venu(e)s	venaient	viendront			viennent	viendraient
voir								
je / j'	vois	ai vu	voyais	verrai			voie	verrais
tu	vois	as vu	voyais	verras		vois	voies	verrais
il / elle / on	voit	a vu	voyait	verra			voie	verrait
nous	voyons	avons vu	voyions	verrons		voyons	voyions	verrions
vous	voyez	avez vu	voyiez	verrez		voyez	voyiez	verriez
ils / elles	voient	ont vu	voyaient	verront			voient	verraient
vouloir								
je / j'	veux	ai voulu	voulais	voudrai			veuille	voudrais
tu	veux	as voulu	voulais	voudras		veuille	veuilles	voudrais
il / elle / on	veut	a voulu	voulait	voudra			veuille	voudrait
nous	voulons	avons voulu	voulions	voudrons		veuillons	voulions	voudrions
vous	voulez	avez voulu	vouliez	voudrez		veuillez	vouliez	voudriez
ils / elles	veulent	ont voulu	voulaient	voudront			veuillent	voudraient

The French-English Vocabulary contains all the words and expressions included in the **Vocabulaire actif** sections at the end of each chapter. Entries are followed by the chapter number (**P** for the Chapitre préliminaire) where they appear. In addition the French-English vocabulary includes all words and expressions used in the **À l'écoute** listening sections and the **Lecture** and **Littérature** reading selections, as well as all words and expressions used in the **Activités** sections.

    The English-French Vocabulary includes words listed in the **Vocabulaire actif** sections, plus many additional words that students might want to use for their speaking or writing assignments.

    Expressions are listed under their key word(s). In subentries, the symbol ~ indicates the repetition of the key word. Regular adjectives are given in the masculine form, with the feminine ending following in parentheses. For irregular adjectives, the irregular ending of the feminine, or the whole word if needed, is given in parentheses. Irregular forms of the plural are also indicated. The gender of each noun is indicated after the noun. If the noun has both a masculine and a feminine form, both are listed in full. If the noun has an irregular form for the plural, this is also indicated in parentheses after the word.

The following abbreviations are used.

adj.	adjective	*m.pl.*	masculine plural
adv.	adverb	*n.*	noun
art.	article	*pl.*	plural
conj.	conjunction	*prep.*	preposition
f.	feminine	*pron.*	pronoun
f.pl.	feminine plural	*rel.pron.*	relative pronoun
inv.	invariable	*sing.*	singular
m.	masculine	*v.*	verb

à to, at, in [3]
~ **bientôt** see you soon [P]
~ **cause de** because of
~ **côté de** next to, beside [3]
~ **domicile** at home
~ **haute voix** aloud
~ **la rigueur** if need be
~ **l'heure** on time [6]
~ **mi-temps** half-time [11]
~ **pied** on foot [7]
~ **plein temps** full-time [11]
~ **tour de rôle** in turn
~ **votre avis** in your opinion
abaisser to lower
abandonner to abandon [C]
abbaye *f.* abbey
abbé *m.* priest
abdominal *m.* (*pl.* **abdominaux**) sit-up
abonnement *m.* subscription
abri *m.* shelter
absent(e) absent [4]
absolu(e) absolute
absolument absolutely [11]
académie *f.* school district
accent *m.* accent [P]
~ **aigu** acute accent [P]
~ **circonflexe** circumflex accent [P]
~ **grave** grave accent [P]
accepter to accept
accessoire *m.* accessory [10]
accident *m.* accident
accompagner to accompany
accomplir to accomplish, to fulfill
accord *m.* agreement
d'~ agreed, OK [3]
accorder to give, grant
accroître to increase
s'~ to grow
accueillir to welcome [C]
accumuler to accumulate
accuser to blame
achat *m.* purchase
acheter to buy [2]
acquérir to acquire
acte *m.* act, action
acteur/actrice *m./f.* actor [1]
actif (-ive) active [1]
activement actively [11]
activité *f.* activity
actualité *f.* current events
actuel(le) current, present-day

actuellement currently, at the present time
addition *f.* bill, check (restaurant) [5]
adepte *m./f.* adherent
adjoint(e) *m./f.* assistant
admirer to admire [2]
admis(e) allowed
adorer to adore [2]
adresse *f.* address
aérobic *m.* aerobics [10]
aéroport *m.* airport
affaires *f.pl.* business [7]
voyage d'~ business trip [7]
affectif (-ive) emotional
affiche *f.* sign; poster
affronter to confront
africain(e) African [1]
Afrique *f.* Africa
âge *m.* age [2]
Quel ~ as-tu/avez-vous? How old are you? [2]
agence *f.* agency
~ **de voyage** *f.* travel agency [7]
~ **matrimoniale** marriage bureau
agir sur to have an effect on
s'agir: il s'agit de it's a question of [9]
agréable pleasant, nice [3]
agrément *m.* amenity
voyage d'~ pleasure trip
agresser to attack
agricole agricultural
agriculture *f.* agriculture
ah bon? really? [4]
aide *f.* aid, help
aider to help
aiguilleur *m.* switchman
ail *m.* garlic [5]
ailleurs elsewhere
aimable nice [9]
aimer to like, to love [2]
air *m.* air
avoir l'~ to look, to seem
en plein ~ outdoor
ajouter add
alcoolisé(e) alcoholic
Algérie *f.* Algeria
algérien(ne) Algerian [1]
aliment *m.* food [5]
alimentaire relating to food
alimentation *f.* food, nutrition

alimenter to feed
Allemagne *f.* Germany
allemand *m.* German (language) [4]
allemand(e) German [1]
aller to go [2]
~ **à la chasse** to go hunting [7]
~ **à la pêche** to go fishing [7]
~ **bien** to feel good; to look good on; to fit [10]
~ **en cours** to go to class
~ **mal** to look bad on; to fit poorly [10]
~-**retour** *m.* round-trip ticket [7]
~ **simple** *m.* one-way ticket [7]
ça va? how are you? [P]
comment allez-vous/vas-tu? how are you? [P]
vous allez bien? how are you? are you well? [P]
allergique allergic [1]
allô? hello (on the telephone) [3]
allons let's go
allumer to turn/switch on
allumette *f.* match
pommes ~s matchstick potatoes
alors so, then
~**?** well?
~ **quand même** but still [11]
~ **que** whereas, while [2]
et ~? Oh yeah? [4]
alpage *m.* mountain pasture
altruiste altruistic [1]
amabilité *f.* kindness, politeness
amande *f.* almond
ambassade *f.* embassy
ambigu (-guë) ambiguous
ambition *f.* ambition [11]
âme *f.* **sœur** soul mate
améliorer to improve
amener to bring
américain(e) American [1]
Amérique *f.* America
ami/amie *m./f.* friend [2]
amicalement (closing to a friendly letter) in friendship
amitié *f.* friendship [8]
~**s** (closing to a friendly letter)
amour *m.* love
roman *m.* **d'~** romantic novel [2]
film *m.* **d'~** romantic movie [2]
amphithéâtre *m.* lecture hall [4]
amusant(e) funny, amusing [1]

amuser to amuse
  s'~ to have fun [8]
an *m.* year [4]
analyse *f.* analysis
ananas *m.* pineapple
ancêtre *m.* ancestor
anchois *m.* anchovy
ancien(ne) ancient; former
  anciens combattants *m.pl.* war
    veterans
anglais *m.* English (language) [4]
anglais(e) English [1]
Angleterre *f.* England
animal *m.* (*pl.* **animaux**) animal
  [12]
animer to make lively
année *f.* year [4]
  les ~s 50 the fifties
anniversaire *m.* birthday;
  anniversary [2]
  bon ~! happy birthday! [9]
annonce *f.* classified ad;
  announcement [3]
  petites ~s classified ads
annoncer to announce
annonceur/annonceuse
  m./f. announcer
annuel(le) annual
annulé(e) cancelled
annuler to cancel
anorak *m.* ski jacket, parka
antan yesteryear
anthractite charcoal gray
antibiotique *m.* antibiotic [12]
anticiper to anticipate
antique ancient
août *m.* August [4]
aphasique aphasic
apostrophe *f.* apostrophe [P]
apparaître to appear
appareil *m.* appliance
  ~ électronique electronic
    appliance
  qui est à l'~? who is calling? [3]
apparence *f.* appearance
apparenté(e) related
  mot ~ cognate
appartement *m.* apartment [3]
appartenir to belong
appel *m.* appeal, call [C]
  faire ~ to appeal
  sur ~ on call
appeler to call
  je m'appelle my name is [P]
  s'~ to be named
appétit *m.* appetite

appliquer to apply
  s'~ to apply oneself
apporter to bring [5]
  pourriez-vous m'~ please bring
    me [5]
apprécier to appreciate [8]
apprendre to learn; to teach [4]
apprivoiser to tame
approprié(e) appropriate
après after [5]
après-midi *m.* afternoon [4]
  de l'~ in the afternoon (time) [4]
arabe *m.* Arabic
arabesque *f.* arabesque
arachide *f.* peanut
araignée *f.* spider [12]
arbitre *m.* referee
arbre *m.* tree
  ~ généalogique family tree
architecte *m./f.* architect [1]
architecture *f.* architecture [4]
argent *m.* money [4]
argenté(e) silver
armée *f.* army
arrêt *m.* stop
arrêter to stop [9]
arrière *m.*: **en ~** backwards
arrivée *f.* arrival [7]
arriver to arrive; to happen
art *m.* art [4]
artichaut *m.* artichoke
artiste *m./f.* artist [1]
ascenseur *m.* elevator [7]
aspirateur *m.* vacuum cleaner [8]
  passer l'~ to vacuum [8]
aspirine *f.* aspirin [12]
assassinat *m.* assassination
s'asseoir to sit down
assez enough [5]; rather
assiette *f.* plate [5]
assis(e) seated [9]
assister à to attend, be present at
associer to match
Assomption *f.* Assumption
s'assumer to take charge (of one's
  life)
assurer to ensure
astuce *f.* astuteness
atout *m.* advantage
attacher to tie, to bind
attaque *f.* **cérébrale** stroke
attaquer to attack
attendre to wait (for) [7]
attentes *f.pl.* expectations [11]
attentif (-ive) careful
attention! be careful! attention!

attirer to attract
attraper to grab
attribuer to award
au (*see* **à**) [3]
  ~ besoin if necessary
  ~ coin de at the corner of [3]
  ~ contraire on the contrary [11]
  ~ lieu de instead of
  ~ moins at least [2]
  ~ revoir good-bye [P]
  ~ sujet de about [3]
au-delà de over; beyond
augmenter to increase
aujourd'hui today [3]
aussi also [1]
  ~... que as . . . as [5]
aussitôt que as soon as
autant de as many . . . as [5]
auteur *m.* author
automne *m.* autumn, fall [6]
autoriser to authorize
autorité *f.* authority
autre other [3]
  l'un l'~ one another
autrefois formerly [8]
autrement differently
avance *f.*: **à l'~** beforehand
  d'~ in advance
  en ~ early [6]
avancer to advance
avant before
  ~ de before
avantage *m.* advantage
avare stingy; greedy
avec with
  ~ plaisir *m.* with pleasure [6]
avenir *m.* future [11]
aventure *f.* adventure [2]
  film *m.* **d'~** adventure movie [2]
avenue *f.* avenue [3]
avion *m.* plane [7]
  en ~ by plane [7]
avis: à mon ~ in my opinion [C]
  à votre ~ in your opinion
avocat *m.* avocado
avocat/avocate *m./f.* lawyer [1]
avoir to have [2]
  ~ _____ ans to be _____ years
    old [2]
  ~ besoin (de) to need [8]
  ~ confiance en soi to be self-
    confident [8]
  ~ de la chance to be lucky
  ~ du mal (à) to have a hard time
  ~ envie de to want to, to feel like
    [6]

~ faim   to be hungry [5]
~ honte (de)   to be ashamed (of) [9]
en ~ marre   to be fed up [4]
~ l'air   to look, to seem
~ l'intention de   to intend to [11]
~ le temps   to have time [4]
~ lieu   to take place
~ mal à la tête   to have a headache
~ peur   to be afraid [4]
~ soif   to be thirsty [5]
~ tort   to be wrong [12]
avouer   to admit, to confess
avril *m.*   April [4]

bac/baccalauréat *m.*   baccalaureate exam
bagages *m.pl.*   luggage [7]
bagarre *f.*   brawl, fight
baguette *f.*   loaf of French bread [5]
baignoire *f.*   bathtub [7]
bâiller   to yawn
bain *m.*   bath(tub)
   salle *f.* **de ~s**   bathroom [3]
baissé(e)   lowered
baisser   to lower [10]
   se ~   to duck
bal *m.*   dance [8]
   ~ costumé   costume ball
baladeur *m.*   Walkman [3]
balle *f.*   ball
ballon *m.*   ball [9]
balnéaire   bathing
banal(e) (*m.pl.* **banals**)   commonplace
banane *f.*   banana [5]
banc *m.*   bench
bande *f.* **dessinée**   comic strip [6]
banlieue *f.*   suburbs [11]
banque *f.*   bank [3]
banquier *m.*   banker [11]
barbare   barbaric
barbare *m./f.*   barbarian
barbe *m.*   beard
   quelle ~!   what a bore!
bardé(e)   covered
bas(se)   low
base-ball *m.*   baseball [2]
basket *m.*   basketball [2]; basketball shoe [10]
   faire du ~   to play basketball [4]
bataille *f.*   battle

bateau *m.* (*pl.* **bateaux**)   boat [7]
   en ~   by boat [7]
   faire du ~   to go boating [7]
bâtiment *m.*   building [3]
bâtir   to build [C]
bâton *m.*   stick
battre   to hit, to beat [9]
   se ~   to fight [8]
bavard(e)   talkative
beau/bel/belle/beaux/belles   handsome, beautiful [3]
   il fait beau   it's nice weather [6]
beau-frère *m.*   brother-in-law [2]
beaucoup   much, many, a lot [2]
beauté *f.*   beauty
bébé *m.*   baby
bédouin(e)   Bedouin
belge   Belgian [1]
Belgique *f.*   Belgium
belle-sœur *f.*   sister-in-law [2]
ben   well, so [1]
bénéfice *m.*   benefit
berger/bergère *m./f.*   shepherd/shepherdess
besoin *m.*   need
   au ~   as needed
   avoir ~ de   to need [8]
bête   stupid [1]
bêtise *f.*   stupidity [12]
   ~s *f.pl.*   nonsense
beurre *m.*   butter [5]
biberon *m.*   baby bottle
bibliothèque *f.*   library [4]
bien   well; fine [P]
   ~ sûr   of course [2]
   c'est ~ que   it's a good thing that [C]
   eh ~   well
bien *m.*   good
bientôt   soon [4]
bière *f.*   beer [5]
bifteck *m.*   steak [5]
bijou *m.* (*pl.* **-bijoux**)   jewel [12]
bijoux *m.pl.*   jewelry
bilingue   bilingual
billet *m.*   ticket [7]
biologie *f.*   biology [4]
biscuit *m.*   cookie [5]
bise: faire la ~   to kiss
blague *f.*   joke [8]
blanc *m.*   white [3]
blanc (blanche)   white [3]
blé *m.*   wheat
blesser   to wound
   se ~   to be injured, to be hurt [12]

blessure *f.*   injury, wound [12]
bleu(e)   blue [2]
   bleu marine   navy blue [10]
bloc *m.* **opératoire**   surgery (department)
blond(e)   blond [1]
blonde *f.*   girlfriend (slang)
blouson *m.*   waist-length jacket [10]
bœuf *m.*   beef [5]
bof!   (expression of indifference) [4]
boire   to drink [5]
bois *m.*   wood [10]; woods
boisson *f.*   drink, beverage [5]
boîte *f.*   can; box [5]
   ~ (de nuit)   nightclub [8]
   en ~   canned [5]
boiter   to limp
bol d'air *m.*   breath of fresh air
bon(ne)   good; right [3]
   bonne ...! (feast day)   happy ...! [9]
   bonne idée *f.*   good idea [6]
   bonne réponse *f.*   correct answer
   de bonne heure   early
bonbon *m.*   (piece of) candy
bonheur *m.*   happiness; good fortune [8]
bonjour   hello; good morning [P]
bonsoir   good evening, good night [P]
bord *m.*   edge
   à ~   on board
   au ~ de la mer   at the shore, seaside
bordeaux (*inv.*)   burgundy (color) [10]
botte *f.*   boot [10]
bottine *f.*   ankle boot [10]
bouche *f.*   mouth [10]
boucher/bouchère *m./f.*   butcher
boucherie *f.*   butcher shop [5]
boucle *f.*   buckle
   ~ d'oreille   earring
bouclier *m.*   shield
bouger   to move
bougie *f.*   candle [9]
boulangerie *f.*   bakery [5]
boule *f.*   ball
boulevard *m.*   boulevard [3]
bouquet *m.*   bouquet [9]
bourse *f.*   scholarship
bout *m.*   end
bouteille *f.*   bottle [5]
bras *m.*   arm [10]

bravo! bravo! [9]
bref (brève) brief
brésilien(ne) Brazilian [1]
brie *m.* Brie cheese [5]
briller to shine
briser to break
broche *f.* brooch, pin
brochette *f.* food on a skewer
bronchite *f.* bronchitis [12]
(se) brosser to brush [10]
brouillard *m.* fog [6]
  il fait du ~ it's foggy [6]
brousse *f.* brush; the bush
  (wilderness)
bruit *m.* noise
brûler to burn
brume *f.* haze
brumeux (-euse) hazy
brun(e) dark-haired, brunette,
  brown [1]
brusquement abruptly
bûche *f.* yule log cake
budget *m.* budget
bulletin *m.* **météo** weather report
bureau *m.* (*pl.* **bureaux**) desk;
  office [P]
  ~ de renseignements
    information desk [7]
  ~ de tabac tobacco/magazine
    shop [3]
businessman *m.* businessman
but *m.* goal
buveur (-euse) *m./f.* drinker

ça this; that
  ~ dépend it depends
  ~ s'appelle it's called [5]
  ~ te dit? are you interested?
  ~ va? How are you? [P]
  ~ va (bien)! I'm fine! [P]
cabane *f.* cabin
cabas *m.* tote bag
cabine *f.* **d'aiguillage** *f.* control
  booth
cabinet *m.* **de toilette** *f.* toilet
caché(e) hidden [12]
cacher to hide
cadeau *m.* (*pl.* **cadeaux**) gift [4]
cadre *m.* executive [11];
  surroundings
  ~ moyen middle manager
  ~ supérieur high-level executive
cafard: avoir le ~ to have the blues

café *m.* café [3]; coffee [5]
  ~ au lait *m.* coffee with milk [5]
  ~ crème *m.* coffee with cream [5]
  ~ décaféiné decaffeinated coffee
caféine *f.* caffeine
cahier *m.* notebook, workbook [P]
caisse *f.* case
caleçon *m.* leggings
calendrier *m.* calendar [4]
calme calm [1]
camarade *m./f.* classmate; friend
  ~ de chambre roommate [2]
camembert *m.* Camembert cheese
  [5]
campagne *f.* country(side)
camping *m.* camping [7]
  faire du ~ to go camping [7]
campus *m.* campus [4]
Canada *m.* Canada
canadien(ne) Canadian [1]
canapé *m.* couch, sofa [3]
cancer *m.* cancer [12]
candidature *f.* candidacy
canne *f.* cane
  ~ à sucre *f.* sugar cane
cannibale *m./f.* cannibal
cantine *f.* cafeteria
capeline *f.* sun hat
capituler to surrender
car for
caractère *m.* character
  ~s gras bold type
caractéristique characteristic
carafe *f.* pitcher [5]
cardigan *m.* button-up sweater [10]
caresser to caress, stroke
carnaval *m.* carnival; period before
  Lent
carotte *f.* carrot [5]
carré *m.* square
carreau *m.* (*pl.* **carreaux**) square
  à carreaux plaid [10]
carrefour *m.* intersection
carrière *f.* career [11]
carte *f.* map [P]; menu [5]; card
  ~ de crédit credit card [7]
cas *m.* case
  en ~ de in case of
  selon le ~ as the case may be
case *f.* hut
casquette *f.* cap
casser to break
cassette *f.* cassette [P]
catastrophe *f.* catastrophe [C]
catégorie *f.* category, class

cathédrale *f.* cathedral [7]
cauchemar *m.* nightmare
cause *f.* cause
  à ~ de because of
causerie *f.* chat
CD *m.* CD [P]
  lecteur *m.* **de ~** CD player [3]
ce/cet/cette/ces this, that; these,
  those [2]
  ~...-ci this, these [2]
  ~ ...-là that, those [2]
ce (*pron.*) this; it [P]
  ~ que what
  ~ sont they are [P]
ceci (*pron.*) this
cédille *f.* cedilla [P]
ceinture *f.* belt [10]
célèbre famous [7]
célébrer to celebrate
célibat *m.* single life
célibataire single, unmarried [8]
célibataire *m./f.* single person
celui/celle/ceux/celles that/that
  one
cent hundred
centième one hundredth
centre *m.* center
centre-ville *m.* downtown [3]
céréale *f.* cereal grain
  ~s cereal [5]
certain(e) some
certainement certainly [11]
cerveau *m.* (*pl.* **cerveaux**) brain
ces (*see* ce/cet/cette/ces)
c'est this is; he/she/it is [P]
c'est-à-dire that is
chacun(e) each one
chaîne *f.* channel [6]
chaise *f.* chair [P]
chalet *m.* chalet
chaleur *f.* heat
chambre *f.* room; bedroom [3]
champ *m.* field
champignon *m.* mushroom
chance *f.* luck
  avoir de la ~ to be lucky
  bonne ~! good luck! [9]
  quelle ~! what luck! [4]
chandail *m.* sweater
changement *m.* change
changer to change [6]
  ~ de chaîne to change the
    channel [6]
  se ~ les idées à to take one's
    mind off things

chanson *f.* song
chanter to sing [2]
chanteur/chanteuse *m./f.* singer [1]
chapeau *m.* (*pl.* **chapeaux**) hat [10]
~! bravo! [9]
chaque each
charcuterie *f.* delicatessen [5]
chargé(e): horaire ~ full schedule
charges *f.pl.* utilities [3]; reponsibilities
charmant(e) charming
chasse *f.* hunting [7]
aller à la ~ to go hunting [7]
chasser to kick out; to chase
chasseur *m.* hunter
chat/chatte *m./f.* cat [8]
château *m.* (*pl.* **châteaux**) castle, château [7]
chaud(e) hot [5]
il fait ~ it's hot (weather) [6]
chaussette *f.* sock [10]
chausson *m.* (culinary) turnover
chaussure *f.* shoe [10]
chef *m.* chief, leader; chef
~ d'entreprise head of company [11]
chef-d'œuvre *m.* (*pl.* **chefs-d'œuvre**) masterpiece
chemin *m.* path
chemise *f.* shirt [10]
~ de nuit nightgown [10]
chemisier *m.* blouse, women's shirt [10]
cher (chère) dear; expensive [5]
chercher to look for [3]
va me ~... go get me . . .
chercheur (-euse) *m./f.* researcher
chéri(e) darling, dear
cheval *m.* (*pl.* **chevaux**) horse
chevelure *f.* head of hair
cheveux *m.pl.* hair [2]
chez at the home of
chic *inv.* chic, sophisticated
~! cool! great!
chien *m.* dog [7]
chiffre *m.* figure, number
chimie *f.* chemistry [4]
Chine *f.* China
chiné(e) mottled
chinois(e) Chinese [1]
chip *m.* chip
choc *m.* shock
chocolat *m.* chocolate [1]; hot chocolate [5]
choisir to choose [10]

choix *m.* choice
cholestérol *m.* cholesterol
chômage *m.* unemployment [11]
chômeur/chômeuse *m./f.* unemployed person
chose *f.* thing
quelque ~ something
chouchou/chouchoute *m./f.* (teacher's) pet
chouette great, neat, cool [4]
chuchoter to whisper
chum *m./f.* friend; boyfriend/girlfriend
chute *f.* **de neige** snowfall
-ci (*see* **ce/cet/cette/ces**)
ci-dessous below
ciel *m.* (*pl.* **cieux**) sky [6]
le ~ est couvert it's cloudy [6]
le ~ est variable it's partly cloudy
cil *m.* eyelash
cimetière *m.* cemetery
ciné *m.* movies [8]
cinéaste *m./f.* filmmaker
cinéma *m.* cinema, movies; movie theater [2]
cinq five [2]
cinquante fifty [2]
circonlocution *f.* circumlocution
circonstance *f.* circumstance
circuit *m.* circuit, route
circuler dans la salle to circulate in the classroom
cirque *m.* circus
citer to cite, to quote
citoyen(ne) *m./f.* citizen [C]
citron *m.* lemon [5]
~ pressé fresh lemonade [5]
clair(e) light, bright; clear [10]
classe *f.* class [P]
classer to classify
classeur *m.* binder [P]
claustrophobe claustrophobic
clé *f.* key [7]
client/cliente *m./f.* client [5]
climat *m.* climate [6]
climatisé(e) air conditioned
coca *m.* cola [5]
cocher to check
cocotier *m.* coconut tree
cœur *m.* heart [8]
de bon ~ heartily
par ~ by heart
cohabitation *f.* cohabitation
coiffure *f.* hairdo
se coiffer to do one's hair [10]

coin *m.* corner [3]
au ~ de at the corner of [3]
boucherie du ~ *f.* neighborhood butcher shop
coincé(e) stuck
col *m.* collar [10]
colère *f.* anger
collection *f.* collection
faire la ~ de to collect
collège *m.* middle school/junior high [4]
collègue *m./f.* colleague
collier *m.* necklace
colline *f.* hill
colon *m.* colonist
colonisation *f.* colonization
colonne *f.* column
coloris *m.* color, shade
combien (de) how much, how many [2]
comédie *f.* comedy [2]
comédien(ne) *m./f.* comedian
comique funny, comical
commander to order [5]
comme like, as; how [12]
~ ci ~ ça so-so [P]
~ d'habitude as usual
commencement *m.* beginning
commencer to begin [4]
comment how [1]
~? what? [P]
~ allez-vous? how are you? [P]
~ ça s'écrit? how do you spell that? [P]
~ ça va? how are you? [P]
~ dit-on... ? how do you say . . . ?
~ est-il? what is he like? [1]
~ s'appelle-t-il? what is his name? [P]
~ tu t'appelles? what is your name? [P]
~ vas-tu? how are you? [1]
~ vous appelez-vous? what is your name? [P]
commerce *m.* business; store
commercial(e) (*m.pl.* **commerciaux**) business (*adj.*)
commettre to commit
commode *f.* chest of drawers; dresser [3]
commun: en ~ in common
commune rurale *f.* rural community; small town [3]
communiquer to communicate [8]
compagne *f.* companion

compagnie *f.* company
comparaison *f.* comparison [5]
comparer to compare
compenser to compensate
compléter to complete
composté(e) validated
comprendre to understand [4]
  se ~ to understand each other [8]
comprimé *m.* pill, tablet [12]
compris(e) included [3]
compromis *m.* compromise
comptabilité *f.* accounting [4]
comptable *m./f.* accountant [11]
compter to count; to intend (to do something) [11]
concerner to concern
concert *m.* concert [2]
concierge *m./f.* caretaker
concordance *f.* **des temps** sequence of tenses
concours *m.* **d'entrée** entrance examination
confisquer to confiscate
confiture *f.* jam
conflit *m.* conflict
conformiste conformist [1]
confort *m.* comfort, ease [8]
  ~ matériel physical comfort [8]
  tout ~ all the conveniences
confortable comfortable [3]
congé *m.*: **jour de ~** day off; holiday [9]
conjoint(e) *m./f.* spouse
conjugaison *f.* conjugation
conjuguer to conjugate
connaissance *f.* knowledge
connaître to know [9]
  se ~ to know each other [9]
  tu connais... ? do you know (so and so)? [1]
conquête *f.* conquest
consacré(e) à devoted to
conseil *m.* advice; council [8]
conseiller/conseillère *m./f.* counsellor, advisor
conseiller to advise
conséquence *f.* consequence
conséquent: par ~ as a result
conservateur (-trice) conservative
conserver to preserve
conserves *f.pl.* preserves
considérer to consider
consigne *f.* baggage checkroom [7]
consommation *f.* consumption
constamment constantly [11]
construire to build

contagieux (-ieuse) contagious [12]
contaminer to contaminate
conte *m.* story
  ~ de fées fairy tale
contenir to contain
content(e) glad, pleased
continuer to continue [3]
contraire *m.* opposite
  au ~ on the contrary [11]
contre against; as opposed to; in exchange for
  par ~ on the other hand [2]
contribuer to contribute
convaincant(e) convincing
convaincre to convince
convaincu(e) convinced
convenir to be appropriate
convention *f.* **collective** collective wage agreement
convoquer to summon
copain/copine *m./f.* friend, pal [1]
coquet(te) dainty
corde *f.* rope
corps *m.* body [10]
corriger to correct
corsage *m.* bodice
cosmonaute *m./f.* astronaut
costume *m.* suit; outfit [10]
côte *f.* coast
côté *m.* side
  à ~ de next to, beside [3]
côtelette *f.* cutlet [5]
coton *m.* cotton [10]
cou *m.* neck [10]
couche *f.* stratum
se coucher to go to bed; to set (sun) [10]
couchette *f.* berth in sleeping compartment [7]
coude *m.* elbow [10]
couler to flow
couleur *f.* color
coulis *m.* type of sauce
coup *m.* blow
  ~ de main helping hand [7]
coupe *f.* **du monde** World Cup
couper to cut
couple *m.* couple [8]
cour *f.* yard
  ~ de récréation schoolyard
courir to run, to go to
courrier *m.* mail
  ~ du cœur advice column
cours *m.* avenue; course, class [4]
  au ~ de during
  aller en ~ to go to class

course *f.* errand; track [6]
  faire des ~s to go shopping [4]
  faire les ~s to go grocery shopping [5]
court(e) short [10]
  à manches courtes short-sleeved [10]
cousin/cousine *m./f.* cousin [2]
couteau *m.* (*pl.* **couteaux**) knife [5]
coûter to cost [3]
coutume *f.* custom
couvert *m.* place setting [5]
couvert(e) covered
  le ciel est ~ it's cloudy [6]
craie *f.* chalk [P]
  morceau *m.* **de ~** piece of chalk
cravate *f.* tie [10]
crayon *m.* pencil [P]
créer to create
crémerie *f.* dairy store
créole Creole
crétin *m.* idiot
crevette *f.* shrimp [5]
cri *m.* shout; cry for help
  pousser des ~s to shout
crier to shout, to yell
crise *f.* crisis [C]
  ~ cardiaque heart attack [12]
  ~ économique depression
critère *m.* criterion
croire to think, to believe [C]
croissant *m.* croissant [5]
croissant(e) growing
cru(e) raw [9]
cuillère *f.* spoon [5]
cuir *m.* leather [10]
cuisine *f.* cooking; kitchen [3]
  faire la ~ to do the cooking [4]
cuisinier/cuisinière *m./f.* cook [11]
cuisse *f.* **de canard** duck leg
cuit(e) cooked [9]
culinaire culinary
curriculum *m.* **vitae** résumé [11]
CV *m.* résumé [11]
cyclisme *m.* cycling [6]

d'abord first [5]
d'accord OK, agreed [3]
  être ~ to agree
dame *f.* lady [1]
dans in [3]
  ~ les nuages in the clouds
danser to dance [2]
date *f.* date [4]
d'autres other; others

d'avance   in advance
de/du/de la/des *art.*   any; some [1]
de/du/de la/des *prep.*   from; of
~ **rien**   you're welcome [P]
débat *m.*   debate
debout   standing [9]
débris *m.*: **un vieux** ~   decrepit old man
début *m.*   beginning
débutant/débutante *m./f.*   beginner [11]
décembre *m.*   December [4]
déception *f.*   disappointment
déchiré(e)   torn
décidément   decidedly
décider   to decide
découper   to cut out
découvrir   to discover
décret *m.*   decree
décrire   to describe
décroissant: par ordre ~   in descending order
déduire   to deduce
défendre   to defend
défenseur *m.*   defender
défier   to defy
défilé *m.*   parade [9]
défiler   to parade
défini(e)   definite
définir   to define
degré *m.*   degree
dehors   outside, outdoors
déjà   already [4]
déjeuner   to have lunch
déjeuner *m.*   lunch [5]
petit ~   breakfast [5]
délinquance *f.*   delinquency, crime [C]
demain   tomorrow [3]
demande *f.* **d'emploi**   job application [11]
faire une ~   to apply for a job [11]
demander   to ask (for)
demeurer   to stay
demi(e) *m./f.*   half
et ~   thirty (minutes past the hour) [4]
demi-pension *f.*   lodging with breakfast and dinner
densément   densely
dent *f.*   tooth [10]
dentaire   dental
dentiste *m./f.*   dentist [1]
départ *m.*   departure [7]
dépassé(e)   outdated
dépasser   to exceed

se dépêcher   to hurry (up) [10]
dépendant(e) *m./f.*   dependent
dépense *f.*   expense; expenditure
dépenser   to spend (money) [12]
se déplacer   to move from one place to another
déposer   to deposit; to drop off
déprimant(e)   depressing
depuis   since; for [7]
~ **combien de temps?**   for how long? [7]
~ **dix ans**   in the last 10 years
~ **quand**   since when [7]
~ **que**   since
député *m.*   deputy
dernier (-ière)   last; latest [4]
derrière   behind [3]
des   (*see* **de**)
dès   from; as early as
~ **maintenant**   starting now
~ **que**   as soon as [11]
désaccord *m.*   disagreement
désagréable   unpleasant [1]
désapprobation *f.*   disapproval
désavantage *m.*   disadvantage
descendre   to go down; to get down; to get off [7]
description *f.*   description [2]
désert *m.*   desert [7]
désert(e)   deserted
désespéré(e)   desperate
désir *m.*   desire; wish
désirer   to want, to wish [5]
vous désirez?   what would you like? [5]
désolé(e)   sorry [3]
désordre *m.*   untidiness
en ~   untidy
désormais   from now on
dessert *m.*   dessert [5]
dessin *m.*   drawing [4]
~ **animé** *m.*   cartoon [6]
dessiner   to draw
dessous *m.pl.*   underside; shady side
détail *m.*   detail
détente *f.*   relaxation, rest
détester   to hate [2]
détruire   to destroy [C]
deux   two [2]
les ~   both [2]
deuxième   second [3]
~ **classe** *f.*   second class [7]
devant   in front of [3]
(se) développer   to develop [8]
devenir   to become [11]

deviner   to guess
devise *f.*   motto
devoir   to have to; must; to owe [8]
j'aurais dû   I should have [12]
je devais   I was supposed to [8]
je devrais   I should [12]
devoir *m.*   duty
~**s**   homework [4]
faire ses ~**s**   to do one's homework [4]
dévorer   to devour
d'habitude   usually [4]
diabétique   diabetic
diagnostic *m.*   diagnosis
diététique   dietetic [5]
différence *f.*   difference
différent(e)   different
difficile   difficult; choosy
difficilement   with difficulty [11]
difficulté *f.*   difficulty
digne   proper, suitable
dimanche *m.*   Sunday [4]
diminuer   to decrease
dinde *f.*   turkey [9]
dîner *m.*   dinner [5]
dîner   to have dinner [2]
diplôme *m.*   diploma, degree
diplômé(e)   graduate
dire   to say [6]
se ~   to say of oneself
direct: en ~   live
direction *f.*   management
~**s**   directions [3]
discipliné(e)   disciplined [10]
discothèque *f.*   discotheque
disponibilité *f.*   availability
disponible   available
disposer de   to have free or available
dispute *f.*   quarrel; argument
se disputer   to argue [8]
disque *m.* **compact**   compact disk
lecteur *m.* **de** ~**s** ~**s**   CD player
distinguer   to distinguish
divers(e)   various
diviser   to divide
divorce *m.*   divorce [8]
dix   ten [2]
dix-huit   eighteen
dix-neuf   nineteen
dix-sept   seventeen
doctorat *m.*   doctorate
doigt *m.*   finger [10]
lever le ~   to raise one's hand [9]
domaine *m.*   field
~ **de spécialisation**   major

domicile: à ~ at home
dommage: c'est ~ que it's too bad that [C]
donc therefore; so [C]
donné(e) given
donner to give [2]
dont of which, of whom; whose [12]
doré(e) golden
dormeur/dormeuse *m./f.* sleeper
dormir to sleep [20]
dos *m.* back [10]
d'où from where [1]
doucement softly
douche *f.* shower [3]
douleur *f.* pain
doute: sans ~ probably
douter to doubt [C]
doux (douce) sweet; mild; soft
douzaine *f.* dozen [5]
douze twelve [2]
drame *m.* drama [6]
drapeau *m.* (*pl.* **drapeaux**) flag
draperie *f.* cloth
drogue *f.* drug, drugs
droit *m.* law (*field of study*) [4]; right (*entitlement*) [C]
droit(e) right
  tout ~ straight ahead
droite *f.* right (*direction*) [3]
  à ~ on the right [3]
drôle funny
du (*see* de)
dur *adv.* hard [10]
durer to last

eau *f.* water [5]
ébloui(e) dazzled
éblouissant(e) dazzling
échancré(e) low-cut
échange *m.* exchange
échanger to exchange
écharpe *f.* scarf, muffler [10]
éclater to explode
école *f.* school [4]
  ~ maternelle kindergarten [4]
  ~ primaire elementary school [4]
  ~ supérieure school of higher education
écolier (-ière) *m./f.* school child
économie *f.* economics [4]
économique economic
écourté(e) shortened
écouter to listen (to) [2]
écraser to crush

écrire to write
  s'~ to write one another [8]
écrit(e) written
écrivain *m.* writer [1]
s'écrouler to crumble
éducation *f.* education
  ~ physique physical education [4]
éduquer to educate
effectivement actually
effectuer to execute, to carry out
égal(e) (*m.pl.* **-aux**) equal
égalité *f.* equality [11]
église *f.* church [3]
égoïste selfish [1]
eh ben well (*colloquial*)
eh bien well, so [11]
élaboré(e) elaborate
élargir to enlarge, to widen
électricité *f.* electricity
électronique: message ~ *m.* e-mail message [6]
élève *m./f.* student, pupil
élevé(e) high
élever to raise
elle she, it [P]; her [11]
  ~s they [1]; them [11]
élu/élue *m./f.* elected official
embauché(e) hired [11]
embaucher to hire [11]
embêtant(e) annoying, irritating [4]
embouteillage *m.* traffic jam
embrasser to kiss
émission *f.* television program [6]
emmener to take along
émouvant(e) emotionally moving
s'emparer de to seize upon
empathique empathic
empêcher to prevent
emplacement *m.* location [3]
emploi *m.* job [11]
  ~ du temps schedule [4]
employé/employée *m./f.* employee [11]
employer to use
employeur *m.* employer [11]
emporter to take away
en *prep.* to, in
  ~ avance early [6]
  ~ boîte canned
  ~ face de across from [3]
  ~ fait actually, in fact
  ~ haut de above
  ~ pratique in practice
  ~ retard late [6]

  ~ théorie in theory
  ~ train de in the process of
en *pron.* of it, of them [12]
enchanté(e) delighted [P]
enclume *f.* anvil
encore again; still
  ~ de more
  pas ~ not yet
encourager to encourage [C]
en-dessous de below
endroit *m.* place, spot, site [12]
  par ~s in places
énergétique energy-producing [5]
énergique energetic [1]
enfant *m./f.* child [2]
enfin finally; after all [5]
enlever to take away, to take off
ennemi *m.* enemy
ennui *m.* boredom [11]
s'ennuyer to be bored [8]
ennuyeux (-euse) boring [1]
enregistré(e) registered
enseignant/enseignante *m./f.* teacher, educator [11]
enseignement *m.* education
  ~ supérieur higher education
ensemble together [8]
ensemble *m.* whole (thing)
ensoleillé(e) sunny [6]
ensuite then [5]
entendre to hear [7]
  s'~ to get along [8]
entendu! agreed! [6]
entier (-ière) entire, whole
entre between [3]
entrecôte *f.* rib steak
entrée *f.* entrance
entreprise *f.* company, firm
entrer (dans) to enter [6]
  ~ à la fac to enroll [4]
entretien *m.* interview [11]
envers toward
envie *f.*: **avoir ~ de** to want to, to feel like [6]
environ approximately
envisager to look upon, consider
envol *m.* take-off
s'envoler to fly away
envoyer to send
épanouir to develop
épanouissement *m.* development, blossoming
épaule *f.* shoulder [10]
épicerie *f.* grocery store [5]
épicier/épicière *m./f.* grocer
épisode *m.* episode

époque: à cette ~-là in those days [8]

à l'~ at the time; at this time

épouser to marry [8]

épouvante *f.*: **film** *m.* **d'~** horror movie

équilibré(e) balanced

équipe *f.* team

érable *m.* maple

ermite hermit

escalader to climb

escalier *m.* staircase, stairs [7]

escargot *m.* snail

esclave *m./f.* slave

espace *m.* space

~ clos closed space

Espagne *f.* Spain

espagnol(e) Spanish [1]

espèce *f.* type, sort [5]

espérer to hope [11]

espoir *m.* hope

esprit *m.* mind

essai *m.* trial

essayer to try

essence *f.* gas

essentiel *m.* essential

est *m.* east [6]

est-ce que (question marker) [1]

estimer to be of the opinion

estomac *m.* stomach

et and [1]

~ vous? And you? [P]

établir to establish

étage *m.* floor, story [7]

étagères *f.pl.* bookcase [3]

étape *f.* step, stage

état *m.* state

États-Unis *m.pl.* United States

été *m.* summer [6]

éteindre to turn off

éternuer to sneeze [12]

étoile *f.* star [12]

étoilé(e) starry

étonnant(e) surprising [C]

étrange strange [12]

étranger (-ère) foreign [4]

langue *f.* **étrangère** foreign language [4]

étranger (-ère) *m./f.* stranger, alien; foreigner [C]

à l'étranger in a foreign country

être to be [1]

~ au régime to be on a diet [5]

~ né(e) to be born

~ pressé(e) to be in a hurry [5]

être *m.* being

étrennes *f.pl.* New Year's gift

études *f.pl.* studies

~ supérieures higher education

étudiant(e) student [P]

étudier to study [2]

euh uh [P]

européen(ne) European

eux *pron. m.pl.* they; them [11]

événement *m.* event

évêque *m.* bishop

évidemment evidently [11]

éviter to avoid [11]

évoluer to evolve

exact(e) precise, correct

exagérer to exaggerate

examen *m.* test, exam [4]

passer un ~ to take a test [4]

rater un ~ to fail a test [4]

réussir à un ~ to pass a test

examiner to examine [12]

excéder to exceed

exception *f.*: **à l'~ de** with the exception of

excès *m.* excess

excusez-moi excuse me [11]

exercer to practice, to carry on, to carry out

exercice *m.* exercise

faire de l'~ to exercise [4]

exigé(e) required

exigence *f.* requirement

exister to exist, to be

il existe en noir it comes in black

exotique exotic

expérience *f.* experiment; experience

explication *f.* explanation

expliquer to explain

exploit *m.* feat

explorateur/exploratrice *m./f.* explorer

exposition *f.* exhibit

expression *f.* expression

exprimer to express

exquis(e) exquisite

extérieur: à l'~ de outside of

extérioriser to externalize

extrait *m.* excerpt

extrait(e) excerpted

fac/faculté *f.* college/university [4]

face: en ~ de across from [3]

fâché(e) angry [9]

se fâcher to get mad/angry [10]

facilement easily [11]

façon *f.* way, manner

de toute ~ in any case

facteur *m.* factor

faible weak

vent ~ light wind

faim *f.* hunger [5]

avoir ~ to be hungry [5]

faire to do, to make [4]

~ attention to pay attention

~ des courses to go shopping [4]

~ fortune to make one's fortune

~ la collection de to collect

~ la connaissance de to meet

~ la cuisine to cook [4]

~ la sieste to take a nap

~ les courses to go grocery shopping [5]

~ le tour de to tour

~ mal à to hurt [10]

~ partie de to be part of

~ peur à to scare [12]

~ son lit to make one's bed [4]

~ une promenade to go for a walk [4]

~ un séjour to stay [7]

~ un voyage to go on a trip [4]

il fait beau/froid, etc. it is nice, cold, etc. (weather) [6]

un et un font deux one and one make two

fait *m.*: **en ~** actually, in fact

falaise *f.* cliff

falloir to be necessary

il faut it is necessary [8]

il faut que (one must) [C]

fameux (-euse) famous

familial(e) (*m.pl.* **-aux**) family

famille *f.* family [2]

fanfaron(ne) boasting

fantasme *m.* fantasy [12]

fantôme *m.* ghost

farci(e) stuffed

fardeau *m.* (*pl.* **fardeaux**) burden

fatigant tiring

fatigué(e) tired [1]

faut (*see* **falloir**)

faute *f.* mistake, error

fauteuil *m.* armchair [3]

faux (fausse) false

faveur *f.*: **en ~ de** in favor of

favori(te) favorite

favoriser to favor

fée *f.*: **bonne ~** fairy godmother

conte de ~s fairy tale

félicitations *f.* congratulations [9]

féliciter to congratulate [9]
femme *f.* woman [1]; wife [2]
  ~ d'affaires businesswoman [11]
  ~ de ménage housekeeper
fenêtre *f.* window [P]
fer *m.* iron
  ~ à repasser *m.* iron (for ironing clothes)
ferme *f.* farm
fermer to close
féroce fierce
fête *f.* saint's day; celebration, party; holiday [9]
  ~ foraine carnival
  ~ nationale national holiday
fêter to celebrate
feu *m.* (*pl.* **feux**) fire [10]
  ~ rouge *m.* traffic light
feuille *f.* leaf
  ~ de papier sheet of paper [P]
feuilleter to leaf through
feuilleton *m.* soap opera [6]
février *m.* February [4]
se ficher de to not care
  je m'en fiche! I don't give a damn! [4]
fidèle faithful
fier (fière) proud
fierté *f.* pride
fièvre *f.* fever
fille *f.* girl [1]; daughter [2]
film *m.* movie [2]
  ~ d'amour romantic film [2]
  ~ d'aventure action film [2]
  ~ d'épouvante horror movie [6]
  ~ policier detective movie [6]
fils *m.* son [2]
fin *f.* end
finalement finally [5]
financier (-ière) financial
finir to finish [10]
fixe fixed
flamand *m.* Flemish
flanelle *f.* flannel [10]
fleur *f.* flower [9]
  à ~s flowered [10]
fleurir to make bloom
fleuve *m.* river
foie *m.* **gras** goose liver pâté
fois *f.* time [2]
  à la ~ at the same time
  une ~ once [2]
foncé(e) dark (color) [10]
fonction *f.* **publique** public office
fonctionnaire *m./f.* civil servant [11]

fonctionner to work (machine)
fondé(e) founded
fontaine *f.* fountain
foot(ball) *m.* soccer [2]
  faire du ~ to play soccer [4]
force *f.* strength
  ~ ouvrière workforce
  de ~ by force
forêt *f.* forest [7]
formation *f.* education, training [11]
forme *f.* shape, figure [10]
  en (bonne) ~ in (good) shape [10]
formidable terrific, great [4]
formulaire *m.* form [11]
formule *f.* formula
  ~s de politesse polite expressions [P]
fort *adv.* loud; hard
fort(e) heavy-set, fat; strong [1]
forteresse *f.* fortress
fortune *f.* fortune
  bonne ~ luck
fou (folle) crazy, foolish [1]; incredible
foulard *m.* scarf [C]
foule *f.* crowd [12]
four *m.* oven
  au ~ baked
fourchette *f.* fork [5]
frais *m.* expense
frais (fraîche) fresh; cool [5]
  il fait frais it's cool (weather) [6]
fraise *f.* strawberry [5]
framboise *f.* raspberry [5]
français *m.* French (language) [4]
français(e) French [1]
France *f.* France
francophone French-speaking
francophonie *f.* French-speaking countries
franchement frankly
frapper to knock; to strike, to hit [9]
fréquemment frequently [11]
frère *m.* brother [2]
frites *f.pl.* French fries [5]
froid(e) cold [5]
  il fait ~ it's cold (weather) [6]
fromage *m.* cheese [5]
front *m.* forehead [10]
frontière *f.* border [C]
fruit *m.* fruit [5]
  ~s de mer *m.pl.* seafood [5]
fuir to flee

fumeurs *m.pl.* smokers; smoking (section) [7]
fusil *m.* gun, rifle

gagner to win; to gain; to earn [11]
  ~ sa vie to earn a living [11]
gagneur/gagneuse *m./f.* winner
gant *m.* glove [10]
garage *m.* garage [7]
garantir to guarantee
garçon *m.* boy [1]
garder to keep
gare *f.* train station [3]
garni(e) served with vegetables
gâteau *m.* (*pl.* **gâteaux**) cake [5]
gâter to spoil
gauche *f.* left [3]
  à ~ to the left, on the left [3]
gênant(e) annoying
généralement generally [11]
généreux (-euse) generous [1]
génial(e) cool, great
genou *m.* (*pl.* **genoux**) knee [10]
genre *m.* type, sort, kind [6]
gens *m.pl.* people [1]
gentil(le) nice [4]
géographie *f.* geography [4]
geste *m.* gesture
gestion *f.* business management [4]
gîte *m.* shelter
glace *f.* ice cream [5]; ice
  ~ à la vanille vanilla ice cream [5]
  ~ au chocolat chocolate ice cream [5]
glacé(e) icy
glacial(e) icy, bitterly cold
glisser to slip
golf *m.* golf [4]
  faire du ~ to play golf [4]
gomme *f.* eraser [P]
gorge *f.* throat [10]
  avoir mal à la ~ to have a sore throat
goût *m.* taste [8]
gouvernement *m.* government
grâce à thanks to
grammaire *f.* grammar
gramme *m.* gram [5]
grand-mère *f.* grandmother [2]
grand-père *m.* grandfather [2]
grand(e) big; tall [1]
  grande personne *f.* grown-up
grandir to grow up

grands-parents *m.pl.* grandparents [2]

gras(se) greasy, fatty [5]
  faire la grasse matinée to sleep in [4]

gratin *m.* dish baked with breadcrumbs or grated cheese on top

gratinée à l'oignon *f.* onion soup

grippe *f.* flu [12]

gris(e) gray [2]

gronder to rumble

gros(se) heavyset [1]; big, great
  grosses bises hugs and kisses

grossièreté *f.* vulgarity

grossir to gain weight [10]

grouper to group

guerre *f.* war [C]
  ~ de Sécession American Civil War
  Première ~ mondiale World War I

guerrier *m.* warrior

guichet *m.* ticket window [7]

guirlande *f.* garland

gymnastique *f.* gymnastics [4]
  faire de la ~ to exercise [4]

s'habiller to get dressed [10]

habitant(e) *m./f.* inhabitant

habiter to live [2]

habitude *f.* habit
  comme d'~ as usual

habituel(le) usual

s'habituer to become accustomed

haltère *f.* dumbbell

***Hanoukka** *f.* Hanukkah

***hanter** to haunt

***haricots** *m.pl.* **verts** green beans [5]

***haut** *m.* upper part

***haut(e)** high [10]
  à haute voix aloud

***hein?** eh? [1]

herbe *f.* grass

héritage *m.* heritage

***héros** *m.* hero

heure *f.* hour, o'clock; time [4]
  à l'~ on time [6]
  à quelle ~? at what time? [4]
  de bonne ~ early

An asterisk (*) indicates an aspirate h: no liaison or elision is made at the beginning of the word.

~s supplémentaires overtime

quelle ~ est-il? what time is it? [4]

tout à l'~ in a little while

heureusement fortunately [11]

heureux (-euse) happy [1]

hier yesterday [5]

histoire *f.* history [4]; story [6]

historique historical [2]

hiver *m.* winter [6]

***hockey** *m.* hockey [6]

***homard** *m.* lobster [5]

homme *m.* man [1]
  ~ d'affaires *m.* businessman [11]

***honte** *f.* shame
  avoir ~ to be ashamed

hôpital *m.* (*pl.* **hôpitaux**) hospital [3]

horaire *m.* timetable, schedule; hours [7]

horloge *f.* clock [P]

***hors de** out of

***hors-d'œuvre** *m.* (*pl.* **hors-d'œuvre**) hors d'œuvre [5]

hôte *m.* host

hôtel *m.* hotel [3]
  ~ particulier mansion

hôtelier (-ière) hotel (*adj.*)

***huit** eight

huître *f.* oyster [5]

humain(e) human

humide damp

hypothèse *f.* hypothesis

hypothétique hypothetical

ici here; this is (on telephone) [3]

idéal(e) ideal [1]

idéaliste idealistic [1]

idée *f.* idea [6]
  se changer les ~s to take one's mind off things

identifier to identify

identité *f.* identity

ignorer to not know

il he, it [P]

il y a there is, there are [2]; ago [6]
  il n'y a pas de quoi you're welcome [P]

île *f.* island [7]

illuminé(e) lit up

illusoire illusory

ils they [1]

image *f.* picture, image [9]

imaginer to imagine

immédiatement immediately

immeuble *m.* apartment building

immigré(e) *m./f.* immigrant [C]

impatiemment impatiently [11]

impatient(e) impatient [1]

imperméable *m.* raincoat [10]

impliquer to involve

s'imposer to be called for; to be essential

impressionniste impressionist

imprévu(e) unexpected

imprimé(e) printed
  tissu *m.* **~** print fabric [10]

impuissant(e) powerless

inattendu(e) unexpected

incarner to embody

incluant including

incontesté(e) uncontested

incrédule skeptical

incroyable incredible [4]

indépendant(e) independent
  entrée indépendante separate entrance

index *m.* index finger

indifférence *f.* indifference [C]

indifférent(e) indifferent [C]

indigène *m./f.* native

indigestion *f.* indigestion [12]

indiquer to indicate

indiscret (-ète) indiscreet

individu *m.* individual

individualiste nonconformist [1]

individuel(le) individual [3]

industriel *m.* industrialist

inférieur(e) inferior

infini(e) infinite

infirmerie *f.* nurse's office

infirmier/infirmière *m./f.* nurse [11]

information *f.* information
  ~s news

informatique *f.* computer science [4]

ingénieur *m.* engineer [1]

injuste unfair

inquiet (-ète) worried

(s')inquiéter to worry [12]

inquiétude *f.* worry

insolite strange

s'installer to settle

instituteur/institutrice *m./f.* grade school teacher

instruction *f.* education

s'intégrer to be integrated [C]

intelligent(e) intelligent [1]

intention: avoir l'~ de to intend to [11]

interdiction *f.* ban
interdire to forbid
interdit(e) forbidden
intéressant(e) interesting [1]
intéresser to interest
  s'~ à to be interested in [10]
  ça vous (t')intéresse? would you like to? [6]
intérêt *m.* interest; advantage
interprète *m./f.* interpreter
interroger to question [9]
interviewer to interview
s'intituler to be entitled
intolérance *f.* intolerance [C]
intolérant(e) intolerant [C]
inutile useless
investir to invest
invité(e) *m./f.* guest
inviter to invite [2]
irisé(e) in rainbow colors
irrité(e) irritated
islamique Islamic
isolé(e) isolated
Italie *f.* Italy
italien(ne) Italian [1]

jaloux (-ouse) jealous
jamais never [2]
  ne... ~ never [5]
jambe *f.* leg [10]
jambon *m.* ham [5]
janvier *m.* January [4]
japonais(e) Japanese [1]
jardin *m.* garden [7]
jardinet *m.* small garden
jaune yellow [3]
jazz *m.* jazz [2]
je I [P]
jean *m.* jeans [10]
jeu *m.* (*pl.* **jeux**) game
jeudi *m.* Thursday [4]
jeune young [3]
jeunesse *f.* youth
jogging *m.* jogging [4]; sweats [10]
  faire du ~ to go jogging [4]
joie *f.* joy
joli(e) pretty [3]
jongleur *m.* juggler
joue *f.* cheek [10]
jouer to play; to gamble [2]
jouet *m.* toy [9]
jour *m.* day; daytime [4]
  de nos ~s today
  ~ chômé public holiday

  ~ d'action de grâces Thanksgiving Day
  ~ de congé day off; holiday [9]
  ~ de fête holiday
  ~ de l'An New Year's Day
  ~ des morts All Souls' Day
  ~ férié public holiday
  par ~ a day (per day)
  tous les jours every day
journal *m.* (*pl.* **journaux**) newspaper [6]
  ~ télévisé *m.* news (TV) [6]
journaliste *m./f.* journalist, reporter [1]
journée *f.* day(time) [4]
  ~ de repos *f.* day of rest
joyeux (-euse) happy; merry [9]
judo *m.* judo [6]
juillet *m.* July [4]
juin *m.* June [4]
jupe *f.* skirt [10]
juridique legal
jus *m.* **de fruits** fruit juice [5]
jusqu'à as far as, up to [3]
jusqu'où how far
juste just; fair
justement exactly

kilo *m.* kilogram [5]
kiosque *m.* newsstand

la (*see* **le/la/l'/les**)
-là (*see* **ce/cet/cette/ces**)
là there [3]
  il est ~ he is in [3]
  il n'est pas ~ he's not in [3]
là-bas there, over there [1]
là-dedans inside
lac *m.* lake [7]
lâcher to let go of
laine *f.* wool [10]
  en ~ wool [10]
laisser to let, to allow
  ~ à l'abandon to abandon
  ~ tomber to drop
lait *m.* milk [5]
  ~ maternisé infant formula
lampe *f.* lamp [3]
lancer to launch
langage *m.* language
langue *f.* language
  ~ étrangère foreign language [4]
lapin *m.* rabbit
laquelle (*see* **lequel**)

larme *f.* tear
lasagne *f.* lasagna
lavabo *m.* bathroom sink [7]
laver to wash [8]
  se ~ to wash (oneself) [10]
le/la/l'/les *art.* the [1]
le/la/l'/les *pron.* him, her, it, them [6]
lecteur/lectrice *m./f.* reader
  lecteur de CD CD player [3]
lecture *f.* reading [6]
légèrement lightly
légume *m.* vegetable [5]
lendemain *m.* the next day [6]
lentement slowly [11]
lequel/laquelle/lesquel(le)s which one(s)
les (*see* **le/la/l'/les**)
lessive *f.* laundry [8]
lettre *f.* letter [6]
  ~ de l'alphabet letter of the alphabet [P]
leur *pron.* (to) them [6]
leur *adj.* their [2]
lever to raise [10]
  ~ le doigt to raise one's hand [9]
  se ~ to get up; to rise [10]
lèvres *f.pl.* lips [10]
libéré(e) freed
libérer to free
liberté *f.* freedom
  ~ d'expression freedom of speech
  ~ d'expression religieuse freedom of religion
libre free [4]
licence *f.* bachelor's degree
lien *m.* tie, bond; link
  ~ de parenté family relationship
lier to link
lieu *m.* (*pl.* **lieux**) place [3]
  avoir ~ to take place
  au ~ de instead of
ligne *f.* **aérienne** airline
lire to read [2]
lit *m.* bed [3]
  faire son ~ to make one's bed [4]
  ~s superposés bunk beds
litre *m.* liter [5]
littérature *f.* literature [2]
livre *f.* pound [5]
livre *m.* book [P]
locataire *m./f.* tenant, renter [3]
logement *m.* lodging [3]
logique logical
logis *m.* lodging

loi *f.*   law [C]
loin   far away; far
  ~ de   far from [3]
loisir *m.*   leisure
  ~s   leisure activities [2]
long(ue)   long [4]
  à manches longues   long-sleeved [10]
  le long de   along
longtemps   a long time [9]
longueur *f.*   length
loterie *f.*   lottery [12]
loto *m.*   bingo
louer   to rent [3]
lugubre   gloomy
lui   he; him; to him/her [6]
lumière *f.*   light
lumineux (-euse)   luminous, bright
lundi *m.*   Monday [4]
lune *f.*   moon [10]
lunettes *f.pl.*   (eye)glasses
  ~ de soleil   sunglasses [10]
lutte *f.*   wrestling
lutter (contre)   to fight (against) [C]
luxe *m.*   luxury
lycée *m.*   high school [4]

ma (*see* **mon/ma/mes**)
macédoine *f.* **de légumes**   mixed vegetables
madame (Mme) (*pl.* **mesdames**)   madam, Mrs. [P]
mademoiselle (Mlle) (*pl.* **mesdemoiselles**)   Miss [P]
magasin *m.*   store [3]
magazine *m.*   magazine [2]
Maghreb *m.*   Maghreb
maghrebin(e)   from the Maghreb
magnétoscope *m.*   video cassette recorder [3]
magnifique   magnificent [9]
magnifiquement   magnificently
mai *m.*   May [4]
maigrir   to lose weight [10]
maille: en ~   knit
maillot *m.* **de bain**   bathing suit [10]
main *f.*   hand [10]
main-d'œuvre *f.*   manpower
maintenant   now [3]
maintenir   to maintain
maire *m.*   mayor

mais   but [1]
  ~ oui   but of course; well, yes [1]
  ~ non   of course not [1]
  ~ si   well, yes [1]
maïs *m.*   corn [5]
maison *f.*   house [3]
  ~ de campagne   country house
maître *m.* **d'hôtel**   butler
maîtresse *f.*   schoolteacher [9]
maîtrise *f.*   master's degree
maîtriser   to master
majeur(e)   main, major
majorité *f.*   majority
  grande ~   vast majority
mal   badly, poorly [2]
mal *m.*   evil
  avoir du ~ à   to have a hard time [C]
  avoir ~ à   to hurt [12]
  ~ à la gorge   sore throat [12]
  ~ à la tête   headache [12]
malade   sick, ill [1]
maladie *f.*   disease, illness [112A]
malaise *m.*   discomfort
malentendu *m.*   misunderstanding
malgré   in spite of
malheur *m.*   misfortune, bad luck
malheureusement   unfortunately [6]
malheureux (-euse)   unfortunate
maman *f.*   mom
manche *f.*   sleeve
  à ~s courtes   short-sleeved [10]
  à ~s longues   long-sleeved [10]
  sans ~s   sleeveless
manger   to eat [2]
  se ~   to be eaten
mangue *f.*   mango
manier   to handle
manière *f.*   way, means
  ~s   manners
manifester   to demonstrate
mannequin *m.*   model
manque *m.*   lack [11]
  un ~ de   a lack of [11]
manquer   to miss
  il manque . . .   is missing
manteau *m.* (*pl.* **manteaux**)   coat [10]
maquillage *m.*   makeup
se maquiller   to put on makeup [10]
marchand(e) *m./f.*   merchant
marche *f.*   walking [4]
  faire de la ~   to go walking [4]

marché *m.*   market
mardi *m.*   Tuesday [4]
  ~ gras *m.*   Shrove Tuesday
mari *m.*   husband [2]
mariage *m.*   marriage [8]
  ~ à l'essai   trial marriage
se marier   to get married; to blend [8]
marine: bleu marine   navy blue [10]
Maroc *m.*   Morocco
marocain(e)   Moroccan [1]
marque *f.*   brand [10]
marqué(e)   marked
marquer un but   to score a goal
marre: j'en ai ~!   I've had it! [4]
marron *inv.*   brown [10]
marron *m.*   chestnut
mars *m.*   March [4]
masque *f.*   mask
match *m.*   match, game [2]
matériel(le)   material
maths *f.pl.*   math [4]
matière *f.*   school subject [4]
  en ~ de   in the matter of [4]
matin *m.*   morning [4]
  du ~   in the morning (time)
matinal(e) (*m.pl.* **-aux**)   morning (*adj.*)
matinée *f.*   morning
  faire la grasse ~   to sleep in [4]
mauvais(e)   bad [3]
  il fait mauvais   it's bad weather [6]
me   me, to me [8]
mécanicien/mécanicienne *m./f.*   mechanic [1]
mécontent(e)   displeased
médecin *m.*   doctor [1]
médecine *f.*   (discipline of) medicine [4]
médias *m.pl.*   (communications) media
médicament *m.*   medicine, medication [12]
meilleur(e)   better (*adj.*) [5]
  le meilleur/la meilleure/les meilleur(e)s   the best [9]
se mêler: De quoi te mêles-tu?   Mind your own business!
membre *m.*   member
même *adj.*   same [7]
  -~   self
même *adv.*   even
mémoire *f.*   memory

menacer   to threaten
ménage *m.*   household
mental(e) (*m.pl.* **-aux**)   mental
menteur/menteuse *m./f.*   liar
mentionné(e)   mentioned [2]
mentir   to lie
menton *m.*   chin
menu *m.*   menu; fixed-price menu [5]
mépriser   to despise, to scorn
mer *f.*   sea [7]
   fruits *m.pl.* **de ~**   seafood [5]
merci   thank you [P]; mercy
   ~ mille fois   many thanks [9]
mercredi *m.*   Wednesday [4]
mère *f.*   mother [2]
mériter   to deserve [12]
merveilleux (-euse)   marvelous
mes (*see* **mon/ma/mes**)
mésaventure *f.*   misadventure
message *m.*   message [6]
   ~ électronique   e-mail message [6]
messe *f.*   Mass
météo(rologique): bulletin *m.*
   ~   weather report [6]
métier *m.*   occupation, career [11]
métro *m.*   subway
mettre   to put; to put on [10]
   ~ au piquet   to put in the corner (punish)
meublé(e)   furnished [3]
   non ~   unfurnished [3]
meubles *m.pl.*   furniture [3]
mexicain(e)   Mexican [1]
Mexique *m.*   Mexico
mi-chemin: à ~   half-way
mi-temps: à ~   half/part-time [11]
miche *f.* **de pain**   loaf of bread
midi *m.*   noon [4]
mieux (*adv.*)   better [5]
   il vaudrait ~   it would be better [C]
   il vaut ~ que   it is better that [C]
   le ~   the best (*adv.*) [9]
migraine *f.*   migraine [12]
mijaurée *f.*   stuck-up woman
milieu *m.*   middle; milieu
   au ~ de   in the middle of
   ~ de travail   workplace
   ~ social   social class
militaire   military
mille *inv.*   thousand [3]
milliard *m.*   billion [3]
million *m.*   million [3]

mince   slender, thin [1]
   ~ (alors)!   drat!, darn it! [4]
minérale: eau *f.* **~**   mineral water [5]
mini-pochette *f.*   small clutch bag
ministre *m.*   cabinet minister
   premier ~   prime minister
minuit *m.*   midnight [4]
mis(e) en conserve   canned
misère *f.*   poverty [C]
mite *f.*   clothes moth
mixte   mixed
se mobiliser   to rally, mobilize [C]
mocassin *m.*   loafer; moccasin [10]
mode *m.*   mood
   sur le ~ rigolo   in a funny way
mode *f.*   fashion; style [10]
modéré(e)   moderate
modeste   modest
moi   me [11]
   ~ non plus   me neither; neither do I [1]
   ~ aussi   me too; so do I [1]
moins (de)   less, fewer [5]
   au ~   at least [2]
   de ~ en ~   less and less
   en ~   less; fewer
   le/la/les ~   the least [9]
   ~ dix   ten minutes to (the hour) [4]
   ~ le quart   quarter to (the hour) [4]
   ~ que   less than [5]
mois *m.*   month [4]
moitié *f.*   half
moment *m.*   moment [3]
   un ~   just a minute [3]
mon/ma/mes   my [2]
monde *m.*   world [7]
   tout le ~   everyone
monotone   monotonous
monsieur/M.   sir, Mr. [P]
montagne *f.*   mountain [6]
   en ~   in the mountains
monter   to go up; to bring up; to climb; to get ahead [6]
montre *f.*   watch
montrer   to show [9]
monture *f.*   eyeglass frame
monument *m.*   monument [7]
moral(e)   moral
morale *f.*   morals, ethics
   faire la ~ à   to lecture
morceau *m.* (*pl.* **morceaux**)   piece [5]
   ~ de craie   piece of chalk [P]

mort(e)   dead [9]
mort *f.*   death [12]
morue *f.*   cod
mosquée *f.*   mosque
mot *m.*   word
   écrire un ~   to write a note
   ~ apparenté   cognate
mot-clé *m.*   key word
motiver   to motivate
mouche *f.*   fly
moulant(e)   tight-fitting
mourir   to die [112A]
mousse *f.* **au chocolat**   chocolate mousse [5]
moyen(ne)   average [8]
   classe moyenne *f.*   middle class
moyenne *f.*   average
   en ~   on average
moyen *m.*   means
municipalité *f.*   town government
mur *m.*   wall [P]
mûrir   to mature
murmurer   to whisper, to murmur [9]
musculation *f.*   weight lifting [10]
musée *m.*   museum [3]
musicien/musicienne *m./f.*   musician [1]
musique *f.*   music [2]
   faire de la ~   to play music [4]
musulman(e)   Moslem

nager   to swim [7]
naïf (naïve)   naive
naissance *f.*   birth
naître   to be born
narrateur/narratrice *m./f.*   narrator
natation *f.*   swimming [4]
   faire de la ~   to swim [4]
nationalité *f.*   nationality [1]
nature *f.*   nature [7]
naturel(le)   natural
nausée *f.*   nausea [12]
   avoir la ~   to be nauseated [12]
navette *f.* **spaciale**   space shuttle
navigateur *m.*   seafarer
ne (n')   not [1]
   ~... jamais   never [5]
   ~... pas   not [1]
   ~... personne   no one, nobody, not anyone [9]
   ~... plus   no more, no longer [5]

~... **que** only
~... **rien** nothing, not anything [9]
né(e) born
néanmoins nevertheless
nécessité *f.* necessity
négatif (-ive) negative
neige *f.* snow [6]
   chute de ~ snowfall
neiger: il neige it's snowing [6]
nerveux (-euse) nervous [1]
n'est-ce pas? isn't it so? [1]
nettoyer to clean
neuf nine
neuf (neuve) (brand-)new
neveu *m.* (*pl.* **neveux**) nephew [2]
nez *m.* nose [10]
   avoir le ~ qui coule to have a runny nose [12]
   ~ bouché stuffy nose [12]
ni: ~ l'un ~ l'autre neither one [2]
nièce *f.* niece [2]
n'importe no matter
niveau *m.* (*pl.* **niveaux**) level
nœud *m.* knot
noir *m.* black [3]
noir(e) black; dark [2]
nom *m.* name
   ~ de famille *m.* surname [P]
nombre *m.* number
   ~s ordinaux ordinal numbers [3]
non-fumeurs non-smoking (section) [7]
nord *m.* north [6]
nos (*see* **notre/nos**)
note *f.* note; grade
notre/nos our [2]
nourrir to feed
nourriture *f.* food
nous we [1]; (to) us [8]
nouveau/nouvel/nouvelle/ nouveaux/nouvelles new [3]
   de nouveau again
nouvelle *f.* (piece of) news
novembre *m.* November [4]
noyade *f.* drowning
nuage *m.* cloud [6]
nuageux (-euse) cloudy [6]
nuit *f.* night [7]
numéro *m.* number
numéroter to number
nylon *m.* nylon [10]

obéir to obey
objectif *m.* goal, objective

objet *m.* object, thing
   ~ d'art art object
   ~s personnels *m.pl.* personal possessions [3]
   ~s trouvés *m.pl.* lost-and-found
obligatoire mandatory
obscurité *f.* darkness [12]
obstinément stubbornly
obtenir to obtain, to get
occasion *f.* opportunity [9]
occupé(e) busy [4]
s'occuper de to be busy with
octobre *m.* October [4]
odeur *f.* odor, smell
odorant(e) fragrant
œil *m.* (*pl.* **yeux**) eye [10]
œuf *m.* egg [5]
officialisation *f.* making official
officiel(le) official
offrir to offer, to give [9]
oie *f.* goose
oignon *m.* onion [5]
oiseau *m.* (*pl.* **oiseaux**) bird
omelette *f.* omelet [5]
on one; people; they; we
oncle *m.* uncle [2]
onze eleven
opéra *m.* opera
opinion *f.* opinion
optimiste optimistic [1]
or *m.* gold
orage *m.* storm [6]
orageux (-euse) stormy [6]
orange *f.* orange [5]
   ~ (adj.) inv. orange
ordinateur *m.* computer [3]
ordre *m.* order
   par ~ décroissant in descending order
oreille *f.* ear [10]
organisation *f.* organization
organiser to organize
origine *f.* origin; source; background [C]
   à l'~ originally
   d'origine africaine of African origin [C]
os *m.* bone
ou or [1]
où where [3]
   le jour ~ the day that
   ~ se trouve... ? where is . . . located? [3]
ouais yeah
oublier to forget [5]
ouest *m.* west [6]

ours *m.* **en peluche** teddy bear
outre-mer overseas
ouvert(e) open [9]
ouvragé(e) worked, decorated
ouvrier/ouvrière *m./f.* factory worker [11]
ouvrir to open
   s'~ to open oneself up

pain *m.* bread [5]
   ~ grillé *m.* toast [5]
paix *f.* peace
palace *m.* luxury hotel
pâlir to pale
palmier *m.* palm tree
pamplemousse *m.* grapefruit
pancarte *f.* sign
panne: tomber en ~ to break down
pansement *m.* bandage [12]
   faire un ~ to bandage [12]
pantalon *m.* pants [10]
   pantalon de survêtement sweatpants
pantoufle *f.* slipper [10]
papa *m.* dad
papier *m.* paper
   ~ à lettres stationery
Pâques *f.pl.* Easter
par by
   ~ contre on the other hand [2]
   ~ jour a (per) day
paraître to appear, to seem
parc *m.* park
parce que because
parcourir to skim
pardon excuse me [3]
   ~? what? excuse me? [P]
pareil(le) equal [8]
parenté *f.* family relationship
parents *m.pl.* relatives; parents [2]
   ~ éloignés distant relatives
paresseux (-euse) lazy [1]
parfait(e) perfect [6]
   c'est parfait! that's perfect! [6]
parfum *m.* perfume; scent
Paris *m.* Paris
parisien(ne) Parisian
parlement *m.* parliament
parler to speak [2]
   se ~ to talk to each other [8]
parmi among
parole *f.* word; lyric
   donner sa ~ to give one's word

part *f.*: **à ~** apart from
  c'est de la ~ de qui? may I ask
    who's calling? [3]
partager to share
partenaire *m./f.* partner [8]
parti *m.* party
particularisme *m.* specific
    characteristics
particulier (-ière) particular,
    private
  hôtel *m.* **~** mansion
particulier: chez un ~ in a private
    house
partie *f.* part; game
partir to leave [7]
partout everywhere [10]
parure *f.* dress, finery
pas *m.* step
pas not [P]
  ~ beaucoup not much, not many
    [2]
  ~ de ... no . . .
  ~ du tout not at all [1]
  ~ mal not bad [P]
  ~ tant de manières! stop fooling
    around!
  ~ trop not very, not too
passé *m.* past
passé(e) last; past
passe-temps *m.* pastime [6]
passeport *m.* passport
passer to take (an exam) [4]; to
    pass (through, by) [6]; to spend
    (time) [7]
  ~ l'aspirateur to vacuum [8]
  ~ par to stop by
se passer to happen [8]
  qu'est-ce qui s'est passé? what
    happened?
passif (-ive) passive [1]
pâté *m.* pâté [5]
pâtes *f.pl.* pasta [5]
patiemment patiently [11]
patient(e) patient [1]
patin *m.* skate
  ~ à roulettes roller skate
patinage *m.* **sur glace** ice skating
patinoire *f.* skating rink
pâtisserie *f.* pastry shop [5]
patrie *f.* country
patron/patronne *m./f.* boss [11]
paupière *f.* eyelid [10]
pause-café *f.* coffee break
pauvre poor [1]
  ~ de moi! woe is me!
pauvre *m./f.* poor person [C]

pauvreté *f.* poverty [C]
payer to pay [5]
pays *m.* country [6]
paysage *m.* countryside, landscape
peau *f.* skin
pêche *f.* peach [5]; fishing [7]
  aller à la ~ to go fishing [7]
péché *m.* sin
pêcheur *m.* fisherman
se peigner to comb one's hair [10]
peine *f.* sorrow, pain
  à ~ barely
peintre *m.* painter [1]
peinture *f.* painting [4]
pelouse *f.* lawn
peluche *f.* stuffed animal [9]
penché(e) sur concerned with
pendant during [7]
  ~ que while
pendant combien de temps for
    how long [7]
pensée *f.* thought
penser to think [2]
  ~ à to think about [2]
  ~ de to think of
pension *f.* **complète** lodging and
    meals
perdre to lose [7]
  ~ du temps to waste time
père *m.* father [2]
père Noël *m.* Santa Claus [9]
période *f.* period
permanence: en ~ permanently
permettre to allow, to permit
perpétuer to carry on
persillade *f.* chopped parsley
personnage *m.* character
personnalité *f.* personality
personne no one, nobody [9]
  ~ ne no one, nobody [9]
  ne... ~ no one, nobody, not
    anyone [9]
personne *f.* person
  grande ~ grown-up
perte *f.* loss
perturbation *f.* weather
    disturbance
peser to weigh
pessimiste [1]
petit(e) short, small, little [1]
  ~ ami(e) *m./f.* boyfriend/
    girlfriend [8]
  ~ déjeuner *m.* breakfast [5]
  ~s pois *m.pl.* peas [5]
petit-fils/petite-fille *m./f.*
    grandson/granddaughter [2]

pétition *f.* petition [C]
pétri(e) de steeped in
peu little, a little [1]
  un ~ a little [5]
  à ~ près almost, nearly
peuplé(e) inhabited
peur *f.* fear [12]
  avoir ~ to be afraid [4]
  faire ~ à to scare [12]
peut-être perhaps, maybe [1]
phare *m.* light
pharmacie *f.* drugstore [3]
pharmacien/pharmacienne *m./f.*
    pharmacist [12]
philosophie *f.* philosophy [4]
phobie *f.* phobia
photo *f.* **de famille** family photo
    [2]
photographie *f.* photograph
phrase *f.* sentence
physique *f.* physics [4]
physique physical
  éducation ~ physical education
    [4]
pièce *f.* room [3]
pied *m.* foot [10]
  à ~ on foot [7]
pilon *m.* pestle
piment *m.* bell pepper
pique-nique *m.* picnic [9]
piqûre *f.* injection [12]
  faire une ~ à to give an injection
    to [12]
pire worse
  le ~ the worst
piscine *f.* pool [7]
pizza *f.* pizza [5]
placard *m.* closet [3]
place *f.* seat, place; room [7];
    square [3]
plage *f.* beach [7]
plainte *f.* complaint
plaire to please [4]
  ça te plaît? do you like that? [4]
plaisance *f.*: **de ~** pleasure related
plaisanter: to kid
  tu plaisantes! you're kidding!
    [4]
plaisir *m.* pleasure [6]
  avec ~ with pleasure [6]
plan *m.* **de la ville** street map [3]
planche *f.* **à voile** sailboarding
planète *f.* planet
plat *m.* course (food), dish [5]
  ~ principal main course [5]
  ~s cuisinés prepared foods

plat(e) flat
plateau *m.* (*pl.* **plateaux**) platter
  à ~ platform (shoe)
plein(e) full
  à ~ temps full-time [11]
  en ~ air outdoor
pléthore *f.* plethora
pleurer to cry [5]
pleut: il ~ it's raining [6]
plié(e) bent
plongée *f.* **sous-marine** diving
pluie *f.* rain [6]
  sous la ~ in the rain
plupart: la ~ de most [9]
pluriel *m.* plural
plus more [5]
  de ~ en ~ more and more
  ne... ~ no more, no longer [5]
  ~ de more [5]
  le/la/les ~ the most [9]
  ~... ~... the more . . . the more
  ~... que more . . . than [5]
  ~ tard later [3]
  ~ tôt earlier [4]
plusieurs several
plutôt instead, rather [2]
  ~ que instead of
pluvieux (-euse) rainy
pneumonie *f.* pneumonia [12]
poche *f.* pocket [10]
poème *m.* poem [6]
poids *m.* weight
poil: de tout ~ of all sorts
poire *f.* pear [5]
pois: à ~ polka dot [10]
  petits ~ peas [5]
poisson *m.* fish [5]
poissonnerie *f.* fishmonger's shop
  [5]
poivre *m.* pepper [5]
poivron *m.* green pepper
pôle *m.* pole
poli(e) polite
policier (-ière) detective [2]
poliment politely [11]
politicien/politicienne *m./f.*
  politician [1]
politique political
polo *m.* polo shirt [10]
polyester *m.* polyester [10]
pomme *f.* apple [5]
  ~ de terre potato [5]
  ~s frites French fries
  tarte *f.* **aux ~s** apple tart [5]
pompes *f.pl.* pushups [10]

population *f.* population
  ~ active workforce
porc *m.* pork [5]
port *m.* wearing; harbor
porte *f.* door [P]
porter to wear; to carry [10]
  se ~ bien to be in good health
poser to place; to put down
  ~ une question to ask a question
  [2]
positif (-ive) positive
position *f.* position, location
posséder to own, to possess, to
  have
possible possible
poste *f.* post office [3]
  par la ~ by mail
poste *m.* job, position [11]
  ~ de télévision television set
poster *m.* poster [3]
postulant/postulante *m./f.*
  applicant
poterie *f.* pottery
poule *f.* hen
poulet *m.* chicken [5]
poupée *f.* doll [9]
  ~ de chiffons rag doll
pour for; to, in order to
  le ~ et le contre pros and cons
  ~ moi in my opinion [C]
pourcentage *m.* percentage
pourquoi why [3]
pourriez-vous... ? could you . . . ?
  [3]
poursuivre to pursue
pourtant yet
pousser to push, to encourage
  ~ des cris to shout
pouvoir to be able to; can [4]
  j'ai pu I succeeded in [9]
  je n'ai pas pu I failed to [9]
pouvoir *m.* power [11]
pratique practical
pratique *f.:* **en ~** in practice
pratiquer to practice
pratiquement practically
précieux (-euse) precious
précis(e) precise
préféré(e) favorite
préférer to prefer [2]
préjugé *m.* prejudice [C]
premier (-ière) first [3]
  premier étage *m.* second floor
  [7]
  première classe *f.* first class [7]

premièrement first [5]
prendre to take [3]; to have (food)
  [5]
  ~ rendez-vous to make an
  appointment [11]
préparer to prepare [4]
  ~ un examen to study for an
  exam [4]
près (de) near [3]
prescrire to prescribe [12]
présent(e) present
présentations *f.pl.* introductions
  [P]
présenter to introduce . . . to . . .
  je te/vous présente let me
  introduce [P]
  se ~ to come to
président(e) *m./f.* president [1]
présider à to preside over
presque almost, nearly [2]
presqu'île *f.* peninsula
pressé(e) in a hurry [5]
pressentir to have a presentiment
prêt(e) ready
prétendre to claim
prêter to lend [8]
preuve *f.* proof
prévu(e) planned
prié(e): est ~ de se présenter is
  asked to come
prier to pray
  je t'/vous en prie you're
  welcome [9]
prière *f.* prayer
prince *m.* prince
princesse *f.* princess
principal(e) (*m.pl.* **-aux**) principal
  plat *m.* **~** main course [5]
principe *m.* principle
printemps *m.* spring [6]
privilégié(e) preferred
prix *m.* price [3]
problème *m.* problem [6]
processus *m.* process
prochain(e) next [6]
proche near (*adj.*)
produit *m.* product [5]
professeur *m.* teacher, professor
  [P]
profession *f.* occupation [1]
  ~ libérale profession [11]
professionnel(le) professional [11]
profiter de to take advantage of
programme *m.* program [6]
progrès *m.* progress

progressivement gradually
proie *f.* prey
projet *m.* plan [4]; project
promenade *f.* walk [4]
  faire une ~ to go for a walk [4]
se promener to go for a walk [10]
promettre to promise
promotion *f.* promotion [11]
se proposer to intend
propre own
propriétaire *m./f.* landlord/
  landlady [3]
protéger to protect
protester to protest [C]
provenance *f.*: **en ~ de** from
provinciaux *m.pl.* French people
  who live outside Paris
provoquer to instigate, to provoke
proximité *f.* proximity
psychologie *f.* psychology [4]
psychologique psychological
psychologue *m./f.* psychologist
pub *f.* commercial [6]
public (-ique) public
publicité *f.* advertisement
publier to publish
puis then [5]
pull *m.* pullover [10]
puni(e) punished [9]
punir to punish
punition *f.* punishment
pureté *f.* purity
pyjama *m.* pyjamas [10]

quand when [3]
  ~ même all the same
quantité *f.* quantity [5]
quarante forty [2]
quart: et ~ fifteen (minutes past the
  hour) [4]
  moins le ~ quarter to (the hour)
    [4]
  ~ de travail *m.* shift
quartier *m.* neighborhood [7]
quatorze fourteen [2]
quatre four [2]
quatre-vingt eighty [3]
quatre-vingt-dix ninety [3]
quatre-vingt-onze ninety-one [3]
quatre-vingt-un eighty-one [3]
que what
  ~ je suis bête! how stupid of me!
    [12]

quel/quelle which, what [2]
  quel âge avez-vous/as-tu? how
    old are you? [2]
  quelle bêtise! how stupid! [12]
  quel temps fait-il? what is the
    weather like?
quelque chose something [5]
  ~ de bon something good
quelquefois sometimes [2]
quelqu'un someone, somebody
    [12]
  ~ de célèbre someone famous
querelle *f.* quarrel
qu'est-ce que what [2]
  ~ c'est? what is it? [P]
  qu'est-ce qu'il y a? what's the
    matter?
  ~ c'est que ça? what is that? [5]
qu'est-ce qui what
  ~ se passe? what's going on?
question *f.* question
qui who [P]
  ~ est à l'appareil? who's calling?
    [3]
quiche *f.* quiche [5]
quinze fifteen
quitter to leave [12]
  ne quittez pas please hold [3]
quoi what
  de la/du ~? some what? [5]
  il n'y a pas de ~ you're welcome
    [9]
quotidien(ne) daily [10]

racisme *m.* racism [C]
raconter to tell, to relate [8]
radio *f.* radio [2]
raffermissement *m.* firming
raffiné(e) refined, cultured
raffinement *m.* refinement
raison *f.* reason
raisonnable reasonable [1]
raisonnablement reasonably
raisonner to reason
Ramadan *m.* Ramadan
ramener to bring back
rang *m.* row
ranger to tidy [8]
rapide fast
rapide *m.* express train
rapidement quickly [11]
rappel *m.* reminder
rappeler to remind (of)

rapport *m.* report [6]; relationship
rarement rarely [11]
se raser to shave [10]
rassuré(e) reassured
rater to miss [7]; to fail (an exam)
    [4]
rattraper to catch up with
ravissant(e) ravishing
rayon *m.* department, counter (in a
  store) [5]
rayure *f.*: **à rayures** striped, with
  stripes
réagir to react
réaliser to accomplish, achieve,
  fulfill [11]
réaliste realistic [1]
réalité *f.* reality [11]
rebrodé(e) embroidered
récemment recently [11]
recensement *m.* census
réceptionniste *m./f.* receptionist
    [7]
recevoir to receive
recherche *f.* research; search
  à la ~ de in search of
rechercher to look for
recommander to recommend [12]
reconnaître to recognize [9]
recouvrir to cover
récréation *f.* recess
recruter to recruit
recycler to recycle
réellement really
refaire to redo
réfléchir to reflect, to think
reflet *m.* reflection
refléter to reflect
  se ~ to be reflected
réflexion *f.* reflection, thought
  à la ~ upon reflection
réforme *f.* reform
refuser to refuse
regard *m.* look, gaze
regarder to look at [2]
régime *m.* diet [5]
  être au ~ to be on a diet [5]
  suivre un ~ to be on a diet
regretter to be sorry; to regret [7]
regroupement *m.* reuniting
réimporter to reimport
reine *f.* queen [9]
rejeter to reject
rejoindre to join
se réjouir to be delighted
relation *f.* relation (not family)

se relever   to pick oneself up; to recover
relier   to connect
religieux (-euse)   religious
relire   to reread
remercier   to thank [9]
remettre   to restore, to return
remplacer   to replace
remplir   to fill out (a form, etc.) [11]
renard *m.*   fox
rencontre *f.*   meeting
rencontrer   to meet [8]
rendre   to make, to render [7]
   ~ malade   to make sick
   ~ visite à   to visit (a person) [7]
renommé   renowned
renseignement *m.*   information
rentrer   to come home; to return; to go back (in) [6]
renvoyer   to fire
répandu(e)   widespread
répartition *f.*   distribution
repas *m.*   meal [5]
repasser   to iron [8]
repenser   to think again
répéter   to repeat
répétition *f.*   repetition
replier   to bend again
répondeur *m.*   answering machine [3]
répondre   to answer, to respond [7]
réponse *f.*   answer; response
repos *m.*   rest
se reposer   to rest [10]
repousser   to push away
représenter   to represent
reprise: à plusieurs ~s   several times
requête *f.*   request
réseau (*pl.* **réseaux**)   network
réservé(e) à   reserved for [11]
résidence *f.* **universitaire**   university dorm [3]
se résigner   to resign oneself
respecter   to respect [C]
responsable   responsible
ressembler (à)   to resemble [2]
   se ~   to look alike
ressentir   to feel
restaurant *m.*   restaurant [2]
   ~ universitaire   university cafeteria [4]
restauration *f.*   restoration
rester   to stay, to remain [6]
   ~ debout   to remain standing [9]

resto-U *m.*   university cafeteria
résultat *m.*   result
résumé *m.*   summary
résumer   to summarize
retard *m.*   lag, delay
   en ~   late [6]
retenir   to keep
retirer   to take off
retour *m.*   return
retourner   to return [6]
   se ~   to turn around
   retraite *f.*   retirement [11]
retrouver   to meet [2]
   se ~   to meet [8]
se réunir   to get together
réussir   to succeed; to make a success of [10]
   ~ à un examen   to pass an exam [4]
réussite *f.*   success [11]
rêve *m.*   dream [12]
(se) réveiller   to wake up [10]
réveillon *m.*   Christmas Eve dinner
révélateur (-trice)   revealing
révéler   to reveal
revenir   to return, to come back [7]
rêver   to dream [12]
   ~ à   to dream of
revêtir   to assume
réviser   to review
revoir   to see again
   se ~   to see each other again [8]
rez-de-chaussée *m.*   ground floor [7]
rhume *m.*   cold [12]
   ~ des foins   hay fever [12]
riche   rich [1]
richesse *f.*   richness
rideaux *m.pl.*   curtains [3]
ridicule   ridiculous
rien   nothing [9]
   ce n'est ~   you're welcome [9]
   de ~   you're welcome [9]
   ne... ~   nothing, not anything [9]
   ~ d'intéressant   nothing interesting
   ~ du tout   nothing at all
rigolo (-ote)   funny
rigoureux (-euse)   harsh
rigueur: à la ~   if need be
rire   to laugh [8]
risque *m.*   risk
rival(e) (*m.pl.* **-aux**)   rival
rivière *f.*   river
riz *m.*   rice [5]

robe *f.*   dress [10]
   ~ de chambre   bathrobe [10]
   ~ du soir   evening dress [10]
rock *m.*   rock music [2]
roi *m.*   king [9]
rôle *m.*   role
   à tour de ~   in turn
romain(e)   Roman
roman *m.*   novel [2]
   ~ d'amour   romantic novel
   ~ policier   detective novel [2]
romanche *m.*   Romansh (language)
rompre   to break
roquefort *m.*   Roquefort cheese [5]
rosbif *m.*   roast beef [5]
roue *f.*   wheel
rouge   red
rouge *m.*   red [3]
route *f.*   road
   ~ en terre   dirt road
routier (-ière)   road (*adj.*)
routine *f.*   routine [10]
roux (rousse)   red (hair) [2]
rue *f.*   street [3]
rupture *f.*   breaking off; breakup
rural(e) (*m.pl.* **ruraux**)   rural
russe   Russian [1]
Russie *f.*   Russia
rythme *m.*   rhythm

sa   (*see* **son/sa/ses**)
sable *m.*   sand
sac *m.* **à dos**   backpack [P]
sacrée   sacred
sacrifier   to sacrifice
sage   quiet, well-behaved; wise
sage-femme *f.*   midwife
saigner   to bleed
sain(e)   healthful [5]
saint(e)   holy
saisir   to seize
saison *f.*   season [6]
salade *f.*   salad; lettuce [5]
salaire *m.*   wages, salary [11]
salle *f.*   room; classroom [P]
   ~ à manger   dining room [3]
   ~ de bains   bathroom [3]
   ~ de classe   classroom [P]
salon *m.*   parlor, living room [3]
salsita *f.*   salsa
salut   hi [P]
salutations *f.pl.*   greetings [P]
samedi *m.*   Saturday [4]

sandale *f.* sandal [10]
sandwich *m.* sandwich [5]
sang *m.* blood
sans without
  ~ doute probably
sans-abri *m./f.* homeless person [C]
santé *f.* health [5]
sapin *m.* fir tree
satisfaire to satisfy
satisfait(e) satisfied [3]
saucisse *f.* sausage [5]
saucisson *m.* salami [5]
sauf except for
sauter to jump
sauvage wild
sauvage *m./f.* savage
sauver to save
savoir to know [9]
  j'ai su I found out [9]
savoir *m.* knowledge
scandaleux (-euse) scandalous [C]
scène *f.* scene
sceptique skeptical
science *f.* science [4]
  ~s politiques political science [4]
scolaire school (*adj.*)
se himself; herself; itself;
  themselves [8]
sec (sèche) dry, dried
secret *m.* secret [8]
secrétaire *m./f.* secretary [1]
sécurité *f.* security
  ~ sociale social security
sein: au ~ de within
seize sixteen
séjour *m.* living room [3]; stay [7]
  faire un ~ to stay [7]
sel *m.* salt [5]
sélectionner to select
selon according to
  ~ vous in your opinion
  ~ le cas as the case may be
semaine *f.* week [4]
  dans une ~ in a week [6]
  une ~ après a week later [6]
semblable similar
sembler to seem [C]
semelle *f.* sole
semestre *m.* semester
sénat *m.* senate
sénateur *m.* senator
Sénégal *m.* Senegal
sénégalais(e) Senegalese [1]
sens *m.* meaning; direction, sense
  ~ inverse opposite direction

sensible sensitive
sensuel(le) sensual
sentimental(e): vie *f.* **sentimentale**
  love life
sentir to smell
  se ~ to feel [8]
  se ~ bien/mal to feel well/ill [12]
séparé(e) separate
séparément separately
séparer to separate
sept seven
septembre *m.* September [4]
série *f.* series
sérieusement seriously [11]
sérieux (-euse) serious [1]
serpent *m.* snake
serré(e) tight
serveur/serveuse *m./f.* waiter/
  waitress [5]
service *m.* service
  ~ compris tip included
  ~ militaire military service
serviette *f.* briefcase [P]; napkin [5]
servir to serve; to be of use [7]
serviteur/servante *m./f.* servant
ses (*see* **son/sa/ses**)
seuil *m.* **de la pauvreté** poverty
  level
seul(e) alone
seulement only [11]
short *m.* shorts [10]
si yes [2]
  mais ~ well, yes [1]
si *adv.* as, so
si conj. if [12]; what if? [8]
sida *m.* AIDS [12]
siècle *m.* century
siège *m.* seat, headquarters
sieste *f.* nap [4]
  faire la ~ to take a nap [4]
signe *m.* sign
signification *f.* meaning
signifier to mean
s'il vous (te) plaît please [P]
singulier *m.* singular
sirop *m.* syrup [12]
sketch *m.* skit
ski *m.* skiing [4]
  faire du ~ to ski [4]
  ~ nautique water skiing [7]
smoking *m.* tuxedo [10]
sociable friendly, outgoing [1]
social(e) (*m.pl.* **sociaux**) social
société *f.* society; company [11]
sociologie *f.* sociology [4]

sociologue *m./f.* sociologist
sœur sister [2]
soi oneself [11]
  à ~ of one's own
soie *f.* silk [10]
soi-même oneself [12]
soif *f.* thirst [5]
  avoir ~ to be thirsty [5]
soigner to take care of
soin *m.* care
soir *m.* evening [4]
  ce ~ tonight
  demain ~ tomorrow night [6]
  du ~ in the evening (time) [4]
  hier ~ last night [6]
soirée *f.* party [8]
soixante sixty [2]
soixante et onze seventy-one [3]
soixante-dix seventy [3]
soixante-douze seventy-two [3]
sol *m.* soil; land
soldat *m.* soldier
solde *m.* sale
  en ~s on sale
soleil *m.* sun [6]
  il fait du ~ it's sunny [6]
solitude *f.* solitude [12]
solution *f.* solution [C]
sombre dark
son *m.* sound
son/sa/ses his/her/its [2]
sondage *m.* survey, poll
sonder to survey
sortie *f.* outing [6]
sortir to go out [7]
souche: de ~ by blood
souci *m.* concern, care [12]
se soucier de to worry about
soudain suddenly
souffle *m.* breath
souffrir to suffer
souhaiter to wish [9]
souligner to underscore
soupçonner to suspect
soupe *f.* soup [5]
  ~ au poulet chicken soup
souper *m.* supper
sourcil *m.* eyebrow
souris *f.* mouse
sous under
  ~ la pluie in the rain
se soustraire à to avoid
sous-vêtements *m.pl.* underwear
soutenir to support
souvenir *m.* souvenir [7]; memory

se souvenir de   to remember [8]
souvent   often [2]
souverain(e)   sovereign
spacieux (-euse)   spacious [3]
spécialiste *m./f.*   specialist [12]
spécialité *f.*   specialty
spectacle *m.*   show, event
   ~ de variétés   variety show
sport *m.*   sports [2]
   faire du ~   to play sports [4]
sportif (-ive)   athletic; sports [1]
stade *m.*   stadium [6]
stage *m.*   internship [11]
standing *m.:* **grand ~**   luxury
station *f.*   resort
station-service *f.*   gas station
statistique *f.*   statistic
statut *m.*   status
stimuler   to stimulate
stress *m.*   stress
strict(e)   strict [4]
studio *m.*   studio (apartment) [3]
stupéfait(e)   astounded
stupide   stupid [1]
stylo *m.*   pen [P]
succès *m.*   success [11]
sucre *m.*   sugar [5]
sucré(e)   sweet [5]
sud *m.*   south [6]
suffire   to suffice, to be enough
   suffit!   that's enough!
suis (*see* **être, suivre**)
Suisse *f.*   Switzerland
suisse   Swiss [1]
suite: tout de ~   right away
suivant(e)   following
suivi(e)   followed
suivre   to follow
   ~ un régime   to be on a diet
sujet *m.*   subject
   au ~ de   about, on the subject of
super   terrific, great [4]
superficie *f.*   area
supérieur(e)   higher, upper
   école supérieure *f.*   school of
      higher education
supermarché *m.*   supermarket [3]
supporter   to stand, to tolerate [12]
suprême *m.* **de volaille**   poultry in
   cream sauce
sur   on [3]
   un ~ dix   one out of ten
sûr(e)   sure, certain
   bien ~   of course [2]
sûrement   surely
surgelé(e)   frozen [5]

surhumain(e)   superhuman
surnaturel(le)   supernatural
surnuméraire   extra
surprenant(e)   surprising [12]
surtout   especially, above all [2]
surveillant/surveillante *m./f.*
   monitor, supervisor
survoler   to get a general view
susceptible de   likely to
sweat *m.*   sweatshirt
sympathique   nice, pleasant [1]
symptôme *m.*   symptom [12]

ta (*see* **ton/ta/tes**)
tabac *m.*   tobacco
   bureau *m.* **de ~**   tobacco/
      magazine shop
table *f.*   table [P]
tableau *m.* (*pl.* **tableaux**)
   chalkboard [P]; chart, table;
   painting [12]
   ~ noir   blackboard
tabouret *m.*   stool
tâche *f.*   task; chore
   ~ domestique   household chore
tâcher   to try
taco *f.*   taco
tactique *f.*   tactic
Tahiti *f.*   Tahiti
tahitien(ne)   Tahitian [9]
taille *f.*   height; waist [10]
tailleur *m.*   women's suit [10]
se taire   to be quiet
tandis que   while, whereas
tant: ~ de   so much, so many
   ~ pis   too bad [4]
tante *f.*   aunt [2]
tantôt... tantôt   now . . . now
tapis *m.*   rug [3]
tard   late [4]
taro *m.*   taro
tarte *f.*   pie, tart
   ~ aux fraises   strawberry tart [5]
   ~ aux pommes   apple tart [5]
tas *m.:* **un ~ de**   lots of [8]
tasse *f.*   cup [5]
taux *m.*   rate
te   you, to you [8]
tee-shirt *m.*   T-shirt [10]
teinté(e)   tinged
tel(le): un(e) ~   such a
télé *f.*   TV
télécommande *f.*   remote control
   [6]
téléphone *m.*   telephone [3]

téléphoner   to telephone [3]
   se ~   to call each other on the
      phone [8]
téléphoniste *m./f.*   telephone
   operator
télévision *f.*   television [2]
tellement   so
   ~ de   so much
température *f.*   temperature [6]
temps *m.*   time; weather [4]; tense
   à ~   in time, on time
   avoir le ~ (de)   to have time (to)
      [4]
   de ~ en ~   from time to time
   du ~ libre   free time [4]
   emploi *m.* **du ~**   schedule [4]
   en ce ~-là   at that time [8]
   en même ~   at the same time
   il est ~ que   it is time that [C]
   quel ~ fait-il?   What is the
      weather like?
tendance *f.*   tendency
tendre   to stretch, to straighten
ténèbres *f.pl.*   darkness
tennis *f.*   sneaker, tennis shoe [10]
tennis *m.*   tennis [2]
   faire du ~   to play tennis [4]
tentative *f.*   attempt
terminaison *f.*   ending
(se) terminer   to end
terrasse *f.*   terrace
terre *f.*   earth; ground
   par ~   on the ground
   route en~   dirt road
terrible   terrific; terrible
territoire *m.*   territory
tes (*see* **ton/ta/tes**)
tête *f.*   head [10]
TGV (train à grande vitesse) *m.*
   high-speed train [7]
thé *m.*   tea [5]
   ~ citron   tea with lemon [5]
   ~ nature   plain tea [5]
théâtre *m.*   theater
théorie *f.:* **en ~**   in theory
thérapeute *m./f.*   therapist
thon *m.*   tuna [5]
tiens!   say! [4]
timide   shy [1]
timidement   shyly
tissu *m.*   fabric [10]
titre *m.*   title
   à ~ de   as
toi   you [11]
toilettes *f.pl.*   toilet [3]
tomate *f.*   tomato [5]

tombe *f.*   grave
tomber   to fall [6]
  laisser ~   to drop
  ~ en panne   to break down
  ~ malade   to become ill [12]
  ~ par terre   to fall on the ground
ton/ta/tes   your [2]
tonnerre *m.*   thunder
tortue *f.*   turtle
tôt   early [4]
toucher   to touch; to affect [10]
  touche pas à...   hands off . . .
toujours   always; still [2]
tour *m.*   tour; turn
  à son ~   in turn
  à ~ de rôle   in turn
  ~ du monde   around-the-world
    trip [12]
tourner   to turn [3]
Toussaint *m.*   All Saints' Day
tousser   to cough [12]
tout *pron.*   everything [4]
tout *adv.*: **~ à l'heure**   in a little
    while
  ~ de suite   immediately, right
    away [7]
  ~ droit   straight ahead [3]
tout/toute/tous/toutes   all, every,
    each; the whole
  tous les deux   both
  tous les jours   every day [2]
  tout le monde   everyone,
    everybody [8]
  de toute façon   in any case
toux *f.*   cough [12]
tradition *f.*   tradition [9]
traditionnel(le)   traditional [9]
traditionnellement   traditionally
tragique   tragic
trahir   to betray
train *m.*   train
  en ~   by train [7]
  en ~ de   in the process of
trait *m.* **d'union**   hyphen [P]
traite *f.* **des esclaves**   slave trade
traitement *m.*   treatment [12]
traiter   to treat
trame *f.*   plot
tranche *f.*   slice [5]
tranquille   calm, tranquil [12]
  laisser ~   to leave alone, to leave
    in peace
transfert *m.*   transfer
travail *m.*   work; job
travailler   to work [2]
traverser   to cross, to go through [3]

tréma *m.*   diaeresis
trembler   to shake
très   very [1]
  ~ bien, merci   fine, thank you [P]
tribu *f.*   tribe
triste   sad [1]
tromper   to deceive
  se ~   to be mistaken
trop   too, too much [3]
trouver   to find [3]; to think
  se ~   to be located
truculent(e)   larger than life
tu   you [P]
tuer   to kill
tunique *f.*   tunic
Tunisie *f.*   Tunisia
tunisien(ne)   Tunisian
type *m.*   type
typique   typical [1]

un(e)   a, an [P]; one [2]
  un à un   one by one
  une fois   once [2]
unanime   unanimous
uni(e)   plain (one color); united
unificatrice   acting to unify
union *f.* **libre**   cohabitation
univers *m.*   universe
universel(le)   universal
université *f.*   university [4]
urbain(e)   urban
usage *m.*   custom
utile   useful [11]
utilisation *f.*   use
utiliser   to use

vacances *f.pl.*   vacation [2]
  bonnes ~!   have a nice vacation!
    [9]
vachement   very
vaincre   to defeat
vaisselle *f.*   dishes [8]
valeur *f.*   value [10]
valise *f.*   suitcase [10]
vallée *f.*   valley
variable   changeable, partly cloudy
    [6]
varier   to vary
variétés *f.pl.*   variety show [6]
vaudrait: il ~ mieux   it would be
    better [C]
vaut: il ~ mieux que   it is better
    that [C]
veau *m.*   veal [5]; calfskin

vedette *f.*   star (celebrity)
végétarien(ne)   vegetarian
vélo *m.*   bicycle [4]
  en ~   by bicycle [7]
  faire du ~   to go biking [4]
velours *m.*   velvet [10]
vendeur/vendeuse *m./f.*
    salesperson [11]
vendre   to sell [7]
vendredi *m.*   Friday [4]
venir   to come [7]
  ~ de   to come from; to have just
    [11]
vent *m.*   wind [6]
  il fait du ~   it's windy [6]
  il y a du ~   it's windy
vente *f.*   sale
ventre *m.*   belly [10]
  mal au ~   bellyache
verbe *m.*   verb
verdure *f.*   greenery
véritable   true, real
vérité *f.*   truth [6]
vernaculaire   vernacular
vernissage *m.*   art exhibit opening
verre *m.*   glass [5]; lens
vers   toward; around (time)
vert(e)   green [2]
  haricots *m.pl.* **verts**   green beans
    [5]
veste *f.*   jacket [10]
vestiaire   clothing *(adj.)*
vestige *m.*   remainder
vêtements *m.pl.*   clothes [8]
vêtu(e)   dressed
vétuste   decrepit
viande *f.*   meat [5]
victime *f.*   victim
victoire *f.*   victory, win
vide   empty
vidéocassette *f.*   video cassette [3]
vie *f.*   life
  ~ sentimentale   love life
vieillir   to age, to grow old
vieux/vieil/vieille/vieux/vieille
    old [3]
vif (vive)   bright
vignoble *m.*   vineyard
vigueur *f.*: **en ~**   in force
villa *f.*   villa
village *m.*   village
ville *f.*   city [3]
  ~ d'origine   hometown
  ~ natale   city of own's birth
vin *m.*   wine [5]
violence *f.*   violence

vis-à-vis toward
viser to focus on
visible visible
visite *f.* visit
   rendre ~ à to visit (a person) [7]
visiter to visit (a place) [7]
vite fast, quickly
vitesse *f.* speed
vitre *f.* windowpane
vivre to live
voici here is, here are [1]
voilà there is, there are; here is, here are [1]
voile *f.* sailing
   planche *f.* **à ~** sailboard
voir to see [3]
   se ~ to see each other [8]
voisin(e) *m./f.* neighbor
voisinage *m.* neighborhood
voiture *f.* car [7]
   en ~ by car [7]
voix *f.* voice
   à haute ~ aloud
vol *m.* flight [7]
volcan *m.* volcano

voleur *m.* thief
volley *m.* volleyball [4]
   faire du ~ to play volleyball [4]
volontiers! with pleasure! [6]
vos (*see* **votre/vos**)
voter to vote
votre/vos your [2]
   votre nom *m.***?** your last name? [P]
   votre prénom *m.***?** your first name? [P]
vouloir to want (to) [4]
   j'ai voulu I tried to [9]
   je n'ai pas voulu I refused to [9]
   je veux bien I'd love to [6]
   je voudrais I would like [3]
vous you [P]; (to) you [8]
   ~ deux both of you
voyage *m.* trip [4]
   bon ~! have a nice trip! [9]
   faire un ~ to go on a trip [4]
   ~ d'affaires business trip [7]
   ~ d'agrément pleasure trip
   ~ organisé package tour [7]
voyager to travel [2]
voyageur/voyageuse *m./f.* traveler

voyons let's see
vrai(e) true [4]
   C'est pas ~! No way! [4]
   C'est ~? Is that right? [4]
vraiment really [1]

W.C. *m.pl.* toilet [3]
week-end *m.* weekend

xénophobe xenophobic

y to there, there [7]
   il ~ a there is, there are [2]; ago [7]
yaourt *m.* yogurt [5]
yeux *m.pl.* (*sing.* **œil**) eyes [2]

zapper to zap, to channel surf [6]
zappeur *m.* channel surfer [6]
zéro zero
zone *f.* zone
   ~ de perturbation area of unsettled weather
zoo *m.* zoo
zut (alors)! rats! nuts! [4]

a/an un(e)
  a little un peu
  a lot (of) beaucoup (de)
abandon abandonner
able: be ~ to pouvoir
about au sujet de
above all surtout
absent absent(e)
absolutely absolument
accent accent *m.*
accept accepter
accessory accessoire *m.*
accident accident *m.*
accompany accompagner
accomplish réaliser
accountant comptable *m./f.*
accounting comptabilité *f.*
accustomed: become ~ s'habituer
across from en face de
action film film *m.* d'aventure
active actif (-ive)
actively activement
actor acteur *m.*
actress actrice *f.*
actually en fait
admire admirer
adore adorer
ads: classified ~ petites annonces *f.*
advantage avantage *m.*
advice conseil *m.*
aerobics aérobic *m.*
African africain(e)
after après
afternoon après-midi *m.*
  3:00 in the ~ 3 heures de l'après-midi
afterwards après, ensuite
again encore
against contre
agency agence *f.*
ago il y a
agreed! entendu! d'accord!
ahead: straight ~ tout droit
AIDS sida *m.*
air air *m.*
air conditioned climatisé(e)
airline ligne *f.* aérienne
alcoholic alcoolisé(e)
  ~ beverage boisson *f.* alcoolisée
Algerian algérien(ne)
alien étranger (-ère) *m./f.*
all *adj.* tout/toute/tous/toutes

all *pron., adv.* tout
allergic allergique
almost presque
alone seul(e)
aloud à haute voix
already déjà
also aussi
altruistic altruiste
always toujours
ambition ambition *f.*
American américain(e)
amusing amusant(e)
ancestors ancêtres *m.pl.*
and et
angry fâché(e)
  get ~ se fâcher
animal animal *m.* (*pl.* animaux)
anniversary anniversaire *m.*
annoying embêtant(e); gênant(e)
answer *n.* réponse *f.*
answer *v.* répondre (à)
answering machine répondeur *m.*
antibiotic antibiotique *m.*
anyone: not ~ ne... personne
anything: not ~ ne... rien
apartment appartement *m.*
  ~ building immeuble *m.*
apostrophe apostrophe *f.*
appeal appel *m.*
apple pomme *f.*
  ~ tart tarte aux pommes
appliance (electronic) appareil *m.* (électronique)
applicant postulant/postulante *m./f.*
apply appliquer
  ~ for a job faire une demande d'emploi
appointment rendez-vous *m.*
  make an ~ prendre rendez-vous
appreciate apprécier
April avril *m.*
architect architecte *m./f.*
architecture architecture *f.*
argue se disputer
arm bras *m.*
armchair fauteuil *m.*
around-the-world trip tour *m.* du monde
arrival arrivée *f.*
arrive arriver
art art *m.*

artist artiste *m./f.*
as aussi, si
  ~ ... ~ aussi... que
  ~ far as jusqu'à
  ~ many as autant de
  ~ soon ~ dès que
  ~ usual comme d'habitude
ashamed: be ~ (of) avoir honte (de)
ask demander
  ~ a question poser une question
aspirin aspirine *f.*
at à, dans, en
  ~ first d'abord
  ~ home à domicile
  ~ least au moins
  ~ that time en ce temps-là
  ~ the corner of au coin de
  ~ the home of chez
  ~ what time? à quelle heure?
athletic sportif (-ive)
attention: pay ~ faire attention
August août *m.*
aunt tante *f.*
author auteur *m.*
autumn automne *m.*
avenue avenue *f.*
average moyen(ne)
avoid éviter

baccalaureate exam bac; baccalauréat *m.*
bachelor's degree licence *f.*
back dos *m.*
background origine *f.*
backpack sac *m.* à dos
bad mauvais(e)
  it's ~ weather il fait mauvais
badly mal
baggage checkroom consigne *f.*
bakery boulangerie *f.*
balanced équilibré(e)
ball balle *f.*; ballon *m.*
banana banane *f.*
bandage *v.* faire un pansement
bandage *n.* pansement *m.*
bank banque *f.*
banker banquier *m.*
barbaric barbare
baseball base-ball *m.*

basketball   basket *m.*
  play ~   faire du basket
  ~ shoe   basket *m.*
bathing suit   maillot *m.* de bain
bathrobe   robe *f.* de chambre
bathroom   salle *f.* de bains
bathtub   baignoire *f.*
be   être
  ~ able   pouvoir
  ~ afraid (of)   avoir peur (de)
  ~ ashamed (of)   avoir honte (de)
  ~ bored   s'ennuyer
  ~ born   naître
  ~ careful!   attention!
  ~ fed up   en avoir marre
  ~ hungry   avoir faim
  ~ hurt   se blesser
  ~ injured   se blesser
  ~ interested in   s'intéresser à
  ~ lucky   avoir de la chance
  ~ mistaken   tromper se
  ~ on a diet   être au régime
  ~ part of   faire partie de
  ~ self-confident   avoir confiance
    en soi
  ~ sorry   regretter
  ~ thirsty   avoir soif
  ~ wrong   avoir tort
  ~ _____ years old   avoir _____
    ans
  I was born   je suis né(e)
beach   plage *f.*
beans: green ~   haricots verts *m.pl.*
beat   battre
beautiful   beau/bel/belle/beaux/
  belles
because   parce que
  ~ of   à cause de
become   devenir
  ~ accustomed   s'habituer
  ~ ill   tomber malade
bed   lit *m.*
  go to ~   se coucher
bedroom   chambre *f.*
beef   bœuf *m.*
beer   bière *f.*
before   avant de
begin   commencer
beginner   débutant/débutante
  m./f.
beginning   début *m.*
behind   derrière
Belgian   belge
believe   croire
belly   ventre *m.*

belt   ceinture *f.*
bench   banc *m.*
berth in sleeping compartment
  couchette *f.*
beside   à côté de
best *adj.*: **the ~**   le meilleur/la
  meilleure/les meilleur(e)s
best *adv.*   le mieux
better *adj.*   meilleur(e)
better *adv.*   mieux
  it is ~ that   il vaut mieux que
  it would be ~ that   il vaudrait
    mieux que
between   entre
bicycle   vélo *m.*
  by ~   en vélo
  ride a ~   faire du vélo
big   grand(e); gros(se)
biking: to go ~   faire du vélo
bill *(restaurant)*   addition *f.*
billion   milliard *m.*
binder   classeur *m.*
biological   biologique
biology   biologie *f.*
birth   naissance *f.*
birthday   anniversaire *m.*
  happy ~!   bon anniversaire!
black   noir(e)
blond   blond(e)
blouse   chemisier *m.*
blue   bleu(e)
  navy ~   bleu marine
boat   bateau *m.* (*pl.* bateaux)
  by ~   en bateau
boating: go ~   faire du bateau
body   corps *m.*
bond   lien *m.*
book   livre *m.*
bookcase   étagères *f.pl.*
boot   botte *f.*
border   frontière *f.*
boredom   ennui *m.*
boring   ennuyeux (-euse)
born   né(e)
boss   patron/patronne *m./f.*
both   (tous) les deux
bottle   bouteille *f.*
boulevard   boulevard *m.*
bouquet   bouquet *m.*
boy   garçon *m.*
boyfriend   petit ami *m.*
brain   cerveau *m.* (*pl.* cerveaux)
bravo!   bravo! chapeau!
brawl   bagarre *f.*
Brazilian   brésilien(ne)

bread   pain *m.*
  loaf of French ~   baguette *f.*
break down   tomber en panne
breakfast   petit déjeuner *m.*
Brie cheese   brie *m.*
briefcase   serviette *f.*
bring   apporter
  please ~ me   pourriez-vous
    m'apporter...
  ~ up   monter
bronchitis   bronchite *f.*
brother   frère *m.*
brother-in-law   beau-frère *m.*
brown   brun(e)
brunette   brun(e)
brush   se brosser
build   bâtir
building   bâtiment *m.*
burgundy (color)   bordeaux *(inv.)*
business   affaires *f.pl.*; commerce *m.*
  ~ trip   voyage *m.* d'affaires
businessman   homme *m.* d'affaires;
  businessman *m.*
businesswoman   femme *f.*
  d'affaires
busy   occupé(e)
but   mais
  ~ still   alors quand même
butcher shop   boucherie *f.*
butter   beurre *m.*
buy   acheter
by   par, en

café   café *m.*
cafeteria   cantine *f.*
cake   gâteau *m.* (*pl.* gâteaux)
calendar   calendrier *m.*
call *n.*   appel *m.*
call *v.*   appeler; (on the phone)
  téléphoner
  it's ~ed   ça s'appelle
calm   tranquille; calme
Camembert cheese   camembert *m.*
camping   camping *m.*
  go ~   faire du camping
campus   campus *m.*
can *n.*   boîte *f.*
can *v.*   pouvoir
  could you ... ?   Est-ce que vous
    pouriez... ? Pourriez-vous... ?
Canadian   canadien(ne)
cancer   cancer *m.*
candle   bougie *f.*

canned en boîte
cannibal cannibale *m./f.*
cap casquette *f.*
car voiture *f.*
care *n.* souci *m.*
care *v.*: **not to ~** s'en ficher
  I don't ~! je m'en fiche! bof!
career carrière *f.*; métier *m.*
carrot carotte *f.*
carry on exercer
cartoon dessin *m.* animé
case cas *m.*
  in any ~ de toute façon
cassette cassette *f.*
cat chat/chatte *m./f.*
catastrophe catastrophe *f.*
cathedral cathédrale *f.*
CD CD *m.*
  ~ player lecteur *m.* de CD
cedilla cédille *f.*
cereal céréales *f.pl.*
certainly certainement
chair chaise *f.*
chalet chalet *m.*
chalk craie *f.*
chalkboard tableau *m.* (*pl.*
  tableaux)
chance occasion *f.*
change changer
  ~ the channel changer de chaîne
changeable variable
channel: TV ~ chaîne *f.*
  ~ surf zapper
  ~ surfer zappeur *m.*
character personnage *m.*
characteristic caractéristique *m.*
château château *m.* (*pl.* châteaux)
check (*restaurant*) addition *f.*
cheek joue *f.*
cheese fromage *m.*
chemistry chimie *f.*
chest of drawers commode *f.*
chicken poulet *m.*
child enfant *m./f.*
chin menton *m.*
Chinese chinois(e)
chip chip *m.*
chocolate chocolat *m.*
  ~ mousse mousse *f.* au chocolat
  hot ~ chocolat *m.*
choice choix *m.*
cholesterol cholestérol *m.*
choose choisir
church église *f.*
cinema cinéma *m.*

citizen citoyen(ne) *m./f.*
city ville *f.*
  ~ of one's birth ville *f.* natale
civil servant fonctionnaire *m./f.*
class classe *f.*; cours *m.*
  first ~ première classe
  second ~ deuxième classe
classical music musique *f.*
  classique
classified ads petites annonces *f.pl.*
classroom salle *f.* de classe
claustrophobic claustrophobe
clean nettoyer
  ~ up ranger
cleaning nettoyage *m.*
client client/cliente *m./f.*
climate climat *m.*
clock horloge *f.*
closet placard *m.*
clothes vêtements *m.pl.*
cloud nuage *m.*
  in the ~s dans les nuages
cloudy nuageux (-euse)
  it's ~ le ciel est couvert
  partly ~ variable
coat manteau *m.* (*pl.* manteaux)
coffee café *m.*
  ~ with cream café crème
  ~ with milk café au lait
cohabitation union libre *f.*,
  cohabitation *f.*
coke coca *m.*
cold *adj.* froid(e)
  it's ~ (*weather*) il fait froid
cold *n.* rhume *m.*
collar col *m.*
colonization colonisation *f.*
comb se peigner
come venir
  ~ back revenir, rentrer
  ~ from venir de
comedy *n.* comédie *f.*
comedy *adj.* comique
comfort confort *m.*
comfortable confortable
comic strip bande *f.* dessinée
commercial pub *f.*
communicate communiquer
communications media médias
  m.pl.
compact disk disque *m.* compact
company compagnie *f.*
  ~ head chef *m.* d'entreprise
comparison comparaison *f.*
complaint plainte *f.*

composition rédaction *f.*
computer ordinateur *m.*
  ~ science informatique *f.*
concern souci *m.*
concert concert *m.*
conflict conflit *m.*
conformist conformiste
congratulate féliciter
congratulations félicitations *f.pl.*
constantly constamment
contagious contagieux (-ieuse)
continue continuer
contrary: on the ~ au contraire
contribute contribuer
cook *n.* cuisinier/cuisinière *m./f.*
cook *v.* faire la cuisine
cooked cuit(e)
cookie biscuit *m.*
cooking cuisine *f.*
  do the ~ faire la cuisine
cool frais (fraîche)
  ~! chouette!
  it's ~ (weather) il fait frais
corn maïs *m.*
corner coin *m.*
  at the ~ of au coin de
cost coûter
cotton *adj.* en coton
cotton *n.* coton *m.*
couch canapé *m.*
cough *n.* toux *f.*
cough *v.* tousser
could you . . . ? pourriez-vous... ?
count compter
country pays *m.*
  ~ house maison *f.* de campagne
countryside campagne *f.*
couple couple *m.*
course (*food*) plat *m.*; (class) cours
  m.
  main ~ plat *m.* principal
cousin cousin/cousine *m./f.*
crazy fou (folle)
create créer
credit card carte *f.* de crédit
Creole créole
crime délinquance *f.*
crisis crise *f.*
criterion critère *m.*
croissant croissant *m.*
cross traverser
crowd foule *f.*
cry pleurer
cup tasse *f.*
curtains rideaux *m.pl.*

custom   coutume *f.*
   ~s   mœurs *f.pl.*
cycling   cyclisme *m.*

daily   quotidien(ne)
dairy   laitier
   ~ store/department   crémerie
dance *n.*   bal *m.*
dance *v.*   danser
dark   sombre; (color) foncé(e)
dark-haired   brun(e)
darkness   obscurité *f.*
date   date *f.*
daughter   fille *f.*
day   jour *m.*; journée *f.*
   ~ off   jour *m.* de congé
   ~ of rest   journée *f.* de repos
   in those ~s   à cette époque-là
   the next ~   le lendemain
daytime   journée *f.*
dead   mort(e)
dear   cher (chère)
death   mort *f.*
decaffeinated   décaféiné
deceive   tromper
December   décembre *m.*
decrease   diminuer
defend   défendre
degree   diplôme *m.*
   bachelor's degree   licence *f.*
   master's degree   maîtrise *f.*
delicatessen   charcuterie *f.*
delighted   enchanté(e)
delinquency   délinquance *f.*
dentist   dentiste *m./f.*
department (in a store)   rayon *m.*
departure   départ *m.*
dependent   dépendant(e) *m./f.*
description   description *f.*
desert   désert *m.*
deserted   désert(e)
deserve   mériter
desk   bureau *m.* (*pl.* bureaux)
desperate   désespéré(e)
dessert   dessert *m.*
destroy   détruire
detective movie/novel   film/
   roman *m.* policier
develop   (se) développer
diabetic   diabétique
diaeresis   tréma *m.*
diagnosis   diagnostic *m.*
die   mourir
diet   régime *m.*
   be on a ~   suivre un régime, être
      au régime

dietetic   diététique
difficulty: with ~   difficilement
dine   dîner
dining room   salle *f.* à manger
dinner   dîner *m.*
   to have ~   dîner
diploma   diplôme *m.*
directions   directions *f.pl.*
disadvantage   désavantage *m.*
disciplined   discipliné(e)
discotheque   discothèque *f.*
disease   maladie *f.*
dishes   vaisselle *f.*
disorder   désordre *m.*
displeased   mécontent(e)
distant relatives   parents *m.pl.*
   éloignés
divorce   divorce *m.*
do   faire
   ~ gymnastics   faire de la
      gymnastique
   ~ one's duty   faire son devoir
   ~ one's homework   faire ses
      devoirs
   ~ the cooking   faire la cuisine
   ~ the dishes   faire la vaisselle
   ~ the laundry   faire la lessive
doctor   médecin *m.*
doctorate   doctorat *m.*
dog   chien *m.*
doll   poupée *f.*
door   porte *f.*
doubt   douter
downtown   centre-ville *m.*
dozen   douzaine *f.*
drama   drame *m.*
drawing   dessin *m.*
dream *n.*   rêve *m.*
dream *v.*   rêver
dress   robe *f.*
   evening ~   robe *f.* du soir
dress   s'habiller
dresser   commode *f.*
dressy   habillé(e)
drink *n.*   boisson *f.*
drink *v.*   boire
drugstore   pharmacie *f.*
during   pendant
duty   devoir *m.*

each   chaque; tout/toute
ear   oreille *f.*
earlier   plus tôt
early   tôt; en avance; de bonne heure
earn   gagner
   ~ a living   gagner sa vie

easily   facilement
east   est *m.*
Easter   Pâques *f.pl.*
eat   manger
ecological   écologique
economic   économique
economics   économie *f.*
education   éducation *f.*; formation *f.*
   higher ~   études *f.pl.* supérieurs
   physical ~   éducation *f.* physique
egg   œuf *m.*
eight   huit
eighteen   dix-huit
eighty   quatre-vingt
elbow   coude *m.*
electronic appliance   appareil *m.*
   électronique
electronic game   jeu *m.*
   électronique
elementary school   école *f.*
   primaire
elevator   ascenseur *m.*
eleven   onze
elsewhere   ailleurs
e-mail message   message *m.*
   électronique
employee   employé/employée
   m./f.
employer   employeur *m.*
empty   vide
encourage   encourager
end *n.*   bout *m.*; fin *m.*
end *v.*   terminer
energetic   énergique
energy-producing   énergétique
engineer   ingénieur *m.*
English *n.*   anglais *m.*
English *adj.*   anglais(e)
enough   assez
enroll   entrer à la fac
enter   entrer dans
environment   environnement *m.*
equal   pareil(le)
equality   égalité *f.*
eraser   gomme *f.*
error   faute *f.*; erreur *f.*
especially   surtout
even   même
evening   soir *m.*
   8:00 in the ~   8 heures du soir
   ~ dress   robe du soir *f.*
   good ~   bonsoir
every   tout/toute/tous/toutes
   ~ day   tous les jours
everybody   tout le monde
everyone   tout le monde

everything　tout
everywhere　partout
evidently　évidemment
exam　examen *m.*
　　fail an ~　rater un examen
　　pass an ~　réussir à un examen
　　take an ~　passer un examen
examine　examiner
excuse me　pardon; excusez-moi
exercise *n.*　exercice *m.*
exercise *v.*　faire de l'exercice; faire
　　de la gymnastique
exotic　exotique
expectations　attentes *f.pl.*
expensive　cher (chère)
explode　éclater
expression　expression *f.*
　　polite ~s　formules *f.pl.* de
　　　politesse
eye　œil *m.* (*pl.* yeux)
eyebrow　sourcil *m.*
eyeglasses　lunettes *f.pl.*
eyelash　cil *m.*
eyelid　paupière *f.*

fabric　tissu *m.*
fact: in ~　en fait
factory worker　ouvrier/ouvrière
　　m./f.
fail (an exam)　rater
fairy tale　conte *m.* de fées
fall *n.*　automne *m.*
fall *v.*　tomber
family　famille *f.*
　　~ member　membre *m.* de la
　　　famille
　　~ photo　photo *f.* de famille
　　~ relationship　lien *m.* de
　　　parenté
　　~ tree　arbre *m.* généalogique
famous　célèbre
fantasy　fantasme *m.*
far　lointain(e)
　　~ from　loin de
fashion　mode *f.*
fat　fort(e); gros(se); gras(se)
father　père *m.*
favor　favoriser
favorite　préféré(e), favori(te)
fear　peur *f.*
feat　exploit *m.*
February　février *m.*
fed up: be ~　en avoir marre
feed　nourrir
feel　ressentir; se sentir
　　~ like　avoir envie de

few　peu (de)
　　a ~　quelques
fewer　moins de
field　champ *m.*
fifteen　quize
fifty　cinquante
fight　se battre; lutter
　　~ against　lutter contre
figure　forme *f.*
fill out (a form, etc.)　remplir
film　film *m.*
finally　enfin, finalement
financial　financier (-ière)
find　trouver
　　I found out　j'ai su
fine: the weather is ~　il fait beau
　　~, thank you　très bien, merci
　　I'm ~!　ça va (bien)!
finger　doigt *m.*
finish　finir
fir tree　sapin *m.*
fire　feu *m.*
first *adj.*　premier (-ière)
　　~ floor　rez-de-chaussée *m.*
first *adv.*　d'abord
　　at ~　d'abord
fish *n.*　poisson *m.*
fish *v.*　aller à la pêche
fishing　pêche *f.*
fishmonger's shop　poissonnerie *f.*
fit　aller bien
　　~ poorly　aller mal à
five　cinq
flannel *adj.*　en flanelle
flannel *n.*　flanelle *f.*
flight　vol *m.*
floor　étage *m.*
flower　fleur *f.*
flowered　à fleurs
flu　grippe *f.*
fog　brouillard *m.*
foggy: it's ~　il fait du brouillard
food　aliment *m.*
foolish　fou (folle)
foot　pied *m.*
　　on ~　à pied
football　football *m.* américain
for　pour
　　~ how long　pendant combien de
　　　temps; depuis combien de
　　　temps
forbid　interdire
forehead　front *m.*
foreign　étranger (-ère)
forest　forêt *f.*
forget　oublier

fork　fourchette *f.*
form　formulaire *m.*
formerly　autrefois
fortune: make one's ~　faire
　　fortune
fortunately　heureusement
forty　quarante
four　quatre
fourteen　quatorze
fox　renard *m.*
frankly　franchement
free　libre
French *n.*　français *m.*
French *adj.*　français(e)
　　~ bread　baguette *f.*
　　~ fries　frites *f.pl.*
frequently　fréquemment
fresh　frais (fraîche)
Friday　vendredi *m.*
friend　ami/amie *m./f.*;
　　copain/copine *m./f.*
friendship　amitié *f.*
friendly　sociable
from　de
　　~ now on　désormais
　　~ where　d'où
front: in ~ of　devant
frozen　surgelé(e)
fruit　fruit *m.*
fruit juice　jus *m.* de fruits
full　plein(e)
full-time　à plein temps
fun: have ~　s'amuser
funny　comique, amusant(e)
furnished　meublé
furniture　meubles *m.pl.*
future　avenir *m.*

gain　gagner
　　~ weight　grossir
game　match *m.*; jeu *m.*
　　~ show　jeu télévisé
garage　garage *m.*
garden　jardin *m.*
garlic　ail *m.*
gas　essence *f.*
generally　généralement
generous　généreux (-euse)
geography　géographie *f.*
German (*language*)　allemand *m.*
German *adj.*　allemand(e)
get: ~ along　s'entendre
　　~ angry　se fâcher
　　~ down　descendre
　　~ dressed　s'habiller
　　~ mad　se fâcher

~ **married**   se marier

~ **up**   se lever

ghost   fantôme *m.*

gift   cadeau *m.* (*pl.* cadeaux)

girl   fille *f.*

girlfriend   petite amie *f.*

give   offrir; donner

glass   verre *m.*

glasses (eye-)   lunettes *f.pl.*

glove   gant *m.*

go   aller

~ **back**   rentrer

~ **boating**   faire du bateau

~ **camping**   faire du camping

~ **fishing**   aller à la pêche

~ **for a walk**   se promener, faire une promenade

~ **hunting**   aller à la chasse

~ **in for sports**   faire du sport

~ **out**   sortir

~ **shopping**   faire des courses

~ **to bed**   se coucher

~ **up**   monter

goal   objectif *m.*; but *m.*

golf   golf *m.*

play ~   faire du golf

good   bon(ne)

~ **evening**   bonsoir

~ **grief!**   mince!

~ **idea!**   bonne idée!

~ **night**   bonsoir

it's a good thing that   c'est bien que

good-bye   au revoir

grab   attraper

grade   note *f.*

grade school teacher   instituteur/institutrice *m./f.*

graduate   diplômé(e)

gram   gramme *m.*

granddaughter   petite-fille *f.*

grandfather   grand-père *m.*

grandmother   grand-mère *f.*

grandparents   grands-parents *m.pl.*

grandson   petit-fils *m.*

gray   gris(e)

greasy   gras (grasse)

great   chouette, super, formidable

green   vert(e)

~ **beans**   haricots *m.pl.* verts

greetings   salutations *f.pl.*

grocery:

go ~ **shopping**   faire les courses

~ **store**   épicerie *f.*

ground: on the ~   par terre

~ **floor**   rez-de-chaussée *m.*

grow: ~ **old**   vieillir

~ **up**   grandir

guess   deviner

gun   fusil *m.*

gymnastics   gymnastique *f.*

do ~   faire de la gymnastique

habit   habitude *f.*

hair   cheveux *m.pl.*

hairdo   coiffure *f.*

ham   jambon *m.*

hand   main *f.*

give someone a ~   donner un coup de main à

on the other ~   par contre

raise one's ~   lever le doigt

shake ~**s**   serrer la main; (se) donner la main

handsome   beau/bel/belle/beaux/belles

Hanukkah   Hanoukka *f.*

happen   se passer

what happened?   qu'est-ce qui s'est passé?

happiness   bonheur *m.*

happy   heureux (-euse)

~ **birthday!**   bon anniversaire!

~ **New Year!**   bonne année!

~ **holidays!**   joyeuses fêtes!

hard   dur *(adv.)*

have a ~ **time**   avoir du mal (à)

hat   chapeau *m.* (*pl.* chapeaux)

hate   détester

have   avoir; posséder

~ **a hard time**   avoir du mal à

~ **dinner**   dîner

~ **(food)**   prendre

~ **fun**   s'amuser

~ **just**   venir de

~ **to**   devoir

hay fever   rhume *m.* des foins

he   il

head   tête *f.*

headache   mal *m.* à la tête

health   santé *f.*

healthful   sain(e)

hear   entendre

heart   cœur *m.*

~ **attack**   crise *f.* cardiaque

heat   chaleur *f.*

heavyset   fort(e); gros(se)

height   taille *f.*

hello   bonjour, salut!; (on the telephone) allô?

help   aider

helping hand   coup *m.* de main

hen   poule *f.*

her *pron.*   la; elle

her *adj.*   son/sa/ses

here   ici

~ **is/are**   voici, voilà

heritage   héritage *m.*

hi   salut

hidden   caché(e)

high school   lycée *m.*

him   le; lui

hire   embaucher

hired   embauché(e)

his   son/sa/ses

historical   historique

history   histoire *f.*

hit   battre

hockey   hockey *m.*

holiday   fête *f.*; jour *m.* de congé

happy ~   joyeuses fêtes

home: at ~   à domicile

at the ~ **of**   chez

in a private ~   chez un particulier

homeless person   sans-abri *m./f.*

hometown   ville *f.* d'origine

homework   devoirs *m.pl.*

hope   espérer

horror movie   film *m.* d'épouvante

hors d'oeuvre   hors-d'œuvre *m.* (*pl.* hors-d'œuvre)

horse   cheval *m.* (*pl.* chevaux)

hospital   hôpital *m.*

host   hôte *m.*

hot   chaud(e)

~ **chocolate**   chocolat *m.*

it's ~ **(weather)**   il fait chaud

hotel   hôtel *m.*

hour   heure *f.*

house   maison *f.*

how   comment; comme

~ **many**   combien (de)

~ **much**   combien (de)

~ **do you spell that?**   comment ça s'écrit?

~ **are you?**   comment allez-vous/vas-tu? (comment) ça va?

~ **old are you?**   quel âge avez-vous/as-tu?

~ **stupid of me!**   que je suis bête!

hundred   cent

hunger   faim *f.*

hungry: be ~   avoir faim

hunter   chasseur *m.*

hunting   chasse *f.*

go ~   aller à la chasse

hurry   se dépêcher

hurry: in a ~   pressé(e)
hurt   avoir mal à; faire mal à
   be ~   se blesser
husband   mari *m.*
hyphen   trait *m.* d'union
hypothesis   hypothèse *f.*

I   je
ice   glace *f.*
   ~ skating   patinage *m.* sur glace
ice cream   glace *f.*
   chocolate ~   glace au chocolat
   vanilla ~   glace à la vanille
idea   idée *f.*
   good ~!   bonne idée!
ideal   idéal(e)
idealistic   idéaliste
identity   identité *f.*
if   si
   ~ need be   à la rigueur
ill   malade
   become ~   tomber malade
illness   maladie *f.*
image   image *f.*
immediately   tout de suite
immigrant   immigré(e) *m./f.*
impatiently   impatiemment
impressionist   impressionniste
in   dans, en, à
   he's (not) in   il (n')est (pas) là
   ~ a private home   chez un
     particulier
   ~ front of   devant
   ~ my opinion   pour moi, à mon
     avis
   ~ practice   en pratique
   ~ theory   en théorie
   ~ those days   à cette époque-là
included   compris(e)
increase   augmenter
incredible   incroyable
indifference   indifférence *f.*
indifferent   indifférent(e)
indigestion   indigestion *f.*
individual *adj.*   individuel(le)
individual *n.*   individu *m.*
information desk   bureau *m.* de
   renseignements
inhabitant   habitant(e) *m./f.*
injection   piqûre *f.*
   give an ~   faire une piqûre (à)
injure oneself   se blesser
injured: be ~   se blesser
injury   blessure *f.*
instead of   au lieu de
instigate   provoquer

integrate: to be ~d   s'intégrer
intelligent   intelligent(e)
intend to   avoir l'intention de
interest *v.*   intéresser
   be interested   s'intéresser
interesting   intéressant(e)
internship   stage *m.*
interview   entretien *m.*, interview *f.*
intolerance   intolérance *f.*
intolerant   intolérant(e)
introductions   présentations *f.pl.*
invest   investir
invite   inviter
iron   repasser
irritating   embêtant(e)
Islamic   islamique
island   île *f.*
isolated   isolé(e)
it   il/elle; le/la
   ~ is   il est, c'est
   ~ is necessary (that)   il faut
     (que)
   ~'s a question of   il s'agit de
   ~'s . . . (weather)   il fait...
   ~'s raining   il pleut
   ~'s snowing   il neige
Italian   italien(ne)
its   son/sa/ses

jacket   veste *f.*; (waist-length)
   blouson *m.*
jam   confiture *f.*
January   janvier *m.*
Japanese   japonais(e)
jazz   jazz *m.*
jeans   jean *m.*
jewel   bijou *m.* (*pl.* bijoux)
jewelry   bijoux *m.pl.*
job   emploi *m.*; poste *m.*
   ~ application   demande *f.*
     d'emploi
jogging   jogging *m.*
   go ~   faire du jogging
joke   blague *f.*
journalist   journaliste *m./f.*
judo   judo *m.*
juice   jus *m.*
July   juillet *m.*
June   juin *m.*
junior high school   collège *m.*
just: have ~   venir de
   ~ a minute   un moment

keep   garder
key   clé *f.*

kidding: be ~   plaisanter!
   you're kidding!   tu plaisantes!
kill   tuer
kilogram   kilo *m.*
kind   genre *m.*
kindergarten   école *f.* maternelle
king   roi *m.*
kitchen   cuisine *f.*
knee   genou *m.* (*pl.* genoux)
knife   couteau *m.* (*pl.* couteaux)
knit   en maille
knock   frapper
knot   nœud *m.*
know   savoir; connaître
   ~ each other   se connaître

lack   manque *m.*
   a ~ of   un manque de
lady   dame *f.*
lake   lac *m.*
lamp   lampe *f.*
landlord/landlady   propriétaire *m./f.*
language   langue *f.*
last   dernier (-ière)
   ~ night   hier soir
late   tard; en retard
later   plus tard
latest   dernier (-ière)
laugh   rire
laundry   lessive *f.*
law   (field of study) droit *m.*;
   (legislation) loi *f.*
lawyer   avocat/avocate *m./f.*
lazy   paresseux (-euse)
leaf   feuille *f.*
learn   apprendre
least: at ~   au moins
   the ~   le/la/les moins
leather *adj.*   en cuir
leather *n.*   cuir *m.*
leave   partir; quitter
lecture hall   amphithéâtre *m.*
left   gauche *f.*
leg   jambe *f.*
leggings   caleçon *m.*
leisure activities   loisirs *m.*
lemon   citron *m.*
lemonade: fresh ~   citron pressé *m.*
lend   prêter
less   moins de
   ~ . . . than   moins... que
   ~ and ~   de moins en moins
let: ~ me introduce you to . . .   je
   te/vous présente...
   ~'s go   allons
   ~'s see   voyons

letter lettre *f.*
  ~ of the alphabet lettre *f.* de
    l'alphabet
lettuce salade *f.*
level niveau *m.* (*pl.* niveaux)
library bibliothèque *f.*
life vie *f.*
light *adj.* clair(e) (color)
light *n.* lumière *f.*
like *prep.* comme
like *v.* aimer
  do you ~ that? ça te plaît?
  I like that Ça me plaît
  what would you ~? vous désirez?
  would you ~ to? ça vous
    (t')intéresse?
lips lèvres *f.pl.*
listen (to) écouter
liter litre *m.*
literature littérature *f.*
little petit(e)
  a ~ un peu
live habiter; vivre
living room séjour *m.*; salon *m.*
loaf of French bread baguette *f.*
loafer mocassin *m.*
lobster homard *m.*
location emplacement *m.*
lodging logement *m.*; logis *m.*
  ~ with breakfast and dinner
    demi-pension *f.*
long long(ue)
longer: no ~ ne... plus
long-sleeved à manches longues
look avoir l'air
  ~ at regarder
  ~ bad on aller mal à
  ~ for chercher
  ~ good on aller bien à
lose perdre
  ~ weight maigrir
lost-and-found objets *m.pl.* trouvés
lot: a ~ (of) beaucoup (de)
lottery loterie *f.*
love *n.* amour *m.*
love *v.* aimer
lower baisser
luck chance *f.*
  good ~! bonne chance!
  what ~! quelle chance!
lucky: be ~ avoir de la chance
luggage bagages *m.pl.*
luminous lumineux (-euse)
lunch déjeuner *m.*

madam madame
magazine magazine *m.*
magnificent magnifique
main course plat *m.* principal
make faire; rendre
  ~ an appointment prendre
    rendez-vous
  ~ one's bed faire son lit
  ~ one's fortune faire fortune
  ~ sick rendre malade
makeup: to put on ~ se maquiller
man homme *m.*
management les cadres *m.pl.*
mandatory obligatoire
manners manières *f.pl.*
many beaucoup de, beaucoup
map carte *f.*; (city) plan
March mars *m.*
marriage mariage *m.*
married: to get ~ se marier
marry épouser
marvelous merveilleux (-euse)
master's degree maîtrise *f.*
match match *m.*
material comfort confort *m.*
  matériel
math maths *f.pl.*
mature mûrir
May mai *m.*
may I . . . ? est-ce que je
  pourrais... ?
maybe peut-être
me me; moi
meal repas *m.*
meat viande *f.*
mechanic mécanicien/
  mécanicienne *m./f.*
medication médicament *m.*
medicine (drug) médicament *m.*;
  (discipline) médecine *f.*
meet retrouver; se retrouver;
  rencontrer
mentioned mentionné(e)
menu menu *m.*; carte *f.*
  fixed-price ~ menu *m.*
merry Christmas joyeux Noël
message message *m.*
  e-mail ~ message électronique
    m.
Mexican mexicain(e)
midday midi *m.*
middle milieu *m.*
midnight minuit *m.*
migraine migraine *f.*

milk *n.* lait *m.*
  milk *adj.* laitier
million million *m.*
mineral water eau minérale *f.*
minutes to (the hour) moins...
miss rater
Miss mademoiselle *f.* (*pl.*
  Mesdemoiselles) (abbr. Mlle/
  Mlles)
mistake faute *f.*; erreur *f.*
misunderstanding malentendu *m.*
mocassin mocassin *m.*
moderate modéré(e)
moment moment *m.*
Monday lundi *m.*
money argent *m.*
month mois *m.*
monument monument *m.*
moon lune *f.*
moral moral(e)
more plus de
  ~ . . . than plus... que
  ~ and ~ de plus en plus
  no ~ ne... plus
  the ~ . . . the ~ plus... plus...
morning matin *m.*
  6:00 in the ~ 6 heures du matin
  tomorrow ~ demain matin
  yesterday ~ hier matin
Moroccan marocain(e)
most la plupart de
  the ~ le/la/les plus
mother mère *f.*
mountain montagne *f.*
mouse souris *f.*
mousse mousse *f.*
  chocolate ~ mousse *f.* au
    chocolat
mouth bouche *f.*
movie film *m.*
  detective ~ film policier
  horror ~ film d'épouvante
  ~s cinéma, ciné *m.*
  ~ theater cinéma *m.*
Mr. monsieur *m.* (*pl.* Messieurs)
  (abbr. M.)
Mrs. madame *f.* (*pl.* Mesdames)
  (abbr. Mme)
much beaucoup
  how ~ combien
  too ~ trop (de)
muffler écharpe *f.*
murmur murmurer
museum musée *m.*

music   musique *f.*
   play ~   faire de la musique
musician   musicien/musicienne *m./f.*
must   il faut (que); devoir
my   mon/ma/mes

name   name *m.*
   first ~   prénom *m.*
   last ~   nom *m.*
   my ~ is   je m'appelle
nap   sieste *f.*
   take a ~   faire la sieste
napkin   serviette *f.*
national holiday   fête *f.* nationale
nationality   nationalité *f.*
nature   nature *f.*
nausea   nausée *f.*
nauseated: to be ~   avoir la nausée
near   près de
neat   chouette
necessary: it is ~ (that)   il faut (que)
neck   cou *m.*
need   avoir besoin
   if ~ be   à la rigueur
neighborhood   quartier *m.*; voisinage *m.*
   ~ shop   magasin *m.* du coin
neither one   ni l'un ni l'autre
nephew   neveu (*pl.* neveux) *m.*
never   jamais; ne... jamais
new   nouveau/nouvel/nouvelle/ nouveaux/nouvelles
   ~ Year's Day   Jour de l'An *m.*
news   nouvelles *f.pl.*
   (TV) ~   journal télévisé *m.*
newspaper   journal *m.* (*pl.* journaux)
next   prochain(e)
   ~ to   à côté de
   the ~ day   le lendemain
nice   gentil(le); agréable; sympathique; aimable
   it's ~ weather   il fait beau
niece   nièce *f.*
night   nuit *f.*
   last ~   hier soir
   tomorrow ~   demain soir
nightclub   boîte *f.* (de nuit)
nightgown   chemise *f.* de nuit
nightmare   cauchemar *m.*
nine   neuf

nineteen   dix-neuf
ninety   quatre-vingt-dix
ninety-one   quatre-vingt-onze
no   non
   ~ longer   ne... plus
   ~ more   ne... plus
   ~ one   personne, personne ne, ne... personne
   ~ way!   c'est pas vrai!
nobody   personne, personne ne, ne... personne
noise   bruit *m.*
nonconformist   individualiste
non-smoking (section)   non-fumeurs
nonsense   bêtises *f.pl.*
noon   midi *m.*
north   nord *m.*
nose   nez *m.*
   runny ~   nez qui coule
   stuffy ~   nez bouché
not   ne... pas; pas
   ~ at all   pas du tout
   ~ bad   pas mal
   ~ much   pas beaucoup; pas grand-chose
   ~ too   pas trop
notebook   cahier *m.*
nothing   rien, ne... rien, rien ne...
novel   roman *m.*
November   novembre *m.*
now   maintenant
   from ~ on   désormais
nurse   infirmier/infirmière *m./f.*
nuts!   zut (alors)! mince!
nylon *adj.*   en nylon
nylon *n.*   nylon *m.*

objective   objectif *m.*
occasion   occasion *f.*
occupation   profession *f.*
o'clock   heure *f.*
October   octobre *m.*
odor   odeur *f.*
of   de
   ~ course   bien sûr
   ~ course not   mais non
offer   offrir
office   bureau *m.* (*pl.* bureaux)
often   souvent
oh yeah?   et alors?
OK   d'accord

old   vieux/vieil/vieille/vieux/ vieilles
   be ... years ~   avoir ... ans
   grow ~   vieillir
   how ~ are you?   quel âge as-tu/ avez-vous?
omelet   omelette *f.*
on   sur
   ~ foot   à pied
   ~ the contrary   au contraire
   ~ the other hand   par contre
once   une fois
one *number; art.*   un(e)
one *pron.*   on
one-color   uni
one-self   soi-même
one-way ticket   aller *m.* simple
onion   oignon *m.*
only   seulement; ne... que
open *adj.*   ouvert(e)
open *v.*   ouvrir
   ~ oneself up   s'ouvrir
opinion   opinion *f.*; avis *m.*
optimistic   optimiste
or   ou
orange *adj. inv.*   orange
orange *n.*   orange *f.*
order *n.*   ordre *m.*
order *v.*   commander
ordinal numbers   nombres *m.pl.* ordinaux
organize   organiser
other   autre
our   notre, nos
outdoors   dehors
outgoing   sociable
outing   sortie *f.*
outside   dehors
over there   là-bas
owe   devoir
own   posséder
owner   propriétaire *m./f.*
oyster   huître *f.*

package tour   voyage *m.* organisé
painter   peintre *m.*
painting   peinture *f.*; tableau *m.*
pal   copain *m.*, copine *f.*
pants   pantalon *m.*
parade   défilé *m.*
parents   parents *m.pl.*
parka   anorak *m.*

part: be ~ of faire partie de
part-time à mi-temps
partner partenaire *m./f.*
party soirée *f.*
pass passer
  ~ an exam réussir à un examen
passive passif (-ive)
passport passeport *m.*
pasta pâtes *f.pl.*
pastime passe-temps *m.* (*pl.* passe-temps)
pastry shop pâtisserie *f.*
pâté pâté *m.*
patient patient(e)
patiently patiemment
pay payer
  ~ attention faire attention
peach pêche *f.*
pear poire *f.*
peas petits pois *m.pl.*
pen stylo *m.*
pencil crayon *m.*
people gens *m.pl.*; on (*pron.*)
pepper poivre *m.*
percentage pourcentage *m.*
perfect parfait(e)
  that's ~! c'est parfait!
perhaps peut-être
person personne *f.*
personal possessions objets *m.pl.* personnels
pessimistic pessimiste
petition pétition *f.*
pharmacist pharmacien/ pharmacienne *m./f.*
philosophy philosophie *f.*
phobia phobie *f.*
phone téléphoner
  ~ each other se téléphoner
physical physique
physics physique *f.*
picnic pique-nique *m.*
picture image *f.*
pie tarte *f.*
piece morceau *m.* (*pl.* morceaux)
  ~ of chalk morceau de craie
pile: a ~ of un tas *m.* de
pill comprimé *m.*
pitcher carafe *f.*
pizza pizza *f.*
place setting couvert *m.*
place lieu *m.* (*pl.* lieux); place *f.*; endroit *m.*
plaid à carreaux

plan projet
plane avion *m.*
  by ~ en avion
plate assiette *f.*
play jouer
  ~ (a sport) faire du/de la (sport)
player: CD ~ lecteur *m.* de CD
pleasant sympathique; agréable
please *v.* plaire
please *adv.* s'il vous plaît
  ~ bring me pourriez-vous m'apporter
  ~ hold (*on the telephone*) ne quittez pas
pleasure plaisir *m.*
  ~ trip voyage *m.* d'agrément
  with ~! volontiers! avec plaisir!
pneumonia pneumonie *f.*
pocket poche *f.*
poem poème *m.*
polite expressions formules *f.pl.* de politesse
politely poliment
political politique
  ~ science sciences *f.pl.* politiques
politician politicien/politicienne *m./f.*
polka dot à pois
polo shirt polo *m.*
polyester *adj.* en polyester
polyester *n.* polyester *m.*
pool piscine *f.*
poor pauvre
poor person pauvre *m./f.*
poorly mal
pork porc *m.*
possess posséder
possessions affaires *f.pl.*; objets personnels *m.pl.*
post office poste *f.*
poster poster *m.*
potato pomme *f.* de terre
pound livre *f.*
poverty pauvreté *f.*; misère *f.*
power pouvoir *m.*
practical pratique
practice *n.* pratique *f.*
  in ~ en pratique
  ~ music faire de la musique
practice *v.* exercer
prefer préférer
prejudice préjugé *m.*
prepare préparer
prescribe prescrire
present présent(e)

president président/présidente *m./f.*
pretty joli(e)
prevent empêcher
price prix *m.*
print imprimé
probably sans doute
problem problème *m.*
product produit *m.*
profession profession *f.* libérale; métier *m.*
professional professionnel(le)
professor professeur *m.*
program programme *m.*; (television) émission *f.*; programme *m.*
promotion promotion *f.*
protest *v.* protester
provoke provoquer
psychological drama drame *m.* psychologique
psychology psychologie *f.*
pullover pull *m.*; chandail *m.*
punish punir
punished puni(e)
pupil élève *m./f.*
pushups pompes *f.pl.*
put mettre
  ~ on (se) mettre
  ~ on makeup se maquiller
pyjamas pyjama *m.*

quantity quantité *f.*
quarter (hour) quart *m.*
  ~ after (the hour) et quart
  ~ to (the hour) moins le quart
queen reine *f.*
question interroger
  it's a ~ of il s'agit de
quiche quiche *f.*
quickly rapidement
quit one's job démissionner

racism racisme *m.*
radio radio *f.*
rain *n.* pluie *f.*
rain *v.*: **it's raining** il pleut
raincoat imperméable *m.*
raise lever; élever
  ~ one's hand lever le doigt
rally se mobiliser

Ramadan   Ramadan *m.*
rarely   rarement
raspberry   framboise *f.*
rather   plutôt
rats!   zut (alors)!; mince!
ravishing   ravissant(e)
raw   cru(e)
read   lire
reading   lecture *f.*
reality   réalité *f.*
really   vraiment
   ~?   ah bon?
reason   raisonner
reasonable   raisonnable
recall   (se) rappeler
receive   recevoir
recently   récemment
receptionist   réceptionniste *m./f.*
recess   récréation *f.*
recognize   reconnaître
recommend   recommander
red   rouge
   ~ hair   roux (rousse)
   ~ light   feu rouge *m.*
referee   arbitre *m.*
refined   raffiné(e)
refuse   refuser
regret   regretter
reject   rejeter
relate   raconter
relationship   rapport *m.*
relatives   parents *m.pl.*
   distant ~   parents éloignés
relaxation   détente *f.*
remain   rester
   ~ standing   rester debout
remember   se souvenir
remind   rappeler
remote control   télécommande *f.*
render   rendre
rent   louer
renter   locataire *m./f.*
report   rapport *m.*
reporter   journaliste *m./f.*
required   exigé(e)
research   recherche *f.*
resemble   ressembler (à)
reserved for   réservé(e) à
respect   respecter
responsible   responsable
rest   se reposer
restaurant   restaurant *m.*
résumé   curriculum *m.* vitae, CV *m.*
retirement   retraite *f.*
return   rentrer; revenir; retourner

review   réviser
rice   riz *m.*
rich   riche
ride *n.*   promenade *f.*, randonnée *f.*
   car ~   promenade en voiture
   train ~   voyage *m.* en train
ride *v.*:   ~ a bike   faire du vélo
   ~ a train   voyager en train
rifle   fusil *m.*
right *adj.*   droit(e); correct(e)
   is that ~?   c'est vrai?
right *adv.*   correctement; à droite
   ~ away   tout de suite
right *n.*   (direction) droite *f.*;
   (entitlement) droit *m.*
rise   se lever
risk   risque *m.*
river   fleuve *m.*
road   route *f.*
roast beef   rosbif *m.*
rock music   rock *m.*
romantic film   film *m.* d'amour
room   pièce *f.*; chambre *f.*
roommate   camarade *m./f.* de
   chambre
rope   corde *f.*
Roquefort cheese   roquefort *m.*
round-trip ticket   aller-retour *m.*
routine   routine *f.*
row   rang *m.*
rug   tapis *m.*
runny nose   nez *m.* qui coule
rural   rural(e) (*m.pl.* ruraux)
   ~ community   commune rurale *f.*
Russian   russe

sad   triste
saint's day   fête *f.*
salad   salade *f.*
salami   saucisson *m.*
salary   salaire *m.*
sale   solde *m.*
   on ~   en soldes
salesperson   vendeur/vendeuse
   m./f.
salt   sel *m.*
sand   sable *m.*
sandal   sandale *f.*
sandwich   sandwich *m.*
Santa Claus   père Noël *m.*
satisfied   satisfait(e)
Saturday   samedi *m.*
sausage   saucisse *f.*

say   dire
   ~!   tiens! dis/dites!
scandalous   scandaleux (-euse)
scare   faire peur à
scarf   écharpe *f.*; foulard *m.*
schedule   emploi *m.* du temps;
   (train) horaire *m.*
school   école *f.*; (at university)
   fac/faculté *f.*
   elementary ~   école primaire
   high ~   lycée *m.*
   junior high/middle ~   collège *m.*
   nursery ~   école maternelle
   ~ subject   matière *f.*
schoolteacher   maître/maîtresse
   m./f.
   primary ~   instituteur/
   institutrice *m./f.*
science   science *f.*
sea   mer *f.*
seafood   fruits *m.pl.* de mer
season   saison *f.*
seat   place *f.*
seated   assis(e)
second   deuxième
secret   secret *m.*
secretary   secrétaire *m./f.*
security   sécurité *f.*
see   voir
   ~ one another   se (re)voir
   ~ you soon   à bientôt
seem   avoir l'air; sembler
selfish   égoïste
sell   vendre
send   envoyer
Senegalese   sénégalais(e)
separate   séparé(e)
September   septembre *m.*
serious   sérieux (-euse)
seriously   sérieusement
serve   servir
seven   sept
seventeen   dix-sept
seventy   soixante-dix
seventy-one   soixante et onze
seventy-two   soixante-douze
several   plusieurs
shame   honte *f.*
shape   forme *f.*
   in good ~   en bonne forme
share   partager
shave   se raser
she   elle
sheet of paper   feuille *f.* de papier
shelter   abri *m.*: gîte *m.*

shirt (*men's*) chemise *f*.; (*women's*) chemisier *m*.
shoes chaussures *f.pl.*
  dressy ~ chaussures habillées
shopping: go grocery ~ faire les courses
  go ~ faire des courses
short petit(e); court(e)
shorts short *m*.
short-sleeved à manches courtes
should (*see* devoir)
  I ~ je devrais
  I ~ have j'aurais dû
shoulder épaule *f*.
shout crier
show montrer
show: game ~ jeu *m*. télévisé
  variety ~ variétés *f.pl.*
shower douche *f*.
shrimp crevette *f*.
shy timide
sick malade
  get ~ tomber malade
side côté *m*.
silk *adj.* en soie
silk *n.* soie *f*.
similar semblable
since depuis
  ~ when depuis quand
sing chanter
singer chanteur/chanteuse *m./f.*
single célibataire
  ~ person célibataire *m./f.*
sink (*bathroom*) lavabo *m*.
sir monsieur
sister sœur
sister-in-law belle-sœur *f*.
six six
sixteen seize
sixty soixante
skate patin *m*.
skating: ice ~ patinage *m*. sur glace
  ~ rink patinoire *f*.
skeptical sceptique
ski faire du ski
skiing ski *m*.
skirt jupe *f*.
sky ciel *m*.
sleep dormir
  ~ in faire la grasse matinée
sleeve manche *f*.
slender mince
slice tranche *f*.
slipper pantoufle *f*.
slowly lentement
small petit(e)

smell odeur *f*.
smoking (section) fumeurs *m.pl.*
snail escargot *m*.
sneaker basket *m*.; tennis *f*.
sneeze éternuer
snow *n.* neige *f*.
snow *v.:* **it's snowing** il neige
so eh bien, ben, alors, donc
soap opera feuilleton *m*.
soccer foot *m*., football *m*.
  play ~ faire du foot
society société *f*.
sociology sociologie *f*.
sock chaussette *f*.
sofa canapé *m*.
solid-color uni(e)
solitude solitude *f*.
solution solution *f*.
some *adj.* des; certain(e)s, quelques
  ~ what? de la/du quoi?
some *pron.* en; certain(e)s; quelques-un(e)s
somebody quelqu'un
someone quelqu'un
something quelque chose
sometimes quelquefois
son fils *m*.
song chanson *f*.
soon bientôt
  as ~ as dès que
sore throat mal *m*. à la gorge
sorry désolé(e); pardon
  be ~ regretter
sort espèce *f*.; genre *m*.
so-so comme ci comme ça
soup soupe *f*.
south sud *m*.
souvenir souvenir *m*.
space espace *m*.
spacious spacieux (-euse)
Spanish espagnol(e)
speak parler
  ~ loudly parler fort
specialist spécialiste *m./f.*
spend (*money*) dépenser; (*time, vacation*) passer
spider araignée *f*.
spoon cuillère *f*.
sports sport *m*.
spouse conjoint/conjointe *m./f.*; époux/épouse *m./f.*
spring printemps *m*.
square place *f*.
stadium stade *m*.
staircase escalier *m*.
stairs escalier *m*.

stand supporter
standing debout
star étoile *f*.
station (train) gare *f*.
  gas ~ station *f*. service
stay *n.* séjour *m*.
stay *v.* rester; faire un séjour
steak bifteck *m*.
stimulate stimuler
stingy avare
stool tabouret *m*.
stop arrêter
store magasin *m*.
storm orage *m*.
stormy orageux (-euse)
story étage *m*.; histoire *f*.
straight ahead tout droit
strange étrange
stranger étranger/étrangère *m./f.*
strawberry fraise *f*.
  ~ tart tarte *f*. aux fraises
street rue *f*.
  ~ map plan *m*. de ville
stress stress *m*.
strict strict(e)
strike frapper
striped à rayures
stroke attaque *f*. cérébrale
strong fort(e)
student élève *m./f.*
  university ~ étudiant/étudiante *m./f.*
studio studio *m*.
study étudier
stuffed animal peluche *f*.
stuffy nose nez *m*. bouché
stupid bête; stupide
  how ~! quelle bêtise!
subject (school) matière *f*.
  the ~ is il s'agit de
suburbs banlieue *f*.
succeed réussir
success réussite *f*.; succès *m*.
suffer souffrir
sugar sucre *m*.
  ~ cane canne *f*. à sucre
suit (*men's*) costume *m*.; (*women's*) tailleur *m*.
suitcase valise *f*.
summer été *m*.
sun soleil *m*.
Sunday dimanche *m*.
sunglasses lunettes *f.pl.* de soleil
sunny ensoleillé(e)
  it's ~ il fait du soleil
supermarket supermarché *m*.

supposed: I was ~ to je devais
surname nom *m.* de famille
surprising étonnant(e); surprenant(e)
sweater chandail *m.*; pull *m.*
  button-up ~ cardigan *m.*
sweats jogging *m.*
sweatshirt sweat *m.*
sweet sucré(e), doux (douce)
swim faire de la natation; nager
swimming natation *f.*
Swiss suisse
symptom symptôme *m.*
syrup sirop *m.*

table table *f.*
tablet comprimé *m.*
taco taco *f.*
Tahitian tahitien(ne)
take prendre
  ~ a trip faire un voyage
  ~ advantage of profiter de
  ~ back ramener
  ~ off enlever
talk to each other se parler
talkative bavard(e)
tall grand(e)
tame apprivoiser
tart: apple ~ tarte *f.* aux pommes
taste goût *m.*
tea thé *m.*
  plain ~ thé nature
  ~ with lemon thé citron
  ~ with milk thé au lait
teacher instituteur/institutrice, professeur *m.*; enseignant/ enseignante *m./f.*
team équipe *f.*
telephone *n.* téléphone *m.*
telephone *v.* téléphoner
television télévision *f.*
  ~ set poste *m.* de télévision
tell raconter
temperature température *f.*
  take one's ~ prendre sa température
ten dix
tenant locataire *m./f.*
tendency tendance *f.*
tennis tennis *m.*
  play ~ faire du tennis
  ~ shoe tennis *f.*
terrace terrasse *f.*
terrible terrible
terrific super, formidable

test examen *m.*: épreuve *f.*
thank remercier
  many ~s merci mille fois
  ~s merci
  ~ you merci
Thanksgiving Day Jour *m.* d'action de grâces
that *adj.* ce/cet/cette... (-ci/-là)
that *conj.* que
that *pron.* ce, cela, ça; *rel. pron.* qui, que
the le/la/l'/les
theater: movie ~ cinéma *m.*
their leur, leurs
them les, leurs
then alors, puis, ensuite
theory: in ~ en théorie *f.*
there là, là-bas; y
  ~ is/are il y a; voilà
therefore donc
these *adj.* ces; ces... (-ci/-là)
these *pron.* ceux/celles-ci; ceux/ celles-là
they ils/elles/on
think penser, trouver, croire
  ~ about penser à
  ~ of penser de
thirst soif *f.*
thirsty: be ~ avoir soif
thirteen treize
thirty trente
  ~ (minutes past the hour) et demie
this *adj.* ce, cet, cette... (-ci/-là)
those *adj.* ces; ces... (-ci/-là)
those *pron.* ceux/celles(-ci); ceux/ celles(-là)
thousand mille *inv.*
three trois
throat gorge *f.*
  sore ~ mal *m.* à la gorge
Thursday jeudi *m.*
ticket billet *m.*
  one-way ~ aller simple *m.*
  round-trip ~ aller-retour *m.*
  ~ window guichet *m.*
tie cravate *f.*; lien *m.*
time heure *f.*; temps *m.*
  a long ~ longtemps
  at that ~ en ce temps-là
  free ~ temps libre *m.*
  from ~ to ~ de temps en temps
  have ~ (to) avoir le temps (de)
  have a hard ~ avoir du mal à
  it is ~ that il est temps de/que
  on ~ à l'heure

timetable horaire *m.*
tired fatigué(e)
title titre *m.*
to à, en, dans
  in order ~ pour
  ~ her lui
  ~ him lui
  ~ them leur
toast pain grillé *m.*
tobacco/magazine shop bureau *m.* de tabac
today aujourd'hui
together ensemble
toilet W.C. *m.pl.*; toilettes *f.pl.*
tomato tomate *f.*
tomorrow demain
too trop; aussi
  ~ bad tant pis
  ~ little trop peu (de)
  ~ much trop (de)
tooth dent *f.*
torn déchiré(e)
touch toucher
tour tour *m.*
town village *m.*; ville *f.*
toy jouet *m.*
track course *f.*
tradition tradition *f.*
traditional traditionnel(le)
traditionally traditionnellement
traffic jam embouteillage *m.*
tragic tragique
train train *m.*
  by ~ en train
  high-speed ~ TGV *m.*
  ~ station gare *f.*
training formation *f.*
tranquil tranquille
travel voyager
  ~ agency agence *f.* de voyage
treatment traitement *m.*
tree arbre *m.*
  family ~ arbre *m.* généalogique
trip voyage *m.*
  ~ around the world tour du monde
  business ~ voyage *m.* d'affaires
  go on a ~ faire un voyage
  have a nice ~! bon voyage!
  pleasure ~ voyage d'agrément
true vrai(e)
truth vérité *f.*
try again later essayer plus tard
T-shirt tee-shirt *m.*
Tuesday mardi *m.*
tuna thon *m.*

turkey dinde *f.*
turn tourner
 ~ off éteindre
 ~ on allumer
tuxedo smoking *m.*
twelve douze
twenty vingt
twenty-one vingt et un
twenty-two vingt-deux
two deux
type espèce *f.*; genre *m.*
typical typique

uh euh
uncivilized person sauvage *m./f.*
uncle oncle *m.*
under sous
understand comprendre
 ~ one another se comprendre
unemployment chômage *m.*
unfortunately malheureusement
unfurnished non meublé
university université *f.*
 ~ cafeteria restaurant *m.*
   universitaire
 ~ dorm résidence *f.* universitaire
unmarried célibataire
unpleasant désagréable
up to jusqu'à
us nous
useful utile
usual: as ~ comme d'habitude
usually d'habitude
utilities charges *f.pl.*

vacation vacances *f.pl.*
 ~ day jour de congé
 have a nice ~! bonnes vacances!
vacuum passer l'aspirateur
 ~ cleaner aspirateur *m.*
value valeur *f.*
variety show variétés *f.pl.*
veal veau *m.*
 ~ cutlet côtelette *f.* de veau
vegetable légume *m.*
vegetarian végétarien(ne)
velvet *adj.* en velours
velvet *n.* velours *m.*
very très; vachement *(slang)*

video cassette vidéocassette *f.*
 ~ recorder magnétoscope *m.*
violence violence *f.*
visible visible
visit (a place) visiter; (a person)
   rendre visite à
visit visite *f.*
voice voix *f.*
volleyball volley *m.*
 play ~ faire du volley
vote voter

wages salaire *m.*
waist taille *f.*
waist-length jacket blouson *m.*
wait (for) attendre
waiter/waitress serveur/serveuse
   m./f.
wake up se réveiller
walk *n.* promenade *f.*
 go for a ~ faire une promenade
walk *v.* marcher; faire de la
   marche
walking marche *f.*
 go ~ faire de la marche
wall mur *m.*
want désirer; vouloir
 ~ to vouloir; avoir envie de
war guerre *f.*
wash laver
 ~ (oneself) se laver
watch montre *f.*
water eau *f.*
 mineral ~ eau *f.* minérale
 ~ skiing ski *m.* nautique
we nous; on
weak faible
wealth richesse *f.*
wear porter
weather temps *m.*
 ~ report bulletin météo *m.*
Wednesday mercredi *m.*
week semaine *f.*
 a ~ later une semaine après
 in a ~ dans une semaine
weekend week-end *m.*
weight lifting musculation *f.*
welcome accueillir
 you're ~ il n'y a pas de quoi; je
   t'/vous en prie; de rien
well alors; bien; ben; eh bien
west ouest *m.*

what qu'est-ce que... ?; que; quel/
   quelle
 ~? Pardon? Comment?
 ~ is he like? comment est-il?
 ~ is his/her name? comment
   s'appelle-t-il/elle?
 ~ is it? qu'est-ce que c'est?
 ~ is that? qu'est-ce que c'est que
   ça?
 ~ is your name? comment tu
   t'appelles? comment vous
   appelez-vous?
 ~ time is it? quelle heure est-il?
 ~ would you like? vous désirez?
wheat blé *m.*
 ~ field champ *m.* de blé
when quand
where où
 from ~ d'où
 ~ is . . . located? où se trouve... ?
which quel/quelle
while alors que
white blanc (blanche)
who qui, qui est-ce qui
 ~ am I? qui suis-je?
 ~ is it? qui est-ce?
 ~'s calling? qui est à l'appareil?
whom . . . ? qui est-ce que... ?
why pourquoi
wife femme *f.*
win gagner
wind vent *m.*
window fenêtre *f.*
windy: it's ~ il fait du vent
wine vin *m.*
winter hiver *m.*
wish désirer; souhaiter
with avec
 ~ difficulty difficilement
 ~ pleasure! volontiers! avec
   plaisir!
woman femme *f.*
wood bois *m.*
wool laine *f.*
work travailler
workbook cahier *m.*
worker ouvrier/ouvrière *m./f.*
world monde *m.*
worried inquiet (-ète)
worry s'inquiéter
would: ~ you know? sauriez-
   vous... ?
 ~ you like to? ça vous
   (t')intéresse?

wound blessure *f.*
write écrire
  ~ one another s'écrire
writer écrivain *m.*
wrong: be ~ avoir tort

xenophobic xénophobe

year an *m.*; année *f.*
  be _____ ~s old avoir _____ ans
  happy New ~ bonne année
yellow jaune
yes oui; si (in response to negative
    question)
  well, ~ mais oui; mais si
yesterday hier
yet déjà

yogurt yaourt *m.*
you vous; tu; te; toi
  ~ can vous pouvez
  ~ would like vous voudriez
  ~'re welcome il n'y a pas de
    quoi; je vous (t') en prie; de rien
young jeune
your ton/ta/tes; votre/vos

Index

à
- contractions with, 106
- \+ geographical names, 200n, 249–251
- \+ persons, 219–220
- \+ time frames, 123
- verbs followed by ~, 144–145, 262, 373

accent marks, 8

accentuation of syllables, 26

accepting
- congratulations, 330
- invitations, 222–223
- thanks, 330

acheter, 58, 159n

adjectives
- agreement of, 22–23, 27–28
- comparative of, 172–174
- demonstrative, 52–53
- descriptive, 25
- **il (elle) est** +, 31
- interrogative, 69–71
- irregular, 27–28, 96–98
- of nationality, 18
- placement of, 96–98
- plural of, 22–23
- plural, after **de,** 97
- possessive, 51
- *See also* colors

adverbs, 404–405
- comparative of, 173–174
- to describe the past, 311
- formation of, 404–405
- of frequency, 134–135, 405
- interrogative, 88, 405
- of manner, 404–405
- placement of, 404–405
- of quantity, 170. *See also* quantity, expressions of
- superlative of, 331–332
- of time, 203, 229, 405

advice, giving, 302

affirmative responses, 39

Africa, 244–248, 334, 434. *See also countries by name*

age, 66–68, 69–70

agreement. *See* adjectives, agreement of; past participles

aller, 104–105, 106, 388, 390

alphabet, 8

an(s), 66–68

analogy (strategy), 445

anticipating questions (strategy), 188

s'appeler, 5, 182

apprendre (à), 144–145

articles. *See* definite articles; indefinite articles; partitive articles

asking questions. *See* interrogative; questions

attention, attracting (strategy), 253–254

au, à la, aux. *See* à; contractions

audience, identifying (strategy), 270–271

aussi, 45
- **aussi... que,** 173–174

autant (de), 173, 405

avoiding repetition (strategy), 43

avoir, 69–70, 321, 389–390
- as auxiliary, 179–180, 209–211, 262
- expressions with, 222–223, 388, 437, 439
- \+ partitive, 163

bac (baccalauréat), 137, 138

bathrooms, 81

(se) battre, 317n

beau (bel, belle), 97–98

bien
- comparative of, 174
- superlative of, 332

body, parts of the, 370–372

boire, 162, 163

bon
- comparative, of, 174
- superlative of, 332

brainstorming (strategy), 150

calendar, 128–129, 326–328

careers, 383–384, 392–395. *See also* professions

ce, cet, cette, ces, 52–53

-cer verbs, 58, 279n

c'est (ce sont), 11–12, 182, 460
- vs. **il/elle est,** 31
- \+ stress pronouns, 397–398

-ci, 53

clarification, asking for (strategy), 181–182

classroom expressions, 13

classroom items, 10

climate, 26

clothing, 358–363, 364

collège, 120

colors, 97–98, 97n

combien (de), 49, 88, 170, 404–405

comment, 69, 88, 404–405

comparative, 172–174

compass points, 196

complimenting, 367

compliments, responding to, 366, 367

comprendre, 144–145

conditional, 421–422
- expressing obligation, disapproval, regret with, 432
- hypothesizing with, 429–430
- vs. imperfect, 422
- of politeness, 104, 254, 422
- with **si** clauses, 429–430

congratulations, expressing (strategy), 330

connaître, 337–338
- **se** ~, 338

consonants. *See* pronunciation

continents, 250–251

contractions of **à** and **de** with definite article, 106

contrasting (strategy), 76

countries. *See* geographical names

courses of study, 120, 122, 139

courtesy
- conditional expressing, 104, 254, 422
- expressions of, 4–6, 84

dates, 128–129, 133–134

dating, 295

days of the week, 128–129, 133–134

de
- contractions with, 106
- expressions with, 437
- \+ geographical names, 21, 249–251
- \+ infinitive, 372–373, 460
- after negative expressions, 69–70, 163, 169
- \+ plural adjectives, 97
- replaced by **dont,** 439–440
- replaced by **en,** 436–437
- \+ time frames, 123

declining invitations (strategy), 222–223

definite articles, 30
- **à/de** +, 106
- **aimer** +, 58

Text and Illustrations

pp. 27, 30, 35, 36 Illustrations from *Le petit Nicolas* by Sempé et Goscinny. Copyright © 1960 Éditions Doenoël. Used by permission.

pp. 35–36, From *Le petit Nicolas* by Sempé et Goscinny. Copyright © 1960 Éditions Doenoël. Used by permission.

p. 42, Jacques Prevert, "L'accent grave" in *Paroles.* © Éditions Gallimard. By permission of the publisher.

p. 74, René Philombe, "L'homme qui te ressemble" from *Petites Gouttes de chant pour créer l'homme* (Éditions Semences Africaines, 1977).

p. 91, Reprinted from "Sondage: Les Français sur le vif," *Journal Français d'Amérique,* 17–30 mai 1991. Copyright © 1991. Reprinted with permission.

pp. 129–130, "École: La semaine des quatre jours" from *L'Express,* 11 décembre 1992 édition, Copyright © 1992, L'Express. Reprinted by permission of New York Times Syndicate.

pp. 167–168, Reprinted from "Vie économique: Que mangent les Français?" *Journal Français d'Amérique,* 9 mars–1 avril 1993. Copyright © 1991. Reprinted with permission.

pp. 186–187, Extrait de *Notre fille ne se mariera pas* by Guillaume Oyônô Mbia.

p. 206, Copyright © Dupuis 1997. First printed in *Ciné télé Revue,* #23, 5 juin 1997. Used by permission.

pp. 226–227, From *Le petit Nicolas et les copains* by Sempé et Goscinny. Copyright © 1960 Éditions Doenoël. Used by permission.

pp. 267–269, Text and illustrations from *Le Petit Prince* by Antoine de Saint-Exupéry. Copyright 1943 by Harcourt Brace & Company and renewed 1971 by Consuelo de Saint-Exupéry. Reprinted by permission of the publisher.

pp. 305, 306–309, Text and illustrations from *Le Petit Prince* by Antoine de Saint-Exupéry. Copyright 1943 by Harcourt Brace & Company and renewed 1971 by Consuelo de Saint-Exupéry. Reprinted by permission of the publisher.

p. 359, © Christine Lerche—Sylvie Poideuir/BIBA. Used with permission.

pp. 376–377, Excerpted from "Une abominable feuille d'érable sur la glace" by Roch Carrier, from *Les Enfants du bonhomme dans la lune.* Copyright © 1979. Used by permission of Les Éditions Stanké, Montréal.

pp. 393–394, From Gérard Mermet, "La régression du carriérisme," printed in Francoscopie 1997, pp. 261–263.

pp. 410–411, Reprinted from *Une si longue lettre* by Mariama Bâ by permission of Les Nouvelles Éditions Africaines.

Photographs

p. 1, Owen Franken/Stock Boston; *p. 2,* Chris Hackett/The Image Bank; *p. 9 (top),* David Frazier; *(bottom),* Hazel Hankin/Stock Boston; *p. 17,* Hazel Hankin/Stock Boston; *p. 20 (top left),* author; *(bottom left),* author; *(bottom right),* Michael Newman/PhotoEdit; *(top right),* Ulrike Welsch; *p. 34 (left),* Ermakoff/The Image Works; *(right),* Beryl Goldberg; *p. 41,* Gamma Liaison; *p. 43 (left),* Joseph Sohm/Stock Boston; *(right),* Owen Franken/Stock Boston; *p. 46,* Ulrike Welsch; *p. 49,* Peter Menzel/Stock Boston; *p. 54,* Beryl

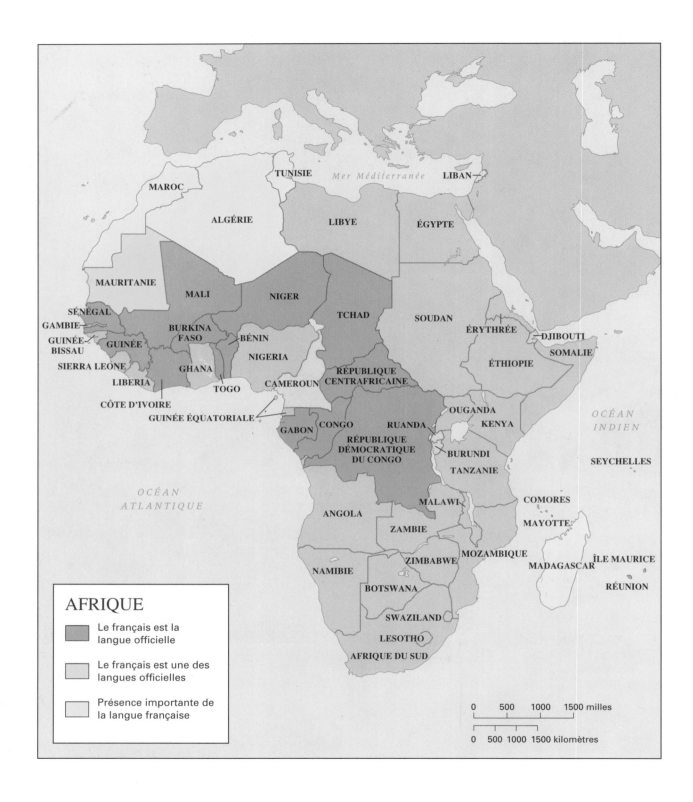

AFRIQUE

- Le français est la langue officielle
- Le français est une des langues officielles
- Présence importante de la langue française

MAROC

TUNISIE

Mer Méditerranée

LIBAN

ALGÉRIE

LIBYE

ÉGYPTE

MAURITANIE

MALI

NIGER

TCHAD

SOUDAN

ÉRYTHRÉE

DJIBOUTI

SÉNÉGAL

GAMBIE

GUINÉE-BISSAU

GUINÉE

SIERRA LEONE

LIBERIA

CÔTE D'IVOIRE

GUINÉE ÉQUATORIALE

BURKINA FASO

BÉNIN

GHANA

TOGO

NIGERIA

CAMEROUN

RÉPUBLIQUE CENTRAFRICAINE

SOMALIE

ÉTHIOPIE

OUGANDA

KENYA

GABON

CONGO

RUANDA

BURUNDI

TANZANIE

RÉPUBLIQUE DÉMOCRATIQUE DU CONGO

SEYCHELLES

OCÉAN ATLANTIQUE

ANGOLA

MALAWI

ZAMBIE

COMORES

MAYOTTE

MOZAMBIQUE

OCÉAN INDIEN

NAMIBIE

ZIMBABWE

MADAGASCAR

ÎLE MAURICE

RÉUNION

BOTSWANA

SWAZILAND

LESOTHO

AFRIQUE DU SUD

0 500 1000 1500 milles

0 500 1000 1500 kilomètres